TWENTY QUESTIONS FOR THE WRITER

TWENTY QUESTIONS FOR THE WRITER

A Rhetoric with Readings

JACQUELINE BERKE Drew University

HARCOURT BRACE JOVANOVICH, INC.
New York Chicago San Francisco Atlanta

ISBN: 0–15–592397–8

Library of Congress Catalog Card Number: 70–181535

Printed in the United States of America

PICTURE CREDITS

52: From *The Book of Popular Science* by permission of the publishers, Grolier Inc., New York

57: Edward Hopper, *Night Shadows.* 1921. Etching. Collection Whitney Museum of American Art, New York. Bequest of Mrs. Josephine N. Hopper

77: © 1967 by George Allen & Unwin. Reprinted by permission of Simon and Schuster, Inc.

123: Nasjonalgalleriet, Oslo

158: Dick Falcon; Dorothy Robbins

417: From Bess Sondel, *Power Steering With Words,* copyright © 1964 Follett Publishing Co.

PREFACE

During my twelve years of teaching writing I have found that procedure in a writing course is as important as content. And the simpler the procedure, the better. For me, then, the ideal text for a writing course would be—first of all—complete and self-contained. The instructor is thereby spared the job of correlating readings in one book with writing assignments in another, with a style guide and exercises in still another, with footnote rules in still another, and so on. Second, the ideal text would be sequentially organized, requiring no complicated rearranging of chapters by the instructor in order to construct a workable frame for his course. The text itself would offer a frame, but, along with this, it would offer sufficient materials and resources to enable the instructor to make a course that would satisfy his own preferences and the needs of his students. That is, the ideal writing text would be flexible as well as clearly organized.

While hardly pretending or even aspiring to write the ideal text, I have nonetheless tried in this book to meet the basic requirements of completeness, simplicity of procedure, and flexibility. *Twenty Questions for the Writer* is self-contained in that it may be used without any additional resources other than a recently edited standard dictionary: included are ample and varied readings; hundreds of suggested writing assignments; practice exercises (for use inside and outside the clasroom); instructions for and illustrations of four different types of term paper; a chapter on research procedure and documentation; two chapters on language; a review of rhetorical principles involving the word, the sentence, and the paragraph.

During a three-year period of testing this text in my own classes at Drew, I have discovered that it can be used simultaneously in two different sections of the course without duplicating either the readings or the writing assignments. To be sure, an instructor using this text may choose to assign additional materials, but for most purposes he will not be forced to do so.

My organizing principle—again in the interest of simplicity and ease—has been sequential, roughly in an order of increasing complexity. Thus, the instructor can move through the chapters of this text as he moves through the weeks of the semester, choosing from among the twenty units of writing assignments those that best serve the needs of his particular class. Each unit of writing assignment, as the Table of Contents indicates, is presented in the form of a question. *The writer invariably begins with a question:* the book is rooted in this observation and the chapters are titled accordingly.

Each unit of writing (i.e., each chapter, each question) includes illustrative essays on a variety of subjects and in a wide range of tones from the very earnest to the matter-of-fact to the frivolous and satiric. In each assignment the student is required to assume the responsibility for answering a given question, but within that mold and the discipline that the mold requires, he may address himself to whatever subject area engages his interest and speak in whatever tone his spirit dictates. I have tried, in other words, to establish in this book a balance between the discipline required to complete even the simplest piece of writing and the feeling of freedom required for a more than pedestrian performance. I consider the striking of such a balance essential to all good writing. Indeed, just as the organizing principle of the book is rooted in the concept of the question, so the basic operating principle (and faith) is rooted in the idea that freedom in writing, as Robert Frost said of freedom in general, means "moving easy in harness."

Applying this metaphor to *Twenty Questions for the Writer,* I would say that the nature of each question provides a particular harness ("How Is X Made or Done?" dictates chronological ordering; "What Are the Types of X?" requires systematic classification; and so on), whereas the discussions within the chapter, the illustrative essays, and the assignments encourage the student to move naturally and easily in a chosen direction within the given confines.

Needless to say, an instructor using this book will impose as loose or tight a harness as he sees fit. Although the thirty or forty suggested assignments at the end of each chapter advise the student to select his own topic, there may well be occasions when an instructor will want the entire class to focus its attention on one topic in particular. And then again maybe not. . . . What applies to students applies equally to instructors: in order to conduct a meaningful and reasonably rewarding course they too must have the opportunity of "moving easy in harness."

I want to thank the following people: for patiently and perceptively reviewing the manuscript at different stages, Barbara McKenzie of the University of Georgia; for mobilizing pages into an expertly turned out manuscript, Ruth Demaree and Nan Lemmerman of Drew University's very expert Stenographic Service; for counsel and guidance in gathering resource materials for Chapter 22, Evelyn Meyer—Reference Librarian at Drew University—herself an extraordinary resource. I also want to thank my students at Drew for their encouraging and constructive responses to preliminary drafts of this material. Finally I want to thank Harcourt editors Ronald Campbell for flexibility and faith, and Mildred Tackett for her consistently incisive and insightful editing throughout and for her particularly rich contribution to Chapter 22.

J. B.

CONTENTS

PREFACE v

Introduction

WRITING AS A HUMAN ACTIVITY 3

Developing the Ability to Write 4
The Qualities of Good Writing 6
Rhetorical Stance 9
"Courtship" Devices 9
The Student Writer 10
Assignments 11

FINDING A SUBJECT 14

Checklist of Subjects 15
Limiting the Subject 16
The Classical Topics 17
The New "Heuristic" 18
Asking the Right Questions 19
Checklist of Twenty Questions 19
Putting Question to Subject-Topic 21
Assignments 22

I Writing a Short Paper

1 WHAT DOES X MEAN? 25

Finding a Subject in Definition 27

Methods of Developing a Definition 28
Formal Definition 34
Experiential Definition 35
Assignments 38

2 HOW CAN X BE DESCRIBED? 41

Sensory Description 41
Technical Description 51
Assignments 53

3 WHAT ARE THE COMPONENT PARTS OF X? 59

Analysis of Physical Structure 59
Analysis of an Intellectual Structure 61
Principles of Analysis 64
Assignments 67

4 HOW IS X MADE OR DONE? 72

Historical-Social Process 75
Technical-Natural Process 76
Intellectual Process 80
Assignments 81

5 HOW SHOULD X BE MADE OR DONE? 85

Qualities of Good "How-to" Writing 86
Variety in "How-to" Writing 87
Carrying the "How-to" Too Far 91
Assignments 92

6 WHAT IS THE ESSENTIAL FUNCTION OF X? 97

The Function of an Institution 97
The Function of a Professional Person 102
Assignments 104

7 WHAT ARE THE CAUSES OF X? 107

The First Principle of Causation: Uniformity 107
The Second Principle of Causation: Sufficiency 110
Cause and Condition 113
Speculating on Reasons 114
Presenting Personal Reasons 117
Assignments 120

8 WHAT ARE THE CONSEQUENCES OF X? 124

Assignments 130

9 WHAT ARE THE TYPES OF X? 132

Classification According to Purpose 133

Complete Classification 134
Organizing the Classification 138
Complex Classification 140
Assignments 142

10 HOW DOES X COMPARE TO Y? 145

Similarity and Difference in Comparison 147
Organization of Comparison 151
Assignments 155

11 WHAT IS THE PRESENT STATUS OF X? 160

Assignments 166

12 HOW SHOULD X BE INTERPRETED? 168

Interpreting an Activity 168
Interpreting a Story 170
Interpreting Symbols 172
Interpreting a Poem 174
Assignments 176

13 WHAT ARE THE FACTS ABOUT X? 184

Range of Subject Matter 184
Range of Purposes 185
Organizing the Fact Piece 191
Assignments 195

14 HOW DID X HAPPEN? 199

Autobiographical Narration 199
Structure in Narration 202
Point of View in Narration 204
Immediacy in Narration 205
Historical Narration 209
The Diary as Narration 211
Assignments 213

15 WHAT KIND OF PERSON IS X? 218

A Member of the Family 218
A Friend or Well-Known Person 227
A Historical Figure 229
A "Type" 232
Assignments 234

16 WHAT IS MY PERSONAL RESPONSE TO X? 237

The Mood Essay 237
The Protest 242
The "Appreciation" 243
Assignments 245

17 WHAT IS MY MEMORY OF X? 249

The Quality of Memory 249
Remembering Childhood Experiences 251
Remembering Episodes 255
Remembering People 256
Assignments 258

18 WHAT IS THE VALUE OF X? 261

Evaluating Man's Behavior 263
Evaluating Books 264
General Reviews 268
Assignments 271

19 HOW CAN X BE SUMMARIZED? 273

Summarizing Ideas 274
Summarizing Data 279
Summarizing Plot 280
Summarizing Events 283
Assignments 284

20 WHAT CASE CAN BE MADE FOR OR AGAINST X? 292

Is and Ought Propositions 293
Locating the Issues 300
Deduction and Induction 305
Argument by Analogy 309
Common Logical Fallacies 313
Substantiating the Argument 315
The Satiric Attack 317
Testing the Argument 319
Assignments 320

II Writing a Long Paper: Research and Organization

21 THE LONG PAPER 329

Form and Function of the Term Paper 329
Extended Analysis 330
Assignments 337
Description-Narration 338
Assignments 345
Extended Characterization 346
Assignments 351
Extended Argument 352
Assignments 363

22 GATHERING INFORMATION 365

The Importance of Facts 365

Remembering Facts 366
Observing Facts 368
Thinking: Drawing Inferences and Interpretations 369
Research 370
Note-Taking 389
Avoiding Plagiarism 393
Footnotes and Bibliography 394
Assignments 399

23 ORGANIZING THE PAPER 400

Natural Order 400
Logical Order 401
The Working Outline 402
Intuitive Order 404
Getting Started 405
Ending the Paper 408
Assignments 409

III Principles of Style: A Guide

24 THE LIMITS OF LANGUAGE 413

Language Is Removed from Reality 413
Words Are Generalizations 415
Language Is Subjective 416
Denotation and Connotation 418
Extending the Limits 419
Using Language to Deceive 421
Developing Semantic Sophistication 421
Writing Versus Speech 422
Assignments 424

25 CHOOSING WORDS 427

The Natural Word 428
The Concrete Word 430
The Right Word 430
Clichés 433
Figures of Speech 434
Assignments 437

26 IMPROVING SENTENCES 439

The Writer's "Style" 439
Working Toward Unity 440
Working Toward Coherence 443
Working Toward Economy 455
Working Toward Emphasis 459
Working Toward Vigor 462

Working Toward Rhythm 464
Punctuation Chart 474
Assignments 474

27 WRITING PARAGRAPHS 478

The Paragraph as a Cage of Form 478
Paragraph Divisions 479
Paragraph Unity 483
Developing the Paragraph 485
Achieving Coherence 497
Assignments 509

TOPIC INDEX 517
SELECTIONS INDEX 525

INTRODUCTION

WRITING AS A HUMAN ACTIVITY

And how is clarity to be acquired? Mainly by taking trouble; and by writing to serve people rather than to impress them.[1]

F. L. Lucas

It is only when we view writing in its broadest perspective—as an instrument through which men communicate with one another in time and space, transmitting their accumulated culture from one generation to another—that we can see how vitally related our written language is not only to the life of the individual but to the total life of the community: "Greece and Rome civilized by language," Ezra Pound tells us. "Rome rose with the idiom of Caesar, Ovid, and Tacitus, she declined in a welter of rhetoric, the diplomat's 'language to conceal thought'!"

Pound uses the term "rhetoric" in the pejorative sense to mean tricks that are designed to deceive and confuse the reader or listener. But the classical meaning of "rhetoric"—and the meaning insisted on by modern rhetoricians—is the art of using language to its best possible effect: to teach, to delight, to win assent, to "energize" the truth, to move an audience to action—not ill-chosen or precipitous action, but considered and significant action. This ancient and modern view is best expressed in Kenneth Burke's deeply moral definition of rhetoric as "the use of language to promote social cooperation in the human jungle." Thus the modern rhetorician—dedicated to the effective and forceful use of language—shuns verbal trickery, sophistry, and all forms of sensationalism and harangue, leaving these to the demagogue, the

[1] From *Style*, by F. L. Lucas. Copyright © 1962, 1955 by F. L. Lucas. Reprinted by permission of The Macmillan Company and Cassell & Co. Ltd.

professional agitator, the propagandist, and the supersalesman. The rest of us—particularly those of us in a college community where our special task is to search out truth—are also expected to make our major appeal to reason rather than emotion: to inform and explain by indicating precisely *how* and *why;* to organize material in logical patterns; to argue by carefully reasoned, consistent procedures; to support, illustrate, demonstrate, amplify, and wherever possible *prove* our points; to express ourselves clearly and accurately. These are the touchstones of responsible writing.

It is imperative, then, that we write clearly, cogently, compellingly; that we build bridges to one another with our written discourse; that we use it to unite and not divide us. Although, thanks to twentieth-century technology, we may be said to live in a global village where electronic media connect us with the most remote areas of the world, we are still tied to the written word as the basic means of human communication and interaction. On a personal and political level we still write *to* and *for* each other, as evidenced by the increasing number of newspapers, magazines, and books that pour off the press. And we are still tied to written communication for conducting the business of the world: the machine makers and button pushers follow written instructions; radio and television programs originate in written proposals, recommendations, and scripts; diplomats negotiate—endlessly—by means of formal correspondence (witness the huge collections of presidential materials now being assembled in the Truman, Eisenhower, Kennedy, and Johnson libraries). Supplemented by film, tape, and record, the written document still provides the copious details that constitute the archives of our civilization.

Developing the Ability to Write

There is no question, then, that the ability to write clearly, cogently, and persuasively is a basic need in our time—a need that, unfortunately, goes largely unfulfilled. For the fact is that most people write poorly—and with great reluctance. (Since they *know* their deficiency, they are understandably unwilling to exhibit it!) As one student complained, pointing first to his head and then to the paper in front of him, "It's all up here; I just can't get it down there." Although he thought this was *his* unique problem, this student was actually voicing everyone's problem. For writing is the act of transmitting thoughts, feelings, and ideas from "up here" in the head to "down there" on paper. Putting "black on white," as one author described his work, is very exacting and—when it is done well—very exciting work that requires many composite skills: (1) *mental*—the writer must be able to think clearly and organize his ideas in an orderly, logical sequence; (2) *psychological*—the writer must feel free and sufficiently relaxed so that ideas will in fact move from head to hand, so that they will not "block" or elude the cast of words; (3) *rhetorical*—the writer must know the fundamentals of the craft: the variety of ways sentences can be put together to make a smoothly flowing, readable composition; (4) *critical*—once he has written something, the writer must be able to judge it, to know whether it is good or bad, and if it is bad, to improve it.

A student often admits that he realizes a paper is poor when he turns it in, but he cannot improve it. He does not know *specifically* what is weak, *specifically* how it can be strengthened. Unless we can evaluate our writing in a concrete and constructive way, unless we learn to be patient and painstaking almost to the limits of endurance, we cannot hope to reach a level of excellence, or even competence. Professional writers who recognize that "hard writing makes easy reading," resign themselves to drudgery: "I can't write five words but that I change seven," complained Dorothy Parker. "There is no good writing, only re-writing," said James Thurber, always witty, urbane, and unbelievably facile (or so it seemed). Surely writing was second nature to him! Quite the opposite, as Thurber himself has said:

> The first or second draft of everything I write reads as if it was turned out by a charwoman. . . . For me it's mostly a question of rewriting. . . . A story I've been working on—"The Train on Track Six,". . . was rewritten fifteen complete times. . . . It's part of a constant attempt on my part to make the finished version smooth, to make it seem effortless.

To make the finished version seem effortless: this is the mark of a supremely good style. It is *unobtrusively* good; it does not call attention to itself. In fact the reader is barely aware of *how* the writer has written; he is aware only of *what* he has written; the subject matter alone stands out, not the writing. The writing flows smoothly, like a river moving with the current—inevitably onward.

Many people who write are simply not aware of what is involved in the writing process: the thinking, planning, assembling, classifying, organizing —in short, the prewriting that is prerequisite to a clear presentation (not to mention the rewriting that comes later). Others realize what is required but stubbornly refuse to take necessary pains. Their writing is obscure and hard to read because they will not submit to the demands of the discipline. Unfortunately, we are sometimes forced to read the work of such authors (they surround us, alas; sometimes they even write textbooks). Reading them means rereading and rereading, for their prose is like an obstacle course through which we wind a weary and uncertain way—as in the following passage from P. A. Sorokin's *Society, Culture, and Personality.*

> In conformity with the preceding point, if all the interacting parties in marriage, in minority-majority groups, in different occupational, religious, political, economic, racial, ethnic, and other interacting groups and persons view the given overtly similar (or dissimilar) traits: A,B,C,D,N (physical, biological, mental, socio-cultural) as negligible values or as no values at all, as comprising even no similarity (or dissimilarity), such overt similarities-dissimilarities are innocuous in the generation of either solidarity or antagonism.[2]

Whenever possible, of course, the sensible reader refuses to read such gibberish, just as the sensible person refuses to visit a doctor who is careless or a lawyer who is incompetent. Clearly, the writer of the above sentence-paragraph is both careless *and* incompetent. To begin with, his thoughts are addled (we wonder, "Does *he* know what he is talking about?"). One phrase

[2] Albert Kitzhaber, *Themes, Theories, and Therapy* (New York: McGraw-Hill, 1963), p. 129.

tumbles out after another in no discernible order; parentheses constantly interrupt the flow of thought; the endless listing of abstract words, curiously hyphenated words, jargon, and unnecessary coding (A,B,C, etc.) makes the head spin. It is impossible to follow or even *guess* at the writer's meaning.

Admittedly you cannot hope that a basic writing course—or even a four-year college education—will make you a first-rate writer, a master of the craft. But you can hope and expect that you will gain important insights into the art of writing, that you will learn how to analyze a page of prose, to see how it works: why it succeeds as a unit of communication or why it projects only a hazy and possibly distorted notion of the intended meaning. Most important you will gain greater control of your own writing; you will learn to write better and still better, with greater fluency and flexibility.

The Qualities of Good Writing

Even before you set out, you come prepared by instinct and intuition to make certain judgments about what is "good." Take the following familiar sentence for example: "I know not what course others may take, but as for me, give me liberty or give me death." Do you suppose this thought of Patrick Henry's would have come ringing down through the centuries if he had expressed this sentiment not in one tight, rhythmical sentence but as follows:

> It would be difficult, if not impossible, to predict on the basis of my limited information as to the predilections of the public, what the citizenry at large will regard as action commensurate with the present provocation, but after arduous consideration I personally feel so intensely and irrevocably committed to the position of social, political, and economic independence, that rather than submit to foreign and despotic control which is anathema to me, I will make the ultimate sacrifice of which man is capable—under the aegis of personal honor, ideological conviction, and existential commitment, I will sacrifice my own mortal existence.

How does this rambling, "high-flown" paraphrase measure up to the bold "Give me liberty or give me death"? Who will deny that something is "happening" in Patrick Henry's rousing challenge that not only fails to happen in the paraphrase but is actually negated there? Would you bear with this long-winded, pompous speaker to the end? If you were to judge his statement strictly on its rhetoric (its choice and arrangement of words), you might aptly call it more boring than brave. Perhaps a plainer version will work better. Let us consider this one:

> Liberty is a very important thing for a man to have. Most people—at least the people I've talked to or that other people have told me about—know this and therefore are very anxious to preserve their liberty. Of course I can't be absolutely sure about what other folks are going to do in this present crisis, what with all these threats and everything, but I've made up my mind that I'm going to fight because liberty is really a very important thing to me; at least that's the way I feel about it.

This flat, "homely" prose, weighted down with what Flaubert called "fatty deposits," is grammatical enough. As in the pompous paraphrase, every verb agrees with its subject, every comma is in its proper place; nonetheless it lacks the qualities that make a statement—of one sentence or one hundred pages—pungent, vital, moving, memorable.

Let us isolate these qualities and describe them briefly. (They will be described in greater detail in Part III, Principles of Style: A Guide.) The first is *economy*. In an appropriately slender volume entitled *The Elements of Style*, authors William Strunk and E. B. White state concisely the case for economy: "A sentence should contain no unnecessary words, a paragraph no unnecessary sentences, for the same reason that a drawing should have no unnecessary lines and a machine no unnecessary parts. This requires not that the writer make all his sentences short or that he avoid all detail . . . but that every word tell." In other words, economical writing is *efficient* and *aesthetically satisfying*. While it makes a minimum demand on the energy and patience of the reader, it returns to him a maximum of sharply compressed meaning. The writer should accept this as his basic responsibility: that he inflict no unnecessary words on the reader—just as a dentist inflicts no unnecessary pain, a lawyer no unnecessary risk. Economical writing avoids strain and at the same time promotes pleasure by producing a sense of form and right proportion, a sense of words that fit the ideas that they embody—with not a line of "deadwood" to dull the reader's attention, not an extra, useless phrase to clog the free flow of ideas, one following swiftly and clearly upon another.

Another basic quality of good writing is *simplicity*. Here again this does not require that the writer make all his sentences primerlike or that he reduce complexities to bare bone, but rather that he avoid embellishment or embroidery. "All affectation is bad," said Cervantes, and most writers agree. The natural, unpretentious style is best. But, paradoxically, simplicity or naturalness does not come naturally. By the time a person is old enough to write, he has usually grown so self-conscious that he stiffens, sometimes to the point of rigidity, when he is called upon to make a statement—in speech or in writing. It is easy to offer the kindly advice "be yourself," but many people do not feel like themselves when they take a pencil in hand or sit down at a typewriter. Thus during the early days of the Second World War when air raids were feared in New York City and "black-outs" instituted, an anonymous writer—probably a young civil service worker at City Hall—produced and distributed to stores throughout the city the following poster:

Illumination
is Required
to be
Extinguished
on These Premises
after Nightfall

What he meant, of course, was simply "Lights Out After Dark"; but apparently that direct imperative—clear and to the point—did not sound "official" enough. And so, under a common misapprehension, the writer resorted to long Latinate words and involved syntax (note the awkward passives "*is* Required" and "*to be* Extinguished") to establish a tone of dignity and authority. In contrast, how beautifully simple are the words of the translators of the King James Version of the Bible, who felt no need for flourish, flamboyance, or grandiloquence. The Lord did not loftily or bombastically proclaim that universal illumination was required to be instantaneously installed. Simply but majestically "God said, Let there be light: and there was light. . . . And God called the light Day, and the darkness he called Night."

In this same tradition most memorable declarations have been spare and direct. Abraham Lincoln and John Kennedy seem to "speak to each other across the span of a century," notes French author André Maurois, for both men embodied noble themes in eloquently simple terms. Said Lincoln in his second Inaugural Address: "With malice towards none, with charity for all, with firmness in the right as God gives us the right, let us strive on to finish the work we are in . . ." One hundred years later President Kennedy made his Inaugural dedication: "With a good conscience our only sure reward, with history the final judge of our deeds, let us go forth to lead the land we love. . . ."

The third fundamental element of good writing is *clarity*—a basic commandment of every responsible writer. Some people question whether it is always possible to be clear; after all, certain ideas are inherently complicated and inescapably difficult. True enough. But the responsible writer recognizes that his writing should not add to the complications nor increase the difficulty; his writing should not set up an additional roadblock to understanding. Indeed, the German philosopher Wittgenstein goes so far as to say that "whatever can be said can be said clearly." If a writer understands his own idea and wants to convey it to others, he is obliged to render it in clear, orderly, readable, understandable prose—else why bother writing in the first place? Actually the writer who is obscure is usually confused himself; uncertain of what he wants to say or what he means, he has not yet completed that process of thinking through and reasoning into the heart of his subject. He is still working toward his thesis; he has not yet discovered it.

Suffice it to say here that whatever the topic, whatever the occasion, expository writing should be readable, informative, and, wherever possible, engaging. At its best it may even be poetic, as Nikos Kazantzakis suggests in *Zorba the Greek*, where he draws an analogy between good prose and a beautiful landscape:

> To my mind the Cretan countryside resembled good prose, carefully ordered, sober, free from superfluous ornament, powerful and restrained. It expressed all that was necessary with the greatest economy. It had no flippancy nor artifice about it. It said what it had to say with a manly austerity. But between the severe lines one could discern an unexpected sensitiveness and tenderness; in the sheltered hollows the lemon and orange trees perfumed the air, and from the vastness of the sea emanated an inexhaustible poetry.

Even in technical fields where the range of styles is necessarily limited (and poetry is neither possible nor appropriate), the writer must always be aware of "the reader over his shoulder." Take such topics as how to follow postal regulations for overseas mail, how to change oil in an engine, how to produce aspirin from salicylic acid. Here are technical expository descriptions that defy a memorable turn of phrase; here is writing that is of necessity cut-and-dried, dispassionate, and bloodless. But it need not be difficult, tedious, confusing, or dull to those who want to find out about mailing letters, changing oil, or making aspirin. Those who seek such information should have reasonably easy access to it, which means that written instructions should be clear, simple, spare, direct, and most of all, *human:* for no matter how technical a subject, all writing is done *for* human beings *by* human beings. Writing in other words, like language itself, is a strictly human enterprise. Machines may stamp letters, measure oil, and convert acids, but only human beings talk and write *about* these procedures so that other human beings may better understand them. It is always appropriate, therefore, to be human in one's statement.

Rhetorical Stance

Part of this humanity must stem from the writer's sense of who his readers are. He must assume a "rhetorical stance." Indeed this is a fundamental principle of rhetoric: *nothing should ever be written in a vacuum.* The writer should identify his audience, hypothetical or real, so that he may speak to them in an appropriate voice. A student, for example, should never "just write," without visualizing a definite group of readers—his fellow students, perhaps, or the educated community at large (intelligent nonspecialists). Without these definite readers in mind, the writer cannot assume a suitable and appropriate relationship to his material, his purpose, and his audience. A proper rhetorical stance, in other words, requires that the writer have an active sense of:

1. Who he is as a writer.
2. Who his readers are.
3. Why he is addressing them and on what occasion.
4. His relationship to his subject matter.
5. How he wants his readers to relate to the subject matter.

"Courtship" Devices

In addition to establishing a rhetorical stance, the writer should draw upon those personal and aesthetic effects that will enhance a statement without distorting it and that will "delight" the reader, or at least sustain his attention. "One's case," said Aristotle, "should, in justice, be fought on the strength of the facts alone." This would be ideal: mind speaking to mind. The truth is, however, that man cannot be appealed to solely on rational grounds, or, to quote Aristotle again in a more cynical mood, "External matters do count much, because of the sorry nature of an audience." Facing the realities, then, the writer tries to "woo" the reader through a kind of "courtship," to use another of Kenneth Burke's expressions. In other words, he tries to break down the natural barriers and fears that separate people, whether their encounter is face-to-face or on the printed page.

What the writer must do is personalize his relationship with the reader by using those rhetorical devices that will enable him to emerge from the page as a fellow human being, with a distinctive voice and, in a broad sense, a personality. Somehow the occasion on which writer and reader come together must be recognized as a special occasion, marked by a special purpose and an element of pleasure.

Rhetoric provides a rich storehouse of "courting" devices, and we shall consider these in Part III. For example, the pleasant rhythm of a balanced antithesis is evident in President Kennedy's immortal statement, "Ask not what your country can do for you; ask what you can do for your country." The lilting suspense of a periodic sentence (one that suspends its predication until the end), appears in Edward Gibbon's delightful account of how he came to write the famous *Decline and Fall of the Roman Empire:*

> It was at Rome, on the 15th of October 1764, as I sat musing amidst the ruins of the Capitol, while the barefooted friars were singing vespers in the temple of Jupiter, that the idea of writing the decline and fall of the city first started to my mind.

Modern scholar Simeon Potter has observed that the word-picture drawn by Gibbon, although brief, is "artistically perfect":

> The rhythm is stately and entirely satisfying. The reader is held in suspense to the end.
>
> Had he wished, and had he been less of an artist, Gibbon might have said exactly the same things in a different way, arranging them in their logical and grammatical order: "The idea of writing the decline and fall of the city first started to my mind as I sat musing amidst the ruins of the Capitol at Rome on the 15th of October 1764, while the barefooted friars were singing vespers in the temple of Jupiter." What has happened? It is not merely that a periodic sentence has been reexpressed as a loose one. The emphasis is now all wrong and the magnificent cadence of the original is quite marred. All is still grammatically correct, but "proper words" are no longer in "proper places." The passage has quite lost its harmonious rhythm.

In addition to economy, simplicity, and clarity, then—the foundations of sound, dependable rhetoric—there is this marvelous dimension of "harmonious rhythm," of proper words in proper places. The writer who is sensitive to these "strategies" will delight as well as inform his reader, and in delighting reinforce his statement.

The Student Writer

As Erich Fromm has said of the child, "He must grow until finally he becomes his own father," so we can say of the student writer: he must grow until he becomes his own teacher, his own critic, his own editor. Slowly he will cultivate a sensitivity to good, clear, unpretentious prose; at the same time, he will develop a negative sensitivity—an intolerance—to prose that is awkward, pompous, jargon-ridden, diffuse, dull. He will, in other words, be able to view a passage of prose, his own or someone else's, with a keen, critical eye, capable of seeing what has gone into it and of judging what has emerged as a finished piece.

Most important, the student who reaches maturity as a writer will know how to go about the job of writing, no matter what his assignment. He will not feel overwhelmed or intimidated by his material any more than the carpenter is overwhelmed or intimidated by the unworked wood from which he must construct a desk or a bookcase. In much the same way the properly trained student-writer acts on his raw material and shapes it in accordance with his will and plan. He knows what he wants to say, even as a carpenter knows before he has taken his saw in hand what his final product is to be; he organizes his ideas in a logical, orderly sequence, even as a carpenter assembles his tools and maps out the steps by which he will convert raw wood into smooth, polished furniture.

Always in control of what he is doing, the writer—like the craftsman and the artist—experiences a sense of creativity. For, in truth, he *is* creating. Indeed, the term "creative writing" should not be limited, as it often is, to fiction alone, i.e., poetry, short stories, novels. *All* writing is creative when the writer forges out of his raw material (poetic images, anecdotes, statistics, a set of facts) a new whole: a poem, an expository article, an essay, a term paper. Any writer who understands language as a medium of expression and uses it in a deliberate and disciplined way to shape his purposes, factual or fictional, and to address an audience of his choice, is working creatively and thereby producing creative writing. All writing assignments, then, expository or otherwise, should be approached as a creative challenge; the writer is being called upon to create out of isolated separate elements (facts, feelings, memories, ideas, and so on) a new whole which will be, like John Stuart Mill's chemical compound, "more than the sum of its parts."

ASSIGNMENTS

I. As a reader, respond to the following passages, indicating whether you think they are well written or poorly written and why.

The data, in general, suggest that neither similarity nor complementarity of needs appears to be particularly meaningful in the determination of adolescent friendships beyond the suggested importance of similarity in a case where an extreme difference in friendship choices exists. However, both of these need patterns are internally consistent phenomena and perhaps are related to other factors. Similarities in perceptual and cognitive phenomena appear to be promising leads for future research in this area.

—Cited in Albert Kitzhaber, *Themes, Theories, and Therapy*
(drawn from a doctor's dissertation in education)

I want to oppose the idea that the school has to teach directly that special knowledge and those accomplishments which one has to use later directly in life. The demands of life are much too manifold to let such a specialized training in school appear possible. Apart from that, it seems to me, moreover, objectionable to treat the individual like a dead tool. The school should always have as its aim that the young man leave it as a harmonious personality, not as a specialist. This in my opinion is true in a certain sense even for technical schools, whose students will devote themselves to a quite definite profession. The development of general ability for independent thinking and judgment should always be placed foremost, not the acquisition of special knowledge. If a person masters the fundamentals of his subject and has learned to think and work independently, he will surely find his way and besides will better be able to adapt himself to progress and changes than the person whose training principally consists in the acquiring of detailed knowledge.[3]

Becoming a doctor is by no means a recent notion, it is a goal which has lingered with me since high school. I am not interested in going into a field of research or teaching, although I am quite aware that without these professions, medicine would not have progressed much from Hippocrates' time. My purpose for obtaining a M.D. is to go into the practice of medicine. To treat patients with the best equipment at my disposal and to establish a personal patient-physician relationship. To me being a doctor is not a five day a week job, one's work is not completed after office hours. A good doctor will be available when he is needed. I want to become a doctor so I can instill a feeling of security and trust in my patients and to convey to them that a doctor can be more than just one who prescribes medication. He can be someone to trust and turn to in times of crisis—a healer in the broadest sense of the word.

A doctor holds an admirable position in today's society and being a physician offers security for the future. There is no worry about having a job for next year or that a bad winter will cause financial difficulties. I am certainly looking forward to having a family some day and expect to send my children through school. As a doctor I would be assured the ability to send my children through school and establish a happy life for my family.

—Student application to medical school

I suspect that we have a good deal to learn from the 18th-century travelers. First, they saw that their books were printed with dignity, with fine type and wide margins on paper that had some texture to it. Second, they took with them an attitude of mind that delighted in the extravagance and eccentricities of the people they met on their journeys; they were far from being moralists. Third, they had a fine feeling for monuments, by which they meant palaces and castles, towers, churches and gateways, and all carved stonework and woodwork wherever it met the eye. Finally, they were in no hurry.

—Robert Payne, "Florence Was Exciting, Venice Overrated,"
The New York Times Book Review, June 5, 1966, p. 3

It is a miracle that New York works at all. The whole thing is implausible. Every time the residents brush their teeth, millions of gallons of water must be drawn from the Catskills and the hills of Westchester. When a young man in Manhattan writes a letter to his girl in Brooklyn, the love message gets blown to her through a pneumatic tube—pfft—just like that. The subterranean system of telephone cable, power lines, steam pipes, gas mains and sewer pipes is reason enough to abandon the island to the gods and the weevils. Every time an incision is made in the pavement, the noisy surgeons expose ganglia that are tangled beyond belief. By rights, New York should have destroyed itself long ago, from panic or fire or rioting or failure of some

[3] From *Out of My Later Years,* by Albert Einstein. Reprinted by permission of the Estate of Albert Einstein.

vital supply line in its circulatory system or from some deep labyrinthine short circuit. Long ago the city should have experienced an insoluble traffic snarl at some impossible bottleneck. It should have perished of hunger when food lines failed for a few days. It should have been wiped out by a plague starting in its slums or carried in by ships' rats. It should have been overwhelmed by the sea that licks at it on every side. The workers in its myriad cells should have succumbed to nerves, from the fearful pall of smoke-fog that drifts over every few days from Jersey, blotting out all light at noon and leaving the high offices suspended, men groping and depressed, and the sense of world's end. It should have been touched in the head by the August heat and gone off its rocker.

—E. B. White, *Here Is New York*

In effect, it was hypothesized that certain physical data categories including housing types and densities, land use characteristics, and ecological location constitute a scalable content area. This could be called a continuum of residential desirability. Likewise, it was hypothesized that several social data categories, describing the same census tracts, and referring generally to the social stratification system of the city, would also be scalable. This scale could be called a continuum of socio-economic status. Thirdly, it was hypothesized that there would be a high positive correlation between the scale types on each continuum.

II. Read the following paragraph and answer the question posed below. Indicate what you think of the quality of the writing.

Of the two types of crime, namely crime as deviant behavior and crime as learned behavior, the theory of deviant behavior is implicit or explicit in most predictive studies. Also, personality differences which are ignored or considered unimportant in the cultural approach to crime are considered relevant in most prediction instruments, whether devised by clinicians or by sociologists. For example, studies have emphasized that delinquent recidivism is the result of failure of personal and/or social controls, whether in the family or in the local community. But from a learning viewpoint of delinquency the emphasis would have been upon accessibility to delinquent associates and upon the continued influence by delinquents as against conventional persons.

According to this paragraph, studies in the prediction of crimes emphasize ____________________. Fill in the correct letter, choosing from the following answers:

A. Complete reliance on measurable community factors in terms of continued relations with delinquent or criminal types.
B. Deviations from conventional behavior as key clues in prediction.
C. Personality factors as more significant than cultural factors.
D. Primarily the direct linkages between learned behavior and crime incidents.
E. The relationships between persons outside the home rather than inside the family.

—From the New York City Civil Service Exam for promotion of police lieutenants to captaincy

FINDING A SUBJECT

It is not true—as is commonly supposed—that the professional writer is someone who has something vital and compelling to say that drives him to the typewriter so that he may say it and be *done* until another idea comes along to drive him to the typewriter again and still again when a third idea crops up, and so on and on. More often, the writer is someone who has chosen to write because he finds writing to be a delight, a disease, or a bit of both. But once having made this decision, he is not perennially brimming over with things to write *about.*

Like the rest of us, the writer who does not (like the reporter) work on a given assignment, is periodically faced with a blank page and an equally blank mind. From the "booming buzzing confusion" of the world around him he must somehow locate and lay claim to one particular self-contained topic. He must, as Cicero said, "hit upon what to say." Once he has done this he can go on to "manage and marshal" his materials and finally "to array them in the adornments of style" (to continue quoting Cicero). But first—there is no getting around this—*first he must hit upon what to say.* It is an obvious first step, and yet until recently, with the revival of rhetoric, it was virtually ignored as an integral part of the composition process. The assumption seemed to be that the getting of an idea was the writer's own private problem. Seek and you shall find. Somehow.

There is some truth to this, of course; getting an idea is, to be sure, a private, inward process; and if you wish to find, you certainly should seek. But *how* to seek? *Where* to find? It is not easy, because in the beginning you don't even know exactly *what* you are seeking—just a good idea. "I wasted the entire week trying to decide what to write about," said a discouraged freshman. True enough: he spent hours at his desk staring into space in morose silence, lamenting his fate, moaning, groaning, and chewing erasers off pencils (a pleasantly self-pitying approach, but not especially productive). He submitted the finished paper disconsolately; it was written between midnight and 4 A.M. and proofread on the way to class. He knew it was not very good, but at least it was *done.* How he hates to write! If only he could think of things to write about. . . .

This student should be introduced to what the ancients called the art of invention—finding something to write about. He should be made to see that this first step in the composition process—hitting upon what to say—is indeed an art in itself that must be consciously and conscientiously cultivated. Briefly, it may be described as knowing how to "invent" or "discover" (the ancients used both terms) the subject of a discourse by putting oneself in the way of stimulation, the kind of stimulation that will actively "generate" ideas in your mind and thereby produce a specific topic and things to say about the topic.

These are the two main aspects of the art of invention: finding a subject and developing it. Like every other stage of the composition process, this first stage of finding something to write about can be dealt with actively and systematically. Even more important, it can and must be dealt with *creatively,* for finding an idea and preparing to mold it into a new and original whole is a distinctly creative process.

The aim of this section, then, is to explain how to go about the creative process of invention with appropriate creative energy and purpose. To help accomplish this aim we shall draw upon basic principles of rhetoric,[1] and concern ourselves with common-sense techniques like trying to find an idea by *looking* for it and by using simple, easily accessible guides such as the dictionary, which—called into service in this behalf—is a rich source of ideas.

Checklist of Subjects

Here, then, are twenty subjects chosen from the most familiar and available of all reference works—the dictionary. (An encyclopedia, reader's guide, or any alphabetically arranged subject index will do as well.) The procedure is simple: thumb through the pages starting with *A* and move on through the alphabet, jotting down whatever terms catch your eye and your interest—whatever you *respond* to. You can be certain that an unconscious as well as a conscious process of selection is at work here, guiding you to one or another term that appeals to you and that will therefore provide a good starting point for the invention process.

1 In Chapter 22, "Gathering Information," we shall deal with methods of probing the mind to gather information for an essay using the insights of depth psychology, for it is from the psychologist rather than the rhetorician that we can learn how to reach into the "inner psyche" and thereby activate a stubborn memory or stimulate a seemingly empty mind. In this process we must learn how to probe our own ideas and feelings; how to concentrate deeply; how to be receptive to images that are "not thought out but beheld." (Wolfgang Pauli, cited in Ira Progoff, *Depth Psychology and Modern Man* [New York: The Julian Press, Inc., 1959], p. 236.)

1. American Indian	11. Nature
2. Assassination	12. Patriotism
3. Books	13. Poetry
4. Creativity	14. Poverty
5. Education	15. Prejudice
6. Family	16. Propaganda
7. Holocaust	17. Science
8. Intellectual	18. Symbol
9. Language	19. Women
10. Literature	20. Writing

Limiting the Subject

Let us begin with the first item on the subject list—American Indian. Surely we cannot approach this subject as such, for it is as vast and formless as the Great Plains the Indians themselves once inhabited. Where should we begin? How could we hope to cover the territory of the American Indian in less than a volume—or several volumes? Clearly, the only sensible procedure is to *limit the subject,* to concentrate on one or another of its many aspects. For instance, we could consider one particular tribe in one particular place (Navajos of New Mexico). We could limit the subject still further (Navajos living in New Mexico *at the present time*). The subject is now more manageable in scope, more amenable to essay form, although it is still not sharply focused in terms of what we will say *about* the Navahos living in New Mexico at the present time. This will come later (as we shall see) when we address a specific question to the limited topic; then and only then will we arrive at the *real* topic—the thesis, the "so-what?"—the *point of the piece.*

Let us move on to the third item on the subject list—Books. Here again you cannot reasonably expect to write a short coherent piece about books in general. Why not reduce the subject numerically, then, to *one particular* book. E. M. Forster once wrote a delightful and engaging essay on "A Book That Influenced Me"; similarly, William Golding has written nostalgically and vividly of his response to one childhood favorite, *The Swiss Family Robinson* (pp. 243–44).

We are not concerned at this point with the actual finding of a real topic, but rather with the preliminary process of narrowing down a subject area to some aspect of itself so that it is feasible and encompassable in a single essay of approximately 500 to 750 words (the average weekly paper in a college writing course). This conscious and deliberate narrowing-down process is an imperative first step in invention; for without it we are likely to wander over a too-large and amorphous field, to never get our bearings. Only if we resist such overwhelming subjects as "Science" and contemplate instead a limited subject such as three specific characteristics of the scientific spirit (Robert Millikan, "The Spirit of Modern Science," pp. 62–64) can we achieve a unified and coherent unit of discourse.

To summarize: in selecting a topic for a paper, we should try to view it in terms of such limiting factors as the following:

1. a specific *kind*	not art in general, but pop art
2. a specific *time*	not art in all periods, but the last decade of twentieth-century art
3. a specific *place*	not universal art but art in America
4. a specific *number*	not all pop artists, but representative pop artists
5. a specific *person*	Roy Lichtenstein, a well-known pop art pioneer
6. a specific *type*	not all kinds of pop art, but serigraphs (silk screen prints)
7. a specific *aspect*	not art as a whole, but art as communication
8. a specific *example*	not pop art, but Andy Warhol's "Marilyn Monroe"
9. a specific *experience*	the first time you saw a pop art exhibit at the Museum of Modern Art

It should be admitted here that there are times when the normal processes of invention are telescoped, as if by miracle, into a sudden flash of inspiration (ah, *this* is what I want to say!), followed by a few blissful hours of pouring forth what you do in fact—and in the innermost recesses of your mind and heart—*want to say at a particular moment.* It is an exhilarating experience, this "having of inspiration," but we cannot *depend* on it. We must proceed by plan and regular procedure—as the ancients did and as writers have done throughout the many centuries when rhetoric was taught as a formal discipline.

The Classical Topics

Having found and limited our subject, we must now go on to the second stage of invention—finding something to say about our subject, developing it. Let us turn to the ancients, for, although they were concerned largely with writing speeches to be delivered in public, they recognized the full sweep of the composition process: that it begins in the mind and the way the mind looks *out* upon its subject matter and *in* upon itself. Thus the orator was encouraged to read widely and to study conscientiously in order to "stock" his mind with subject matter. Cicero specified that the ideal orator was a man of vast learning and liberal education. In addition, he was trained in techniques to set his mind in motion, to entreat thinking, to stir memory, to coax imagination. Through these concrete procedures he was spared the torments of the blank page, the frustration of just sitting back and waiting for a topic to present itself. Aristotle went so far as to codify the invention procedure by reducing all possible topics to four categories:

1. what is possible or impossible
2. what happened or did not happen
3. what will happen
4. questions of degree (greatness or smallness)

Aristotle's list may seem absurdly oversimplified, but notice that on any subject these four categories are excellent places to begin thinking about what a writer might want to say (thus the ancient designation "topoi": a place or region of thinking where an argument might be located and developed). Take an example of "topoi"—or, as we now say, topic—#1 (what is possible or impossible): "By mining the resources of the sea, we can derive more than sufficient foodstuff to feed the hungry peoples of the world." The writer is asserting that something is possible—a familiar type of proposition. Topic #2 (what happened) also provides a familiar proposition: "The Treaty of Versailles laid the groundwork for the Second World War. Either this *did* or *did not* happen; the writer who asserts either position must prepare an argument. Topic #3 (what will happen) characterizes all prophetic writing, from the simple weather forecast to full-scale analyses of future developments in any sphere: why candidate X will win the election, why urban areas are heading for decentralization. The possibilities are endless. Finally there is topic #4 (questions of degree): "Human organ transplants are too widely and sensationally publicized, thereby creating a circuslike atmosphere around a serious new medical specialty." The proposition stands as an argument for *less* of something and, by implication, *more* of something else—privacy, dignity.

Aristotle's four basic categories plus certain other modes of analysis recognized among the ancients—cause-effect (X causes Y); similarity (X is like Y); dissimilarity (X is unlike Y); example (X illustrates Y); consequence (X is a result of Y)—provided a kind of checklist of mental acts the orator could perform when investigating and collecting arguments on a subject. Having this checklist available, the classical orator was never at a loss, never driven to passive despair; on the contrary, he always had before him the prescribed "discovery procedures" that he could calmly and confidently follow, secure in the knowledge that by doing so he would locate his argument and line up his proofs.

The New "Heuristic"

Wisely, then, the ancients refused to leave the matter of invention to chance and haphazard improvisation. They insisted on a formal "heuristic," that is, a systematic inquiry into a subject matter—and into one's mind as well—in order to discover the best possibilities for discourse. Modern rhetoricians are evolving a comparable heuristic, rooted in the classical system but strongly influenced by new concepts drawn from modern science, especially linguistic theory. We shall not describe this new heuristic here but simply incorporate some of its more helpful features into a heuristic of our own—a method suited to our needs in this text.

Asking the Right Questions

Actually the substance of our approach can be summed up in a single phrase: asking the right questions. By using the question as a probing instrument—turned inward to the mind (a repository of dormant ideas) and outward to the subject matter (a source of data and information)—we are able to make discoveries, ultimately to "generate" a sharply focused idea. In every case, as we shall see, *it is the question, posed and answered, that is at the heart of any single piece of discourse.* For what else does the writer do but ask questions and then answer them?

He may be telling a newspaper reader who robbed whose house and what was stolen; he may be explaining in a magazine advertisement why Brand X cosmetic cream will prevent "crow's feet" around the eyes; he may be describing in a long controversial book the death of a president or the reasons for violence in American cities; he may be analyzing the lost generation of the 1920s or simply telling its story in novel or play form; he may be revealing secret military alliances in the Middle East or rhapsodizing over the song of a skylark. Whatever his subject, whatever the temper and tone of the piece, the writer is forever answering questions. "And a writer cannot answer a question," as one journalist points out, "unless he has first asked it." [2] Nor can he achieve a sharp focus or a unified thrust in a piece of writing unless he is aware of exactly what question or questions he is posing, making certain he holds firmly throughout to a steady line of development, so that the finished piece answers precisely that single question or those several questions he has posed.

Like the journalist, then, applying to all events his perennial "who-what-when-where-why?" the writer must always be prepared with the right set of questions if he expects to find his way into a topic, to stimulate his thinking, to stake out his special area of interest, and to glean enough information about it to make a new whole—a unified piece of writing that is distinctly his own.

What are the right questions specifically? We shall consider them in a moment and elaborate on the many ways they may "generate" and focus a piece of discourse. But first it will be well to caution against viewing a modern set of topoi with the same complacency Aristotle felt toward the "commonplaces," i.e., the common places where one might go in order to invent an argument. For the seeming completeness of Aristotle's survey of topics was, as we now know, largely illusory. There is no fixed number of topics nor of topic categories; the number is endless. Discourse is a process; one idea generates another in ongoing, open-ended progression.

Checklist of Twenty Questions

In this cycle of question-generating-idea, idea-generating-question, then further questions generating further ideas, and so on and on, the following

[2] Norman Lobsenze, *Writing as a Career* (New York: Henry Z. Walck, Inc., 1963), p. 15.

twenty basic questions have been compiled. Although they have been stripped of all concrete subject reference, you should not be put off by their faceless aspect: "X" is used in order to keep the discussion on an abstract level. For these twenty questions present ways of *observing* or *thinking about* a subject as "thought starters" to set the wheels of invention turning. As such they apply to any subject matter.

Suppose, for example, you have been asked to write a paper on anything that interests you. *Where* will you find a wedge into *what* subject? We have already considered ways of locating and limiting a subject; now let us examine this checklist of questions, each of which can provide the final, focal point of departure for your essay.

1. What does X mean?	Definition
2. How can X be described?	Description
3. What are the component parts of X?	Simple Analysis
4. How is X made or done?	Process Analysis
5. How *should* X be made or done?	Directional Analysis
6. What is the essential function of X?	Functional Analysis
7. What are the causes of X?	Causal Analysis
8. What are the consequences of X?	Causal Analysis
9. What are the types of X?	Classification
10. How does X compare with Y?	Comparison
11. What is the present status of X?	Comparison
12. How can X be interpreted?	Interpretation
13. What are the facts about X?	Reportage
14. How did X happen?	Narration
15. What kind of person is X?	Characterization
16. What is my personal response to X?	Reflection
17. What is my memory of X?	Reminiscence
18. What is the value of X?	Evaluation
19. How can X be summarized?	Summary
20. What case can be made *for* or *against* X?	Argumentation

Before we proceed to put flesh and bone on X by referring to specific subjects, a few important points should be made about the questions themselves. First of all, as you can see, they are not comprehnesive. There are more questions you can ask of a subject than have been indicated here. So be it; even the newest of the new heuristics does not pretend to cover *all* possible approaches. In this case your imagination can fill in any gaps you may encounter. You may, in other words, invent your own questions or frame them somewhat differently if that helps you to focus your idea more precisely.

Furthermore it must be admitted that there is some overlapping within the twenty questions themselves. This is inevitable, as every list compiler ultimately discovers, whether the list contains principles, rules, regulations, or questions. (Even the Ten Commandments overlap to some extent, as do the seven deadly sins.)

Admittedly then, these questions are not meant to be complete but only suggestive of the way the mind regularly and automatically goes about its business of thinking and thereby exploring the universe. Like Aristotle's "commonplaces," these questions represent some of the common places that the mind naturally travels to when it encounters a person, object, event, or idea in the outside world, or an experience, thought, feeling, or sensation within. "What is it?" we wonder. "How does it work?" "Why?" We are forever wondering about things and searching for answers and explanations; this is a natural, ongoing process of the human mind.

Putting Question to Subject-Topic

As we have said, the special job of invention is to start up a specific line of questioning *at a given time* when the mind may not necessarily be ready to perform; when it may be tired or simply lazy; but when there are, nonetheless, demands on it to "think up something to write about." For it is by asking a question that we find a topic and by answering it that we compose our paper. Our paper, in other words, is the reply we make to the question we pose. No question, no paper.

In Part I, the heart of this book, each chapter is concerned with one of the twenty questions posed above. The essays in each illustrate answers to the question. For example, in response to question 1, What does X mean? psychologist Gordon Allport addresses himself to the problem of prejudice (subject #15 on the checklist of subjects). He answers the question in terms of four specific instances (pp. 36–38). Look now at Chapter 2, "How can X be described?" The essay "Moonrise over Monument Valley" (pp. 42–43) is a narrowed-down, sharply focused presentation of the broad subject area "Nature" (subject #11 on the checklist):

Nature:	limited to one type of habitat	the desert
	limited to one country	United States
	limited to one state	Arizona
	limited to one place in one state	Monument Valley
	limited to one time	when the moon rises

To this narrowed-down aspect of his subject area the writer addresses the questions, "What does it look like? How can it be described?" His answer is given in the very striking and evocative description of the moon rising over the "limitless expanse" of the "tawny desert."

It is not necessary at this point to review the many ways in which the writer has *invented* or *located* his topic by addressing a pertinent question to some aspect of a subject area. The table of contents for Part I provides abundant illustrations of how this "heuristic" works. Suffice it to say here that the "heuristic" (indeed, the art of invention itself) is not so much a formal technique as it is plain common sense. But, it is common sense *applied in a deliberate and disciplined manner* to help you fulfill a particular assignment at a particular time and to make you relatively independent of "inspiration"; to show you how to find a topic when you *need* one, not merely when the spirit moves you.

It neither demeans the art of invention nor the question "heuristic" to admit that these are essentially intuitive processes; you have been asking similar questions and inventing topics all your life. The aim of the procedure described here is to help you invent topics "on call," with more precision, originality, and ease. Hopefully you will come to feel toward the heuristic (i.e., the question procedure) something of the confidence and assurance that the classical orators felt toward Aristotle's "commonplaces." Hopefully they will serve you in the same efficient and dependable manner.

ASSIGNMENTS

I. Using a dictionary or any reference work of comparable scope make up a list of twenty subjects that interest you. They may be fields of study, (astronomy, astrology); hobbies (glassblowing, raising guppies); sports (rugby, ice hockey, tennis). Almost any subject area—provided you are interested in it or know something about it—will offer a good starting point for the invention process.

II. Using the list of limiting factors cited on page 17, narrow each of your subjects to one aspect of itself (one specific kind, time, place, experience).

III. Select *five* of your subjects and carry them through progressive stages of limitation (p. 21). Formulate your *real* topic by posing a specific question chosen from the list on page 20 to some aspect of your limited topic.

WRITING A SHORT PAPER

1 WHAT DOES X MEAN?

Cicero said that every discourse should begin with a definition in order to make clear what the subject under consideration *is*. True enough: whether the subject is basically a matter of dispute or merely of discussion, a definition helps to clarify the issues. Definition, then, is important when the discourse depends on a term or terms whose meaning must be understood if the rest of the piece is to make sense, if the writer and reader are to stand on common ground. Thus many essays, articles, and books begin with a statement indicating how the author intends to use a given word, *what he means* by it.

In his introduction to *A History of Western Philosophy*, for example, Bertrand Russell states that since the term "philosophy" is used in many different ways, he will explain what *he* means by it:

A DEFINITION OF PHILOSOPHY

BERTRAND RUSSELL

"Philosophy" is a word which has been used in many ways, some wider, some narrower. I propose to use it in a very wide sense, which I will now try to explain.

Philosophy, as I shall understand the word, is something intermediate between theology and science. Like theology, it consists of speculations on matters as to which definite knowledge has, so far, been unascertainable; but like science, it appeals to human reason rather than to authority, whether that of tradition or that of revelation. All *definite* knowledge—so I should contend—belongs to science; all *dogma* as to what surpasses definite knowledge belongs to theology. But between theology and science there is a No Man's Land, exposed to attack from both sides; this No Man's Land is philosophy. Almost all the questions of most interest to speculative minds are such as science cannot answer, and the confident answers of theologians no longer seem too convincing as they did in former centuries. Is the world divided into mind and matter, and, if so, what is mind and what is matter? Is mind subject to matter, or is it possessed of independent powers? Has the universe any unity or purpose? Is it evolving towards some goal? Are there really laws of nature, or do we believe in them only because of our innate love of order? Is man what he seems to the astronomer, a tiny lump of impure carbon and water impotently crawling on a small and unimportant planet? Or is he what he appears to Hamlet? Is he perhaps both at once? Is there a way of living that is noble and another that is base, or are all ways of living merely futile? If there is a way of living that is noble, in what does it consist, and how shall we achieve it? Must the good be eternal in order to deserve to be valued, or is it worth seeking even if the universe is inexorably moving towards death? Is there such a thing as wisdom, or is what seems such merely the ultimate refinement of folly? To such questions no answer can be found in the laboratory. Theologies have professed to give answers, all too definite; but their very definiteness causes modern minds to view them with suspicion. The study of these questions, if not the answering of them, is the business of philosophy.[1]

Russell has done more here than look up the word "philosophy" in the dictionary (that repository of all accepted, conventional meanings of words) and set forth the *one* meaning he liked best or found most useful. In a sense, Russell has gone beyond conventional meaning in this definition; certainly he has particularized and elaborated on the conventional meaning in a way that is both inventive and illuminating. Thus, we do not receive from Russell any of the routine dictionary definitions:

1. Philosophy is the love or pursuit of wisdom.
2. Philosophy is the search for underlying causes.
3. Philosophy is a critical examination of fundamental beliefs.
4. Philosophy is the study of the principles of human nature and conduct.

Instead, Russell begins by locating the word with almost geographical precision. Philosophy stands midway between theology and science. We can almost *see* it:

This spatial placement of a word accords with the original meaning of "definition," for the term is derived from the Latin *definire:* to put boundaries around. Thus when we define a term we set up boundaries or limits that separate it from other terms, just as a fence separates one piece of land from another. An agricultural metaphor lurks in the background here; it is appropriate since the definer does in fact "stake out" for his term a special territory of meaning. Under the "No Man's Land" of philosophy, for example, Russell has very skillfully included all the traditional concerns of the discipline: questions relating to the nature of reality ("Is the world divided into

[1] From *A History of Western Philosophy,* by Bertrand Russell. Reprinted by permission of Simon & Schuster, Inc., and George Allen & Unwin Ltd.

mind and matter?"); the problem of good and evil ("Is there a way of living that is noble and another that is base?"); the possibility of knowledge ("Is there such a thing as wisdom?"). Russell concludes his definition by further restricting the domain of the discipline by indicating that it is the *studying* of these questions rather than the *answering* of them that is "the business of philosophy."

Russell's definition, as stated above, is part of an introduction to a book. This is true of many definitions; they are really miniature *introductory* essays to larger units of discourse, ranging in length from one paragraph to several pages. At the same time, the definition can exist as an independent form—an essay in definition. This too may be relatively short (200–800 words) like the essays reprinted in this section or longer like the essay "What Is Pain" (pp. 330–37).

Finding a Subject in Definition

Whatever its form or length, however, definition offers vast possibilities to the student writer, for he can "hit upon" his topic simply by asking the questions "What does it mean?" or "What *should* it mean?" of any term that seems to him uncertain, mystifying, curious, provocative, troublesome, or simply in need of refurbishing (one might strip away a hard crust of connotation, for example, to find a more fundamental meaning). As we shall see (Chapter 24, "The Limits of Language"), there are many abstract and ambiguous words in our language that mean different things to different people: a word like "excellence," for example, about which John Gardner said, "It is a little like those ink blots that psychologists use to interpret personality. As the individual contemplates the word 'excellence' he reads into it his own aspirations, his own conceptions of high standards, his hopes for a better world." [2] The same is true of words such as "honor," "loyalty," "liberty," "progress," "courage," "justice," "democracy," "capitalism," "communism," (any –ism). They are all "ink blots" and create an opportunity for an essay in which the writer either establishes common criteria of meaning or offers his own personal meaning, as E. B. White does below in his essay "Democracy" (p. 36).

In addition to ambiguous terms, a writer may contemplate words that are, in his opinion, not widely or well understood either because their meaning has changed or because they have acquired connotations. Linguists have shown that language grows organically, moved by its own inner forces. No external pressure—not even the most determined efforts of the strictest purists—can dictate its destiny. This does not imply, however, that users of the language may not concern themselves with the way specific words are faring. Since meanings often "blur," it is appropriate that periodically someone reappraise a word by recognizing and redefining its boundaries. It may even happen, as in the case of the word "grammar," that in the course of its development a word will radiate so widely from its original sense that it will come to mean several different things, thereby requiring several different definitions. W. Nelson Francis' essay "Three Meanings of Grammar" illustrates this point.

[2] John Gardner, *Excellence* (New York: Harper & Row, 1961), pp. xii–xiii.

"What does X mean?" The writer may address this question to a word that he believes should be "recalled to itself"; its original and potential fullness of meaning reviewed and restored. An essay could be written on the word "discipline," for example, in which the commonly used negative and restrictive notion of punishment would be replaced by the wider meaning of training. In actual, etymological fact the derivation of "discipline" is the same as that of "disciple": "one who learns or voluntarily follows a leader." Seen in this light, the word "discipline" carries no stigma; it means "making a disciple." Similarly the words "welfare" (welfare state), "charity" (handout), "intellectual" (egghead), and "politician" (opportunist), have all taken on negative connotations that a writer may decide are objectionable. Thus in answer to the question "What does it mean?" a writer may try to rescue a word from its progressive "degradation" by redefining it in a more affirmative context. A dictionary definition merely sums up and informs, but an essay in definition may agitate for reform.

Methods of Developing a Definition

There are many ways to develop a definition. Bertrand Russell, as we have seen, lists the questions that—in his view—constitute the subject matter or "business" of philosophy. Allan Nevins, as we will note below, develops his definition of "history" by contrasting it with what it is *not*. Thus these writers establish the boundaries of their subject. The essays that follow illustrate various methods whereby the writer may set boundaries and in so doing answer the question, "What does X mean?" It is worth noting also that most of the essays are structured—roughly—in three parts:

1. The need for a definition is stated.
2. Past or current uses are reviewed and shown to be inadequate, inappropriate, or confusing.
3. The writer's definition (often a restatement of diversely held notions) is offered, showing how it applies in this case—why it has value; why it is *better*.

By Citing Different Meanings

THREE MEANINGS OF GRAMMAR

W. NELSON FRANCIS

Need for definition stated

A curious paradox exists in regard to grammar. On the one hand it is felt to be the dullest and driest of academic subjects, fit only for those in whose veins the red blood of life has long since turned to ink. On the other, it is a subject upon which people who would scorn to be professional grammarians hold very dogmatic opinions, which they will defend with considerable emotion. Much of this prejudice stems from the usual sources of prejudice—ignorance and confusion. Even highly educated people seldom have a clear idea of what grammarians do, and there is an unfortunate confusion about the meaning of the term "grammar" itself.

Hence it would be well to begin with definitions. What do people mean when they use the word "grammar"? Actually the word is used to refer to three different things, and much of the emotional thinking about matters grammatical arises from confusion among these different meanings.

Current uses are confusing

The first thing we mean by "grammar" is "the set of formal patterns in which the words of a language are arranged in order to convey larger meanings." It is not necessary that we be able to discuss these patterns self-consciously in order to be able to use them. In fact, all speakers of a language above the age of five or six know how to use its complex forms of organization with considerable skill; in this sense of the word—call it "Grammar 1" —they are thoroughly familiar with its grammar.

Three meanings isolated

The second meaning of "grammar"—call it "Grammar 2"—is "the branch of linguistic science which is concerned with the description, analysis, and formulization of formal language patterns." Just as gravity was in full operation before Newton's apple fell, so grammar in the first sense was in full operation before anyone formulated the first rule that began the history of grammar as a study.

The third sense in which people use the word "grammar" is "linguistic etiquette." This we may call "Grammar 3." The word in this sense is often coupled with a derogatory adjective: we say that the expression "he ain't here" is "bad grammar." What we mean is that such an expression is bad linguistic manners in certain circles. From the point of view of "Grammar 1" it is faultless; it conforms just as completely to the structural patterns of English as does "he isn't here." The trouble with it is like the trouble with Prince Hal in Shakespeare's play—it is "bad," not in itself, but in the company it keeps.

Why the new 3-part definition is better (it unravels confusion)

As has already been suggested, much confusion arises from mixing these meanings. One hears a good deal of criticism of teachers of English couched in such terms as "they don't teach grammar any more." Criticism of this sort is based on the wholly unproved assumption that teaching Grammar 2 will increase the student's proficiency in Grammar 1 or improve his manners in Grammar 3. Actually the form of Grammar 2 which is usually taught is a very inaccurate and misleading analysis of the facts of Grammar 1; and it therefore is of highly questionable value in improving a person's ability to handle the structural patterns of his language. It is hardly reasonable to expect that teaching a person some inaccurate grammatical analysis will either improve the effectiveness of his assertions or teach him what expressions are acceptable to use in a given social context.

Summary

These, then, are the three meanings of "grammar": Grammar 1, a form of behavior; Grammar 2, a field of study, a science; and Grammar 3, a branch of etiquette.[3]

[3] From "Revolution in Grammar," by W. Nelson Francis. Reprinted from *The Quarterly Journal of Speech,* October 1954 by permission of W. Nelson Francis and Speech Communication Association.

By Citing Examples

WHAT IS A SYMBOL?

M. H. ABRAMS

Definition

A symbol, in the broadest use of the term, is anything which signifies something else; in this sense, all words are symbols. As commonly used in criticism, however, "symbol" is applied only to a word or phrase signifying an object which itself has significance; that is, the object referred to has a range of meaning beyond itself. Some symbols are "conventional," or "public"; thus "the Cross," "the Red, White, and Blue," "the Good Shepherd" are terms which signify objects of which the symbolic meanings are widely known. Poets, like all of us, use these conventional symbols; but some poets also use "private symbols," which are not widely known, or which they develop for themselves (usually by expanding and elaborating pre-existing associations of an object), and these set a more difficult problem in interpretation.

Examples of public symbols

Take as an example the word "rose," which in its literal meaning is a kind of flower. In Burns's line, "O my love's like a red, red rose," the word is used as a simile, and in the version "O my love is a red, red rose," it is used as a metaphor. William Blake wrote:

Example of private symbol

O Rose, thou art sick!
The invisible worm
That flies in the night,
In the howling storm,

Has found out thy bed
Of crimson joy,
And his dark secret love
Does thy life destroy.

This rose is not the vehicle for a simile or a metaphor, because it lacks the paired subject—"my love," in the examples just cited—which is characteristic of these figures. . . . Blake's rose *is* a rose—yet it is also something more; words like "bed," "joy," "love," indicate that the described object has a further range of significance which makes it a symbol. But Blake's rose is not, like the symbolic rose of Dante's *Paradise* and other medieval poems, an element in a complex set of traditional religious symbols which were widely known to contemporary readers. Only from the clues in Blake's poem itself, supplemented by a knowledge of parallel elements in his other poems, do we come to see that Blake's worm-eaten rose symbolizes such matters as the destruction wrought by furtiveness, deceit, and hypocrisy in what should be a frank and joyous relationship of physical love.[4]

[4] From *A Glossary of Literary Terms*, by Meyer H. Abrams. Reprinted by permission of Holt, Rinehart and Winston, Inc.

By Contrasting X With What It Is Not

WHAT IS HISTORY?

ALLAN NEVINS

Need for definition

Because history has been approached from many different points of view, it has received more amusingly varied definitions than even the novel. The cynic's definition of it as a *mensonge convenu*, a lie agreed upon, may harmonize with the statement attributed to Disraeli that he preferred romances to history because they told more truth; but it is a piece of baseless flippancy. It is precisely the fact that historians are always ready to disagree with each other which makes any persistence of lies in history—that is, true history—unlikely. Carlyle, approaching the subject from his special predilection, which emphasized the role of the individual, termed history the essence of innumerable biographies. But obviously it is a good deal more than that; it takes account of many forces which are not personal at all. John Cotter Morison defined it as "the prose narrative of past events, as probably true as the fallibility of human testimony will allow." Good so far as it goes, that definition is too pedestrian to be wholly satisfactory. Conversely, a familiar modern statement that history is the record of everything in the past which helps explain how the present came to be, is too philosophical and priggish. It emphasizes too much the utilitarian role of history, which we often wish to read without any reference whatever to the present—even to get entirely away from the present.

What history is *not*

Inadequate definitions

New definition

History is any integrated narrative or description of past events or facts written in a spirit of critical inquiry for the whole truth. A definition which attempts to be more precise than this is certain to be misleading. For above all, it is the historical point of view, the historical method of approach—*that is, the spirit of critical inquiry for the whole truth*—which, applied to the past, makes history. It will not do to lay down a more exclusive formula. There are as many different schools and theories of history as the schools of philosophy, of medicine, and of painting. But it will be agreed that a newspaper report of some current event, a debate in Congress, a diplomatic exchange between France and Germany, is not history, because it cannot be written as an inquiry into the *whole* truth. Only superficial sources of information, generally speaking, are open to newspapermen. It will also be agreed that a Democratic or Republican campaign-book reviewing events of the four years just preceding publication is not history; it is not written as a *critical* inquiry into the truth. A careful historical novel, like Charles Reace's *Cloister and the Hearth,* holds many historical values. But it will be agreed that it is not history, for it is not written primarily as an inquiry into past *truth* at all, but primarily to entertain and please by an artistic use of the imagination.[5]

[5] From *The Gateway to History* by Allan Nevins. Reprinted by permission of D. C. Heath and Company.

By Citing Origin and Development

WORLD A AND WORLD B

C. S. LEWIS

In the earliest recorded period of our language this noun "world" has two senses which we may call *World A* and *World B*.

(A.) In Alfred's version of Boethius we read that children die and the parents 'mourn for it all their *woruld*.' This clearly means 'all their life.' But to cover all the shades of the A-sense we had better say that *World A* means something like age or *durée*. In Aelfric's homily on the Assumption of St. John we find 'through endless *worulda*' (plural), through ages without end. In Alfred again 'will stand to *worulda*,' will last forever. The A-sense long survived the Anglo-Saxon period. In the thirteenth-century *Sawles Warde* comes 'praise thee from worlde into worlde,' from age to age, representing *in saecula saeculorum*. By an unusual archaism, the A-sense is preserved in the Prayer Book, where it probably mystifies many church-goers. . . .

(B.) The *B*-sense is that which the word most naturally suggests to a modern speaker. The poet who did the Metres of Boethius into Anglo-Saxon writes 'in those days there were no great houses in the *weoruld*e.' Here we could translate it 'earth.' But whenever the distinction between the earth and the universe is present to the mind, *World B* can mean either, and the context usually shows which. Thus Gower writes

> Tofore the creacion
> Of eny worldes stacion,
> Of hevene, or erthe, or eke of helle
> (VII, 203)

—'before the creation of any place in the universe, e.g. of heaven, earth or hell.' *World B* may loosely be defined as the region that contains all regions; if all absolutely, then it means universe; if 'all that usually concern us humans,' then it means earth.

Since *World A* is something in time and *World B* something in space, it is not at once easy to see the semantic trunk out of which two such different branches have grown. But the very form of the word provides a probable cue. *Worold,* like its Old Norse equivalent *veroldr,* appears to be built out of two elements. The first is *wer* (a man), related to Latin *vir* and Irish *fir,* and fossilised in *wer-wolf,* the man-wolf. The second is something like *ald,* age or period. But what would 'man-age' mean? Something, I believe, which all our attempts at translation will make too precise. The generations of men? Human history? The common lot of men, the sort of life they have? Anyway, 'all this' in which we find ourselves embedded. Perhaps 'human life' will serve us best.

Now when we turn from considering words in isolation and look at them in concrete sentences, we discover that 'human life' is not nearly so distinguishable from *World B* (the region of regions) as we had supposed. In *Beowulf* 'parting from *woruld*e' (3068) means death; to enjoy or share in or have *woruld*e (1061–2) means to be alive; 'they woke into *worold*' (60) means 'they were born.' Whether we translate *woruld* by 'human life' or 'earth' or 'universe,' we shall make equally good sense, and very nearly the same sense, of all three. And good reason why. To be alive and to be in the region of regions are the same thing; we seem to enter both when we are born and perhaps leave both simultaneously when we die. Sense A and Sense B were not before the poet's mind as alternatives at all; just as, if we say 'He left the College in 1930,' we do not always know whether we mean primarily that he relinquished his status as a member of it or that he moved his belongings out of his rooms and went away by a taxi. Here, as not seldom, we begin by thinking that we have met a semantic chasm which has to be bridged and then discover that we were digging the chasm.[6]

By Enlarging the Meaning

ON PEDANTRY

JOSEPH ADDISON

A man who has been brought up among books, and is able to talk of nothing else, is a very indifferent companion, and what we call a pedant. But methinks we should enlarge the title, and give it every one that does not know how to think out of his profession and particular way of life.

What is a greater pedant than a mere man of the town? Bar him the playhouses, a catalogue of the reigning beauties, and an account of a few fashionable distempers that have befallen him, and you strike him dumb. How many a pretty gentleman's knowledge lies all within the verge of the court? He will tell you the names of the principal favourites, repeat the shrewd sayings of a man of quality, whisper an intrigue that is not yet blown upon by common fame; or, if the sphere of his observations is a little larger than ordinary, will perhaps enter into all the incidents, turns, and revolutions in a game of *ombre*. When he has gone thus far, he has shown you the whole circle of his accomplishments, his parts are drained, and he is disabled from any farther conversation. What are these but rank pedants? and yet these are the men who value themselves most on their exemption from the pedantry of colleges.

I might here mention the military pedant who always talks in a camp, and in storming towns, making lodgments and fighting battles from one end of the year to the other. Everything he speaks smells of gunpowder; if you take away his artillery from him, he has not a word to say for himself. I might likewise mention the law pedant, that is perpetually putting cases, repeating the transactions of Westminster-hall, wrangling with you upon the most indifferent circumstances of life, and not to be convinced of the distance of a place, or of the most trivial point in conversation, but by dint of argument. The state pedant is wrapt up in news, and lost in politics. If you mention either of the kings of Spain or Poland, he talks very notably; but if you go out of the *Gazette* you drop him. In short, a mere courtier, a mere soldier, a mere scholar, a mere anything, is an insipid pedantic character, and equally ridiculous.

Of all the species of pedants which I have mentioned, the book pedant is much the most supportable; he has at least an exercised understanding, and a head which is full though confused, so that a man who converses with him may often receive from him hints of things that are worth knowing, and what

6 From *Studies in Words*, by C. S. Lewis. Reprinted by permission of Cambridge University Press.

he may possibly turn to his own advantage, though they are of little use to the owner. The worst kind of pedants among learned men are such as are naturally endued with a very small share of common sense, and have read a great number of books without taste or distinction.

The truth of it is, learning like travelling, and all other methods of improvement, as it finishes good sense, so it makes a silly man ten thousand times more insufferable, by supplying variety of matter to his impertinence, and giving him an opportunity of abounding in absurdities.[7]

You will agree that Addison's enlargement of the term "pedant" is not altogether out of bounds; it does not strain either our credibility or the limits of language itself. This is a prerequisite, of course, of all definition: although it may depart from ordinary meaning, it must remain in the neighborhood of common usage. Because Humpty Dumpty's definition of "glory" in *Through the Looking-Glass* was *not* within the neighborhood of common usage ("I meant," he told Alice, " 'there's a nice knockdown argument for you!' "), Alice was forced to reject the word. Even in Wonderland it carried too private a meaning to have any exchange value.

Thus in trying to control or qualify the common meaning of a word, we may attempt to restore its original luster; or we may attempt to sharpen, deepen, enlarge, or enrich its current domain of denotation and connotation; but we may *not* try to rewrite the dictionary.

Formal Definition

If you examine the above definitions carefully, you will note that at the core of most of them is a three-part "formal" or "logical" definition (so called by rhetoricians). According to this pattern, a term to be defined is placed in a larger category or class; it is then distinguished from other members of the class by noting "differentiae." This process is illustrated below:

Term (to be defined)	*Class* (or genus)	*Differentiae* (distinguishing characteristics)
philosophy	is a field of study	that speculates on matters for which there is no definite knowledge and that appeals to reason rather than authority
grammar 1	is a set of formal patterns	whereby the words of a language are arranged to convey a larger meaning
grammar 2	is a branch of linguistic science	concerned with the description, analysis, and formularization of formal language patterns
grammar 3	is a branch of language study	concerned with etiquette
a symbol	is any "thing"	that stands for something else
history	is an integrated narrative of past events	written in a spirit of inquiry for the whole truth
a pedant	is a person	who knows nothing but his own profession or way of life

[7] From *The Spectator*, 30 June 1711.

Unlike the logician, the writer is not obliged to follow the logical formula *exactly*. Yet most good expository definitions have the three-part formal pattern, even if it is implicit rather than explicit. And most rhetorical definitions satisfy the basic *logical* prerequisites of a good definition: that the differentiae be neither too broad nor too narrow and that the definition be the equivalent of the term defined.

In any case, it is helpful for both the writer and reader to search out and apply to the rhetorical definition the basic logical patterning of a term, for nothing marks off an area of meaning with greater precision than the formal, one-sentence definition. It often provides a foundation and "thesis" for the entire piece that may then be extended, as we have seen in the illustrations above, by any number of methods. Thus it may be stated as a general principle that whenever possible, answer the question "What does X mean?" in terms of a formal, logical definition.

Experiential Definition

Admittedly this is not always possible, however; some words are too inextricably tied to an individual vantage point: too subjective, too relative, too experiential. One such word—as Abraham Lincoln pointed out—is "liberty."

> The world has never had a good definition of the word liberty. . . . We all declare for liberty, but using the same word we do not mean the same thing. With some, the word liberty may mean for each man to do as he pleases with himself and the product of his labor; while with others the same word may mean for some men and the product of other men's labor. . . .
>
> The shepherd drives the wolf from the sheep's throat, for which the sheep thanks the shepherd as his liberator, while the wolf denounces him for the same act. . . . Plainly the sheep and the wolf are not agreed upon a definition of liberty.

What should the writer do, then, with such subjective words? The answer is simple. He can write an essay containing *not* a formal definition, worked out against fixed, objective standards, but rather a personal definition worked out in terms of his own beliefs, feelings, and experiences. Thus the late and eloquent Judge Learned Hand had this to say about the spirit of liberty:

> What then is the spirit of liberty? I cannot define it; I can only tell you my own faith. The spirit of liberty is the spirit which is not too sure that it is right; the spirit of liberty is the spirit which seeks to understand the minds of other men and women; the spirit of liberty is the spirit which weighs their interests alongside its own without bias; the spirit of liberty remembers that not even a sparrow falls to earth unheeded; the spirit of liberty is the spirit of Him who, near two thousand years ago, taught mankind that lesson it has never learned, but has never quite forgotten: that there may be a kingdom where the least shall be heard and considered side by side with the greatest.

Similarly, E. B. White was moved, during the Second World War, to define "democracy" *not* in terms of formal procedures, but in terms of his own personal experiences and associations.

DEMOCRACY

We received a letter from the Writers' War Board the other day asking for a statement on "The Meaning of Democracy." It presumably is our duty to comply with such a request, and it is certainly our pleasure.

Surely the Board knows what democracy is. It is the line that forms on the right. It is the don't in don't shove. It is the hole in the stuffed shirt through which the sawdust slowly trickles; it is the dent in the high hat. Democracy is the recurrent suspicion that more than half of the people are right more than half of the time. It is the feeling of privacy in the voting booths, the feeling of communion in the libraries, the feeling of vitality everywhere. Democracy is a letter to the editor. Democracy is the score at the beginning of the ninth. It is an idea that hasn't been disproved yet, a song the words of which have not gone bad. It's the mustard on the hot dog and the cream in the rationed coffee. Democracy is a request from a War Board, in the middle of a morning in the middle of a war, wanting to know what democracy is.[8]

According to political scientist Anatol Rapoport, the personal definition is no less valuable than the formal; in fact, it is sometimes the best, perhaps the *only* way to formulate certain definitions—by indicating the feelings, experiences, and ideas associated with the term in question. What *happens* in connection with it? What is done? What is thought, felt? In Rapoport's view the question "What do you mean?" is essentially a request to share the experiences associated with the words you are using. In the following definition of "prejudice," for example, psychologist Gordon Allport achieves this form of "sharing" by citing four instances in which prejudice was "happening." Thus he establishes—as no formal definition alone could—the experiential common denominator of "prejudice":

THE NATURE OF PREJUDICE

GORDON ALLPORT

Before I attempt to define prejudice, let us have in mind four instances that I think we all would agree *are* prejudice.

The first is the case of the Cambridge University student, who said, "I despise all Americans. But," he added, a bit puzzled, "I've never met one that I didn't like."

The second is the case of another Englishman, who said to an American, "I think you're awfully unfair in your treatment of Negroes. How *do* Americans feel about Negroes?" The American replied, "Well, I suppose some Americans feel about Negroes just the way you feel about the Irish." The Englishman said, "Oh, come now! The Negroes are human beings!"

Then there's the incident that occasionally takes place in various parts of

[8] This editorial first appeared in *The New Yorker*. It is reprinted with permission of the author from his book, *The Wild Flag*, Houghton Mifflin 1946. Copyright by E. B. White, 1943–46.

the world (in the West Indies, for example, I'm told). When an American walks down the street the natives conspicuously hold their noses till the American gets by. The case of odor is always interesting. Odor gets mixed up with prejudice because odor has great associative power. We know that some Chinese deplore the odor of Americans. Some white people think Negroes have a distinctive smell and vice versa. An intrepid psychologist recently did an experiment; it went as follows. He brought to a gymnasium an equal number of white and colored students and had them take shower baths. When they were nice and clean he had them exercise vigorously for fifteen minutes. Then he put them in different rooms, and he put a clean white sheet over each one. Then he brought his judges in, and each went to the sheeted figures and sniffed. They were to say, "white" or "black," guessing at the identity of the subject. The experiment seemed to prove that when we are sweaty we all smell bad in the same way. It's good to have experimental demonstration of the fact.

The fourth example I'd like to bring before you is a piece of writing that I quote. Please ask yourselves who, in your judgment, wrote it. It's a passage about the Jews.

> The synagogue is worse than a brothel. It's a den of scoundrels. It's a criminal assembly of Jews, a place of meeting for the assassins of Christ, a den of thieves, a house of ill fame, a dwelling of iniquity. Whatever name more horrible to be found, it could never be worse than the synagogue deserves.
>
> I would say the same things about their souls. Debauchery and drunkenness have brought them to the level of lusty goat and pig. They know only one thing; to satisfy their stomachs and get drunk, kill, and beat each other up. Why should we salute them? We should have not even the slightest converse with them. They are lustful, rapacious, greedy, perfidious robbers.

Now who wrote that? Perhaps you say Hitler, or Goebbels, or one of our local anti-Semites? No, it was written by Saint John Chrysostom, in the fourth century A.D. Saint John Chrysostom, as you know, gave us the first liturgy in the Christian church still used in the Orthodox churches today. From it all services of the Holy Communion derive. Episcopalians will recognize him also as the author of that exalted prayer that closes the offices of both matin and evensong in the *Book of Common Prayer*. I include this incident to show how complex the problem is. Religious people are by no means necessarily free from prejudice. In this regard be patient even with our saints.

What do these four instances have in common? You notice that all of them indicate that somebody is "down" on somebody else—a feeling of rejection, or hostility. But also, in all these four instances, there is indication that the person is not "up" on his subject—not really informed about Americans, Irish, Jews, or bodily odors.

So I would offer, first a slang definition of prejudice: *Prejudice is being down on somebody you're not up on.* If you dislike slang, let me offer the same thought in the style of St. Thomas Aquinas. Thomists have defined prejudice as *thinking ill of others without sufficient warrant*.

You notice that both definitions, as well as the examples I gave, specify two ingredients in prejudice. First there is some sort of faulty generalization in thinking about a group. I'll call this the process of *categorization*. Then there is the negative, rejective, or hostile ingredient, a *feeling* tone. "Being down on something" is the hostile ingredient; "that you're not up on" is the categorization ingredient; "Thinking ill of others" is the hostile ingredient; "without sufficient warrant" is the faulty categorization.

Parenthetically I should say that of course there is such a thing as *positive* prejudice. We can be just as prejudiced *in favor of* as we are *against*. We can be biased in favor of our children, our neighborhood or our college. Spinoza makes the distinction neatly. He says that *love prejudice* is "thinking well of others, through love, more than right." *Hate prejudice,* he says, is "thinking ill of others through hate, more than is right." [9]

In summary it might be said that the way you answer the question "What does X mean?" depends on what X *is* and what your purpose is in defining it. If you are trying to communicate the feel of a thing, what "prejudice" means *experientially,* then of course illustrations will best serve your purpose, for they bridge the gap most directly between words and experience. If, however, your purpose is to evaluate an alleged violation of the Fair Employment Practices Act, you need a general, working definition of "prejudice"; not the feeling or experience of prejudice, but the category of practice into which it may be classified and further described in terms of its "differentiae" (i.e., those distinguishing characteristics that added together could be fairly viewed as constituting "prejudicial treatment" of a job applicant). In this instance, formal, fixed, and objective criteria must be set up to indicate what constitutes prejudice toward a job applicant—formally, logically, and legally.

ASSIGNMENTS

Reminder: A definition, as pointed out above, is never written in a vacuum but always within a specific rhetorical stance, i.e., a given context established by the writer to meet the needs of a given occasion. Thus, before you begin an assignment in definition you should visualize, or (if the assignment is merely an exercise) *invent* the occasion that calls it forth. As a writer you should keep in mind a particular problem or situation, a specific audience, and a fixed point of view.

I. Write a one-sentence formal or logical definition of each of the following words:

lawyer	idiot	jet
doctor	imbecile	star
rhetoric	needle	book
biology	pencil	navy
botany	rock	marines
archeology	rock music	psychotic
photosynthesis	radar	neurotic
fireplace		

II. Compare Bertrand Russell's definition of "philosophy" with Allan Nevins' definition of "history." How are they similar? dissimilar? Note their basic organization or structure. In a comparable form style write a definition (500–750 words) of one of the following disciplines:

[9] From "Reading the Nature of Prejudice," by Gordon W. Allport, in the *Claremont College Reading Conference 17th Yearbook.* Reprinted by permission of The Claremont College Curriculum Laboratory.

literature	geology
music	archeology (or any science)
history	sociology
economics	anthropology
chemistry	political science
physics	

III. Write a definition (500–750 words) of one of the following general terms using the one-sentence, formal definition (explicitly stated or implicit) as a base or thesis:

patriotism	public opinion	mass media
plagiarism	libel	isolationist
atheism	heresy	internationalist
communism	reactionary	myth
(any) –ism	liberal	jazz
censorship	radical	temperance
poverty	religion	nature

IV. In an essay (500–750 words) restore one of the following words to respectability by stripping it of negative connotations and redefining it in a more respectable light:

gang	cliché
politician	informer
bookworm	gossip
shrewd	censorship
manipulator	slang
idle	militarist
exploit	welfare
charity	intellectual

V. In the manner of C. S. Lewis' "World A and World B," write an essay (500–750 words) tracing the history of one of the following words:

romance	grammar	hussy	serious
tragedy	citizen	pride	undertaker
comedy	boor	science	scruple
epic	boycott	atomic	lynch
gossip	affair	bunk	corporation
logic	cad	scissors	rifle
rhetoric			

VI. In a paragraph (150–250 words) trace recent changes in the meaning of one of the following words:

survey	affluent	computer
recession	retarded	beat
stoned	cool	tough
center	liquidate	loophole

VII. In an essay (500–750 words) written in the manner of Joseph Addison suggest an enlarged definition of one of the following terms:

politician	bookworm	atheist
miser	cheat	agnostic

preacher	hero	religious person
soldier	coward	heretic
militarist	explorer	adventurer

VIII. In an essay (500–750 words) written in the manner of Gordon Allport's essay on prejudice establish the common denominator for a term by citing three or four instances in which it clearly has application:

courage	wisdom	freedom
cowardice	intelligence	oppression
wit	genius	tyranny
love	patriotism	maturity
hate	discrimination	beauty
happiness	peace	violence

IX. About the spirit of liberty, Judge Learned Hand said "I cannot define it; I can only tell you my own faith." In a paragraph (150–300 words) tell your "own faith" in the spirit of one of the following words:

justice	loyalty
courage	charity
love	brotherhood
freedom	democracy
honor	idealism
sportsmanship	neighborliness

2 HOW CAN X BE DESCRIBED?

For the student who reportedly said that he would "have to run out and get run over by a truck in order to find something to write about," there is a simpler and safer alternative: address the question "How can it be described?" to some aspect of the environment—a person, a place, an object, or an event. Look at the sky and the stars; look at the school gymnasium and the used-car lot at the edge of town (you do not need a poetic subject). Indeed, look up from your desk, look across the room, look at the window, look *out* the window, look out and *beyond*. Look and then answer the question "What does it look like?" Describe what you see, hear, smell, feel. Describe your sensations and impressions. Is it a dark and eerie night (scary?); a gray and bleak day (depressing?); a sunny and warm day, alive with people and laughter? Whatever is happening out there, take careful note; for as poet John Ciardi has said, whatever is looked at carefully is worth looking at—and as he might have added—worth writing about as well.

Like a definition, a description may be an essay in itself or part of a longer work (short story, novel, article, biography, etc.). Description is a necessary adjunct to all types of writing since it reconstructs for the reader how something or someone *appears*. This above all, then, in writing description: the writer must have a keen eye; in fact, all his senses must be alert if he is to take in the scene and then reproduce it in a verbal picture that will come alive for the reader.

Sensory Description

More than that, the conscientious writer tries to probe beneath the surface not only to see what is there, but also to discover what can only be felt or surmised: the underlying mood or atmosphere, the sense as well as the sight of his subject.

Creating Mood in Description

Notice how successfully, yet how simply, the writer of the following essay has accomplished this deeper dimension of description through his skillful use of words that communicate not merely the visual and physical quality of the event being experienced but also its underlying mood and magic.

Words such as "mysterious" and "lonely," for example, evoke in their very sound a sense of mystery and loneliness; the descriptive term "diminutive wraith" (a succession of short, light "i's" followed by the emphatic and vaguely archaic monosyllable "wraith") suggests—somehow—a small other-worldly creature, a wisp and not an overweight chunk of a girl. Similarly, words such as "fantastically," "limitless," "towering," "enormous," and "massive" introduce a scene that is unmistakably larger than life, a blow-up of the ordinary in which time itself is extended far back to an "ancient sea." Note the color words at work in this description: "red and yellow sandstone," "tawny desert," "silver ornaments," "darkening shades of orange," "pale saffron." Note the very precise shapes: "giant's chess pieces," "twin pinnacles," "miniature ocean waves," a "golden globe," a "massive disk," a "ragged skyline."

All these details, embedded in the sound and contour as well as in the meaning of the words, contribute to the total impact of the piece: we *see* the colors; we *hear* the rustle of the night wind (the ear as well as the eye is accosted); we *feel* the texture of the surrounding sandstone; we *sense* in our own body muscles the relentless thrust upward to the sky where, shortly, the moon will rise.

MOONRISE OVER MONUMENT VALLEY

JOHN V. YOUNG

We were camped here in early spring, by one of those open-faced shelters that the Navajos have provided for tourists in this part of their vast tribal park on the Arizona-Utah border, 25 miles north of Kayenta. It was cool but pleasant, and we were alone, three men in a truck.

We were here for a purpose: to see the full moon rise over this most mysterious and lonely of scenic wonders, where fantastically eroded red and yellow sandstone shapes soar to the sky like a giant's chess pieces and where people—especially white strangers—come quickly to feel like pretty small change indeed.

Because all Navajo dwellings face east, our camp faced east—toward the rising sun and the rising moon and across a limitless expanse of tawny desert, that ancient sea, framed by the towering nearby twin pinnacles called The Mittens. We began to feel the magic even before the sun was fully down. It occurred when a diminutive wraith of a Navajo girl wearing a long, dark, velvet dress gleaming with silver ornaments drifted silently by, herding a flock of ghostly sheep to a waterhole somewhere. A bell on one of the rams tinkled faintly, and then its music was lost in the soft rustle of the night wind, leaving us with an impression that perhaps we had really seen nothing at all.

Just then, a large woolly dog appeared out of the gloom, seeming to materialize on the spot. It sat quietly on the edge of the glow from our camp-fire, its eyes shining like mirrors. It made no sound but when we offered food, it accepted the gift gravely and with much dignity. The dog then vanished again, probably to join the girl and her flock. We were not certain it was not part of the illusion.

As the sun disappeared entirely, the evening afterglow brush tipped all the spires and cliffs with magenta, deepening to purple and the sand ripples stood out like miniature ocean waves in darkening shades of orange. Off to the east on the edge of the desert, a pale saffron glow told us the moon was about to rise behind a thin layer of clouds, slashed by the white contrail of an invisible jet airplane miles away.

We had our cameras on tripods and were fussing with light meters, making casual bets as to the exact place where the moon would first appear, when it happened—instant enchantment. Precisely between the twin spires of The Mittens, the enormous golden globe loomed suddenly, seeming as big as the sun itself, behind a coppery curtain on the rim of creation.

We were as totally unprepared for the great size of the moon as we were for its flaming color, nor could we have prepared ourselves for the improbable setting. We felt like the wizards of Stonehenge, commanding the planets to send their light through the magic orifices in line at the equinox. Had the Navajo medicine men contrived this for our benefit?

The massive disk of the moon seemed to rise very fast at first, an optical effect magnified by the crystalline air and the flatness of the landscape between us and the distant, ragged skyline. Then it seemed to pause for a moment, as if it were pinioned on one of the pinnacles or impaled on a sharply upthrusting rocky point. Its blazing light made inky shadows all around us, split by the brilliant wedge of the moon's path between the spires. The wind had stopped. There was not a sound anywhere, nor even a whisper. If a drum had sounded just then, it would not have been out of place, I suppose, but it would have frightened us half to death.

Before the moon had cleared the tops of The Mittens, the show was over and the magic was gone. A thin veil of clouds spread over the sky, ending the spell as suddenly as it had come upon us. It was as if the gods had decided that we had seen enough for mere mortals on one spring night, and I must confess it was something of a relief to find ourselves back on mundane earth again, with sand in our shoes and a chill in the air.[1]

In this strikingly vivid description we are there with the writer, sharing his campsite and his physical point of view—i.e., his angle of vision, "facing east" across the limitless expanse of tawny desert. With him, we are turned toward the "rising moon," and never—from the opening to the closing paragraph—do we turn away. Our position in relation to the subject is fixed throughout, even when we are momentarily distracted from the scenery by the appearance of a young Navajo girl "wearing a long, dark, velvet dress gleaming with silver ornaments." Note that these few selected details of her outfit enable us to see her as the writer saw her; note also that she reinforces the mood that is beginning to overtake the writer as he settles down in this "mysterious and lonely" place.

The girl could have been a distraction if the writer had presented her as

[1] "When the Full Moon Shines Its Magic Light Over Monument Valley," by John V. Young. © 1965–69 by The New York Times Company. Reprinted by permission.

clomping onto the scene. Instead she is silent throughout; her sheep are a "ghostly" flock, and the small bell on the neck of a ram tinkles only "faintly." (We can *hear* it blending with "the soft rustle of the night wind.") No wonder, then, that as she vanishes into the distance followed by the large, woolly dog—silent, grave, and dignified, with "its eyes shining like mirrors" as if to foreshadow the still brighter shining to come—we are left with the impression that they never in actual fact passed by; they were illusions, the work of a magician.

As the sun begins to sink there is a sudden cascade of color: magenta, purple, darkening shades of orange, and a pale saffron "glow." The stage is set for the instant enchantment that will accompany the rise—at long last—of the full moon, an "enormous golden globe . . . as big as the sun itself." The writer is obviously moved at this point, but happily he does not rhapsodize nor lapse into purple prose (". . . its blinding light burned deep into my eyes with its illimitable luster and swept through my being like a spear of fire . . ."). Instead, he gives a calm, controlled, accurate, and unembellished report that rings true:

> We were as totally unprepared for the great size of the moon as we were for its flaming color, nor could we have prepared ourselves for the improbable setting. We felt like the wizards of Stonehenge, commanding the planets to send their light through the magic orifices in line at the equinox.

How apt is the analogy to the "wizards of Stonehenge"; how well it develops the sense of mystery and magic.

So too does the sudden "still picture" of the moon as it seems to pause for a moment "pinioned on one of the pinnacles." (Note the arresting alliteration of "p's" that themselves cause a moment's pause.) We move in, as if for a camera close-up, to see what it looks like: "Its blazing light made inky shadows all around us, split by the brilliant wedge of the moon's path between the spires."

The massive disk of the moon clears the tops of The Mittens and abruptly disappears: "The show was over and the magic was gone." As a thin veil of clouds passes over, the writer returns us to earth, telling us that we are "mere mortals" after all, and proving his point by evoking the concrete image (and thereby the tactile sensation) of "sand in our shoes and a chill in the air."

Effective Selection of Detail

Clearly, a good description must evoke sense impressions, for only then can the reader begin to respond totally. Although several senses may be called into play, however, the visual will usually predominate, since most of us use our eyes as a primary guide and as a check or verifier of our other senses. (Thus Shakespeare, in *A Midsummer Night's Dream,* has Bottom rush into the woods "to see a noise that he heard.") It is not surprising, then, that most descriptions focus on how something or someone looked.

Take Sophia, for example, the lovely heroine of *Tom Jones:*

> Sophia, then, the only daughter of Mr. Western, was a middle-sized woman; but rather inclining to tall. Her shape was not only exact, but

> extremely delicate; and the nice proportion of her arms promised the truest symmetry in her limbs. Her hair, which was black, was so luxuriant that it reached her middle, before she cut it to comply with the modern fashion; and it was now curled so gracefully in her neck that few could believe it to be her own. If envy could find any part of the fact which demanded less commendation than the rest, it might possibly think her forehead might have been higher without prejudice to her. Her eyebrows were full, even, and arched beyond the power of art to imitate. Her black eyes had a lustre in them which all her softness could not extinguish.

Fielding does not give all the details of Sophia's physical appearance (an overly detailed listing becomes tedious and dull); instead he gives what contributes to the total effect, just as in "Moonrise over Monument Valley" the writer selects those details that help to create the dominant mood of the piece.

Similarly, in the description of Sophia we are given a selection of details that enables us to see her in our mind's eye: she is tall, with nice proportions (the over-all contour of the person); she is delicate (the texture or "aura" of her); her black hair curls gracefully on her neck; she has a relatively low forehead (perhaps a *slight* imperfection to make her seem more human); she has lovely arched eyebrows and lustrous black eyes (proverbially "the windows of the soul"). One need not carry the description further; Sophia, for all practical purposes, has been described.

Similarly in the following description of an old beggar couple encountered during his travels in Persia, Justice William O. Douglas selects only those features that most economically represent the picture originally presented to his view:

TWO BEGGARS

These people were beggars of low estate. The man was dressed in rags. His coat was not merely patched; it was made of patches, pieces cut from old blankets, gunny sacks, and canvas. I did not at first notice his finely chiseled features because of the heavy stubble of his gray beard and the streaks of dirt on his face. His hands were long, thin, and sensitive. A typical Azerbaijan felt hat without a brim sat on the back of his head. Gnarled toes stuck out from a pair of decrepit leather sandals.

He and his wife were Christians. She stood unveiled before me, a grimy tan-colored cotton shawl draped over her head. Her face was pinched and drawn, partly from a total absence of teeth, partly from hunger. Her skin was parched and dry like leather, her hands were as thin and skinny as talons. She talked in a shrill voice, nervously twirling the ends of her shawl.[2]

Note that the features selected reveal aspects not only of these beggars' appearance but also of their cruelly deprived lives: the gnarled toes that stick out from the man's sandals; the woman's hands, so skinny and everlastingly in motion that we are reminded of an emaciated bird of prey, fran-

[2] From pp. 46–47 in *Strange Lands and Friendly People* by William O. Douglas. Copyright, 1951 by William O. Douglas. Reprinted by permission of Harper & Row, Publishers.

tically clawing at the earth with its talons. Here are human embodiments of hunger, poverty, and deprivation rendered alive by the selected details that collectively sum them up and project their essence. The first principle of description, then, is careful selection of detail.

Arrangement: Physical Point of View

The second basic principle of description is to arrange details methodically, not in haphazard or random fashion, but in a given order that is either inherent to the subject or dictated by the context. The beggars, for example, are described in terms of prominent characteristics, moving from the more obvious (the gray stubble and dirt on the man's face) to the less noticeable, subtle, or partially hidden (the finely chiseled features). Similarly the woman is first described in terms of how she looked (unveiled and grimy), then how she sounded (a shrill voice), and finally how she moved (twirling her shawl). In "Moonrise over Monument Valley," the description is organized differently in that the writer relates "what it looked like" in terms of "how it happened," a step-by-step description of a process (the rising of the moon) *necessarily* arranged in chronological order.

Another important aspect of arrangement of details is to maintain a consistent physical point of view—that is, the description is written as it is observed and includes only what can be observed. There are basically two physical points of view: the fixed and the moving. Justice Douglas' description of the beggars, for example, is written from the point of view of a person standing in front of them (a fixed observer); Douglas does not tell us what the backs of the beggars look like. The following short passage, "View from Rochester Bridge," presents a scene from the viewpoint of an observer whose eyes move spatially from left to right. (An example of the moving observer will be found in the Mark Twain selection reprinted below.)

VIEW FROM ROCHESTER BRIDGE

CHARLES DICKENS

On the left of the spectator lay the ruined wall, broken in many places, and in some, overhanging the narrow beach below in rude and heavy masses. Huge knots of sea-weed hung upon the jagged and pointed stones, trembling in every breath of wind; and the green ivy clung mournfully round the dark and ruined battlements. Behind it rose the ancient castle, its towers roofless, and its massive walls crumbling away, but telling us proudly of its own might and strength, as when, seven hundred years ago, it rang with the clash of arms, or resounded with the noise of feasting and revelry. On either side, the banks of the Medway, covered with corn-fields and pastures, with here and there a windmill, or a distant church, stretched away as far as the eye could see, presenting a rich and varied landscape, rendered more beautiful by the changing shadows which passed swiftly across it, as the thin and half-formed clouds skimmed away in the light of the morning sun. The river, reflecting the clear blue of the sky, glistened and sparkled as it flowed noiselessly on; and the oars of the fishermen dipped into the water with a clear and liquid sound, as the heavy but picturesque boats glided slowly down the stream.

Tone: Psychological Point of View

In addition to maintaining a consistent physical point of view toward his subject, the writer of description must maintain a consistent attitude—a psychological point of view—to ensure unity of effect. In the following passage from *Life on the Mississippi* note first how Mark Twain uses the physical point of view of the moving observer. We move at his elbow on a tour of the "house beautiful" of the Midwest in mid-nineteenth-century America; we move from outside to inside from hallway to parlor to bedrooms. Unlike Dickens surveying Rochester Bridge, from one stationary point, or Justice Douglas, standing still before his subjects, Twain keeps us moving.

Note also that the details in this sketch are overwhelming—and deliberately so. For the house itself, certainly the main parlor, is overwhelmingly and outrageously overcrowded, incredibly elaborate, and essentially uncomfortable (with its horsehair sofa "which keeps sliding from under you"), lacking in taste, originality, or restraint—plainly phony. Nothing less than a total description will reveal it for what it is: a middle-class monstrosity. This description, then—amusing and entertaining as it is—is actually more than description; it presents an attitude toward and a commentary on a way of life. And these, in turn, establish the special tone of the piece.

HOUSE BEAUTIFUL

MARK TWAIN

Every town and village along that vast stretch of double river-frontage had a best dwelling, finest dwelling, mansion—the home of its wealthiest and most conspicuous citizen. It is easy to describe it: large grassy yard, with paling fence painted white—in fair repair; brick walk from gate to door; big, square, two-story "frame" house, painted white and porticoed like a Grecian temple —with this difference, that the imposing fluted columns and Corinthian capitals were a pathetic sham, being made of white pine, and painted; iron knocker; brass door-knob—discolored, for lack of polishing. Within, an uncarpeted hall, of planed boards; opening out of it, a parlor, fifteen feet by fifteen—in some instances five or ten feet larger; ingrain carpet; mahogany center-table; lamp on it, with green-paper shade—standing on a gridiron, so to speak, made of high-colored yarns, by the young ladies of the house, and called a lamp-mat; several books, piled and disposed, with cast-iron exactness, according to an inherited and unchangeable plan; among them, Tupper, much penciled; also, *Friendship's Offering*, and *Affection's Wreath*, with their sappy inanities illustrated in dieaway mezzotints; also, Ossian; *Alonzo and Melissa*, maybe *Ivanhoe*, also "Album," full of original "poetry" of the Thou-hast-wounded-the-spirit-that-loved-thee breed; two or three goody-goody works—*Shepherd of Salisbury Plain*, etc.; current number of the chaste and innocuous *Godey's Lady's Book*, with painted fashion-plate of wax-figure women with mouths all alike—lips and eye-lids the same size—each five-foot woman with a two-inch wedge sticking from under her dress and letting on to be half of her foot. Polished air-tight stove (new and deadly invention), with pipe passing through a board which closes up the discarded good old fireplace. On each end of the wooden mantel, over the fireplace, a large basket of peaches and other fruits, natural size, all done in plaster, rudely, or in wax, and painted to resemble the originals—which they don't. Over middle of mantel, engraving—"Washington Crossing the Delaware"; on the wall by the door, copy of it done in thunder-and-lightning crewels by one of the young ladies—work of art which would have made Washington hesitate about crossing, if he could have foreseen what advantage was going to be taken of it. Piano—kettle in disguise—with music, bound and unbound, piled on it, and on a stand near by: "Battle of Prague"; "Bird Waltz"; "Arkansas Traveler"; "Rosin the Bow"; "Marseillaise Hymn"; "On a Lone Barren Isle" (St. Helena); "The Last Link is Broken"; "She Wore a Wreath of Roses the Night When Last we Met"; "Go, Forget me, Why Should Sorrow o'er That Brow a Shadow Fling"; "Hours That Were to Memory Dearer"; "Long, Long Ago"; "Days of Absence"; "A Life on the Ocean Wave, a Home on the Rolling Deep"; "Bird at Sea"; and spread open on the rack where the plaintive singer has left it, "*Ro*-holl on, silver *moo*-hoon, guide the *trav*-el-err on his way," etc. Tilted pensively against the piano, a guitar—guitar capable of playing the Spanish fandango by itself, if you give it a start. Frantic work of art on the wall—pious motto, done on the premises, sometimes in colored yarns, sometimes in faded grasses: progenitor of the "God Bless Our Home" of modern commerce. Framed in black moldings on the wall, other works of art, conceived and committed on the premises, by the young ladies; being grim black-and-white crayons; landscapes, mostly: lake, solitary sailboat, petrified clouds, pregeological trees on shore, anthracite precipice; name of criminal conspicuous in the corner. Lithograph, "Napoleon Crossing the Alps." Lithograph, "The Grave at St. Helena." Steel plates, Trumbull's "Battle of Bunker Hill," and the "Sally from Gibraltar." Copper plates, "Moses Smiting the Rock," and "Return of the Prodigal Son." In big gilt frame, slander of the family in oil: papa holding a book ("Constitution of the United States"); guitar leaning against mamma, blue ribbons fluttering from its neck; the young ladies, as children, in slippers and scalloped pantalettes, one embracing toy horse, the other beguiling kitten with ball of yarn, and both simpering up at mamma, who simpers back. These persons all fresh, raw, and red—apparently skinned. Opposite, in gilt frame, grandpa and grandma, at thirty and twenty-two, stiff, old-fashioned, high-collared, puff-sleeved, glaring pallidly out from a background of solid Egyptian night. Under a glass French clock dome, large bouquet of stiff flowers done in corpsy-white wax. Pyramidal what-not in the corner, the shelves occupied chiefly with bric-a-brac of the period, disposed with an eye to best effect: shell, with the Lord's Prayer carved on it; another shell—of the long-oval sort, narrow, straight orifice, three inches long, running from end to end—portrait of Washington carved on it; not well done; the shell had Washington's mouth, originally—artist should have built to that. These two are memorials of the long-ago bridal trip to New Orleans and the French Market. Other bric-a-brac: California "Specimens"—quartz, with gold wart adhering; old Guinea-gold locker, with circlet of ancestral hair in it; Indian arrowheads, of flint; pair of bead moccasins, from uncle who crossed the Plains; three "alum" baskets of various colors—being skeleton-frame of wire, clothed on with cubes of crystalized alum in the rock-candy style—works of art which were achieved by the young ladies; their doubles and duplicates to be found upon all what-nots in the land; convention of desiccated bugs and butterflies pinned to a card; painted toy dog, seated upon bellows attachment—drops its under-jaw and squeaks when pressed upon; sugar-candy rabbit—limbs and features merged together, not strongly defined; pewter presidential-campaign medal; miniature cardboard wood-sawyer, to be attached to the stovepipe and operated by the heat; small Napoleon, done in wax; spread-open daguerreotypes of dim children, parents, cousins, aunts, and friends, in all attitudes but customary ones; no templed portico at back, and manufactured landscape stretching away in the distance—that came in later, with the photograph; all these vague figures lavishly chained and ringed gold bronze; all of them too much combed, too much fixed up; and all of them uncomfortable in inflexible Sunday clothes of a pattern which the spectator cannot realize could ever have been in fashion; husband and wife generally grouped together—husband sitting, wife standing, with hand of wife on his shoulder—and both preserving, all these fading years, some traceable effect of the daguerreotypist's brisk "Now smile, if you please!" Bracketed over what-not—place of social sacredness—an outrage in water color done by the young niece that came on a visit long ago, and died. Pity, too; for she might have repented of this in time. Horsehair chairs, horsehair sofa which keeps sliding from under you. Windowshades, of oil stuff, with milkmaids and ruined castles stenciled on them in fierce colors. Lambrequins dependent from gaudy boxings of beaten tin, gilded. Bedrooms with rag carpets; bedsteads of the "corded" sort, with a sag in the middle, the cords needing tightening; snuffy feather-bed—not aired often enough; cane-seat chairs, splint-bottomed rocker; looking-glass on wall, school-slate size, veneered frame; inherited bureau; wash-bowl and pitcher, possibly—but not certainly; brass candlestick, tallow candle, snuffers. Nothing else in the room. Not a bathroom in the house; and no visitor likely to come along who has ever seen one.

That was the residence of the principal citizen, all the way from the suburbs of New Orleans to the edge of St. Louis.

This type of total (or seemingly total) tongue-in-cheek description—used for satiric effect—is represented in a modern idiom by Tom Wolfe, whose description below of "Baby" Jane Holzer's birthday party (replete with sound effects and mock asides) includes a roll call of guests (Shrimp, Nicky, Jerry, Barbara, Lennie, Sally, Catherine—"everybody but Bailey, who is off in Egypt or something . . .") and a wealth of trivia and details (*exactly* what Baby Jane is wearing and who designed it, Shrimp's textured stockings, Goldie's gold lamé tights, and Lennie's British suit and dark blue shirt "bought on 42nd Street for this party").

Wolfe may seem to be throwing everything into his description, including the most minute and insignificant details, but actually his listing makes an important point. He is describing a way of life in which *everything* (the most petty piece of gossip or feature of apparel) is important because *nothing* is important. The people being described do not and cannot distinguish the serious from the silly, the authentic from the spurious, the relevant from the irrelevant, the worthy from the worthless. In fact, these people (the sophisticated jet set) move in a herd, following one another blindly and blithely, as conditioned in their responses as Pavlov's famous dogs who salivated when the bell rang. Thus the title "The Girl of the Year" is as ironic in its tone and implications as is the adjective "beautiful" in Mark Twain's "House Beautiful." It expresses the writer's personal attitude toward his subject, an attitude that is maintained consistently throughout the piece, giving it its distinctive satiric tone.

THE GIRL OF THE YEAR

TOM WOLFE

ooooooooooooosh! Baby Jane blows out all the candles. It is her twenty-fourth birthday. She and everybody, Shrimp, Nicky, Jerry, everybody but Bailey, who is off in Egypt or something, they are all up in Jerry Schatzberg's . . . *pad* . . . his lavish apartment at 333 Park Avenue South, up above his studio. There is a skylight. The cook brings out the cake and Jane blows out the candles. Twenty-four! Jerry and Nicky are giving a huge party, a dance, in honor of the Stones, and already the people are coming into the studio downstairs. But it is also Jane's birthday. She is wearing a black velvet jump suit by Luis Estevez, the designer. It has huge bell-bottom pants. She puts her legs together . . . it looks like an evening dress. But she can also spread them apart, like so, and strike very Janelike poses. This is like the Upper Room or something. Downstairs, they're all coming in for the party, all those people one sees at parties, everybody who goes to the parties in New York, but up here it is like a tableau, like a tableau of . . . Us. Shrimp is sitting there with her glorious pout and her textured white stockings. Barbara Steele, who was so terrific in *8½*, with thin black lips and wrought-iron eyelashes. Nicky Haslam is there with his Byron shirt on and his tiger skin vest and blue jeans and boots. Jerry is there with his hair flowing back in curls. Lennie, Jane's husband, is there in a British suit and a dark blue shirt he bought on 42nd Street for this party, because this is a party for the Rolling Stones. The Stones are not here yet, but here in the upper room are Goldie and the Gingerbreads, four girls in gold lamé tights who will play the rock and roll for the party. Nicky discovered them at the Wagon Wheel. Gold lamé, can you imagine? Goldie, the leader, is a young girl with a husky voice and nice kind of slightly thick—you know—glorious sort of *East End* features, only she is from New York—ah, the delicacy of minor grossness, unabashed. The Stones' music is playing over the hi-fi.

Finally the Stones come in, in blue jeans, sweat shirts, the usual, and people get up and Mick Jagger comes in with his mouth open and his eyes down, faintly weary with success, and everybody goes downstairs to the studio, where people are now piling in, hundreds of them. Goldie and Gingerbreads are on a stand at one end of the studio, all electric, electric guitars, electric bass, drums, loudspeakers and a couple of spotlights exploding off the gold lamé. *Baby baby baby where did our love go.* The music suddenly fills up the room like a giant egg slicer. Sally Kirkland, Jr., a young actress, is out on the studio floor in a leopard print dress with her vast mane flying, doing the frug with Jerry Schatzberg. And then the other Girl of the Year, Catherine Milinaire, is out there in a black dress, and then Baby Jane is out there with her incredible mane and her Luis Estevez jump suit, frugging, and then everybody is out there. Suddenly it is very odd. Suddenly everybody is out there in the gloaming, bobbing up and down with the music plugged into *Baby baby baby.* The whole floor of the studio begins to bounce up and down, like a trampoline, the whole floor, some people are afraid and edge off to the side, but most keep bobbing in the gloaming, and—pow!—glasses begin to hit the floor, but everyone keeps bouncing up and down, crushing the glass underfoot, while the brown whiskey slicks around. So many heads bobbing, so many bodies jiggling, so many giblets jiggling, so much anointed flesh shaking and jiggling, this way and that, so many faces one wanted so desperately to see, and here they are, red the color of dried peppers in the gloaming, bouncing up and down with just a few fights, wrenching in the gloaming, until 5 A.M.—gleecang—Goldie pulls all the electric cords out and the studio is suddenly just a dim ochre studio with broken glass all over the floor, crushed underfoot, and the sweet high smell of brown whiskey rising from the floor.

Monday's papers will record it as the Mods and Rockers Ball, as the Party of the Year, but that is Monday, a long way off. So they all decide they should go to the Brasserie. It is the only place in town where anybody would still be around. So they all get into cabs and go up to the Brasserie, up on 53rd Street between Park and Lexington. The Brasserie is the right place, all right. The Brasserie has a great entrance, elevated over the tables like a fashion show almost. There are, what?, 35 people in the Brasserie. They all look up, and as the first salmon light of dawn comes through the front window, here come . . . four teen-age girls in gold lamé tights, and a chap in a tiger skin vest and blue jeans and a gentleman in an English suit who seems to be wearing a 42nd Street hood shirt and a fellow in a sweater who has flowing curly hair . . . and then, a girl with an incredible mane, a vast tawny corona wearing a black velvet jump suit. One never knows who is in the Brasserie at this hour—but are there any so dead in here that they do not get the point? Girl of the Year? Listen, they will *never* forget.[3]

To produce a unified effect, then, a description should embody a consistent psychological as well as physical point of view—i.e., the writer should generate throughout his piece a particular tone and a consistent attitude toward his subject: a sense of awe and wonder ("Moonrise over Monument Valley"); of appreciative delight ("Sophia"); of compassion ("Two Beggars"); of amusement ("House Beautiful"). Obviously there are no restrictions as to tone; the only imperative is that it be maintained consistently throughout.

Technical Description

In addition to sensory or impressionistic description there is another type: technical or scientific description, which focuses its attention exclusively on what is literally, physically, and palpably there; what can be objectively perceived, measured, checked, and verified. The describer tries to be objective, dispassionate, reliable, and fair, respecting the subject as it is for what it is, adding no comments or asides; offering no personal interpretation or aesthetic judgment. Technical description appeals to the understanding rather than the senses or the emotions. It is limited in scope, but it is also very useful and important, especially for students in the sciences, technology, and business, for they will be asked to describe subjects such as an amoeba under a microscope, a Diesel engine, a computer program. Each of these requires a detached approach, a clear eye, and an equally clear, direct, matter-of-fact style of writing—with no rhetorical flourishes or personal digressions. Just the facts as observed.

Take the following description, for example. This, says the writer, is what the common grasshopper looks like:

[3] Reprinted with the permission of Farrar Straus & Giroux, Inc. from *The Kandy-Kolored Tangerine-Flake Streamline Baby* by Tom Wolfe, copyright © 1964 by the New York Herald Tribune, Inc.

Grasshopper species are distributed in a wide belt around the world, extending from the cold regions of the north to those of the south. They range up to the snow fringes of mountains and have reached many isolated oceanic islands. These insects are generally large, averaging about two inches in length; the range is from a half inch to six inches. About 18,000 species are known.

The head is rather large and solidly built; the forewings are usually strong. There are two rather compound eyes, three ocelli (simple eyes), two short antennae—less than half the length of the body—and a powerful set of jaws. The front wings cover the more delicate rear wings when the insect is at rest. The front and middle pair of legs are short and are used for walking. The rear legs, which serve for leaping, are large and strongly muscled. They catapult the insect several feet into the air. Here the powerful wings take over, sometimes for extended flights of many miles. The legs are armed with rows of spines. These aid the insect in pushing through thick vegetation and also serve as defensive armament against a pursuing enemy.

Along the inner surface of each upper hind leg of many grasshoppers is an elevated, sharp ridge. This may be smooth or notched. There is also a raised vein on each tegmen, or forewing. When the grasshopper scrapes his legs against his tegmina, he produces the familiar rasping noise we associate with his kind.[4]

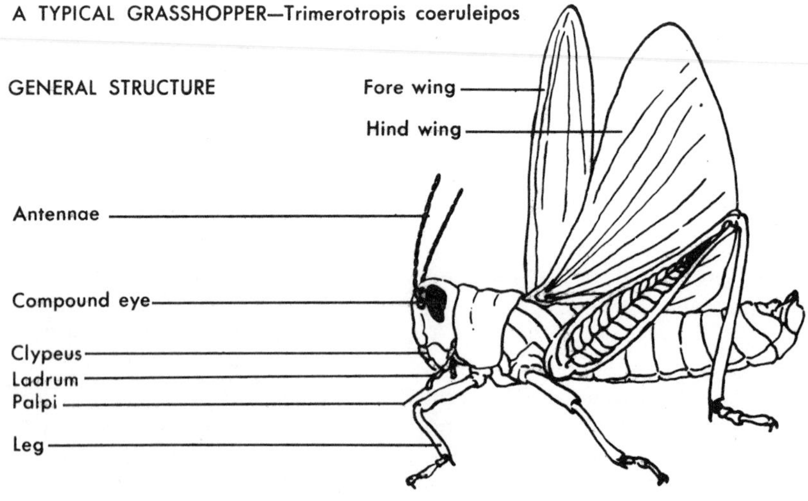

In contrast, then, to the sensory or impressionistic description, the technical description addresses itself exclusively to the mind, providing data that even a camera would miss: the ridge on the inner surface of each of the grasshopper's upper hind legs. It omits details that would strike us immediately in a photograph or that would be essential in a sensory description:

[4] Reprinted from *The Book of Popular Science* by permission of the publishers, Grolier Incorporated, New York.

the color and texture of the skin, the shape of the eyes. Although the technical description does not give us a visual impression of the grasshopper, it serves its own unique purpose. It enables us, without any further aids but the attributes included in the description, to identify an unknown insect as a grasshopper.

It is worth noting, finally, that like many technical or scientific descriptions this one uses an illustration to supplement the verbal picture, providing both an overall perspective and a set of details that words alone cannot communicate. Thus, whenever possible, the writer of a technical description should try to include a diagrammatic representation or illustration of what he is describing. One such diagram or sketch will often be worth the proverbial "thousand words."

As is true of many types of writing, the distinction between technical and sensory description is not always sharp. Occasionally, in a scientific description the writer uses details mainly for sensory effect, and more frequently the writer of a sensory description includes technical details that appeal to our understanding rather than our senses. In James Agee's description of a Southern cemetery below, the details are so strange and unfamiliar as to be barely believable. Yet we are moved to belief because the painstakingly rendered details and the matter-of-fact tone give the piece a documentary solidness. On the one hand, the description offers objective data ("The graveyard is about fifty by a hundred yards . . ."); on the other hand, it offers vivid sense impressions ("It is heavily silent and fragrant and all the leaves are breathing slowly . . ."). For many reasons, and on many levels, this essay in description will repay close study.

ASSIGNMENTS

I. A. Read the following descriptive essay:

SHADY GROVE, ALABAMA, JULY 1936

JAMES AGEE

The graveyard is about fifty by a hundred yards inside a wire fence. There are almost no trees in it: a lemon verbena and a small magnolia; it is all red clay and very few weeds.

Out at the front of it across the road there is a cornfield and then a field of cotton and then trees.

Most of the headboards are pine, and at the far end of the yard from the church the graves are thinned out and there are many slender and low pine stumps about the height of the headboards. The shadows are all struck sharp lengthwise of the graves, toward the cornfield, by the afternoon sun. There is no one anywhere in sight. It is heavily silent and fragrant and all the leaves are breathing slowly without touching each other.

Some of the graves have real headstones, a few of them so large they must be the graves of landowners. One is a thick limestone log erected by the Woodmen of the World. One or two of the others, besides a headpiece, have a flat of stone as large as the whole grave.

On one of these there is a china dish on whose cover delicate hands lie crossed, cuffs at their wrists, and the nails distinct.

On another a large fluted vase stands full of dead flowers, with an inch of rusty water at the bottom.

On others of these stones, as many as a dozen of them, there is something I have never seen before: by some kind of porcelain reproduction, a photograph of the person who is buried there; the last or the best likeness that had been made, in a small-town studio, or at home with a snapshot camera. I remember one well of a fifteen-year-old boy in Sunday pants and a plaid pullover sweater, his hair combed, his cap in his hand, sitting against a piece of farm machinery and grinning. His eyes are squinted against the light and his nose makes a deep shadow down one side of his chin. Somebody's arm, with the sleeve rolled up, is against him; somebody who is almost certainly still alive: they could not cut him entirely out of the picture. Another is a studio portrait, close up, in artificial lighting, of a young woman. She is leaned a little forward, smiling vivaciously, one hand at her cheek. She is not very pretty, but she believed she was; her face is free from strain or fear. She is wearing an evidently new dress, with a mail-order look about it; patterns of beads are sewn over it and have caught the light. Her face is soft with powder and at the wings of her nose lines have been deleted. Her dark blonde hair is newly washed and professionally done up in puffs at the ears which in that time, shortly after the first great war of her century, were called cootie garages. This image of her face is split across and the split has begun to turn brown at its edges.

I think these would be graves of small farmers.

There are others about which there can be no mistake: they are the graves of the poorest of the farmers and of the tenants. Mainly they are the graves with the pine headboards; or without them.

When the grave is still young, it is very sharply distinct, and of a peculiar form. The clay is raised in a long and narrow oval with a sharp ridge, the shape exactly of an inverted boat. A fairly broad board is driven at the head; a narrower one, sometimes only a stob, at the feet. A good many of the headboards have been sawed into the flat simulacrum of an hourglass; in some of these, the top has been roughly rounded off, so that the resemblance is more nearly that of a head and shoulders sunken or risen to the waist in the dirt. On some of these boards names and dates have been written or printed in hesitant letterings, in pencil or in crayon, but most of them appear never to have been touched in this way. The boards at some of the graves have fallen slantwise or down; many graves seem never to have been marked except in their own carefully made shape. These graves are of all sizes between those of giants and of newborn children; and there are a great many, so many they seem shoals of minnows, two feet long and less, lying near one another; and of these smallest graves, very few are marked with any wood at all, and many are already so drawn into the earth that they are scarcely distinguishable. Some of the largest, on the other hand, are of heroic size, seven and eight feet long, and of these more are marked, a few, even, with the smallest and plainest blocks of limestone, and initials, once or twice a full name; but many more of them have never been marked, and many, too, are sunken half down and more and almost entirely into the earth. A great many of these graves, perhaps half to two thirds of those which are still distinct, have been decorated, not only with shrunken flowers in their cracked vases and with bent targets of blasted flowers, but otherwise as well. Some have a line of white clamshells planted along their ridge; of others, the rim as well is garlanded with these shells. On one large grave, which is otherwise completely plain, a blown-out electric bulb is screwed into the clay at the exact center. On another, on the slop of clay just in front of the headboard, its feet next the board, is a horseshoe; and at its center a blown bulb is stood upright. On two or three others there are insulators of blue-green glass. On several graves, which I presume to be those of women, there is at the center the prettiest or the oldest and most valued piece of china: on one, a blue glass butter dish whose cover is a setting hen; on another, an intricate milk-colored glass basket; on others, ten-cent-store candy dishes and iridescent vases; on one, a pattern of white and colored buttons. On other graves there are small and thick white butter dishes of the sort which are used in lunch-rooms, and by the action of rain these stand free of the grave on slender turrets of clay. On still another grave, laid carefully next the headboard, is a corncob pipe. On the graves of children there are still these pretty pieces of glass and china, but they begin to diminish in size and they verge into the forms of animals and into homuncular symbols of growth; and there are toys: small autos, locomotives and fire engines of red and blue metal; tea sets for dolls, and tin kettles the size of thimbles: little effigies in rubber and glass and china, of cows, lions, bulldogs, squeaking mice, and the characters of comic strips; and . . . what two parents have done here for their little daughter: not only a tea set, and a cocacola bottle, and a milk bottle, ranged on her short grave, but a stone at the head and a stone at the foot, and in the headstone her six month image as she lies sleeping dead in her white dress, the head sunken delicately forward, deeply and delicately gone, the eyes seamed, as that of a dead bird, and on the rear face of this stone the words:

> We can't have all things to please us,
> Our little Daughter, Joe An, has gone to Jesus.[5]

B. Consider and evaluate this description of Shady Grove cemetery in terms of the following:

1. technical elements that give the piece documentary solidness
2. sensory images, personal impressions, judgments
3. point of view
4. selection, arrangement, and significance of details
5. organization
6. dominant mood or atmosphere
7. choice of words and images
8. tone
9. aptness of subject (Do you agree with poet John Ciardi that anything looked at carefully is worth looking at?)

C. Do you think this cemetery is worth looking at? Why?

D. Do you think a larger comment ("thematic statement") on human nature or life in general is being made in this essay?

[5] From *Let Us Now Praise Famous Men* by James Agee and Walker Evans. Copyright © renewed 1969 by Mia Fritsch Agee. Reprinted by permission of the publisher, Houghton Mifflin Company.

A. Point to the humorous and ironic details in "House Beautiful" that reveal Mark Twain's attitude toward this "residence of the principal citizen." Include such mocking touches (evident in the "voice" of the author) as "Pity, too; for she might have repented of this in time . . ."

B. Do the same with "The Girl of the Year."

III. A. Evaluate the following descriptions in terms of the dominant mood or impression the writer creates and how he creates it (choice of words, sounds, sense images, projection of feeling):

THE HOUSE OF USHER

EDGAR ALLAN POE

During the whole of a dull, dark, and soundless day in the autumn of the year, when the clouds hung oppressively low in the heavens, I had been passing alone, on horseback, through a singularly dreary tract of country; and at length found myself, as the shades of evening drew on, within view of the melancholy House of Usher. I know not how it was—but, with the first glimpse of the building, a sense of insufferable gloom pervaded my spirit. . . . I looked upon the scene before me—upon the mere house, and the simple landscape features of the domain—upon the bleak walls—upon the vacant eyelike windows—upon a few rank hedges—and upon a few white trunks of decaying trees—with an utter depression of soul which I can compare to no earthly sensation more properly than to the afterdream of the reveller upon opium—the bitter lapse into everyday life—the hideous dropping off of the veil. There was an iciness, a sinking, a sickening of the heart—an unredeemed dreariness of thought which no goading of the imagination could torture into aught of the sublime.

OCTOBER

THOMAS WOLFE

October had come again, and that year it was sharp and soon: frost was early, burning the thick green on the mountain sides to massed brilliant hues of blazing colors, painting the air with sharpness, sorrow and delight—and with October. Sometimes, and often, there was warmth by day, an ancient drowsy light, a golden warmth and pollenated haze in afternoon, but over all the earth there was the premonitory breath of frost, an exultancy for all the men who were returning, a haunting sorrow for the buried men, and for all those who were gone and would not come again.[6]

B. Describe a *person, place, setting,* or *event* (500–750 words) in such a way that you project the mood or atmosphere of one of the following:

bustling activity	luxury
calm and quiet	fear
sloppiness	suspicion

[6] Reprinted with the permission of Charles Scribner's Sons from *Of Time and The River*, pages 156–57, by Thomas Wolfe. Copyright 1935 Charles Scribner's Sons; renewal copyright © 1963 Paul Gitlin, Administrator, C.T.A.

cleanliness	loneliness
deprivation	despair
poverty	gaiety
beauty	ugliness

C. In 150–250 words, describe a season of the year, an aspect of a season, or a particular mood or emotion associated with a particular month ("April is the cruelest month," said T. S. Eliot, "mixing Memory and desire.").

D. In the manner of "Moonrise over Monument Valley," write a description (500–750 words) of a natural event as you watch it happen or as you imagine it, organizing your material chronologically.

IV. A. Write a technical description (250–300 words) comparable to "The Grasshopper." Illustrate if you wish.

B. As Louis Agassiz urged his students to "look at your fish" (pp. 368–69), so you are urged to study the picture below, noting every possible feature and detail. Then write a one-paragraph objective or technical description (250–500 words) in which you describe the "facts" of the picture: what it looks like to an objective observer who adds no personal opinion or judgment.

C. Write a second description (500–750 words) in which you respond personally and emotionally to the picture, projecting into it your own thoughts and feelings (in the style of Agee and Poe).

V. A. Write a descriptive essay (500–750 words) in which you adopt a suitable psychological point of view and maintain this attitude throughout.

B. Adopt the satirical point of view of the observer-commentator, in the manner of Tom Wolfe describing "The Girl of the Year," or Twain in "House Beautiful." Describe an "event"—a party, a person, a meeting, a family gathering, a class session—that you think lends itself to satire (500–750 words).

VI. A. Write a description of a room, a building, a street, a lake, a mountain, or the like from two different physical points of view (250 words each):

1. regarding your subject from a fixed position ("View from Rochester Bridge").

and

2. moving *through* your subject, beginning with an overall view from the perimeter (a long shot), and then coming progressively closer to note the finer details ("House Beautiful").

3 WHAT ARE THE COMPONENT PARTS OF X?

To ask about the component parts of something, to find out what they are and how they are related to one another—this is analysis. We are, of course, forever analyzing things simply because the only way to understand a person, an object, an idea, an event, a process, an organization is to take it apart in a systematic manner to try to see what makes it "tick," what made it happen, why it is as it is. Thus analysis is a natural function of the human mind, going on all the time as we explore the world around us in order to understand it better. Thinking itself is impossible without analysis; every subject we contemplate with any seriousness—whether we write or talk about it—is necessarily analyzed.

All the questions in this book, but particularly the next ten, deal with analysis in that they attempt to break down a total subject into its parts. Logicians call this process "division"; it is a necessary first step in problem-solving and in writing as well. Before we can deal with a subject we must see its internal divisions.

Analysis of a Physical Structure

The following essay asks, "What are the component parts of X?" Note that the organization of an analysis is more or less "given" to the writer; once he has answered the question "What are the component parts?" he has already outlined his essay: the parts of the subject become the parts of his piece. In this case, as you will see, the three components of blood plus the plasma constitute the four basic units of the discourse, which are in turn broken down into subunits, as each of the components is analyzed into *its* respective parts.

THE COMPOSITION OF BLOOD

LOUIS FAUGERES BISHOP

Introduction (states component elements)

Under the microscope we can see that [blood] is composed of a watery fluid called plasma, in which certain formed elements are suspended. The formed elements are different types of cells —red blood cells, white blood cells and platelets.

1. Red blood cells

The red blood cells are the most numerous of the formed elements. There are normally about 5,000,000 in each cubic millimeter of blood in men and about 4,500,000 in women during the child bearing years. Each cell is about 1/3500 of an inch in diameter. Normally the cells are in the form of disks, both sides of which are concave.

Red blood cells are developed in the red marrow, found in the ends of the long bones and throughout the interior of flat bones, such as the vertebrae and ribs. The cells have definite nuclei in the early stages of their formation; in man and the other mammals the nuclei are lost by the time the cells have become mature and before they are released into the blood stream.

(Broken down into their elements)

Each mature red blood cell has a structural framework called the stroma, which is made up chiefly of proteins and fatty materials. It forms a mesh extending into the interior of the cell; it gives the cell its shape and flexibility. The most important chemical substance in the cell is hemoglobin, which causes blood to have a red color. Hemoglobin is composed of an iron-containing pigment called heme and a protein called globin; there are about four parts of heme to ninety-six parts of globin. In man the normal amount of hemoglobin is 14 to 15.6 grams per 100 cubic centimeters of blood; in woman it is 11 to 14 grams.

Hemoglobin combines with oxygen in the lungs after air has been inhaled; the resulting compound is called oxyhemoglobin. When the red blood cells later make their way to other parts of the body deficient in oxygen, the oxygen in the compound breaks its bonds and makes its way by diffusion to the tissues of the oxygen-poor areas. Thus the red blood cells draw oxygen from the lungs, transport it in the blood stream and release it to the tissues as needed.

2. White blood cells

The white blood cells are the body's military force, attacking disease organisms such as staphylococci, streptococci and meningococci. These cells are far less numerous than the red variety; the proportion of white to red under normal conditions is 1 to 400 or 500. The white cells are semitransparent bodies. They differ from red cells in several important respects; among other things, they contain no hemoglobin and they always have nuclei.

(Indication of the varieties)

There are several easily distinguished varieties of white cells: neutrophils, lymphocytes, basophils, eosinophils and monocytes. Neutrophils, basophils and eosinophils are formed in the bone marrow. Lymphocytes are made in the lymphatic tissues; monocytes, in the reticulo-endothelial system.

The neutrophils are by far the most numerous of the white blood cells, making up from 65 to 70 per cent of the total. They derive their name from the fact that they readily take the color of a neutral dye. These cells are about half as large again as red blood cells.

3. Platelets

Platelets are tiny circular or oval disks, which are derived from certain giant cells in the bone marrow, called megakaryocytes. Their number ranges from 200,000 per cubic millimeter to 500,000 or more. The platelets, which are much smaller than the blood cells, serve several useful purposes. When they disintegrate, they liberate a substance called thrombokinase or thromboplastin, which is vital in the blood-clotting process. They also help to plug leaks in the tiny blood vessels called capillaries.

4. Analysis of plasma

The plasma is the watery part of the blood, making up from 50 to 60 per cent of the total. It is a clear yellow fluid, serving as a vehicle for the transportation of red blood cells, white blood cells, platelets and various substances necessary for the vital functioning of the body cells, for clotting and for the defense of the body against disease. After clotting occurs, a straw-colored fluid called serum is left; this retains its liquid form indefinitely.

About 90 per cent of plasma is water, in which a great variety of substances are held in suspension or in solution. These include proteins, such as fibrinogen, albumin and the globulins, and also sugar, fat and inorganic salts derived from food or from the storage depots of the body. Plasma contains urea, uric acid, creatine and other products of the breakdown of proteins. There are enzymes, such as adrenal hormones, thyroxine and insulin, derived from the glands of internal secretion. There are also various gases: oxygen and nitrogen, diffused into the blood from the lungs; and carbon dioxide, diffused into the blood from the tissues.[1]

Analysis of an Intellectual Structure

Just as objects and substances may be broken down into their physical parts, ideas and concepts may be divided into their conceptual and psychological components: the thoughts, attitudes, and feelings that make up the idea or concept of "patriotism," for example. Conceptual analysis is more common than physical analysis. Most people regularly try to "figure things out" in their heads, whereas relatively few want to know about "taking things apart" (like a television set or a clock).

Ultimately, if one is determined enough, no concept is too abstract for analysis. The renowned physicist, Robert Andrew Millikan, for example, believed that most people do not understand the conceptual whole called the "scientific spirit," and he wrote the following essay to analyze what it is in terms of its three basic elements.

[1] "The Life Stream: What Blood Is and What It Does," *The Book of Popular Science* (Canada: The Grolier Society, 1971), III, 325–31.

THE SPIRIT OF MODERN SCIENCE

ROBERT ANDREW MILLIKAN

The spirit of modern science is something relatively new in the history of the world, and I want to give an analysis of what it is. I want to take you up in an aeroplane which flies in time rather than in space, and look down with you upon the high peaks that distinguish the centuries, and let you see what is the distinguishing characteristic of the century in which we live. I think there will be no question at all, if you get far enough out of it so that you can see the woods without having your vision clouded by the proximity of the trees, that the thing which is characteristic of our modern civilization is the spirit of scientific research,—a spirit which first grew up in the subject of physics, and which has spread from that to all other subjects of modern scientific inquiry.

That spirit has three elements. The first is a philosophy; the second is a method; and the third is a faith.

Look first at the philosophy. It is new for the reason that all primitive peoples, and many that are not primitive, have held a philosophy that is both animistic and fatalistic. Every phenomenon which is at all unusual, or for any reason not immediately intelligible, used to be attributed to the direct action of some invisible personal being. Witness the peopling of the woods and streams with spirits, by the Greeks; the miracles and possession by demons, of the Jews; the witchcraft manias of our own Puritan forefathers, only two or three hundred years ago.

That a supine fatalism results from such a philosophy is to be expected; for, according to it, everything that happens is the will of the gods, or the will of some more powerful beings than ourselves. And so, in all the ancient world, and in much of the modern, also, three blind fates sit down in dark and deep inferno and weave out the fates of men. Man himself is not a vital agent in the march of things; he is only a speck, an atom which is hurled hither and thither in the play of mysterious, titanic, uncontrollable forces.

Now, the philosophy of physics, a philosophy which was held at first timidly, always tentatively, always as a mere working hypothesis, but yet held with ever increasing conviction from the time of Galileo, when the experimental method may be said to have had its beginnings, is the exact antithesis of this. Stated in its most sweeping form, it holds that the universe is rationally intelligible, no matter how far from a complete comprehension of it we may now be, or indeed may ever come to be. It believes in the absolute uniformity of nature. It views the world as a mechanism, every part and every movement of which fits in some definite, invariable way into the other parts and the other movements; and it sets itself the inspiring task of studying every phenomenon in the confident hope that the connections between it and other phenomena can ultimately be found. It will have naught of caprice. Such is the spirit, the attitude, the working hypothesis of all modern science; and this philosophy is in no sense materialistic, because good, and mind, and soul, and moral values,—these things are all here just as truly as are any physical objects; they must simply be inside and not outside of this matchless mechanism.

Second, as to the method of science. It is a method practically unknown to the ancient world; for that world was essentially subjective in all its thinking, and built up its views of things largely by introspection. The scientific method, on the other hand, is a method which is ready for the discard the very minute that it fails to work. It is the method which believes in a minute, careful, wholly dispassionate analysis of a situation; and any physicist or engineer who allows the least trace of prejudice or preconception to enter into his study of a given problem violates the most sacred duty of his profession. This present cataclysm, which has set the world back a thousand years in so many ways, has shown us the pitiful spectacle of scientists who have forgotten completely the scientific method, and who have been controlled simply by prejudice and preconception. This fact is no reflection on the scientific method; it merely means that these men have not been able to carry over the methods they use in their science into all the departments of their thinking. The world has been controlled by prejudice and emotionalism so long that reversions still occur; but the fact that these reversions occur does not discredit the scientist, nor make him disbelieve in his method. Why? Simply because that method has worked; it is working to-day, and its promise of working to-morrow is larger than it has ever been before in the history of the world.

Do you realize that within the life of men now living, within a hundred years, or one hundred and thirty years at most, all the external conditions under which man lives his life on this earth have been more completely revolutionized than during all the ages of recorded history which preceded? My great-grandfather lived essentially the same kind of life, so far as external conditions were concerned, as did his Assyrian prototype six thousand years ago. He went as far as his own legs, or the legs of his horse, could carry him. He dug his ditch, he mowed his hay, with the power of his own two arms, or the power of his wife's two arms, with an occasional lift from his horse or his ox. He carried a dried potato in his pocket to keep off rheumatism, and he worshipped his God in almost the same superstitious way. It was not until the beginning of the nineteenth century that the great discovery of the ages began to be borne in upon the consciousness of mankind through the work of a few patient, indefatigable men who had caught the spirit which Galileo perhaps first notably embodied, and passed on to Newton, to Franklin, to Faraday, to Maxwell, and to the other great architects of the modern scientific world in which we live,—the discovery that man is not a pawn in a game played by higher powers, that his external as well as his internal destiny is in his own hands.

You may prefer to have me call that not a discovery but a faith. Very well! It is the faith of the scientist, and it is a faith which he will tell you has been justified by works. Take just this one illustration. In the mystical, fatalistic ages, electricity was simply the agent of an inscrutable Providence: it was Elijah's fire from Heaven sent down to consume the enemies of Jehovah, or it was Jove's thunderbolt hurled by an angry god; and it was just as impious to study so direct a manifestation of God's power in the world as it would be for a child to study the strap with which he is being punished, or the mental attributes of the father who wields the strap. It was only one hundred and fifty years ago that Franklin sent up his famous kite, and showed that thunderbolts are identical with the sparks which he could draw on a winter's night from his cat's back. Then, thirty years afterward Volta found that he could manufacture them artificially by dipping dissimilar metals into an acid. And, thirty years farther along, Oersted found that, when tamed and running noiselessly along a wire, they will deflect a magnet: and with that discovery the electric battery was born, and the erstwhile blustering thunderbolts were set the inglorious task of ringing house bells, primarily for the convenience of womankind. Ten years later Faraday found that all he had to do to obtain a current was to move a wire across the pole of a magnet, and in that discovery the dynamo was born, and our modern electrical age, with its electric transmission of power, its electric lighting, its electric telephoning, its electric toasting, its electric foot warming, and its electric milking. All that is an immediate and inevitable consequence of that discovery,—a discovery which grew out of the faith of a few physicists that the most mysterious, the most capricious, and the most terrible of natural phenomena is capable of a rational explanation, and ultimately amenable to human control.

At the [Pennsylvania state] Capitol in Harrisburg is a picture by Sir Edwin Abbey, which is entitled, "Wisdom, or the Spirit of Science." It consists of a veiled figure with the forked lightnings in one hand, and in the other, the owl and the serpent, the symbols of mystery; and beneath is the inscription:

I am what is, what hath been, and what shall be.
My veil has been disclosed by none.
What I have brought forth is this: The sun is born.

It is to lighten man's understanding, to illuminate his path through life, and not merely to make it easy, that science exists.[2]

Here again the essay—like most essays in simple analysis—is organized at the moment the writer indicates what his component parts are: the elements of the "spirit" are also the units of the piece. Thus Millikan's essay can be outlined as follows:

INTRODUCTION:

The spirit of modern science is relatively new; has three elements: philosophy, method, and faith.

I. Philosophy

II. Method

III. Faith

CONCLUSION:

As the picture "Wisdom, or the Spirit of Science" illustrates, science exists to illuminate life, not merely make it easy.

Principles of Analysis

Analysis is a challenging and demanding form of writing in that it requires systematic and rigorously logical thinking conducted in the light of clear and consistent principles. We cannot concern ourselves here with formal logic, but neither can we ignore three basic logical principles that are fundamental to all analysis, whether performed by a logician or by a writer:

1. Analysis (or division) must be made according to the structure of the thing analyzed. In logical terms, to smash a glass is not to divide it because a glass is not composed of fragments of glass. To determine the component parts of a glass it is necessary to make a chemical analysis.

[2] From pp. 311–12 in *Science in Literature,* edited by Frederick H. Law (Harper, 1929). Reprinted by permission of Harper & Row, Publishers.

2. The kind of structure being analyzed depends on the interest of the analyzer. Thus, English literature can be analyzed as a chronological structure into Old, Middle, Modern, or it can be analyzed into various genres—poetry, drama, essays and so on. Whatever structure the writer chooses to work with, he must be consistent if he is to achieve the primary purpose of analysis: to keep component parts clear and distinct. Thus, he cannot analyze literature into Old, Middle, and poetry. This analysis shifts its basis of division from chronology to genre.

3. A logical analysis should also be complete—i.e., X should be divided into *all* its component parts, not just some of them. In scientific or technical analysis this is mandatory; in a general essay on a nonscientific subject, however, the writer need not be quite as strict. He may choose to deal with only the main part or selected aspects of his subject, in which case he should indicate that the analysis is partial and incomplete, thereby letting the reader know he has not inadvertently overlooked the elements he has not mentioned. One simple device for completing a division with dispatch is to include the category "others" or "miscellaneous." Thus, in analyzing the body of an author's works, we might divide them into novels, plays, short stories, and "miscellaneous writings." In this way nothing is left out.

Notice that the two essays so far cited in this section amply fulfill these prerequisites of logical analysis. In "The Composition of Blood" Bishop analyzes blood in terms of its natural components; he never shifts the basis of division (to "rich" or "poor" blood, color of blood, rate of flow). The analysis is also complete; although Bishop does not name every protein or enzyme found in plasma, he indicates that there are others ("also various gases") that fall into the explicitly stated main categories. Similarly in his essay on modern science, Millikan analyzes this vast and complex subject in terms of his special interest—i.e., its spirit. At no point does he shift his ground to contemplate the various types of sciences (biology, chemistry), their degree of "purity," their difficulty. And here again, in terms of *how* he analyzes his subject, Millikan is complete: as he sees it there are three and no more than three "basic elements."

Skillfully written, analysis can reveal the essence of a seemingly difficult or esoteric subject. Take music, for example, which many people enjoy, but relatively few understand. Hoping to increase enjoyment by promoting understanding, musicologist David Randolph wrote the following analysis in which he views the totality "music" in terms of his chosen interest or point of view: what the listener responds to. The analysis is strictly logical in that Randolph sticks scrupulously throughout to the special ground on which the analysis rests. He never shifts to types of music, individual instruments, etc. There is also no question as to whether it is complete. There are five and only five important elements to respond to in music. Even "if we wanted to be rigid about definitions," Randolph assures us, "we could say that music consists of nothing but the manipulation of the five elements."

FIVE BASIC ELEMENTS OF MUSIC

DAVID RANDOLPH

Let us see what it is that you respond to in music.

Do you find something appealing about the famous tune from Schubert's Unfinished Symphony? If so, then you are responding to one of the most important elements of music—*melody*.

Do you find that you feel like tapping your foot during the march movement of Tchaikovsky's Pathetique Symphony? If so, then you are responding to another extremely important element—*rhythm*.

Yet observe that rhythm is present in the melody of Schubert's Unfinished (just tap out the melody on a table with your finger, without singing, and you will isolate the rhythm), and that melody is present in even the most rhythmic portion of the Tchaikovsky march. Therefore, in the process of merely "liking" one of these works, you are actually appreciating *two* musical elements at once. While this example may not impress you by its profundity, the *principle* —being aware of what it is that you respond to—is at the root of all genuine music appreciation.

Now imagine how much less satisfying Schubert's melody would be if it were buzzed through a tissue-papered comb, instead of being played by the entire cello section of an orchestra. The melody and the rhythm would still be present as before; the difference would lie only in the quality of the sound that reached your ears. Therefore, when you enjoy the richness of the sound of the massed cellos playing the melody, you are responding to another of the basic elements—*tone color*. Your appreciation, then, really involves *three* elements.

Now, let us suppose that a pianist is playing one of your favorite songs—the melody in the right hand, the accompanying chords in the left. Suppose that his finger slips as he plays one of the chords, causing him to play a sour note. Your immediate awareness of that wrong note comes from your response to another of the basic elements—*harmony*.

Let us briefly consider the more positive implications of harmony. Whether you are attracted by barbershop-quartet singing, or by an atmospheric work by Debussy, or by the powerful, forthright ending of Beethoven's Fifth Symphony, *part* of your reaction stems from your response to the harmony, which may be defined as the simultaneous sounding of two or more notes (usually more than two, as in these three examples). Thus we have found a *fourth* element in your appreciation.

Do you have a sense of completeness at the conclusion of a performance of (we will use only one of countless possible examples) Beethoven's Ninth Symphony? Are you left with a feeling of satisfaction as well as of elation? If so, part of that sense of satisfaction—of completion—comes from your feeling for *form,* which is the last of the five basic elements of music. . . .

If we wanted to be rigid about definitions, we could say that music consists of nothing but the manipulation of the five elements. The statement is correct in that there is no music in the world, regardless of the time or place of its origin, that can be based upon anything other than some combination of these five elements. Thus, to offer the most extreme contrast possible, what we may imagine as the ritual stamping on the ground by the savage appealing to his gods partakes of some the same basic elements as does Bach's

Passion According to St. Matthew, notably rhythm and tone color, and certainly, to a degree, form.[3]

ASSIGNMENTS

I. Analyze the three essays in this section in terms of the following rhetorical issues:

A. As you can infer it from the essays themselves, describe the rhetorical stance of each writer: his purpose and his relationship to subject, occasion, and reader. Is each identical to, similar to, or different from the other two?

B. Evaluate paragraph structure according to where "breaks" occur. Indicate how they do or do not coincide with steps in the unfolding and development of the ideas in each essay. Are the paragraphs themselves unified? internally consistent? Explain.

C. Comment on the appropriateness of tone in these essays.

(*Note:* In order to deal effectively with the above questions it is advisable that you read the following sections: Introduction, p. 9 and Chapter 27.)

II. Assuming a rhetorical stance similar to Randolph and using the informal direct "you" address to the reader, write an essay (500–750 words) in which you isolate the elements of one of the following:

Arts	*Sports*
ballet	baseball
painting	football
architecture	soccer
photography	tennis
opera	golf
literature	skiing

III. As Robert Millikan analyzes the spirit of modern science by breaking it down into its three elements, write an essay (500–750 words) in which you describe the "spirit" of one of the following by analyzing it in terms of its basic elements—features, qualities, beliefs.

the spirit of modern art
the spirit of the new morality
the spirit of dissent
the spirit of revolution
the spirit of liberal education

IV. A. Read the essay below and answer the questions that follow:

[3] From *This Is Music: A Guide to the Pleasures of Listening,* by David Randolph. Copyright © 1964 by David Randolph. Used with permission of McGraw-Hill Book Company.

THE CREDO OF THE INTELLECTUALS (1920's)

FREDERICK LEWIS ALLEN

What was the credo of the intellectuals during these years of revolt? Not many of them accepted all the propositions in the following rough summary; yet it suggests, perhaps, the general drift of their collective opinion:

They believed in a greater degree of sex freedom than had been permitted by the strict American code; and as for discussion of sex, not only did they believe it should be free, but some of them appeared to believe it should be continuous. They formed the spearhead of the revolution in manners and morals. . . . From the early days of the decade, when they thrilled at the lackadaisical petting of F. Scott Fitzgerald's young thinkers and at the boldness of Edna St. Vincent Millay's announcement that her candle burned at both ends and could not last the night, to the latter days when they were all agog over the literature of homosexuality and went by the thousand to take Eugene O'Neill's five-hour lesson in psychopathology, *Strange Interlude,* they read about sex, talked about sex, thought about sex, and defied anybody to say No.

In particular, they defied the enforcement of propriety by legislation and detested all the influences to which they attributed it. They hated the Methodist lobby, John S. Sumner, and all other defenders of censorship; they pictured the Puritan, even of Colonial days, as a blue-nosed, cracked-voiced hypocrite; and they looked at Victorianism as half indecent and half funny. The literary reputations of Thackeray, Tennyson, Longfellow, and the Boston *literati* of the last century sank in their estimation to new lows for all time. Convinced that the era of short skirts and literary dalliance had brought a new enlightenment, the younger intellectuals laughed at the "Gay Nineties" as depicted in *Life* and joined Thomas Beer in condescending scrutiny of the voluminous dresses and fictional indirections of the Mauve Decade. Some of them, in fact, seemed to be persuaded that all periods prior to the coming of modernity had been ridiculous—with the exception of Greek civilization, Italy at the time of Casanova, France at the time of the great courtesans, and eighteenth-century England.

Most of them were passionate anti-prohibitionists, and this fact, together with their dislike of censorship and their skepticism about political and social regeneration, made them dubious about all reform movements and distrustful of all reformers. They emphatically did not believe that they were their brothers' keepers; anybody who did not regard tolerance as one of the supreme virtues was to them intolerable. If one heard at a single dinner party of advanced thinkers that there were "too many laws" and that people ought to be let alone, one heard it at a hundred. In 1915 the word reformer had been generally a complimentary term: In 1925 it had become—among the intellectuals, at least—a term of contempt.

They were mostly, though not all, religious skeptics. If there was less shouting agnosticism and atheism in the nineteen-twenties than in the eighteen-nineties it was chiefly because disbelief was no longer considered sensational and because the irreligious intellectuals, feeling no evangelical urge to make over others in their own image, were content quietly to stay away from church. It is doubtful if any college undergraduate of the nineties or of any other previous period in the United States could have said "No intelligent person believes in God any more" as blandly as undergraduates said it during the discussions of compulsory college chapel which raged during the 'twenties. Never before had so many books addressed to the thinking public assumed at the outset that their readers had rejected the old theology.

They were united in a scorn of the great bourgeois majority which they held responsible for prohibition, censorship, Fundamentalism, and other repressions. They emulated Mencken in their disgust at Babbitts, Rotarians, the Ku Klux Klan, Service-with-a-Smile, boosters, and super-salesmen. Those of them who lived in the urban centers prided themselves on their superiority to the denizens of the benighted outlying cities and towns where Babbittry flourished; witness, for example, the motto of the *New Yorker* when it was first established in the middle of the decade: "Not for the old lady from Dubuque." Particularly did they despise the mobs of prosperous American tourists which surged through Europe; one could hardly occupy a steamer chair next to anybody who had Aldous Huxley's latest novel on his lap without being told of a delightful little restaurant somewhere in France which was quite "unspoiled by Americans."

They took a particular pleasure in overturning the idols of the majority; hence the vogue among them of the practice for which W. E. Woodward, in a novel published in 1923, invented the word "debunking." Lytton Strachey's *Queen Victoria,* which had been a best seller in the United States in 1922, was followed by a deluge of debunking biographies. Rupert Hughes removed a few coats of whitewash from George Washington and nearly caused a riot when he declared in a speech that "Washington was a great card-player, a distiller of whisky, and a champion curser, and he danced for three hours without stopping with the wife of his principal general." Other American worthies were portrayed in all their erring humanity, and the notorious rascals of history were rediscovered as picturesque and glamorous fellows; until for a time it was almost taken for granted that the biographer, if he were to be successful, must turn conventional white into black and vice versa.

They feared the effect upon themselves and upon American culture of mass production and the machine, and saw themselves as fighting at the last ditch for the right to be themselves in a civilization which was being leveled into monotony by Fordismus and the chain-store mind. Their hatred of regimentation gave impetus to the progressive school movement and nourished such innovations in higher education as Antioch, Rollins, Meiklejohn's Experimental College at Wisconsin, and the honors plan at Swarthmore and elsewhere. It gave legal impetus to the little-theater movement, which made remarkable headway from coast to coast, especially in the schools. The heroes of current novels were depicted as being stifled in the air of the home town, and as fleeing for their cultural lives either to Manhattan or, better yet, to Montparnasse or the Riviera. In any café in Paris one might find an American expatriate thanking his stars that he was free from standardization at last, oblivious of the fact that there was no more standardized institution even in the land of automobiles and radio than the French sidewalk café. The intellectuals lapped up the criticisms of American culture offered them by foreign lecturers imported in record-breaking numbers, and felt no resentment when the best magazines flaunted before their eyes, month after month, titles like "Our American Stupidity" and "Childish Americans." They quite expected to be told that America was sinking into barbarism and was an altogether impossible place for a civilized person to live in—as when James Truslow Adams lamented in the *Atlantic Monthly*, "I am wondering, as a personal but practical question, just how and where a man of moderate means who prefers simple living, simple pleasures, and the things of the mind is going to be able to live any longer in his native country."

Few of the American intellectuals of the nineteen-twenties, let it be repeated, subscribed to all the propositions in this credo, but he or she who accepted none of them was suspect among the enlightened. He was not truly civilized, he was not modern. The prosperity band-wagon rolled on, but by the wayside stood the highbrows with voices upraised in derision and dismay.[4]

1. What is a "credo"?
2. Into how many constituent parts is this subject divided? What are they?
3. Is the division complete? or complete *enough?*
4. Are the parts arranged logically? Can you detect any particular principle of order?
5. Comment on the organization of the essay.
6. Is there a single quality or "spirit" that runs through all the parts?
7. Does the credo of the intellectuals appear to be *thoughtful, moderate, fair-minded?* or *pretentious, close-minded, intolerant?* What qualities of heart and mind do you feel run through the separate "propositions" of this credo? Cite specific words and phrases that seem to be clues.
8. Can you detect the writer's attitude toward the intellectuals from his manner of writing? Would you say his tone is reverent? amused? disdainful? flippant? angry? Again cite specific clues: words, phrases, images, manner of expressions that create the special "tone of voice" that emerges in this piece.

B. Write an essay (500–750 words) analyzing the credo of the intellectuals today (or of the "hippies," "radicals," or any special group in which you have an interest).

[4] From pp. 234–38 in *Only Yesterday* by Frederick Lewis Allen. Copyright, 1931 by Frederick Lewis Allen; renewed, 1959 by Agnes Rogers Allen. Reprinted by permission of Harper & Row, Publishers, Inc.

4 HOW IS X MADE OR DONE?

If you were to ask how something is done or made, you would be entering into a special form of analysis that rhetoricians call "process analysis." Here, instead of dividing a given subject into its component parts, you divide an ongoing process into its successive stages.

An essay of this kind presents an orderly, step-by-step, chronologically arranged description of how a process of some kind takes place, how it is conducted, how it functions, how a poem is written (a creative process); how a clock keeps time (a mechanical process); how plants make chlorophyll (a natural process); how bread is baked (a manufacturing process); how women won the franchise (a social process); how the Russian Revolution began (a historical process). An essay in process analysis is apt to be readable and lively, for by its very nature it keeps moving from stage one, to stage two, to stage three, and so on.

Suppose, for example, you address the question "How is X done?" to some aspect of creativity (subject #4 on the checklist): the creative art of choreography. In this case you might write an essay like the following vividly descriptive analysis by choreographer Agnes DeMille of how she composes a ballet.

COMPOSING A BALLET

AGNES DEMILLE

To make up a dance, I still need . . . a pot of tea, walking space, privacy and an idea. . . .

When I first visualize the dance, I see the characters moving in color and costume. Before I go into rehearsal, I know what costumes the people wear and generally what color and texture. I also, to a large extent, hear the orchestral effects. Since I can have ideas only under the stress of emotion, I must create artificially an atmosphere which will induce this excitement. I shut myself in a studio and play gramophone music, Bach, Mozart, Smetana, or almost any folk music in interesting arrangements. At this point I avoid using the score because it could easily become threadbare.

I start sitting with my feet up and drinking pots of strong tea, but as I am taken into the subject I begin to move and before I know it I am walking the length of the studio and acting full out the gestures and scenes. The key dramatic scenes come this way. I never forget a single nuance of them afterwards; I do usually forget dance sequences.

The next step is to find the style of gesture. This is done standing and moving, again behind locked doors and again with a gramophone. Before I find how a character dances, I must know how he walks and stands. If I can discover the basic rhythms of his natural gesture, I will know how to expand them into dance movements.

It takes hours daily of blind instinctive moving and fumbling to find the revealing gesture, and the process goes on for weeks before I am ready to start composing. Nor can I think any of this out sitting down. My body does it for me. It happens. That is why the choreographic process is exhausting. It happens on one's feet after hours of work, and the energy required is roughly the equivalent of writing a novel and winning a tennis match simultaneously. This is the kernel, the nucleus of the dance. All the design develops from this.

Having established a scenario and discovered the style and key steps, I then sit down at my desk and work out the pattern of the dances. If the score is already composed, the dance pattern is naturally suggested by and derived from the pattern of the music. If it remains to be composed as it does in all musical comedies, the choreographer goes it alone. This, of course, is harder. Music has an enormous suggestive power and the design of the composer offers a helpful blueprint. . . .

Through practice I have learned to project a whole composition in rough outline mentally and to know exactly how the dancers will look at any given moment moving in counterpoint in as many as five groups. As an aid in concentration, I make detailed diagrams and notes of my own arbitrary invention, intelligible only to me and only for about a week, but they are not comparable in exactness to music notation.

At this point, I am ready, God help me, to enter the rehearsal hall.[1]

Obviously it is not difficult to organize an essay in process analysis because it generally organizes itself in a time sequence. What *is* difficult is dividing the process into logical sequential stages, and making certain that each stage is accurately described, for if there is one weak link in the chain, the entire explanation can collapse, leaving the reader in confusion.

Notice how carefully Agnes DeMille has "divided" the choreographic act into its component parts—i.e., the six successive steps through which it is "carried out":

step one: getting the ideas (and the conditions for developing them: a pot of tea, walking space)

[1] Copyright 1951, 1952 by Agnes DeMille. From *Dance to the Piper* by Agnes De Mille, by permission of Atlantic-Little, Brown and Co.

step two: visualizing the dancers "moving" in color and costume and "hearing" the music
step three: establishing key dramatic scenes
step four: discovering the basic gestures, rhythms, and style of character ("My body does it for me.")
step five: writing down the pattern of the dances (detailed diagrams and notes)
step six: entering the rehearsal hall (with God's help!)

Notice also that the six steps *flow* into one another. At no point does the reader wonder what stage he is at, for "time" words (plus "place" words, pronouns that refer to earlier nouns, repetitions of key words) keep him oriented and moving steadily *ahead:*

When I first visualize the dance . . .
Before I go into rehearsal . . .
At this point I avoid using the score . . .
I *begin* to move and *before* I know it . . .
I never forget a single nuance . . . *afterwards* . . .
The *next* step is to find the style . . .
. . . *again* behind locked doors and *again* with a gramophone . . .
Before I find how a character dances . . .
. . . the process *goes on for weeks* . . .
. . . *after* hours of work . . .
I *then* sit down at my desk . . .
At this point, I am ready . . .

The creative process, as it has been described by many scientists and artists, falls roughly into four stages: *preparation*—the stage of deliberate and conscious planning, training, and effort; *incubation*—the stage in which one is not *consciously* dwelling on a problem but is nonetheless "mulling it over" on an unconscious level; *illumination*—the "flash" wherein one sees, as Bertrand Russell tells us in the following essay, "exactly what I had to say."; *verification*—the stage in which one checks and tests his newly discovered hypothesis and reviews and revises what he has "made."

HOW I WRITE

BERTRAND RUSSELL

I cannot pretend to know how writing ought to be done, or what a wise critic would advise me to do with a view to improving my own writing. The most that I can do is to relate some things about my own attempts.

Until I was twenty-one, I wished to write more or less in the style of John Stuart Mill. I liked the structure of his sentences and his manner of developing a subject. I had, however, already a different ideal, derived, I suppose, from mathematics. I wished to say everything in the smallest number of words in which it could be said clearly. Perhaps, I thought, one should imitate Baedeker rather than any more literary model. I would spend hours trying to find the shortest way of saying something without ambiguity, and to this aim I was willing to sacrifice ali attempts at aesthetic excellence.

At the age of twenty-one, however, I came under a new influence, that of my future brother-in-law, Logan Pearsall Smith. He was at that time exclusively interested in style as opposed to matter. His gods were Flaubert and Walter Pater, and I was quite ready to believe that the way to learn how to write was to copy their technique. He gave me various simple rules, of which I remember only two: "Put a comma every four words," and "never use 'and' except at the beginning of a sentence." His most emphatic advice was that one must always re-write. I conscientiously tried this, but found that my first draft was almost always better than my second. This discovery has saved me an immense amount of time. I do not, of course, apply it to the substance, but only to the form. When I discover an error of an important kind, I re-write the whole. What I do not find is that I can improve a sentence when I am satisfied with what it means.

Very gradually I have discovered ways of writing with a minimum of worry and anxiety. When I was young each fresh piece of serious work used to seem to me for a time—perhaps a long time—to be beyond my powers. I would fret myself into a nervous state from fear that it was never going to come right. I would make one unsatisfying attempt after another, and in the end have to discard them all. At last I found that such fumbling attempts were a waste of time. It appeared that after first contemplating a book on some subject, and after giving serious preliminary attention to it, I needed a period of sub-conscious incubation which could not be hurried and was if anything impeded by deliberate thinking. Sometimes I would find, after a time, that I had made a mistake, and that I could not write the book I had had in mind. But often I was more fortunate. Having, by a time of very intense concentration, planted the problem in my sub-consciousness, it would germinate underground until suddenly the solution emerged with blinding clarity, so that it only remained to write down what had appeared as if in a revelation.

The most curious example of this process, and the one which led me subsequently to rely upon it, occurred at the beginning of 1914. I had undertaken to give the Lowell Lectures at Boston, and had chosen as my subject "Our Knowledge of the External World." Throughout 1913 I thought about this topic. In term time in my rooms at Cambridge, in vacations in a quiet inn on the upper reaches of the Thames, I concentrated with such intensity that I sometimes forgot to breathe and emerged panting as from a trance. But all to no avail. To every theory that I could think of I could perceive fatal objections. At last, in despair, I went off to Rome for Christmas, hoping that a holiday would revive my flagging energy. I got back to Cambridge on the last day of 1913, and although my difficulties were still completely unresolved I arranged, because the remaining time was short, to dictate as best I could to a stenographer. Next morning, as she came in at the door, I suddenly saw exactly what I had to say, and proceeded to dictate the whole book without a moment's hesitation.

I do not want to convey an exaggerated impression. The book was very imperfect, and I now think that it contains serious errors. But it was the best that I could have done at that time, and a more leisurely method (within the time at my disposal) would almost certainly have produced something worse. Whatever may be true of other people, this is the right method for me. Flaubert and Pater, I have found, are best forgotten so far as I am concerned.

Although what I now think about how to write is not so very different from what I thought at the age of eighteen, my development has not been by any means rectilinear. There was a time, in the first years of this century, when I had more florid and rhetorical ambitions. This was the time when I wrote *The Free Man's Worship,* a work of which I do not now think well. At that time I was steeped in Milton's prose, and his rolling periods reverberated through the caverns of my mind. I cannot say that I no longer admire them, but for me to imitate them involves a certain insincerity. In fact, all imitation is dangerous. Nothing could be better in style than the Prayer Book and the Authorized Version of the Bible, but they express a way of thinking and feeling which is different from that of our time. A style is not good unless it is an intimate and almost involuntary expression of the personality of the writer, and then only if the writer's personality is worth expressing. But although direct imitation is always to be deprecated, there is much to be gained by familiarity with good prose, especially in cultivating a sense of prose rhythm.[2]

Historical-Social Process

As mentioned above, process analysis is relatively easy to organize since it falls naturally into a chronological progression. What happens, however, when the progress being analyzed is so complex (as in many historical events or in complicated scientific processes) that dozens, maybe hundreds, of stages are involved? In such a case, it would be unwieldy, if not impossible, to analyze each stage. One solution is to "block out" the process in terms of three or four key units around which a multitude of actions can be arranged.

In historical analysis, then, the main challenge is to find an appropriate way of grouping the stages of a given action, for the limitless day-by-day, minute-by-minute details involved in any historical occurrence could easily swamp the writer. Certainly he cannot include everything. He must group his facts around given "centers"; he must also be scrupulously clear about chronology. Notice how the writer of the following historical process sweeps through centuries of history in a single paragraph by clustering all the events of the prehistoric period around three main groups of migrants who arrived in Britain in three waves (note also the time transitions: *first, next,* and *later*).

First wave

First were the paleolithic men, or men of the rough-stone age, who used rude weapons, ornaments, and implements of stone and bone. They probably lived in caves and depended for their subsistence on the wild beasts they captured and the vegetable prod-

Second wave

ucts they found growing wild. *Next* were the neolithic men, or men of the polished-stone age, who used the well-shaped stone, bone, and horn implements that are frequently found, and probably lived in some kind of artificial buildings, raised crops, kept domestic animals, knew how to weave cloth and to make pottery, and perhaps traded with other peoples. They built and deposited their dead in long burial mounds such as those whose remains still

2 From *Portraits from Memory,* by Bertrand Russell. Copyright © 1951, 1952, 1953, 1956 by Bertrand Russell. Reprinted by permission of Simon and Schuster and George Allen & Unwin Ltd.

Third wave

exist. They were small men, perhaps of the same race as is now represented by the Basques of Spain. *Later* than these came a race who knew the use of bronze, who buried their dead in small, round burial mounds, and who were probably the builders of Stonehenge, Kit's Coty House, and the other mysterious groups of standing stones which are found scattered through England. These are known as men of the bronze age, and may have been the earliest immigrants of the race dominant in Britain when our written knowledge of it begins.[3]

Technical-Natural Process

Still another recurrent type of process analysis involves description of natural or technical operations. Here again transitional devices are especially important, for they link the stages of a process that might otherwise seem fragmented or discontinuous. What keeps the stages clearly sequential are "time" words, "place" words (such as "here"), pronouns that refer to nouns in preceding sentences, and repetition of key words. Observe how these several factors work in the following paragraph, a brief—but clear and precise—analysis of a physiological process: how blood circulates. (Key transitions and repetitions are italicized.)

Part of the *blood* in the heart [receives] a fresh store of *oxygen* from the *lungs*. This *blood* is pumped into a large *artery—the aorta*—and from the aorta it is carried into a branched system of smaller *arteries*. From the *arteries* it passes into the capillaries. *Here oxygen* and food materials (which have been absorbed from the small intestine and liver) are given up to the tissues. Waste materials, including the gas carbon dioxide, are received. The *blood then* passes to the veins. It is returned to the heart by way of two large veins.

Next, the *blood* is pumped from the heart through the large *pulmonary artery* to the *lungs*. (*Pulmonary* comes from the Latin *pulmo*: "lung.") In the *lungs* carbon dioxide is discharged and *oxygen* is received. The *blood* is *then* returned to the heart through the *pulmonary* veins, and another cycle *begins*.[4]

The two analyses that follow are also technical, although they are very different in both tone and style. The first is a straightforward factual explanation of the working of a thermostat, described in terms of the natural laws that underlie it—specifically the fact that liquid expands when it is heated. This account is dry and somewhat difficult to read (the average person may need to read it more than once), for it is an uncompromisingly detailed description of an uncompromisingly natural-mechanical process.

The second analysis, "The Process of Riveting," while technical, is easier to read because *the process is humanized.* It is written from the point of view of the people involved in the process. Thus the collective effort of the riveters at each step of the way—their skillful and risky manipulation of

[3] From *A Short History of England* revised and enlarged editic 1 by Edward P. Cheyney. Reprinted by permission of Ginn and Company.

[4] Reprinted from *The Book of Popular Science* by permission of the publishers, Grolier Incorporated, New York.

the rivet—introduces an element of life and suspense into an otherwise mechanical procedure.

THE WAY THINGS WORK: A THERMOSTAT

A thermostat is a device for maintaining a temperature constant at a desired value. For this purpose it is equipped with a temperature sensing unit which detects any deviation of the actual temperature from the desired value and transmits information on this to a device which cancels the deviation. The sensing unit may be a tube filled with a liquid, a bimetallic strip or a spring bellows. The simplest device of this kind is the direct-acting thermostat. It makes use of the fact that nearly all liquids expand on heating (Fig. 1). The thermostat itself consists of a tube filled with a liquid which expands very considerably when it is heated (Fig. 2). The connection to the control device which actuates the valve in the hot-water supply pipe (for example) is established by a capillary tube which is also filled with liquid. If the air temperature in the room under thermostatic control rises above the desired level, the liquid in the sensing unit expands, overcomes the restraining force of a spring

Fig. 1 PRINCIPLE OF THERMOSTATIC CONTROL

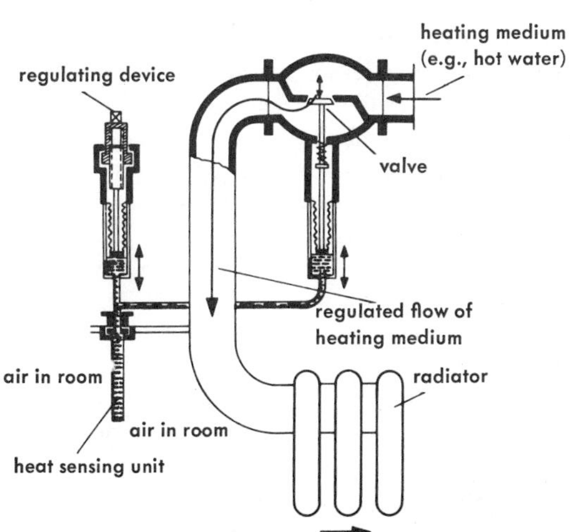

Fig. 2 THERMOSTAT FOR SPACE HEATING CONTROL (*direct action*)

on the valve, and throttles or closes the latter. As a result of this, the flow of hot water (or other heating medium) is reduced and less heat is supplied to the room. Because of this the temperature in the room will go down after a time, so that the liquid cools and contracts. The spring load on the valve once again exceeds the pressure exerted by the liquid and opens the valve. In this way the temperature in the room is kept constant within fairly narrow limits. The desired value of the temperature is set on a graduated scale which has been calibrated by the makers. By rotation of the screw on the control device the valve spring is compressed to a greater or less extent by the liquid, so that the valve correspondingly opens more or less. The low rate of the hot water thus increases or decreases, causing the temperature level in the room to rise or to fall (Fig. 2).[5]

THE PROCESS OF RIVETING

The actual process of riveting is simple—in description. Rivets are carried to the job by the rivet boy, a riveter's apprentice whose ambition it is to replace one of the members of the gang—which one, he leaves to luck. The rivets are dumped into a keg beside a small coke furnace. The furnace stands on a platform of loose boards roped to steel girders which may or may not have been riveted. If they have not been riveted there will be a certain amount of play in the temporary bolts. The furnace is tended by the heater or passer. He wears heavy clothes and gloves to protect him from the flying sparks and intense heat of his work, and he holds a pair of tongs about a foot and a half long in his right hand. When a rivet is needed, he whirls the furnace blower until the coke is white-hot, picks up a rivet with his tongs, and drives it into the coals. His skill as a heater appears in his knowledge of the exact time necessary to heat the steel. If he overheats it, it will flake, and the flakes will permit the rivet to turn in its hole. And a rivet which gives in its hole is condemned by the inspectors.

When the heater judges that his rivet is right, he turns to face the catcher, who may be above or below him or fifty or sixty or eighty feet away on the same floor level with the naked girders between. There is no means of handing the rivet over. It must be thrown. And it must be accurately thrown. And if the floor beams of the floor above have been laid so that a flat trajectory is essential, it must be thrown with considerable force. The catcher is therefore armed with a smallish, battered tin can, called a cup, with which to catch the red-hot steel. Various patented cups have been put upon the market from time to time but they have made little headway. Catchers prefer the ancient can.

The catcher's position is not exactly one which a sportsman catching rivets for pleasure would choose. He stands upon a narrow platform of loose planks laid over needle beams and roped to a girder near the connection upon which the gang is at work. There are live coils of pneumatic tubing for the rivet gun around his feet. If he moves more than a step or two in any direction, he is gone, and if he loses his balance backward he is apt to end up at street level without time to walk. And the object is to catch a red-hot iron rivet weighing anywhere from a quarter of a pound to a pound and a half and capable, if he

[5] From *The Way Things Work: An Illustrated Encyclopedia of Technology.* Copyright © 1967, by George Allen & Unwin, Ltd. Reprinted by permission of Simon and Schuster.

lets it pass, of drilling an automobile radiator or a man's skull 500 feet below as neatly as a shank of shrapnel. Why more rivets do not fall is the great mystery of skyscraper construction. The only reasonable explanation offered to date is the reply of an erector's foreman who was asked what would happen if a catcher on the Forty Wall Street job let a rivet go by him around lunch hour. "Well," said the foreman, "he's not supposed to."

There is practically no exchange of words among riveters. Not only are they averse to conversation, which would be reasonable enough in view of the effect they have on the conversation of others, but they are averse to speech in any form. The catcher faces the heater. He holds his tin can up. The heater swings his tongs, releasing one handle. The red iron arcs through the air in one of those parabolas so much admired by the stenographers in the neighboring windows. And the tin can clanks.

Meantime the gun-man and the bucker-up have prepared the connection—aligning the two holes, if necessary, with a drift pin driven by a pneumatic hammer—and removed the temporary bolts. They, too, stand on loose-roped boards with the column or the beam between them. When the rivet strikes the catcher's can, he picks it out with a pair of tongs held in his right hand, knocks it sharply against the steel to shake off the glowing flakes, and rams it into the hole, an operation which is responsible for his alternative title of sticker. Once the rivet is in place, the bucker-up braces himself with his dolly bar, a short heavy bar of steel, against the capped end of the rivet. On outside wall work he is sometimes obliged to hold on by one elbow with his weight out over the street and the jar of the riveting shaking his precarious balance. And the gun-man lifts his pneumatic hammer to the rivet's other end.

The gun-man's work is the hardest work, physically, done by the gang. The hammers in use for steel construction work are supposed to weigh around thirty pounds and actually weigh about thirty-five. They must not only be held against the rivet end, but held there with the gun-man's entire strength, and for a period of forty to sixty seconds. (A rivet driven too long will develop a collar inside the new head.) And the concussion to the ears and to the arms during that period is very great. The whole platform shakes and the vibration can be felt down the column thirty stories below. It is common practice for the catcher to push with the gun-man and for the gun-man and the bucker-up to pass the gun back and forth between them when the angle is difficult. Also on a heavy rivet job the catcher and the bucker-up may relieve the gun-man at the gun.

The weight of the guns is one cause, though indirect, of accidents. The rivet set, which is the actual hammer at the point of the gun, is held in place, when the gun leaves the factory, by clips. Since the clips increase the weight of the hammer, it is good riveting practice to knock them off against the nearest column and replace them with a hank of wire. But wire has a way of breaking, and when it breaks there is nothing to keep the rivet set and the pneumatic piston itself from taking the bucker-up or the catcher on the belt and knocking him into the next block.[6]

6 "Riveting a Skyscraper," by the Editors of *Fortune* (October 1930). Courtesy of *Fortune* magazine.

Intellectual Process

When you try to present a "train of thought" or a line of reasoning—in order to explain your views, or to argue a case for or against something—you are attempting to describe an intellectual or logical process, one which is based on the laws of reasoning. No finer essay has been written in this category than Thomas Huxley's eminently readable analysis of the act of thinking itself: how we use the inductive and deductive modes in our everyday lives.

THINKING SCIENTIFICALLY

THOMAS HENRY HUXLEY

There is a well-known incident in one of Molière's plays, where the author makes the hero express unbounded delight on being told that he had been talking prose during the whole of his life. In the same way, I trust, that you will take comfort, and be delighted with yourselves, on the discovery that you have been acting on the principles of inductive and deductive philosophy during the same period. Probably there is not one here who has not in the course of the day had occasion to set in motion a complex train of reasoning, of the very same kind, though differing of course in degree, as that which a scientific man goes through in tracing the causes of natural phenomena.

A very trivial circumstance will serve to exemplify this. Suppose you go into a fruiterer's shop, wanting an apple,—you take up one, and, on biting it, you find it sour; you look at it, and see that it is hard and green. You take up another one, and that too is hard, green, and sour. The shopman offers you a third; but, before biting it, you examine it, and find that it is hard and green, and you immediately say that you will not have it, as it must be sour, like those that you have already tried.

Nothing can be more simple than that, you think; but if you will take the trouble to analyse and trace out into its logical elements what has been done by the mind, you will be greatly surprised. In the first place you have performed the operation of induction. You found that, in two experiences, hardness and greenness in apples went together with sourness. It was so in the first case, and it was confirmed by the second. True, it is a very small basis, but still it is enough to make an induction from; you generalise the facts, and you expect to find sourness in apples where you get hardness and greenness. You found upon that a general law, that all hard and green apples are sour; and that, so far as it goes, is a perfect induction. Well, having got your natural law in this way, when you are offered another apple which you find is hard and green, you say, "All hard and green apples are sour; this apple is hard and green, therefore this apple is sour." That train of reasoning is what logicians call a syllogism, and has all its various parts and terms,—its major premiss, its minor premiss, and its conclusion. And, by the help of further reasoning, which if drawn out, would have to be exhibited in two or three other syllogisms, you arrive at your final determination, "I will not have that apple." So that, you see, you have, in the first place, established a law by induction, and upon that you have founded a deduction, and reasoned out the special conclusion of the particular case. Well now, suppose, having got your law, that at some time afterwards, you are discussing the qualities of apples with a friend: you will say to him, "It is a very curious thing,—but I find that all hard and green apples are sour!" Your friend says to you, "But how do you know that?" You at once reply, "Oh, because I have tried them over and over again, and have always found them to be so." Well, if we were talking science instead of common sense, we should call that an experimental verification. And if still opposed, you go further, and say, "I have heard from the people in Somersetshire and Devonshire, where a large number of apples are grown, that they have observed the same thing. It is also found to be the case in Normandy, and in North America. In short, I find it to be the universal experience of mankind wherever attention has been directed to the subject." Whereupon, your friend, unless he is a very unreasonable man, agrees with you, and is convinced that you are quite right in the conclusion you have drawn. He believes, although perhaps he does not know he believes it, that the more extensive verifications are,—that the more frequently experiments have been made, and results of the same kind arrived at,—that the more varied the conditions under which the same results are attained, the more certain is the ultimate conclusion, and he disputes the question no further. He sees that the experiment has been tried under all sorts of conditions, as to time, place and people, with the same result; and he says with you, therefore, that the law you have laid down must be a good one, and he must believe it.

In science we do the same thing;—the philosopher exercises precisely the same faculties, though in a much more delicate manner. In scientific inquiry it becomes a matter of duty to expose a supposed law to every possible kind of verification, and to take care, moreover, that this is done intentionally, and not left to a mere accident, as in the case of the apples. And in science, as in common life, our confidence in a law is in exact proportion to the absence of variation in the result of our experimental verifications. For instance, if you let go your grasp of an article you may have in your hand, it will immediately fall to the ground. That is a very common verification of one of the best established laws of nature—that of gravitation. The method by which men of science establish the existence of that law is exactly the same as that by which we have established the trivial proposition about the sourness of hard and green apples. But we believe it in such an extensive, thorough, and unhesitating manner because the universal experience of mankind verifies it, and we can verify it ourselves at any time; and that is the strongest possible foundation on which any natural law can rest.[7]

ASSIGNMENTS

I. Creative Process

A. Write an essay (500–750 words) describing a creative experience you have had—the composition of a poem, story, or piece of music; the painting of a picture; the design of a room or a piece of furniture.

or

B. Describe the process of learning how to do something (as Russell learned to write). Any accomplishment will provide a suitable topic:

[7] From *Collected Works*, by Thomas H. Huxley.

how you learned to swim, ski, speak French, play bridge—maybe even how you learned "to think," i.e., to think *rigorously*. (Assignment IV, p. 84).

II. Historical Process

A. Write an essay (500–750 words) on one of the following topics, chosen from one of the following groups:

1. Discoveries and Inventions

How Schliemann discovered Troy
How Columbus discovered America
How Salk discovered the polio vaccine
How Pasteur discovered the pasteurization process
How the Curies discovered radium
How Bell invented the telephone
How Edison invented the electric light

2. General Historical Events

Beginnings:

How Alaska became a state
How the Great Wall of China was built
How the Third Reich rose

Endings:

How Belgium lost the Belgian Congo
How the French Revolution ended
How the Roman Empire fell

3. Social and Political Process

How Congress investigates
How a U.S. president is elected
How women won the vote
How the Eighteenth Amendment was repealed

4. General Enterprises

How a newspaper or magazine is "put to bed"
From press to doorstep: the paper is delivered
How a class is conducted
How a party is organized
How a paper is written
How a trip is planned
How traffic is regulated
How a university is run (or any part thereof)

III. Technical-Natural Process

A. Answer the following questions based on the essay "The Way Things Work: A Thermostat."

1. Describe the stages in the action of a thermostat.
2. Are they clearly indicated in this essay, or must they be inferred?
3. Before describing the *action* of a thermostat, what information must the writer offer?
4. What purpose do the illustrations serve?

5. Does this description of a process convey *attitudes* of any kind?
6. Write a short essay comparable to this one (150–250 words) in which you describe (in terms of the natural laws underlying the process) how one of the following works:

a camera	a radio
a microscope	a barometer
a telegraph	a parachute
a magnet	a mirror

B. Answer the following questions based on the essay "The Process of Riveting."

1. Outline the main stages involved in riveting steel.
2. How does the writer move us through the stages? (Note his point of view.)
3. What additional information, i.e., additional to the "outline of stages," does the writer include in this analysis (biographical data, descriptive details, suggestion of attitudes, anecdotes, description of people)? Why does he include them?
4. Comment on the writer's style: length of paragraphs and unity; choice of words (technical? plain?); length and difficulty of sentences; transitional devices; general flow and readability, appropriateness of tone.
5. Comment specifically on the following sentences. In what way do they contribute to the overall tone of the piece?
   a. "It must be thrown. And it must be accurately thrown."
   b. "Catchers prefer the ancient can."
   c. "The catcher's position is not exactly one which a sportsman catching rivets for pleasure would choose."
   d. "Well, he's not supposed to."
   e. "And the tin can clanks."
6. Do you agree with the rhetorician who called this "a justly admired example of description of a process"?
7. In the style of this article, write an essay (500–750 words) in which you humanize one of the following complex processes, showing how people participate in it:

   How explosives are manufactured
   How glass is blown
   How skyscraper windows are washed
   How paintings are restored
   How tobacco is cured

C. Write an essay (500–750 words) explaining one of the following natural processes:

1. Physiology (how X functions)

   How we see
   How we hear
   How we maintain balance
   How we breathe
   How we digest food
   How we think
   How we remember
   How we fall asleep

2. Botany (how X is made)

How plants manufacture chlorophyll
How plants manufacture oxygen
How plants manufacture food
How plants reproduce
How plants evolve
How trees develop "rings"

IV. "Thinking Scientifically"

A. Write an essay (350–500 words) called "Thinking Scientifically," in which you illustrate your own everyday use of inductive and deductive reasoning.

B. Write another essay of equal length supporting Dr. Johnson's counter observation that "most men think indistinctly." In this instance cite illustrations of the illogical, the irrational, the impulsive, the half-thought-through. Suggested title: "Thinking Unscientifically."

5 HOW SHOULD X BE MADE OR DONE?

With this question we come to the most practical type of writing: the "how-to" piece, a form of process analysis that tells the reader not only how a particular process *is* made or done, but how it *should be* made or done. Thus it becomes a set of directions from the writer to his reader, telling him precisely how to move through a series of steps toward a given goal. All recipes are clearly instances of the "how-to" form, as are all inside-the-package instructions. We conduct much of the business of the world by means of this kind of writing. Here, for example, is a straightforward account of how to acquire a relatively simple skill.

BEGINNER'S RECIPE FOR WALKING

AARON SUSSMAN AND RUTH GOODE

Take (as the recipes say) a comfortable pair of shoes. In a man's wardrobe any daytime pair will do for a beginning, but a woman may have to hunt through the closet for shoes low in the heel and broad in the toe.

Take comfortable clothes, suitable for the season, light rather than heavy. Again, a man is ordinarily dressed for a first try at walking, but a woman will have to look in her wardrobe for a wide enough skirt or, better yet, slacks. What you wear depends on where you walk; look at Chapter II, "Walking Comfort," for more on clothes and shoes. There is no doubt that dressing especially for a walk puts us in the right frame of mind for good walking, but we want to fit walking into our daily lives, and we will not do that if we insist on too many special trimmings.

And here is a negative: *Do not take your dog.* That is, not unless he (or she) is trained as a walking companion. An animal pulling or dragging on a leash, or running free and into trouble, is no pleasure on a walk. If your dog is young enough, take it to an obedience school. When it has passed the course, both of you will enjoy your walks together. . . .

Take a time. Any time that you fit into your daily round is a good time for walking. If you have only twenty minutes, you can walk a mile.

Take a place. Any place will do that is pleasant. Look for places convenient to your daily tasks and customary ways. If you go to an office or job, find a part of the route that you can walk. Walk to the train if you commute. Walk to the second or third bus stop or subway station from your house; get off, as Paul Dudley White does, a stop or two before your usual one. Park your car ten blocks farther away and walk the half mile to and from it. Walk ten blocks to and from lunch. Go out and walk after dinner, before you sit down to the television, a book, or the work you brought home. . . .

Walk a modest distance at first. If you walk a mile out, you have to walk a mile back, and that's two miles. Walking in the city, you have the streets to tell you how far you have gone, but in the country you can go farther than you realize and the return trip can take you past your fatigue point. Even the shoes that were so comfortable can pinch and chafe on the way back. As you walk day by day, your limit stretches. Your watch will tell you how long you have walked but not how far, unless you know your rate of speed. So add this ingredient to the recipe:

Take a pedometer. . . . Set it to your stride and register the distance of your walk while you measure the time by your watch. You will be walking farther and farther without fatigue, and with pedometer and watch you can readily see after each walk where your fatigue point is. Use your pedometer as a safety device, until you are a seasoned walker who can go for miles without tiring.

Comfortably dressed and shod, a person in ordinary health can walk a mile without fatigue. At three miles an hour, a brisk but not strenuous pace for most people, that's a twenty-minute walk. After you have walked a mile a day for a week, and enjoyed it, you will be looking for ways to steal twenty minutes more for another mile. The time will soon come when five miles (one hour and forty minutes) is your weekend treat, and the daily mile or two miles is a walk you hardly even notice.[1]

Qualities of Good "How-to" Writing

"How-to" or directional writing automatically puts the writer into the authoritative position of instructor, telling his "less informed" reader-students exactly what to do and how to do it. Imperatives are common in a "how-to" piece: *take* a time; *take* a place; *do not take* your dog. With the sense of self-importance that inevitably accompanies this form of writing, however, the writer should feel an equal sense of responsibility, for in assuming the role of teacher and counselor, he must make certain he is teaching well and counseling wisely.

[1] From *The Magic of Walking*, by Aaron Sussman and Ruth Goode. Copyright © 1967, by Aaron Sussman and Ruth Goode. Reprinted by permission of Simon and Schuster.

The writer's first responsibility, of course, is to be accurate and clear. If, for example, he is instructing the reader in "the art of winning at bridge," he has to be absolutely certain first that he has his facts right, and second that he explains them clearly, not leaving out a single step or important detail, taking nothing for granted; allowing for no uncertainties or ambiguities as to what is meant. These are the cardinal virtues of directional writing: accuracy, clarity, and still another quality—*conciseness.* No extra words should clog the free-flow of information. Instructions should be written in a systematic, absolutely lucid, and readable manner.

"How-to" pieces present no serious organizational problems since directions must be given in strict chronological order (first do this, then that, etc.) and the mode of address, as we have seen, is invariably imperative.

Variety in "How-to" Writing

The "how-to" form clearly lends itself to an extraordinarily wide range of subject matter and an equally wide variety of tones. In general, the writer and reader are brought together in intimate contact (direct address from *me* to *you*), thereby establishing a situation in which the deeper humanistic purposes of writing have an excellent opportunity to fulfill themselves: increasing understanding among men; sharing knowledge and skills; helping one another.

The most helpful "how-to" pieces often deal with concrete and important activities that people should know about. Thus a book like *What To Do Till the Doctor Comes* performs a public service by providing a series of "how-to" essays explaining the essentials of first-aid treatment for a variety of ills—such as bleeding.

HOW TO CONTROL BLEEDING BY PRESSURE BANDAGE

As a rule, bleeding which is not severe can be controlled by placing a compress (pad of sterile gauze, clean handkerchief, or similar material) over the wound and applying pressure by means of a bandage or adhesive-tape strapping. If the pressure bandage does not control the bleeding, hand pressure applied on the compress directly over the wound may stop it. When bleeding has been controlled by a pressure bandage, do not remove the dressing if it soaks through. By doing so you will disturb the blood clots which are forming and may hurt the patient, thus increasing the danger of shock. Put another dressing on top of the first one and bandage tightly.[2]

Less concrete in terms of physical action, but useful in their own way (provided they are not too "pat") are advice pieces such as the following:

[2] *What To Do Till the Doctor Comes,* by Donald B. Armstrong, M.D. and Grace T. Hallock. Copyright © 1943, by Simon and Schuster, Inc. Reprinted by permission of the publisher.

HOW TO GET MORE WORK DONE

JOHN KORD LAGEMANN

Whenever I meet anyone with a special flair for getting things done, I make a point of asking, "How do you do it?" The answers, I have found, are rules of thumb which belong in the category of practical wisdom rather than scientific research—but they work. Here are the techniques that busy men and women in a wide variety of professions have told me that are most helpful.

Get started. "There are two steps in getting any task done," said the late Adlai Stevenson when I asked him how he managed to write all his own speeches in addition to carrying on his official duties as U.S. Ambassador to the United Nations. "The first step is to begin. The second is to begin again. The first is the hardest."

Making a good start on any new project is like taking your first parachute jump—it requires boldness. At 40, Winston Churchill took up painting as a hobby. "Very gingerly," Churchill recalled, "I mixed a little blue paint with a very small brush, and then with infinite precaution made a mark about as big as a small bean upon the affronted snow-white shield." At that moment, a friend who was a painter's wife entered the room and exclaimed, "But what are you hesitating about?" Seizing a brush, she walloped the canvas with large, fierce strokes. "The spell was broken," Churchill concluded. "I have never felt any awe of a canvas since. This beginning with audacity is a great part of the art of painting." It is also a large part of tackling and mastering any new job.

Just getting into the posture for work may put you in the mood. Pianist Ania Dorfman said that the hardest part of practicing was sitting down at the keyboard. After that, habit and discipline took over and set her in motion. . . .

Choose a pacesetter. Every coach knows that the best way to improve the performance of a player is to expose him to pacesetters—outstanding players who set high standards of skill and endurance. In tennis, for example, it is impossible for even an ace to show what he can do if he is matched with a dud. Dennis Ralston, three times the top-ranking U.S. amateur tennis player before recently turning pro, says, "In training, the main problem is to find the opponent who is a little better than you are, and learn how to beat him at his own game." . . .

Manage your time. Time is our working capital. "Managing it is everybody's No. 1 problem," says the well-known management consultant, Peter F. Drucker, in his recent book, *The Effective Executive.* "Those who really get things done don't start with their work; they start with their time."

Like money, time has a way of disappearing—a dribble here, a dribble there, until you find yourself asking at the end of a busy day, "Where did it go?" It's only by budgeting the hours and minutes of the day that you can have time left over for your own personal use. It's this "discretionary time" that buys freedom from harassment and a sense of mastery in getting a job done.

One of the most effective techniques of time management is the simple one of setting a deadline. Once my two sons and I spent a week by ourselves in the country. We had to do all the housework, but we put off doing the domestic chores until the house was a mess. One night I bet the boys a dollar

I could do the supper dishes in ten minutes. They took me up on it, and I finished just under the wire. Next night my sons shaved two minutes off my record. We assigned time limits to the other daily housekeeping tasks, and found that we could keep things shipshape with no more than an hour of concentrated work. The rest of the day was ours to do with as we pleased.

. . . One day the editor dropped in to see how the work was going and, realizing that I was getting nowhere, said, "Did you ever notice that one of the first things that strikes you about a girl is her perfume? After you've been with her a while, the perfume seems to disappear. But if you leave her and come back, the scent is as vivid as ever. Maybe that's what you should do with this article. Leave it for a while and do something else. Then come back to it."

I took his advice, and the article was finished. Since then, I've noticed that most people who work with ideas use this same device. They work on one problem until they start losing the feel of it, then turn to something else. Later they return to the first problem with fresh interest.

Filter out the irrelevant. Imagine yourself surrounded by an invisible bubble within which you are shielded from distraction. The outside world is still there, but the wall of your bubble filters out everything irrelevant to the task at hand.

Concentration doesn't mean a narrowing down of interest. It means the widening out and fullest use of all one's powers—a comprehensive problem under consideration. Emerson called this kind of concentration "the secret of strength in politics, in war, in trade—in short, in all management of human affairs."

Find your own work rhythm. The conventional way of breaking up the day is so many hours for work and so many for play, relaxation and sleep. But if you feel like working after dinner—or, for that matter, at 3 A.M.—why not? A lot of creative work can be done at odd times and places.

The great Canadian physician Sir William Osler, between his teaching, his medical writings and practice, had very little time to pursue his lifelong interest in books. However, he set aside 15 minutes every night to compile an annotated bibliography of his huge library. When he died his ambitious *Bibliotheca Osleriana* contained 7787 entries.

Finish the job. Jobs, like stories, have a beginning, a development and an end. Having started work on a project, many of us don't know when or where to stop. The solution is to plan your work in advance so that when you come to the point where your plan is fulfilled, you can say, "That's that."

Don't be like the futile politician of whom philosopher George Santayana once said, "Having lost sight of his goal, he redoubles his effort." Define your goal precisely, so that once it is attained you can move on to other projects. . . .[3]

For humorists as well as serious advice-givers, the "how-to" piece opens up vast possibilities, as can be seen in the delightfully zany piece that follows:

[3] Reprinted with permission from the May 1967 *Reader's Digest.* Copyright 1967 by the Reader's Digest Assn., Inc. Also reprinted by permission of Mrs. John Kord Lagemann.

HOW TO BE EFFICIENT WITH FEWER VIOLINS

The following is the report of a Work Study Engineer after a visit to a symphony concert at the Royal Festival Hall in London:

For considerable periods the four oboe players had nothing to do. The number should be reduced and the work spread more evenly over the whole of the concert, thus eliminating peaks of activity.

All the twelve violins were playing identical notes; this seems unnecessary duplication. The staff of this section should be drastically cut. If a larger volume of sound is required, it could be obtained by means of electronic apparatus.

Much effort was absorbed in the playing of demi-semi-quavers; this seems to be an unnecessary refinement. It is recommended that all notes should be rounded up to the nearest semi-quaver. If this were done it would be possible to use trainees and lower-grade operatives more extensively.

There seems to be too much repetition of some musical passages. Scores should be drastically pruned. No useful purpose is served by repeating on the horns a passage which has already been handled by the strings. It is estimated that if all redundant passages were eliminated the whole concert time of 2 hours could be reduced to 20 minutes and there would be no need for an interval.

The conductor agrees generally with these recommendations, but expresses the opinion that there might be some falling off in box-office receipts. In that unlikely event, it should be possible to close sections of the auditorium entirely, with a consequential saving of overhead expenses, lighting, attendance, etc. If the worst came to the worst, the whole thing could be abandoned and the public could go to the Albert Hall instead.

Following the principle that "There is always a better method," it is felt that further review might still yield additional benefits. For example, it is considered that there is still wide scope for application of the "Questioning Attitude" to many of the methods of operation, as they are in many cases traditional and have not been changed for several centuries. In the circumstances it is remarkable that Methods Engineering principles have been adhered to as well as they have. For example, it was noted that the pianist was not only carrying out most of his work by two-handed operation, but was also using both feet for pedal operations. Nevertheless, there were excessive reaches for some notes on the piano and it is probable that re-design of the keyboard to bring all notes within the normal working area would be of advantage to this operator. In many cases the operators were using one hand for holding the instrument, whereas the use of a fixture would have rendered the idle hand available for other work.

It was noted that excessive effort was being used occasionally by the players of wind instruments, whereas one air compressor could supply adequate air for all instruments under more accurately controlled conditions.

Obsolescence of equipment is another matter into which it is suggested further investigation could be made, as it was reputed in the program that the leading violinist's instrument was already several hundred years old. If normal depreciation schedules had been applied the value of this instrument should have been reduced to zero and it is probable that purchase of more modern equipment could have been considered.[4]

[4] From *Ministry of Transport Bulletin.*

Carrying the "How-to" Too Far

Some people feel that as a prose form, "how-toism" has been extended to ridiculous extremes, that it threatens to run our lives: "How to eat, talk, breathe, sleep, cook with sour cream, play canasta, give a church supper, raise parakeets, and bet on the horses. How to be healthy, wealthy, wise, and happily married. How to become popular, articulate, refined, charming, virile, cultured, and couth. How to cope with children, sex, religion, old age, Christmas, in-laws, and other common problems of life."[5]

More disturbing, "how-toism" often distorts a difficult process by depicting it in a rosy glow of simplicity ("there's nothing to it!"). Two actual titles establish this point clearly enough: "You Can Make a Stradivarius Violin" and "The Art of Becoming an Original Writer in Three Days."

Most of us have read similar pieces that simplify, to the point of simple-mindedness, the intricacies of real life. Take, for example, the following:

HOW TO STOP WORRYING

DALE CARNEGIE

Rule 1: Get the facts. Remember that Dean Hawks of Columbia University said that "half the worry in the world is caused by people trying to make decisions before they have sufficient knowledge on which to base a decision."

Rule 2: After carefully weighing all the facts, come to a decision.

Rule 3: Once a decision is carefully reached, act! Get busy carrying out your decision—and dismiss all anxiety about the outcome.

Rule 4: When you, or any of your associates, are tempted to worry about a problem, write out and answer the following questions:

a. What is the problem?
b. What is the cause of the problem?
c. What are all possible solutions?
d. What is the best solution?[6]

There is probably nothing wrong with these suggestions as sensible, thumb-nail guides for the average "worry wart." But in the face of the complexities of human nature and human predicaments, such guides are pathetically pat and superficial. Indeed, anyone who sincerely believes that he can solve the problem of worrying simply by following Dale Carnegie's four basic rules has in fact something to worry about!

[5] Dwight Macdonald, *Against the American Grain* (New York: Random House, 1962), p. 361.

[6] From *How to Stop Worrying and Start Living* by Dale Carnegie. Copyright © 1944, 1945, 1946, 1947, 1948 by Dale Carnegie. Reprinted by Simon and Schuster, Inc.

ASSIGNMENTS

I. Evaluate the five "how-tos" in this section ("Beginner's Recipe for Walking," "How to Control Bleeding," "How to Get More Work Done," "How to Be Efficient with Fewer Violins," and "How to Stop Worrying") in terms of the following principles of writing:

A. *accuracy* (Are the facts correct? Indicate in what ways the writer may have oversimplified or overcomplicated the process.)

B. *clarity* (Are the steps clearly presented?)

C. *economy* (Are there any unnecessary words or information?)

D. *rhetorical stance* (To whom is the writer addressing himself? What is his point of view? tone? purpose in writing the piece?)

II. Write an essay (500–750 words) in which you present "A Beginner's Recipe" for one of the following:

stamp collecting
bird watching
folk dancing
tightrope walking
hunting an alligator
bicycle riding
serving a tennis ball
playing billiards
diving
hiking
pitching horseshoes
mountain climbing
kite flying
pitching a tent
fishing

III. Write a short self-help piece (150–250 words) in which you:

A. Offer concrete suggestions on how to treat the following physical ills:

high fever
cold
frostbite
poison ivy
acne
athlete's foot
hangover
first-degree burn
bee sting
dog bite
muscle strain

B. Offer concrete, sensible, and restrained suggestions on how to deal with the following psychological problems:

attempts to stop smoking
insomnia
hysteria

shock
depression
anxiety
dreams
fatigue
guilt
drugs

C. Offer sweepingly oversimplified advice on the problems listed above.

IV. The agony of figuring out so-called "easy-to-follow" instructions in order to "do-it-yourself" has never been more eloquently described than in the following essay by one of America's best-known humorists.

INSERT FLAP A

S. J. PERELMAN

One stifling summer afternoon last August, in the attic of a tiny stone house in Pennsylvania, I made a most interesting discovery: the shortest, cheapest method of inducing a nervous breakdown ever perfected. In this technique (eventually adopted by the psychology department of Duke University, which will adopt anything), the subject is placed in a sharply sloping attic heated to 340° F. and given a mothproof closet known as the Jiffy-Cloz to assemble. The Jiffy-Cloz, procurable at any department store or neighborhood insane asylum, consists of half a dozen gigantic sheets of red cardboard, two plywood doors, a clothes rack, and a packet of staples. With these is included a set of instructions mimeographed in pale-violet ink, fruity with phrases like "Pass Section F through Slot AA, taking care not to fold tabs behind washers (see Fig. 9)." The cardboard is so processed that as the subject struggles convulsively to force the staple through, it suddenly buckles, plunging the staple deep into his thumb. He thereupon springs up with a dolorous cry and smites his knob (Section K) on the rafters (RR). As a final demonic touch, the Jiffy-Cloz people cunningly omit four of the staples necessary to finish the job, so that after indescribable purgatory, the best the subject can possible achieve is a sleazy, capricous structure which would reduce any self-respecting moth to helpless laughter. The cumulative frustration, the tropical heat, and the soft, ghostly chuckling of the moths are calculated to unseat the strongest mentality.

In a period of rapid technological change, however, it was inevitable that a method as cumbersome as the Jiffy-Cloz would be superseded. It was superseded at exactly nine-thirty Christmas morning by a device called the Self-Running, 10-Inch Scale-Model Delivery-Truck Kit Powered by Magic Motor, costing twenty-nine cents. About nine on that particular morning, I was spread-eagled on my bed, indulging in my favorite sport of mouth-breathing, when a cork fired from a child's air gun mysteriously lodged in my throat. The pellet proved awkward for a while, but I finally ejected it by flailing the little marksman (and his sister, for good measure) until their welkins rang, and sauntered in to breakfast. Before I could choke down a healing fruit juice, my consort, a tall, regal creature indistinguishable from Cornelia, the Mother of the Gracchi, except that her foot was entangled in a roller skate, swept in. She extended a large, unmistakable box covered with diagrams.

"Now don't start making excuses," she whined. "It's just a simple cardboard toy. The directions are on the back—"

"Look, dear," I interrupted, rising hurriedly and pulling on my overcoat, "it clean slipped my mind. I'm supposed to take a lesson in crosshatching at Zim's School of Cartooning today."

"On Christmas?" she asked suspiciously.

"Yes, it's the only time they could fit me in," I countered glibly. "This is the big week for crosshatching, you know, between Christmas and New Year's."

"Do you think you ought to go in your pajamas?" she asked.

"Oh, that's O.K.," I smiled. "We often work in our pajamas up at Zim's. Well, goodbye now. If I'm not home by Thursday, you'll find a cold snack in the safe-deposit box." My subterfuge, unluckily, went for naught, and in a trice I was sprawled on the nursery floor, surrounded by two lambkins and ninety-eight segments of the Self-Running, 10-Inch Scale-Mode Delivery-Truck Construction Kit.

The theory of the kit was simplicity itself, easily intelligible to Kettering of General Motors, Professor Millikan, or any first-rate physicist. Taking as my starting point the only sentence I could comprehend, "Fold down on all lines marked 'fold down'; fold up on all lines marked 'fold up,' " I set the children to work and myself folded up with an album of views of Chili Williams. In a few moments, my skin was suffused with a delightful tingling sensation and I was ready for the second phase, lightly referred to in the directions as "Preparing the Spring Motor Unit." As nearly as I could determine after twenty minutes of mumbling, the Magic Motor ("No Electricity—No Batteries—Nothing to Wind—Motor Never Wears Out") was an accordion-pleated affair operating by torsion, attached to the axles. "It is necessary," said the text, "to cut a slight notch in each of the axles with a knife (see Fig. C). To find the exact place to cut this notch, lay one of the axles over diagram at bottom of page."

"Well *now* we're getting someplace!" I boomed, with a false gusto that deceived nobody. "Here, Buster, run in and get Daddy a knife."

"I dowanna," quavered the boy, backing away. "You always cut yourself at this stage." I gave the wee fellow an indulgent pat on the head that flattened it slightly, to teach him civility, and commandeered a long, serrated bread knife from the kitchen. "Now watch me closely, children," I ordered. "We place the axle on the diagram as in Fig. C, applying a strong downward pressure in the knife handle at all times." The axle must have been a factory second, because an instant later I was in the bathroom grinding my teeth in agony and attempting to stanch the flow of blood. Ultimately, I succeeded in contriving a rough bandage and slipped back into the nursery without awakening the children's suspicions. An agreeable surprise awaited me. Displaying a mechanical aptitude clearly inherited from their sire, the rascals had put together the chassis of the delivery truck.

"Very good indeed," I complimented (naturally, one has to exaggerate praise to develop a child's self-confidence). "Let's see—what's the next step? Ah, yes. 'Lock into box shape by inserting tabs C, D, E, F, G, H, J, K, and L into slots C, D, E, F, G, H, J, K, and L. Ends of front axle should be pushed through holes A and B.' " While marshaling the indicated parts in their proper order, I emphasized to my rapt listeners the necessity of patience and perseverance. "Haste makes waste, you know," I reminded them. "Rome wasn't built in a day. Remember, your daddy isn't always going to be here to show you."

"Where *are* you going to be?" they demanded.

"In the movies if I can arrange it," I snarled. Poising tabs C, D, E, F, G, H, J, K and L in one hand and the corresponding slots in the other, I essayed a union of the two, but in vain. The moment I made one set fast and tackled another, tab and slot would part company, thumbing their noses at me. Although the children were too immature to understand, I saw in a flash where the trouble lay. Some idiotic employee at the factory had punched out the wrong design, probably out of sheer spite. So that was his game, eh? I set my lips in a grim line and, throwing one hundred and fifty-seven pounds of fighting fat into the effort, pounded the component parts into a homogeneous mass.

"There," I said with a gasp, "that's close enough. Now then, who wants candy? One, two, three—everybody off to the candy store!"

"We wanna finish the delivery truck!" they wailed. "Mummy, he won't let us finish the delivery truck!" Threats, cajolery, bribes were of no avail. In this jungle code, a twenty-nine-cent gewgaw bulked larger than a parent's love. Realizing that I was dealing with a pair of monomaniacs, I determined to show them who was master and wildly began locking the cardboard units helter-skelter, without any regard for the directions. When sections refused to fit, I gouged them with my nails and forced them together, cackling shrilly. The side panels collapsed; with a bestial oath, I drove a safety pin through them and lashed them to the roof. I used paper clips, bobby pins, anything I could lay my hands on. My fingers fairly flew and my breath whistled in my throat. "You want a delivery truck, do you?" I panted. "All right, I'll show you!" As merciful blackness closed in, I was on my hands and knees, bunting the infernal thing along with my nose and whinnying, "Roll, confound you, roll!"

"Absolute quiet," a carefully modulated voice was saying, "and fifteen of the white tablets every four hours." I opened my eyes carefully in the darkened room. Dimly I picked out a knifelike character actor in pince-nez lenses and a morning coat folding a stethoscope into his bag. "Yes," he added thoughtfully, "if we play our cards right, this ought to be a long, expensive recovery." From far away, I could hear my wife's voice bravely trying to control her anxiety.

"What if he becomes restless, Doctor?"

"Get him a detective story," returned the leech. "Or better still, a nice, soothing picture puzzle—something he can do with his hands." [7]

Write an essay of 350–500 words describing your difficulties trying to follow the instructions in an instruction kit; or to carry out the intricate steps in a complicated recipe (or some such). Describe your problem in narrative form, as Perelman does.

V. Write a set of instructions (500–750 words) for improving any skill, craft, art, sports in which you feel sufficiently proficient to qualify as "instructor."

[7] From *The Most of S. J. Perelman.* Copyright © 1930, 1931, 1932, 1933, 1935, 1936, 1953, 1955, 1956, 1957, 1958 by S. J. Perelman. Reprinted by permission of Simon and Schuster, Inc.

VI. The following essay by Benjamin Franklin describes a technical process for which he was famous.

HOW TO MAKE LIGHTNING RODS

BENJAMIN FRANKLIN

Prepare a steel rod about five or six feet long, about half an inch thick at its largest end, and tapering to a sharp point. This point should be gilded to prevent its rusting. Secure to the big end of the rod a strong eye or a ring half an inch in diameter. Fix the rod upright to the chimney or the highest part of a house. It should be fixed with some sort of staples or special nails to keep it steady. The pointed end should extend upward, and should rise three or four feet above the chimney or building to which the rod is fixed. Drive into the ground an iron rod about one inch in diameter, and ten or twelve feet long. This rod should also have an eye or ring fixed to its upper end. It is best to place the iron rod some distance from the foundation of the house. Ten feet away is a good distance, if the size of the property permits. Then take as much length of iron rod of a smaller diameter as will be necessary to reach from the eye on the rod above to the eye of the rod below. Fasten this securely to the fixed rods by passing it through the eyes and bending the ends to form rings too. Then close all the joints with lead. This is easily done by making a small bag of strong paper around the joints, tying it tight below, and then pouring in the molten lead. It is useful to have these joints treated in this way so that there will be a considerable area of contact between each piece. To prevent the wind from shaking this long rod, it may be fastened to the building by several staples. If the building is especially large or long, extending more than one hundred feet for example, it is wise to erect a rod at each end. If there is a well sufficiently near to the building to permit placing the iron rod in the water, this is even better than the use of the iron rod in the ground. It may also be wise to paint the iron to prevent it from rusting. A building so protected will not be damaged by lightning.[8]

Write an essay (150–250 words) comparable to this one, in which you explain to a friend (as Franklin was explaining to his friend David Hume) how to make something. Suggestions:

a loudspeaker	a ceramic bowl
a bookcase	a decal
a tray	a blanket
a wax figure	a basket
a lamp	a bracelet
pickles (or any food)	a string of beads
a sweater	a leather belt
a slipcover	a dress (or any article of clothing)
a potholder	

[8] From a letter to David Hume, dated in London, January 24, 1762.

6 WHAT IS THE ESSENTIAL FUNCTION OF X?

In questions 3, 4, and 5 above we dealt with various kinds of analysis: breaking something down into its component parts; describing the steps in a process; explaining "how to" go about a process. There is still another kind of analysis, especially useful in dealing with a complex concept or entity, in which we seek to explain our subject by locating its essential function.

The Function of an Institution

Let us take subject #5, for example, on the checklist of subjects—Education, narrow this down to *College* Education, and ask: "What is its essential function?" What main purpose does—and *should*—a college education serve, particularly a liberal arts education? Consider the three different replies to this question cited below. Sociologist Daniel Bell explains his view by distinguishing between secondary and graduate schools; poet-educator John Ciardi develops his "enrichment of life principle" through a long and lively illustration; William James speaks with eloquence and passion in behalf of education as biography.

WHAT IS A COLLEGE EDUCATION *FOR?*

DANIEL BELL

The distinctive function of the college must be to teach modes of conceptualization, explanation, and verification of knowledge. As between the secondary school, with its emphasis on primary skills and factual data, and the graduate or professional school, whose necessary concern is with specialization

and technique, the distinctive function of the college is to deal with the grounds of knowledge: not what one knows but how one knows. The college can be the unique place where students acquire self-consciousness, historical consciousness, and methodological consciousness.

Liberal education, for me, is more than the cultivation of the humanities, although it is certainly that. It is an emphasis on the grounds of knowledge. For this reason I reject the commonly made distinction between general education as dealing with broad relationships, and specialized instruction as presenting detailed material within an organized discipline. The relevant distinction, I feel, lies in the way a subject is introduced. When a subject is presented as received doctrine or fact, it becomes an aspect of specialization and technique. When it is introduced with an awareness of its contingency and of the conceptual frame that guides its organization, the student can then proceed with the necessary self-consciousness that keeps his mind open to possibility and to reorientation. All knowledge, thus, is liberal (that is, it enlarges and liberates the mind) when it is committed to continuing inquiry.[1]

JOHN CIARDI

Let me tell you one of the earliest disasters in my career as a teacher. It was January of 1940 and I was fresh out of graduate school starting my first semester at the University of Kansas City. Part of the reading for the freshman English course was *Hamlet*. Part of the student body was a beanpole with hair on top who came into my class, sat down, folded his arms, and looked at me as if to say: "All right, damn you, teach me something." Two weeks later we started *Hamlet*. Three weeks later he came into my office with his hands on his hips. It is easy to put your hands on your hips if you are not carrying books, and this one was an unburdened soul. "Look," he said, "I came here to be a pharmacist. Why do I have to read this stuff?" And not having a book of his own to point to, he pointed at mine which was lying on the desk.

New as I was to the faculty, I could have told this specimen a number of things. I could have pointed out that he had enrolled, not in a drugstore-mechanics school, but in a college, and that at the end of his course he meant to reach for a scroll that read Bachelor of Science. It would not read: Qualified Pill-Grinding Technician. It would certify that he had specialized in pharmacy and had attained a certain minimum qualification, but it would further certify that he had been exposed to some of the ideas mankind has generated within its history. That is to say, he had not entered a technical training school but a university, and that in universities students enroll for both training and education.

I could have told him all this, but it was fairly obvious he wasn't going to be around long enough for it to matter: at the rate he was going, the first marking period might reasonably be expected to blow him toward the employment agency.

Nevertheless, I was young and I had a high sense of duty and I tried to put it this way: "For the rest of your life," I said, "your days are going to average out to about twenty-four hours. They will be a little shorter when you are in

[1] From *The Reforming of General Education,* by Daniel Bell (New York: Columbia University Press, 1966).

love, and a little longer when you are out of love, but the average will tend to hold. For eight of these hours, more or less, you will be asleep, and I assume you need neither education nor training to manage to get through that third of your life.

"Then for about eight hours of each working day you will, I hope, be usefully employed. Assume you have gone through pharmacy school—or engineering, or aggie, or law school, or whatever—during those eight hours you will be using your professional skills. You will see to it during this third of your life that the cyanide stays out of the aspirin, that the bull doesn't jump the fence, or that your client doesn't go to the electric chair as a result of your incompetence. These are all useful pursuits, they involve skills every man must respect, and they can all bring you good basic satisfactions. Along with everything else, they will probably be what sets your table, supports your wife, and rears your children. They will be your income, and may it always suffice.

"But having finished the day's work what do you do with those other eight hours—with the other third of your life? Let's say you go home to your family. What sort of family are you raising? Will the children ever be exposed to a reasonably penetrating idea at home? We all think of ourselves as citizens of a great democracy. Democracies can exist, however, only as long as they remain intellectually alive. Will you be presiding over a family that maintains some basic contact with the great continuity of democratic intellect? Or is your family life going to be strictly penny-ante and beer on ice? Will there be a book in the house? Will there be a painting a reasonably sensitive man can look at without shuddering? Will your family be able to speak English and to talk about an idea? Will the kids ever get to hear Bach?"

That is about what I said, but this particular pest was not interested. "Look," he said, "you professors raise your kids your way; I'll take care of my own. Me, I'm out to make money."

"I hope you make a lot of it," I told him, "because you're going to be badly stuck for something to do when you're not signing checks."

Fourteen years later, I am still teaching, and I am here to tell you that the business of the college is not only to train you, but to put you in touch with what the best human minds have thought. If you have no time for Shakespeare, for a basic look at philosophy, for the continuity of the fine arts, for that lesson of man's development we call history—then you have no business being in college. You are on your way to being that new species of mechanized savage, the Push-button Neanderthal. Our colleges inevitably graduate a number of such life-forms, but it cannot be said that they went to college; rather, the college went through them—without making contact.

No one gets to be a human being unaided. There is not time enough in a single lifetime to invent for oneself everything one needs to know in order to be a civilized human.

Assume, for example, that you want to be a physicist. You pass the great stone halls of, say, M.I.T., and there cut into the stone are the names of the master scientists. The chances are that few of any of you will leave your names to be cut into those stones. Yet any one of you who managed to stay awake through part of a high school course in physics, knows more about physics than did many of those great makers of the past. You know more because they left you what they knew. The first course in any science is essentially a history course. You have to begin by learning what the past learned for you. Except as a man has entered the past of the race he has no function in civilization.

And as this is true of the techniques of mankind, so is it true of mankind's spiritual resources. Most of these resources, both technical and spiritual, are stored in books. Books, the arts, and the techniques of science, are man's peculiar accomplishment. When you have read a book, you have added to your human experience. Read Homer and your mind includes a piece of Homer's mind. Through books you can acquire at least fragments of the mind and experience of Virgil, Dante, Shakespeare—the list is endless. For a great book is necessarily a gift: it offers you a life you have not time to live yourself, and it takes you into a world you have not time to travel in literal time. A civilized human mind is, in essence, one that contains many such lives and many such worlds. If you are too much in a hurry, or too arrogantly proud of your own limitations, to accept as a gift to your humanity some pieces of the minds of Sophocles, of Aristotle, of Chaucer—and right down the scale and down the ages to Yeats, Einstein, E. B. White, and Ogden Nash—then you may be protected by the laws governing manslaughter, and you may be a voting entity, but you are neither a developed human being nor a useful citizen of a democracy.

I think it was La Rochefoucauld who said that most people would never fall in love if they hadn't read about it. He might have said that no one would ever manage to become human if he hadn't read about it.

I speak, I am sure, for the faculty of the liberal arts college and for the faculties of the specialized schools as well, when I say that a university has no real existence and no real purpose except as it succeeds in putting you in touch, both as specialists and as humans, with those human minds *your* human mind needs to include. The faculty, by its very existence, says implicitly: "We have been aided by many people, and by many books, and by the arts, in our attempt to make ourselves some sort of storehouse of human experience. We are here to make available to you, as best we can, that experience." [2]

WILLIAM JAMES

The sifting of human creations!—nothing less than this is what we ought to mean by the humanities. Essentially this means biography; what our colleges should teach is, therefore, biographical history, . . . not of politics merely, but of anything and everything so far as human efforts and conquests are factors that have played their part. Studying in this way, we learn what types of activity have stood the test of time; we acquire standards of the excellent and durable. All our arts and sciences and institutions are but so many quests of perfection on the part of men; and when we see how diverse the types of excellence may be, how various the tests, how flexible the adaptations, we gain a richer sense of what the terms "better" and "worse" may signify in general. Our critical sensibilities grow both more acute and less fanatical. We sympathize with men's mistakes even in the act of penetrating them; we feel the

[2] "Another School Year—Why?" by John Ciardi from the *Rutgers Alumni Monthly*, November 1954. Reprinted by permission.

pathos of lost causes and misguided epochs even while we applaud what overcame them.

Such words are vague and such ideas are inadequate, but their meaning is unmistakable. What the colleges—teaching humanities by examples which may be special, but which must be typical and pregnant—should at least try to give us, is a general sense of what, under various disguises, *superiority* has always signified and may still signify. The feeling for a good human job anywhere, the admiration of the really admirable, the disesteem of what is cheap and trashy and impermanent—this is what we call the critical sense, the sense for ideal values. It is the better part of what men know as wisdom. Some of us are wise in this way naturally and by genius; some of us never become so. But to have spent one's youth at college, in contact with the choice and rare and precious, and yet still to be a blind prig or vulgarian, unable to scent out human excellence or to divine it amid its accidents, to know it only when ticketed and labelled and forced on us by others, this indeed should be accounted the very calamity and shipwreck of a higher education.

The sense for human superiority ought, then, to be considered our line, as boring subways is the engineer's line and the surgeon's is appendicitis. Our college ought to have lit up in us a lasting relish for the better kind of man, a loss of appetite for mediocrities, and a disgust for cheapjacks. We ought to smell, as it were, the difference of quality in men and their proposals when we enter the world of affairs about us. Expertness in this might well atone for some of our awkwardness at accounts, for some of our ignorance of dynamos. The best claim we can make for the higher education, the best single phrase in which we can tell what it ought to do for us, is then, exactly what I said: it should enable us to *know a good man when we see him*. . . .

The notion that a people can run itself and its affairs anonymously is now well known to be the silliest of absurdities. Mankind does nothing save through initiatives on the part of inventors, great or small, and imitation by the rest of us—these are the sole factors active in human progress. Individuals of genius show the way, and set the patterns, which common people then adopt and follow. *The rivalry of the patterns is the history of the world*. Our democratic problem thus is statable in ultra-simple terms: Who are the kind of men from whom our majorities shall take their cue? Whom shall they treat as rightful leaders? We and our leaders are the x and the y of the equation here; all other historic circumstances, be they economical, political, or intellectual, are only the background of occasion on which the living drama works itself out between us.

In this very simple way does the value of our educated class define itself: we more than others should be able to divine the worthier and better leaders. The terms here are monstrously simplified, of course, but such a bird's-eye view lets us immediately take our bearings. In our democracy, where everything else is shifting, we alumni and alumnae of the colleges are the only permanent presence that corresponds to the aristocracy in older countries. We have continuous traditions, as they have; our motto, too, is *noblesse oblige*; and, unlike them, we stand for ideal interests solely, for we have no corporate selfishness and wield no powers of corruption. We ought to have our own class-consciousness. "Les intellectuels"! What prouder club-name could there be than this one, used ironically by the party of "red blood," the party of every stupid prejudice and passion, during the anti-Dreyfus craze, to satirize the men in

France who still retained some critical sense and judgment! Critical sense, it has to be confessed, is not an exciting term, hardly a banner to carry in processions. Affections for old habit, currents of self-interest, and gales of passion are the forces that keep the human ship moving; and the pressure of the judicious pilot's hand upon the tiller is a relatively insignificant energy. But the affections, passions, and interest are shifting, successive, and distraught; they blow in alternation, while the pilot's hand is steadfast. He knows the compass, and, with all the leeways he is obligated to tack toward, he always makes some headway. A small force, if it never lets up, will accumulate effects more considerable than those of much greater forces if these work inconsistently. The ceaseless whisper of the more permanent ideals, the steady tug of truth and justice, give them but time, *must* warp the world in their direction.[3]

The Function of a Professional Person

Let us address the question of function to another aspect of the general subject of Education: What is the function of a critic—a man educated beyond the level of most men, an interpreter and evaluator, a taste maker. How does he serve the ordinary man? Poet W. H. Auden has answered this question simply and practically, by pointing out, first of all, what he believes to be the critic's essential function, and then by developing his opinion, point by point. Most of the essays in this section follow this organizational procedure.

THE FUNCTION OF A CRITIC

W. H. AUDEN

What is the function of a critic? So far as I am concerned, he can do me one or more of the following services:

1. Introduce me to authors or works of which I was hitherto unaware.
2. Convince me that I have undervalued an author or a work because I had not read them carefully enough.
3. Show me relations between works of different ages and cultures which I could never have seen for myself because I do not know enough and never shall.
4. Give a "reading" of a work which increases my understanding of it.
5. Throw light upon the process of artistic "Making."
6. Throw light upon the relation of art to life, to science, economics, ethics, religion, etc.

The first three of these services demand scholarship. A scholar is not merely someone whose knowledge is extensive; the knowledge must be of value to others. One would not call a man who knew the Manhattan Telephone Directory by heart a scholar, because one cannot imagine circumstances in which he would acquire a pupil. Since scholarship implies a relation between one who knows more and one who knows less, it may be temporary; in relation to

[3] From "The Social Value of the College Bred" from *Memories and Studies* by William James.

the public, every reviewer is, temporarily, a scholar, because he has read the book he is reviewing and the public has not. Though the knowledge a scholar possesses must be potentially valuable, it is not necessary that he recognize its value himself; it is always possible that the pupil to whom he imparts his knowledge has a better sense of its value than he. In general, when reading a scholarly critic, one profits more from his quotations than from his comments.

The last three services demand, not superior knowledge, but superior insight. A critic shows superior insight if the questions he raises are fresh and important, however much one may disagree with his answers to them. Few readers, probably, find themselves able to accept Tolstoi's conclusions in "What is Art?", but, once one has read the book, one can never again ignore the questions Tolstoi raises.

The one thing I most emphatically do not ask of a critic is that he tell me what I "ought" to approve of or condemn. I have no objection to his telling me what works and authors he likes and dislikes; indeed, it is useful to know this for, from his expressed preferences about works which I have read, I learn how likely I am to agree or disagree with his verdicts on works which I have not. But let him not dare to lay down the law to me. The responsibility for what I choose to read is mine, and nobody else on earth can do it for me.[4]

Related to both the educated man and the critic, as Auden points out above, is the scholar. No man has described the scholar's role with greater eloquence or a firmer grasp of the "ideal" to be aspired to than has Ralph Waldo Emerson in his famous Phi Beta Kappa address of 1837, an address that Oliver Wendell Holmes called "our intellectual Declaration of Independence."

THE ROLE OF THE SCHOLAR

RALPH WALDO EMERSON

The office of the scholar is to cheer, to raise, and to guide men by showing them facts amidst appearances. He plies the slow, unhonored, and unpaid task of observation. Flamsteed and Herschel, in their glazed observatories, may catalogue the stars with the praise of all men, and, the results being splendid and useful, honor is sure. But he, in his private observatory, cataloguing obscure and nebulous stars of the human mind, which as yet no man has thought of as such,—watching days and months, sometimes, for a few facts; correcting still his old records;—must relinquish display and immediate fame. In the long period of his preparation, he must betray often an ignorance and shiftlessness in popular arts, incurring the disdain of the able who shoulder him aside. Long he must stammer in his speech; often forego the living for the dead. Worse yet, he must accept,—how often! poverty and solitude. For the ease and pleasure of treading the old road, accepting the fashions, the education, the religion of society, he takes the cross of making his own, and, of course, the self-accusation, the faint heart, the frequent uncertainty and loss of time, which are the nettles and tangling vines in the way of the self-relying and self-directed; and the state of virtual hostility in which he seems to stand to society, and especially to educated society. For all this loss and scorn,

[4] From *The Dyer's Hand and Other Essays*, by W. H. Auden.

what offset? He is to find consolation in exercising the highest functions of human nature. He is one, who raises himself from private considerations, and breathes and lives on public and illustrious thoughts. He is the world's eye. He is the world's heart. He is to resist the vulgar prosperity that retrogrades ever to barbarism, by preserving and communicating heroic sentiments, noble biographies, melodious verse, and the conclusions of history. Whatsoever oracles the human heart, in all emergencies, in all solemn hours, has uttered as its commentary on the world of actions,—these he shall receive and impart. And whatsoever new verdict Reason from her inviolable seat pronounces on the passing men and events of to-day,—this he shall hear and promulgate.

These being his functions, it becomes him to feel all confidence in himself, and to defer never to the popular cry. He and he only knows the world. The world of any moment is the merest appearance. Some great decorum, some fetish of a government, some ephemeral trade, or war, or man, is cried up by half mankind and cried down by the other half, as if all depended on this particular up or down. The odds are that the whole question is not worth the poorest thought which the scholar has lost in listening to the controversy. Let him not quit his belief that a popgun is a popgun, though the ancient and honorable of the earth affirm it to be the crack of doom. In silence, in steadiness, in severe abstraction, let him hold by himself; add observation to observation, patient of neglect, patient of reproach, and bide his own time,—happy enough, if he can satisfy himself alone, that this day he has seen something truly. Success treads on every right step. For the instinct is sure, that prompts him to tell his brother what he thinks. He then learns, that in going down into the secrets of his own mind, he has descended into the secrets of all minds. He learns that he who has mastered any law in his private thoughts, is master to that extent of all men whose language he speaks, and of all into whose language his own can be translated. The poet, in utter solitude remembering his spontaneous thoughts and recording them, is found to have recorded that, which men in crowded cities find true for them also. The orator distrusts at first the fitness of his grand confession,—his want of knowledge of the persons he addresses,—until he finds that he is the complement of his hearers;—that they drink his words because he fulfills for them their own nature; the deeper he dives into his privatest, secretest presentiment, to his wonder he finds, this is the most acceptable, most public, and universally true. The people delight in it; the better part of every man feels, This is my music; this is myself.

ASSIGNMENTS

I. A. Compare the essays by Daniel Bell, John Ciardi, and Henry James, each of which asks the question "What is a college education for?"

1. In a sentence or two apiece, summarize each writer's view of the function or purpose of education.
2. Are the views mutually exclusive or do they overlap? Compare them.
3. Is there one view you subscribe to more than the others? Explain.
4. Consider the following statement by Carl Becker: The chief merit of any college course is "that it unsettles students, makes them ask

questions." How does this observation relate to the essays considered here?

5. Compare the three essays in terms of
   readability
   tone
   style

B. In an essay (500–750 words) describe the main function of higher education as you view it, drawing on the essays reprinted here and on any other sources you wish to consult.

II. A. Consider the Auden essay on "The Function of a Critic."

1. Do you agree with the six basic services of the critic as Auden states them? Explain.
2. Compare Auden's critic with Bennett's "passionate few" (Arnold Bennett, "Why a Classic Is a Classic," pp. 114–17). What is the relation of both the critic and the passionate few to the general reader?
3. In what category do you think Auden belongs: critic, passionate few, general reader?
4. Comment on Auden's statement: "But let him [the critic] not dare to lay down the law to me."

B. As Auden describes the function of the critic, write an essay (500–750 words) in which you describe the function of one of the following professionals:

the scientist	the clergyman
the artist	the policeman
the musician	the lawyer
the writer	the doctor
the teacher	the philosopher

III. A. There is much to contemplate in Emerson's statement on the function of the scholar.

1. Do you agree that it is the scholar's "office . . . to cheer, to raise, and to guide men by showing them facts amidst appearances"?
2. To what do "facts" and "appearances" refer?
3. In what sense is the scholar "the world's eye" and "the world's heart"?
4. To what sort of "oracles" uttered by the human heart is Emerson referring?
5. Considering Emerson's description of the functions of the scholar, do you agree with him that the scholar should "defer never to the popular cry"? Is this a democratic principle?
6. Does the statement "he and he only knows the world" refer to *all* knowledge?
7. Do you think it is true of the scholar today (as Emerson says of the scholars of his time) that he will be "happy enough, if he can satisfy himself alone, that this day he has seen something truly"?
8. Do you agree that the scholar fulfills for his public "their own nature"?
9. Do you think the scholar described by Emerson is a real person or an ideal?

10. Comment on Emerson's prose style, noting sentence structure, rhythm and flow of sentences, choice of words, images, and tone. (Note especially the last two sentences.)

B. In an essay (500–750 words) compare the function of James' educated man with that of Emerson's scholar, showing how they are alike and unlike one another. You may wish to add a third person, for example, a member of Bennett's "passionate few," for example.

7 WHAT ARE THE CAUSES OF X?

Surely there is no more provocative question than the simple "*Why?*" Why is the sky dark at night? Why are we *more* or *less* intelligent? Why is a classic a classic?

When he asks "Why?" the writer is preparing, as we shall see, to write a causal analysis—i.e., he is seeking to locate and explain the causes for a given act, idea, feeling, condition, or event. As Aristotle pointed out, man is *naturally* curious; almost as soon as he begins to think, he begins to wonder "Why?" As early as the fifth century B.C., the Greek philosopher Leucippus said: "Nothing happens without a ground but everything through a cause and of necessity." Here, then, is the "principle of universal causation," believed to run through all things, confirming us in our impulse to ask "*Why?*"

The First Principle of Causation: Uniformity

Why, for instance, do natural events occur as they do—why the tides of the sea, why the movement of the planets, why the cycle of seasons? There will be little guesswork or speculation in answering these questions, for the course of nature is regarded as uniform: natural events proceed by natural, uniform law. Thus, under the same circumstances, the same things will always happen in the same way. The leaves fall from the trees every autumn, and the first leaf and the last fall for the same reasons as all the billions of leaves in between.

We refer, then, to the "law of causation" that establishes that two events (X and Y) are so closely and unconditionally connected that one *cannot* occur without the other—i.e., Y can take place only if X has previously occurred; if X occurs, then Y necessarily and inevitably follows. In such an instance we say that X is the cause of Y.

In writing about natural events, the writer's first responsibility is to familiarize himself fully with the uniform laws that govern the event in question. Firmly in command of this information, he can then explain the event clearly and engagingly so that the reader can understand and enjoy the explanation, even if it is necessarily complicated—as are many scientific explanations. Certainly the writer of the following essay (not a scientist but a journalist) has managed to render an extraordinarily lucid and vivid account of a complicated natural process.

WHY IS THE SKY DARK AT NIGHT?

BRUCE BLIVEN

Since the childhood of our race, mankind has accepted the darkness of the nighttime sky as an unquestioned commonplace fact of life on earth. The sun rises each morning, bringing with it daylight. When the sun sets, the one major source of light is gone. Hence the sky can no longer be bright. So have reasoned generation upon generation of men—but their reasoning overlooked something.

The first man who seems to have thought deeply about this phenomenon was a German physician, Heinrich W. M. Olbers, who lived in Bremen and who, in 1826, set out to produce a scientific and mathematical answer to the question: *Why is the world dark at night?*

Dr. Olbers had a lifelong passion for astronomy. Even during the years when he was practicing medicine he spent the greater part of each night in his homemade observatory on top of his house, studying the heavens. He located the comet of 1815, which was named for him; he took part in the rediscovery of Ceres and discovered Pallas and Vesta—three tiny planets that circle the sun. But his greatest achievement was to ask this seemingly obvious question.

The sun, Olbers figured, provides only about half the light we on earth should theoretically be receiving; the other half should come from the billions of stars in the heavens. With all that starlight, why is midnight not as bright as day?

Dr. Olbers would have been even more puzzled had he had today's knowledge of the incredible vastness of the universe, the uncounted billions of light-giving stars in the depths of space. Our sun and its planets are only a microscopic part of the Milky Way, an average-size galaxy containing 100 billion stars—which are on the average as bright as our sun. And the Milky Way itself is only one of a seemingly limitless number of galaxies. Radio telescopes can now "hear" several billion light-years out into space; and however far they penetrate, in every direction, the galaxies continue to appear.

The number of the stars is, in fact, far beyond the power of the mind to grasp; yet so great is space that it is sparsely populated.

Though he was aware of only a small part of the stellar universe, the total number of stars known to Dr. Olbers was yet huge indeed. Taking into account their numbers, brightness and distance, making painstaking calculations, he came to an amazing conclusion: with light streaming from so many stars, the sky should *not* be dark at night. The earth even at midnight should be blazing with light and heat. It should, in fact, be frying.

How did he figure this? Suppose, said Dr. Olbers, you think of the universe as a vast hollow ball studded with stars and trillions of miles in diameter, with the earth at its center. Light will reach the earth from a multitude of stars; and while the rays from those far away will be very faint, this will be offset because the farther out you go, the greater the number of stars. In fact, the number of stars increases much faster than the distance (just as the volume of a sphere increases in proportion to its radius). Thus the weakening of the light at greater distances is *more than offset* by the greater number of stars there are when such distances are taken into account. No matter how weak the effect of any one star, therefore, if the number is large enough and the elapsed time long enough, the planet at the center should be ablaze with light and heat.

Why is this not so? Why then *is* the sky dark at night? The good doctor thought that interstellar fog must absorb almost all the starlight. But other astronomers were not satisfied that this was a sufficient explanation, and the question became famous as "Olbers' paradox."

For 100 years astronomers tried to solve the paradox. A clue came only 16 years after Olbers had raised the question, but nobody at the time recognized its relevance.

In 1842, an Austrian professor of mathematics, Christian Doppler, discovered what has ever after been known as the Doppler effect. Stand by a railroad track; as a train comes toward you the pitch of its whistle sounds high, but after it has passed, the whistle sounds lower. Doppler found the clue. As the train approaches, the sound waves it sends toward you seem, to you, shortened or "crowded"—and since short-wave sounds are higher pitched, the whistle sounds higher. Conversely, when the train speeds *away* from you, the sound waves must travel a greater distance; so they seem to you to be farther apart and therefore sound lower.

The Doppler effect applies to light waves, too. Light waves appear to the eye as longer when they come from an object moving away from us; they seem shorter and "crowded" if the object is approaching us.

With light the effect shows up in color. Light waves are longer (and weaker) at the red end of the color spectrum, shorter at the violet end. So light waves from a source that is moving away tend to be shifted down the spectrum toward the red end, a phenomenon called the "Red Shift." Thus astronomers came to realize that a slight redness in the light coming from a celestial body means that it is moving away from the observer.

Among those in this century who pondered Olbers' paradox, knowing there *must* be an answer to it, was Dr. Edwin P. Hubble of California's Mount Wilson Observatory. In 1924, with the superior instruments available, Dr. Hubble found that light from distant sources, from distant galaxies outside the Milky Way, showed the Red Shift. This, he reasoned, could only mean that their light waves were being stretched out—hence these stars, these whole galaxies of stars, must be traveling away from us at tremendous speed.

Could it be? Hubble continued to watch the sky, and the evidence mounted that this was so. He found that the farther out he looked, the redder was the light that his telescope picked up. In fact, he saw, the galaxies were escaping from us with speeds that increased in a mathematically precise manner with their distance.

Hubble concluded that the whole universe is expanding—everything in it is moving farther and farther apart from everything else. Other observers confirmed his theory, and "the expanding universe" became the fundamental, though almost unbelievable, discovery of modern astronomy.

With this discovery Dr. Olbers' question at last was answered. *The sky is dark at night because the universe expands!* The galaxies are moving away from us so fast as to weaken the radiation we receive from them. This is what gives us our restful nocturnal darkness, and also saves us from being vaporized in the never-ending shower of hot starlight. Were it not for this fact, life on earth would not be possible.[1]

Note that in this essay the author explains the astronomical phenomenon (the dark sky) in terms of three natural laws: the Doppler effect, the Red Shift, and, underlying both, the expanding universe. It is possible, of course, to extend the principle of uniformity beyond scientific causal analysis. Thus, even in everyday reasoning, we tend to search for a principle of uniformity: "Why did Johnny break his truck?" "Because he was tired." Generalization (principle of uniformity): "Tired children tend to break their toys."

The Second Principle of Causation: Sufficiency

Cause and effect sequences are of several types.

1. Cause ⟶ Effect (Single cause, Single effect)

2. Cause 1 ⟶ / Cause 2 ⟶ / Cause 3 ⟶ Effect (Multiple causes, Single effect)

3. Cause ⟶ Effect 1 / Effect 2 / Effect 3 (Single cause, Multiple effects)

4. Cause 1 → Cause 2 → Cause 3 → Effect (Causal chain)

The following essay begins by suggesting the possibility of one cause for a given effect, but demonstrates that on the basis of the evidence, one cause is not sufficient explanation for the event in question. There are, in fact, *two* equally important causes at work.

[1] Reprinted with permission from the July 1963 *Reader's Digest*. Copyright 1963 by the Reader's Digest Assn., Inc. Also reprinted by permission of Bruce Bliven.

THE DEVELOPMENT OF INTELLIGENCE: HEREDITY OR ENVIRONMENT?

DONALD OLDING HEBB

The classical view in psychology held that intelligence is determined essentially by heredity. This view seemed to be supported by such experiments as the following.

Learning ability was tested in a large number of laboratory rats. The brightest males and females, those with the fewest errors, were then bred with each other, and the dullest likewise. The second generation was tested and the brightest offspring of the bright group were bred, and the dullest offspring of the dull group. This was continued, until by the seventh generation it was found that there was little or no overlap in the scores of the bright and dull groups; practically all of the bright made better scores in maze learning than any of the dull.

This seems to show that intelligence is not dependent on environment, but on heredity alone. However, there are other experiments that contradict this. One experimenter equated heredity in two groups of infant rats by the *split-litter* method: taking several litters of pups, he put half of each litter into one group, half into the other. One group was reared in a restricted environment, each animal in a small cage which he could not see out of, containing no objects and presenting no opportunity for problem-solving. The other group was reared in a "free environment," a very large cage which was a sort of amusement park for rats, containing a variety of objects, and barriers which gave experience with varied paths (direct and indirect) from one point in the cage to another. The two groups were tested at maturity for problem-solving ability, and the ones reared in the free environment had a lasting superiority to those reared in the restricted environment. Similarly, dogs reared in rather extreme isolation in small cages show marked deficiencies in learning and problem-solving; physically, they are healthy and vigorous, so the deficiencies are not attributable to a failure of bodily development. These experiments show that intelligence is a matter of environment, not heredity.

But do they? Let us look again at the two kinds of experiments. In the breeding experiment, all the animals are brought up in identical small cages, effectively equating environmental factors and keeping them from influencing the results. In the second kind, the rearing experiments, hereditary variables are equated, which removes their influence. The two results therefore are not contradictory at all. Both these influences are important; if one is held constant, it does not affect the outcome of the experiment—and thus is easily forgotten; but it must not be forgotten.

With this point in mind, we can examine the result of a related investigation of human intelligence. Identical twins are ones which, according to genetics, originate from a single fertilized ovum and thus have the same hereditary characteristics. If they are brought up in different environments, we should be able to see what kind of effect variations of environment have upon intelligence. Psychologists have therefore been very interested in identical-twin orphans adopted in different families. It has been found that the IQ's are very similar, and this fact has sometimes been used as argument that man's adult intelligence is determined by heredity and not by environment.

But if we examine the evidence, we find that most of these pairs of children have been brought up in very similar environments. When a pair of twins is orphaned, one of two things happens. They may be adopted by the neighbors, which implies similar environments—the same community, plus the fact that all the families in one neighborhood are apt to have about the same economic and social status. Or the twins may be taken charge of by a social agency, to oversee adoption, and this again means that they will get into environments that have much in common, social workers having strong ideas about who is fit to bring up children. In this kind of "experiment" differential effects of environment are minimized, and it is hardly surprising to find similar IQ's in identical twins with similar environments. The fact that identical twins have IQ's which are more alike than those of fraternal twins is a valid argument that heredity is important, just as the rat-breeding experiment was a valid demonstration of the same point; but it does not show that heredity is the *only* variable. To show this we need to have one of each pair of twins brought up in the worst possible environment, the other in the best possible one: if then there was no significant difference in IQ, we could conclude that intelligence is unaffected by the sensory environment. This experiment however is not likely to be done, and in the meantime there is a great deal of evidence to indicate that such a result is in the highest degree improbable.

Sometimes it is recognized that heredity and environment both affect intelligence, but the writer then goes on to say *how* important each is. The student may find it said for example that 80 per cent of intelligence is determined by heredity, 20 per cent by environment. This statement is, on the face of it, nonsense. It means that a man would have 80 per cent of the problem-solving ability he would otherwise have had, if he were never given the opportunity to learn a language, never learned how people behave, and so forth. Conversely, it means that 20 per cent of a man's problem-solving capacity will result from a good environment, no matter *what* heredity is involved, which we know of course is not true. What we must say is that both these variables are of 100 per cent importance: their relation is not additive but multiplicative. To ask how much heredity contributes to intelligence is like asking how much the width of a field contributes to its area.

It is reasonable to ask how much the *variations* in intelligence are determined by variations of heredity, or of environment, but this is a very different question, and the answer cannot be generalized. In a very homogeneous community, culturally, practically all the variability of intelligence might be determined by heredity, but this would only occur when environmental variation in the group studied is at a minimum. It has been found repeatedly that cultural differences can affect intelligence-test scores to a very marked degree. For example, children growing up on canal boats in England, thus removed from many of the normal experiences of other children, showed a sharp decline in intelligence: IQ 90 at age 6, 77 at age 7½, 60 at age 12. An IQ below 70 is ordinarily considered to mean mental deficiency, whereas 90 is within the range of normal ability. Again, a very similar picture (IQ 84 at 7, IQ 60 at 15) has been found for growing children in isolated mountain communities in the United States. The higher IQ's for the younger children show that the low scores, at later ages, do not mean deficient heredities—otherwise all the IQ's would be low. Instead, it appears that the social and cultural environment is sufficiently stimulating for a normal development of intelligence in the first four or five years of life, but progressively inadequate from then on.

None of this means, of course, that the child's heredity is unimportant. Intelligence is the joint product of heredity and of the physical and social environments. Emphasizing the importance of one of these factors does not reduce the importance of the others.[2]

In establishing causal connections, the writer must think carefully and rigorously, recognizing that it is easy to fall into such common fallacies as *post hoc ergo propter hoc* (after this, therefore because of this). To the simple mind (or the mind intent on deceiving), any event that follows another is necessarily the *result* of it. Thus as Mark Twain once pointed out in a humorous *post hoc* application: "I joined the Confederacy for two weeks. Then I deserted. The Confederacy fell."

Most superstitions grow out of this fallacy: "A black cat crossed my path. Later that day I twisted my ankle. The black cat *caused* my twisted ankle. Black cats are therefore 'unlucky.'" And: "John eats a lot of fish. John is smart. Eating fish is good for the brain."

The writer who wishes to be taken seriously must guard against superstitious, oversimplified cause-effect connections. The first question a critical mind addresses to an assertion of causal relationship should be: "Was the supposed cause *sufficient* to produce the given effect?" Obviously a black cat cannot be sufficient cause for a twisted ankle, fish cannot stimulate the brain, and a four-leaf clover cannot bring luck. In each case the stated cause (however colorful) is *insufficient* to produce the given effect.

Cause and Condition

Thus the careful thinker and writer makes certain that he considers *all* possible causes for any given event. He recognizes not only that there *can* be more than one cause behind any given situation (the Vietnam war, the recession, racial unrest), but that there usually *is*. Indeed, the careful thinker and writer recognizes that the world of events is rarely characterized by

Single Cause → Single Effect

More than that, he sees that for every individual effect there are—in addition to multiple causes—countless *conditions* that must also be taken into account if a causal explanation is to be reasonably accurate and complete. Let us say that the direct cause of my answering the telephone is that it rings:

Cause ——————→ Effect
(telephone ringing)   (I answer the telephone)

One could view this event in this linear manner; roughly it is true, but only roughly. In actual fact there are countless conditions that enter into this situation that enable it to occur: the telephone is in good repair (each small part is in working order); my ears are "attuned" (here again, each small part is working); I am within hearing distance (I might have stepped outside for a moment). And so on and on. If any one of these numerous small conditions had not held to its exact course at the precise moment the tele-

[2] From *A Textbook of Psychology*, second edition, by Donald Olding Hebb. Reprinted by permission of W. B. Saunders Company and the author.

phone rang, I would not have answered it: the given effect (B) would *not* have followed the supposed cause (A).

With this in mind, we can look back to the Bliven essay on nighttime darkness and note that many conditions had to remain equal and constant in order for the law of causation to operate in its ordinary manner. Of course the sun rises each morning, as stated—but only if no untoward occurrences take place in the solar system that might throw the entire causal chain out of gear. Similarly, the environment, as described in the Hebb essay, will influence the development of certain individuals in certain ways—but here again, only if the individual nervous system remains broadly within the normal range of functioning, and the environment continues to be the environment as we know it.

The careful thinker and writer, then, will take into account not only the basic *causes* of a given effect, but the surrounding *conditions* as well.

Speculating on Reasons

Many essays in causal analysis are little more than nonsense because they assert causal connections that have no basis in fact or logical inference. The two essays reprinted above are not guilty of what logicians call "forced" or unwarranted hypotheses since the explanation (Why darkness? Why intelligence?) is based on concrete evidence drawn from the orderly realm of science and not merely from heady speculation.

In contrast, the following essay is based on speculation. Novelist Arnold Bennett tries to explain how and why a classic becomes and remains a classic, how it is kept alive. He cannot *know* for certain since there are no controlled studies, surveys, or experiments yielding definite information or objective data on this subject. Thus Bennett has no alternative but to speculate, and he does this by establishing a causal sequence that (according to his observation and experience) seems accurate:

Cause A → Cause B → Cause C → Effect

As you read, note that Bennett begins with Cause C and works backward. Classics survive, he tells us, because of a devoted minority, the "passionate few," who love literature (Cause C). And *why* do they love literature? Because they find in it the kind of "keen and lasting pleasure" that some men find in beer. It is the "recurrence of this pleasure" that keeps their interest in literature alive (Cause B).

And *why* does literature give this pleasure? No answer! Bennett tells us that the passionate few can no more resist literature than the bee can neglect a flower. *But they can no more tell you why!* In other words causation breaks down at this point.

WHY A CLASSIC IS A CLASSIC

ARNOLD BENNETT

Introduction: the problem stated

The large majority of our fellow citizens care as much about literature as they care about archaeology or the program of the Legislature. They do not ignore it; they are not quite indifferent to it. But their interest in it is faint and perfunctory; or, if their interest happens to be violent, it is spasmodic. Ask the two hundred thousand persons whose enthusiasm made the vogue of a popular novel ten years ago what they think of that novel now, and you will gather that they have utterly forgotten it, and that they would no more dream of reading it again than of reading Bishop Stubb's *Select Charters*. Probably if they did read it again they would not enjoy it—not because the said novel is a whit worse now than it was ten years ago; not because their taste has improved—but because they have not had sufficient practice to be able to rely on their taste as a means of permanent pleasure. They simply don't know from one day to the next what will please them.

The question posed: *why?*

In the face of this one may ask: Why does the great and universal fame of classical authors continue? The answer is that the fame of classical authors is entirely independent of the majority. Do you suppose that if the fame of Shakespeare depended on the man in the street it would survive a fortnight? The fame of classical authors is originally made, and it is maintained, by a passionate few. Even when a first-class author has enjoyed immense success during his lifetime, the majority have never appreciated him so sincerely as they have appreciated second-rate men. He has always been reinforced by the ardor of the passionate few. And in the case of an author who has emerged into glory after his death the happy sequel has been due solely to the obstinate perseverance of the few. They could not leave him alone; they would not. They kept on savoring him, and talking about him, and buying him, and they generally behaved with such eager zeal, and they were so authoritative and sure of themselves, that at last the majority grew accustomed to the sound of his name and placidly agreed to the proposition that he was a genius; the majority really did not care very much either way.

Cause C (described)

And it is by the passionate few that the renown of genius is kept alive from one generation to another. These few are always at work. They are always rediscovering genius. Their curiosity and enthusiasm are exhaustless, so that there is little chance of genius being ignored. And, moreover, they are always working either for or against the verdicts of the majority. The majority can make a reputation, but it is too careless to maintain it. If, by accident, the passionate few agree with the majority in a particular instance, they will frequently remind the majority that such and such a reputation has been made, and the majority will idly concur: "Ah, yes. By the way, we must not forget that such and such a reputation exists." Without that persistent memory-jogging the reputation would quickly fall into the oblivion which is death. The passionate few only have their way by reason of the fact that they are genuinely interested in literature, that literature matters to them. They conquer by their obstinacy alone, by their eternal repetition of the same statements. Do you suppose they could prove to the man in the street that Shakespeare was a great artist? The said man would not even understand the terms they employed. But when he is told ten thousand times, and generation after generation, that Shakespeare was a great artist, the said man believes—not by reason, but by faith. And he too repeats that Shakespeare was a great artist, and he buys the complete works of Shakespeare and puts them on his shelves, and he goes to see the marvellous stage effects which accompany *King Lear* or *Hamlet,* and comes back religiously convinced that Shakespeare was a great artist. All because the passionate few could not keep their admiration of Shakespeare to themselves. This is not cynicism; but truth. And it is important that those who wish to form their literary taste should grasp it.

Cause B (described)

What causes the passionate few to make such a fuss about literature? There can be only one reply. They find a keen and lasting pleasure in literature. They enjoy literature as some men enjoy beer. The recurrence of this pleasure naturally keeps their interest in literature very much alive. They are forever making new researches, forever practising on themselves. They learn to understand themselves. They learn to know what they want. Their taste becomes surer and surer as their experience lengthens. They do not enjoy today what will seem tedious to them tomorrow. When they find a book tedious, no amount of popular clatter will persuade them that it is pleasurable; and when they find it pleasurable no chill silence of the street crowds will affect their conviction that the book is good and permanent. They have faith in themselves. What are the qualities in a book which give keen and lasting pleasure to the passionate few? This is a question so difficult that it has never yet been completely answered. You may talk lightly about truth, insight, knowledge, wisdom, humor, and beauty, but these comfortable words do not really carry you very far, for each of them has to be defined, especially the first and last. It is all very well for Keats in his airy manner to assert that beauty is truth, truth beauty, and that that is all he knows or needs to know. I, for one, need to know a lot more. And I shall never know. Nobody, not even Hazlitt nor Sainte-Beuve, has ever finally explained why he thought a book beautiful. I take the first fine lines that come to hand—

Cause A

> The woods of Arcady are dead,
> And over is their antique joy—

and I say that those lines are beautiful, because they give me pleasure. But why? No answer! I only know that the passionate few will, broadly, agree with me in deriving this mysterious pleasure from those lines. I am only convinced that the liveliness of our pleasure in those and many other lines by the same author will ultimately cause the majority to believe, by faith, that W. B. Yeats is a genius. The one reassuring aspect of the literary affair is that the passionate few are passionate about the same things. A continuance of interest does, in actual practice, lead ultimately to the same judgments. There is only the difference in width of interest. Some of the passionate few lack catholicity, or, rather,

(Declared a mystery)

the whole of their interest is confined to one narrow channel; they have none left over. These men help specially to vitalize the reputations of the narrower geniuses: such as Crashaw. But their active predilections never contradict the general verdict of the passionate few; rather they reinforce it.

A classic is a work which gives pleasure to the minority which is intensely and permanently interested in literature. It lives on because the minority, eager to renew the sensation of pleasure, is eternally curious and is therefore engaged in an eternal process of rediscovery. A classic does not survive for any ethical reason. It does not survive because it conforms to certain canons, or because neglect would not kill it. It survives because it is a source of pleasure, and because the passionate few can no more neglect it than a bee can neglect a flower. The passionate few do not read "the right things" because they are right. That is to put the cart before the horse. "The right things" are the right things solely because the passionate few *like* reading them. Hence—and I now arrive at my point—the one primary essential to literary taste is a hot interest in literature. If you have that, all the rest will come. It matters nothing that at present you fail to find pleasure in certain classics. The driving impulse of your interest will force you to acquire experience, and experience will teach you the use of the means of pleasure. You do not know the secret ways of yourself: that is all. A continuance of interest must inevitably bring you to the keenest joys. But, of course, experience may be acquired judiciously or injudiciously, just as Putney may be reached via Walham Green or via Moscow.[3]

Presenting Personal Reasons

A still more subjective type of causal analysis is that in which the writer tries to explain why he feels or acts a certain way. In this case the causes are personal and therefore cannot be evaluated in the same terms as objective analysis—i.e., as accurate or inaccurate—but rather as sincere or insincere, convincing or unconvincing, logically consistent or inconsistent, and *reasonable* or unreasonable in terms of themselves.

Sometimes the presentation of reasons to explain a particular action takes on the character of a "defense" and thereby becomes an "argument" (Chapter 20, "What Case Can Be Made *For* or *Against* X?"). A fine example of a causal analysis that is also defense and argument is the following essay by actor-playwright Ossie Davis, one of the first men to publicly praise Malcolm X, the controversial Black Muslim leader, after his assassination. When asked by a magazine editor *why* he had done so, Davis replied as follows:

[3] From *Literary Taste and How to Form It* by Arnold Bennett, 1927, reprinted by permission of Doubleday & Company, Inc.

WHY I EULOGIZED MALCOLM X

OSSIE DAVIS

You are not the only person curious to know why I would eulogize a man like Malcolm X. Many who know and respect me have written letters. Of these letters I am proudest of those from a sixth-grade class of young white boys and girls who asked me to explain. I appreciate your giving me this chance to do so.

You may anticipate my defense somewhat by considering the following fact: no Negro has yet asked me that question. (My pastor in Grace Baptist Church where I teach Sunday school preached a sermon about Malcolm in which he called him a "giant in a sick world.") Every one of the many letters I got from my own people lauded Malcolm as a man, and commended me for having spoken at his funeral.

At the same time—and this is important—most all of them took special pains to disagree with much or all of what Malcolm said and what he stood for. That is, with one singing exception, they all, every last, black, glory-hugging one of them knew that Malcolm—whatever else he was or was not—*Malcolm was a man!*

White folks do not need anybody to remind them that they are men. We do! This was his one incontrovertible benefit to his people.

Protocol and common sense require that Negroes stand back and let the white man speak up for us, defend us, and lead us from behind the scene in our fight. This is the essence of Negro politics. But Malcolm said to hell with that! Get up off your knees and fight your own battles. That's the way to win back your self-respect. That's the way to make the white man respect you. And if he won't let you live like a man, he certainly can't keep you from dying like one!

Malcolm, as you can see, was refreshing excitement; he scared hell out of the rest of us, bred as we are to caution, to hypocrisy in the presence of white folks, to the smile that never fades. Malcolm knew that every white man in America profits directly or indirectly from his position vis-à-vis Negroes, profits from racism even though he does not practice it or believe it.

He also knew that every Negro who did not challenge on the spot every instance of racism, overt or covert, committed against him and his people, who chose instead to swallow his spit and go on smiling, was an Uncle Tom and a traitor, without balls or guts, or any other commonly accepted aspects of manhood!

Now, we knew all these things as well as Malcolm did, but we also knew what happened to people who stick their necks out and say them. And if all the lies we tell ourselves by way of extenuation were put into print, it would constitute one of the great chapters in the history of man's justifiable cowardice in the face of other men.

But Malcolm kept snatching our lies away. He kept shouting the painful truth we whites and blacks did not want to hear from all the housetops. And he wouldn't stop for love nor money.

You can imagine what howling, shocking nuisance this man was to both Negroes and whites. Once Malcolm fastened on you, you could not escape. He was one of the most fascinating and charming men I have ever met, and never hesitated to take his attractiveness and beat you to death with it. Yet his irritation, though painful to us, was most salutary. He would make you angry as hell, but he would also make you proud. It was impossible to remain defensive and apologetic about being a Negro in his presence. He wouldn't let you. And you always left his presence with the sneaky suspicion that maybe, after all, you were a man!

But in explaining Malcolm, let me take care not to explain him away. He had been a criminal, an addict, a pimp, and a prisoner; a racist, and a hater, he had really believed the white man was a devil. But all this had changed! Two days before his death, in commenting to Gordon Parks about his past life he said: "That was a mad scene. The sickness and madness of those days! I'm glad to be free of them."

And Malcolm was free. No one who knew him before and after his trip to Mecca could doubt that he had completely abandoned racism, separatism, and hatred. But he had not abandoned his shock-effect statements, his bristling agitation for immediate freedom in this country not only for blacks, but for everybody.

And most of all, in the area of race relations, he still delighted in twisting the white man's tail, and in making Uncle Toms, compromisers and accommodationists—I deliberately include myself—thoroughly ashamed of the urbane and smiling hypocrisy we practice merely to exist in a world whose values we both envy and despise.

But even had Malcolm not changed, he would still have been a relevant figure on the American scene, standing in relation as he does, to the "responsible" civil rights leaders, just about where John Brown stood in relation to the "responsible" abolitionist in the fight against slavery. Almost all disagreed with Brown's mad and fanatical tactics which led him foolishly to attack a Federal arsenal at Harpers Ferry, to lose two sons, and later to be hanged for treason.

Yet, today the world, and especially the Negro people, proclaim Brown not a traitor, but a hero and a martyr in a noble cause. So in future, I will not be surprised if men came to see that Malcolm X was, within his own limitations and in his own inimitable style, also a martyr in that cause.

But there is much controversy still about this most controversial American, and I am content to wait for history to make the final decision.

But in personal judgment, there is no appeal from instinct. I knew the man personally, and however much I disagreed with him, I never doubted that Malcolm X, even when he was wrong, was always that rarest thing in the world among us Negroes: a true man.

And if, to protect my relations with the many good white folks who make it possible for me to earn a fairly good living in the entertainment industry, I was too chicken, too cautious, to admit that fact when he was alive, I thought at least that now, when all the white folks are safe from him at last, I could be honest with myself enough to lift my hat for one final salute to that brave, black, ironic gallantry, which was his style and hallmark, that shocking zing of fire-and-be-damned-to-you, so absolutely absent in every other Negro man I know, which brought him, too soon, to his death.[4]

It is interesting to note that even in this kind of analysis the principle of uniformity may be applied. There are constant factors in the black experi-

[4] From *Black on Black*, cited by Arnold Adoff. Reprinted by permission of Ossie Davis.

ence, for example, that made the qualities of Malcolm X important to the blacks and representative of the race. If Davis' reasoning is valid, then, the cause of his action goes beyond personal experience to the experience of the black people as a whole.

ASSIGNMENTS

I. A. While keeping in mind the fact that the writer of an informal causal analysis is permitted more latitude than formal logic would allow, we should nonetheless carefully examine the basic assumptions and reasoning of Bennett's "Why a Classic Is a Classic."

1. Do you think Bennett's basic assumption is sound—that the majority of people do not know or care about literature and that they are simply intimidated by the reputation of a Shakespeare? Do *you* like Shakespeare? Why or why not?
2. Do you agree that only the "passionate few" are genuinely appreciative of literature and that it is preserved only through their zealous support?
3. Is Bennett correct in his assertion that most people have not read enough to rely on their own taste either as a standard of judgment or as a means of pleasure ("They simply don't know from one day to the next what will please them.") Do you think you have read enough to trust your own taste? Do you feel that the observation made about a liberal education—that it aims to increase the area of potential appreciation—is relevant here? How so?
4. Do you know anybody who "enjoys literature as some men enjoy beer"? Do you? If not, do you think anybody does?
5. Is it, as Bennett asserts, impossible to analyze completely the reasons why a book gives pleasure or why it is great? ("Nobody has ever finally explained why he thought a book beautiful.") Can you explain why you thought a given work was beautiful? Are there human (in addition to literary) reasons Bennett has not indicated (perhaps not thought of) that contribute to making a book "great," valued by generations of readers?
6. How do you interpret Bennett's term "hot interest in literature"? Do you agree that "if you have that, all the rest will come"?
7. Do you agree with Bennett's definition of a classic as "a work which gives pleasure to the minority which is intensely and permanently interested in literature"? Could this definition be seen as "begging the question" (see Logical Fallacies, pp. 312–15)? Suggest your own definition and cite examples.

B. Write an essay (500–750 words) in which you support Bennett's reasoning or show it to be inadequate.

or

Write an essay of equal length in which you explain why you regard one of the following works as a classic:

The Adventures of Huckleberry Finn
David Copperfield
Pride and Prejudice

Romeo and Juliet
Peter Pan
(or a suitable equivalent)

II. A. Since "Why I Eulogized Malcolm X" is in many important respects an argument as well as an explanation and causal analysis, it will be worthwhile at this point to foreshadow Chapter 20 by examining some of the techniques Davis uses to "make his case":

1. To what larger audience is this essay addressed?
2. Does Davis build a solid, convincing case in behalf of his action?
    a. Are his reasons reasonable?
    b. What type of evidence does he cite to support his statements—objective or subjective?
    c. Does he have *many* reasons, or do they all "boil down" to one comprehensive reason?
    d. Are his points arranged in ascending order of importance?
    e. Does Davis' refusal to "explain away" Malcolm's faults ("He had been a criminal, an addict, a pimp . . .") weaken the defense?
    f. Explain the significance and impact of the following statements:

        . . . no Negro has yet asked me that question.
        And he wouldn't stop for love nor money.
        I deliberately include myself [among Uncle Toms, compromisers]
        to exist in a world whose values we both envy and despise.
        . . . I am content to wait for history to make the final decision.

    g. Characterize the tone of this essay (aggressive, apologetic, sad, bitter, matter-of-fact, angry, restrained).
    h. What larger social purpose does this eulogy serve?

B. Write an essay (500–750 words) in which you explain why—in a controversial situation—you acted as you did. Try to make your explanation as reasonable and convincing as possible.

III. Write an essay (500–750 words) indicating the main causes for any one of the following:

A. Natural phenomena

green grass
rain
blue sky
white clouds
appearance of stars at night
revolution of the earth around the sun
sunrise
sunset
movement of the tides

B. Biological-Psychological conditions

Disorders

headaches
arteriosclerosis

high blood pressure
diabetes
cirrhosis
epilepsy
hiccoughing
hay fever
stuttering
schizophrenia
homosexuality
suicide
aphasia
amnesia

Accidents

automobile accidents
home accidents
fires
airplane crashes
mining accidents

C. Architecture

the construction of one of the Seven Wonders of the World
the construction of cathedrals (or one particular cathedral) in the Middle Ages
the popularity of prefabricated houses
the evolution of the skyscraper in the United States
the belief that Frank Lloyd Wright was a great architect

IV. Write an essay (500–750 words) in which you explain why you believe or disbelieve in any one of the following:

A. Law

capital punishment
legal abortion
civil rights legislation
present divorce laws
alimony
the jury system
current immigration quotas
a man is innocent until he's proven guilty
diplomatic immunity
present income tax laws
inheritance tax
the justice of the Nuremberg Trials
treating prostitution as a crime
treating drug use as a crime
conscientious objectors

B. Religion

religion *per se*
God as "giver"
going to church
the Bible as revelation
the Bible as literature

the Immaculate Conception
immortality
heaven and hell
missionaries
papal infallibility
the Trinity
salvation
Day of Judgment
original sin
free will
doctrine of the elect

V. Study the following picture, and write an essay (250 words) in which you try to imagine or infer the causes of the "cry":

8 WHAT ARE THE CONSEQUENCES OF X?

Just as we are naturally curious about the causes of various ideas, acts, or events, so we are naturally curious about consequences—i.e., linking X with the inevitable sequelae of X.[1] Thus whereas the previous question ("What Causes X?") started with *effects* and traced them back to *causes*, we now start with *causes* and trace them forward to *effects*. In the following essay, for example, we contemplate the consequences of a new and somewhat frightening medical specialty—transplantation of human organs. In this case the writer (a layman writing in consultation with a doctor and a biochemist) considers a not-too-distant prospect—what effect will transplantation of the brain have on *identity?*

BRAIN TRANSPLANTATION AND PERSONAL IDENTITY

ROLAND PUCCETTI

I begin without introduction. We have a patient dying of some wasting general disease, such as cancer, which as far as we can tell has not yet affected his brain. Let us call him X. At the same time we have an emergency admission, Y, where massive cerebral damage was incurred in an accident, though his body is unhurt and in good general health. We keep Y alive for hours using a respirator machine, adrenalin injections, and so on, but it is quite clear he will never recover consciousness or control over his body. X and Y

[1] In tracing consequences, as in tracing reasons, it is important to establish a clear cause-effect relationship, especially when dealing with social and historical topics. For a consideration of the logical foundations for sound causal analysis, see the previous section, pp. 107–14.

are of the same blood group. So with X's consent, and with permission of Y's nearest kin, we prepare to transplant X's brain into Y's body, sacrificing thereby one fatally-diseased body and one fatally-damaged brain. On the level of medical ethics I cannot see how this is much different from heart transplantation. However, there are formidable surgical and logical differences, as we shall see.

The actual operation is easier stated than described, but I shall give its general lines. First we cut the vertebral artery and clamp it in both X and Y. We do the same with the carotid artery, except that in X's case we withdraw blood from the brain, chill it, and pump it back. This freezes the hypothalamus slightly, lowers the temperature and metabolic rate within the brain, and reduces danger of tissue damage by oxygen starvation. Then we cut through X's scalp, lay it back, and section the cranium in large arcs. Next the brainstem is severed in the *medulla oblongata,* where it passes through the *foramen magnum* and merges with the spinal cord. Finally we cut all twelve cranial nerves where they join the brainstem, and lift X's brain out. Exactly the same having been done with Y's brain, we now place X's brain in Y's empty cranial cavity. Y's brain, of course, we discard along with X's body. The ends of the two arteries are now sutured, the twelve cranial nerves are butted and sheathed in arterial tubes made for this purpose, and the lower brainstem–spinal cord fitted together. Then we rewire the sections of Y's cranium, replace the cerebrospinal fluid by injection, sew back the scalp, and dose Y's body heavily with immuno-suppressive drugs. . . .

We now have X's brain comfortably installed in Y's body, hooked up and ready to go. This is where our logical difficulties begin. To avoid prejudicing the outcome, let us call the composite organism Z. The question arises, *Who* is Z? Is Z just Y with a new brain? Or X with a new body? Or have we created a third person, "Z"? And depending on our answer here, to what extent is our concept of a particular person linked to possession of a particular body or brain? To a particular sex, for that matter?

I. ARE PEOPLE WHAT YOU MEET?

Suppose we let six months go by, during which time Z heals nicely and is discharged from the hospital. We now find Z in his favourite pub of a late afternoon, toasting his new health. A youngish man enters, slaps him on the back, and starts addressing him as Y.

> Joel Andrews, you say? I'm terribly sorry. My name is Weatherby.
> Oh, come off it, Joel. I know you like a brother.
> Clarence Weatherby.
> We roomed together at school!
> I had all my schooling in Australia.
> But I was best man at your wedding, just two years ago!
> Two years ago I was in South Africa, long since married.
> This is incredible! You even have that scar on the bridge of your nose.
> What about it?
> I gave it to you, with a cricket bat. Don't you remember?
> Never played cricket in my life.

Nothing in this dialogue comes as a surprise. After all, how *could* Z, i.e. Y's body with X's brain, remember things Y did? Memories are stored in the cerebral cortex and brainstem, not the body. What the young man is asking Z to remember perished with Y's brain. So Z cannot be Y, even if he has Y's body. You might say, Yes, but people sometimes lose memories—even all memories prior to a cerebral accident—yet they are the same people. True, but Z is not a general amnesiac. Unless he's lying he has a very definite set of memory traces to draw upon, quite different from Y's.

To whom do these memories belong? Surely not to Z as a distinct person. If Z were a distinct person, newly created by the juncture of X's brain and Y's body, his memory could extend no further back in time than six months ago. Indeed, as a new person he would not even have the store of unconscious traces the amnesiac has. He would not know how to walk and talk, for example. He would be on the intellectual level of the infant toddler. But Z is not like that at all. Thus Z cannot be "Z," that is a novel person, any more than he can be Y. Then who *is* Z? Only one alternative remains. He must be X.

> Look, I think there's something you should know. Your friend is dead.
> Joel dead? Good God! How did it happen?
> I'm told he dived into an empty swimming pool on his head.
> How did you learn this? Did you know him?
> We never actually met. I mean, we weren't introduced.
> How's Kitty taking it?
> His wife? I owe my life to that woman.
> I don't follow.
> You've heard of brain transplantation, haven't you? Well . . .

Will the young man accept Z as X, even if he hears the whole story from Y's lips? Or will he think he is the victim of some kind of elaborate joke? No one can say in advance, but assuming that brain transplants are not unknown by this time, it seems to me he would.

> So there she sat, vaguely hoping I was her husband after all.
> Poor Kitty.
> Yes, she even kissed me goodbye on her last visit. I actually cried.
> And your own wife? It must have been equally weird to her.
> Well, of course. (*Smiling.*) But on the whole I'd say she's pleased with the change.
> What do you mean?
> I was 48 and your friend only 29. A most vigorous young man too, if I must say so.
> Joel was an excellent skier.
> That won't help me. I don't know how to stand in the bloody things.
> Do you like any sports?
> Tennis. I can play a match of singles without breathing hard now.
> That's funny. Joel never played tennis.
> Should have taken it up. What stamina! And his reflexes.

Everything above is consistent with the hypothesis of brain transplantation, once one realises exactly what is being transplanted.

For instance, while he's talking Z will probably reveal a slight Australian accent. When appropriate he would throw in some Australian expression. But his voice production would be Y's, because that's not in X's brain. Similarly, his sexual interests and associations would remain X's, but reinforced by Y's hormone production and better general health. Since the memory storage is in the brain, he could hardly be expected to have acquired Y's learned responses along with that body. These are stored in the reticular activating system in the upper brainstem, and in the cerebellum. Thus he wouldn't be able to ski, though if he knew tennis he would find he has become a better player because the reflexes, muscle response to nerve impulses, and supporting organ efficiency—heart, lungs, *etc.*—would be far superior to what he had before he acquired Y's body. No doubt the first few months of post-operative recovery would require Z to get used to these differences. Where he used to drag himself out of bed he will now bound, as if he had been transported to a planet subject to lesser gravitational forces. It is the reverse of a healthy person having to walk very carefully after a long confinement in bed, when his muscular response, *etc.*, became weakened. Since the reticular activating system and cerebellum embody a feedback mechanism enabling us to make adjustments between sensory input and motor output unconsciously, the new situation requires conscious adjustment. But soon it is effected. X learns, in brief, to take over Y's body successfully.

But then why should we continue to speak of Z? Z is not, as we saw, really "Z," a new person. Z is the organic composite of X's brain and Y's body, which in terms of personal identity is really X. We sometimes say someone is "a new person" where we mean he's undergone *sauna* treatments, psychoanalysis, Dr. Reich's orgone box, transcendental meditation, hormone injections, conversion to Roman Catholicism, Communism, Zen Buddhism or what have you. These are all weak senses of the term "new person." In the strong sense they remain the same person nevertheless. So does X, even though his transformation is more drastic on the corporeal side. Old acquaintances who knew him not long before the transplant would find it hard, as his wife did, to believe this is Clarence Weatherby. But he could provide convincing evidence he is, in the form not only of specific memories but also of continued likes and dislikes, emotional responses, character traits—everything that goes to make up a real individual person.

One can fancy X standing in the graveyard, in Y's body, watching a double funeral. Alongside him are Y's wife and his son. There are two coffins being lowered into the grave together. One is very small—shoebox size. That is Y's dead brain. The other is very big, X's former body. Everyone is grieving. But not for X. Why should they, since he is standing there, alive and happier than he has been for years? Only Y is being buried, in that tiny box. If you asked X how it felt to witness his own funeral he would perhaps laugh, and rightly so. He might even point to the shoebox-sized coffin and say "ask Y that." [2]

By addressing the question of consequences to almost any subject, the writer locates a topic, as Rousseau did in his *Confessions.* Looking back upon an early episode in his life, he traced its consequences upon himself and an "innocent victim."

[2] From *Analysis,* Vol. 29, No. 3, January 1969. Reprinted by permission of Basil Blackwell, Publisher.

A SHAMEFUL ACT

JEAN-JACQUES ROUSSEAU

Would that I had finished all that I had to say about my stay at Madame de Vercellis's! But, although my condition apparently remained the same, I did not leave the house as I entered it. I carried away from it lasting recollections of crime and the insupportable weight of remorse, which, after forty years, still lies heavy on my conscience; while the bitterness of it, far from growing weaker, makes itself more strongly felt with my advancing years. Who would believe that a childish fault could have such cruel consequences? For these more than probable consequences my heart is inconsolable. I have, perhaps, caused the ruin of an amiable, honest, and estimable girl, who certainly was far more worthy than myself, and doomed her to disgrace and misery.

It is almost unavoidable that the break up of an establishment should cause some confusion in the house, and that several things should get lost; however, the servants were so honest, and the Lorenzis so watchful, that nothing was missing when the inventory was taken. Only Mademoiselle Pontal had lost a piece of old red and silver-coloured ribbon. Many other things of greater value were at my disposal; this ribbon alone tempted me; I stole it, and, as I took no trouble to conceal it, it was soon found. They wanted to know how it had come into my possession. I became confused, stammered, blushed, and at last said that Marion had given it to me. Marion was a young girl from Maurienne, whom Madame de Vercellis had taken for her cook, when she left off giving dinner and discharged her own, as she had more need of good soup than of fine stews. Marion was not only pretty but had a fresh colour, only found on the mountains, and, above all, there was something about her so gentle and modest, that it was impossible for anyone to see her without loving her; in addition to that, she was a good and virtuous girl, and of unquestionable honesty. All were surprised when I mentioned her name. We were both equally trusted and it was considered important to find out which of us two was really the thief. She was sent for; a number of people were assembled, amongst them the Comte de la Roque. When she came, the ribbon was shown to her. I boldly accused her; she was astounded, and unable to utter a word; looked at me in a manner that would have disarmed the Devil himself, but against which my barbarous heart was proof. At last, she denied the theft firmly, but without anger, addressed herself to me, exhorted me to reflect, and not to disgrace an innocent girl who had never done me any harm; but I, with infernal impudence, persisted in my story, and declared to her face that she had given me the ribbon. The poor girl began to cry, and only said to me: "Ah! Rousseau, I thought you were a good man. You make me very unhappy, but I should not like to be in your place." That was all. She proceeded to defend herself with equal simplicity and firmness, but without allowing herself to utter the slightest reproach against me. This moderation, contrasted with my decided tone, did her harm. It did not seem natural to suppose, on the one side, such devilish impudence, and, on the other, such angelic mildness. Although the matter did not appear to be absolutely settled, they were prepossessed in my favour. In the confusion which prevailed, they did not give themselves time to get to the bottom of the affair; and the Comte de la Roque, in dismissing us both, contented himself with saying that the conscience of the guilty one would amply avenge the innocent. His prediction has been fulfilled; it fulfils itself every day.

I do not know what became of the victim of my false accusation; but it is not likely that she afterwards found it easy to get a good situation. She carried away with her an imputation upon her honesty which was in every way cruel. The theft was only a trifling one, but still it was a theft, and, what is worse, made use of to lead a young man astray; lastly, lying and obstinacy left nothing to be hoped from one in whom so many vices were united. I do not even consider misery and desertion as the greatest danger to which I exposed her. At her age, who knows to what extremes discouragement and the feeling of ill-used innocence may have carried her? Oh, if my remorse at having, perhaps, made her unhappy is unendurable, one may judge what I feel at the thought of having, perhaps, made her worse than myself!

This cruel remembrance at times so sorely troubles and upsets me, that in my sleepless hours I seem to see the poor girl coming to reproach me for my crime, as if it had been committed only yesterday. As long as I have lived quietly, it has tormented me less; but in the midst of a stormy life it robs me of the sweet consolation of persecuted innocence, it makes me feel what I think I have said in one of my books, that "Remorse goes to sleep when our fortunes are prosperous, and makes itself felt more keenly in adversity." However, I have never been able to bring myself to unburden my heart of this confession to a friend. The closest intimacy has never led me so far with anyone, not even with Madame de Warens. All that I have been able to do has been to confess that I had to reproach myself with an atrocious act, but I have never stated wherein it consisted. This burden has remained to this day upon my conscience without alleviation; and I can affirm that the desire of freeing myself from it in some degree, has greatly contributed to the resolution I have taken of writing my Confessions.

Like most questions, "What are the consequences?" lends itself to a variety of treatments, lighthearted as well as serious. In the following sketch, humorist Art Buchwald wonders: What would happen if paperback publications decided to "spice up" the old childhood favorites with a "dash" of pornography? It is amusing to contemplate the consequences.

SUBTITLES FOR OLD BOOKS

ART BUCHWALD

There was a time when the only way you could get a pornographic book was to smuggle it in from Paris. But in recent years the paperback book industry in the United States has been outdoing anything you could bring in from Paris. I feel everyone has a right to make a dollar under our free enterprise system and if people want to buy pornographic literature that is their business. What I object to is the publishers making non-pornographic books pornographic by putting half-naked women on the covers of good books and printing descriptions of the contents which give an entirely different idea of the plot.

If the trend continues, here is how our paperback publishers will soon describe some books familiar to all of us:

Snow White and the Seven Dwarfs—The story of a ravishing blond virgin who was held captive by seven deformed men, all with different lusts.

Cinderella—A beautiful passionate woman bares her naked foot to the man she loves while her stepmother and stepsisters plot to cheat her out of the one memorable night in her life.

Alice in Wonderland—A young girl's search for happiness in a weird depraved world of animal desires. Can she ever return to a normal happy life after falling so far?

Huckleberry Finn—A wild youth runs away from his home to help a Negro slave escape from the ravishing Miss Watson.

Little Women—Four teen-agers, wise beyond their years, are caught up in the throbbing tumult of the Civil War. Read what happens to them when a rich old gentleman and his greedy grandson take rooms as boarders in a house without men.

Tom Brown's Schooldays—For the first time we look beyond the locked doors of an English boarding school to reveal the truth about a life that one talks about and only a few will whisper.

Treasure Island—The crew of a ship bent on rape and plunder land on an island inhabited by sex-crazed cannibals. An innocent boy finds the secret of growing up.

Little Red Riding Hood—A girl goes to visit her grandmother only to discover a wolf in her bed. Read what happens when the girl refuses to get into bed with the wolf.

Tom Sawyer—A gang of subteen-age hoodlums paint the town white, and commit mayhem and murder to satisfy their desires.

Heidi—A young lady caught up in the wild life of Switzerland fights for love.

Babar the Elephant—Life in the raw.

And so it goes. As for the covers, I'll have to leave that up to the publishers. I hate to think what the paperback artists will do with *Wind in the Willows*.[3]

ASSIGNMENTS

I. Write an essay (500–750 words) indicating what you think were, are, or will be the major effects or consequences of any one of the following (on the individual, the family, or society at large):

A. Inventions

the automobile
the telephone
the television
the airplane
the electric light

B. Social changes

space travel
human transplants

[3] Reprinted by permission of G. P. Putnam's Sons from *And Then I Told the President* by Art Buchwald. Copyright © 1964, 1965 by Art Buchwald.

war on poverty
fight against pollution
increased drug usage
increased divorce rate
increased mixed marriages
increased urbanization
increased automation
increased income tax
increased leisure time
the new morality

II. In an essay (500–750 words) describe the effect on your mind or sensibilities of one of the following:

the moon
the sun
long hair and beards
hot weather
cold weather
noise
silence
prejudice
current fashions
nightmares
fatigue
religion
advertising

III. As Rousseau has described the "cruel consequences" of a "childish fault," write an essay (500–750 words) in which you describe some "shameful act" for which you have suffered remorse. Or, if you wish, describe the consequences of some act which had happy, rather than dire, consequences.

IV. Write a humorous essay (250–500 words) in the manner of Art Buchwald, in which you continue to speculate on what will happen to childhood favorites if the paperback publishers continue the trend toward pornographic advertising.

or

Write an essay, humorous or satirical in tone, in which you answer the question "What would happen if . . ."

9 WHAT ARE THE TYPES OF X?

Another common and popular type of analysis is classification: seeing something in terms of its classes or "types."

Classification is a highly methodical and sophisticated form of analysis and an indispensable condition of systematic thought, for it involves a sorting process that groups things into categories based on similar characteristics, thereby bringing order out of chaos. Indeed, Adam did precisely this—fashioned order out of chaos—when he classified the beasts of the field and the fowl of the air; he saw the multiplicity of creatures on the earth in terms of common characteristics that entitled them to be grouped together.

Ever since then, man has been classifying, i.e., arranging things in order to see them more clearly in terms of their similarities and differences, and in that way learn more about them.

We frequently use classification in our daily living; for example, we may sort our daily mail into three categories: bills, junk mail, and letters (an incomplete but still useful system of classification). We put the bills to one side, throw away the junk mail unopened, and give our time to the letters. Or a friend may say to us: "I have just met your neighbor Joe Smith. What kind of man is he?" The friend is asking us to classify Joe Smith. We may reply: "Oh, Joe is the aggressive junior executive-on-the-make type, but very friendly." If our friend knows other junior executives-on-the-make, he will have some idea of the characteristics of Joe Smith.

In using classification we can either start with the individual and put him into a class (as we did with Joe Smith), or, as in the following piece, we can start with a class and divide it into its constituent members. Thus, Paul Bohannan observes that there are—roughly—three kinds of human needs:

> When a baby is born he is a bundle of needs [which] must be satisfied. The psychiatrist, Harry Stack Sullivan, has divided the needs of the human infant (and, indeed, of all human beings) into three main groups. The first of these is the need for the chemicals and the proper temperature to maintain life and growth. The infant [like] any other human being, feels these needs as the tensions of hunger and cold, and as the need for oxygen.
>
> The second type of need is . . . for sleep. This need is one that we do not yet understand totally, although our present scientific knowledge of sleep is more extensive than it was even a few years ago. This is a difficult subject, and I shall say no more about the need for sleep than that it includes a need to dream, that the proportion of time one spends sleeping is reduced as one grows older, and that the way in which people sleep is greatly affected by their cultural customs.
>
> The third kind of need has been called many things, but there is no real need for a euphemism—it is the need for love. This need is a response to a kind of tension quite different from the tensions of chemical demands. It is what doctors call the tension of anxiety. The tension of anxiety does not pertain to physical needs, but to the fear of punitive social relationships or of the loss of gratifying relationships.
>
> The personality of the human animal is rooted as deeply in this need for love—at least, personal interaction—as his physical well-being is rooted in his chemical needs.[1]

Bohannan equates the third need, for love, with the first two because like them it is "a response to tension." That is, the common characteristic that makes these needs a genuine class is that they are all "responses to tension." But it might be argued that since the need for love does not, like the other needs, have a purely physical basis, Bohannan's classification is not valid, and his discussion falls apart.

This is the essential point about classification: it must be based on shared characteristics of the individual members of the class. Simply grouping things is not to classify them. If we put 100 people in a room, we do *not* have a class; if we put 100 airline pilots or 100 engineers or 100 Americans of Italian descent in a room, then we *do* have a class.

Classification According to Purpose

What characteristics we use as the basis of a classification depend on our own interest and purpose. Thus, we can classify our 100 people politically, socially, economically, even by the color of their eyes, depending on what special point we want to make.

The writer, of course, is free to choose whatever basis of classification best suits his purpose, but once he has chosen he must not switch midway to a different ground. If he does, he will commit the logical error of cross-ranking, i.e., producing overlapping rather than mutually exclusive categories. Someone who classifies the types of houses in a town as Victorian, colonial,

[1] From *Love, Sex, & Being Human* by Paul Bohannan, copyright © 1969 by Paul Bohannan. Reprinted by permission of Doubleday & Company, Inc.

ranch, and "two-story" is guilty of cross-ranking because Victorian and colonial style houses can have two stories.

When properly "envisioned," classification is an extraordinarily useful method of inventing an essay, for there is always a "story" in the designation of types—as the writer chooses to depict them. And the choice will depend on *why* the writer is making the classification in the first place, and on what new insights or refinements of understanding he hopes to provide by analyzing his subject in terms of a given set of categories.

Complete Classification

In the following paragraph, Joseph Addison divides bodily labor into two kinds; he makes a dichotomous (two-part) classification. All labor is either of one kind or the other.

> Bodily labor is of two kinds, either that which a man submits to for his livelihood, or that which he undergoes for his pleasure. The latter of them generally changes the name of labor for that of exercise, but differs only from ordinary labor as it rises from another motive.
>
> A country life abounds in both these kinds of labor, and for that reason gives a man a greater stock of health, and consequently a more perfect enjoyment of himself, than any other way of life.[2]

A dichotomous classification is necessarily complete because it divides everything into either A or B (X or not X). However, completeness is more difficult to achieve in a complex classification such as a scientific classification or the Dewey decimal system for classifying books in a library.

A scientific classification—like a simple analysis—must be complete, i.e., each separate item must fall into its designated group with no "loose ends." Thus a zoologist finds a place in his classification for *all* forms of animal life; a botanist does the same for plant life. Similarly, under the Dewey decimal system a library assigns every one of its holdings a general "number" heading: 900 if it is a history book, 700 if it deals with the arts, etc. These numbers are then broken down further: 930 for ancient history; 940 for medieval and modern European history. And so on. A good classification embodies the dictum "a place for everything and everything in its place." Thus in the Dewey system, small items that are too specialized to have individual headings are grouped into categories such as "General Works," "Miscellaneous," and "Literature of Other Languages." (The "other" includes all languages that have not been specifically named, so that no language spoken or written anywhere is overlooked; each has a theoretical "place" into which it "fits" within the library's classification system.) Notice, then, in the list below that the classification is *complete* and the groups are *mutually exclusive* (there is no overlapping).

[2] "Recreation," *The Spectator*, No. 115, July 12, 1711.

CLASSIFICATION SYSTEM

000 GENERAL WORKS

010 Bibliography. Classified catalogues
020 Library science
030 Encyclopedias
040 General collected essays
050 General periodicals
060 General societies. Museums
070 Newspapers
080 Collected works
090 Manuscripts and rare books

100 PHILOSOPHY

110 Metaphysics
120 Other metaphysical theories
130 Branches of psychology and pseudopsychology
140 Psychology of religious experience
150 Psychology
160 Logic
170 Ethics
180 Ancient and medieval philosophy
190 Modern Western philosophy

200 RELIGION

210 Natural theology
220 Bible
230 Doctrinal theology
240 Devotional and practical theology
250 Pastoral theology
260 Christian church. Christian sociology
270 Christian church history
280 Christian churches and sects
290 Other religions

300 SOCIAL SCIENCES

310 Statistics
320 Political science
330 Economics
340 Law. Constitutional history
350 Public administration
360 Social welfare
370 Education
380 Public services; public utilities
390 Customs and folklore

400 LANGUAGE

410 Comparative linguistics
420 English

430 German
440 French
450 Italian
460 Spanish
470 Latin
480 Greek
490 Other languages

500 PURE SCIENCE

510 Mathematics
520 Astronomy and allied sciences
530 Physics
540 Chemistry
550 Earth sciences
560 Paleontology
570 Anthropological and biological sciences
580 Botanical sciences
590 Zoological sciences

600 TECHNOLOGY (Applied science)

610 Medical sciences
620 Engineering
630 Agriculture
640 Home economics
650 Business and business methods
660 Chemical technology (Industrial chemistry)
670 }
680 } Manufactures
690 Building construction

700 THE ARTS

710 Landscape and civic art
720 Architecture
730 Sculpture
740 Drawing and decorative arts
750 Painting
760 Prints and print making
770 Photography
780 Music
790 Recreation

800 LITERATURE

810 American (U.S.) literature
820 English literature
830 German literature
840 French literature
850 Italian literature
860 Spanish literature

870 Latin literature
880 Greek literature
890 Literature of other languages

900 HISTORY

910 Geography, travels, description of places
920 Biography
930 Ancient history
940 Medieval and modern history of Europe
950 Medieval and modern history of Asia
960 Medieval and modern history of Africa
970 Medieval and modern history of North America
980 Medieval and modern history of South America
990 Medieval and modern history of Pacific Ocean islands

In using classification for rhetorical reasons—as the formal basis of an essay—we are, of course, allowed more latitude than the scientist will permit. Even so, note that in the following essay—a nonscientific classification—the author makes a gesture toward "completeness":

DIFFERENT TYPES OF COMPOSERS

AARON COPLAND

I can see three different types of composers in musical history, each of whom conceives music in a somewhat different fashion.

The type that has fired public imagination most is that of the spontaneously inspired composer—the Franz Schubert type, in other words. All composers are inspired, of course, but this type is more spontaneously inspired. Music simply wells out of him. He can't get it down on paper fast enough. You can almost tell this type of composer by his prolific output. In certain months, Schubert wrote a song a day. Hugo Wolf did the same.

In a sense, men of this kind begin not so much with a musical theme as with a completed composition. They invariably work best in the shorter forms. It is much easier to improvise a song than it is to improvise a symphony. It isn't easy to be inspired in that spontaneous way for long periods at a stretch. Even Schubert was more successful in handling the shorter forms of music. The spontaneously inspired man is only one type of composer, with his own limitations.

Beethoven symbolizes the second type—the constructive type, one might call it. This type exemplifies my theory of the creative process in music better than any other, because in this case the composer really does begin with a musical theme. In Beethoven's case there is no doubt about it, for we have the notebooks in which he put the themes down. We can see from his notebooks how he worked over his themes—how he would not let them be until they were as perfect as he could make them. Beethoven was not a spontaneously inspired composer in the Schubert sense at all. He was the type that begins with a theme; makes it a germinal idea; and upon that constructs a musical work, day after day, in painstaking fashion. Most composers since Beethoven's day belong to this second type.

The third type of creator I can only call, for lack of a better name, the traditionalist type. Men like Palestrina and Bach belong in this category. They both exemplify the kind of composer who is born in a particular period of musical history, when a certain musical style is about to reach its fullest development. It is a question at such a time of creating music in a well-known and accepted style and doing it in a way that is better than anyone has done it before you.

Beethoven and Schubert started from a different premise. They both had serious pretensions to originality: After all, Schubert practically created the song form singlehanded; and the whole face of music changed after Beethoven lived. But Bach and Palestrina simply improved on what had gone before them.

The traditionalist type of composer begins with a pattern rather than with a theme. The creative act with Palestrina is not the thematic conception so much as the personal treatment of a well-established pattern. And even Bach, who conceived forty-eight of the most varied and inspired themes in his *Well Tempered Clavichord*, knew in advance the general formal mold that they were to fill. It goes without saying that we are not living in a traditionalist period nowadays.

One might add, for the sake of completeness, a fourth type of composer—the pioneer type: men like Gesualdo in the seventeenth century, Moussorgsky and Berlioz in the nineteenth, Debussy and Edgar Varese in the twentieth. It is difficult to summarize the composing methods of so variegated a group. One can safely say that their approach to composition is the opposite of the traditionalist type. They clearly oppose conventional solutions of musical problems. In many ways, their attitude is experimental—they seek to add new harmonies, new sonorities, new formal principles. The pioneer type was the characteristic one at the turn of the seventeenth century and also at the beginning of the twentieth century, but it is much less evident today.[3]

Organizing the Classification

We can see that an essay concerned with "the types of X" presents no serious problem in organization since—here again—the organization is more or less *given:* the three or four (or however many) designated "types" generally make up the three of four sections of the piece.

This organization underlies the Copland essay reprinted above (each type of composer is reviewed, one after another) and the essay that follows, a description of Carl Jung's classic two-part division of people into personality types (extrovert and introvert). It is interesting to note that in this essay, even more than in Copland's, the types are regarded not as mutually exclusive, with discernibly "fixed" personalities (an imperative of the scientific or technical classification), but rather as poles on the scale of personality (people are *predominantly* one or the other, no one is purely extrovert or introvert). Thus, in this essay—as in all rhetorical rather than strictly logical classifications—the categories may allowably interpenetrate to some extent.

[3] From *What to Listen For in Music*, Revised Edition by Aaron Copland, copyright © 1957 by McGraw-Hill, Inc., used with permission of McGraw-Hill Book Company.

JUNG'S PSYCHOLOGICAL TYPES

FRIEDA FORDHAM

Introduction

Jung's contribution to the psychology of the conscious mind is largely embodied in his work on psychological types. The attempt to classify human beings according to type has a long history; it is nearly two thousand years since the Greek physician, Galen, tried to distinguish four fundamental temperamental differences in men, and his descriptive terms (though psychologically naive)—the sanguine, the phlegmatic, the choleric, and the melancholic—have passed into common speech. There have been various attempts which, taking modern knowledge into account, aim at a more precise formulation—for instance, Kretschmer's—and [Carl] Jung's division of people into extraverts and introverts has already come to be widely known, if not fully understood. Jung distinguishes two differing attitudes to life, two modes of reacting to circumstances which he finds sufficiently marked and widespread to describe as typical.

> There is a whole class of men [he says] who at the moment of reaction to a given situation at first draw back a little as if with an unvoiced "No," and only after that are able to react; and there is another class who, in the same situation, come forward with an immediate reaction, apparently confident that their behavior is obviously right. The former class would therefore be characterized by a certain negative relation to the object, and the latter by a positive one . . . the former class corresponds to the introverted and the second to the extraverted attitude.

Type one

The extraverted attitude is characterized by an outward flowing of libido, an interest in events, in people and things, a relationship with them, and a dependence on them; when this attitude is habitual to anyone Jung describes him or her as an *extraverted type*. This type is motivated by outside factors and greatly influenced by the environment. The extraverted type is sociable and confident in unfamiliar surroundings. He or she is generally on good terms with the world, and even when disagreeing with it can still be described as related to it, for instead of withdrawing (as the opposite type tends to do) they prefer to argue and quarrel, or try to reshape it according to their own pattern.

Type two

The introverted attitude, in contrast, is one of withdrawal; the libido flows inward and is concentrated upon subjective factors, and the predominating influence is "inner necessity." When this attitude is habitual Jung speaks of an "introverted type." This type lacks confidence in relation to people and things, tends to be unsociable, and prefers reflection to activity. Each type undervalues the other, seeing the negative rather than the positive qualities of the opposite attitude, a fact which has led to endless misunderstanding and even in the course of time to the formulation of antagonistic philosophies.

Conclusion

In the West we prefer the extraverted attitude, describing it in such favourable terms as outgoing, well-adjusted, &c., while on

> the other hand, in the East, at least until recent times, the introverted attitude has been the prevailing one. On this basis one may explain the material and technical development of the Western Hemisphere as contrasted with the material poverty but greater spiritual development of the East.[4]

Complex Classification

Finally it is worth noting that there are occasions when the writer may apply to his subject not one but *many* grounds of classification; not because he is carelessly prone to cross-ranking but rather because this is his main intention: to exhibit the infinite complexity of his subject; to demonstrate that it cannot be encompassed in any one set of categories. Thus in the following essay on excellence, John Gardner classifies this concept according to a great variety of categories.

THE MANY KINDS OF EXCELLENCE

JOHN GARDNER

There are many varieties of excellence. This is one of those absurdly obvious truths of which we must continually remind ourselves. The Duke of Wellington, in a famous incident, revealed an enviable understanding of it. The government was considering the dispatch of an expedition to Burma to take Rangoon. The Cabinet summoned Wellington and asked him who would be the ablest general to head such an undertaking. He said, "Send Lord Combermere." The government officials protested: "But we have always understood that your Grace thought Lord Combermere a fool." The Duke's response was vigorous and to the point. "So he is a fool, and a damned fool, but he can take Rangoon."

In the intellectual field alone there are many kinds of excellence. There is the kind of intellectual activity that leads to a new theory, and the kind that leads to a new machine. There is the mind that finds its most effective expression in teaching and the mind that is most at home in research. There is the mind that works best in quantitative terms, and the mind that luxuriates in poetic imagery.

And there is excellence in art, in music, in craftsmanship, in human relations, in technical work, in leadership, in parental responsibilities.

Some kinds of excellence can be fostered by the educational system, and others must be fostered outside the educational system. Some kinds—e.g., managerial—may lead to worldly success, and others—e.g., compassion—may not.

There are types of excellence that involve doing something well and types that involve being a certain kind of person. There are kinds of excellence so subjective that the world cannot even observe much less appraise them. Montaigne wrote, "It is not only for an exterior show or ostentation that our soul must play her part, but inwardly within ourselves, where no eyes shine but ours."

[4] From *An Introduction to Jung's Psychology* by Frieda Fordham. Copyright 1953, 1959, 1966 by Frieda Fordham.

There is a way of measuring excellence that involves comparison between people—some are musical geniuses and some are not; and there is another that involves comparison between myself at my best and myself at my worst. It is this latter comparison which enables me to assert that I am being true to the best that is in me—or forces me to confess that I am not.

Definitions of excellence tend to be most narrow at the point where we are selecting individuals, or testing them, or training them. In the course of daily life, mature people recognize many varieties of excellence in one another. But when we are selecting, testing or training we arbitrarily narrow the range. The reasons for doing so are practical ones. Narrowing the grounds for selection is one way of making the selection process manageable. To the extent that we admit a great variety of kinds of excellence we make the task of testing virtually impossible.

Consider the relatively narrow bottleneck through which most youngsters enter a career as a scientist. What they need to a very high degree is the capacity to manipulate abstract symbols and to give the kind of intellectual response required on intelligence tests. This capacity for abstract reasoning, and for the manipulation of mathematical and verbal symbols, is useful not only on the tests but in every course they take. The capacity to understand these symbols in various combinations and to reproduce them on paper in other combinations is priceless. There are other factors which contribute to success in graduate school, but most graduate students would agree that this is the heart and soul of the matter.

On the other hand, if one looks at a group of mature scientists—in their fifties, let us say—one finds that those who are respected have gained their reputations through exercising a remarkable variety of talents. One is honored for his extraordinary gifts as a teacher: his students are his great contribution to the world. Another is respected for the penetrating ideas he puts into the stream of the science. Another is respected—though perhaps not loved—for his devastating critical faculties. And so the list goes. Some are specialists by nature, some generalists; some creative, some plodding; some gifted in action, some in expression.

Anyone who looks at the way in which the world judges his own contemporaries will recognize the varied standards of judgment which come into play. But though in daily life we recognize a good many kinds of high performance, we rarely make this variety explicit in our thinking about excellence.

And though we admit a considerable range of excellences, we are still narrower in this respect than we should be. One way to make ourselves see this is to reflect on the diverse kinds of excellence that human beings have honored at different times and places. At any given time in a particular society, the idea of what constitutes excellence tends to be limited—but the conception changes as we move from one society to another or one century to another. Baltasar Gracián said:

> It is not everyone that finds the age he deserves. . . . Some men have been worthy of a better century, for every species of good does not triumph. Things have their period; even excellences are subject to fashion.

Taking the whole span of history and literature, the images of excellence are amply varied: Confucius teaching the feudal lords to govern wisely . . . Leonidas defending the pass at Thermopylae . . . Saint Francis preaching to the birds at Alviano . . . Lincoln writing the second inaugural "with malice toward none". . . Mozart composing his first oratorio at the age of eleven . . . Galileo dropping weights from the Tower of Pisa . . . Emily Dickinson jotting her "letters to the world" on scraps of paper . . . Jesus saying, "Father forgive them; for they know not what they do" . . . Florence Nightingale nursing the wounded at Balaclava . . . Eli Whitney pioneering the manufacture of interchangeable parts . . . Ruth saying to Naomi, "Thy people shall be my people."

The list is long and the variety is great. Taken collectively, human societies have gone a long way toward exploring the full range of human excellences. But a particular society at a given moment in history is apt to honor only a portion of the full range. And wise indeed is the society that is not afraid to face hard questions about its own practices on this point. Is it honoring the excellences which are most fruitful for its own continued vitality? To what excellences is it relatively insentive; and what does this imply for the tone and texture of its life? Is it squandering approbation on kinds of high performance which have nothing to contribute to its creativity as a society?

If any one among us can contemplate those questions without uneasiness, he has not thought very long nor very hard about excellence in the United States.[5]

ASSIGNMENTS

I. A. Evaluate Aaron Copland's essay on "Different Types of Composers."

1. Is the classification complete?
2. Comment on the repetition of the words "type" and "composer." Could you eliminate any of this repetition? Would this improve the piece rhetorically?
3. Note the repetition of the word "case" in paragraph four, sentences two and three. Is it necessary? Could you eliminate one use of "case"? What would you substitute? Would it be better?
4. Compare Copland's rhetorical stance in this piece with that of Randolph in "Five Basic Elements of Music" (pp. 66–67).

B. Using Aaron Copland's first sentence, "I can see three different types of composers in musical history, each of whom conceives music in a somewhat different fashion," substitute for "composers in musical history" one of the following and write an essay (500–750 words). You may have to vary the number of types.

painters	architects
dancers	photographers
poets	artists
playwrights	teachers
novelists	doctors

II. In an essay (500–750 words) classify people you know or know of into Jung's *extrovert-introvert* types. You may wish to add a third category,

[5] From pp. 127–31 in *Excellence: Can We Be Equal and Excellent Too?* by John W. Gardner. Copyright © 1961 by John W. Gardner. Reprinted by permission of Harper & Row, Publishers.

the *ambivert* (one who balances or oscillates between extroversion and introversion).

III. A. Analyze John Gardner's essay "The Many Types of Excellence" in terms of the following:

1. In attempting to encompass "the full range of human excellence," Gardner has given us *many* classifications, not just one. What are they? Does he thereby violate a logical principle; i.e., does he thoughtlessly shift the ground of his classification? Explain.
2. Is Gardner's classification technically complete? Are the groupings mutually exclusive or do they overlap?
3. Comment on the function of the Duke of Wellington anecdote in paragraph one.
4. Analyze paragraph structure in this essay in terms of length and number of paragraphs. How do paragraph breaks coincide with turns of thought? Could you justify more or fewer breaks? Point to specific paragraphs that could conceivably be joined.

B. Gardner's essay describes many types of excellence in the hope that we will not oversimplify this complex quality or overlook important distinctions within the concept itself. Write an essay (500–750 words) in which you warn against oversimplification by describing the many types of one of the following (as you have observed or experienced it):

intelligence	beauty
freedom	goodness
truth	loyalty
happiness	charity
love	courage

IV. In an essay (500–750 words) indicate the "common types" of any one of the following:

A. Psychology/Sociology

dreams	propaganda
memories	conformity
mental disturbances	class conflict
talent or aptitude	fads
ambition	pressure groups
success	communities
prejudice	status seekers

B. Anthropology

marriage customs	(in a given group)
mourning	(in a given group)
burial	(in a given group)
dating	(in a given group)
suicide	(in a given group)
drinking	(in a given group)
hospitality	(in a given group)
taboos	(in a given group)

C. Travel

railroad
road

ship
airplane
motor vehicle

D. Law

law courts in the United States
law specialties
crimes
prisons
crime prevention
assaults
evidence
misdemeanors

E. Zoology

whales
goats
crabs
elephants
reptiles
monkeys
snakes
ants

10 HOW DOES X COMPARE TO Y?

Take any two people, objects, events, ideas, books, disciplines, countries, continents, planets; take any two periods of time, works of art, artists, *anything* (provided they are in comparable categories, i.e., that there is a logical basis of comparison), and ask of your double subject: How does one compare with the other? How are they similar? How different? In this way you will be "inventing" a study in comparative analysis.[1] Read the following example, a short comparison of two presidents that shows how they were *alike:*

> Kennedy has been compared to Franklin Delano Roosevelt and he liked to pose in front of an F.D.R. portrait. In fact, some of his qualities more nearly recall Theodore Roosevelt, the apostle of the big stick, the strenuous life and the bully pulpit. Like T.R., for instance, Kennedy has a perhaps undue regard for Harvard and a craving for its approval. The only election he ever lost was one of the ones he wanted most to win—his first try for a seat on the Harvard Board of Overseers. He grimly ran again and his election to the Board was a cherished triumph. Like T.R., too, Kennedy fancied himself in the role of national taste maker—Roosevelt picked up Edwin Arlington Robinson and Kennedy

[1] Strictly speaking, *comparison* refers to the drawing of similarities and *contrast* to dissimilarities; but in popular usage the term "comparison" encompasses both processes and means "bringing things together in order to examine them and to see how they are related to one another." Also strictly speaking, a comparison may involve more than two subjects: X could theoretically be set alongside not only Y but also S, T, U, and V. Or—to cite further possibilities—X could be compared with Y in the light of Z. And so on. . . . The possibilities are legion. We will confine ourselves to the double-subject, since most of what should be said about comparison fits under this heading.

> adopted Robert Frost. Roosevelt let his rather rigid literary ideas get about and the Kennedys thought they ought to provide White House examples—Casals, Shakespeare and opera in the East Room—for the cultural uplift of the nation. . . .[2]

Note that in this paragraph the two men are compared not merely *in general* but on the basis of *two specific qualities.* This is the basis of all good comparison. The writer does not simply say X is like Y; instead he says—with precision—X is like Y on the basis of the following points: 1, 2, 3, etc., which is to say, in this case:

Kennedy was like Theodore Roosevelt in that both

1. were apostles of the big stick.
2. were apostles of the strenuous life.
3. were apostles of the bully pulpit.
4. regarded Harvard highly.
5. regarded themselves as tastemakers.

Now note another comparison, this one showing—through an analogy—how two men (again two presidents) were *different:*

> Lyndon Johnson's father once told him that he did not belong in politics unless he could walk into a roomful of men and tell immediately who was for him and who was against him. In fact, even the shrewd LBJ has not quite such occult power, but his liking for the story tells us something useful about him: he sets much store by instinct. No wonder, then, that it would be to his instincts—honed in the Texas hill country, sharpened in a life of politics, confirmed in his successful Congressional career—that he would often turn in the White House.
>
> This reliance on instinct enabled Johnson to put on the Presidency like a suit of comfortable old clothes. John Kennedy, on the other hand, came to it with a historical, nearly theoretical view of what was required of a strong President; he knew exactly what Woodrow Wilson had said about the office and he had read Corwin and Neustadt and he was unabashedly willing to quote Lincoln: "I see the storm coming and I know His hand is in it. If He has a place and work for me, I believe that I am ready."
>
> And Kennedy would add: "Today I say to you that if the people of this nation select me to be their President, I believe that I am ready." With eager confidence, Kennedy acquired a Presidential suit off the rack and put on a little weight to make himself fit it.[3]

[2] From *Kennedy Without Tears: The Man Beneath the Myth* by Tom Wicker. Copyright © 1964 by Tom Wicker. First published in *Esquire Magazine.* Reprinted by permission of William Morrow and Company, Inc.

[3] Reprinted by permission of William Morrow and Company, Inc. from *JFK and LBJ: The Influence of Personality Upon Politics* by Tom Wicker, copyright © 1968 by Tom Wicker.

Similarity and Difference in Comparison

As a form of analysis, comparison is not merely a rhetorical technique; it is a natural, instinctive process that goes on constantly in everyone's mind. It is the way we think and learn—by comparing the unfamiliar with the familiar; it is the way we come to terms with a new situation—by comparing it with an old one. We get our bearings by comparing the past with the present. Whether we are more impressed by the *similarities* between two situations or the *differences* depends, of course, on the situations themselves. The ability to see through the differences to the underlying similarities—or conversely, through the similarities to the underlying differences—is not only the mark of critical intelligence but of the creative mind at work. Psychologist William James tells us that "some people are far more sensitive to resemblances and far more ready to point out wherein they consist, than others are. They are the wits, the poets, the inventors, the scientific men, the practical geniuses." Speaking specifically of Newton and Darwin, James says, "The flash of similarity between an apple and the moon, between the rivalry for food in nature and the rivalry for man's selection, was too recondite to have occurred to any but exceptional minds."

One need not be a Newton or a Darwin, however, to be discriminating, to cut through "to the heart of the matter." Thus the writer, concentrating full attention on his topic, may note that two seemingly similar things are, in one or more discernible and significant respects, *different* (X is *not* like Y). Literary critic Mark Schorer makes this point in connection with two southern writers, Truman Capote and Carson McCullers, whose names, he tells us, are "frequently coupled." The fact is, however, that "the differences are greater than the similarities." Schorer documents this observation by citing several specific points of contrast, beginning with the doctrine of "love."

TWO "SOUTHERN" WRITERS

First point of difference

If Truman Capote is also a writer who comes from the South, he is not a "Southern writer" in the sense that Mrs. McCullers is: he is equally at home and perhaps even more at home in very different settings. The doctrine of love [is] given different interpretations. In Capote's *The Grass Harp,* the Judge speaks as follows:

> "We are speaking of love. A leaf, a handful of seed—begin with these, learn a little what it is to love. First, a leaf, a fall of rain, then someone to receive what a leaf has taught you, what a fall of rain has ripened. No easy process, understand, it would take a lifetime, it has mine; and still I've never mastered it—I only know how true it is: that love is a chain of love, as nature is a chain of life."

And later in the novel, Dolly recalls this speech:

> "Charlie said that love is a chain of love. I hope you listened and understood him. Because when you can love one thing," she held the blue egg as preciously as the Judge had held a leaf, "you can love another, and that is owning, that is something to live with. You can forgive everything."

The difference is that in the Capote world, love does make for communion and even community in a way that Mrs. McCullers can rarely permit. His is the gentler view, hers the more disabused.

Second point of difference

And if both like to write about children and grotesques, freaks and cripples and perverts, Mrs. McCullers seems to view them as representative of the human race whereas for Capote they are exemplars of a private world within the world at large, and of a private view.

Third point of difference

And finally, if both are novelists of sensibility, Mrs. McCullers' sensibility, as we have observed, expresses itself most fully in the objective forms of parable and fable, while Capote's sensibility moves in two different directions—into the most subjective drama of all, the psychic drama far below the level of reason, on the one hand, and, on the other, into objective social drama, often fanciful, and always indifferent to "social problems" in the usual sense.

Conclusion

Close readers could probably find many minor similarities of detail (the crossed eyes of Miss Amelia Evans [in McCullers' *Ballad of a Sad Cafe*], for example, "exchanging with each other one long and secret gaze of grief," and the crossed eyes of Verena in *The Grass Harp,* peering "inward upon a stony vista"), but these make for no important similarity. In the end they are two quite different writers.[4]

In the same way, the writer may make the point that apparent opposites are reconciled on a deeper level by common, shared qualities. Such is the case, says Civil War historian Bruce Catton, with Generals Ulysses S. Grant and Robert E. Lee—"oddly different" men on the surface, representing "two conflicting currents," but "under everything else" the same type of man.

GRANT AND LEE: A STUDY IN CONTRASTS

BRUCE CATTON

When Ulysses S. Grant and Robert E. Lee met in the parlor of a modest house at Appomattox Court House, Virginia, on April 9, 1865, to work out the terms for the surrender of Lee's Army of Northern Virginia, a great chapter in American life came to a close, and a great new chapter began.

These men were bringing the Civil War to its virtual finish. To be sure, other armies had yet to surrender, and for a few days the fugitive Confederate government would struggle desperately and vainly, trying to find some way to go on living now that its chief support was gone. But in effect it was all over when Grant and Lee signed the papers. And the little room where they wrote out the terms was the scene of one of the poignant, dramatic contrasts in American history.

They were two strong men, these oddly different generals, and they represented the strengths of two conflicting currents that, through them, had come into final collision.

[4] Reprinted by permission of Farrer, Straus & Giroux, Inc. from *The World We Imagine* by Mark Schorer. Copyright © 1963, 1968 by Mark Schorer.

Back of Robert E. Lee was the notion that the old aristocratic concept might somehow survive and be dominant in American life.

Lee was tidewater Virginia, and in his background were family, culture, and tradition . . . the age of chivalry transplanted to a New World which was making its own legends and its own myths. He embodied a way of life that had come down through the age of knighthood and the English country squire. America was a land that was beginning all over again, dedicated to nothing much more complicated than the rather hazy belief that all men had equal rights and should have an equal chance in the world. In such a land Lee stood for the feeling that it was somehow of advantage to human society to have a pronounced inequality in the social structure. There should be a leisure class, backed by ownership of land; in turn, society itself should be keyed to the land as the chief source of wealth and influence. It would bring forth (according to this ideal) a class of men with a strong sense of obligation to the community; men who lived not to gain advantage for themselves, but to meet the solemn obligations which had been laid on them by the very fact that they were privileged. From them the country would get its leadership; to them it could look for the higher values—of thought, of conduct, of personal deportment—to give it strength and virtue.

Lee embodied the noblest elements of this aristocratic ideal. Through him, the landed nobility justified itself. For four years, the Southern states had fought a desperate war to uphold the ideals for which Lee stood. In the end, it almost seemed as if the Confederacy fought for Lee; as if he himself was the Confederacy . . . the best thing that the way of life for which the Confederacy stood could ever have to offer. He had passed into legend before Appomattox. Thousands of tired, underfed, poorly clothed Confederate soldiers, long past the simple enthusiasm of the early days of the struggle, somehow considered Lee the symbol of everything for which they had been willing to die. But they could not quite put this feeling into words. If the Lost Cause, sanctified by so much heroism and so many deaths, had a living justification, its justification was General Lee.

Grant, the son of a tanner on the Western frontier, was everything Lee was not. He had come up the hard way and embodied nothing in particular except the eternal toughness and sinewy fiber of the men who grew up beyond the mountains. He was one of a body of men who owed reverence and obeisance to no one, who were self-reliant to a fault, who cared hardly anything for the past but who had a sharp eye for the future.

These frontier men were the precise opposites of the tidewater aristocrats. Back of them, in the great surge that had taken people over the Alleghenies and into the opening Western country, there was a deep, implicit dissatisfaction with a past that had settled into grooves. They stood for democracy, not from any reasoned conclusion about the proper ordering of human society, but simply because they had grown up in the middle of democracy and knew how it worked. Their society might have privileges, but they would be privileges each man had won for himself. Forms and patterns meant nothing. No man was born to anything, except perhaps to a chance to show how far he could rise. Life was competition.

Yet along with this feeling had come a deep sense of belonging to a national community. The Westerner who developed a farm, opened a shop, or set up in business as a trader, could hope to prosper only as his own community prospered—and his community ran from the Atlantic to the Pacific and from Canada down to Mexico. If the land was settled, with towns and highways and accessible markets, he could better himself. He saw his fate in terms of the nation's own destiny. As its horizons expanded, so did his. He had, in other words, an acute dollars-and-cents stake in the continued growth and development of his country.

And that, perhaps, is where the contrast between Grant and Lee becomes most striking. The Virginia aristocrat, inevitably, saw himself in relation to his own region. He lived in a static society which could endure almost anything except change. Instinctively, his first loyalty would go to the locality in which that society existed. He would fight to the limit of endurance to defend it, because in defending it he was defending everything that gave his own life its deepest meaning.

The Westerner, on the other hand, would fight with an equal tenacity for the broader concept of society. He fought so because everything he lived by was tied to growth, expansion, and a constantly widening horizon. What he lived by would survive or fall with the nation itself. He could not possibly stand by unmoved in the face of an attempt to destroy the Union. He would combat it with everything he had, because he could only see it as an effort to cut the ground out from under his feet.

So Grant and Lee were in complete contrast, representing two diametrically opposed elements in American life. Grant was the modern man emerging; beyond him, ready to come on the stage, was the great age of steel and machinery, of crowded cities and a restless, burgeoning vitality. Lee might have ridden down from the old age of chivalry, lance in hand, silken banner fluttering over his head. Each man was the perfect champion of his cause, drawing both his strengths and his weaknesses from the people he led.

Yet it was not all contrast, after all. Different as they were—in background, in personality, in underlying aspiration—these two great soldiers had much in common. Under everything else, they were marvelous fighters. Furthermore, their fighting qualities were really very much alike.

Each man had, to begin with, the great virtue of utter tenacity and fidelity. Grant fought his way down the Mississippi Valley in spite of acute personal discouragement and profound military handicaps. Lee hung on in the trenches at Petersburg after hope itself had died. In each man there was an indomitable quality . . . the born fighter's refusal to give up as long as he can still remain on his feet and lift his two fists.

Daring and resourcefulness they had, too; the ability to think faster and move faster than the enemy. These were the qualities which gave Lee the dazzling campaigns of Second Manassas and Chancellorsville and won Vicksburg for Grant.

Lastly, and perhaps greatest of all, there was the ability, at the end, to turn quickly from war to peace once the fighting was over. Out of the way these two men behaved at Appomattox came the possibility of a peace of reconciliation. It was a possibility not wholly realized, in the years to come, but which did, in the end, help the two sections to become one nation again . . . after a war whose bitterness might have seemed to make such a reunion wholly impossible. No part of either man's life became him more than the part he played in their brief meeting in the McLean house at Appomattox. Their behavior there put all succeeding generations of Americans in their debt. Two great Americans, Grant and Lee—very different, yet under everything very much alike. Their encounter at Appomattox was one of the great moments of American history.[5]

Organization of Comparison

It is worth pausing here to review the basic organizational possibilities of the essay in comparison, for there are several recurrent forms into which comparative analysis may conveniently be cast. There are also many variations within each form, for the forms are flexible, giving the writer ample freedom to shape his essay as he wishes. But the important thing is that the essay should always *have a shape*—a definite plan or pattern of development so that it does not shift back and forth: from X to Y; back to *part* of X; then more about Y; back to *another* part of X, and so on. Whatever shifting takes place must follow an orderly procedure.

The Grant-Lee piece, for example, represents a "comparison of wholes" wherein one total subject is compared with another total subject, so that the two may be regarded side-by-side, as follows:

I. Lee
  A. personal background
  B. leadership of the Confederate army

II. Grant
  A. personal background
  B. leadership of the Union army

If the writer's main intention is not to compare two total subjects one against the other (Grant and Lee), but rather to demonstrate how parts of one "play off" against parts of the other (Grant's strengths of character as opposed to Lee's), then he will structure his piece according to the specific points of concern.

Thus in the final third of the Grant-Lee piece the writer considers—point by point—the fighting qualities of the two men, noting that they are remarkably similar in regard to:

1. tenacity
2. fidelity to cause
3. daring
4. resourcefulness
5. ability to convert from war to peace

This type of structure is called "comparison of parts," and it generally involves many parts, one following another in rapid succession with intricate (though always orderly) weaving back and forth between X and Y, sometimes within a single sentence, as in the following essay about two well-known explorers:

[5] From *The American Story* edited by Earl S. Miers. Copyright 1956 by Broadcast Music, Inc. Reprinted by permission of Broadcast Music, Inc.

STANLEY AND LIVINGSTONE

EMIL LUDWIG

If we compare Stanley with Livingstone, it is hard to say which of them gains by the comparison.

Both were self-made men, the one beginning as a cotton spinner, the other as a shepherd, sailor, and clerk. The one was a missionary, the other a journalist. But when they got down to work, Stanley remained what he was whereas Livingstone forgot the missionaries for his mission.

Both explored great rivers. Livingstone was a monomaniac in the grip of a misanthropic passion for the Nile, and he even had a peculiar love for its name. Stanley on the other hand was always actuated by some specific purpose.

Livingstone groped with a mystical urge towards enigmatic headwaters; Stanley broke himself a new path to an unpeopled estuary. Stanley was trying to fulfill a task; Livingstone was in search of Africa's marvels. The two men are alike in that they followed the two largest streams of a continent, the one going upstream to the source, the other going downstream to the mouth. Livingstone, loving Africa, wanted to explore. Stanley, loving his work, wanted to have explored.

Livingstone went for years without uttering a word. He wanted to remain alone with his savages, whom he loved as fellow beings. His wife traveled with him for twelve years, until she died in the wilderness—and thereafter he remained alone. When he heard that white men were near, he would retire deeper into the interior. It is amusing to observe the elaborate precautions which Stanley took to keep his expedition in search of Livingstone a secret, lest his quarry should learn of it in time to escape. Stanley drew a breath of relief each time he left Africa. Livingstone firmly refused to accompany Stanley to England or to the coast.

Stanley always sent word—and as promptly as possible. He was continually writing, whereas Livingstone hardly ever wrote. He was taciturn, and grew old and gray in the wilderness while maintaining silence. Stanley also possessed the great virtue of silence, but only when some important undertaking had to be kept in the dark. Livingstone's silence was philosophical, Stanley's was shrewd.

Stanley advanced by force of arms, a whole train of people surrounding him. He nearly always looked upon the black man as an enemy. But Livingstone, when a negro became angry, acted like a wise old gentleman who merely frowned to show that he was offended.

Stanley gives a famous account of their meeting, when he finally came upon Livingstone after an eight months' march: "As I advanced towards him I noticed he was pale, looked wearied. . . . I would have run to him, only I was a coward in the presence of such a mob—would have embraced him, only, he being an Englishman, I did not know how he would receive me." Stanley took off his cap and said:

"Dr. Livingstone, I presume?"

"Yes."

"I thank God, Doctor, I have been permitted to see you."

"I feel thankful that I am here to welcome you."

Livingstone records the incident in his journal: "It was Henry Moreland Stanley, the traveling correspondent of the New York 'Herald,' sent by James Gordon Bennett, junior, at an expense of more than £4000, to obtain accurate information about Dr. Livingstone if living, and if dead, to bring home my bones."

The seeker: young, ambitious, optimistic, thoroughly pleased with his job. The sought: an old explorer, skeptical, mature, misanthropic, kind-hearted, eternally restless. The messenger of God, and the messenger of America.

Soon after this Livingstone died, alone in the primitive forests, at the heart of Africa. Black men brought his body to the coast, but England buried him in Westminster Abbey. Stanley died near London fifteen years after leaving Africa for the last time. He died well off, with wife and child at his bedside. But England refused to bury him.

Which of them should be ranked the higher?

From the standpoint of drama, it could only be Livingstone. Yet if I had the palm to award, I should lay it upon that rough stone on which is inscribed. . . .

HENRY MORTON STANLEY
BULA–MATARI
1841–1904
AFRICA [6]

In the following essay we find a variation of these two basic organizational patterns. There is first a comparison for similarities, then for differences.

In most cases the writer will present the position he wants to stress in the second, more emphatic, half of the essay, following a principle that applies at all levels of English discourse whether it be sentence, paragraph, or whole essay—that which comes last is fixed more forcibly in the reader's mind. Observing this psychological truth, Northrop Frye moves from the obvious similarities between myth and folk tale to the not-so-obvious differences.

MYTH AND FOLK TALE

NORTHROP FRYE

Similarities noted

By a myth . . . I mean primarily a certain type of story . . . in which some of the chief characters are gods or other beings larger in power than humanity. Very seldom is it located in history: its action takes place in a world above or prior to ordinary time. . . . Hence, like the folk tale, it is an *abstract story-pattern.* The characters can do what they like, which means what the story-teller likes: there is no need to be plausible or logical in motivation. The things that happen in myth are things that happen only in stories; they are in a self-contained literary world. Hence myth would naturally have the same kind of appeal for the fiction writer that folk tales have. It presents him with a ready-made framework, hoary with antiquity, and allows him to devote all his energies to elaborating its design. Thus the use of myth in Joyce or Cocteau, like the use of folk tale in Mann, is parallel to the use

[6] From *Genius and Character* by Emil Ludwig, copyright, 1927, by Harcourt Brace Jovanovich, Inc.; renewed 1955, by Kenneth Burke. Reprinted by permission of the publisher.

of abstraction and other means of emphasizing design in contemporary painting; and a modern writer's interest in primitive fertility rites is parallel to a modern sculptor's interest in primitive woodcarving.

Differences noted

The differences between myth and folk tale, however, also have their importance. Myths, as compared with folk tales, are usually in a special category of seriousness: they are believed to have "really happened," or to have some exceptional significance in explaining certain features of life, such as ritual. Again, whereas folk tales simply interchange motifs and develop variants, myths show an odd tendency to stick together and build up bigger structures. We have creation myths, fall and flood myths, metamorphosis and dying-god myths, divine-marriage and hero-ancestry myths, etiological myths, apocalyptic myths; and writers of sacred scriptures or collectors of myth like Ovid tend to arrange these in a series. And while myths themselves are seldom historical, they seem to provide a kind of containing form of tradition, one result of which is the obliterating of boundaries separating legend, historical reminiscence, and actual history that we find in Homer and the Old Testament.

As a type of story, myth is a form of verbal art, and belongs to the world of art. Like art, and unlike science, it deals, not with the world that man contemplates, but with the world that man creates. The total form of art, so to speak, is a world whose content is nature but whose form is human; hence when it "imitates" nature it assimilates nature to human forms. The world of art is human in perspective, a world in which the sun continues to rise and set long after science has explained that its rising and setting are illusions. And myth, too, makes a systematic attempt to see nature in human shape: it does not simply roam at large in nature like the folk tale.[7]

Note that in contrasting the two types of stories, myth and folk tale, Frye accentuates the qualities of each. This is one of the important rhetorical advantages of the comparative approach: each side of the comparison is more clearly delineated as a result of the other, each *highlights* the other by bringing out distinctive points of similarity or difference.

Because the mind naturally works in terms of comparison, because comparative situations are common in everyday life (before and after, then and now, loss and gain, promise and fulfillment), and because there is no clearer indication of how well a person has grasped his subject than his ability to detect similarities and differences among its parts (thus the popularity of "How does X compare to Y?" as an essay-type examination question), the student writer should make an extra effort to master this form of discourse. It is not a difficult form if it is approached systematically, and it produces predictably interesting and engaging essays.

[7] From "Myth, Fiction, and Displacement," by Northrop Frye. Reprinted by permission from *Daedalus*, Journal of the American Academy of Arts and Sciences, Boston, Massachusetts, Volume 90, Number 1.

ASSIGNMENTS

I. Read the essay reprinted below and answer the following questions:

A. What two things are being compared in this essay?

B. What is the structural plan of the essay?

C. Is the comparison apt? How do X and Y illuminate each other?

D. Comment on the tone of the essay.

DETACHING FROM REALITY

RUSSELL BAKER

Assignment: Compose a short theme on the topic, "What I Did on My Summer Vacation."

Execution: When I began my summer vacation I had an extensive list of vital and fascinating things to do, not to mention a number of fashionable things—such as getting a sun tan—which seemed obligatory. I spent my sume vacation not doing any of these things.

I began almost immediately (the second day away) by not reading "Steppenwolf" by Hermann Hesse, a work so popular with today's youth this year that no one can speak with authority about the young until he has read it.

Not reading "Steppenwolf" was remarkably easy. I began, of course, by actually reading page one while lying in the grass in the shade of a privet hedge. By page two my attention had shifted to a magnificent cumulous cloud drifting overhead and on page three, as I drifted off to sleep, I perceived with remarkable clarity that the certain way to ruin a vacation would be to spend my time preparing to speak with authority on today's youth.

Having not read "Steppenwolf" with such ease on the second day, I awoke on the third day feeling unusually refreshed. If not reading "Steppenwolf" left me feeling that good, I reflected, there was no telling what benefits might flow from not reading "Remembrance of Things Past," by Marcel Proust, and "Pendennis" by Thackeray.

I immediately took both books to the shade of my privet hedge and didn't read them. The brief nap that resulted left me feeling like a new man. That evening I didn't make that extra effort to catch up on the ABM debate which had previously seemed so essential to a successful vacation, and the next morning I began an intensive program of not reading anything whatsoever about President Nixon.

Not learning to sail was much harder and required almost a week. Each morning for six days I awoke feeling that I must learn to sail, not only so that I could talk knowledgeably about splicing the main brace, but also because of a sense that one should learn something new on a vacation.

On the seventh day, while eating a banana royal in the ice cream parlor, I dealt directly with the problem. A companion asked me if I wanted to join him in learning how to splice the main brace. I said it sounded like a lot of work and that I would almost certainly never be any good at it and that, anyhow, I really had an idiotic urge to sit in the flower bed and pull weeds.

Not learning to sail was intensely satisfying. In fact, not doing things on my summer vacation was creating such serenity of spirit that I began searching for things not to do. I took up smoking so that I could have the satisfaction of spending my summer vacation not trying to quit smoking.

My pre-vacation list naturally included—it was point number three in fact—the resolution to "get a sun tan." After the first few days of miserable broiling and basting on a plastic lounge in the back yard, I began asking sensible questions.

This may have been the result of all the not reading about President Nixon I had been doing. In any case, it suddenly occurred to me that once I had got this sun tan, at great expense in misery and toil, there would be nothing to do with it.

A sun tan cannot be taken home and hung in the closet. It cannot be put in the safe deposit box, nor sold, nor willed to one's children in the estate. There is only one thing anybody can do with a sun tan and that is, lose it. It became obvious that one of the most senseless ways imaginable to spend a vacation was in getting a sun tan, so I spent the rest of my summer vacation not getting one.

For much the same reason I spent a lot of my summer vacation not getting into shape. After a man has labored and suffered and made his summer vacation an agony in order to get into shape, he goes home. And what does he do? He gets out of shape.

My summer vacation eventually reached such a pleasant stage because of all the things I was not doing that I decided this was the way life should be lived. I announced that I would make it a perfect summer by not doing the last thing on my list; to wit, "Return to work."

That very evening psychiatrists, statesmen, generals, capitalists and President Nixon notified me confidentially that I might be carrying an infection more deadly to mankind than anything that could conceivably be brought back from the moon. Now I read about the ABM and President Nixon every day and am halfway through "Steppenwolf." Soon I will be able to speak with authority about the young. Won't that be something? [8]

II. In "Grant and Lee: A Study in Contrasts" the two generals are shown to be different *and* alike. Cite the specific points of difference and likeness, indicating whether they are organized methodically and logically. Do the same with "Stanley and Livingstone," indicating whether they are organized methodically and logically.

III. Write an essay (500–750 words) in which you compare two men or two women, using as your ground plan either of the patterns described above: comparison of wholes or comparison of parts.

IV. Write a one-paragraph essay (150–250 words) showing that X is *not* like Y, on the basis of specific points. Choose one pair of topics from one of the following categories:

A. Warfare

conventional/guerrilla
Korea/Vietnam
atomic weapons/conventional weapons

[8] "Observer: Detaching from Reality" by Russell Baker. © 1965–69 by The New York Times Company. Reprinted by permission.

atomic warfare/germ warfare
offensive/defensive

B. Astronomy

astronomy/astrology
Ptolemaic theory/Copernican theory
dawn/dusk
sun/moon
Earth/Mars
planet/star

C. Eating

appetite/hunger
home cooking/college cafeteria
eating to live/living to eat
eating in the tropics/eating in the Arctic
eating/dining
an ordinary diner/a gourmet

D. Fact and Fiction

detectives/detectives in movies and television
American Indians/Indians in movies and television
family life/family life on a television series
Marine Corps/movie marines
courtroom/courtroom on television

(Note: The specific points of difference need not be factual details in every case; a "point" may be an example, an analogy, an attitude, as in the comparison of Kennedy and Johnson. The "points" may also be *one* main point discussed in terms of its ramifications.)

V. Choose either one following pair of poems or the pair of pictures and write an essay (300–500 words) showing that X is both *like* Y (on the basis of specific points) and *unlike* Y (again on the basis of specific points). For greater emphasis, be sure to place your more important observations at the end of the essay.

A. 1.

DEATH BE NOT PROUD

JOHN DONNE

Death, be not proud, though some have called thee
Mighty and dreadful, for thou art not so;
For those whom thou think'st thou dost overthrow
Die not, poor Death, nor yet canst thou kill me.
From rest and sleep, which but thy pictures be,
Much pleasure; then from thee much more must flow,
And soonest our best men with thee do go,
Rest of their bones, and soul's delivery.
Thou art slave to fate, chance, kings, and desperate men,
And dost with poison, war, and sickness dwell,
And poppy or charms can make us sleep as well
And better than thy stroke; why swell'st thou then?
One short sleep past, we wake eternally
And death shall be no more; Death, thou shalt die.

2. DO NOT GO GENTLE INTO THAT GOOD NIGHT

DYLAN THOMAS

Do not go gentle into that good night,
Old age should burn and rave at close of day;
Rage, rage against the dying of the light.

Though wise men at their end know dark is right,
Because their words had forked no lightning they
Do not go gentle into that good night.

Good men, the last wave by, crying how bright
Their frail deeds might have danced in a green bay,
Rage, rage against the dying of the light.

Wild men who caught and sang the sun in flight,
And learn, too late, they grieved it on its way,
Do not go gentle into that good night.

Grave men, near death, who see with blinding sight
Blind eyes could blaze like meteors and be gay,
Rage, rage against the dying of the light.

> **And you, my father, there on the sa**
> **Curse, bless, me now with your fie**
> **Do not go gentle into that good**
> **Rage, rage against the dying o**

VI. The paired terms listed below are close to be distinguished from one another tively). Write an essay (250–350 wor difference or differences between the ter.

talent/genius
aptitude/talent
conscience/guilt
knowledge/wisdom
intelligence/knowledge
cooperate/collaborate
induction/deduction
libel/slander
liberty/license
class/caste
dissent/rebellion
wit/humor

VII. Drawing on your own experience, write an essay (500–750 words) on one of the following topics:

A. Two things mistakenly believed to be alike

B. What you expected or planned (the dream) versus what happened (the reality) as in Russell Baker, "Detaching from Reality" (pp. 155–56)

C. A similarity (or difference) between two authors or two literary works (or two *anything*) that has not, to your knowledge, been observed before

[9] Dylan Thomas, *Collected Poems.* Copyright 1952 by Dylan Thomas. Reprinted by permission of New Directions Publishing Corporation, J. M. Dent & Sons Ltd., and the Trustees for the Copyrights of the late Dylan Thomas.

11 WHAT IS THE PRESENT STATUS OF X?

In every professional field or discipline, as well as in every area of ordinary life, we are periodically required to bring things up-to-date, to ask "What is the present status of X?" or, in words we are more likely to use, "What is new about X?" or "What is happening with X?" or "How do people feel about X at the present moment?" How do *I* feel at the present time? The question clearly leads us to a special kind of comparison (Chapter 10, "How Does X Compare to Y?"), in which the two items being compared are time oriented—*then* versus *now*.

For example, in the 1920s, when science was making a sharp spurt forward, philosopher Bertrand Russell wrote an essay deploring the loss of the old comfortable "simplicities" such as the belief in man's immortal soul. "What is the current status of this belief?" asked Russell, beginning with a conventional comparison between the good old days "when I was young" and the existence of a "soul was thought to be indubitable," and "nowadays" when all such consolations are called into question.

ON THE STATUS OF THE SOUL

BERTRAND RUSSELL

One of the most painful circumstances of recent advances in science is that each one of them makes us know less than we thought we did. When I was young we all knew, or thought we knew, that a man consists of a soul and a body; that the body is in time and space, but the soul is in time only. Whether the soul survives death was a matter as to which opinions might differ, but that there is a soul was thought to be indubitable. As for the body, the plain man of course considered its existence self-evident, and so did the man of science, but the philosopher was apt to analyse it away after one fashion or another, reducing it usually to ideas in the mind of the man who had the body and anybody else who happened to notice him. The philosopher, however, was not taken seriously, and science remained comfortably materialistic, even in the hands of quite orthodox scientists.

Nowadays these fine old simplicities are lost: physicists assure us that there is no such thing as matter, and psychologists assure us that there is no such thing as mind. This is an unprecedented occurrence. Who ever heard of a cobbler saying that there was no such thing as boots, or a tailor maintaining that all men are really naked? Yet that would have been no odder than what physicists and certain psychologists have been doing. To begin with the latter, some of them attempt to reduce everything that seems to be mental activity to an activity of the body. There are, however, various difficulties in the way of reducing mental activity to physical activity. I do not think we can yet say with any assurance whether these difficulties are or are not superable. What we can say, on the basis of physics itself, is that what we have hitherto called our body is really an elaborate scientific construction not corresponding to any physical reality. The modern would-be materialist thus finds himself in a curious position, for, while he may with a certain degree of success reduce the activities of the mind to those of the body, he cannot explain away the fact that the body itself is merely a convenient concept invented by the mind. We find ourselves thus going round and round in a circle: mind is an emanation of body, and body is an invention of mind. Evidently this cannot be quite right, and we have to look for something that is neither mind nor body, out of which both can spring.

Let us begin with the body. The plain man thinks that material objects must certainly exist, since they are evident to the senses. Whatever else may be doubted, it is certain that anything you can bump into must be real; this is the plain man's metaphysic. This is all very well, but the physicist comes along and shows that you never bump into anything: even when you run your head against a stone wall, you do not really touch it. When you think you touch a thing, there are certain electrons and protons, forming part of your body, which are attracted and repelled by certain electrons and protons in the thing you think you are touching, but there is no actual contact. The electrons and protons in your body, becoming agitated by nearness to the other electrons and protons, are disturbed, and transmit a disturbance along your nerves to the brain; the effect in the brain is what is necessary to your sensation of contact, and by suitable experiments this sensation can be made quite deceptive. The electrons and protons themselves, however, are only a crude first approximation, a way of collecting into a bundle either trains of waves or the statistical probabilities of various different kinds of events. Thus matter has become altogether too ghostly to be used as an adequate stick with which to beat the mind. Matter in motion, which used to seem so unquestionable, turns out to be a concept quite inadequate for the needs of physics.

Nevertheless modern science gives no indication whatever of the existence of the soul or mind as an entity; indeed the reasons for disbelieving in it are of very much the same kind as the reasons for disbelieving in matter. Mind and matter were something like the lion and the unicorn fighting for the crown; the end of the battle is not the victory of one or the other, but the discovery that both are only heraldic inventions. The world consists of events, not of things that endure for a long time and have changing properties. Events can be collected into groups by their causal relations. If the causal relations are of one sort, the resulting group of events may be called a physical object, and if the causal relations are of another sort, the resulting group may be called a mind. Any event that occurs inside a man's head will belong to groups of both kinds; considered as belonging to a group of one kind, it is a constituent of his brain, and considered as belonging to a group of the other kind, it is a constituent of his mind.

Thus both mind and matter are merely convenient ways of organizing events. There can be no reason for supposing that either a piece of mind or a piece of matter is immortal. . . .[1]

We may properly ask the question, "What is its present status?" of almost any thing, idea, habit, custom, condition, or belief. Is it "in" or "out"? Timely or obsolete? How is it different from or similar to what it was—and why? As Heraclitus pointed out more than two thousand years ago, the world is in a constant state of flux; nothing stands still; one never steps into the same stream twice. Thus there is always a "story" in an assessment of the "present status" of something. For example, another major belief of mankind is "My country right or wrong." The following essay reassesses this "comfortable simplicity" and decides that its present status is highly questionable. Note that the writer assumes that the reader is familiar with one term of the comparison—the *then*—and therefore concentrates most of his attention on the second term—the *now:*

A CHANGING PATRIOTISM

LOUDON WAINWRIGHT

My Fourths of July all run together, a parade of twilights where I sit expectantly on grassy hillsides waiting for enough darkness for the first big rocket; where little children, the hot, white glow of sparklers against their half-thrilled, half-frightened faces, spin their magic sticks into hoops of fire and toss them, dying, as high as they can. Late arrivals pick their way through the tangle of seated forms, bending over now and then as they look for the faces of friends in the fading light. Then there is the great whoosh, and the crowd is frozen in the brilliance of the first cascade of stars and roars its delight at a bang that makes the hillside tremble.

This has always been for me among the most pleasant of our patriotic tribal rituals. For those evenings I and all the others with me on the grass become willing figures in one of those freckled old cover illustrations by Norman Rockwell, good, clean Americans all, open-mouthed at the booming of the rockets, exhilarated by the thunder of the explosions, warmed by the shower of red, white and blue sparks that drip to the ground in the finale's huge firework flag. Stirred by the incendiary symbolism of an old liberation, we march ragtag home to inaudible fifes and drums.

Over this past weekend of the Fourth of July, I attended an old-fashioned hillside display witnessed by thousands. There, before things got booming in

[1] From *In Praise of Idleness* by Bertrand Russell. Reprinted by permission of George Allen & Unwin Ltd.

the clear sky, a speaker reminded the crowd, as surely hundreds of speakers did all over the country, that a lot of citizens were at that moment dangerously engaged in the service of the country whose independence we were so happily marking and that we should think of them. This reference to Americans in Vietnam struck me as entirely called for; in fact, I think an omission of something like it would have been quite wrong. Yet the man's words and the fireworks that followed set me to wondering about the meanings of patriotism in these times. What is it now? Has it changed? And what responses should calls for it bring from anyone who thinks of himself as loyal?

Obviously—at least in regard to our national involvement in Vietnam—patriotism has changed. The time was when it was enough for a patriot to say, "My country, right or wrong." Now, whatever solidarity of thinking anyone might wish for, the hard fact is that we watchers of fireworks are sharply divided and that one man's patriotism can seem foolish, reprehensible or even traitorous to his neighbor. The simplistic call for stiffened backbones just doesn't produce them. Instead, it heightens a dissent that, in its turn, reinfuriates the militant.

A lot of the current problem over patriotism, it seems to me, is caused by people who appear to take great pleasure in cloaking themselves in the flag, a use for which it was not intended. For example, in a burst of legislative hysteria late last month the House of Representatives voted by an overwhelming 385 to 16 to make it a federal crime to publicly mutilate or otherwise desecrate the American flag. In the face of evidence presented by the U.S. Attorney General, who pointed out that there are already laws in every state which may be enforced against the "infinitesimal" number of people who engage in such acts, the members of the House were adamant in their righteous anger and one congressman suggested that flag burners should be taken 500 miles out to sea, be handcuffed, have anchor chains tied around their necks and then dumped overboard. Hopefully the Senate will either ignore or vote down this nonsense; even so, its partial passage seems a ludicrous tolling of the Liberty Bell.

From still higher places the calls come for old-style flag-waving. In his meeting with Chairman Kosygin, President Johnson appeared to have accomplished something truly substantial by way of lessening tensions between the U.S. and the Soviet Union. Though Kosygin returned from the smiles of Glassboro to his familiar stone-faced line, the man-to-man confrontation between him and the President seemed a real achievement and one from which Mr. Johnson gained big stature in his own country. Yet no sooner had Kosygin flown away than the President let loose with a whopping fruit salad of a speech about the glories of America. To a safe, tame and enthusiastic audience of Jaycees in Baltimore, Mr. Johnson advised his listeners to return to their own communities and ". . . say to them that it's not absolutely essential; it's not a prerequisite; it's not required that you tear our country down and our flag down in order to lift them up." Attacking the press's distortion in coverage of protest, he lauded American progress in a catalogue that included everything from the obliteration of measles to the ownership of half the trucks in the world. He pointed out that there were 10,000 first-term enlistments per week, and evoking the virtually religious application of his efforts at "the house called Holly Bush," he told the Jaycees that if they were determined enough and supportive enough of his efforts ". . . you can, in the words of your own creed, help us unlock earth's great treasure, human personality, then the cussers and the doubters will be relegated to the rear. And the doers and the builders will take up the front line."

I have no doubt that it lies within a President's duty to be exhortative of his people in troubled times. Yet in Mr. Johnson's calls for patriotism there is a certain manifest demagoguery. Who says it's absolutely necessary, a prerequisite, that country and flag be torn down in order to be lifted up? The distortion here is the President's, for he knows—perhaps more precisely than anyone else—that the elements of sober and influential dissent in this country are just as loyal and just as unlikely to damn country and desecrate flag as any official of the Jaycees or the American Legion. And as for the cussers and doubters who will be relegated to the rear, what's that all about? The annals of patriotism are packed with names of cussers and doubters and the last place an enlightened leadership would want them is in the rear. In fact, the next time we gather on hillsides to watch the pinwheels and the rockets, it might be appropriate to recall not only the current sacrifices of our patriots but the doubters who first made the day something to remember.[2]

Because people are naturally curious, they want and need to be brought up-to-date on all sorts of subjects, even those that take them into the darkest corners of the human spirit. Not surprisingly, then, in the summer of 1958 —thirteen years after the defeat of Nazi Germany—an American correspondent went to Auschwitz, the most hideous of the Nazi concentration camps (where four million prisoners, mostly Jews, were murdered during the Second World War), to describe its present status. What is it like *now?* This was the question that he answered in the following news story, whose impact rests on the contrast between the ghastly activity of the past and the peaceful stillness of the present.

NO NEWS FROM AUSCHWITZ

A. M. ROSENTHAL

August 31, 1958

The most terrible thing of all, somehow, was that at Brzezinka the sun was bright and warm, the rows of graceful poplars were lovely to look upon and on the grass near the gates children played.

It all seemed frighteningly wrong, as in a nightmare, that at Brzezinka the sun should ever shine or that there should be light and greenness and the sound of young laughter. It would be fitting if at Brzezinka the sun never shone and the grass withered because this is a place of unutterable terror.

And yet, every day, from all over the world, people come to Brzezinka, quite possibly the most grisly tourist center on earth. They come for a variety of reasons—to see if it could really have been true, to remind themselves not to forget, to pay homage to the dead by the simple act of looking upon their place of suffering.

Brzezinka is a couple of miles from the better-known southern Polish town of Oswiecim. Oswiecim has about 12,000 inhabitants, is situated about 171

[2] "A Changing Patriotism," by Loudon Wainwright, *Life* magazine, July 14, 1967, © 1967 Time, Inc.

miles from Warsaw and lies in a damp, marshy area at the eastern end of the pass called the Moravian Gate. Brzezinka and Oswiecim together formed part of that minutely organized factory of torture and death that the Nazis called Konzentrationslager Auschwitz.

By now, fourteen years after the last batch of prisoners was herded naked into the gas chambers by dogs and guards, the story of Auschwitz has been told a great many times. Some of the inmates have written of those events of which sane men cannot conceive. Rudolf Franz Ferdinand Hoess, the superintendent of the camp, before he was executed wrote his detailed memoirs of mass exterminations and the experiments on living bodies. Four million people died here, the Poles say.

And so there is no news to report about Auschwitz. There is merely the compulsion to write something about it, a compulsion that grows out of a restless feeling that to have visited Auschwitz and then turned away without having said or written anything would be a most grievous act of discourtesy to those who died here.

Brzezinka and Oswiecim are very quiet places now; the screams can no longer be heard. The tourist walks silently, quickly at first to get it over with and then, as his mind peoples the barracks and the chambers and the dungeons and flogging posts, he walks draggingly. The guide does not say much either, because there is nothing much for him to say after he has pointed.

For every visitor, there is one particular bit of horror that he knows he will never forget. For some it is seeing the rebuilt gas chamber at Oswiecim and being told that this is the "small one." For others it is the fact that at Brzezinka, in the ruins of the gas chambers and the crematoria the Germans blew up when they retreated, there are daisies growing. There are visitors who gaze blankly at the gas chambers and the furnaces because their minds simply cannot encompass them, but stand shivering before the great mounds of human hair behind the plate glass window or the piles of babies' shoes or the brick cells where men sentenced to death by suffocation were walled up.

One visitor opened his mouth in a silent scream simply at the sight of boxes —great stretches of three-tiered boxes in the women's barracks. They were about six feet wide, about three feet high, and into them from five to ten prisoners were shoved for the night. The guide walks quickly through the barracks. Nothing more to see here.

A brick building where sterilization experiments were carried out on women prisoners. The guide tries the door—it's locked. The visitor is grateful that he does not have to go in, and then flushes with shame.

A long corridor where rows of faces stare from the walls. Thousands of pictures, the photographs of prisoners. They are all dead now, the men and women who stood before the cameras, and they all knew they were to die.

They all stare blank-faced, but one picture, in the middle of a row, seizes the eye and wrenches the mind. A girl, 22 years old, plumply pretty, blonde. She is smiling gently, as at a sweet, treasured thought. What was the thought that passed through her young mind and is now her memorial on the wall of the dead at Auschwitz?

Into the suffocation dungeons the visitor is taken for a moment and feels himself strangling. Another visitor goes in, stumbles out and crosses herself. There is no place to pray at Auschwitz.

The visitors look pleadingly at each other and say to the guide, "Enough."

There is nothing new to report about Auschwitz. It was a sunny day and the trees were green and at the gates the children played.[3]

ASSIGNMENTS

I. A. Evaluate the rhetorical effectiveness of Bertrand Russell's essay "On the Status of the Soul" in terms of the

1. opening sentence
2. second paragraph (unity and development, variety in sentence construction)
3. third paragraph (transitions, unity, development)
4. fourth paragraph (transitions, use of analogy)

B. Russell tells us that we are losing such "fine old simplicities" as the belief in an immortal soul. In an essay (500–750 words) describe the present status, as you view it, of one of the following established "simplicities":

Be it ever so humble there's no place like home.
Honor thy father and mother.
Love conquers all.
You can't keep a good man down.
There's always room at the top.
Cleanliness is next to godliness.
heaven and hell

II. A. Answer the following questions based on the essay "A Changing Patriotism."

1. Which of the following rhetorical-poetic devices are used by Loudon Wainwright, and how do they function to produce a given effect:

metaphor	allusion
alliteration	rhythm
onomatopoeia	connotation of words
variations in sentence structure	use of examples
use of parallelism	word repetition
transitions	

2. Show how Wainwright uses tone and levels of usage as strategies—i.e., as ways of establishing contact with his readers and making them receptive to what he has to say.
3. As an example of organization, outline this essay into its main headings and subheadings. Check your outline against the outline on page 401.

B. Write an essay (500–750 words) comparable to Wainwright's in which you describe a changing code of honor, loyalty, morality, courage.

[3] "No News from Auschwitz" by A. M. Rosenthal.

III. A. Answer the following questions based on the essay "No News from Auschwitz."

1. In A. M. Rosenthal's grimly moving essay what is the basic and ironic contrast that makes everything seem "frighteningly wrong"?
2. Point to other contrasting elements in this piece and show how they function as an organizing principle.
3. Evaluate the function and effectiveness of the opening and closing paragraphs.
4. In what way is the tone of this essay subdued?
5. Discuss "restraint" as the fundamental rhetorical device of this essay. Cite specific examples of understatement, and speculate on what the piece might be like if the writer had not exercised restraint. Explain why the story would have been more or less effective.
6. Discuss the simplicity of diction and the structure of the following sentences. Explain why you do or do not find them powerful.

   And so there is no news to report about Auschwitz.

   The guide does not say much either, because there is nothing much for him to say after he has pointed.

   Nothing more to see here.
7. Explain the grammatical structure of the following sentences and indicate what rhetorical function they serve:

   A brick building where sterilization experiments were carried out on women prisoners.

   A long corridor where rows of faces stare from the walls.

   Thousands of pictures, the photographs of prisoners.
8. Why does the writer single out and ponder the photograph of *one* prisoner—the "plumply pretty" blonde?
9. What is the significance of the visitor who "crosses herself"? What extra dimension of meaning is introduced by this detail?

B. In an essay (500–750 words) describe the present status of a place that has changed drastically—for good or ill—since you first knew or heard about it.

12 HOW SHOULD X BE INTERPRETED?

Beyond definition, description, and analysis—and to a large extent dependent on these basic processes—is the more subtle and complex business of interpretation, explaining what is not immediately apparent: the deeper meaning or significance of a subject, the relation of particulars to a general principle, the truth that lies beneath the surface.

Interpreting an Activity

Take the subject of football, for example. On the face of it football is simply a popular spectator sport, a national pastime, a "he-man" game filled with action and excitement. On a deeper level, however—as the writer of the following essay points out—football is more than a game. It is an acting out of basic and primitive human aggression, of man's "territorial instinct," his compulsive drive to gain and hold on to property. Note how the writer supports his interpretation by explaining explicit facts about the game in terms of an implicit general principle.

FOOTBALL—THE GAME OF AGGRESSION

GEORGE STADE

There are many ways in which professional football is unique among sports, and as many others in which it is the fullest expression of what is at the heart of all sports. There is no other major sport so dependent upon raw force, nor any so dependent on a complex and delicate strategy; none so wide in the range of specialized functions demanded from its players; none so dependent upon the undifferentiated athletic *sine qua non,* a quickwitted body; none so primitive; none so futuristic; none so American.

Football is first of all a form of play, something one engages in instinctively and only for the sake of performing the activity in question. Among forms of play, footba'l is a game, which means that it is built on communal needs, rather than on private evasions, like mountain climbing. Among games it is a sport; it requires athletic ability, unlike croquet. And among sports, it is one whose mode is violence and whose violence is its special glory.

In some sports—basketball, baseball, soccer—violence is occasional (and usually illegal); in others, like hockey, it is incidental; in others still, car racing, for example, it is accidental. Definitive violence football shares alone with boxing and bullfighting, among major sports. But in bullfighting a man is pitted not against another man, but against an animal, and boxing is a competition between individuals, not teams, and that makes a great difference. If shame is the proper and usual penalty for failures in sporting competitions between individuals, guilt is the consequence of failing not only oneself and one's fans, but also one's teammates. Failure in football, moreover, seems more related to a failure of courage, seems more unmanning than in any other sport outside of bullfighting. In other sports one loses a knack, is outsmarted, or is merely inferior in ability, but in football, on top of these, a player fails because he "lacks desire," or "can't take it anymore," or "hears footsteps," as his teammates will put it.

Many sports, especially those in which there is a goal to be defended, seem enactments of the games animals play under the stimulus of what ethologists, students of animal behavior, call *territory*—"the drive to gain, maintain, and defend the exclusive right to a piece of property," as Robert Ardrey puts it. The most striking symptom of this drive is aggressiveness, but among social animals, such as primates, it leads to "amity for the social partner, hostility for the territorial neighbor." The territorial instinct is closely related to whatever makes animals establish pecking orders: the tangible sign of one's status within the orders is the size and value of the territory one is able to command. Individuals fight over status, groups over *lebensraum* and a bit more. These instincts, some ethologists have claimed, are behind patriotism and private property, and also, I would add, codes of honor, as among ancient Greeks, modern Sicilians, primitive hunters, teen-age gangs, soldiers, aristocrats, and athletes, especially football players.

The territorial basis of certain kinds of sports is closest to the surface in football, whose plays are all attempts to gain and defend property through aggression. Does this not make football *par excellence* the game of instinctual satisfactions, especially among Americans, who are notorious as violent patriots and instinctive defenders of private property? (At the same time, in football this drive is more elaborated than in other sports by whatever turns instinct into art; football is more richly patterned, more formal, more complex in the functions of its parts, which makes football *par excellence* the game of esthetic satisfactions.) Even the unusual amity, if that is the word, that exists among football players has been remarked upon, notably by Norman Mailer. And what is it that corresponds in football to the various feathers, furs, fins, gorgeous colors by means of which animals puff themselves into exaggerated gestures of masculine potency? The football player's equipment, of course.

His cleats raise him an inch off the ground. Knee and thigh pads thrust the force lines of his legs forward. His pants are tight against his rump and the back of his thighs, portions of his body which the requirements of the game stuff with muscle. Even the tubby guard looks slim of waist by comparison with his shoulders, extended half a foot on each side by padding. Finally the helmet, which from the esthetic point of view most clearly expresses the genius of the sport. Not only does the helmet make the player inches taller and give his head a size proportionate to the rest of him; it makes him anonymous, inscrutable, more serviceable as a symbol. The football player in uniform strikes the eye in a succession of gestalt shifts: first a hooded phantom out of the paleolithic past of the species; then a premonition of a future of spacemen.

In sum, and I am almost serious about this, football players are to America what tragic actors were to ancient Athens and gladiators to Rome: models of perennially heroic, aggressive, violent humanity, but adapted to the social realities of the times and places that formed them.[1]

Interpreting a Story

Whereas analysis breaks down a subject, interpretation synthesizes or puts together. To formulate a convincing interpretation, then, the writer must see the single, scattered parts of a subject as contributing on a deeper level to a unified whole. Seen in this light, all of literary criticism involves interpretation, a probing into the single elements of a poem or story to see how they are related to each other and to the whole. What is the writer trying to tell us beyond the surface details? What larger statement is he making? How do the single details contribute to that statement? Take a relatively simple short story such as the following, for example, and then judge one critic's interpretation of what the surface details "add up to": what they mean in terms of how the characters relate to one another; who is victim, who victimized. Do you think it would be possible to defend an entirely different (maybe even an opposite) interpretation of this story?

BIRTHDAY PARTY

KATHERINE BRUSH

They were a couple in their late thirties, and they looked unmistakably married. They sat on the banquette opposite us in a little narrow restaurant, having dinner. The man had a round, self-satisfied face, with glasses on it; the women was fadingly pretty, in a big hat. There was nothing conspicuous about them, nothing particularly noticeable, until the end of their meal, when it suddenly became obvious that this was an Occasion—in fact, the husband's birthday, and the wife had planned a little surprise for him.

It arrived, in the form of a small but glossy birthday cake, with one pink candle burning in the center. The headwaiter brought it in and placed it before the husband, and meanwhile the violin-and-piano orchestra played "Happy Birthday to You" and the wife beamed with shy pride over her little

[1] From "Game Theory" by George Stade. Reprinted from *The Columbia Forum*, Fall 1966, Volume IX, Number 4. Copyright 1966 by The Trustees of Columbia University in the City of New York.

surprise, and such few people as there were in the restaurant tried to help out with a pattering of applause. It became clear at once that help was needed, because the husband was not pleased. Instead he was hotly embarrassed, and indignant at his wife for embarrassing him.

You looked at him and you saw this and you thought, "Oh, now, don't be like that!" But he was like that, and as soon as the little cake had been deposited on the table, and the orchestra had finished the birthday piece, and the general attention had shifted from the man and woman, I saw him say something to her under his breath—some punishing thing, quick and curt and unkind. I couldn't bear to look at the woman then, so I stared at my plate and waited for quite a long time. Not long enough, though. She was still crying when I finally glanced over there again. Crying quietly and heartbrokenly and hopelessly, all to herself, under the gay big brim of her best hat.[2]

AN INTERPRETATION OF "BIRTHDAY PARTY"

B. BERNARD COHEN

In "Birthday Party," the private emotions of an inconspicuous couple burst momentarily into public view. From the point of view of the observer we learn the circumstances which ignite the emotional tension. But, more important, the narrator's observations prepare us for the conflicting responses of the husband and wife.

In fact, the narrator's first impressions of the couple are remarkably sound without his realizing their validity. The husband's face is classified as "self-satisfied" with the clear implication of an egotistical and possibly arrogant character behind it. The wife, on the other hand, is extremely feminine and both fragile and meek. She is "fadingly pretty," an indication that she is like a beautiful piece of fragile china somewhat marred by aging. In addition, when the cake is presented and the birthday song is played, the wife is pictured as beaming with "shy pride." These details clearly stress the subdued nature of her character. Obviously the occasion is a sentimental one for her, yet her emotions in responding to her prepared surprise are not excessive.

Her husband's reactions to her "little surprise" are excessive: he is "hotly embarrassed" and indignant at his wife for embarrassing him. In his reaction there is something cruel—something sadistic—for when he feels affronted by her public display of the occasion, he deliberately hurts her with a statement described as "some punishing thing, quick and curt and unkind." Thus the meek, shy fragility of the wife is crushed by the overwhelmingly powerful emotional response of the husband.

Only when she is terribly hurt by his actions and words, do her emotions pour forth in tears. Yet her tears are fully understandable: what she had intended as a sentimental tribute to her husband has turned into a bruising emotional nightmare. The reversal is painfully ironic and is graphically described in the last sentence: ". . . crying quietly and heartbrokenly and hopelessly, all to her herself, under the gay big brim of her best hat." She is not big but beaten; she is not gay; the word "best" may be applicable to her hat, but not to her life.

That "gay big brim" is obviously a cover-up, a symbol perhaps of a hopeless attempt by the wife to conceal the basic incompatibility of two people whose characters and emotional make-up are vastly different. The story as presented through the observer is thus a conflict between her fragile meekness and his hard-heartedness, her sentimentality and his cold fury, her feeble attempt to please him and his sadistic desire to crush her. Behind this incompatibility there must be a long untold series of similar expressions of arrogance by the husband, who apparently knows that there is one person whom his ego can dominate and destroy—his wife. Even during his birthday party he defeats her.[3]

Interpreting Symbols

Sometimes an element in a story seems on the surface to be just another element, but proves on closer examination to have wider significance. In the following essay, for example, author William Saroyan explains the significance in one of his novels of a simple, superficially unimportant detail—an egg. When viewed on a literal level it is simply an object; but when interpreted on a deeper level, it is seen to be *more* than an egg. It is also a symbol, i.e., it has a range of meaning and significance beyond itself.

THE EGG

WILLIAM SAROYAN

I sometimes *actually* answer kids in English classes . . . who want to know the real meaning of something in *The Human Comedy*.

For instance, Ulysses goes running home from the railroad track where he waved to a singing Negro riding a freight train. The man not only waved back to him, which the engineer had not done, but also called out to him. Ulysses runs straight to the chicken coop in the yard of his house, and to the laying nest there, where he finds one egg. He picks up the egg and runs to his mother, who is hanging clothes on the line in the yard, and he looks at her but doesn't say anything. He just hands her the egg. Well, now, the whole class talked about that for some time, and so on behalf of the class Ava Gardner (yes, she has the same name as the movie actress but doesn't want a career in the movies, only wants to be as intelligent as possible and some day be a good wife and mother) sends a letter to the writer, and the letter is forwarded to three old addresses and finally reaches the writer in Paris.

Ava wants to know "What did Ulysses mean by handing his mother that egg?"

Dear Ava Gardner: Thank you very much for your kind letter, which I am sorry to say wandered around for six weeks, so that I am only now able to try to answer it, when it's too late for the writing of the term papers for your English class at Lincoln High School in Fargo, North Dakota.

To begin with, I think you ought to know that a writer may not know what something he has written means, although this doesn't necessarily mean that it doesn't mean anything.

[3] From *Writing About Literature* by B. Bernard Cohen. Copyright © 1963 by Scott, Foresman and Company.

The obvious meaning of course is that a boy of three or four, speechless with gladness because a total stranger, traveling away, saw him, answered his wave, and called out to him in the voice of a friend, again has found an egg in the nest where miraculously eggs keep appearing. Now, an egg is white, it is whole, and the shape of it is quite startling in its simplicity and flawlessness. An egg is good to see. To some people it is as good to see, again and again, as a great work of sculpture, for it is in fact the greatest of such works, the first of them, and of course we know an egg is not shaped by a sculptor, it is laid by a hen. Or at any rate the egg the little boy found *was.* At his age he may not have known that. He may not have suspected any connection between the ten or eleven hens and the one rooster and the appearance of eggs in the laying nest. He may not have known at all how the eggs got there. He may only have known that if he went to the nest often enough he would see an egg, and he liked going, and he liked seeing an egg. The same thing, almost, every time, but each egg is a new egg, each egg is itself. He may even have believed that his going *made* each egg, that an egg was out there as a reward to him for being alive, for being interested in everything, for not understanding very much, and for many other reasons which only little children know.

Now, of course, little children don't know very many words, they're not very good at language, they don't know how to say what they feel and believe and know, or think they know, as the rest of us do. Having greeted the traveler, who was going home, far away, and having become filled with a mixture of gladness and solemnity, and a little loneliness, by the sight and sound and gesture of the traveler, and by his warmth and understanding and swift friendship, Ulysses may have felt that now, for sure, he would be rewarded with an egg, a new egg, the egg of the mixture, of having been seen by a total stranger, a big man with a big voice and a dark skin, of having been astonished by the man's swift acceptance of him, a small boy standing among weeds watching another train go by, of feeling suddenly a part of the traveler, a part of all travelers, of all strangers, of the whole human race. He may have felt that he would find the egg of many meanings, the egg perhaps of all meanings, the gathering together in one small white real thing that you could pick up with your hand and look at, a gathering together into a perfect form of all mute truth, the truth of the eye, which all creatures have, but children most of all.

And the egg *was* there, and Ulysses was there, and the traveler was gone. Ulysses may have felt a touch of loneliness, not for members of his family alone when he was away from them, or for people he had met and known enough to like and had thought about ever since, but for any people, all people, going, gone, and perhaps never to be seen again. And his mother was there, and of course every man's mother *is* his mother, a wonderful and astonishing gift, but his father *wasn't* there, his father was gone, perhaps he had gone as the traveler on the freight train had gone, and the boy may have felt a renewal of his longing to see his father because of his separation from the traveler. He didn't understand about death, he didn't know he would never see his father again, and he took the egg to his mother, and looked at her again, at the marvel and miracle of her, and for all I know, Ava, in handing her the egg he meant that he hoped the traveler would get safely home, that his own father would come walking down the street soon and be home again, and that he loved his mother, but he loved his father, he loved his brothers and sisters, and the traveler, and the whole strange business of being himself, named Ulysses, in the world, a part of it now and forever, and a part of all of the people in it.

But he didn't know how to say so much. Perhaps the egg would say it for him.

It is possible that *that* might be something like what Ulysses meant by handing his mother the egg.[4]

Interpreting a Poem

Since poetry is the most compressed and cryptic of all literary forms, it must be carefully interpreted in order to be experienced in its deepest and fullest sense. The e. e. cummings poem reprinted below, for example, may appear on the surface to be mere nonsense, yet as critic R. W. Stallman points out, it is actually "rich in meanings." At the literal level it is a miniature short story; at the thematic level it makes a profound observation about how we live and how we love.

AN INTERPRETATION OF E. E. CUMMINGS' "ANYONE LIVED IN A PRETTY HOW TOWN"

R. W. STALLMAN

ANYONE LIVED IN A PRETTY HOW TOWN

anyone lived in a pretty how town
(with up so floating many bells down)
spring summer autumn winter
he sang his didn't he danced his did.

Women and men(both little and small)
cared for anyone not at all
they sowed their isn't they reaped their same
sun moon stars rain

children guessed(but only a few
and down they forgot as up they grew
autumn winter spring summer)
that noone loved him more by more

when by now and tree by leaf
she laughed his joy she cried his grief
bird by snow and stir by still
anyone's any was all to her

someones married their everyones
laughed their cryings and did their dance
(sleep wake hope and then)they
said their nevers they slept their dream

[4] From *Here Comes There Goes You Know Who* by William Saroyan.

stars rain sun moon
(and only the snow can begin to explain
how children are apt to forget to remember
with up so floating many bells down)

one day anyone died i guess
(and noone stooped to kiss his face)
busy folk buried them side by side
little by little and was by was

all by all and deep by deep
and more by more they dream their sleep
noone and anyone earth by april
wish by spirit and if by yes.

Women and men(both dong and ding)
summer autumn winter spring
reaped their sowing and went their came
sun moon stars rain [5]

This poem, apparently obscure nonsense, is rich in meanings; and though it may appear difficult at first glance, it is actually very simple to understand. Cummings uses language "reflexively," every word being counterpointed against another. At the literal level of the language there is a narrative plot, a miniature short story. What makes the poem seem so strange or seemingly incomprehensible is its uncommon arrangement of common words, its wrenched syntax, and its coining of new words from old ones by reconverting their dictionary meaning and usage.

Cummings's case study is a certain anonymous fellow, a citizen of How * Town. The town disowns him. Why? Well, for one thing their conventions are shocked by his unconventional way of life. He simply does not conform. Of course they don't care for Mr. Anyone because they "cared for anyone not at all" (line 6); they care only selfishly for themselves alone. These people "both little [*i.e.*, children] and small" (5) are small spiritually; which is why "noone loved him more by more" (12). And socially he didn't count because "anyone" married "noone." As for Miss "noone," she "loved him more by more." The non-lovers are the Someones who "married their everyones" (17). They play the social game, which is why they are Someones, but in conforming like "everyones" they have lost out in living, in loving life for its own sake. These Someones and Everyones do the conventional things in the conventional ways, and their life is a deadness and a monotony—"sleep wake hope and

* The dictionary lists eight variant meanings for the word *how*, and all eight reverberate throughout the poem. Cummings uses the word as a noun. In the noun-sense the word means manner or method. But the meanings of *how* as adverb equally apply:—1. In what manner or way; 2. to what number or degree; 3. in what state or condition; 4. for what reason; 5. with what meaning, to what effect; 6. at what price, how dear; and 7. *how* meaning "what," as how about it? How Town is the conventional town of conformity to convention, where what counts is social manner or method, social degree, state or condition. In How Town what counts is how you do it, and the price is dear. In the sense of *how* as "why," the question asked by the person is what meaning has this way of life?

then"—because they live not at all spontaneously. And that is what sets them apart from Mr. Anyone. They "*did* their dance" (18), whereas he "*danced* his did" (4). They "*said* their nevers" (20), said their neverthelesses, talked about what they didn't do and made excuses; whereas he "*sang* his didn't" (4). In short, "anyone *lived*." For him How Town was "pretty how town," beautiful; beautiful "with up so floating many bells down"—life in both its up's and down's, it was all singsong to him. Anyone and Noone lived happily forever in the point-present now—not in How Town so much as in Now Town. She loved him "by now and tree by leaf" (13), all of him by every part of him; "anyone's any [thing] was all to her" (16). She "laughed his joy she cried his grief" (14); whereas the Someones married to their Everyones "laughed [at] their cryings" (18); their marriage is no marriage, merely an empty form. Even in death the lovers "dream their sleep" (30), belong to eternity and are reborn ("earth by april"); whereas the non-lovers even while living seem dead —"they slept their dream" (20). Caring "for anyone not at all/they sowed their isn't they reaped their same" (6–8). Their routine clocked existence repeats itself through the cycles of time—"autumn winter spring summer"—with one season the same as another and later generations repeating the same old stenciled way of life (stanza 9). Time passes, mechanical time clocked by "sun moon stars rain" (lines 8 and 36), with the variant—"stars rain sun moon" (21)—to indicate the passing of time. The life of Someones and Everyones is never punctuated by memorable moments. No comma halts these "busy folk." And their children repeat the same blurred, indiscriminate, humdrum existence; they too "went their came" (35), wasting their coming by their busy going. Thus the bells, symbolizing Time, sound to them only as "dong and ding" (33), which is as dead men hear it, hollow; whereas to Mr. Anyone the bells sang, and he danced his life in lilt with them. Himself childlike in spontaneity, "children guessed" *how to live,* by his example—"but only a few/and down they forgot as up they grew" (9–10). Living is by loving, and loving is by losing oneself in another:

> little by little and was by was
>
> all by all and deep by deep
> and more by more they dream their sleep
> noone and anyone

But like Someones and Everyones, children become time-busy and "forget to remember" how to live, how to love. And that is how it goes in How to Live Town. The day Anyone died (stanza 7) "noone stooped to kiss his face." [6]

ASSIGNMENTS

I. Freud said that all behavior is a gesture—an "acting out" of deep-seated feelings and needs. Thus what we see on the surface is often (if not always) a symptom of "deeper meanings" lying beneath. In an interpretive essay (500–750 words) contemplate one of the "states" or activities listed below in terms of its possible expressive function (as foot-

[6] R. W. Stallman and R. T. Watters: *The Creative Reader,* second edition. Copyright © 1962, The Ronald Press Company, New York. Used by permission.

ball "expresses" aggression). Speculate on what larger human purposes are being "acted out"—and satisfied—in the following:

stealing	baseball	kite flying
suicide	knitting	wrestling
alcoholism	dancing	ventriloquism
stuttering	sailing	Bingo
lying	automobile racing	bullfighting
swearing	skiing	fishing
dreaming	gambling	playing pool
smoking	hunting	mountain climbing
promiscuity	boxing	singing
ice skating	hiking	working out a crossword puzzle
playing a musical instrument		

II. A. Like "Birthday Party," the following short story involves two people, a man and wife. Here again it is possible to interpret the story in more than one way, i.e., to see in it various meanings. Read the story carefully (at least twice), noting as many details of character and plot as possible.

THE GIRLS IN THEIR SUMMER DRESSES

IRWIN SHAW

Fifth Avenue was shining in the sun when they left the Brevoort. The sun was warm, even though it was February, and everything looked like Sunday morning—the buses and the well-dressed people walking slowly in couples and the quiet buildings with the windows closed.

Michael held Frances' arm tightly as they walked toward Washington Square in the sunlight. They walked lightly, almost smiling, because they had slept late and had a good breakfast and it was Sunday. Michael unbuttoned his coat and let it flap around him in the mild wind.

"Look out," Frances said as they crossed Eighth Street. "You'll break your neck." Michael laughed and Frances laughed with him.

"She's not so pretty," Frances said. "Anyway, not pretty enough to take a chance of breaking your neck."

Michael laughed again. "How did you know I was looking at her?"

Frances cocked her head to one side and smiled at her husband under the brim of her hat. "Mike, darling," she said.

"O.K.," he said. "Excuse me."

Frances patted his arm lightly and pulled him along a little faster toward Washington Square. "Let's not see anybody all day," she said. "Let's just hang around with each other. You and me. We're always up to our neck in people, drinking their Scotch or drinking our Scotch; we only see each other in bed. I want to go out with my husband all day long. I want him to talk only to me and listen only to me."

"What's to stop us?" Michael asked.

"The Stevensons. They want us to drop by around one o'clock and they'll drive us into the country."

"The cunning Stevensons," Mike said. "Transparent. They can whistle. They can go driving in the country by themselves."

"Is it a date?"

"It's a date."

Frances leaned over and kissed him on the tip of his ear.

"Darling," Michael said, "this is Fifth Avenue."

"Let me arrange a program," Frances said. "A planned Sunday in New York for a young couple with money to throw away."

"Go easy."

"First let's go to the Metropolitan Museum of Art," Frances suggested, because Michael had said during the week he wanted to go. "I haven't been there in three years and there're at least ten pictures I want to see again. Then we can take the bus down to Radio City and watch them skate. And later we'll go down to Cavanagh's and get a steak as big as a blacksmith's apron, with a bottle of wine, and after that there's a French picture at the Filmarte that everybody says—say, are you listening to me?"

"Sure," he said. He took his eyes off the hatless girl with the dark hair, cut dancer-style like a helmet, who was walking past him.

"That's the program for the day," Frances said flatly. "Or maybe you'd just rather walk up and down Fifth Avenue."

"No," Michael said. "Not at all."

"You always look at other women," Frances said. "Everywhere. Every damned place we go."

"No, darling," Michael said, "I look at everything. God gave me eyes and I look at women and men in subway excavations and moving pictures and the little flowers of the field. I casually inspect the universe."

"You ought to see the look in your eye," Frances said, "as you casually inspect the universe on Fifth Avenue."

"I'm a happily married man." Michael pressed her elbow tenderly. "Example for the whole twentieth century—Mr. and Mrs. Mike Loomis. Hey, let's have a drink," he said stopping.

"We just had breakfast."

"Now listen, darling," Mike said, choosing his words with care, "it's a nice day and we both felt good and there's no reason why we have to break it up. Let's have a nice Sunday."

"All right. I don't know why I started this. Let's drop it. Let's have a good time."

They joined hands consciously and walked without talking among the baby carriages and the old Italian men in their Sunday clothes and the young women with Scotties in Washington Square Park.

"At least once a year everyone should go to the Metropolitan Museum of Art," Frances said after a while, her tone a good imitation of the tone she had used at breakfast and at the beginning of their walk. "And it's nice on Sunday. There're a lot of people looking at the pictures and you get the feeling maybe Art isn't on the decline in New York City, after all—"

"I want to tell you something," Michael said very seriously. "I have not touched another woman. Not once. In all the five years."

"All right," Frances said.

"You believe that, don't you?"

"All right."

They walked between the crowded benches, under the scrubby city-park trees.

"I try not to notice it," Frances said, "but I feel rotten inside, in my stomach, when we pass a woman and you look at her and I see that look in your eye and that's the way you looked at me the first time. In Alice Maxwell's house. Standing there in the living room, next to the radio, with a green hat on and all those people."

"I remember the hat," Michael said.

"The same look," Frances said. "And it makes me feel bad. It makes me feel terrible."

"Sh-h-h, please, darling, sh-h-h."

"I think I would like a drink now," Frances said.

They walked over to a bar on Eighth Street, not saying anything, Michael automatically helping her over curbstones and guiding her past automobiles. They sat near a window in the bar and the sun streamed in and there was a small, cheerful fire in the fireplace. A little Japanese waiter came over and put down some pretzels and smiled happily at them.

"What do you order after breakfast?" Michael asked.

"Brandy, I suppose," Frances said.

"Courvoisier," Michael told the waiter. "Two Courvoisiers."

The waiter came with the glasses and they sat drinking the brandy in the sunlight. Michael finished half his and drank a little water.

"I look at women," he said. "Correct. I don't say it's wrong or right. I look at them. If I pass them on the street and I don't look at them, I'm fooling you, I'm fooling myself."

"You look at them as though you want them," Frances said, playing with her brandy glass. "Every one of them."

"In a way," Michael said, speaking softly and not to his wife, "in a way that's true. I don't do anything about it, but it's true."

"I know it. That's why I feel bad."

"Another brandy," Michael called. "Waiter, two more brandies."

He sighed and closed his eyes and rubbed them gently with his fingertips. "I love the way women look. One of the things I like best about New York is the battalions of women. When I first came to New York from Ohio that was the first thing I noticed, the million wonderful women, all over the city. I walked around with my heart in my throat."

"A kid," Frances said. "That's a kid's feeling."

"Guess again," Michael said. "Guess again. I'm older now. I'm a man getting near middle age, putting on a little fat, and I still love to walk along Fifth Avenue at three oclock on the east side of the street between Fiftieth and the Fifty-seventh Streets. They're all out then, shopping, in their furs and their crazy hats, everything all concentrated from all over the world into seven blocks—the best furs, the best clothes, the handsomest women, out to spend money and feeling good about it."

The Japanese waiter put the two drinks down, smiling with great happiness. "Everything is all right?" he asked.

"Everything is wonderful," Michael said.

"If it's just a couple of fur coats," Frances said, "and forty-five dollar hats—"

"It's not the fur coats. Or the hats. That's just the scenery for that particular kind of women. Understand," he said, "you don't have to listen to this."

"I want to listen."

"I like the girls in the offices. Neat, with their eyeglasses, smart, chipper, knowing what everything is about. I like the girls on Forty-fourth Street at lunchtime, the actresses, all dressed up on nothing a week. I like the salesgirls in the stores, paying attention to you first because you're a man, leaving lady customers waiting. I got all this stuff accumulated in me because I've been thinking about it for ten years and now you've asked for it and here it is."

"Go ahead," Frances said.

"When I think of New York City, I think of all the girls on parade in the city. I don't know whether it's something special with me or whether every man in the city walks around with the same feeling inside him, but I feel as though I'm at a picnic in this city. I like to sit near the women in the theatres, the famous beauties who've taken six hours to get ready and look it. And the young girls at the football games, with the red cheeks, and when the warm weather comes, the girls in their summer dresses." He finished his drink. "That's the story."

Frances finished her drink and swallowed two or three times extra. "You say you love me?"

"I love you."

"I'm pretty, too," Frances said. "As pretty as any of them."

"You're beautiful," Michael said.

"I'm good for you," Frances said, pleading. "I've made a good wife, a good housekeeper, a good friend. I'd do any damn thing for you."

"I know," Michael said. He put his hand out and grasped hers.

"You'd like to be free to—" Frances said.

"Sh-h-h."

"Tell the truth." She took her hand away from under his.

Michael flicked the edge of his glass with his finger. "O.K.," he said gently. "Sometimes I feel I would like to be free."

"Well," Frances said, "any time you say."

"Don't be foolish." Michael swung his chair around to her side of the table and patted her thigh.

She began to cry silently into her handkerchief, bent over just enough so that nobody else in the bar would notice. "Someday," she said, crying, "you're going to make a move."

Michael didn't say anything. He sat watching the bartender slowly peel a lemon.

"Aren't you?" Frances asked harshly. "Come on, tell me. Talk. Aren't you?"

"Maybe," Michael said. He moved his chair back again. "How the hell do I know?"

"You know," Frances persisted. "Don't you know?"

"Yes," Michael said after a while. "I know."

Frances stopped crying then. Two or three snuffles into the handkerchief and she put it away and her face didn't tell anything to anybody. "At least do me one favor," she said.

"Sure."

"Stop talking about how pretty this woman is or that one. Nice eyes, nice breasts, a pretty figure, good voice." She mimicked his voice. "Keep it to yourself. I'm not interested."

Michael waved to the waiter. "I'll keep it to myself," he said.

Frances flicked the corners of her eyes. "Another brandy," she told the waiter.

"Two," Michael said.

"Yes, Ma'am, yes, sir," said the waiter, backing away.

Frances regarded Michael coolly across the table. "Do you want me to call the Stevensons?" she asked. "It'll be nice in the country."

"Sure," Michael said. "Call them."

She got up from the table and walked across the room toward the telephone. Michael watched her walk, thinking what a pretty girl, what nice legs.[7]

B. According to one well-known interpretation of this story, its "deeper meaning," the *point* it is making beyond the events narrated, is the sad recognition

> and the bitter acceptance—of the fact that the couple really mean nothing to each other. Each is, as it were, merely a convenience to the other. This is, of course, especially true of Michael's attitude toward Frances. Despite his actual faithfulness, Frances is just another girl, the one he "happens" to have married.[8]

This interpretation has been challenged as an oversimplification of human nature and a misreading "of meaningful pattern in the details of the short story." Yes, a marriage is faltering in this story; that is clear. According to the second interpretation, however, Michael is not the prime cause of the couple's plight.

> Each is equally "guilty" of the problem which faces them. Michael is, of course, "guilty" of being too insensitive to his wife's feelings, a fact . . . quite different from the assertion that his wife is to him "just another girl." Frances is, on the other hand, "guilty" of assuming marriage to be the portal beyond which all desire, without deviation, is centered upon the one object, any breach of which necessarily suggests sexual promiscuity and failure of love for the proper love partner.[9]

In preparation for writing your own interpretation, consider the opposing views summarized above; also evaluate the importance of the following details quoted from the story (cite other details equally significant):

> Michael held Frances' arm tightly. . . . (Is this a genuinely felt gesture?)
> Michael laughed and Frances laughed with him. (Is there a real community of feeling between them at this point?)
> I want to go out with my husband all day long. I want him to talk only to me and listen only to me. (Do you think this is the only time Frances has said this, or felt this way?)
> Michael said, "I look at everything. . . . I casually inspect the universe." (Is this merely an excuse to distract Frances? Is Mike "casual"?)

[7] Copyright 1939 and renewed 1967 by Irwin Shaw. Reprinted from *Selected Short Stories of Irwin Shaw* by permission of Random House, Inc.

[8] Cleanth Brooks and Robert Penn Warren, *Understanding Fiction* (New York: Appleton-Century-Crofts, Inc., 1959), p. 89.

[9] Joe L. Baird and Ralph Grajeda, "A Shaw Story and Brooks and Warren," *The CEA Critic*, 28:5 (Feb. 1966), 1.

"A kid," Frances said. "That's a kid's feeling."
"I feel as though I'm at a picnic in this city." (What do you think is the significance of the "picnic" image?)

C. Just as words can have "layers of meaning," so can stories. Describe the layers of meaning in this story in terms of the conflict:
1. between two people
2. between husband and wife
3. within the individual person
4. between the individual and the human, universal "condition"

D. Write an essay (750–1,000 words) in which you interpret the meaning, or theme, of this story. Be certain to support your interpretation with specific citations (evidence) from the story itself.

III. It is possible to interpret "Birthday Party" in a different way in which the husband, rather than the wife, is viewed sympathetically. Write an essay (500–750 words) defending this interpretation and citing evidence in the story that supports it.

IV. In an essay (500–750 words) show how an object or image (like Saroyan's "egg") has functioned in a story, play, or poem as a symbol (e.g., the whale in *Moby Dick*, the albatross in "The Rime of the Ancient Mariner").

V. A. Write an interpretation (350–500 words) of the following poem (in the manner of R. W. Stallman's interpretation of the cummings poem):

THE THOUGHT–FOX

TED HUGHES

I imagine this midnight moment's forest:
Something else is alive
Beside the clock's loneliness
And this blank page where my fingers move.

Through the window I see no star:
Something more near
Thought deeper within darkness
Is entering the loneliness:

Cold, delicately as the dark snow,
A fox's nose touches twig, leaf;
Two eyes serve a movement, that now
And again now, and now, and now

Sets neat prints into the snow
Between trees, and warily a lame
Shadow lags by stump and in hollow
Of a body that is bold to come

Across clearings, an eye,
A widening deepening greenness,
Brilliantly, concentratedly,
Coming about its own business

Till, with a sudden sharp hot stink of fox
It enters the dark hole of the head.
The window is starless still; the clock ticks,
The page is printed.[10]

B. In framing your interpretation, consider the following questions:
1. How do the verb "imagine" and the adjective "midnight" (l. 1) help to establish the central metaphor of the poem?
2. What does the "forest" (l. 1) refer to? How is it an appropriate image?
3. What is the "something else . . . alive" in line 2?
4. Suggest symbolic implications for the "clock" (l. 3) and state the importance of these implications in clarifying the development of the poem.
5. What does the contrast between the starless night and the deeper darkness (stanza 2) suggest about the sources of the act being performed, an act completed only when "The page is printed" (l. 24)?
6. How does stanza 6 amplify this point?
7. How do the fox's habits and movements (stanzas 3–5) provide effective images for the action taking place on the "blank page where my fingers move"?

[10] "The Thought-Fox" from *The Hawk in the Rain* by Ted Hughes. Copyright © 1957 by Ted Hughes. Reprinted by permission of Harper & Row, Publishers, Inc.

13 WHAT ARE THE FACTS ABOUT X?

An essay presenting "the facts about X" will be basically informative (as compared to descriptive, narrative, argumentative). Neither systematic nor complete in the formal sense, it is not strictly speaking analysis; yet in a looser sense it serves the same purpose. The facts—as a reporter or researcher sees or knows them—represent a breaking down of a subject into *some* of its important parts.

Range of Subject Matter

There are countless sources for a factual or informative essay, ranging from matters of historical significance ("The Facts About the Cuban Crisis"), to the timely and newsworthy ("The Facts About Mercury Poisoning"), to the seemingly trivial (Montaigne's essay on "Thumbs"). The obvious prerequisite of a good fact piece is that the writer know how to track down "the facts" (Chapter 22, "Gathering Information"). Equally important, he must be able to get his facts straight; accuracy is a prime virtue in this type of reportorial writing. So are genuine interest and enthusiasm, for as one wise observer remarked, "There are no boring subjects, only boring writers." The writer, then, must play to his own strengths, sticking to subject matter that he either knows something about or would like to know something about. An informed essay on bowling by someone who bowls and enjoys the sport has infinitely more merit than a listlessly written survey of a so-called "important" topic of presumed "social significance."

Range of Purposes

In writing a factual essay the writer must also know how to select his facts judiciously. Since he cannot tell everything, he must include only those details that promote his particular purpose. In this sense the purpose of the essay determines what specific facts the writer will present and *how* he will present them (seriously, satirically, calmly, angrily). Since the purpose of the fact essay gives it its distinctive shape and tone, it will be helpful to review certain recurrent purposes—the four basic reasons why writers might approach a subject with this question in mind: "What are the facts about X?"

To Clear Up Misconceptions

Every year tourists from all over the United States flock to the southwest to view the remnants of what they take to be a vanishing breed—the American Indian. And every year, as a New Mexico newspaper editor observes in the essay below, the tourists ask the same uninformed questions, revealing the "wild superstitions" they still entertain about this minority group. To forestall these questions and to clear up major misconceptions, Oliver LaFarge, a noted expert on Indian affairs, tries to present the facts. By doing so in a dispassionate manner (by keeping a "straight face"), by adopting an uncomplicated one-two-three format, by keeping his style simple and economical (appropriate to his medium, a newspaper; and to his audience, the reading public), LaFarge succeeds, does he not?, in convincing us that he is, in fact, giving us *facts*—unvarnished and unbiased.

THE AMERICAN INDIAN: FALSEHOODS AND TRUTHS

OLIVER LAFARGE

Now that Santa Fe is in the season of many visitors, it seems appropriate to answer some of the many wild superstitions about Indians; not only among Easterners, but among a great many of our permanent residents. The notes below are in essence answers to questions—or, often enough, dogmatic statements—encountered in the past year.

1. Indians are citizens and they have the right to vote. Charles Curtis, vice president of the United States, was an Indian, with the same status as any Indian you see when you visit a pueblo.

2. Indians can leave their reservations whenever they please, go where they wish, live where they choose and engage in any business they think they are competent to handle.

3. Indians do not receive a pension from the government. They have to earn their own livings. If they do well enough, they must pay income tax like anybody else.

4. It is not true that, if you give an Indian a lift and he is hurt in an accident while in your car, the federal government will sue you. If the accident occurs on Indian land, and the Indian is smart and mean enough to sue, the action will come up in federal court; otherwise the state court. Mr. Indian in either case will have to find and pay his own attorney, just like anyone else.

5. Indians are not oil-rich. Out of some 450,000 of them, about 3,000 have individual incomes from oil, and most of these have less than $2,500 a year. Some tribes have income from oil, gas, mines, and so forth, such as the Nava-

hos and Jicarilla Apaches in this vicinity. If their annual take were divided among all members of the tribe, there would hardly be enough for one good meal per person. The tribes use income of this kind for public purposes of various sorts, such as drought relief, pay of tribal police, and hiring business advisers.

6. Pueblo Indians do not have to get permission from the governor of their pueblo before having a baby.

7. The word pueblo is pronounced "pwayblow" and not "pee-eeblow," or "pew-eeblow" or "MacGarnigle."

8. The word Apache is pronounced "Apatchee." The French "apaches" took their name from the American tribe and Gallicized the word. Referring to those tribes as "Apash" may be intended to show off the speaker's profound dunking in French cultuah; what it does is show off the speaker's ignorance (sometimes pronounced "igger-ance").

9. The word Navaho—oh well, let's don't go into that.

10. The dancers who take part in ceremonies at the various pueblos do so without pay. They dance because they believe in the ceremonies, and because they are proud of their traditions and their art. If, on the side, the community can make a little money out of letting you take pictures, that is to the public good. Minor dances are also performed commercially, such as the dances at Tesuque for the American Express tours. Sometimes such dances are authentic, sometimes they are not.

11. The money you pay when you visit Taos Pueblo does not mean that Taos is "degenerate" or "commercialized." Having been plagued by visitors for years, the Indians had sense enough to cash in on the plague. The money is scrupulously accounted for and used for civic purposes.

12. Your behavior in the presence of Indians, loud or quiet, rude or polite, prying or considerate, will govern their opinion of you exactly as when you are in the presence of other Americans.[1]

To Satisfy Natural Curiosity

The fact piece need not serve any larger purpose beyond itself. Facts for their own sake are justification enough for an essay, provided that the facts are interesting and that they satisfy "natural curiosity."

Certainly the following piece fulfills these conditions. *Everyone* is interested in the weather—especially its more violent moods. Here, then, are the facts about hurricanes.

HURRICANES

Hurricanes are tropical cyclones in which winds reach speeds of 74 miles per hour or more, and blow in a large spiral around a relatively calm center—the eye of the hurricane. Every year, these violent storms bring destruction to coastlines and islands in their erratic path. Tropical cyclones of the same type are called typhoons in the North Pacific, baguios in the Philippines, and cyclones in the Indian Ocean.

Stated very simply, hurricanes are giant whirlwinds in which air moves in a large, tightening spiral around a center of extreme low pressure, reaching

[1] From *The Man With the Calabash Pipe* by Oliver LaFarge.

maximum velocity in a circular band extending outward 20 or 30 miles from the rim of the eye. This circulation is counterclockwise in the Northern Hemisphere, and clockwise in the Southern Hemisphere. Near the eye, hurricane winds may gust to more than 200 miles per hour, and the entire storm dominates the ocean surface and lower atmosphere over tens of thousands of square miles.

The eye, like the spiral structure of the storm, is unique to hurricanes. Here, winds are light and skies are clear or partly cloudy. But this calm is deceptive, bordered as it is by hurricane-force winds and torrential rains. Many persons have been killed or injured when the calm eye lured them out of shelter, only to be caught in the hurricane winds at the far side of the eye, where the wind blows from a direction opposite to that in the leading half of the storm.

Hurricane winds do much damage, but drowning is the greatest cause of hurricane deaths. As the storm approaches and moves across the coastline, it brings huge waves, raising tides some 15 feet or more above normal. The rise may come rapidly, and produce flash floods in coastal lowlands, or may come in the form of giant waves—which are mistakenly called "tidal waves." Waves and currents erode beaches and barrier islands, undermine waterfront structures, and wash out highway and railroad beds. The torrential rains produce sudden flooding; as the storm moves inland and its winds diminish, floods constitute the hurricane's greatest threat.

The hurricanes that strike the eastern United States are born in the tropical and subtropical North Atlantic Ocean, the Caribbean Sea, and the Gulf of Mexico. Most occur in August, September, and October, but the six-month period from June 1 to November 30 is considered the Atlantic hurricane season.

The principal regions of tropical cyclone origin vary during the season. Most early (May and June) storms originate in the Gulf of Mexico and western Caribbean. In July and August, the areas of most frequent origin shift eastward, and by September are located over the larger area from the Bahamas southeastward to the Lesser Antilles, and thence eastward to south of the Cape Verde Islands, near the west coast of Africa. After mid-September, the principal areas of origin shift back to the western Caribbean and Gulf of Mexico.

On average, six Atlantic hurricanes occur per year. However, there are significant deviations from this average. In 1916 and 1950, 11 hurricanes were observed, and no hurricanes were observed in 1907 and 1914. During 1893, 1950, and 1961 seasons, four hurricanes were observed in progress at the same time.

Hurricanes also form along the west coast of Mexico and Central America, but their effects are seldom felt as far north as California. These threaten shipping and aviation, however, and are watched as carefully as their Atlantic cousins.

Hurricanes begin as relatively small tropical cyclones which drift gradually to the west-northwest (in the Northern Hemisphere), imbedded in the westward-blowing tradewinds of the tropics. Under certain conditions these disturbances increase in size, speed, and intensity until they become full-fledged hurricanes.

The storms move forward very slowly in the tropics, and may sometimes hover for short periods of time. The initial forward speed is usually 15 miles per hour or less. Then, as the hurricane moves farther from the Equator, its forward speed tends to increase; at middle latitudes it may exceed 60 miles per hour in extreme cases.

The great storms are driven by the heat released by condensing water vapor, and by external mechanical forces. Once cut off from the warm ocean, the storm begins to die, starved for water and heat energy, and dragged apart by friction as it moves over the land.[2]

To Entertain

The question "What are the facts about X?" may be addressed to a subject as fragile and unlikely as "thumbs." In the hands of a master essayist, like Montaigne, there is engaging material here for a short piece, designed exclusively to divert or entertain.

OF THUMBS

MONTAIGNE

Tacitus reports that, with certain barbarian kings, their manner of making a binding obligation was to clasp their right hands tightly together and intertwist their thumbs; and when, by dint of squeezing them, the blood came to the tip, they pricked them lightly, and then each sucked the other's. Physicians say that the thumb is the master-finger of the hand, and that the word *pouce* is derived from the Latin *pollere,* which signifies to surpass others in excellence. And it seems that the Latins, too, sometimes use it in the sense of the whole hand:—

> No soft persuasion, or of voice or thumb
> Will make him rise to the occasion.

In Rome it was a sign of favour to put the thumbs together and turn them down,—

> Your companion will applaud your sport with both thumbs,—

and of disfavour to raise them and turn them outward,—

> the populace, with thumbs reversed, kill indiscriminately.

The Romans released from military service those who were wounded in the thumb, because they were no longer able to grasp their weapons firmly enough. Augustus confiscated the property of a Roman knight who had treacherously cut off the thumbs of his young sons, to excuse them from going into the army; and before that, the Senate, at the time of the Italian war, had condemned Caius Vatienus to life-long imprisonment and had confiscated all his property, for having intentionally cut off the thumb of his left hand, to exempt himself from that expedition. Some one, who it was I do not recall, having won a naval battle, had the thumbs of his vanquished foes cut off, to deprive them of the means of fighting and of handling the oars. The Athenians cut off the thumbs of the Aeginetans, to take away their superiority in the art

[2] From *Hurricane,* United States Department of Commerce, Environmental Science Services Administration, 1969.

of seamanship. In Lacedaemon the schoolmaster punished the children by biting their thumbs.[3]

To Make a Social Comment

Frequently, of course, informative essays do more than simply inform. Woven into the facts is a social commentary, an aside to the reader (only partly explicit), that nudges him slightly and asks, "Isn't this absurd?" In the following essay, reporter Joan Didion gives us "the facts about" the wedding business in Las Vegas. Although she occasionally interjects an editorial comment ("it is merchandising 'niceness'"), the facts are allowed, for the most part, to speak for themselves, and in so speaking a social commentary inevitably emerges.

MARRYING ABSURD

JOAN DIDION

To be married in Las Vegas, Clark County, Nevada, a bride must swear that she is eighteen or has parental permission and a bridegroom that he is twenty-one or has parental permission. Someone must put up five dollars for the license. (On Sundays and holidays, fifteen dollars. The Clark County Courthouse issues marriage licenses at any time of the day or night except between noon and one in the afternoon, between eight and nine in the evening, and between four and five in the morning.) Nothing else is required. The State of Nevada, alone among these United States, demands neither a premarital blood test nor a waiting period before or after the issuance of a marriage license. Driving in across the Mojave from Los Angeles, one sees the signs way out on the desert, looming up from that moonscape of rattlesnakes and mesquite, even before the Las Vegas lights appear like a mirage on the horizon: "GETTING MARRIED? Free License Information First Strip Exit." Perhaps the Las Vegas wedding industry achieved its peak operational efficiency between 9:00 P.M. and midnight of August 26, 1965, an otherwise unremarkable Thursday which happened to be, by Presidential order, the last day on which anyone could improve his draft status merely by getting married. One hundred and seventy-one couples were pronounced man and wife in the name of Clark County and the State of Nevada that night, sixty-seven of them by a single justice of the peace, Mr. James A. Brennan. Mr. Brennan did one wedding at the Dunes and the other sixty-six in his office, and charged each couple eight dollars. One bride lent her veil to six others. "I got it down from five to three minutes," Mr. Brennan said later of his feat. "I could've married them *en masse*, but they're people, not cattle. People expect more when they get married."

What people who get married in Las Vegas actually do expect—what, in the largest sense, their "expectations" are—strikes one as a curious and self-contradictory business. Las Vegas is the most extreme and allegorical of American settlements, bizarre and beautiful in its venality and in its devotion to immediate gratification, a place the tone of which is set by mobsters and call girls and ladies' room attendants with amyl nitrite poppers in their uni-

[3] From *The Essays of Michel Montaigne*, translated by George B. Ives. Reprinted by permission of Harvard University Press.

form pockets. Almost everyone notes that there is no "time" in Las Vegas, no night and no day and no past and no future (no Las Vegas casino, however, has taken the obliteration of the ordinary time sense quite so far as Harold's Club in Reno, which for a while issued, at odd intervals in the day and night, mimeographed "bulletins" carrying news from the world outside); neither is there any logical sense of where one is. One is standing on a highway in the middle of a vast hostile desert looking at an eighty-foot sign which blinks "STARDUST" or "CAESAR'S PALACE." Yes, but what does that explain? This geographical implausibility reinforces the sense that what happens there has no connection with "real" life; Nevada cities like Reno and Carson are ranch towns, Western towns, places behind which there is some historical imperative. But Las Vegas seems to exist only in the eye of the beholder. All of which makes it an extraordinarily stimulating and interesting place, but an odd one in which to want to wear a candlelight satin Priscilla of Boston wedding dress with Chantilly lace insets, tapered sleeves and a detachable modified train.

And yet the Las Vegas wedding business seems to appeal to precisely that impulse. "Sincere and Dignified Since 1954," one wedding chapel advertises. There are nineteen such wedding chapels in Las Vegas, intensely competitive, each offering better, faster, and, by implication, more sincere services than the next: Our Photos Best Anywhere, Your Wedding on a Phonograph Record, Candlelight with Your Ceremony, Honeymoon Accommodations, Free Transportation from Your Motel to Courthouse to Chapel and Return to Motel, Religious or Civil Ceremonies, Dressing Rooms, Flowers, Rings, Announcements, Witnesses Available, and Ample Parking. All of these services, like most others in Las Vegas (sauna baths, payroll-check cashing, chinchilla coats for sale or rent) are offered twenty-four hours a day, seven days a week, presumably on the premise that marriage, like craps, is a game to be played when the table seems hot.

But what strikes one most about the Strip chapels, with their wishing wells and stained-glass paper windows and their artificial bouvardia, is that so much of their business is by no means a matter of simple convenience, of late-night liaisons between show girls and baby Crosbys. Of course there is some of that. (One night about eleven o'clock in Las Vegas I watched a bride in an orange minidress and masses of flamecolored hair stumble from a Strip chapel on the arm of her bridegroom, who looked the part of the expendable nephew in movies like *Miami Syndicate*. "I gotta get the kids," the bride whimpered. "I gotta pick up the sitter, I gotta get to the midnight show." "What you gotta get," the bridegroom said, opening the door of a Cadillac Coupe de Ville and watching her crumple on the seat, "is sober.") But Las Vegas seems to offer something other than "convenience"; it is merchandising "niceness," the facsimile of proper ritual, to children who do not know how else to find it, how to make the arrangements, how to do it "right." All day and evening long on the Strip, one sees actual wedding parties, waiting under the harsh lights at a crosswalk, standing uneasily in the parking lot of the Frontier while the photographer hired by The Little Church of the West ("Wedding Place of the Stars") certifies the occasion, takes the picture: the bride in a veil and white satin pumps, the bridegroom usually in a white dinner jacket, and even an attendant or two, a sister or a best friend in hot-pink *peau de soie*, a flirtation veil, a carnation nosegay. "When I Fall in Love It Will Be Forever," the organist plays, and then a few bars of Lohengrin. The mother cries; the stepfather, awkward in his role, invites the chapel hostess to join them for a drink at the Sands. The hostess declines with a professional smile; she has already transferred her interest to the group waiting outside. One bride out, another in, and again the sign goes up on the chapel door: "One moment please—Wedding."

I sat next to one such wedding party in a Strip restaurant the last time I was in Las Vegas. The marriage had just taken place; the bride still wore her dress, the mother her corsage. A bored waiter poured out a few swallows of pink champagne ("on the house") for everyone but the bride, who was too young to be served. "You'll need something with more kick than that," the bride's father said with heavy jocularity to his new son-in-law; the ritual jokes about the wedding night had a certain Panglossian character, since the bride was clearly several months pregnant. Another round of pink champagne, this time not on the house, and the bride began to cry. "It was just as nice," she sobbed, "as I hoped and dreamed it would be." [4]

Organizing the Fact Piece

The fact essay, like any other piece of expository writing, requires careful organization (see Chapter 23, "Organizing the Paper"). Sometimes, if there is an overwhelming number of small, separate facts to contend with, the writer may have trouble trying to fit everything in, finding a format to accommodate the host of details. Here again, as always, the writer's purpose and his overall rhetorical stance must be his guide. In his piece on the American Indian, as pointed out above, Oliver LaFarge's main intention was to expose a series of false beliefs. Quite sensibly, then, he organized his piece in terms of the beliefs themselves, considering them one-by-one, replacing each specific falsehood with a specific truth.

The essay on hurricanes is more subtly organized, yet it too has an appropriately simple format that might be outlined as follows:

1. What hurricanes are
2. Dangers of the hurricane
3. Location and frequency of occurrence
4. How hurricanes form

In each of these sections the writer has included numerous details, which are easy to follow because of their logical arrangement and intrinsic interest.

The Didion essay, "Marrying Absurd," has a far more subtle and intricate organization that will repay close study (Assignment IV, p. 197).

Another method of organizing a fact piece is through "question and answer" presentation, a lively approach to a subject (everyone is stirred to curiosity by the presentation of a question) and serviceable in that the reader can turn immediately to the specific aspect of the subject he is interested in. The following essay on marijuana is published by the National Institute of Mental Health:

[4] Reprinted with the permission of Farrar, Straus & Giroux, Inc. from *Slouching Towards Bethlehem* by Joan Didion, copyright © 1967, 1968 by Joan Didion.

WHAT IS MARIHUANA?

Marihuana is a drug found in the flowering tops and leaves of the Indian hemp plant, *cannabis sativa*. The plant grows in mild climates in countries around the world, especially in Mexico, Africa, India, and the Middle East. It also grows in the United States, where the drug is known as pot, tea, grass, weed, Mary Jane, and by other names.

For use as a drug, the leaves and flowers of the plant are dried and crushed or chopped into small pieces. This green product is usually rolled and smoked in short cigarettes or in pipes, or it can be taken in food. The cigarettes are commonly known as reefers, joints, and sticks. The smoke from marihuana is harsh, and smells like burnt rope or dried grasses. Its sweetish odor is easily recognized.

The strength of the drug differs from place to place, depending on where and how it is grown, how it is prepared for use, and how it is stored. The marihuana available in the United States is much weaker than the kind grown in Asia, Africa, or the Near East.

HOW DOES THE DRUG WORK?

When smoked, marihuana quickly enters the bloodstream and acts on the brain and nervous system. It affects the user's mood and thinking. Its pathway into the brain is not yet understood. Some scientists report that the drug accumulates in the liver. Because it may cause hallucinations when taken in very large doses, it is classed as a mild "hallucinogen." Just how the drug works in the body and how it produces its effects have not yet been discovered by medical science.

WHAT ARE ITS PHYSICAL EFFECTS?

The long-term physical effects of taking marihuana are not yet known. The kind of research needed to learn the results of chronic use has not yet been done.

The more obvious physical reactions include rapid heart beat, lowering of body temperature, and sometimes reddening of the eyes. The drug also changes blood sugar levels, stimulates the appetite, and dehydrates the body. Users may get talkative, loud, unsteady, or drowsy, and find it hard to coordinate their movements.

WHAT IS ITS USE?

Although it has been known to man for nearly 5,000 years, marihuana is one of the least understood of all natural drugs. In China, very early in history, it was given to relieve pain during surgery and, in India, as a medicine. Unlike other drugs, it has no known use in modern medicine. It is used mainly for its intoxicating effects. According to a United Nations survey, it has been most widely used in Asia and Africa.

Traffic in and use of drugs from the cannabis plant is now legally restricted in nearly every civilized country in the world, including countries where marihuana is used in religious ceremonies or as a native medicine.

HOW WIDELY IS IT USED
IN THE UNITED STATES?

The use of marihuana as an intoxicating drug was introduced in the United States in 1920. In 1937, its general use was outlawed by the Federal Marihuana Tax Act, followed by strict laws and enforcement in every State. In the mid-1960's, authorities reported a sharp increase in the use of marihuana. Arrests on marihuana charges have more than doubled since 1960, according to the President's Commission on Crime.

The exact extent of marihuana use in the United States is not known. Some health authorities believe that 4 to 5 million Americans may have used the drug at least once in their lives. Other estimates are as high as 20 million. Research studies are underway to determine more precisely just how widely the drug is used.

WHAT ARE ITS OTHER EFFECTS?

The drug's effects on the emotions and senses vary widely, depending on the amount and strength of the marihuana used. The social setting in which it is taken and what the user expects also influence his reaction to the drug.

Usually, when it is smoked, marihuana's effect is felt quickly, in about 15 minutes. Its effects can last from 2 to 4 hours. The range of effects can vary from depression to a feeling of excitement. Some users, however, experience no change of mood at all. The sense of time and distance of many users frequently becomes distorted. A minute may seem like an hour. Something near may seem far away.

WHY IS SO LITTLE KNOWN
ABOUT THE DRUG?

Medical science does not yet know enough about the effects of marihuana use because its active ingredient—*tetrahydrocannabinol*—was produced in pure form only recently. In the summer of 1966 the chemical, first synthesized by an NIMH-supported scientist in Israel, was made available for research purposes. Now for the first time researchers can accurately measure the drug's effects and study its short- and long-term action on the body.

WHAT RESEARCH IS BEING DONE?

The National Institute of Mental Health, an agency of the Public Health Service, is responsible for supporting and conducting research to learn more about marihuana and to present this knowledge to the public.

The program of the NIMH Center for Studies of Narcotic and Drug Abuse includes surveys of how people get the drug, how widely students and others use it, and what effects different amounts and periods of use have upon people, physically and psychologically. With NIMH support, scientists are now studying the special drug qualities of marihuana, and its physical effects on the body.

The NIMH Addiction Research Center in Lexington, Kentucky, plans research to discover exactly how marihuana affects memory, perception (or awareness), mood, and physical movement. Other studies are planned to learn more about the drug's long-range effects on the body and mind.

HOW DOES MARIHUANA AFFECT JUDGMENT?

A person using marihuana finds it harder to make decisions that require clear thinking. And he finds himself more easily open to other people's suggestions. Doing any task that takes good reflexes and thinking is affected by the drug. For this reason it is dangerous to drive while under the influence of the drug.

WHAT ARE THE LATEST FINDINGS ABOUT THE DRUG?

Working with man-made tetrahydrocannabinol, one of the active ingredients of marihuana, a leading scientist recently found that high dosages of the drug brought on severe reactions in every person tested. The National Institute of Mental Health study also showed that psychotic reactions sometimes occur, for unknown reasons, in some individuals who take smaller amounts.

The scientist observed that a dose equal to one cigarette of the United States type can make the smoker feel excited, gay, or silly. After an amount equal to four, the user notices changes in what he can perceive. He reports that colors seem brighter, his sense of hearing keener. After a dose equal to 10 cigarettes, other reactions set in. He experiences visual hallucinations (seeing things that are not there), or delusions (beliefs not based in reality). His mood may swing from great joy to extreme anxiety. He may become deeply depressed, or have feelings of uneasiness, panic, or fear.

IS MARIHUANA ADDICTING?

Authorities now think in terms of drug "dependence" rather than "addiction." Marihuana, which is not a narcotic, does not cause physical dependence as do heroin and other narcotics. This means that the body does not become dependent on continuing use of the drug. The body probably does not develop a tolerance to the drug, either, which would make larger and larger doses necessary to get the same effects. Withdrawal from marihuana does not produce physical sickness.

A number of scientists think the drug can cause psychological dependence, however, if its users take it regularly. All researchers agree that more knowledge of the physical, personal, and social consequence of marihuana use is needed before more factual statements can be made.

DOES IT LEAD TO USE OF NARCOTICS?

A 1967 study of narcotic addicts from city areas showed that more than 80 percent had previously used marihuana. Of the much larger number of persons who use marihuana, scientists agree that few go on to use morphine and heroin. No direct cause-and-effect link between the use of marihuana and narcotics has been found. Researchers point out, however, a person predisposed to abuse one drug may be likely to abuse other, stronger drugs. Also, users of one illicit drug may be exposed to a variety of them through contacts with drug sellers and other users.

WHAT ARE THE LAWS DEALING WITH MARIHUANA?

Under Federal law, to have, give or sell marihuana in the United States is a felony, which is a serious crime. Federal and many State laws deal with the drug as severely as if it were a narcotic.

The Federal penalty for possessing the drug is 2 to 10 years imprisonment for the first offense, 5 to 20 years for the second offense, and 10 to 40 years for further offenses. Fines of up to $20,000 for the first or subsequent offenses may be imposed. State laws also control the illicit use of these drugs. For transfer or sale of the drug, the first offense may bring a 5- to 20-year sentence and a fine of up to $20,000; two or more offenses, 10 to 40 years in prison. If a person over 18 sells to a minor under 18 years of age, he is subject to a fine of up to $20,000 and/or 10 to 40 years in prison for the first offense, with no suspension of sentence, probation, or parole.

WHAT ARE THE SPECIAL RISKS FOR YOUNG USERS?

Breaking the laws dealing with marihuana can have serious effects on the lives of young people. They may find their education interrupted and their future shadowed or altered by having a police record. An arrest or conviction for a felony can complicate their life and plans at many turns. For example, in many States, a person with a police record must meet special conditions to obtain or renew a driver's license. Conviction can prevent a person from being able to enter a profession such as medicine, law, or teaching. It can make it difficult for him to get a responsible position in business or industry. Special hearings are necessary before he can hold a government job. Before a student tries marihuana, he should be aware of the social and legal facts about getting involved with the drug.

Other risks are pointed out by experts on human growth and development. They say that a more subtle result of drug abuse on the young person is its effect on his personality growth and development. For young people to experiment with drugs at a time when they are going through a period of many changes in their transition to adulthood is a seriously questionable practice.

"It can be especially disturbing to a young person who is already having enough of a task getting adjusted to life and establishing his values," says an NIMH scientist engaged in studies of young marihuana users.

Another reason for caution: Statements being reported by students that the use of marihuana is "medically safe," are not supported by scientific evidence. It is hoped that research now underway may add to the little currently known about the effects of the use of marihuana.

ASSIGNMENTS

I. A. In the spirit of Oliver LaFarge's factual piece on American Indians, write an essay (500–750 words) clearing up misconceptions about any minority group in the United States with which you are familiar.

Puerto Ricans
Negroes
Jews

Catholics
Polish-Americans
Japanese-Americans
Chinese-Americans
Mexican-Americans

B. Write the same type of essay on one of the following topics (see Chapter 22, "Gathering Information"). Organize your essay either in lists (like LaFarge's) or in question-and-answer form (like the marijuana piece).

hypnotism
group therapy
missionaries
conscientious objectors
alcoholism
drug addiction
Zen
pollution
homosexuality
conservation
capital punishment
abortion
chemical warfare
DAR (Daughters of the American Revolution)
parochical schools
sex education
pesticides
smoking

C. Write a short essay (250–500 words) correcting the causal fallacies at the root of the medical superstitions listed below, i.e., cite the *facts* behind the superstition:

Night air is unhealthy.
Fish is brain food.
Insanity is inherited.
Green apples cause a stomach ache.
Children born of cousins will be defective or deformed.
Frogs and toads cause warts.
Feed a cold, starve a fever.

II. Write a fact piece on one of the following (500–750 words) designed to entertain or inform.

cosmic rays	buried treasure
inertia	dwarfs and midgets
gravity	giants
mirages	lullabies
cyclotrons	gypsies
glaciers	magic
earthquakes	voodoo
Arctic Ocean	fire
wind	haunted houses
cave men	tobacco
cave women	Hara-Kiri
chromosomes	sea serpents
digestion	falling stars

coral reefs	clowns
opera	astrology
pigeons	sundials
drought	ice fishing

III. Write an essay in the style of Montaigne (150–250 words) on a subject comparable to "Thumbs."

IV. A. Consider the Didion essay, "Marrying Absurd."

1. What is suggested by the simple declarative sentence early in the piece: "Nothing else is required"?
2. What is ironic about the statement by the justice of the peace: "I could've married them *en masse,* but they're people, not cattle. People expect more when they get married."
3. Why do you suppose the writer put quotation marks around the word "expectations" ("What people who get married in Las Vegas actually do expect—what, in the largest sense, their 'expectations' are . . .")?
4. What is "curious and self-contradictory" about these expectations?
5. In what sense does the writer mean that what happens here has no connection with " 'real' life"?
6. In what sense does Las Vegas exist "in the eye of the beholder"?
7. Explain the contradiction: it is "an extraordinarily stimulating and interesting place, but an odd one in which to want to wear a candlelight satin Priscilla of Boston wedding dress with Chantilly lace insets, tapered sleeves and a detachable modified train."
8. Why do you think the writer describes the wedding dress in such detail? Do you know exactly what "a candlelight satin Priscilla of Boston" is? What "Chantilly lace" is? Does it matter whether you know or not? Do these details create a rhetorical effect independent of literal meaning? Comment on the following words:

candlelight	Chantilly
satin	lace
Priscilla of Boston	modified

9. Does the listing of chapel advertisements (Our Photos Best Anywhere, Your Wedding on a Phonograph Record, etc.) become tedious? Does it serve any purpose?
10. Evaluate the effectiveness of the simile ". . . marriage, like craps, is a game to be played when the table seems hot."
11. There are two illustrative incidents in this essay; comment on their rhetorical impact—i.e., indicate how they develop and reinforce the point the writer is trying to make throughout her exposition.
12. Comment on the effectiveness of the phrases "merchandising 'niceness' " and "the facsimile of proper ritual."
13. Discuss irony as the prevailing tone and unifying principle of this essay.

B. In an essay (750–1,000 words) describe a place, procedure, situation, event that you have observed or have participated in, characterizing it indirectly through your presentation of the objective, observable facts rather than through explicit comment (as in "Marrying Absurd"). The tone of your piece should be appropriate to the subject matter and to the conclusion you want the reader to draw.

V. One of the great compilers of facts was the journalist John Gunther (*Inside Europe, Inside U.S.A.*) who tells us, in his autobiography, how he regarded and approached facts.

I try to report facts as I see them and to tell the truth, but truth is an elusive concept. I think it was Frank Lloyd Wright who once said, "The truth is more important than the facts." I would hesitate to recommend this maxim unreservedly to a school of journalism, but surely what Mr. Wright meant is clear —that selection of facts can be as important as the facts themselves. No man, not even Christopher Isherwood, is a camera—and the camera, as a matter of fact, is one of the greatest liars of our time. There is no such thing as *purely* objective journalism, although plenty of us try to get close. A reporter with no bias at all would be a vegetable. I myself have always had a strong, unalterable liberal bent; I believe in decency and progress, in tomorrow as against yesterday. But I am not often swayed or shaken by events. I have little messianic blood in my veins, and I seldom editorialize. On most issues I take a somewhat detached, even cold, old-fashioned middle view, although I stand more to the left than to the right. *Why* do I write? I suppose the best answer to this is that basically I write for myself, to satisfy my own multiple curiosities. In other words, my work has been a kind of exercise in self-education at the public's expense. I myself am a fairly good average guinea pig, and if something interests me I am reasonably sure it will interest the general reader too. I can only hope that the public has had its money's worth.

My colleague the late Raymond Clapper once said, "Never underestimate a reader's intelligence; never overestimate what he knows." I always try to be readable (and readability, to repeat, depends on pace and euphony) and I greatly enjoy making lists and summaries in my attempts to synthesize large masses of material, but I want to be solid as well and I do not believe in being too simple. It is a good thing to make the reader reach up. On the other hand, he has an absolute right to have terms defined; I try hard never to use a word or a phrase, from "apartheid" to "Common Market," without doing my best to explain exactly what it means.[5]

A. Comment on the following statements. Do you think they represent healthy attitudes on the part of the writer?

1. The truth is more important than the facts.
2. No man . . . is a camera. . . . There is no such thing as *purely* objective journalism. . . .
3. . . . basically I write for myself, to satisfy my multiple curiosities. (Discuss the difference between "expression" and "communication." Does Gunther take both into account?)
4. . . . if something interests me I am reasonably sure it will interest the general reader too.
5. Never underestimate a reader's intelligence; never overestimate what he knows.
6. I always try to be readable. . . .
7. . . . readability . . . depends on pace and euphony. . . .
8. . . . I greatly enjoy making lists and summaries. . . .

B. Would you be inclined to trust the facts set forth in Gunther's writings? Explain.

[5] From pp. 112–13 in *A Fragment of Autobiography* by John Gunther. Copyright © 1961, 1962 by John Gunther. Reprinted by permission of Harper & Row, Publishers.

14 HOW DID X HAPPEN?

When you ask the question "How Did X Happen?" you are preparing to write narration, a story about how something happened. We shall confine our attention here (as elsewhere in this text) to what *actually did happen*—not in the imagination of the writer but in real life—i.e., we shall deal with factual rather than fictional narrative. In both kinds of narrative there are characters and ongoing actions: a series of events unfolding against a specific setting, causally related and moving steadily forward in time and through stages of action. Unlike process analysis which merely *explains*, narration attempts to *re-create* a happening by putting the reader in the very flux and flow of the happening, so that he may see and hear and feel exactly what it was like; so that he may—vicariously—*have* the experience, not merely learn about it. To achieve this, the narrator must present the events in the form of a story; there must be both a teller and a tale. For a piece of writing to qualify as narrative, no more and no less than this is required.

Autobiographical Narration

The following selection tells how hate and shame entered the life of Dick Gregory, comedian and black-rights spokesman. In a good narrative such as this, note how the story flows smoothly and easily—as if the events were taking place at the very moment of telling—and how the dialogue "rings true": The easy colloquial speech of the narrator, the cold unbending tones of the teacher, the flustered repetitions of the child.

NOT POOR, JUST BROKE

DICK GREGORY

I never learned hate at home, or shame. I had to go to school for that. I was about seven years old when I got my first big lesson. I was in love with a little girl named Helene Tucker, a light-complected little girl with pigtails and nice manners. She was always clean and she was smart in school. I think I went to school then mostly to look at her. I brushed my hair and even got me a little old handkerchief. It was a lady's handkerchief, but I didn't want Helene to see me wipe my nose on my hand. The pipes were frozen again, there was no water in the house, but I washed my socks and shirt every night. I'd get a pot, and go over to Mister Ben's grocery store, and stick my pot down into his soda machine. Scoop out some chopped ice. By evening the ice melted to water for washing. I got sick a lot that winter because the fire would go out at night before the clothes were dry. In the morning I'd put them on, wet or dry, because they were the only clothes I had.

Everybody's got a Helene Tucker, a symbol of everything you want. I loved her for her goodness, her cleanness, her popularity. She'd walk down my street and my brothers and sisters would yell, "Here comes Helene," and I'd rub my tennis sneakers on the back of my pants and wish my hair wasn't so nappy and the white folks' shirt fit me better. I'd run out on the street. If I knew my place and didn't come too close, she'd wink at me and say hello. That was a good feeling. Sometimes I'd follow her all the way home, and shovel the snow off her walk and try to make friends with her Momma and her aunts. I'd drop money on her stoop late at night on my way back from shining shoes in the taverns. And she had a Daddy, and he had a good job. He was a paper hanger.

I guess I would have gotten over Helene by summertime, but something happened in that classroom that made her face hang in front of me for the next twenty-two years. When I played the drums in high school it was for Helene and when I broke track records in college it was for Helene and when I started standing behind microphones and heard applause I wished Helene could hear it, too. It wasn't until I was twenty-nine years old and married and making money that I finally got her out of my system. Helene was sitting in that classroom when I learned to be ashamed of myself.

It was on a Thursday. I was sitting in the back of the room, in a seat with a chalk circle drawn around it. The idiot's seat, the troublemaker's seat.

The teacher thought I was stupid. Couldn't spell, couldn't read, couldn't do arithmetic. Just stupid. Teachers were never interested in finding out that you couldn't concentrate because you were so hungry, because you hadn't had any breakfast. All you could think about was noontime, would it ever come? Maybe you could sneak into the cloakroom and steal a bite of some kid's lunch out of a coat pocket. A bite of something. Paste. You can't really make a meal of paste, or put it on bread for a sandwich, but sometimes I'd scoop a few spoonfuls out of the paste jar in the back of the room. Pregnant people get strange tastes. I was pregnant with poverty. Pregnant with dirt and pregnant with smells that made people turn away, pregnant with cold and pregnant with shoes that were never bought for me, pregnant with five other people in my bed and no Daddy in the next room, and pregnant with hunger. Paste doesn't taste too bad when you're hungry.

The teacher thought I was a troublemaker. All she saw from the front of the room was a little black boy who squirmed in his idiot's seat and made noises and poked the kids around him. I guess she couldn't see a kid who made noises because he wanted someone to know he was there.

It was on a Thursday, the day before the Negro payday. The eagle always flew on Friday. The teacher was asking each student how much his father would give to the Community Chest. On Friday night, each kid would get the money from his father, and on Monday he would bring it to the school. I decided I was going to buy me a Daddy right then. I had money in my pocket from shining shoes and selling papers, and whatever Helene Tucker pledged for her Daddy I was going to top it. And I'd hand the money right in. I wasn't going to wait until Monday to buy me a Daddy.

I was shaking, scared to death. The teacher opened her book and started calling out names alphabetically.

"Helene Tucker?"

"My Daddy said he'd give two dollars and fifty cents."

"That's very nice, Helene. Very, very nice indeed."

That made me feel pretty good. It wouldn't take too much to top that. I had almost three dollars in dimes and quarters in my pocket. I stuck my hand in my pocket and held onto the money, waiting for her to call my name. But the teacher closed her book after she called everybody else in the class.

I stood up and raised my hand.

"What is it now?"

"You forgot me."

She turned toward the blackboard. "I don't have time to be playing with you, Richard."

"My Daddy said he'd . . ."

"Sit down, Richard, you're disturbing the class."

"My daddy said he'd give . . . fifteen dollars."

She turned around and looked mad. "We are collecting this money for you and your kind, Richard Gregory. If your Daddy can give fifteen dollars you have no business being on relief."

"I got it right now, I got it right now, my Daddy gave it to me to turn in today, my Daddy said . . ."

"And furthermore," she said, looking right at me, her nostrils getting big and her lips getting thin and her eyes opening wide, "we know you don't have a Daddy."

Helene Tucker turned around, her eyes full of tears. She felt sorry for me. Then I couldn't see her too well because I was crying, too.

"Sit down, Richard."

And I always thought the teacher kind of liked me. She always picked me to wash the blackboard on Friday, after school. That was a big thrill, it made me feel important. If I didn't wash it, come Monday the school might not function right.

"Where are you going, Richard?"

I walked out of school that day, and for a long time I didn't go back very often. There was shame there.

Now there was shame everywhere. It seemed like the whole world had been inside that classroom, everyone had heard what the teacher had said, everyone had turned around and felt sorry for me. There was shame in going to the Worthy Boys Annual Christmas Dinner for you and your kind, because everybody knew what a worthy boy was. Why couldn't they just call it the Boys Annual Dinner, why'd they have to give it a name? There was shame in wearing the brown and orange and white plaid mackinaw the welfare gave to 3,000 boys. Why'd it have to be the same for everybody so when you walked down the street the people could see you were on relief? It was a nice warm mackinaw and it had a hood, and my Momma beat me and called me a little rat when she found out I stuffed it in the bottom of a pail full of garbage way over on Cottage Street. There was shame in running over to Mister Ben's at the end of the day and asking for his rotten peaches, there was shame in asking Mrs. Simmons for a spoonful of sugar, there was shame in running out to meet the relief truck. I hated that truck, full of food for you and your kind. I ran into the house and hid when it came. And then I started to sneak through alleys, to take the long way home so the people going into White's Eat Shop wouldn't see me. Yeah, the whole world heard the teacher that day, we all know you don't have a Daddy.[1]

Structure in Narration

A narrative begins at a specifically designated point in time ("Once upon a time" is the best-known fictional opening) and ends at an equally specific time. In the following episode drawn from *Report to Greco,* by Nikos Kazantzakis, the action of the story begins at nightfall and ends the next morning. In between, the author provides us with "markers" indicating where we are located in the progression of the incident (*almost nightfall, suddenly, finally, as soon as*). Note how at the very outset Kazantzakis establishes a mood of tension, anxiety, and suspense by describing the deserted streets, bolted doors, and atmosphere of enveloping gloom. We are being prepared for a conflict that the narrator fearfully anticipates, and we follow him with mounting suspense as he moves into danger—or is it danger? The story unfolds quietly toward its gentle climax, revealed in the last line.

A NIGHT IN A CALABRIAN VILLAGE

NIKOS KAZANTZAKIS

It was almost nightfall. The whole day: rain, torrents of rain. Drenched to the bone, I arrived in a little Calabrian village. I had to find a hearth where I could dry out, a corner where I could sleep. The streets were deserted, the doors bolted. The dogs were the only ones to scent the stranger's breath; they began to bark from within the courtyards. The peasants in this region are wild and misanthropic, suspicious of strangers. I hesitated at every door, extended my hand, but did not dare to knock.

O for my late grandfather in Crete who took his lantern each evening and made the rounds of the village to see if any stranger had come. He would take him home, feed him, give him a bed for the night, and then in the morn-

[1] From *nigger: An Autobiography* by Dick Gregory with Robert Lipsyte. Copyright, ©, 1964, by Dick Gregory Enterprises, Inc. Reprinted by permission of E. P. Dutton & Co., Inc.

ing see him off with a cup of wine and a slice of bread. Here in the Calabrian villages there were no such grandfathers.

Suddenly I saw an open door at the edge of the village. Inclining my head, I looked in: a murky corridor with a lighted fire at the far end and an old lady bent over it. She seemed to be cooking. Not a sound, nothing but the burning wood. It was fragrant; it must have been pine. I crossed the threshold and entered, bumping against a long table which stood in the middle of the room. Finally I reached the fire and sat down on a stool which I found in front of the hearth. The old lady was squatting on another stool, stirring the meal with a wooden spoon. I felt that she eyed me rapidly, without turning. But she said nothing. Taking off my jacket, I began to dry it. I sensed happiness rising in me like warmth, from my feet to my shins, my thighs, my breast. Hungrily, avidly, I inhaled the fragrance of the steam rising from the pot. The meal must have been baked beans; the aroma was overwhelming. Once more I realized to what an extent earthly happiness is made to the measure of man. It is not a rare bird which we must pursue at one moment in heaven, at the next in our minds. Happiness is a domestic bird found in our own courtyards.

Rising, the old lady took down two soup plates from a shelf next to her. She filled them, and the whole world smelled of beans. Lighting a lamp, she placed it on the long table. Next she brought two wooden spoons and a loaf of black bread. We sat down opposite each other. She made the sign of the cross, then glanced rapidly at me. I understood. I crossed myself and we began to eat. We were both hungry; we did not breathe a word. I had decided not to speak in order to see what would happen. Could she be a mute, I asked myself—or perhaps she's mad, one of those peaceful, kindly lunatics so much like saints.

As soon as we finished, she prepared a bed for me on a bench to the right of the table. I lay down, and she lay down on the other bench opposite me. Outside the rain was falling by the bucketful. For a considerable time I heard the water cackle on the roof, mixed with the old lady's calm, quiet breathing. She must have been tired, for she fell asleep the moment she inclined her head. Little by little, with the rain and the old lady's rhythmical respiration, I too slipped into sleep. When I awoke, I saw daylight peering through the cracks in the door.

The old lady had already risen and placed a saucepan on the fire to prepare the morning milk. I looked at her now in the sparse daylight. Shriveled and humped, she could fit into the palm of your hand. Her legs were so swollen that she had to stop at every step and catch her breath. But her eyes, only her large, pitch-black eyes, gleamed with youthful, unaging brilliance. How beautiful she must have been in her youth, I thought to myself, cursing man's fate, his inevitable deterioration. Sitting down opposite each other again, we drank the milk. Then I rose and slung my carpetbag over my shoulder. I took out my wallet, but the old lady colored deeply.

"No, no," she murmured, extending her hand.

As I looked at her in astonishment, the whole of her bewrinkled face suddenly gleamed.

"Goodbye, and God bless you," she said. "May the Lord repay you for the good you've done me. Since my husband died I've never slept so well." [2]

[2] From *A Report to Greco* by Nikos Kazantzakis. Copyright © 1965 by Simon and Schuster, Inc. Reprinted by permission of the publisher.

Although the action of Kazantzakis' little tale is low-keyed and essentially leisurely, it moves steadily toward its culmination. This is a basic element of good narration: the story must move steadily forward. It should never slacken or bog down under the weight of unessential details or issues not directly related to what it is primarily about. Some beginning writers deliberately try to "draw the story out," on the mistaken notion that this creates suspense. On the contrary, suspense is created (indeed, interest can only be maintained) when the story has pace, i.e., when it moves without undue interruption toward its climax—the revelation of what happened.

Point of View in Narration

In narration as in description, the writer must clearly establish his point of view, the vantage point from which he is telling the story: What is his relation to the events? How much does he know? What is his purpose in telling the story? The narrator may assume any one of several points of view. He may be an outsider, telling his story in the third person and knowing everything that is happening, including what goes on in everybody's head. This is called the *omniscient* point of view, and has generally been used by writers of fiction rather than nonfiction (obviously, since no one is really omniscient). Recently, however, a group of "new nonfiction" writers such as Tom Wolfe in *The Electric Kool-Aid Acid Test* and Truman Capote in *In Cold Blood* have borrowed the techniques of the novelist and short story writer in order to give their reportage a deeper dimension of vitality and reality. Thus they either speculate on what various personages are thinking, or find out (through interviews, etc.) what they actually were thinking and feeling during the time of a reported happening.

A narrator may also tell his story from the viewpoint of one character, seeing and knowing only what that character sees and knows. This is called the *limited* point of view. Or again, he may tell his story in the first person; or he may move like a sound camera, recording only what can be seen and heard, never delving into anyone's mind or heart—the *objective* or *dramatic* point of view.

It is a truism to say that the same events seen through different eyes or from different perspectives produce a different story. Thus no single element in a narrative is more significant than the narrator himself; he is part of the story, the lens through which "what happens" is refracted. Consider the following brief yet complete narrative, for example, in which the "me" is obviously a child. The last "exclamatory" line, followed by three ellipses and three question marks, suggests a child's bewilderment and confusion at an unanswered question. Indeed, the whole context of the story points to a child at the center. Still it is clear that a child is not telling the story at this moment (a child does not use words such as "illicit" and "awkward," or refer to a "foreboding pang"), but rather an adult who is recalling how—in the innocence of her youth—she viewed a strange happening.

THE GIRL IN THE TOBACCONIST SHOP

ROSAMUND LEHMANN

Black-eyed Dora in the tobacconist-cum-sweet-shop bestows her smiles on one and all. She is a beauty, and everybody's favourite. She is so welcoming, and my craving for sweets so compulsive that my visits are constant, and make her laugh. Sometimes she slips me an extra something with my penny bar, and then her full lips widen secretly, like an amused Madonna of the chocolates. One day I run, with sixpence, intending to place half of my treasure in a tin and bury it in a pit I have digged in the shrubbery, against a rainy day; but the shop is shut. Why? It isn't Wednesday. And the next day. And the next. Since my visits are illicit, it is awkward to inquire. When the shop reopens, there is no Dora but someone quite different behind the counter. Next time I accompany my father to buy his evening paper I remark to him that Dora seems to have gone away. He agrees in a voice that gives me a foreboding pang. Subsequently comes yet another of the times when a school friend draws me aside and asks me if I can keep a secret. The secret is that Dora is dead; she has been murdered. She went out one evening with her True Love, and in the field where the old brick-kilns stand he cut her throat.

Her True Love . . . ??? [3]

Immediacy in Narration

As pointed out earlier, narration enables the writer to do more than talk about his subject. Through a well-chosen illustration, ranging in length from a paragraph, or even a few lines, to a full-length factual narrative, the writer can *embody* his points in a dramatic presentation which, in many cases, is far more meaningful and memorable than simple analysis. For this is what "sticks" in a reader's mind: the concrete living example, the *story*, rather than the discussion. Thus narrative is important and engaging not only in and of and for itself—to tell us how X happened—but also as an aid and adjunct to other kinds of writing.

In the following essay, for example, George Orwell is able to say more about the inhumanity of capital punishment by presenting his point in a brief narrative account than he might have said in a long treatise on the subject. Similarly, the essay indicts the dehumanizing effect of colonialism on the colonizers as well as the subjugated colonials, an effect that finds devastating expression in the irritable complaint of the supervising army doctor who is anxious to "get on" with the execution (then to breakfast). "For God's sake," he says to his lackey, "the man ought to have been dead by this time."

A HANGING

GEORGE ORWELL

It was in Burma, a sodden morning of the rains. A sickly light, like yellow tinfoil, was slanting over the high walls into the jail yard. We were waiting

[3] From *The Swan in the Evening*, © 1967, by Rosamund Lehmann. Reprinted by permission of Harcourt Brace Jovanovich, Inc., Rosamund Lehmann, and The Society of Authors.

outside the condemned cells, a row of sheds fronted with double bars, like small animal cages. Each cell measured about ten feet by ten and was quite bare within except for a plank bed and a pot for drinking water. In some of them brown silent men were squatting at the inner bars, with their blankets draped round them. These were the condemned men, due to be hanged within the next week or two.

One prisoner had been brought out of his cell. He was a Hindu, a puny wisp of a man, with a shaven head and vague liquid eyes. He had a thick, sprouting moustache, absurdly too big for his body, rather like the moustache of a comic man on the films. Six tall Indian warders were guarding him and getting him ready for the gallows. Two of them stood by with rifles and fixed bayonets, while the others handcuffed him, passed a chain through his handcuffs and fixed it to their belts, and lashed his arms tight to his sides. They crowded very close about him, with their hands always on him in a careful, caressing grip, as though all the while feeling him to make sure he was there. It was like men handling a fish which is still alive and may jump back into the water. But he stood quite unresisting, yielding his arms limply to the ropes, as though he hardly noticed what was happening.

Eight o'clock and a bugle call, desolately thin in the wet air, floated from the distant barracks. The superintendent of the jail, who was standing apart from the rest of us, moodily prodding the gravel with his stick, raised his head at the sound. He was an army doctor, with a grey toothbrush moustache and a gruff voice. "For God's sake hurry up, Francis," he said irritably. "The man ought to have been dead by this time. Aren't you ready yet?"

Francis, the head jailer, a fat Dravidian in a white drill suit and gold spectacles, waved his black hand. "Yes sir, yes sir," he bubbled. "All iss satisfactorily prepared. The hangman iss waiting. We shall proceed."

"Well, quick march, then. The prisoners can't get their breakfast till this job's over."

We set out for the gallows. Two warders marched on either side of the prisoner, with their rifles at the slope; two others marched close against him, gripping him by arm and shoulder, as though at once pushing and supporting him. The rest of us, magistrates and the like, followed behind. Suddenly, when we had gone ten yards, the procession stopped short without any order or warning. A dreadful thing had happened—a dog, come goodness knows whence, had appeared in the yard. It came bounding among us with a loud volley of barks, and leapt round us wagging its whole body, wild with glee at finding so many human beings together. It was a large woolly dog, half Airedale, half pariah. For a moment it pranced round us, and then, before anyone could stop it, it had made a dash for the prisoner and, jumping up, tried to lick his face. Everyone stood aghast, too taken aback even to grab at the dog.

"Who let the bloody brute in here?" said the superintendent angrily. "Catch it, someone!"

A warder, detached from the escort, charged clumsily after the dog, but it danced and gambolled just out of his reach, taking everything as part of the game. A young Eurasian jailer picked up a handful of gravel and tried to stone the dog away, but it dodged the stones and came after us again. Its yaps echoed from the jail walls. The prisoner, in the grasp of the two warders, looked on incuriously, as though this was another formality of the hanging. It was several minutes before someone managed to catch the dog.

Then we put my handkerchief through its collar and moved off once more, with the dog still straining and whimpering.

It was about forty yards to the gallows. I watched the bare brown back of the prisoner marching in front of me. He walked clumsily with his bound arms, but quite steadily, with that bobbing gait of the Indian who never straightens his knees. At each step his muscles slid neatly into place, the lock of hair on his scalp danced up and down, his feet printed themselves on the wet gravel. And once, in spite of the men who gripped him by each shoulder, he stepped slightly aside to avoid a puddle on the path.

It is curious, but till that moment I had never realized what it meant to destroy a healthy, conscious man. When I saw the prisoner step aside to avoid the puddle I saw the mystery, the unspeakable wrongness of cutting a life short when it is in full tide. This man was not dying, he was alive just as we are alive. All the organs of his body were working—bowels digesting food, skin renewing itself, nails growing, tissues forming—all toiling away in solemn foolery. His nails would still be growing when he stood on the drop, when he was falling through the air with a tenth-of-a-second to live. His eyes saw the yellow gravel and the grey walls, and his brain still remembered, foresaw, reasoned—reasoned even about puddles. He and we were a party of men walking together, seeing, feeling, understanding the same world; and in two minutes, with a sudden snap, one of us would be gone—one mind less, one world less.

The gallows stood in a small yard, separate from the main grounds of the prison, and overgrown with tall prickly weeds. It was a brick erection like three sides of a shed, with planking on top, and above that two beams and a crossbar with the rope dangling. The hangman, a grey-haired convict in the white uniform of the prison, was waiting beside his machine. He greeted us with a servile crouch as we entered. At a word from Francis the two warders, gripping the prisoner more closely than ever, half led half pushed him to the gallows and helped him clumsily up the ladder. Then the hangman climbed up and fixed the rope around the prisoner's neck.

We stood waiting, five yards away. The warders had formed in a rough circle round the gallows. And then, when the noose was fixed, the prisoner began crying out to his god. It was a high, reiterated cry of "Ram! Ram! Ram! Ram!" not urgent and fearful like a prayer or cry for help, but steady, rhythmical, almost like the tolling of a bell. The dog answered the sound with a whine. The hangman, still standing on the gallows, produced a small cotton bag like a flour bag and drew it down over the prisoner's face. But the sound, muffled by the cloth, still persisted, over and over again: "Ram! Ram! Ram! Ram! Ram!"

The hangman climbed down and stood ready, holding the lever. Minutes seemed to pass. The steady, muffled crying from the prisoner went on and on, "Ram! Ram! Ram!" never faltering for an instant. The superintendent, his head on his chest, was slowly poking the ground with his stick; perhaps he was counting the cries, allowing the prisoner a fixed number—fifty, perhaps, or a hundred. Everyone had changed color. The Indians had gone grey like bad coffee, and one or two of the bayonets were wavering. We looked at the lashed, hooded man on the drop, and listened to his cries—each cry another second of life; the same thought was in all our minds: oh, kill him quickly, get it over, stop that abominable noise!

Suddenly the superintendent made up his mind. Throwing up his head he made a swift motion with his stick. "Chalo!" he shouted almost fiercely.

There was a clanking noise, and then dead silence. The prisoner had vanished, and the rope was twisting on itself. I let go of the dog, and it galloped immediately to the back of the gallows; but when it got there it stopped short, barked, and then retreated into a corner of the yard, where it stood among the weeds, looking timorously out at us. We went round the gallows to inspect the prisoner's body. He was dangling with his toes pointed straight downwards, very slowly revolving, as dead as a stone.

The superintendent reached out with his stick and poked the bare brown body; it oscillated slightly. "*He's* all right," said the superintendent. He backed out from under the gallows, and blew out a deep breath. The moody look had gone out of his face quite suddenly. He glanced at his wrist-watch. "Eight minutes past eight. Well, that's all for this morning, thank God."

The warders unfixed bayonets and marched away. The dog, sobered and conscious of having misbehaved itself, slipped after them. We walked out of the gallows yard, past the condemned cells with their waiting prisoners, into the big central yard of the prison. The convicts, under the command of warders armed with lathis, were already receiving their breakfast. They squatted in long rows, each man holding a tin panikin, while two warders with buckets marched round ladling out rice; it seemed quite a homely, jolly scene, after the hanging. An enormous relief had come upon us now that the job was done. One felt an impulse to sing, to break into a run, to snigger. All at once everyone began chattering gaily.

The Eurasian boy walking beside me nodded toward the way we had come, with a knowing smile: "Do you know, sir, our friend [he meant the dead man] when he heard his appeal had been dismissed, he pissed on the floor of his cell. From fright. Kindly take one of my cigarettes, sir. Do you not admire my new silver case, sir? From the boxwalah, two rupees eight annas. Classy European style."

Several people laughed—at what, nobody seemed certain.

Francis was walking by the superintendent, talking garrulously: "Well, sir, all hass passed off with the utmost satisfactoriness. It was all finished—flick! like that. It iss not always so—oah, no! I have known cases where the doctor wass obliged to go beneath the gallows and pull the prissoner's legs to ensure decease. Most disagreeable!"

"Wriggling about, eh? That's bad," said the superintendent.

"Ach, sir, it iss worse when they become refractory! One man, I recall, clung to the bars of hiss cage when we went to take him out. You will scarcely credit, sir, that it took six warders to dislodge him, three pulling at each leg. We reasoned with him. 'My dear fellow,' we said, 'think of all the pain and trouble you are causing to us!' But no, he would not listen! Ach, he wass very troublesome!"

I found that I was laughing quite loudly. Everyone was laughing. Even the superintendent grinned in a tolerant way. "You'd better all come out and have a drink," he said quite genially. "I've got a bottle of whisky in the car. We could do with it."

We went through the big double gates of the prison into the road. "Pulling at his legs!" exclaimed a Burmese magistrate suddenly, and burst into a loud chuckling. We all began laughing again. At that moment Francis' anecdote seemed extraordinarily funny. We all had a drink together, native and European alike, quite amicably. The dead man was a hundred yards away.[4]

Historical Narration

All historical accounts are, in a sense, answers to the question "How did it happen?" But only some historical accounts can be called "narrative," for only some writers present history not merely as a record of the past (wars, treaties, dates) but as an unfolding drama, a direct presentation of human experience. One master of historical narrative was Winston Churchill, whose four-volume *A History of the English-Speaking Peoples* moves with novellike rapidity across the centuries, to describe the sweep and flow of events that shaped the English nation.

In the first volume, Churchill describes the Battle of Hastings (1066), in a passage reprinted below. He brings this military action—the climax of William the Conqueror's invasion—to life through the steady accumulation of concrete details that dramatize the butchery of battle; the slyness of William's feigned retreat; the terrible bloodiness of Harold's defeat; the pathos of his death—as his naked body is "wrapped only in a robe of purple," and as his grief-stricken mother pleads in vain for permission to bury her son in holy ground. Note also a masterful touch: Churchill opens the battle scene by focusing (as in a movie close-up) on the fate of one man—Ivan Taillefer, "the minstrel knight who had claimed the right to make the first attack." With the "astonished English," we watch this impetuous adventurer fling his sword into the air and catch it again with all the jauntiness of a juggler performing before a wide-eyed audience. As he charges into the English ranks, he is immediately slain. Thus, in a five-line vignette, Churchill creates an unforgettable paradigm of human pride and futility.

IN THE BATTLE OF HASTINGS

WINSTON CHURCHILL

At the first streak of dawn William set out from his camp at Pevensey, resolved to put all to the test; and Harold the Saxon King, eight miles away, awaited him in resolute array.

As the battle began Ivan Taillefer, the minstrel knight who had claimed the right to make the first attack, advanced up the hill on horseback, throwing his lance and sword into the air and catching them before the astonished English. He then charged deep into the English ranks, and was slain. The cavalry charges of William's mail-clad knights, cumbersome in manoeuvre, beat in vain upon the dense, ordered masses of the English. Neither the arrow hail nor the assaults of the horsemen could prevail against them. William's left wing of cavalry was thrown into disorder, and retreated rapidly down the

[4] From *Shooting an Elephant and Other Essays* by George Orwell, copyright 1945, 1946, 1949, 1950 by Sonia Brownell Orwell. Reprinted by permission of Harcourt Brace Jovanovich, Inc. Also reprinted by permission of A. M. Heath.

hill. On this the troops on Harold's right, who were mainly the local "fyrd," broke their ranks in eager pursuit. William, in the centre, turned his disciplined squadrons upon them and cut them to pieces. The Normans then reformed their ranks and began a second series of charges upon the English masses, subjecting them in the intervals to severe archery. It has often been remarked that this part of the action resembles the afternoon at Waterloo, when Ney's cavalry exhausted themselves upon the British squares, torn by artillery in the intervals. In both cases the tortured infantry stood unbroken. Never, it was said, had the Norman knights met foot-soldiers of this stubbornness. They were utterly unable to break through the shield-walls, and they suffered serious losses from deft blows of the axe-men, or from javelins, or clubs hurled from the ranks behind. But the arrow showers took a cruel toll. So closely were the English wedged that the wounded could not be removed, and the dead scarcely found room in which to sink upon the ground.

The autumn afternoon was far spent before any result had been achieved, and it was then that William adopted the time-honoured ruse of a feigned retreat. He had seen how readily Harold's right had quitted their positions in pursuit after the first repulse of the Normans. He now organised a sham retreat in apparent disorder, while keeping a powerful force in his own hands.

The house-carls around Harold preserved their discipline and kept their ranks, but the sense of relief to the less trained forces after these hours of combat was such that seeing their enemy in flight proved irresistible. They surged forward on the impulse of victory, and when half-way down the hill were savagely slaughtered by William's horsemen. There remained, as the dusk grew, only the valiant bodyguard who fought round the King and his standard. His brothers, Gyrth and Leofwine, had already been killed. William now directed his archers to shoot high into the air, so that the arrows would fall behind the shield-wall, and one of these pierced Harold in the right eye, inflicting a mortal wound. He fell at the foot of the royal standard, unconquerable except by death, which does not count in honour. The hard-fought battle was now decided. The last formed body of troops was broken, though by no means overwhelmed. They withdrew into the woods behind, and William, who had fought in the foremost ranks and had three horses killed under him, could claim the victory. Nevertheless the pursuit was heavily checked. There is a sudden deep ditch on the reverse slope of the hill of Hastings, into which large numbers of Norman horsemen fell, and in which they were butchered by the infuriated English lurking in the wood.

The dead king's naked body, wrapped only in a robe of purple, was hidden among the rocks of the bay. His mother in vain offered the weight of the body in gold for permission to bury him in holy ground. The Norman Duke's answer was that Harold would be more fittingly laid upon the Saxon shore which he had given his life to defend. The body was later transferred to Waltham Abbey, which he had founded. Although here the English once again accepted conquest and bowed in a new destiny, yet ever must the name of Harold be honoured in the Island for which he and his famous house-carls fought indomitably to the end.[5]

[5] From *A History of the English-Speaking Peoples: The Birth of Britain* by Sir Winston Churchill. Reprinted by permission of Dodd, Mead & Company, Inc. and The Canadian Publishers, McClelland and Stewart Limited, Toronto.

The Diary as Narration

Of the several types of narrative essay—personal, reportorial, biographical, and historical—the personal is probably the most common and popular. Certainly it is the most intimate, for in it the writer talks directly to his readers of his own experiences. Especially intimate is the "journal" or "diary" which is sometimes written to be read by others (for publication after the author's death in some cases) and sometimes "just written" with no audience in mind.

Clearly it was chance that brought to light the diary of Carolina Maria De Jesus, a short section of which is reprinted below. This is one of the strangest diaries ever written, for Carolina originally set down her words on scraps of paper and litter picked up in the gutters and garbage pails of a Brazilian *favela* (slum). In the diary she tells how she lives with her three children (each born of a different father), trying day-by-day to scrape together enough food to keep the family alive. One of the most compelling documents of human poverty ever published, it was written by a woman with only two years of schooling.

THE DIARY OF CAROLINA MARIA DE JESUS

May 2, 1958 I'm not lazy. There are times when I try to keep up my diary. But then I think it's not worth it and figure I'm wasting my time.

I've made a promise to myself. I want to treat people that I know with more consideration. I want to have a pleasant smile for children and the employed.

I received a summons to appear at 8 P.M. at police station number 12. I spent the day looking for paper. At night my feet pained me so I couldn't walk. It started to rain. I went to the station and took José Carlos with me. The summons was for him. José Carlos is nine years old.

May 3 I went to the market at Carlos de Campos Street looking for any old thing. I got a lot of greens. But it didn't help much, for I've got no cooking fat. The children are upset because there's nothing to eat.

May 6 In the morning I went for water. I made João carry it. I was happy, then I received another summons. I was inspired yesterday and my verses were so pretty, I forgot to go to the station. It was 11:00 when I remembered the invitation from the illustrious lieutenant of the 12th precinct.

My advice to would-be politicians is that people do not tolerate hunger. It's necessary to know hunger to know how to describe it.

They are putting up a circus here at Araguaia Street. The Nilo Circus Theater.

May 9 I looked for paper but I didn't like it. Then I thought: I'll pretend that I'm dreaming.

May 10 I went to the police station and talked to the lieutenant. What a pleasant man! If I had known he was going to be so pleasant, I'd have gone on the first summons. The lieutenant was interested in my boys' education. He said the favelas have an unhealthy atmosphere where the people have more chance to go wrong than to become useful to state and country. I thought: if he knows this why doesn't he make a report and send it to the politicians? To Janio Quadros, Kubitschek,* and Dr. Adhemar de Barros? Now he tells me this, I a poor garbage collector. I can't even solve my own problems.

Brazil needs to be led by a person who has known hunger. Hunger is also a teacher.

Who has gone hungry learns to think of the future and of the children.

May 11 Today is Mother's Day. The sky is blue and white. It seems that even nature wants to pay homage to the mothers who feel unhappy because they can't realize the desires of their children.

The sun keeps climbing. Today it's not going to rain. Today is our day.

Dona Teresinha came to visit me. She gave me 15 cruzeiros and said it was for Vera to go to the circus. But I'm going to use the money to buy bread tomorrow because I only have four cruzeiros.

Yesterday I got half a pig's head at the slaughterhouse. We ate the meat and saved the bones. Today I put the bones on to boil and into the broth I put some potatoes. My children are always hungry. When they are starving they aren't so fussy about what they eat.

Night came. The stars are hidden. The shack is filled with mosquitoes. I lit a page from a newspaper and ran it over the walls. This is the way the favela dwellers kill mosquitoes.

May 13 At dawn it was raining. Today is a nice day for me, it's the anniversary of the Abolition. The day we celebrate the freeing of the slaves. In the jails the Negroes were the scapegoats. But now the whites are more educated and don't treat us any more with contempt. May God enlighten the whites so that the Negroes may have a happier life.

It continued to rain and I only have beans and salt. The rain is strong but even so I sent the boys to school. I'm writing until the rain goes away so I can go to Senhor Manuel and sell scrap. With that money I'm going to buy rice and sausage. The rain has stopped for a while. I'm going out.

I feel so sorry for my children. When they see the things to eat that I come home with they shout:

"Viva Mama!"

Their outbursts please me. But I've lost the habit of smiling. Ten minutes later they want more food. I sent João to ask Dona Ida for a little pork fat. She didn't have any. I sent her a note:

"Dona Ida, I beg you to help me get a little pork fat, so I can make soup for the children. Today it's raining and I can't go looking for paper. Thank you, Carolina."

It rained and got colder. Winter had arrived and in winter people eat more. Vera asked for food, and I didn't have any. It was the same old show. I had two cruzeiros and wanted buy a little flour to make a virado.** I went to ask Dona Alice for a little pork. She gave me pork and rice. It was 9 at night when we ate.

And that is the way on May 13, 1958 I fought against the real slavery—hunger! [6]

* President of Brazil from 1956 to 1961.

** A dish of black beans, manioc flour, pork, and eggs.

[6] From *Child of the Dark: The Diary of Carolina Maria De Jesus* translated by David St. Clair. Copyright, ©, 1962 by E. P. Dutton & Co., Inc. and Souvenir Press, Ltd. Reprinted by permission of the publishers. (Published in England as *Beyond All Pity.*)

How Carolina's diary was discovered and brought to publication, and what happened to Carolina as a result, constitutes a story in itself, part of which is reprinted below.

THE STORY OF CAROLINA MARIA DE JESUS

DAVID ST. CLAIR

In April of 1958, Audalio Dantas, a young reporter, was covering the inauguration of a playground near Caninde for his newspaper. When the politicians had made their speeches and gone away, the grown men of the favela began fighting with the children for a place on the teeter-totters and swings. Carolina, standing in the crowd, shouted furiously: "If you continue mistreating these children, I'm going to put all your names in my book!"

Interested, the reporter asked the tall black woman about her book. At first she didn't want to talk to him, but slowly he won her confidence and she took him to her shack. There is the bottom drawer of a dilapidated dresser she pulled out her cherished notebooks. . . .

. . . Published, her diary became the literary sensation of Brazil. Over a thousand people swamped the bookshop on the first day of sales. . . . Carolina signed 600 copies that afternoon, and would have done more if she hadn't stopped to talk to each of the buyers. She asked what their names were, where they lived, and if they were happy. When a state senator appeared with flash bulbs popping, Carolina wrote in his book: "I hope that you give the poor people what they need and stop putting all the tax money into your own pocket. Sincerely, Carolina Maria De Jesus."

Never had a book such an impact on Brazil. In three days the first printing of 10,000 copies was sold out in São Paulo alone. In less than six months 90,000 copies were sold in Brazil and today it is still on the best-seller list, having sold more than any other Brazilian book in history.

Carolina was invited to speak about the favela problem on radio and television, and she gave lectures on the problem in Brazilian universities. Her book has become required reading in sociology classes and the São Paulo Law University has given her the title of "Honorary Member," the first such person so honored who has not had a university education. The title was originally slated for Jean Paul Sartre, but the students decided that Carolina was "far worthier in the fight for freedom" than the French philosopher.[7]

ASSIGNMENTS

I. A. Evaluate Dick Gregory's "Not Poor, Just Broke" in terms of the following:

1. Why does Gregory use this title? Does "Broke" have more than one meaning here?
2. How do the two opening sentences function in the story?
3. Are the characters convincingly drawn? Cite specific details.

[7] From *Child of the Dark: The Diary of Carolina Maria De Jesus* translated by David St. Clair. Copyright, ©, 1962 by E. P. Dutton & Co., Inc. and Souvenir Press, Ltd. Reprinted by permission of the publishers. (Published in England as *Beyond All Pity.*)

4. Outline the "plot." What is the central conflict? What additional conflicts are implied in the story?
5. How does the writer establish and maintain an element of suspense?
6. How does paragraph three function? What rhetorical device unifies the second sentence? What rhetorical purpose does it serve?
7. List descriptive details that seem to you especially well-selected and evocative in helping you to see, hear, feel, and understand what is going on.
8. Does the crucial event or climax of the story have sufficient impact? Explain.
9. Where and how does the mood of the story change? Is there a reversal?

B. Write a narrative essay (850–1,200 words) in which you describe how some dimension of feeling or understanding entered your life—as in Dick Gregory's "Not Poor, Just Broke." Make certain your description is cast within the frame of a *story* in which there is a specific setting, characters (let them speak in normal, natural tones), and action. You may wish to follow the general structure of Gregory's essay:

Introduction
Background situation described (conflict)
Crucial incident (climax)
Long-term effect (resolution)

Be sure to choose an appropriate tone for your narrative.

II. A. An interesting companion piece to Kazantzakis' "A Night in a Calabrian Village," is John Steinbeck's "A Night in a Maine Motel." It is taken from *Travels With Charley*, an account of Steinbeck's cross-country tour "in search of America." Like Kazantzakis, Steinbeck is "on the road" when we meet him, in need of shelter for the night.

A NIGHT IN A MAINE MOTEL

JOHN STEINBECK

Not far outside of Bangor I stopped at an auto court and rented a room. It wasn't expensive. The sign said "Greatly Reduced Winter Rates." It was immaculate; everything was done in plastics—the floors, the curtain, table tops of stainless burnless plastic, lamp shades of plastic. Only the bedding and the towels were of natural material. I went to the small restaurant run in conjunction. It was all plastic too—the table linen, the butter dish. The sugar and crackers were wrapped in cellophane, the jelly in a small plastic coffin sealed with cellophane. It was early evening and I was the only customer. Even the waitress wore a sponge-off apron. She wasn't happy, but then she wasn't unhappy. She wasn't anything. But I don't believe anyone is a nothing. There has to be something inside, if only to keep the skin from collapsing. This vacant eye, listless hand, this damask cheek dusted like a doughnut with plastic powder, had to have a memory or a dream.

On a chance I asked, "How soon you going to Florida?"

"Nex' week," she said listlessly. Then something stirred in that aching void. "Say, how do you know I'm going?"

"Read your mind, I guess."

She looked at my beard. "You with a show?"

"No."

"Then how do you mean read my mind?"

"Maybe I guessed. Like it down there?"

"Oh, sure! I go every year. Lots of waitress jobs in the winter."

"What do you do down there, I mean for fun?"

"Oh, nothing. Just fool around."

"Do you fish or swim?"

"Not much. I just fool around. I don't like that sand, makes me itch."

"Make good money?"

"It's a cheap crowd."

"Cheap?"

"They rather spen' it on booze."

"Than what?"

"Than tips just the same here with the summer."

Strange how one person can saturate a room with vitality, with excitement. Then there are others, and this dame was one of them, who can drain off energy and joy, can suck pleasure dry and get no sustenance from it. Such people spread a grayness in the air about them. I'd been driving a long time, and perhaps my energy was low and my resistance down. She got me. I felt so blue and miserable I wanted to crawl into a plastic cover and die. What a date she must be, what a lover! I tried to imagine that last and couldn't. For a moment I considered giving her a five-dollar tip, but I knew what would happen. She wouldn't be glad. She'd just think I was crazy.

I went back to my clean little room. I don't ever drink alone. It's not much fun. And I don't think I will until I am an alcoholic. But this night I got a bottle of vodka from my stores and took it to my cell. In the bathroom two water tumblers were sealed in cellophane sacks with the words: "These glasses are sterilized for your protection." Across the toilet seat a strip of paper bore the message: "This seat has been sterilized with ultraviolet light for your protection." Everyone was protecting me and it was horrible. I tore the glasses from their covers. I violated the toilet-seat seal with my foot. I poured half a tumbler of vodka and drank it and then another. Then I lay deep in hot water in the tub and I was utterly miserable, and nothing was good anywhere.[8]

Compare the two essays on the basis of the following:

1. point of view (voice, tone, rhetorical stance)
2. setting (locale, atmosphere)
3. characters (compare their respective moods at the beginning and end of the narrative)
4. action (sequence and development of events, climax)
5. theme (suggestions about human nature, economic values, and the impact of chance encounters)
6. style (sentence structure, choice of words, images)

B. Write an essay (750–1,000 words) in which you tell the story of your encounter with another person, describing how you were affected, for either good or ill.

[8] From *Travels With Charley in Search of America* by John Steinbeck. Copyright © 1961, 1962 by The Curtis Publishing Co., Inc. Copyright © 1962 by John Steinbeck. Reprinted by permission of the Viking Press, Inc.

III. In 250–300 words rewrite the story of "The Girl in the Tobacconist Shop" as it might have been written from the point of view of one of the following:

the narrator's father
the owner of the tobacconist shop
the girl's "True Love"

IV. A. Show how the following images from "A Hanging" contribute to the total effect and thesis of the piece:

1. A "sickly light" slants into the jail yard.
2. The prisoner is held as if he were "a fish which is still alive and may jump back into the water."
3. ". . . a bugle call, desolately thin in the wet air, floated from the distant barracks."
4. The dog ("half Airedale, half pariah") licks the prisoner's face.
5. The prisoner cries "Ram! Ram! Ram! Ram!"
6. The superintendent examines the body and says, "*He's* all right."
7. ". . . everyone began chattering gaily."

B. Why do you suppose George Orwell does not indicate what crime the prisoner committed? Is it important?

C. How effective is the one paragraph of explicit protest against capital punishment? Explain its rightness or wrongness in the middle of the narrative. Does it contribute to the horror of what is happening?

D. What mood do you feel upon reading of the laughing and drinking that follow the hanging? Explain.

E. Write a dramatization (500–750 words) of an event you have witnessed, in which you suggest rather than explicitly state your judgment of its meaning and moral significance.

V. Write a narrative essay (750–1,000 words) in which you describe a historical event using the panoramic point of view as Winston Churchill does in "The Battle of Hastings." He sweeps across the battlefield, moving from one event to another, closing in briefly here and there for a close-up, then moving on again.

A. Historic Incident:

Boston Tea Party
Chicago Fire
the signing of the Declaration of Independence
Pocahontas saves John Smith (fact and fiction)
"Star-Spangled Banner" is composed
man walks on the moon
Charlemagne is crowned emperor of the Holy Roman Empire
Napoleon dies
Balboa views the Pacific Ocean
Fulton takes his steamboat up the Hudson
the Wright brothers fly at Kitty Hawk

B. Battles

Gettysburg
Bull Run
Shiloh

Crécy
Poitiers
Waterloo
Bunker Hill
Thermopylae
Dunkirk

VI. A. Consider the diary of Carolina Maria De Jesus.

1. List the reasons why you think Carolina's diary became a best-seller. ("Never had a book such an impact on Brazil.") Do you think its relevance extends beyond Brazil? Explain.
2. In what ways would a formal tract against poverty be more or less effective?
3. What aspects of Carolina's style suggest a "natural" rather than a trained writer? Evaluate the effectiveness of her writing.
4. Comment on the personality, character, and attitudes of Carolina. Is she bitter, resigned, hopeful?
5. What qualities contribute to making this a "touchingly beautiful" document (as one critic has called it)?

B. Write an entry or a series of entries in a diary (750–1,000 words), describing in narrative fashion your activities (and/or state of mind) over the period of a week.

15 WHAT KIND OF PERSON IS X?

Many artists can create the "sense" of a person by simply setting down on their sketch pads a few swift, well-placed lines, thereby pictorially answering the question, "What kind of person is X?" So it is with the writer. By concentrating on a few well-selected, representative characteristics of his subject (a few broad brush strokes), he gives a character sketch, a word-picture, of what that person essentially is—or what he is from the writer's point of view.

To write of a person so that the reader can "see him live, and 'live o'er each scene with him, as he actually advanced through the several stages of his life' ": this is Boswell's definition of biography. Clearly, the essayist cannot do as much, although he must obviously try to bring his subject to life on the pages. The character essay can merely point to the thread that runs through a life and that thereby defines it, or to the single quality that seems to sum it up—what Mary McCarthy calls (in reference to her fictional characters) the "key" that turns the lock.

Writing a character study is, then, another form of analysis, for it involves breaking down an individual personality into its component parts in order to discover its motivating forces. Thus the writer draws upon those questions we have considered that deal with analysis—for example, question 2, "How can X be described?" or question 3, "What are the component parts of X?"

A Member of the Family

The following three essays deal with uncles. In each the writer tries to sum up his uncle in terms of one dominant characteristic; one is the classic "average" man; another is a fiery Horatio Alger-like immigrant; the third is a smug, mean-spirited bully. Note that in their essays all three writers blend description and narration in varying proportions: the first essay is almost totally descriptive; the third is cast within a narrative frame; and the second draws on both modes.

MY AVERAGE UNCLE

ROBERT P. TRISTRAM COFFIN

He stood out splendidly above all my uncles because he did not stand out at all. That was his distinction. He was the averagest man I ever knew.

You would never pick him out in a crowd. He became just another man the minute he was in one. So many more pounds of man. Good solid pounds, but just pounds. You would never remember his hair or his chin, or the shape of his ears. If he said something, you would agree with it, and, an hour later, you would be sure you had said it yourself.

Sometimes I think men like that get along about the best. They are the easiest on their houses, their wives, and their children. They are easiest on the world. They slide along without having to do anything about it as small boys do on their breeches after they have slid on them enough to wear them down smooth. The world is all so much pine needles under them.

Uncle Amos was easy on his wives and children. He had three of them, in all. Wives, I mean. I never did get the count of his children straight, there were too many assortments of them. Three wives. It seemed surprising to me at the time. With all the trouble I had, myself, having to stand on my head and work my legs, or bung stones at cherrybirds, to keep the attention of just one girl for a month, I often wondered how Uncle Amos, who never stood on his head or whittled out even a butterpat, could attract so many women as he did. With hair a little thin on his head, and legs that could not possibly do more than three and a half miles an hour on the road, there he was, with three families behind him. Of course, he had the families spaced. The wives of Uncle Amos did not come all at once. They were drawn out. One batch of children grew pretty well up by the time the next batch hove in sight, waddling and falling on their faces—to save their hands—as waddling children do.

I knew my *Bible,* especially the marital parts, in which I took deep interest. I had read the *Bible* through many times under the eye of one particular aunt. I knew a lot about matrimony from that. But Uncle Amos had me puzzled. He had broken no commandments. All his marriages were open and aboveboard. He wasn't like the patriarchs who didn't always wait for one wife to go before another came. Yet Uncle Amos's status and his children's status were rather complicated.

The women must have been drawn to him because he was so much like what an average fair husband would seem to a woman to be.

This man made no flourishes to attract anybody. He never drove a fast horse. He never wore trousers with checks any larger than an inch square—which, for the time, was conservative. His house never got afire and burned down just after the fire insurance had run out. Not one of his boys and girls ever got drowned or run over by the steam-cars. The few that died growing up died of diphtheria or scarlet fever, which were what children died of then, the usual ways.

Uncle Amos never had a fight.

Uncle Amos never lost a pocket-book. At least not one with much money in it.

Uncle Amos never went even as far as Boston.

But there he was, never making much money, but with all the comforts of home around him, eating his stewed eels, sitting in his galluses out in the orchard in the cool of the evening, with a plump baby to climb up in his lap, whenever he felt like having a baby on his lap and had his old trousers on and didn't care much what happened to him. There he was, shingling his house only when it got to leaking so it put the kitchen fire out. Drinking a little ale now and then, when he came by it easy. No big hayfields to worry about. No wife that craved more than one new dress a year, and that one she generally ran up herself on her sewing machine. One best pair of trousers to his name, which the moths got into, but not so deep but what they could be healed up with a needle. Not many books to excite him and keep him awake nights, or put ideas into his head and make him uneasy. No itch ever spreading out upon him to go out and take the world by its horns. There he was, in clover!

Amos was a Republican. But then, most everybody around was. It was an average condition. Uncle Amos didn't have much to do except carry a torchlight when the Republican Presidents got elected, as they did regularly. And if Uncle Amos got grease on him, it never was very much grease, and his current wife took it out of him with her hot iron. Politics passed him by. Great events passed him by. And big taxes.

But we nephews did not pass him by. We were strangely drawn to him. Especially when some of our specialist uncles wore us down with their crankiness and difference. I spent some of the quietest Sundays of my life in Uncle Amos's yard, lying under apple trees and listening to bees and not listening to Uncle Amos who was bumbling away at something he did not expect me to listen to at all. And caterpillars came suddenly down on fine wires shining like gold, and hit Uncle Amos on his bald spot, and he brushed them off and went on bumbling. The heat was a burden, and the apple blossoms fell to pieces and drifted down on me, and I could see the roof of the world over the black twigs they came from. These were my solidest hours of pure being. I did not have to do anything to live up to this quiet, friendly man. He did not expect me to stand on my head and show off, or go after his pipe, or keep the flies from lighting on his bald spot. And he always had lemon drops somewhere deep in his roomy pockets, fore or aft, and he liked to give them to me.

The only trouble Uncle Amos had in his life was after he had got through with it. When they came to bury him, they could not fix it so he could lie next to all his three women. He had liked them all equally well. But there was not enough of Uncle Amos to go round. So they put him on the end of the row.

Uncle Amos did not mind, I am sure. I am sure he sleeps average well.[1]

[1] Reprinted with permission of The Macmillan Company from *Book of Uncles* by Robert P. Tristram Coffin. Copyright 1942 by The Macmillan Company, renewed 1970 by Margaret Coffin Halvosa.

MY UNCLE KOPPEL AND FREE ENTERPRISE

HARRY GOLDEN

My uncle Koppel (K. Berger) was twenty years old when he came to America. The day after his arrival he opened a small butcher shop on Scammel Street, on New York's Lower East Side. For the next three years he opened up his shop at six o'clock in the morning, worked till after dark, cooked his meals on a stove in the back of the store, and pushed the meat block up against the front door to sleep. What English he learned he picked up from the truck drivers, who delivered the meat and the poultry. There was nothing unusual about this. There were thousands of immigrants who lived, worked, and died within the confines of a few city blocks. But with Koppel Berger it was to be different, because Uncle Koppel had imagination, courage, ability, and, above all, he seemed to know what America was all about.

It was 1904 and all America was singing, "Meet me in St. Louey, Louey, meet me at the Fair . . ." and my immigrant Uncle took the lyrics literally. He arrived in St. Louis, Missouri, with five hundred dollars, a wife, and a vocabulary of about thirty words of broken English. He acquired a lease on a rooming house, which accommodated thirty guests. Again he worked night and day. His wife did the laundry, cleaned the rooms, and made the beds; Uncle Koppel carried the baggage, roomed the guests, kept the accounts, carried the coal, made the hot water, and told his guests that he was an employee so that he could also run all their errands. The St. Louis Fair was a success, and so was Koppel Berger. After two years, he and his wife and infant son returned to New York with a little over eight thousand dollars.

Up on Broadway at 38th Street was the old Hotel Normandie, which was not doing so well under the management of the great prize fighter, the original Kid McCoy (Norman Selby).

With a vocabulary of about seventy-five words of broken English, Uncle Koppel took over the lease on this 250-room hotel in the heart of the theatrical district. Of course, even a genius must have some luck, too, and we must concede that Koppel Berger acquired the Hotel Normandie at exactly the right moment. New York and America were becoming "hotel-minded"; in addition, the theatre was entering upon its greatest era, a "golden age" such as we shall never see again. Between 1907 and 1927, there were literally hundreds and hundreds of road shows and stock companies; burlesque was in all its glory; dozens of opera "extravaganzas" were playing all over the country; vaudeville was at its all-time peak; and on Broadway itself, there were at least one hundred and fifty attractions produced each year.

In those days, "actors" and "actresses" were not particularly welcome at the best hotels. In fact, many New Yorkers will remember the signs on some small hotels and rooming houses, "Actors Accommodated."

In various stages of their careers, Uncle Koppel's Hotel Normandie was "home" to such players as Nat Wills, Wilton Lackaye, Cissie Loftus, Grant Mitchell, Lionel and John Barrymore, Otto Kruger, Doc Rockwell, W. C. Fields, Julian Eltinge, Tully Marshall, Tyrone Power, Sr., Dustin Farnum, Marie Cahill, and, of course, hundreds of lesser-known personalities. They had fun with Koppel Berger. They mimicked his accent; they made jokes of his hotel from the vaudeville stage; and they played tricks on the live fish he had swimming in a bathtub every Friday. Mike Jacobs, too, got started at the Hotel Normandie under Uncle Koppel. The man who later controlled the champion, Joe Louis, as well as the "prize-fight" business itself, started with a small ticket stand at the hotel, and the first time I ever saw Mike, he was sliding down the lobby bannister like a kid, with his brother Jake "catching" him. I used to go to the Normandie once a week after school. My older brother, Jack, was the night clerk, and my mother insisted that he have a "Jewish" meal every Friday night, so I took the Broadway streetcar to 38th Street, carrying a large carton which included a pot of chicken soup, gefilte fish, horseradish, boiled chicken, and "tsimmiss." My mother had arranged with the chef at old Offer's Restaurant to let me use his stove to get the stuff hot again. It was quite a Friday afternoon, all around.

My brother, who later acquired some hotels of his own, coined the phrase about "sleeping on the sign." A guest came in and was told that the only room available would cost $2.50. The guest said, "You've got $1.50 on the sign," and my brother told him, "Try and sleep on the sign."

Most of the one million dollars Uncle Koppel made in the Hotel Normandie came during World War I, when he put dozens of cots in the lobby and in the upstairs hallways, to take care of the tremendous influx of job-seekers and servicemen. The elevator in the Normandie was the old cable variety, with the operator sitting in a swivel chair and pulling the cable up and down.

One night Uncle Koppel rented the swivel chair to a guest who had to get a few hours' sleep.

During this fabulous era of profits at the Normandie, Uncle Koppel was acquiring other hotels—the old Calvert, the Nassau, the Aberdeen, the Riviera in Newark; and, finally, the famous old Martinique Hotel at the intersection of Broadway and Sixth Avenue.

On the day that Koppel Berger took possession of the Martinique, he stopped talking Yiddish. No one will ever know why he stopped talking Yiddish, or how he expected to get along on a vocabulary of about one hundred and fifty words of broken English; but he saw it through to the bitter end. My mother tried to trap him many times into using a Yiddish word, but he never fell for the bait. Not only did he stop talking Yiddish, but he no longer "understood" it.

My mother would say something to him and he'd look at her with big innocent eyes and motion to one of us in a helpless sort of way to act as an "interpreter." She would become exasperated, call to him in Yiddish, and when he turned to one of his "interpreters," she would rattle off a string of "klulas" (Yiddish curse words), each of which was a masterpiece; but old Koppel Berger did not move a muscle or bat an eye. He simply smiled tolerantly, turned to one of us children and asked, "Vot did she set?"

As you would expect, Uncle Koppel liquidated the Hotel Normandie at the very "top." A year before the crash, he sold the hotel to a fellow (a Mr. Lefcourt), who couldn't wait to put up a forty-story building, but who met the terrible depression before he reached the twenty-fifth floor. In his last years, K. Berger retired to California, but he never stopped making money. At the age of eighty-three, he closed a deal for a large and profitable citrus business on the Coast. . . .[2]

[2] Reprinted by permission of The World Publishing Company from *Only in America* by Harry Golden. Copyright © 1958, 1957, 1956, 1955, 1954, 1953, 1951, 1949, 1948, 1944 by Harry Golden.

UNCLE ARAM AND THE POEM

WILLIAM SAROYAN

I had fought everybody for so long at school, at home, and everywhere else that I was sick of it, and sick of myself. I believed the way to become healed was to get out of town.

It was July, 1926.

Soon I'd be eighteen years old, but still I was in Fresno, which I now hated.

I went up to Aram's office to see about getting paid for the occasional office work I had done for a year or more, which I can't pretend I had especially *minded* doing, which in fact I had enjoyed doing. It had been better than nothing, so to say, but at the same time I had actually written a great many letters for him on the typewriter, I had run errands for him, I had announced his clients, I had asked them to wait when he was busy, and in general I had made myself useful.

Still, he hadn't ever handed me any money, except when he had sent me out for a cold watermelon from Long John, or a pound of pistachio nuts, or a leg of lamb for him to take home. Even when I had handed him the change he had invariably accepted all of it.

He was alone in his office when he looked up and saw me. I couldn't help noticing that he knew my visit was not a routine one. And I knew he was ready for me.

"Sit down," he said. "What's on your mind?"

"I want to get out of town."

"I think that's a good idea. You've been giving my sister a bad time long enough. Get out and stay out. When are you leaving?"

"Right away, but I haven't got any money."

"You don't need any money. Bums don't need any money. Go out to the S.P. and grab a freight, the way all the bums do."

"I thought you might pay me."

"For what?"

"For the work I did for you."

"Work *you* did for *me*? This place has been a college for you. You should pay me."

"Well, maybe, then, you'd *lend* me five dollars."

Well, here, for some reason, he went a little berserk, shouting first in English, then in Armenian, and finally in Turkish and Kurdish.

His voice was being heard all over the Rowell Building. The dentist next door stuck his head into the office expecting to say he had a very delicate piece of work to do and Aram was disturbing his patient, but Aram shouted at him before he could open his mouth, which soon enough fell open with astonishment.

"Get out, you dentist. Don't come into this office. This is a place of business. Get back where you belong, and drill your rotten teeth."

And now he felt required to imitate the sound of the drill, saying, "Bzzzz, bzzzz, bzzzz, all day long. Open wider, please. Wider, please. Bzzzz, bzzzz, bzzzz. Get out of here with your dainty little washed hands."

The instant the dentist's face disappeared, before the door was even fully shut, he came right back at me.

Inside, in spite of the anger I felt, I was laughing, because the man was crazy, but very funny.

Now, though, when he renewed the attack, I couldn't take it in silence any more, and I began to shout back at him, only louder than he was shouting.

"For God's sake, what kind of a man are you, anyway? You made a fortune last year and you're going to make a bigger fortune this year. I worked for you. Every penny I've earned I gave to my mother. I can't go to her and ask her for money. What are you shouting at me for?"

Now, after I said each of these things, he shouted a nullifying reply, making a kind of ridiculous duet.

All of the windows on the court of the Rowell Building were being lifted by typists, bookkeepers, dentists, lawyers, fruit shippers, and others, and everybody knew who was shouting: the Armenians, the Saroyans, Aram and his nephew Willie.

When I said, "For God's sake, what kind of a man are you?", Aram said, "A great man, you jackass, not a jackass like you."

"You made a fortune last year."

"Bet your life I did, more than you or anybody else will ever know."

"And you're going to make a bigger fortune this year."

"The biggest yet in every way, shape, manner and form."

"I worked for you."

"You *shit—that's* what you did."

"Every penny I've ever earned I gave to my mother."

"That poor girl has been driven mad by your foolishness. You want to be a writer. Get money in a bank and write *checks,* that's the way to be a writer. That's the kind of writer *I* am, not a stupid poem writer. *The moon is sinking in the sea.* The moon is sinking in your empty head, that's where the moon is sinking. (This of course was his swiftest idea of poetry, and of course there's no telling where he had gotten it from.) You gave her a few pennies, so you could eat six or seven times a day; and sleep in a warm bed in your own room, and get free hotel service. Don't talk to me about giving my sister money. Your *pennies?*"

"I can't go to her and ask her for money."

"Bet your life you can't. You've got to go to the bank for money, the way I do. Tell them what you want it for—to be a bum—and they'll give it to you. But if they don't, they'll give you a blotter. You can always use a blotter, can't you?"

"What are you shouting at me for?"

"Because you're a disgrace to my family. To my sister. To the Saroyan family. Now, get out of here."

For some reason all of a sudden I thought of my father. Surely nobody had ever spoken to him that way, if in fact anybody had ever shouted at him, but I got the feeling that they had actually. Who wanted *The moon is sinking in the sea?* Who wanted any part of such nonsense? This was America. This was California. This was Fresno. This was the real world, not the world of the moon and the sea.

I knew I wasn't going to get any money, so there was no point in shouting any more. I just didn't know how to get money, even money I had earned, or at any rate *believed* I had earned, but perhaps I was mistaken, perhaps he was right, perhaps I owed him money for having gone to college in his office, and so the first thing I must do is earn some money and pay him. It didn't help at all that he was famous all over town as the most open-handed man of wealth among the Armenians. He donated, officially, to everything that came along, and he made generous handouts to all kinds of needy Armenians because they knew how to get money from him. They knew how to get him to write a check, and they always cried out with feigned astonishment, "A hundred dollars, Aram? Really, I had hoped for no more than ten."

Hushed, earnest, a little astonished, but still respectful, I left his office and sneaked out of the building, taking the stairs so I wouldn't have to face the elevator operator or anybody who might be in the elevator.[3]

Despite their feelings about their uncles, writers Robert Coffin, Harry Golden, and William Saroyan were able to achieve a degree of objectivity, to stand back and observe their subjects' strengths and weaknesses. In writing about a closer relative—a parent, for example—such detachment is rarely possible, for in viewing them the writer sees and feels the edges of his own life. Thus, a character sketch of a father or grandfather is likely to be emotional—a paean of praise, perhaps, as in the e. e. cummings piece or a projection of past miseries, as in Yeats' essay about his grandfather. Interestingly and typically, both essays tell us something about the writers as well as about the persons being written about.

MY FATHER

E. E. CUMMINGS

My father . . . was a New Hampshire man, 6 foot 2, a crack shot & a famous fly-fisherman & a firstrate sailor (his sloop was named The Actress) & a woodsman who could find his way through forests primeval without a compass & a canoeist who'd still-paddle you up to a deer without ruffling the surface of a pond & an ornithologist & taxidermist & (when he gave up hunting) an expert photographer (the best I've ever seen) & an actor who portrayed Julius Caesar in Sanders Theatre & a painter (both in oils & watercolors) & a better carpenter than any professional & an architect who designed his own houses before building them & (when he liked) a plumber who just for the fun of it installed all his own waterworks & (while at Harvard) a teacher with small use for professors—by whom (Royce, Lanman, Taussig, etc.) we were literally surrounded (but not defeated)—& later (at Doctor Hale's socalled South Congregational really Unitarian church) a preacher who announced, during the last war, that the Gott Mit Uns boys were in error since the only thing which mattered was for man to be on God's side (& one beautiful Sunday in Spring remarked from the pulpit that he couldn't understand why anyone had come to hear him on such a day) & horribly shocked his pewholders by crying "the Kingdom of Heaven is no spiritual roofgarden: it's inside you" & my father had the first telephone in Cambridge & (long before any Model T Ford) he piloted an Orient Buckboard with Friction Drive produced by the Waltham watch company & my father sent me to a certain public school because its principal was a gentle immense coalblack negress & when he became a diplomat (for World Peace) he gave me & my friends a tremendous party up in a tree at Sceaux Robinson & my father was a servant of the people who

[3] From *Here Comes There Goes You Know Who* by William Saroyan. Copyright © 1961, by William Saroyan. Reprinted by permission of Trident Press, division of Simon & Schuster, Inc.

fought Boston's biggest & crookedest politician fiercely all day & a few evenings later sat down with him cheerfully at the Rotary Club & my father's voice was so magnificent that he was called on to impersonate God speaking from Beacon Hill (he was heard all over the common) & my father gave me Plato's metaphor of the cave with my mother's milk.[4]

GRANDFATHER

WILLIAM BUTLER YEATS

Some of my misery was loneliness and some of it fear of old William Pollexfen my grandfather. He was never unkind, and I cannot remember that he ever spoke harshly to me, but it was the custom to fear and admire him. He had won the freedom of some Spanish city, for saving life perhaps, but was so silent that his wife never knew it till he was near eighty, and then from the chance visit of some old sailor. She asked him if it was true and he said it was true, but she knew him too well to question and his old shipmate had left the town. She too had the habit of fear. We knew that he had been in many parts of the world, for there was a great scar on his hand made by a whaling-hook, and in the dining-room was a cabinet with bits of coral in it and a jar of water from the Jordan for the baptizing of his children and Chinese pictures upon rice-paper and an ivory walking-stick from India that came to me after his death. He had great physical strength and had the reputation of never ordering a man to do anything he would not do himself. He owned many sailing ships and once, when a captain just come to anchor, at Rosses Point reported something wrong with the rudder, had sent a messenger to say "Send a man down to find out what's wrong." "The crew all refuse" was the answer, and to that my grandfather answered, "Go down yourself," and not being obeyed, he dived from the main deck, all the neighbourhood lined along the pebbles of the shore. He came up with his skin torn but well informed about the rudder. He had a violent temper and kept a hatchet at his bedside for burglars and would knock a man down instead of going to law, and I once saw him hunt a party of men with a horsewhip. He had no relation for he was an only child and, being solitary and silent, he had few friends. He corresponded with Campbell of Islay who had befriended him and his crew after a shipwreck, and Captain Webb, the first man who had swum the Channel and who was drowned swimming the Niagara Rapids, had been a mate in his employ and a close friend. That is all the friends I can remember and yet he was so looked up to and admired that when he returned from taking the waters at Bath his men would light bonfires along the railway line for miles; while his partner William Middleton whose father after the great famine had attended the sick for weeks, and taken cholera from a man he carried in his arms into his own house and died of it, and was himself civil to everybody and a cleverer man than my grandfather, came and went without notice. I think I confused my grandfather with God, for I remember in one of my attacks of melancholy praying that he might punish me for my sins, and I was shocked and astonished when a daring little girl—a cousin I think—having waited under a group of trees in the avenue, where she knew he would pass near four

[4] Reprinted by permission of the publishers from e. e. cummings, *i: Six Nonlectures.* Cambridge, Mass.: Harvard University Press, Copyright, 1953, by E. E. Cummings.

o'clock on the way to his dinner, said to him, "If I were you and you were a little girl, I would give you a doll."

Yet for all my admiration and alarm, neither I nor any one else thought it wrong to outwit his violence or his rigour; and his lack of suspicion and something helpless about him made that easy while it stirred our affection. When I must have been still a very little boy, seven or eight years old perhaps, an uncle called me out of bed one night, to ride the five or six miles to Rosses Point to borrow a railway-pass from a cousin. My grandfather had one, but thought it dishonest to let another use it, but the cousin was not so particular. I was let out through a gate that opened upon a little lane beside the garden away from ear-shot of the house, and rode delighted through the moonlight, and awoke my cousin in the small hours by tapping on his window with a whip. I was home again by two or three in the morning and found the coachman waiting in the little lane. My grandfather would not have thought such an adventure possible, for every night at eight he believed that the stable-yard was locked, and he knew that he was brought the key. Some servant had once got into trouble at night and so he had arranged that they should all be locked in. He never knew, what everybody else in the house knew, that for all the ceremonious bringing of the key the gate was never locked.

Even to-day when I read *King Lear* his image is always before me and I often wonder if the delight in passionate men in my plays and in my poetry is more than his memory. He must have been ignorant, though I could not judge him in my childhood, for he had run away to sea when a boy, "gone to sea through the hawse-hole" as he phrased it, and I can but remember him with two books—his Bible and Falconer's *Shipwreck*, a little green-covered book that lay always upon his table.[5]

A Friend or Well-Known Person

It is not clear whether the author of the following essay had ever met Billie Holiday. But he knew her work intimately and was well acquainted with the circumstances of her life. Through this knowledge he was able to find the "key" that turns the lock and reveals the person. Billie Holiday, born in the "rat-run Negro slums of Baltimore," who rose to great heights as a jazz singer, was never able to transcend "her life in conflict with society." Ultimately, it sent her into drug addiction and an untimely, sordid death—all of which is evoked in this deeply compassionate and affectionate portrait.

LADY (FOR A) DAY

RICHARD GEHMAN

Billie Holiday, who was born Eleanora Fagan in the rat-run Negro slums of Baltimore on April 7, 1915, and who changed her name to Billie (after Billie Dove, the movie star) Holiday because she loathed everything about her background or for that matter herself, died in Metropolitan Hospital in New York at 3:10 A.M. on July 17, 1959. Her death came as no surprise to anyone who had followed her career even casually during the past few years. Indeed,

[5] Reprinted with permission of The Macmillan Company from *Autobiographies* by William Butler Yeats. Copyright 1916, 1936 by The Macmillan Company, renewed 1944 by Bertha Georgie Yeats.

early in June, soon after she had been admitted to the hospital and the police arrested her there for possessing heroin and posted a guard outside her door ("Why, they even took away her comic books and her *Confidential,*" someone close to her said angrily), it appeared to many of her friends that the end was near.

I myself thought she died in mid-June. I was driving into New York City one morning at around 6:15, fiddling with the automobile radio, when the startling sound of Billie singing "Lover Man" (the old Decca record, with Camarata's band behind her) came out of the set. New York early-morning disc jockeys simply do not play Billie Holiday records. They play records by people who stole her techniques and tricks and machine-tooled all the emotion out of them, they play records by the Four Shames and the Four Horrors and the Sub-Debs, but they shrink from playing anything as raw and truthful and full of genuine beauty as Billie Holiday's voice. Therefore, when I heard the record that morning, I assumed automatically she had died and some disc jockey was living his three minutes of atonement. I switched off the set. Later I learned that she had not died, and still later, when she finally did, I learned that I had been wrong about the early-morning men. They all spoke of her in that flat, supersentimental, elliptical, and meaningless argot of the network newswriters, and to hear them mouth their clichés one would have supposed that Doris Day, or Sarah Vaughan, or possibly even the Four Freshmen, had passed on, so sad did they seem to sound.

If the preceding lines seem to have been written by a man slightly overwrought, I do not apologize, but I do explain that it has to be impossible for anyone who loved the work of Billie Holiday to write about her in the objective, pipe-smoking manner of, say, Brooks Atkinson. Some of what she was at bottom transmitted itself into her listeners, whether they wanted it or not. Her biographer and friend, William Dufty, wrote a short series about her for *The New York Post* soon after she died; in it he kept hammering away at her honesty and passion for the truth. It struck me, as I read his pain-wracked pieces, that perhaps part of the reason she turned to heroin was that her inability to be anything but truthful may have been more than even she could endure; the drugs may have helped her believe she had found the truth as she wished it had been. I don't know about that. I do know that her agonized outcries on her early records, the bawls and shouts that came not from her mouth but from everything inside her, offended more people than they pleased. Her voice was harsh; it rasped at words like a tool to tell the truth, bending them to the truth as she felt it, and that may have been why she never achieved the audience that, say, the sweet-voiced (and all but emotionless) Ella Fitzgerald or the pseudopassionate (and all but tuneless) Sarah Vaughan, both had.

It was no accident that she began to call herself Lady Day. It was only natural for her to want to think of herself as a queen, and her imperious entries into nightclubs (dog at her side), her demands for treatment worthy of a regal personage, plus some of the scenes she made when she felt she was not getting her due, can be explained not by her addiction but by those drives she took the heroin to cover up. The irony need not be stated. Her life in conflict with society sent her into addiction, and society then punished her. The various arrests, the periods in hospitals, the denial of the right to work were all mere symptoms of something wrong, not only with her but with a good many of us. The French and English have many a good laugh over our unconsciously satirical behavior. We produce the tensions that make our only native American music, we enjoy the music up to a point, and then, as though we were at bottom afraid to see ourselves, we punish those who react to the tensions.

Enough speculation. We couldn't punish the music out of her. It is there on records for all to hear. There were those who felt, in the two years before her death, that she was singing better than ever. Certainly in the past twenty years she had absorbed enough to release emotions that were more intense than those she felt when first she began to sing.

She died the way too many pioneers of jazz apparently have to die (how did Bessie Smith die? Bix Beiderbecke? Charlie Parker? Lester Young?), except that she had a little more money than they; she had, Dufty wrote, seventy cents in the bank and $750 in $50 bills taped to her leg. They laid her out in an undertaker's parlor and put a gardenia in her hair (she always wore one when she sang). About 1,000 people turned up to view the body, and another time that many went to her funeral. "It was a lot like Bird's funeral," one jazz critic said bitterly. "The kind of thing where a lot of people went to be seen." Unlike the last rites for Charlie Parker, to which he was referring, it was not marked by squabbles (two of Parker's wives argued over the possession of his body, which had lain unclaimed in the city morgue for twenty-four hours). It was a conventionally solemn occasion, but there were those who felt that it was not quite fitting; that none of the usual clichés were proper for this immensely talented, admirably rebellious, appallingly honest and hysterically self-destructive woman. Someone recalled the remark that Eddie Condon once made about Bix Beiderbecke. "Bix died of *everything,*" he said. So did Billie.[6]

A Historical Figure

In a remarkable and highly original series of essays called *In the American Grain,* poet William Carlos Williams tried to probe beneath the surface of historical events and personalities to where "the true character lies hid." ("History! History!" he says in an Introduction to the volume, "We fools, what do we know or care?") Williams himself obviously cares, and at the same time tries to know—and pass along to us—some notion of the "unique force" and "configuration" that characterized a man like George Washington. What was this man like as a human being, rather than as a schoolbook legend? What, Williams asks, was "the strange phosphorus of the life, nameless under an old misappellation."

Washington is shown as "the typically good man" whose code was "resistance" ("He couldn't give in"). Yet he always yearned for "home and quiet," his "vine and figtree." He was also one of the "great wench lovers." And "he was hated, don't imagine he was not." As you can see, this is no cliché account of the man who never told a lie. Williams answers the question "What kind of person was X?" in a poetic prose style that is distinctly and splendidly his own.

[6] "Lady (for a) Day," by Richard Gehman, *Saturday Review,* August 29, 1959. Copyright 1959 Saturday Review, Inc. Reprinted by permission of *Saturday Review* and Richard Gehman.

GEORGE WASHINGTON

WILLIAM CARLOS WILLIAMS

Washington was, I think, the typically good man: take it as you please. But, of course, a remarkable one. No doubt at all he, personally, was ninety percent of the force which made of the American Revolution a successful issue. Know of what that force consisted, that is, the intimate character of its makeup, that is, Washington himself, and you will know practically all there is to understand about the beginnings of the American Republic. You will know, also, why a crown was offered this great hero at the conclusion of hostilities with Great Britain, and with what a hidden gesture he rejected the idea. Therein you have it: it was unthinkable—or he might have taken it.

Here was a man of tremendous vitality buried in a massive frame and under a rather stolid and untractable exterior which the ladies somewhat feared, I fancy. He must have looked well to them, from a distance, or say on horseback—but later it proved a little too powerful for comfort. And he wanted them too; violently. One can imagine him curiously alive to the need of dainty waistcoats, lace and kid gloves, in which to cover that dangerous rudeness which he must have felt about himself. His interest in dress at a certain period of his career is notorious.

The surveying contract which took him to Duquesne and the wilderness thereabouts was, however, the other side of the question. In this he must have breathed a more serious air which cannot but have penetrated to the deepest parts of his nature. The thing is, however, that in his case it did not, as it might have done, win him permanently to that kind of existence. There was in his nature a profound spirit of resignation before life's rich proposals which disarmed him. As he expressed it, to him it was always his "vine and figtree," home and quiet, for which he longed. Stress he could endure but peace and regularity pleased him better. There must have been within him a great country whose wild paths he alone knew and explored in secret and at his leisure.

Patience, horses or a fine carriage, a widow to wive, a sloping lawn with a river at the bottom, a thriving field, an adopted daughter—that was as far as his desire wandered. All the rest he accepted as put upon him by chance.

Resistance was, I believe, his code. Encitadeled. A protector of the peace, or at least, keeper of the stillness within himself. He was too strong to want to evade anything. That's his reputation for truthtelling. It was a good scratching to him to take it on and see himself through. He knew he would come through.

There was his club life in Alexandria, as a Mason; the ten-mile ride to Church: it warmed him up a little.

As for rebellion, I don't think it entered his mind. I don't see how it could, except from the rear, subconsciously—that fire was too subdued in him. As commander of the troops he resisted, struck and drew back, struck and doubled on his tracks and struck and struck again, then rested.

He couldn't give in. He couldn't give in without such a ruffling within himself that he had no choice but to continue. That's the secret of Valley Forge and the valor and patience of his battle, as great as the other, against an aimless, wavering Congress at Philadelphia. He couldn't give in. I believe he would have gone out and battled it alone if he had felt his army wasted from under him or even left the country. Or else—

Well, there is the night he wandered off alone near Morristown, I think, off toward the British lines on horseback, impatient of warning—to air himself, so to speak, under the stars. Something angry was stirred there.

But seven days in the week it was for him: resist, be prudent, be calm—with a mad hell inside that might rise, might one day do something perhaps brilliant, perhaps joyously abandoned—but not to be thought of.

Such men suffering thus a political conversion of their emotions are, I suppose, always the noteworthy among us. Battle to them must be the expression of that something in themselves which they fear. Washington's calmness of demeanor and characteristics as a military leader were of that cloth.

Some girl at Princeton, was it? had some joke with him about a slipper at a dance. He was full of it. And there was the obscene anecdote he told that night in the boat crossing the Delaware.

But apparently the one man who got it full, who saw him really roused was General Lee—the one who wanted to replace him in command. That was all right. Washington could understand that and forgive it in another. He forgave Lee and restored him to his division with full trust after his return from capture by the British. But when, subsequently, Lee, in direct disobedience of orders, forgetting his position and risking his own whim on an important decision before Monmouth, lost the chance for an important victory—that was different. Immediately after, Washington met him by chance at a country cross road and Lee got it.

It is said no man, before or after, saw Washington in such a rage. This sort of thing Lee had done, he, Washington, knew from top to bottom. It was the firmly held part of himself which had broken loose—in another. Should he, Washington, stop that resistance in himself, what would happen?

No use to ask that now. Here it was: disaster. To Lee then in a fury, he opened the gates of his soul and Lee saw such hell fire that it was the end of him—retired muttering and half silly to his farm in Virginia where he stayed.

The presidency could not have meant anything to Washington. I think he spoke the candid truth about it when he said he neither desired it nor sought it. He merely did his duty. He did it with wisdom since he couldn't do it any other way. He wasn't enough interested to be scheming. Resist and protect: that was the gist of most that he said. Don't go looking for trouble. Stay home. In his very face, even, it was said in Congress he had turned monster under the name of prudence: "a sort of non-describable chameleon-colored thing called prudence." Alexander Hamilton, a type that needed power, found all this quite to his liking. Washington let him do. He wanted to get back to Mt. Vernon.

America has a special destiny for such men, I suppose, great wench lovers—there is the letter from Jefferson attesting it in the case of Washington, if that were needed—terrible leaders they might make if one could release them. It seems a loss not compensated for by the tawdry stuff bred after them—in place of a splendor, too rare. They are a kind of American swan song, each one.

The whole crawling mass gnaws on them—hates them. He was hated, don't imagine he was not. The minute he had secured their dung heap for them—he had to take their dirt in the face.

From deep within, you may count upon it, came those final words when, his head in a friend's lap, he said with difficulty: "Doctor, I am dying, and have been dying for a long time. . . ." adding to reassure them, "but I am not afraid to die."

He is the typical sacrifice to the mob—in a great many ways thoroughly disappointing.[7]

A "Type"

Up to this point, the essays cited in this chapter have dealt with individuals; we have yet to examine the "type" or "character." Character writing is a very old and popular literary form, going back to the fourth century B.C. when the Greek philosopher Theophrastus wrote probing analyses of the different types of people he observed around him—"both good and bad." Unfortunately, the good portraits have been lost, and we are left with such tiresome but familiar types as the following:

THE UNSEASONABLE MAN

THEOPHRASTUS

Unseasonableness is an annoying faculty for choosing the wrong moment.

The unseasonable man is the kind who comes up to you when you have no time to spare and asks your advice. He sings a serenade to his sweetheart when she has influenza. Just after you have gone bail for somebody and had to pay up, he approaches you with a request that you will go bail for him. If he is going to give evidence he turns up when judgement has just been pronounced. When he is a guest at a wedding he makes derogatory remarks about the female sex. When you have just reached home after a long journey he invites you to come for a stroll. He is certain to bring along a buyer who offers more, when you have just sold your house. When people have heard a matter and know it by heart, he stands up and explains the whole thing from the beginning. He eagerly undertakes a service for you which you don't want performed but which you have not the face to decline. When people are sacrificing and spending money, he arrives to ask for his interest on a loan. When a friend's slave is being beaten he will stand there and tell how he once had a slave who hanged himself after a similar beating. If he takes part in an arbitration, he will set everyone at blows again just when both sides are ready to cry quits. And after dancing once he will seize as partner another man who is not yet drunk.[8]

In the seventeenth century, character writing was revived, and numerous books of "characters" appeared. One of them, Joseph Hall's *Character's of Vertues and Vices* (1608), included—as the title indicates—such virtuous types as "A Patient Man," reprinted below:

[7] William Carlos Williams, *In the American Grain.* Copyright 1925 by James Laughlin, copyright 1933 by William Carlos Williams. Reprinted by permission of New Directions Publishing Corporation.

[8] From *The Characters* by Theophrastus translated by Philip Vellacott. Copyright 1967 by Philip Vellacott. Reprinted by permission of Penguin Books Ltd.

A PATIENT MAN

JOSEPH HALL

The Patient man is made of a mettall, not so hard as flexible: his shoulders are large, fit for a load of injuries; which he beares not out of basenesse and cowardlinesse, because he dare not revenge, but out of Christian fortitude, because he may not: hee hath so conquered himself, that wrongs can not conquer him; and heere in alone findes, that victorie consists in yeelding. Hee is above nature, while hee seemes below himselfe. The vilest creature knowes how to turne againe; but to command himselfe not to resist, being urged, is more than heroicall. His constructions are ever full of charitie and favor; either this wrong was not done, or not with intent of wrong, or if that, upon misinformation; or if none of these, rashnesse (tho a fault) shall serve for an excuse. Himselfe craves the offenders pardon, before his confession; and a slight answer contents where the offended desires to forgive. Hee is Gods best witnesse; and when hee stands before the barre for trueth, his tongue is calmly free, his forhead firme, and hee with erect and setled countenance heares his unjust sentence, and rejoyces in it. The Jailers that attend him, are to him his pages of honour; his dungeon, the lower part of the vault of heaven; his racke or wheele, the staires of his ascent to glorie: he challengeth his executioners, and incounters the fiercest paines with strength of resolution, and while he suffers, the beholders pitie him, the tormentours complaine of wearinesse, and both of them wonder. No anguish can master him, whether by violence or by lingring. He accounts expectation no punishment, and can abide to have his hopes adjourned till a new day. Good lawes serve for his protection, not for his revenge; and his own power, to avoid indignities, not to returne them. His hopes are so strong, that they can insult over the greatest discouragements; and his apprehensions so deepe, that when hee hath once fastened, hee sooner leaveth his life than his hold. Neither time nor perversnesse can make him cast off his charitable endevors, and despaire of prevailing; but in spight of all crosses, and all denials, hee redoubleth his beneficiall offers of love. Hee trieth the sea after many ship-wracks, and beates still at that doore which hee never saw opened. Contrarietie of events doth but exercise, not dismay him; and when crosses afflict him, he sees a divine hand invisibly striking with these sensible scourges: against which hee dares not rebell, not murmure. Hence all things befall him alike; and hee goes with the same minde to the shambles and to the folde. His recreations are calme and gentle; and not more full of relaxation than void of fury. This man onely can turne necessitie into vertue, and put evill to good use. Hee is the surest friend, the latest and easiest enemie, the greatest conqueror, and so much more happie than others, by how much hee could abide to be more miserable.

ASSIGNMENTS

I. Compare the sketches of the three uncles in terms of the following:

A. What kind of person was each (personality, distinctive traits of character)?
B. What was the impact of each uncle on his nephew's life?
C. What is the tone and style of each essay?

II. In an essay (750–1,000 words) explain what kind of person someone you know is—a friend or relative. Since space is limited, try to focus on one dominant quality that, in your view, characterizes the total person (as avariciousness characterized Uncle Aram and resourcefulness Uncle Koppel). Present your "character" in action (as did Saroyan) or in a series of actions (as did Golden). In other words, set your character sketch within the form of narration.

III. A. Contemplate and comment upon cummings' virtuoso sentence in "My Father," noting in particular the striking selection of details, the parenthetic additions, and the final statement: "my father gave me Plato's metaphor of the cave with my mother's milk." What does this mean?

B. Write a one-sentence paragraph characterizing an extraordinary person you know.

IV. A. Consider Yeats' "Grandfather."

1. What is formidable and what is helpless about him?
2. What does the "daring little girl" who asks for a doll contribute to the narration?
3. In what ways is the grandfather like King Lear?

B. Write an essay (500–750 words) about someone you both fear and admire.

V. A. Answer the following questions based on Richard Gehman's article "Lady (for a) Day."

1. In what ways is this an unconventional eulogy? (Consider content and tone.)
2. What is the "key" to Billie Holiday's character, as it is described here?
3. What is the organizing principle of this essay?
4. What is the rhetorical stance?
5. Evaluate the following sentences in terms of their rhetorical effectiveness. Consider length, choice of words, and tone.

> They all spoke of her in that flat, supersentimental, elliptical, and meaningless argot of the network newswriters, and to hear them mouth their clichés one would have supposed that Doris Day, or Sarah Vaughan, or possibly even the Four Freshmen, had passed on, so sad did they seem to sound.
>
> Her voice was harsh; it rasped at words like a tool to tell the truth, bending them to the truth as she felt it, and that may have been why she never achieved the audience that, say, the sweet-voiced (and all but emotionless) Ella Fitzgerald or the

> pseudopassionate (and all but tuneless) Sarah Vaughan, both had.
>
> Enough speculation. We couldn't punish the music out of her.
>
> Someone recalled the remark that Eddie Condon once made about Bix Beiderbecke. "Bix died of *everything*," he said. So did Billie.

B. Write an essay (750–1,000 words) about some other well-known person (Edgar Allan Poe, Stephen Foster) or about someone known to you personally who, like Billie Holiday, "died of everything."

VI. A. Answer the following questions based on William Carlos Williams' sketch of George Washington.

1. Identify the "voice" narrating this essay. Does the writer base his account on facts? What kind of relationship is set up between writer and reader? Cite specific passages to support your answers.
2. Cite details about Washington that you would not find in an ordinary historical account. In what way do they contribute to Williams' purpose in this piece?
3. How do the following sentences achieve their special rhetorical effects?

> Stress he could endure but peace and regularity pleased him better.
>
> There must have been within him a great country whose wild paths he alone knew and explored in secret and at his leisure.
>
> As commander of the troops he resisted, struck and drew back, struck and doubled on his tracks and struck and struck again, then rested.
>
> Or else—
>
> He was full of it.
>
> I think he spoke the candid truth . . . when he said he neither desired it nor sought it.
>
> They [Jefferson and Washington] are a kind of American swan song, each one.
>
> He was hated, don't imagine he was not.

B. In the dramatically rendered, poetic style of William Carlos Williams, write a "sketch" of a historic figure (750–1,000 words).

any president or president's wife
Daniel Boone
Robert Fulton
Benjamin Franklin
Eli Whitney
Ulysses S. Grant
Robert E. Lee
Harriet Beecher Stowe
Benedict Arnold
Nathan Hale
Betsy Ross

VII. A. Write a twentieth-century version of the "Unseasonable Man" or the "Patient Man" (250–500 words).

B. Write a character sketch based on one of the following types (of man or woman) using seventeenth-century style, if you choose.

Virtues	*Vices*
The Reliable	The Fool
The Efficient	The Opportunist
The Mature	The Chronic Complainer
The Generous	The Calamity Jane
The Sincere	The Hypocrite
The Learned	The Bore
The Wise	The Flirt
The Helpful	
The Fun-loving	
The Courageous	
The Independent	

16 WHAT IS MY PERSONAL RESPONSE TO X?

One of the most common and popular types of writing is the so-called personal or familiar essay, in which the writer describes his response to some aspect of his surroundings—an object, situation, or event; a fleeting, fugitive thought or observation that has engaged his attention; an emotion, opinion, or reaction. Any of these provide subject matter for an informal, discursive piece—friendly, perhaps intimate in tone; personal, perhaps even confessional. In this type of essay the writer himself, rather than the subject of the essay, is of central significance. Indeed the success of a personal essay depends largely on the personality of the writer. Is he sensitive and perceptive? Does he see things with a fresh eye and clear spirit? Does he respond in a recognizably human way? Can we feel for him—and with him?

An essay revolving around one's own personal responses is not easy to write, but it is generally rewarding and may even be therapeutic. People need to "talk"; to tell the secrets within the frame of literary form. Here, then, is another human use of writing: the personal or familiar essay. At its best it may promote "social cooperation in the human jungle" by enabling people to see the many ways in which they are—at heart—alike.

The Mood Essay

Consider the following essay, for example, by a master of the form, J. B. Priestley. A curious and fragile situation has created a mood of deep melancholy. Through an open window he has heard the strains of a harmonica, or "mouth organ" as the British call it. Somehow he is filled with indescribable longing and sadness, the kind all of us have felt—inexplicably—at different times. He cannot analyze the mood nor can he "shake it off," not even when he deliberately tries to concentrate on "some fairly cheerful matter." As he reflects on his response to the "doleful tones" of the mouth organ, he realizes that for him the world has been dyed "a ghastly blue."

ON A MOUTH–ORGAN

J. B PRIESTLEY

For the past half hour, someone, probably a small boy, has been playing a mouth-organ underneath my window. I know of no person under this roof peculiarly susceptible to the sound of a mouth-organ, so that I cannot think that the unknown musician is serenading. He is probably a small boy who is simply hanging about, after the fashion of his mysterious tribe, and whiling away the time with a little music. Why he should choose a raw day like this on which to do nothing but slide his lips over the cold metal of a mouth-organ must remain a mystery to me; but I have long realised that unfathomable motives may be hidden away behind the puckered fact and uncouth gestures of small boyhood.

I have not been able to recognise any of the tunes, or the snatches of tunes, which have come floating up to my window. Possibly they are all unknown to me. But I think it is more likely that they are old acquaintances, coming in such a questionable shape that my ear cannot find any familiar cadence; they have been transmuted by the mouth-organ into something rich and strange; for your mouth-organ is one of the great alchemists among musical instruments and leaves no tune as it finds it.

It has been pointed out that whatever material Dickens used, however rich and varied it might be, it was always mysteriously transformed into the Dickens substance, lengths of which he cut off and called Novels. It seems to me that the mouth-organ, though a mechanical agent, has something of this strange power of transformation; whatever is played upon it seems to come out all of a piece; whatever might be the original character of the tunes, gay, fantastical, meditative, stirring, as their sounds are filtered through the little square holes of the instrument, their character changes, and they all become more or less alike. "Rule, Britannia!" "Annie Laurie," and the latest ditty of the music-halls somehow or other lose their individuality and flow into one endless lament, one lugubrious strain, that might very well go on for ever.

For this reason, the sound of a mouth-organ has always succeeded in depressing me. It must have been invented by an incorrigible pessimist, who sought to create a musical instrument that would give to every tune, no matter how lively, some touch of his own hopeless view of life; and probably the only time that he laughed was when he realised that he could leave this thing as a legacy to the world. I have never played a mouth-organ because I know that my own native optimism would not be strong enough to resist the baneful influence of the music it makes. To hear it now and again is more than enough for me.

To one who is filled with the joy of life—a small boy, for example—such hopeless strains may prove only invigorating, may serve as a wholesome check upon his ebullient spirits, like the skeleton at the Egyptian feasts. But to most of us weaker brethren, frail in spirit, music that is unillumined by even a glimmer of hope is intolerable.

For the past half hour, I have been trying to concentrate all my attention upon some fairly cheerful matter, and I have failed. It has been impossible to keep out the sound of this mouth-organ. Its formless, unknown, unending tune, only fit for bewailing a ruined world, has gradually invaded my room, penetrated through the ear into my brain, and coloured or discoloured all the thoughts there. There is in it no trace of that noble sadness which great music, like great poetry, so often brings with it; the mouth-organ knows nothing of "divine despair." It seems to whimper before "the heavy and the weary weight of all this unintelligible world."

"Oh de-ar!" I seem to hear it crying, "No hope for yo-ou and yo-ours; me-eserable world! Oh de-ear!" It has brought with it a fog of depression; my spirits have been sinking lower and lower; and under the influence of this evil mangler of good, heartening tunes I have begun to think that life is not worth living.

Most music worthy of the name has such beauty that it will either raise us to a kind of ecstasy or give us a feeling of vague sadness, which some delicate persons prefer to wild joy. Sir Thomas Browne, you remember, has something to say on this point, in a passage that can never become hackneyed no matter how many times it is quoted: "Whosoever is harmonically composed delights in harmony; which makes me much distrust the symmetry of those heads which declaim against all church music. For myself, not only from my obedience, but my particular genius, I do embrace it; for even that vulgar and tavern-music, which makes one man merry, another mad, strikes in me a deep fit of devotion, and a profound contemplation of the first composer."

But these mouth-organ strains will make a man neither mad nor merry, nor yet strike in him a deep fit of devotion; but if his ear is like mine, they will make him sink into depression and dye his world a ghastly blue.

It is curious that certain other popular musical instruments seem to have the same characteristics as the mouth-organ. The concertina and the accordion, good friends of the sailor, the lonely colonist, and rough, kindly fellows the world over, seem to me to possess the same power of transforming all the tunes played upon them into one long wail. I have read about their "lively strains," but I have never heard them. The sound of a concertina a quarter of a mile away is enough to shake my optimism. An average accordion could turn the Sword Theme from *Siegfried* into a plea for suicide. A flageolet or a tin-whistle has not such a shattering effect; nevertheless, both of them can only give a tune a certain subdued air, which is certainly preferable to the depressing alchemy of the other instruments, but which certainly does not make for liveliness.

The bagpipe, which has been so long the companion of the lonely folk of northern moors and glens, can produce at times a certain rousing martial strain, but, even then, a wailing air creeps into the music like a Scotch mist. Its very reels and strathspeys, which ought to be jolly enough, only sound to me like elaborate complaints against life; their transitory snatches of gaiety are obviously forced. At all other times, the bagpipe is frankly pessimistic, and laments its very existence.

There is probably some technical reason why these instruments produce such doleful tones. Perhaps our sophisticated ears rebel against their peculiar harmonies and discords. But it is certainly curious that mouth-organs, concertinas, tin-whistles, and the rest, so beloved of simple people, should be intolerable to so many of us. Is it that we have no miseries to express in sound? Or is it that our optimism is so brittle that we dare not submit it to the onslaught of this strange music? I do not know.

All that I do know is that at the present moment I am sitting in my armchair before a bright fire, depressed beyond belief by the sound that floats through my window; while outside, in the cold, there stands a small boy, holding a mouth-organ in his numbed hands and bravely sliding his lips over the cold metallic edges of the thing; and by this time he is probably as gay as I am miserable.[1]

Thus the personal essayist talks to us. He is our friend; he need not stand on ceremony. Loosely organized, flowing smoothly as the mind and pen flow, the personal essay is a relaxed form, usually brief and tentative in tone. For the writer is searching for answers, not giving them. He is sharing his innermost thoughts with us; they may not even be rational thoughts and this he will freely admit. Why should the "strange music" of a mouth organ send one into a "fog of depression"? "I do not know," says Priestley, implicitly returning the question: Do *you* know? Have *you* ever been unaccountably moved by some slight, seemingly innocuous circumstance? The personal essay may leave its musings trailing behind in the mind of the reader.

To say that the personal essay is a relaxed form is not to say that it is formless, rather that it proceeds according to a psychological rather than a logical movement. There is an idea, a mood, or a feeling lurking unexpressed in the writer's mind. He does not know exactly what it is, but he tries to recreate it on paper. The words tumble forth. They make patterns; hopefully these patterns will correspond to the pattern of the experience.

Critic Herbert Read tells us that this process is comparable to musical improvisation. It is also "the counterpart of the lyric in poetry." [2] Thus we have such utterances—spontaneous, intimate, evanescent—as Logan Pearsall Smith's *Trivia,* reprinted below. These are miniature essays that capture, in brief space, a fleeting moment of time, a mood, a state of mind, an unexpected but unforgettable upsurge of feeling. Note that sometimes the writer addresses us directly ("I fade from your vision, Reader . . ."); sometimes he soliloquizes, as in a diary ("I secretly write this Book, which They will never read"). In either case, we *hear* the writer's voice.

UNDER AN UMBRELLA

From under the roof of my umbrella I saw the washed pavement lapsing beneath my feet, the news-posters lying smeared with dirt at the crossings, the tracks of the busses in the liquid mud. On I went through this world of wetness. And through what long perspectives of the years shall I still hurry down wet streets—middle-aged, and then, perhaps, very old? And on what errands?

[2] Herbert Read, *Modern Prose Style* (Boston: Beacon Press, 1952), p. 66.

Asking myself this question I fade from your vision, Reader, into the distance, sloping my umbrella against the wind.

THE EVIL EYE

Drawn by the unfelt wind in my little sail over the shallow estuary, I lay in my boat, lost in the dream of mere existence. The cool water glided through my trailing fingers; and leaning over, I watched the sands that slid beneath me, the weeds that languidly swayed with the boat's motion. I was the cool water, I was the gliding sand and the swaying week, I was the sea and sky and sun, I was the whole vast Universe.

DISSATISFACTION

For one thing I hate spiders: I hate most kinds of insects. Their cold intelligence, their stereotyped, unremitting industry repel me. And I am not altogether happy about the future of the human race. When I think of the earth's refrigeration, and the ultimate collapse of our Solar System, I have grave misgivings. And all the books I had read and forgotten—the thought that my mind is really nothing but an empty sieve—often this, too, disconcerts me.

THEY

Their taste is exquisite; They live in Palladian houses, in a world of ivory and precious china, of old brickwork and stone pilasters. In white drawing-rooms I see Them, or on blue, bird-haunted lawns. They talk pleasantly of me, and Their eyes watch me. From the diminished, ridiculous picture of myself which the glass of the world gives me, I turn for comfort, for happiness to my image in the kindly mirror of those eyes.

Who are They? Where, in what paradise of palace, shall I ever find Them? I may walk all the streets, ring all the door-bells of the World, but I shall never find Them. Yet nothing has value for me save in the crown of Their approval for Their coming—which will never be—I build and plant, and for Them alone I secretly write this Book, which They will never read.

GREEN IVORY

What a bore it is, waking up in the morning always the same person. I wish I were Unflinching and emphatic, and had big, bushy eyebrows and a Message for the Age. I wish I were a deep Thinker, or a great Ventriloquist.

I should like to be refined-looking and melancholy, the victim of a hopeless passion; to love in the old, stilted way, with impossible Adoration and Despair under the pale-faced Moon.

I wish I could get up; I wish I were the world's greatest living Violinist. I wish I had lots of silver, and first Editions, and green ivory.

THINGS TO WRITE

What things there are to write, if one could only write them! My mind is full of gleaming thoughts; gay moods and mysterious, moth-like meditations hover in my imagination, fanning their painted wings. They would make my fortune if I could catch them; but always the rarest, those freaked with azure and the deepest crimson, flutter away beyond my reach.

The ever-baffled chase of these filmy nothings often seems, for one of sober years in a sad world, a trifling occupation. But have I not read of the great Kings of Persia who used to ride out to hawk for butterflies, nor deemed this pastime beneath their royal dignity? [3]

The Protest

Another kind of personal response involves a protest, a sounding-off against something going on in the world—an issue, an attitude—that the writer finds objectionable. One such piece, humorous in tone, is James Thurber's personal response to a verbal custom that clearly "got under his skin." In this essay Thurber establishes a tone of dour humor, thereby maintaining that double vision that characterized his general response to life: he was forever laughing with tears in his eyes or bristling with amused and amiable irritation.

THE SPREADING "YOU KNOW"

JAMES THURBER

The latest blight to afflict the spoken word in the United States is the rapidly spreading reiteration of the phrase "*you* know." I don't know just when it began moving like a rainstorm through the language, but I tremble at its increasing garbling of meaning, ruining of rhythm, and drumming upon my hapless ears. One man, in a phone conversation with me last summer, used the phrase thirty-four times in about five minutes, by my own count; a young matron in Chicago got seven "*you* knows" into one wavy sentence, and I have also heard it as far west as Denver, where an otherwise charming woman at a garden party in August said it almost as often as a whippoorwill says, "Whippoorwill." Once, speaking of whippoorwills, I was waked after midnight by one of those feathered hellions and lay there counting his chants. He got up to one hundred and fifty-eight and then suddenly said, "Whip—" and stopped dead. I like to believe that his mate, at the end of her patience, finally let him have it.

My unfortunate tendency to count "*you* knows" is practically making a female whippoorwill out of me. Listening to a radio commentator, not long ago, discussing the recent meeting of the United Nations, I thought I was going mad when I heard him using "you know" as a noun, until I realized that he had shortened United Nations Organization to UNO and was pronouncing it, you know, as if it were "*you* know."

A typical example of speech *you*-knowed to death goes like this. "The other day I saw, you know, Harry Johnson, the, you know, former publicity man for, you know, the Charteriss Publishing Company, and, you know, what he wanted to talk about, strangely enough, was, you know, something you'd never guess. . . ."

This curse may have originated simultaneously on Broadway and in Holly-

[3] From *All Trivia* by Logan Pearsall Smith, copyright, 1933, 1934, by Harcourt Brace Jovanovich, Inc.; copyright, 1961, 1962 by John Russell. Reprinted by permission of the publisher.

wood, where such curses often originate. About twenty-five years ago, or perhaps longer, theatre and movie people jammed their sentences with "you know what I mean?" which was soon shortened to "you *know?*" That had followed the over-use, in the 1920's of "you see?" or just plain "see?" These blights often disappear finally, but a few have stayed and will continue to stay, such as "Well" and "I mean to say" and "I mean" and "The fact is." Others seem to have mercifully passed out of lingo into limbo, such as, to go back a long way, "Twenty-three, skiddoo" and "So's your old man" and "I don't know nothin' from nothin' " and "Believe you me." About five years ago both men and women were saying things like "He has a new Cadillac job with a built-in bar deal in the back seat" and in 1958 almost everything anybody mentioned, or even wrote about, was "triggered." Arguments were triggered, and allergies, and divorces, and even love affairs. This gun-and-bomb verb seemed to make the jumpiest of the jumpy even jumpier, but it has almost died out now, and I trust that I have not triggered its revival.

It was in Paris, from late 1918 until early 1920, that there was a glut—an American glut, to be sure—of "You said it" and "You can say that again," and an American Marine I knew, from Montana, could not speak any sentence of agreement or concurrence without saying, "It *is*, you *know*." Fortunately, that perhaps original use of "*you know*" did not seem to be imported into America.

I am reluctantly making notes for a possible future volume to be called *A Farewell to Speech* or *The Decline and Fall of the King's English*. I hope and pray that I shall not have to write the book. Maybe everything, or at least the language, will clear up before it is too late. Let's face it, it better had, that's for sure, and I don't mean maybe.[4]

The "Appreciation"

In an opposite temper, the writer may express his warm personal response to an aspect of life—a book, for example, read in childhood and remembered warmly and with more insight in later years. Books are frequently the subject of a personal essay, for they tend to elicit strong feelings and long-lasting attachments. We are reminded, for example, of A. A. Milne's tribute to *The Wind in the Willows* as the kind of book a young man gives to his fiancée—and if she does not like it, he breaks the engagement. In this spirit of appreciation, rather than criticism, William Golding has written about one of his childhood favorites.

SWISS FAMILY ROBINSON

WILLIAM GOLDING

Has anyone ever resisted the charm of the Swiss Family? Indeed, can anyone think of it as just another book? Someone once likened Chaucer's stories to an English river, slow, quietly beautiful, and winding all the way. In the same terms, *The Swiss Family Robinson* is like a mountain lake. It is contained and motionless. It does not go anywhere. It has no story. Details, and detached incidents, are looked at separately without regard to what is coming next. This is how children live when they are happy, and this is why children will read *The Swiss Family Robinson* backwards and forwards and not bother about the end. To the adult eye, very little seems intended for out-and-out realism. When father Robinson puts together his boat of tubs with the ease and speed of a Popeye who has just eaten spinach, we, and children too, accept a literary convention. Nor are the vague people at all convincing. For Johann Wyss began, not by writing for a wide public but for his children who knew him and his wife and themselves too well to bother about characterization, even if he had been capable of it. Having isolated his characters, Wyss used the book from then onwards as a sort of holdall for conveying moral instruction and scientific information. He did not foresee the outcome of the book. One feels that the lively and capable Miss Montrose was brought in at the end because Wyss's eldest son had got engaged and Wyss wanted to bring his fiancée into the family. The charm of the book, then, lies precisely in the absence of story. The days are endless and time has no meaning. We sink completely into the milieu of these people who are not going anywhere and do not mind. Time is bright and uncomplicated as holidays spent by the sea in childhood.

At the back of the book stands the determination of Wyss to make and keep his family secure. How safe the Swiss Family Robinson is! That omniscient and omnipotent father, God's representative on earth to his family; that mild, womanly and devoted mother who is nevertheless so competent in her defined sphere—there is no hint that they can be anything but perfect. There is no flaw in their parental authority. This makes it disconcerting, in the new illustrated edition, to find father Robinson red-headed, and a fit hero for a Western, while Mother is a slim and beautiful girl, only a year or two older than her eldest child. I can't help feeling, if the illustrations are anything to go by, that *this time* family life may not be so uncomplicated and placid.

In the text, as ever, the children take a child's place. There is simply no possibility of juvenile delinquency. The guiding hand is gentle but adamant. The children are not allowed to overshadow their parents and save the day, perhaps because these are not the sort of days that have to be saved. It may be that the convention of children knowing more than their parents, being heroic and returning to a saved and admiring father, was a reaction against that gentle but adamantine hand. You can have too much of a good thing after all; and sometimes even a child's eye detects the absurdities in that godlike father-figure.

But no one, either child or adult, laughs at Johann Wyss without affection. He achieved more than he hoped or imagined possible. He gave his own family, and a good slice of European youth, total security between the covers of a book. For the great strength of *The Swiss Family Robinson* is not the brilliantly evoked spirit of place (the crystal cavern, the lobster pools, the grove of trees); it is not even the details held up to the eye and exactly observed (the tools and weapons, the plants and rocks, the good, earned meals). What Wyss captured effortlessly because it was so familiar to him was that family sense—the period when children are no longer babies and not yet young men; the period when a family, if it is lucky and emotionally stable, can look in on itself and be a whole world.[5]

[5] From *The Hot Gates and Other Occasional Pieces*, © 1965, by William Golding. Reprinted by permission of Harcourt Brace Jovanovich, Inc., and Faber and Faber Ltd.

ASSIGNMENTS

I. Rhetorical Analysis

The effectiveness of a personal essay depends on the authenticity of the writer's voice: Does he speak in a natural rhythm that you can *hear*? Is his voice distinctively and recognizably his own? Does he establish and maintain a suitable tone throughout the essay? How do you derive from this tone a sense of how the writer feels about his subject and how he wants *you* to feel?

Since the writer himself is the unifying thread running through the piece, it is important that he cast himself in a clear and consistent role. Before attempting to write your own personal essays, it will be helpful to analyze those in this chapter so that you can see exactly how these writers, each a master craftsman, have achieved their special effects and made their essays "work."

A. In a sentence or two summarize the substance and what you believe to be the writer's purpose in each essay.

B. In a sentence tell why you think the writer has or has not succeeded in achieving his purpose.

C. In terms of the following rhetorical features, show how the writer establishes and maintains an attitude and tone of voice appropriate to his purpose.

1. words
   - precision of nouns, verbs, abjectives
   - concreteness
   - levels of usage
   - connotation
   - repetition
   - sound
2. sentences
   - construction (word order, economy, emphasis, main and subordinate ideas)
   - length
   - variety
   - rhythm and balance (use of parallelism, antithesis)
   - texture
   - opening and closing sentences
3. choice of examples and illustrations
4. citing of authorities
5. use of images
6. use of figurative language
7. use of irony
8. use of allusions
9. smoothness of transitions

II. As J. B. Priestley describes his emotional response to a strain of music, describe in an essay (500–750 words) some chance occurrence that elicited a strong emotional response from you.

III. Write a series of three or four short, personal essays in the manner of Logan Pearsall Smith's *Trivia*. Use his titles, as listed below, or your own.

Happiness
The Busy Bees
The Sound of a Voice
In a Church
The Great Work
At the Window
Self-Control
A Fancy
Things to Say
Joy
Terror
The Rose
Faces
Dining Out
The Suburbs
Ask Me No More
Interruption
Reflections
My Mission
The Birds
A Precaution
The Stars
The Spider
The Age
At the Bank
In the Street
Social Success
Appearance and Reality
Self-Analysis
A Grievance
Comfort
In a Fix
Talk
The Incredible
Evasion
The Great Adventure
Chairs
Somewhere
The Echo
The Pear
Joy
Life Enhancement

IV. As James Thurber "sounds off" against the spreading "you know," write an essay (500–750 words) describing your negative response to some trend or innovative aspect of our culture.

V. In an essay (500–750 words), write a response to a book that was a childhood favorite. Show *why* you responded favorably to that book (as William Golding does in "Swiss Family Robinson") by indicating its distinctive appeal.

VI. In addition to one- and two-paragraph essays, Logan Pearsall Smith wrote "short shorts" of only a few lines—such as the following:

THE MOON

I went in and shook hands with my hostess, but no one else took any special notice; no one screamed or left the room; the quiet murmur of talk went on. I suppose I seemed like the others; observed from outside no doubt I looked like them.

But inside, seen from within . . . ? Or was it a conceivable hypothesis that we were all really alike inside also,—that all these quietly-talking people had got the Moon too, in their heads?

SHRINKAGE

Sometimes my soul floats out beyond the constellations; then all the vast life of the Universe is mine. Then again it evaporates, it shrinks, it dwindles; and of that flood which over-brimmed the bowl of the great Cosmos there is hardly enough now left to fill a teaspoon.

DELAY

I was late for breakfast this morning, for I had been delayed in my heavenly hot bath by the thought of all the other Earnest Thinkers, who, at that very moment—I had good reason to believe it—were soaking the time away in hot baths all over London.[6]

Write a series of five or six "reflections," each of which is no more than six or seven lines long.

VII. A. William Hazlitt (1778–1830) was an early master of the familiar essay who recorded and defined the familiar style as follows:

It is not easy to write a familiar style. Many people mistake a familiar for a vulgar style, and suppose that to write without affectation is to write at random. On the contrary, there is nothing that requires more precision, and, if I may so say, purity of expression, than the style I am speaking of. It utterly rejects not only all unmeaning pomp, but all low, cant phrases, and loose, unconnected, *slipshod* allusions. It is not to take the first word that offers, but the best word in common use; it is not to throw words together in any combinations we please, but to follow and avail ourselves of the true idiom of the language. To write a genuine familiar or truly English style, is to write as any one would speak in common conversation, who had a thorough command and choice of words, or who could discourse with ease, force and perspicuity, setting aside all pedantic and oratorical flourishes.

Comment on Hazlitt's description of the familiar style, explaining what is meant by the following terms:

1. familiar versus vulgar
2. unmeaning pomp
3. low, cant phrases
4. slipshod allusions
5. the true idiom of our language
6. ease, force, and perspicuity
7. pedantic and oratorical flourishes

B. During his lifetime Hazlitt wrote essays on the subjects listed below, most of them collected in his *Table Talk: Opinions on Books, Men, and Things*. Choose one topic and write your own piece (500–750 words).

Why the Heroes of Romances are Insipid
Why Distant Objects Please
On People with One Idea
On Consistency of Opinion
On Prejudice
On Disagreeable People
On Thought and Action
On the Want of Money
On Reading Old Books
On Reading New Books
Of Persons One Would Wish to Have Seen
On the Feeling of Immortality in Youth
On Going on a Journey
On the Pleasure of Painting
On the Ignorance of the Learned

[6] From *All Trivia* by Logan Pearsall Smith, copyright, 1933, 1934, by Harcourt Brace Jovanovich, Inc.; copyright, 1961, 1962 by John Russell. Reprinted by permission of the publisher.

On the Fear of Death
On Sitting for One's Picture
On Fashion
On Nicknames
On Public Opinion
On Personal Identity
On Means and Ends
Consistency of Opinion
Dreams
The Qualifications Necessary to Success in Life
Self-love and Benevolence (a Dialogue)
Envy
Egotism
Hot and Cold
The Pleasure of Hating
The Spirit of Obligations

17 WHAT IS MY MEMORY OF X?

"It is necessary to remember and necessary to forget, but it is better for a writer to remember." So said William Saroyan in a truism worth repeating, for it points to a large body of literature built upon "remembrance of things past."

The Quality of Memory

No writer had a more prodigious memory than Thomas Wolfe, whose novels are distinguished by his genius for conjuring up sense impressions from the past: sounds, sights, odors, colors, shapes—the very texture of experience reexperienced in memory. In a remarkable and revealing account of his creative process, Wolfe described the compulsive memory that drove him "night and day" by its shattering intensity.

THE QUALITY OF MEMORY

THOMAS WOLFE

The quality of my memory is characterized, I believe, in a more than ordinary degree by the intensity of its sense impressions, its power to evoke and bring back the odors, sounds, colors, shapes, and feel of things with concrete vividness. Now [during a summer in Paris] my memory was at work night and day, in a way that I could at first neither check nor control and that swarmed unbidden in a stream of blazing pageantry across my mind, with the million forms and substances of the life that I had left, which was my own, America. I would be sitting, for example, on the terrace of a cafe watching the flash and play of life before me on the Avenue de l'Opéra and suddenly I would remember the iron railing that goes along the boardwalk at Atlantic City. I could see it instantly just the way it was, the heavy iron pipe; its raw, galvanized look; the way the joints were fitted together. It was all so vivid and concrete that I could feel my hand upon it and know the exact dimensions, its size and weight and shape. And suddenly I would realize that I had never seen any railing that looked like this in Europe. And this utterly familiar, common thing would suddenly be revealed to me with all the wonder with which we discover a thing which we have seen all our life and yet have never known before. Or again, it would be a bridge, the look of an old iron bridge across an American river, the sound the train makes as it goes across it; the spoke-and-hollow rumble of the ties below; the look of the muddy banks; the slow, thick, yellow wash of an American river; an old flat-bottomed boat half filled with water stogged in the muddy bank; or it would be, most lonely and haunting of all the sounds I know, the sound of a milk wagon as it entered an American street just at the first gray of the morning, the slow and lonely clopping of the hoof upon the street, the jink of bottles, the sudden rattle of a battered old milk can, the swift and hurried footsteps of the milkman, and again the jink of bottles, a low word spoken to his horse, and then the great, slow, clopping hoof receding into silence, and then quietness and a bird song rising in the street again. Or it would be a little wooden shed out in the country two miles from my home town where people waited for the street car, and I could see and feel again the dull and rusty color of the old green paint and see and feel all of the initials that had been carved out with jackknives on the planks and benches within the shed, and smell the warm and sultry smell so resinous and so thrilling, so filled with a strange and nameless excitement of unknown joy, a coming prophecy, and hear the street car as it came to a stop, the moment of brooding, drowzing silence; a hot thrum and drowsy stitch at three o'clock; the smell of grass and hot sweet clover; and then the sudden sense of absence, loneliness and departure when the street car had gone and there was nothing but the hot and drowsy stitch at three o'clock again.

Or again, it would be an American street with all its jumble of a thousand ugly architectures. It would be Montague Street or Fulton Street in Brooklyn, or Eleventh Street in New York, or other streets where I had lived; and suddenly I would see the gaunt and savage webbing of the elevated structure along Fulton Street, and how the light swarmed through in dusty, broken bars, and I could remember the old, familiar rusty color, that incomparable rusty color that gets into so many things here in America.[1]

Wolfe's memory was, of course, a phenomenon, a miracle—cited here simply to indicate the far reaches of an ability all of us possess to some degree. Most of us can *remember*, in other words, but only vaguely and in snatches. Images do not ordinarily loom up on their own, "in a stream of blazing pageantry." If we ask ourselves the question "What is my memory of X?" we must make a conscious and sustained effort to recover the past. It is not

[1] Reprinted with the permission of Charles Scribner's Sons from *The Story of a Novel*, pages 31–35, by Thomas Wolfe.

waiting on the surface of the mind, ready to be recalled in all its original concreteness and intensity.

Even so, those of us with a less natural endowment than Wolfe's can—by probing and pondering and determinedly digging beneath the surface layers of consciousness—recapture scattered episodes and experiences; they are there to be recalled if bidden. They do need prodding, however, and in Chapter 22, "Gathering Information," specific methods of prodding are discussed (Remembering Facts, pp. 366–67).

Remembering Childhood Experiences

But even without prodding is there anyone who does not remember at least one teacher, classmate, incident, event, feeling or fear, pleasure or pain associated with that most impressionable period of life—that central experience of childhood—going to school?

Notice that in the essay that follows, the writer, Laurie Lee, has vividly recounted his rural boyhood. He has done this through the judicious selection of descriptive details: the particular chants actually recited in his small "village school," the exact roll call of classmates (Walt Kerry, Bill Timbrell, Spadge Hopkins); you can hear the names resounding in the long-ago air). By such descriptive devices—i.e., the use of concrete sensory details (Chapter 2, "How Can X Be Described?") the writer evokes a past reality: the "lively reek of steaming life" (". . . boys' boots, girls' hair, stoves and sweat . . ."), the very *feel* of an experience as it was originally experienced. Only in this way can the writer put us into the very situation he is describing so that we can experience it ourselves, somewhat in the way that he did.

THE VILLAGE SCHOOL

LAURIE LEE

The village school [in Gloucestershire in the 1920s] provided all the instruction we were likely to ask for. It was a small stone barn divided by a wooden partition into two rooms—the Infants and the Big Ones. There was one dame teacher, and perhaps a young girl assistant. . . . Our village school was poor and crowded, but in the end I relished it. It had a lively reek of steaming life: boys' boots, girls' hair, stoves and sweat, blue ink, white chalk and shavings. We learnt nothing abstract or tenuous there—just simple patterns of facts and letters, portable tricks of calculation, no more than was needed to measure a shed, write out a bill, read a swine-disease warning. Through the dead hours of the morning, through the long afternoons, we chanted away at our tables. Passers-by could hear our rising voices in our bottled-up room on the bank: "Twelve-inches-one-foot. Three-feet-make-a-yard. Fourteen-pounds-make-a-stone. Twelve-stone-a-hundred-weight." We absorbed these figures as primal truths declared by some ultimate power. Unhearing, unquestioning, we rocked to our chanting, hammering the gold nails home. "Twice-two-are-four. One-God-is-Love. One-Lord-is-King. One-King-is-George. One-George-is-Fifth . . ." So it was always, had been, would be for ever; we asked no questions; we didn't hear what we said; yet neither did we ever forget it.

So do I now, through the reiterations of those days, recall that school-room which I scarcely noticed—Miss Wardley in glory on her high desk throne, her long throat tinkling with glass. The bubbling stove with its chink of red fire, the old world map as dark as tea; dead field-flowers in jars on the windowsills; the cupboard yawning with dog-eared books. Then the boys and the girls, the dwarfs and the cripples; the slow fat ones and the quick bony ones; giants and louts, angels and squinters—Walt Kerry, Bill Timbrell, Spadge Hopkins, Clergy Green, the Ballingers and Browns, Betty Gleed, Clarry Hogg, Sam and Sixpence, Rose and Jo—were ugly and beautiful, scrofulous, warted, ring-wormed and scabbed at the knees; we were noisy, crude, intolerant, cruel, stupid and superstitious. But we moved together out of the clutch of the fates, inhabitors of a world without doom; with a scratching, licking and chewing of pens, a whisper and passing of jokes, a titter of tickling, a grumble of labour, a vague stare at the wall in a dream.[2]

As we remember school days, so we may remember those interludes separating school years one from another—the summers of our childhood. If there was a sameness about them (every year at the beach, or at camp, or at home) they may seem, in retrospect, one single happy (or unhappy) blur. But if, as in the case of playwright Moss Hart, one summer was marked off from the others by an "electric" discovery, then that summer will stand out from the rest—never to be forgotten. To share that memorable experience with others, the writer must try not merely to tell about it, but rather to render it dramatically, in narrative form, as it happened. He must also try to conjure up, as Laurie Lee did, many descriptive details in order to give his piece the closest possible semblance of reality; once again, to make the reader feel that "he is there."

A MEMORABLE SUMMER

MOSS HART

A city child's summer is spent in the street in front of his home, and all through the long summer vacations I sat on the curb and watched the other boys on the block play baseball or prisoner's base or gutter hockey. I was never asked to take part even when one team had a member missing—not out of any special cruelty, but because they took it for granted I would be no good at it. They were right, of course. Yet much of the bitterness and envy and loneliness I suffered in those years could have been borne better if a single wise teacher or a knowledgeable parent had made me understand that there were compensations for the untough and the nonathletic; that the world would not always be bounded by the curbstone in front of the house.

One of those compensations I blundered into myself, and its effect was electric on both me and the tough world of the boys on the block. I have never forgotten the joy of that wonderful evening when it happened. There was no daylight-saving in those days, and the baseball and other games ended about eight or eight thirty, when it grew dark. Then it was the custom of the boys

[2] From *The Edge of Day: A Boyhood in the West of England* by Laurie Lee. Copyright © 1959 by Laurie Lee. Reprinted by permission of William Morrow and Company, Inc. and The Hogarth Press. (First published in Great Britain under the title *Cider with Rosie.*)

to retire to a little stoop that jutted out from the candy store on the corner and that somehow had become theirs through tribal right. No grownup ever sat there or attempted to. There the boys would sit, talking aimlessly for hours on end. There were the usual probings of sex and dirty jokes, not too well defined or clearly understood; but mostly the talk was of the games played during the day and of the game to be played tomorrow. Ultimately, long silences would fall and then the boys would wander off one by one. It was just after one of those long silences that my life as an outsider changed, and for one glorious summer I was accepted on my own terms as one of the tribe. I can no longer remember which boy it was that summer evening who broke the silence with a question; but whoever he was, I nod to him in gratitude now. "What's in those books you're always reading?" he asked idly. "Stories," I answered. "What kind?" asked somebody else without much interest.

Nor do I know what impelled me to behave as I did, for usually I just sat there in silence, glad enough to be allowed to remain among them; but instead of answering his question, I launched full tilt into the book I was immersed in at the moment. The book was *Sister Carrie* and I told them the story of Sister Carrie for two full hours. They listened bug-eyed and breathless. I must have told it well, but I think there was another and deeper reason that made them so flattering an audience. Listening to a tale being told in the dark is one of the most ancient of man's entertainments, but I was offering them as well, without being aware of doing it, a new and exciting experience.

The books they themselves read were the *Rover Boys* or *Tom Swift* or G. A. Henty. I had read them too, but at thirteen I had long since left them behind. Since I was much alone I had become an omnivorous reader and I had gone through the books-for-boys-series in one vast gulp. In those days there was no intermediate reading material between children's and grownups' books, or I could find none, and since there was no one to say me nay, I had gone right from *Tom Swift and His Flying Machine* to Theodore Dreiser and *Sister Carrie*. Dreiser had hit my young mind and senses with the impact of a thunderbolt, and they listened to me tell the story with some of the wonder that I had had in reading it.

It was, in part, the excitement of discovery—the discovery that there could be another kind of story that gave them a deeper kind of pleasure than the *Rover Boys*—blunderingly, I was giving them a glimpse of the riches contained outside the world of *Tom Swift*. Not one of them left the stoop until I had finished, and I went upstairs that wonderful evening not only a member of the tribe but a figure in my own right among them.

The next night and many nights thereafter, a kind of unspoken ritual took place. As it grew dark, I would take my place in the center of the stoop and, like Scheherazade, begin the evening's tale. Some nights, in order to savor my triumph more completely, I cheated. I would stop at the most exciting part of a story by Jack London or Frank Norris or Bret Harte, and without warning tell them that that was as far as I had gone in the book and it would have to be continued the following evening. It was not true, of course; but I had to make certain of my new-found power and position, and with a sense of drama that I did not know I possessed, I spun out the long summer evenings until school began again in the fall. Other words of mine have been listened to by larger and more fashionable audiences, but for that tough and grimy one that huddled on the stoop outside the candy store, I have an unreasoning affection that will last forever. It was a memorable summer, and it was the last I was to spend with the boys on the block.[3]

Similarly Nikos Kazantzakis, in his autobiographical "odyssey," *Report to Greco,* recalls a period that left its mark on his later life—childhood.

REPORT TO GRECO

NIKOS KAZANTZAKIS

I spent my adolescent years beset by youth's customary difficulties. Two huge beasts awoke inside me, that leopard the flesh, and that insatiable eagle which devours a man's entrails and the more it eats the more it hungers—the mind.

When I was still very young, only three or four years old, I was overcome by a violent curiosity to untangle the mystery of birth. I asked my mother and aunts, "How are babies born, how do they suddenly enter the house? Where do they come from?" I reasoned that some verdant country must exist, perhaps Paradise, where children sprouted like red poppies; every so often a father entered Paradise, picked one, and brought it home. This I turned over and over in my mind without giving it very much credence. As for my mother and aunts, they either failed to answer me at all or else told me fairy tales. But I understood more than they thought, more than I myself thought, and did not believe their tales.

One day during the same period our neighbor Madame Katina died, although still a young woman. When I saw her brought out of her house lying on her back and followed by a large group of people who turned hurriedly into a lane and disappeared, I was seized by terror. "Why did they take her away?" I asked. "Where are they bringing her?" "She died," I was told. "Died? What does that mean?" But no one offered me an explanation. Huddling in a corner behind the sofa and covering my face with a pillow, I began to cry, not from sorrow or fear, but because I did not understand. When my teacher Krasákis died a few years later, however, death had ceased to astonish me. I felt that I understood what it was, and I did not ask.

These two, birth and death, were the very first mysteries to throw my childish soul into a ferment; I kept beating my tender fist against this pair of closed doors to make them open. I saw that I could expect help from nobody. Everyone either remained silent or laughed at me. Whatever I was to learn I would have to learn by myself.

Gradually the flesh awoke also. My kingdom, which had been composed of premonitions and clouds, began to solidify. I overheard street talk. Although I had no clear understanding what these overheard expressions meant, some of them seemed to be filled with secret and forbidden matter. Thus I set them apart, marked them out in my mind, and repeated them over and over—always to myself—so that I would not forget them. One day however, one of them escaped me; I pronounced it aloud in my mother's presence. She winced from fright.

"Who told you that naughty word?" she shouted. "Don't say it again!"

Going to the kitchen, she got some ground pepper and rubbed it thor-

[3] From *Act One,* by Moss Hart. Copyright © 1959 by Catherine Carlisle Hart and Joseph M. Hyman, Trustees. Reprinted by permission of Random House, Inc.

oughly into my mouth. I began to howl; my mouth was on fire. But then and there, to spite her, I secretly vowed that I would continue to say those words, though to myself. For I felt great pleasure in pronouncing them.

Ever since then, however, every forbidden word has burned my lips and smelled of pepper—even now, after so many years and so many sins! [4]

Remembering Episodes

Memories, as we can see, may provide us with short narratives—single, self-contained episodes such as Jan Myrdal relates below in his *Confessions of a Disloyal European*, an autobiographical work that has been characterized as "a montage of memories." Among them are the four episodes reprinted below, which in many respects resemble short stories (what the fiction writer would call a "short short"), for each one, brief as it is, encompasses character, setting, incident, and—in its own subtle way—theme.

FOUR EPISODES

JAN MYRDAL

I

Nic.

I met her in Gothenburg as the European war was ending. Her hair was short; she had been in a concentration camp. Her hair had the colour of many dyes; she had worked underground. The last time I saw her was in Oslo in 1956:

—You want to be happy? Why? You are supposed to work.

Her last letter reached me in Kabul in 1959. After that she didn't answer any letters. Coming to Scandinavia I called and asked:

—How is Nic?

—She is dead.

II

As a child when I lived in central Stockholm I was once playing in the doorway of another house. The caretaker saw me. When I heard him coming down the stairs I ran. He caught me in the street and started hitting me. He struck me in the face.

—I'll teach you, he said. You bastard.

Then he kicked me and left.

Close by a man was beating his Airedale terrier. A woman screamed at him:

—I will report you to the police.

I thought a lot about this the following days.

III

A gypsy family had tried to settle in the small town of Mariefred (Peace to Mary) where I was living. The good citizens, afraid of a drop in land prices, had tried to get them to move. The press in Stockholm had written about it.

[4] From *Report to Greco* by Nikos Kazantzakis. Copyright © 1965 by Simon and Schuster, Inc. Reprinted by permission of the publisher.

The citizens became afraid of scandal. Now there was a meeting of the town council to decide what to do. Reluctantly it was decided that they would get a house. On the way out from the meeting a middle-aged man turned to me and said:

—Gypsies! One ought to get rid of people like that.

—Fine, I said. You gas them and I will heat up my furnace.

As he was a Social Democrat, the Labour people said after that that I was antilabour.

IV

In the fall of 1947 I was in love with B. She was good-looking, intelligent and we said we thought that we had much in common. We were going steady for some time, but she did not allow me to sleep with her. In December that year I left for Belgrade. When I came back to Sweden I married another girl. In February 1949 I came to Stockholm by train from Herrljunga. Met B. Having met again we both realized that we actually were very much in love with each other. I followed her to her room and now she wanted "to give herself to me," as she expressed it.

Suddenly I remembered that I had not washed my feet for several days. There were reasons for this. I had hitchhiked up through Sweden, had spent the night at the county jail of Herrljunga, and had been put on the train to Stockholm. It was in the middle of winter and it was cold.

But as I was afraid that my feet stank—which would not correspond to the image I wanted B to have of me—I tried to find a way to escape from the situation. Unfortunately the fact that my feet (probably) stank did not strike me until B had started to undress. I could not find anything more convincing to say than that I seemed to love the girl I was married to. B was very understanding and we sat for a long time talking about self, soul and love.

And all this because I had forgotten to wash my feet. Or was it? [5]

Remembering People

In addition to the memory of a particular period or event, the writer may recall a particular person, for people are important links tying us to the past. Our fading memories of forms and faces can actually bring the past back to us. Sometimes the memory is dim, such as the elusive and haunting "first friend" of Eli Wiesel's childhood, the "orphan" described below, who comes to symbolize—in retrospect—the writer's own fate.

THE ORPHAN

ELI WIESEL

My first friend was an orphan. That is about all I remember about him. I have forgotten his name, how he looked, what he was like. The color of his eyes, the rhythm of his walk: these too, forgotten. Did he like to sing, to laugh, to play in the sun, to roll in the snow? I cannot remember and, sometimes, I feel a vague remorse, as if it were a rejection.

[5] From *Confessions of a Disloyal European*, by Jan Myrdal.

I sometimes search my memory hoping to find him again, to save him, or, at least, to restore to him a face, a past: I emerge empty-handed. While I have no difficulty seeing myself as a child again, he, the orphan, remains unreachable: an echo without voice, a shadow without reflection. Of our friendship, all that has been preserved is the sadness his presence inspired in me. Even now, discovering the orphan in each human being is enough to reopen an old wound, never fully healed.

I must have been five, maybe a little older. I had scarcely begun to go to primary school, to *heder*. Among the children whom I did not know and did not want to know, I felt myself to be, like each of them, no doubt, the victim of my parents' injustice. I made up countless illnesses so that I could stay home with my mother for just one more day, to hear her say she still loved me, that she was not going to turn me over to strangers.

Obstinate, I resisted the efforts of my old white-bearded schoolmaster, who gently persisted in wanting to teach me the Hebrew alphabet. I think it was because, like all children, I preferred remaining a child. I dreaded the universe of rigid laws which I sensed were inside those black letters whose mysterious power seizes hold of the imagination like a defenseless prey. Whoever says *a* will say *b* and before one notices it, one is already caught up in the machinery: one begins to find words satisfying, one makes gods of them. I had an obscure premonition that, once this threshold were crossed, it would be the letters of the alphabet that would, in the end, undo my innocence, impose itself between my desires and their realization.

The other pupils, as recalcitrant as I, showed the same distrust. Only the orphan was of a different breed. He never acted spoiled; he never tried the patience and kindness of our teacher. First to arrive, he was always the last to leave. He was not rowdy, he did not have tantrums. Diligent, obedient, in contrast to us, he did not feel uprooted in the narrow room with its damp walls, that room where we spent endless hours around a rectangular table, worn down by three generations of unhappy schoolboys.

His exemplary behavior could only annoy us: why did he insist on being different? After a while, I understood: he was different. His mother had died giving birth to him.

I did not know then what it meant to die. In fact, to be an orphan had, in my eyes, a kind of distinction, an honor that did not fall to everyone. Secretly, I began to envy him. Yet my attitude toward him changed. To win his trust, I shared my possessions with him, my little snacks, my presents. At home no one understood: all of a sudden I who refused to eat at every meal, began carrying off double portions.

My mother was alive and that seemed to me unjust. When I was with the orphan, I felt at fault: I possessed a wealth denied to him. And neither one of us had anything to do with it. I would have given everything to restore the balance. To redeem myself, I was ready to become not only his debtor but his admirer as well, his benefactor. For his part, he accepted my sacrifices, and I no longer remember if he thanked me for them, if he really needed them. I do not know why, but I thought he was poor. Or rather—yes, I do know why: spoiled child that I was, I saw every orphan as a *poor* orphan. I could not conceive of misfortune except in its totality: whoever lost one portion of affection, one possibility of love, lost everything.

His birthday coinciding with the anniversary of his mother's death, I heard him saying *Kaddish* in the synagogue. I had to restrain myself with all my might to keep from tearing myself away from my father and rushing over to my friend to embrace him, weeping, and repeat with him word by word the prayer which gives praise to God, who must know what he is doing when he takes away the joy of little children.

Over the years our paths separated. The orphan went his own way. I made new friends, and today I have other reasons for assuming my share of guilt, but at the root of this feeling it is always him I find.

Still I know very well that my first friend long ago ceased to be a unique case: we all belong to a generation of orphans, and the *Kaddish* has become our daily prayer. But each time death takes someone away from me, it is him, my forgotten friend, I mourn. Sometimes I wonder if he did not have my face, my fate perhaps, and if he was not already what I was about to become. Then I tell myself that I should set myself to learning the alphabet, diligently, if only to resemble him the more.[6]

ASSIGNMENTS

I. Rhetorical Analyses:

A. Read Thomas Wolfe's "The Quality of Memory" and answer the following questions:

1. Identify and comment on the sense impressions described by Wolfe.
2. Evaluate the choice of words (nouns, verbs, adjectives).
3. What special rhetorical devices (alliteration, repetition) contribute to the rhythm and impetus of Wolfe's sentences?

B. Read Laurie Lee's "The Village School" and evaluate his description in terms of the following rhetorical features:

1. selection of details
2. choice of adjectives
3. repetition of words
4. sensory images
5. metaphors
6. use of parallelism
7. rhythm
8. inversion of word order
9. suspended sentences
10. voice

C. Read Moss Hart's "A Memorable Summer" and evaluate the quality of this narrative (Does it hold your interest? Is it a good story?) in terms of the following:

1. point of view
2. conflict
3. expository passages
4. suspense
5. climax

[6] From "The Orphan" from *Legends of Our Time* by Eli Wiesel. Copyright © 1968 by Eli Wiesel. Reprinted by permission of Holt, Rinehart and Winston, Inc.

6. use of "tribe" analogy
7. sentence construction
8. sentence rhythm
9. narrative pace
10. selection of details
11. use of dialogue

D. Read Nikos Kazantzakis' "Report to Greco" and answer the following questions:

1. Does the central character in this reminiscence "come alive" as a person? Can you respond to him? Can you identify with him?
2. Describe the organization of this piece.
3. Observe and comment on the writer's manner of combining inner and outer experiences.
4. In what ways is this prose essay poetic?

E. Read Jan Myrdal's "Four Episodes" and answer the following questions:

1. Characterize these "short short" narratives in terms of character, setting, incident, and theme.
2. What special stylistic features distinguish these essays?
3. Explain the impact of these pieces on you, as a reader.

F. Read Eli Wiesel's "The Orphan" and answer the following questions:

1. Trace the steps of this reminiscence that lead to the writer's conclusion that "we all belong to a generation of orphans." Does this conclusion seem justified to you?
2. Comment on point of view and voice. How do they contribute to the total impact of Wiesel's "message"?

II. Writing Assignments:

A. Write an essay (500–750 words) dealing with an early memory connected with going to school.

B. In an essay (500–750 words) describe a time in your life, during childhood or adolescence, that remains "marked off" from other times by specific events, experiences, or feelings that you associate with it (like Hart's memorable summer or Kazantzakis' childhood years).

C. In another section of "Report to Greco" Kazantzakis says this of his childhood:

> Whatever fell into my childhood mind was imprinted there with such depth and received by me with such avidity that even now in my old age I never grow tired of recalling and reliving it. With unerring accuracy I remember my very first acquaintance with the sea, with fire, with woman, and with the odors of the world.

Write an essay (500–750 words) in which you recall your earliest memories, developing them separately in three or four succeeding paragraphs.

D. Write four episodes based on remembered experiences, incidents, people—each "a short short story" in the manner of Myrdal's "Four Episodes."

E. In an essay (500–750 words) similar to Wiesel's "The Orphan," describe your first friend or any friend whose memory has had an impact on your life.

F. In a classic essay by Charles Lamb, "Dream Children: A Reverie" (too well-known to be reprinted here), Lamb (the narrator), who is a bachelor, has a dream-experience—or reverie—in which his imagined grandchildren cluster about him to hear tales of their forebears. It is a heart-warming description, in many ways the typical fantasy of what "might have been" had circumstances worked out differently. In an essay (500–750 words), write a "reverie" in which you place yourself in a situation that "might have been." End your reverie as Lamb ends his: ". . . I found myself quietly seated in my . . . chair, where I had fallen asleep. . . ."

G. Read Dylan Thomas' "A Child's Christmas in Wales" and write an essay (750–1,000 words) describing any holiday as you remember it being celebrated by your family.

18 WHAT IS THE VALUE OF X?

When we ask about the "value" of something we are moving still further beyond basic explanation into the greater complexities of judgment, whereby we ask not merely "What does X do?" but "What does X do worth doing?" and "How well does X do it?" Here the purpose is not merely to inform but to appraise something in terms of its worth, utility, importance, excellence, distinction, truth, beauty, goodness. To what extent does X meet—or fail to meet—specific standards? In an evaluative essay it is always the writer who sets the standards. Even if they are standards adopted from someone else, the writer has adopted them and made them his own. Thus, the moment he addresses himself to this question "What is the value of X?" he becomes a critic. Whether the subject is books, movies, art, or society at large, the writer evaluates it in the light of his own notion of what it is and *should* be. As you can see, then, writing an evaluation is a special challenge, for the evaluation will have value only if the writer is open-minded, well informed, and fair—ready to back up his opinions, but not opinionated. In the following essay, for example, the writer places a high value on a form of exuberance that most people, raised in a Puritan ethic, either frown upon or regard as frivolous. Virtue may be its own reward, but, as Eric Hoffer tells us, the spirit of playfulness—the indulgence in "trivial joys"—yields rewards far beyond its selfish, surface value. Hoffer supports his thesis by citing many momentous contributions to society that have issued from "idle musing"—what he calls a "playful mood."

Evaluating Man's Behavior

THE PLAYFUL MOOD

ERIC HOFFER

I have always felt that the world has lost much by not preserving the small talk of its great men. The little that has come down to us is marked by a penetration and a directness not usually conspicuous in formal discourse or writing; and one is immediately aware of its universality and timelessness. It seems strange that men should so effortlessly attain immortality in their playful moments. Certainly, some have missed immortality as writers by not writing as they talked. Clemenceau is a case in point. His books make dull and difficult reading, yet he could not open his mouth without saying something memorable. The few scraps we have of his small talk throw a more vivid light on the human situation than do shelves of books on psychology, sociology, and history. Toward the end of his life Clemenceau is reported to have exclaimed: "What a shame that I don't have three or four more years to live—I would have rewritten my books for my cook." It is also worth noting that the New Testament and the Lun Yu are largely records of impromptu remarks and sayings, and that Montaigne wrote as he spoke. ("I speak to my paper as I speak to the first person I meet.")

We are told that a great life is "thought of youth wrought out in ripening years"; and it is perhaps equally true that "great" thinking consists in the working out of insights and ideas which come to us in playful moments. Archimedes' bathtub and Newton's apple suggest that momentous trains of thought may have their inception in idle musing. The original insight is most likely to come when elements stored in different compartments of the mind drift into the open, jostle one another, and now and then coalesce to form new combinations. It is doubtful whether a mind that is pinned down and cannot drift elsewhere is capable of formulating new questions. It is true that the working out of ideas and insights requires persistent hard thinking, and the inspiration necessary for such a task is probably a by-product of single-minded application. But the sudden illumination and the flash of discovery are not likely to materialize under pressure.

Men never philosophize or tinker more freely than when they know that their speculation or tinkering leads to no weighty results. We are more ready to try the untried when what we do is inconsequential. Hence the remarkable fact that many inventions had their birth as toys. In the Occident the first machines were mechanical toys, and such crucial instruments as the telescope and microscope were first conceived as playthings. Almost all civilizations display a singular ingenuity in toy making. The Aztecs did not have the wheel, but some of their animal toys had rollers for feet. It would not be fanciful to assume that in the ancient Near East, too, the wheel and the sail made their first appearance as playthings. We are told that in one of the oldest cemeteries in the world the skeletons showed that the average age of the population at death was less than twenty-five—and there is no reason to assume that the place was particularly unhealthy. Thus the chances are that the momentous discoveries and inventions of the Neolithic Age which made possible the rise of civilization, and which formed the basis of everyday life until yesterday, were made by childlike, playful people. It is not unlikely that the first domesticated animals were children's pets. Planting and irrigating, too, were probably first attempted in the course of play. (A girl of five once advised me to plant hair on my bald head.) Even if it could be shown that a striking desiccation of climate preceded the first appearance of herdsmen and cultivators it would not prove that the conception of domestication was born of a crisis. The energies released by a crisis usually flow toward sheer action and application. Domestication could have been practiced as an amusement long before it found practical application. The crisis induced people to make use of things which amuse.

When we do find that a critical challenge has apparently evoked a marked creative response there is always the possibility that the response came not from people cornered by a challenge but from people who in an exuberance of energy went out in search of a challenge. It is highly doubtful whether people are capable of genuine creative responses when necessity takes them by the throat. The desperate struggle for existence is a static rather than a dynamic influence. The urgent search for the vitally necessary is likely to stop once we have found something that is more or less adequate, but the search for the superfluous has no end. Hence the fact that man's most unflagging and spectacular efforts were made not in search of necessities but of superfluities. It is worth remembering that the discovery of America was a by-product of the search for ginger, cloves, pepper, and cinnamon. The utilitarian device, even when it is an essential ingredient of our daily life, is most likely to have its ancestry in the nonutilitarian. The sepulchre, temple, and palace preceded the utilitarian house; ornament preceded clothing; work, particularly teamwork, derives from play. We are told that the bow was a musical instrument before it became a weapon, and some authorities believe that the subtle craft of fishing originated in a period when game was abundant—that it was the product not so much of grim necessity as of curiosity, speculation, and playfulness. We know that poetry preceded prose, and it may be that singing came before talking.

On the whole it seems to be true that the creative periods in history were buoyant and even frivolous. One thinks of the lightheartedness of Periclean Athens, the Renaissance, the Elizabethan Age, and the age of the Enlightenment. Mr. Nehru tells us that in India "during every period when her civilization bloomed, we find an intense joy in life and nature and a pleasure in the art of living." One suspects that much of the praise of seriousness comes from people who have a vital need for a façade of weight and dignity. La Rochefoucauld said of solemnity that it is "a mystery of the body invented to conceal the defects of the mind." The fits of deadly seriousness we know as mass movements, which come bearing a message of serious purpose and weighty ideals, are usually set in motion by sterile pedants possessed of a murderous hatred for festive creativeness. Such movements bring in their wake meagermindedness, fear, austerity, and sterile conformity. Hardly one of the world's great works in literature, art, music, and pure science was conceived and realized in the stern atmosphere of a mass movement. It is only when these movements have spent themselves, and their pattern of austere boredom begins to crack, and the despised present dares assert its claims to trivial joys, that the creative impulse begins to stir amidst the grayness and desolation.

Man shares his playfulness with other warm-blooded animals, with mammals and birds. Insects, reptiles, etc., do not play. Clearly, the division of the forms of life into those that can play and those that cannot is a significant one. Equally significant is the duration of the propensity to play. Mammals and birds play only when young, while man retains the propensity throughout life. My feeling is that the tendency to carry youthful characteristics into adult life, which renders man perpetually immature and unfinished, is at the root of his uniqueness in the universe, and is particularly pronounced in the creative individual. Youth has been called a perishable talent, but perhaps talent and originality are always aspects of youth, and the creative individual is an imperishable juvenile. When the Greeks said, "Whom the gods love die young" they probably meant, as Lord Sankey suggested, that those favored by the gods stay young till the day they die; young and playful.[1]

Obviously "What is the value of X?" is the guiding question behind most examples of critical writing and review. Whether he is concerned with books, movies, theater, music, or dance, the writer of an evaluation is expected to tell his reader whether the offering in question is any good. Naturally the reviewer's opinion is exactly that—*his subjective opinion* for the most part. This does not mean, however, that a good review cannot be objective as well. "I personally do not like courtroom drama," a reviewer might state, adding—if he wants to be fair and to inform his audience of a truth larger and more important than his own likes and dislikes—that the courtroom scenes in one particular play are extraordinarily well done. The good reviewer manages somehow to "get outside himself" so that he has a double vision and a double standard; he sees through his own eyes but he also sees through the eyes of others—or at least he tries.

Evaluating Books

To cite an example, in the following straightforward review of a book on the conservation of natural resources the reviewer, though obviously impressed with the book's thesis and style, does not directly exhort us to read the book and "join the cause." Instead he gives us sufficient information about its content so that we may decide for ourselves whether we want to pursue the subject further.

NOT SO RICH AS YOU THINK: A REVIEW

EDWARD WEEKS

California, with its ever increasing population, presents the most critical battleground of all the states. George R. Stewart is a California naturalist who in his earlier books, *Storm, Fire, Earth Abides,* and *Ordeal by Hunger,* has dramatized the great changes which man has to contend with in his environment. Now in *Not so Rich as You Think* (Houghton Mifflin, $5.00) he confronts us with as difficult and disagreeable a subject as any American can face up to—the devastation which we have lazily, greedily, destructively inflicted on our own country. No more realistic horror story will be published this year.

[1] "The Playful Mood" from *The Ordeal of Change* by Eric Hoffer. Copyright © 1961 by Eric Hoffer. Reprinted by permission of Harper & Row, Publishers, Inc.

His reasoning is irrefutable; we worship the twin gods Production and Invention, and our sacrifices for them are hysterical. Everyone needs an automobile, and hopefully a new one every second year. If beer bottles are a nuisance, devise a can—it is so easy to throw out the window. If the land must give a higher yield, drench it with pesticides; if we need more power, look to the atomic energy plants with their fallout. This has been our success story for too many years. Now it is time to pay the bill, because the sewage, the factory effluents which have been poisoning our rivers, the garbage which we have been stuffing into holes, the tin cans and the rusty cars which won't dissolve, the smog, the pesticide runoffs, and the atomic poisons add up to an enormity of neglect which must be taken seriously. Matter cannot be annihilated; and if we do not begin to control it, it will overwhelm us.

Without wit and a good patient sense of humor, Mr. Stewart's story would have been too dreary to bear. But he makes it readable and concise; he places us against our vivid, reckless, historical background; he plays on our native pride; and in the three final chapters of his short book he suggests a more responsible alternative than apathy.

In the ten chapters of his main argument he considers what happens to matter which is primarily "committed" to water, or to land, or to air, and what happens in each area *after* the processes of nature take over. He tells us that "riversfull" of water pour into factories, are contaminated, and then released again into the stream with results which have caused Mark Twain's River, the Mississippi, to be termed "the colon of the Middle West." He says that the list of the country's dirty industries, according to Secretary Udall, is headed by a large paper company in Detroit involved in the manufacture of toilet tissue. He has some hopeful things to say about our automobile graveyards and the recycling of metal scrap, but no hope whatever for the exhaust control of the internal-combustion engine. He tells us fifty millions are spent annually to remove litter from our main highways and believes that the beer can should be outlawed. In a brief but fascinating chapter entitled "The Ultimates," he studies the tyranny of power: waterpower is by all odds the neatest, he says, but there can never be enough of it to run civilization. He then goes on to assess the atomic power plants and tells how to dispose of atomic wastes. Man's part in all this devastation has been sardonically delineated in the black and white drawings by Robert Osborn.[2]

A good book review poses and answers at least three questions:

1. It indicates the content and presumed purpose of the book (the ability to write a good summary is important here, Chapter 19, "How Can X Be Summarized?")
2. It describes the style of the book (how well or badly the writer has executed his purpose).
3. It judges the value of the book in terms of whether or not its purpose was *worth* achieving. (Should the book have been written? Should it be read?)

Obviously only the first two questions can be answered by relatively objective analysis and interpretation; the third—What is the book's value or worth?—depends on the reviewer's judgment, his opinion of what is valuable

[2] From *The Atlantic Monthly*, February 1968. Reprinted by permission of Edward Weeks.

and worthy. However he deals with the necessarily subjective aspects of reviewing, one thing is certain: he should not use the review as a showcase for his own personal tastes and preferences, featuring these (plus his own barbed wit and clever "asides") at the expense of the book itself. A review should focus on what is being reviewed, not on the reviewer. His function is to illuminate the work so that the reader can better understand and appreciate it. Indeed, as W. H. Auden points out in his essay "The Function of a Critic" (pp. 102–03), the critic's *main* responsibility is to indicate the broader and deeper significance of the work in question.

This assumes, of course, that there is a broader and deeper significance to be appreciated. In some cases, however, this is not so—at least not in the critic's opinion. He may feel that the work has no value at all; he may stress instead the *badness* of the book. Thus in the following review of a history text, the reviewer expresses indignation at the author's misleading title, his oversimplification and inaccurate treatment of the subject, his jargon-ridden writing. This book, says the reviewer—in plain and uncompromising language—is without value. Indeed he lists ten steps—negative and derisive in tone—that helped to make this a poor book.

TEN COMMANDMENTS FOR THE NEW BEHAVIORAL SCIENTIST—A REVIEW

RONALD HILTON

Political History of Latin America by Ronald M. Glassman. 324 pp. New York: Funk & Wagnalls. $7.95.

Perhaps the most remarkable phenomenon in academe during the last decade has been the explosion of the behavioral sciences. The Ford Foundation lit the match; that should have been sufficient warning. It was assumed that the behavioral sciences would help society to solve its problems. University administrators, for whom there is no more potent argument than money and the fashions which attract it, were easily convinced. Those of us who are sympathetic to the social sciences and feel the need for academic renewal welcomed the newcomers. Then everything went sour.

Academic programs which represented decades of devoted work were neglected or wrecked. The social science departments throughout the country became havens for all kinds of idealists and misfits who were looking for a refuge within a refuge (the university) from which to launch their attacks on society. They incited physical violence on the university administrations which had encouraged them, and then turned on their departmental mentors, accusing them of irrelevance. More serious perhaps than these surface eruptions is the effect the behavioral sciences have had on scholarship. That is the subject of this review, since the book here examined provides us with a case study. Here are the characteristics of the new learning.

1. Take a limited subject but make it appear that it is of immense importance. Choose an appropriate, or rather inappropriate title: this book is certainly not a political history of Latin America. The first part deals with medieval Spain, the second with the quasi-feudal society of colonial America, the third with the origin of Latin American cities. A more exact title would have been "Some considerations about the transfer of characteristics of medieval Iberian society to the New World."

2. Claim that your work brings new insights into social problems. The author asserts: "This kind of analysis has never been extended in depth to any of the underdeveloped countries, although some rudimentary attempts have been made in studying the Middle East and Africa. . . . No attempt to apply this model to Latin America has been made at all." In reality the book tells us little that a competent historian does not know already.

3. Invoke the name of Max Weber, as a Soviet Marxist invokes those of Marx and Lenin. This proves that you are orthodox and respectable. The name of Weber appears three times on the first page of the Foreword.

4. Show that you belong to a scientific élite by using strange words even though there is a more common synonym. If these words were used by Weber, so much the better. "Charismatic" used to be an esoteric term, but now it is common coin. So our author repeatedly uses "kingship" instead of "king," "monarchy" or "government." Why "legist" instead of "jurist," "lawmaker" or "lawyer"? If a person withdraws into his own private world, this is "retreatism." Throw in words like "surrogate" and "clan" whenever possible. What on earth is "dereified"? My dictionaries don't give it, and my sociology colleagues at Stanford don't know it. Although "charismatic" has lost its charisma, try it in exotic combinations like "law charisma" or "clan-charismatic." Combinations like "clan-heritable" are favored.

5. Prove your expertise by writing an English which is not only cumbersome but positively unpleasant to anyone who has a sense of style. In his acknowledgments the author thanks two colleagues who made the book more readable. Yet the style is still utterly lacking in "charisma."

6. Claim that you have a model that will bring order into a confused mass of facts. In this book the model is not clear, and after struggling through some 300 pages, the reader is left in a state of obfuscation, longing for an old-fashioned book which is well organized and in which ideas are expressed lucidly.

7. Don't bother too much about facts. At the recent annual meeting of the International Studies Association, a behavioral scientist pontificated: "Models without facts are no vice, facts without models are no virtue." It sounded as if he were reading from the Little Red Book of the Behavioral Scientist. The author of this book asserts airily that "the empirical data on Latin America have been available for almost a century—they are easily obtainable." Having thus dismissed the problem of "empirical data," he proceeds to make one mistake after another.

A whole review could be filled with the factual errors in the book; to mention but one, the author thinks that Havana was the seat of a vice-royalty. Anyone with experience in the field should know how extremely difficult it is to assemble facts about the political history of Latin America. Since the Hispanic American Report disappeared, we have had no good source for contemporary Latin America, and the situation is worse regarding other areas. Our ignorance of the facts is one reason why we make such mistakes in foreign policy. It is much easier to play with models. If an old-fashioned scholar stresses the extreme difficulty of checking and assembling facts, this is dismissed as "busy work" unworthy of a creative scholar. This, incidentally is the rationale of the lazy and essentially mediocre students who wish to reduce classes to muddled, uninformative bull-sessions.

8. Since old-fashioned scholarship is "out," the author tells us at the begin-

ning of his bibliography that he will not list many books specifically on Latin America. He does list a number of them, but he seems to have depended largely on Jean Mariéjol's "The Spain of Ferdinand and Isabella" (in the English translation), Eyler N. Simpson's "The Ejido: Mexico's Way Out" (which is out of date—1937—and frequently wrong), and two books by George M. McBride, "The Land Systems of Mexico" (1923) and "Chile, Land and Society" (1936). McBride's studies were good for their time, but they are quite inadequate for present needs. From these four books, the author quotes frequently verbatim. There is no mention of the vast periodical literature without which it is impossible to write the political history of Latin America.

9. Acquiring the necessary linguistic mastery to study a foreign area takes a lifetime. As a defense mechanism, belittle the study of languages or say you have satisfied the requirement by taking an N.D.E.A.-sponsored summer course. A study of the political history of Latin America would require a detailed study of books, articles and newspapers at least in Spanish and Portuguese. The bibliography does not list a single item in any foreign language. A favorite insult of the behavioral scientists is to call old-fashioned scholars "culture-bound." Who in reality could be more culture-bound than the student of a foreign area who relies essentially on sources in English?

10. If the scholarly study of foreign languages is "out," a display of mathematics is "in." Here our author disappoints us; this book contains absolutely no mathematics. Yet it is impossible to write the political history of Latin America without statistics, and while the use of mathematical formulae by behavioral scientists is often dust in the reader's eyes, some of the most important work in the Latin-American field today is being done in the compilation of historical statistics by scholars like Woodrow Borah and Sherburne F. Cook of Berkeley, James W. Wilkie of U.C.L.A., and Frederic Mauro of the University of Paris-Nanterre. Any substantial political history of Latin America should contain at least some reference to this work.

Such are the Ten Commandments for the new behavioral scientist. And while the behavioral scientists are engaging in their games (game theory being very much "in" and also more fun than the despised empirical facts), our young men are dying in Vietnam and Western civilization is beset by corruption within and a battering from without. This is not 1985, it is 1453.[3]

General Reviews

The three reviews that follow—of a restaurant, a record album, and a movie—are all good examples of their type: clear, informative, and readable. Like a good book review, they provide facts about their subjects, i.e., relatively objective, concrete data. The writers are reporters, in other words, as well as reviewers. Indeed it is only by citing specific details ("dim lighting," "white napery," "the usual murals of French country life") that the writer can convince the reader that he knows what he is talking about; he has paid close attention to the experience he is describing (whether it is eating, listening to a record, or watching a movie); and he is anxious to share that experience—for good or ill—with those who have not yet had it.

[3] From the *New York Times*, August 3, 1969.

DIRECTORY OF DINING

CRAIG CLAIBORNE

Cafe du Soir, 322 East 86th Street, 289–9996. This pleasantly decorated bistro is on a street that is known but certainly not celebrated for its heavy-handed, pseudo-German cooking. By comparison to those pork-hocks-mit-sauerkraut establishments, the Cafe du Soir is a joy. It has dim lighting, tables with white napery, and the usual murals of French country life. The bistro-type menu is predictable, and the kitchen comes off creditably.

The offerings include trout amandine, fillet of sole meunière, coq au vin and boeuf bourguignon, all the well-known standbys. There is a very good creation, a sauté of shrimp maison.

Among the regrettable things, however, list the butter that recently had a refrigerator taste, the not-freshly-made-and-old-garlic-taste of the salad dressing and the American-style coffee.

There are complete luncheons at the Cafe du Soir priced from about $2.25 to $4.25; à la carte dishes from about $1.75 to $3.25. Complete dinners priced from about $4.25 to $6.95; à la carte items from about $2.75 to $5.50. Cocktails, wines. Closed Monday.[4]

THE WIZARDRY OF OZ SMITH

MARTIN WILLIAMS

According to the liner notes of his LP, *The Wizardry of Oz Smith* (Capitol T/ST 2288), Osborne Smith is a singer, actor, composer, and ex-student at the Sorbonne. His program includes "Keys to the Highway," "Midnight Special," and "Careless Love."

Another coffee-house folknik dipping, with all the virility of an antiquarian, into the Leadbelly repertory? Not at all. A vocalist peddling the posturing rusticity of the "soul" jazzman? Again, emphatically not. Oz Smith is, for one thing, one of the most straightforwardly honest singers I have ever heard. He is also powerful and in exceptionally mature and disciplined command of his vocal and histrionic equipment.

Oz Smith approaches this traditional repertory of blues, work songs, and Gospel music with respect, and, more important, he finds in it a personal musical inspiration. His interpretations echo many decades of Afro-American musical tradition with sympathy and with love, yet they are decidedly those of a young contemporary.

I said that Smith is honest. But honesty is not enough for art, and I am sure that Oz Smith is an artist. His version of "Careless Love," for example, is the most beautiful reading of that touching melody, with its highly complex ethnic origins, that I have ever heard. And to have followed it, as was done on this LP, with the rousing Gospel "Twelve Gates to the City" is a superb piece of programing.

I have entertained a possibility that actually Osborne Smith is a fine actor, here doing an expert impression of a singer. But, no, his musical sensibilities are entirely authentic, as authentic as they are exceptional. I find only about

[4] From the *New York Times*, January 19, 1968. © 1968 by The New York Times Company. Reprinted by permission.

one and a half of the ten selections on this LP not up to the level of the rest of it, and I will therefore not say which one and a half.

Oz Smith is abetted by accompaniments of arranger Robert Smith that are stirringly appropriate. They, too, take traditional material and develop it in contemporary terms with generally keen understanding of the beauties and the possibilities implicit in its honorable past. From among the individual players involved, I will single out particularly the trumpet of Thad Jones, who sometimes gets an anguish unheard in blues accompaniments since King Oliver; the ringing guitar of Wally Richardson; and the supple guitar and banjo of Barry Kornfeld.[5]

A FINE, FAMILY–SIZE ENTERPRISE: GYPSY GIRL WITH HAYLEY MILLS

RICHARD SCHICKEL

Introduction: movie is evaluated

The title could not be more fatuous or misleading. There are no hot-blooded passions, ancient curses, mysterious kidnapings, not even so much as a flamenco dance in *Gypsy Girl*. It is, instead, a sensitive study of a child's innocent obsession with death, her relations with a community that fears her strangeness, and her ultimate release from her obsession through the accident of love. It is both original in its theme and refreshingly direct in the way it handles it. In the good taste and sense of its writing, direction and acting, in the non-gypsy spell it casts, it is one of the season's more affecting films.

Gypsy Girl is a family enterprise, starring Hayley Mills in a script co-authored by her mother, Mary Hayley Bell, and directed by her father, John Mills, all of whom have sensibly conspired to hold their film to a scale a family can easily handle. The setting is an English village, the characters are few and the plot, though intricate to recount, is straightforward, crystalline in its motivations and intelligently willing to stretch probability up to but never beyond the breaking point. It does so not for the sake of sensation but rather to stress its essential quality, which is that of a tale such as old men tell in rural lounging places, the kind of story that is motivated not by their desire to gossip but rather by their awe of the infinitude of small strangenesses the human world contains.

Outline of plot

The situation is that Brydie White (Miss Mills) once witnessed the death of a playmate in a shooting accident in which she was also wounded. Now an amnesiac and somewhat retarded, she has become a pariah to most of the town's adults but an enchanted creature to their children. The death of some pet rabbits reawakens the fascination with death that has intermittently preoccupied her, and she founds a cemetery for all the animal "deaders" of the village. The other kids enthusiastically join the project but it reawakens adult unease over Brydie's continued presence.

In effect driven from the community, she is rescued from drowning in a woodland stream by a gypsy boy (Ian McShane) who has

[5] "Oz Smith, Remarkable Singer," by Martin Williams. *Saturday Review*, August 28, 1965. Copyright 1965 Saturday Review, Inc. Reprinted by permission of *Saturday Review* and Martin Williams.

been hovering mysteriously about, an earth-bound guardian angel, full of strange frets and odd angers—and just as much a mistrusted outsider as Brydie. In the end she is given a choice between being institutionalized or marrying her inarticulately loving protector.

Specific reasons cited to support the initial evaluation

Very well then, this is obviously a simple tale of simple hearts and minds grappling with matters that seem rather simple to an audience accustomed to a greater degree of complexity in both their lives and their films. What—beyond the unfamiliarity of its material—accounts for the way the movie worms its way into your consciousness and thereafter tugs with such pleasant insistence at memory?

There is, to begin with, Director Mills's fine sense of the pastoral mood, captured with careful, comfortable color camera work, and his shrewd, quiet eye for rustic types. Combined, these qualities give this film an easy, delicately balanced naturalism which a cruder director could easily have spoiled.

Then there is the authenticity of Hayley Mills's performance. There is something in her that has resisted Hollywood's attempts to turn her into a conventionally cute and kookie adolescent and which causes her to respond very strongly to the challenge of portraying the genuinely odd child, as she did in *Tiger Bay* and *The Chalk Garden*. She knows that in the disturbed mind there resides truth, humor and those pools of strange calmness that are created when consciousness is stretched as far out as it can go.

Finally, the Millses have resisted at every turn the temptation to convert their small miracle into a larger one. They are content to show us that misfits, too, can find love and build lives on it, and that is enough for them. There is no implication here of divine intervention, marvelous cures or even an especially golden future. In short, *Gypsy Girl* is a film with very little fashionable resonance about it. Unambiguous, it will not support much exploration of its meanings or many generalizing speculations about the nature of the human condition. It is merely what it is—an atypical film about atypical people living in what is now an atypical environment. But it is also, as movies run today, atypically honest, modest and humane.[6]

ASSIGNMENTS

I. A. Consider the following questions on Eric Hoffer's "The Playful Mood":

1. State the thesis of the piece in a single sentence.
2. In what way is the opening sentence provocative? What two key words are significantly set against each other?
3. What concrete evidence does Hoffer cite to support his thesis?

4. How would you characterize the tone of this piece—authoritative, tentative, serious? Explain your answer by citing specific phrases and passages.

B. Write an essay (500–750 words) in which you support or criticize Hoffer's evaluation.

C. Write an evaluative essay (750–1,000 words) dealing with some neglected aspect of man's behavior or state of being (boredom as a motivating force) or with some changing aspect of our culture or society (style in dress, the new morality, nudity in films). Organize your essay as follows:

Introduction

I. General evaluation
II. Examples and details supporting the evaluation

Conclusion

II. Analyze and evaluate the formal reviews in this chapter in terms of the following:

A. Do they provide the reader with sufficient information to make a sound judgment of his own?

B. In what ways do the reviewers support their own evaluations (evidence, logical reasoning)?

C. Describe the tone of each review and indicate whether it is appropriate. Does it win the reader's "good will"?

D. Comment on the effectiveness of Ronald Hilton's "Ten Commandments." Do you think a straight criticism would have had as strong an impact as the derisive commandments? Explain.

E. Comment on the writers' style and the overall readability of each review.

III. A. Write a review (500–750 words) dealing with any book you liked and would recommend to others, indicating its

1. content and purpose
2. style and quality
3. value (is its purpose *justified?*)

B. Write a review (500–750 words) in which you condemn a book as having little or no value. In the manner of Hilton's essay, list a series of "commandments."

IV. Write a review (300–500 words) of one of the following:

a restaurant
a record album
a play
a movie
a concert
a television program
a radio show

19 HOW CAN X BE SUMMARIZED?

How to restate briefly and accurately the main points in a body of information; how to see through to its "essence"; how to strip it bare of details and implications; how to condense and communicate its core meaning: this is the intellectual challenge of summarizing, a skill that some people regard as mechanical and routine, not at all "creative." The truth is, however, that there is no greater challenge to the intellect and no more accurate test of understanding than the ability to filter an idea through your mind and "say it over" briefly in your own words. Indeed it can be stated as a general truth: to read and study efficiently; to do research; to take satisfactory notes; to write papers, critiques, and examinations; to grasp an idea and hold it in the mind—all require the ability to "boil down" materials to manageable scope and see them in terms of their basic intention, their main points, and the relation of these points to each other. A summary, in other words, is a demanding exercise in analysis and interpretation (seeing the parts and judging which are *more* or *less* important).

Let us approach this as a significant and recurrent question, then: "How can X be summarized?" Most often the answer will constitute a *section* of an essay rather than a whole essay, although there are occasions when summary is the purpose of a piece of writing: in "The News of the Week in Review" section of the *New York Times*, for example, and in weekly issues of *Time* and *Newsweek* magazines.

Before considering the summary as an independent form, however, we will note how it is used as a supplement to expository writing of all kinds: in a factual essay we summarize background information (related data and ideas, past history of our subject); in concluding an argument we recapitulate its main points; in a literary review or critique we provide a plot summary or "synopsis" of the work in question.

It will be helpful, then, to review the different situations and types of material that call for summary, observing at the outset that the basis of all summary—whatever the subject matter or occasion—is careful and repeated reading of the text to be summarized and sustained critical thinking about what has been read: a process of probing to the "heart of the matter" so that it may be rendered in a clear, concise restatement.

Summarizing Ideas

Ideas and concepts often need brief restatement so that they may be reexamined in a new context. Take the following paragraph by John Stuart Mill, for example, drawn from his famous essay "On Liberty." Assume that you are writing a paper on freedom of the press and you have turned to Section II of this essay ("Of the Liberty of Thought and Discussion") to examine Mill's ideas on the subject with an eye toward summarizing Mill's ideas in your own paper. You would then read and reread the passage reprinted below, analyzing it carefully in terms of Mill's total statement, trying to abstract the main idea from that total statement.

OF THE LIBERTY OF THOUGHT AND DISCUSSION

JOHN STUART MILL

The time, it is to be hoped, is gone by, when any defence would be necessary of the 'liberty of the press' as one of the securities against corrupt or tyrannical government. No argument, we may suppose, can now be needed, against permitting a legislature or an executive, not identified in interest with the people, to prescribe opinions to them, and determine what doctrines or what arguments they shall be allowed to hear. This aspect of the question, besides, has been so often and so triumphantly enforced by preceding writers, that it need not be specially insisted on in this place. Though the law of England, on the subject of the press, is as servile to this day as it was in the time of the Tudors, there is little danger of its being actually put in force against political discussion, except during some temporary panic, when fear of insurrection drives ministers and judges from their propriety; and, speaking generally, it is not, in constitutional countries, to be apprehended, that the government, whether completely responsible to the people or not, will often attempt to control the expression of opinion, except when in doing so it makes itself the organ of the general intolerance of the public. Let us suppose, therefore, that the government is entirely at one with the people, and never thinks of exerting any power of coercion unless in agreement with what it conceives to be their voice. But I deny the right of the people to exercise such coercion, either by themselves or by their government. The power itself is illegitimate. The best government has no more title to it than the worst. It is as noxious, or more noxious, when exerted in accordance with public opinion, than when in opposition to it. If all mankind minus one, were of one opinion, and only one person were of the contrary opinion, mankind would be no more justified in silencing that one person, than he, if he had the power, would be justified in silencing man-

> kind. Were an opinion a personal possession of no value except to the owner; if to be obstructed in the enjoyment of it were simply a private injury, it would make some difference whether the injury was inflicted only on a few persons or on many. But the peculiar evil of silencing the expression of an opinion is, that it is robbing the human race; posterity as well as the existing generation; those who dissent from the opinion, still more than those who hold it. If the opinion is right, they are deprived of the opportunity of exchanging error for truth: if wrong, they lose, what is almost as great a benefit, the clearer perception and livelier impression of truth, produced by its collision with error.[1]

Several careful readings make it clear that Mill has set forth in this paragraph one single important idea about liberty of the press, which may be summarized as follows:

> Except during time of panic, liberty of the press is reasonably safe from corrupt or tyrannical government. A greater present danger is from an intolerant majority who might try—on their own or through government pressure—to silence dissent, thereby robbing society of possible truth (if the dissenters are right), or (if they are wrong) of that clearer, livelier view of truth which emerges when it collides with error.

Sometimes the writer will make our job easier by summarizing his own main idea, in which case we are wise to quote him directly. The following is a summary of William James' essay on the function of higher education (pp. 100–02):

> James tells us in this essay that the humanities should teach biography ("the sifting of human creations!") because through this study we develop a "critical sense" which enables us "to know a good man when we see him."

In the expression "to know a good man when we see him" ("the best single phrase in which we can tell what [education] ought to do for us") James sums up approximately four hundred words of discourse, enabling us—by quoting him—to achieve an equivalent economy and precision of restatement.

In trying to summarize highly complex ideas—a proposal that contains several parts and a rationale—we must again resign ourselves to several readings. We must again carefully search for the main points and the key terms that embody them, noting also recurrent words and phrases and "summing-up" sentences that might profitably serve as quotations. In the following proposal, educator James B. Conant suggests a new approach to an introductory science course. The title (often a clue to what a piece of writing is about) provides us with two key terms.

[1] From *Essential Works of John Stuart Mill*, edited by Max Lerner.

THE TACTICS AND STRATEGY OF SCIENCE

JAMES B. CONANT

Let me now be specific as to my proposal for the reform of the scientific education of the layman. What I propose is the establishment of one or more courses at the college level on the Tactics and Strategy of Science. The objective would be to give a greater degree of understanding of science by the close study of a relatively few historical examples of the development of science. I suggest courses at the college level, for I do not believe they could be introduced earlier in a student's education; but there is no reason why they could not become important parts of programs of adult education. Indeed, such courses might well prove particularly suitable for older groups of men and women.

The analogy with the teaching of strategy and tactics of war by examples from military history is obvious. And the success of that educational procedure is one reason why I venture to be hopeful about this new approach to understanding science. I also draw confidence from the knowledge of how the case method in law schools and a somewhat similar method in the Harvard Business School have demonstrated the value of this type of pedagogic device. The course would not aim to teach science—not even the basic principles or simplest facts—though as a by-product considerable knowledge of certain sciences would be sure to follow. Of course, some elementary knowledge of physics would be a prerequisite, but with the improvement in the teaching of science in high schools which is sure to come, this should prove no serious obstacle.

The case histories would almost all be chosen from the early days in the evolution of the modern discipline. Certain aspects of physics in the seventeenth and eighteenth centuries; chemistry in the eighteenth and nineteenth; geology in the early nineteenth; certain phases of biology in the eighteenth; others in the nineteenth. The advantages of this method of approach are twofold: first, relatively little factual knowledge is required either as regards the science in question or other sciences, and relatively little mathematics; second, in the early days one sees in clearest light the necessary fumblings of even intellectual giants when they are also pioneers; one comes to understand what science is by seeing how difficult it is in fact to carry out glib scientific precepts.

A few words may be in order as to the principles which would guide me in selecting case histories for my course in the Tactics and Strategy of Science. I should wish to show the difficulties which attend each new push forward in the advance of science, and the importance of new techniques: how they arise, are improved, and often revolutionize a field of inquiry. I should hope to illustrate the intricate interplay between experiment, or observation, and the development of new concepts and new generalizations; in short, how new concepts evolve from experiments, how one conceptual scheme for a time is adequate and then is modified or displaced by another. I should want also to illustrate the interconnection between science and society about which so much has been said in recent years by our Marxist friends. I should have very little to say about the classification of facts, unless it were to use this phrase as a straw man. But I should hope that almost all examples chosen would show the hazards which nature puts in the way of those who would examine the facts impartially and classify them accurately. The "controlled experiment" and the planned or controlled observation would be in the forefront of every discussion. The difference in methods between the observational sciences of astronomy, geology, systematic biology on the one hand, and the experimental sciences of physics, chemistry, and experimental biology on the other should be emphasized.

To what extent a course in the Tactics and Strategy of Science should take cognizance of the existence of problems in metaphysics and epistemology would depend on the outlook of the instructor and the maturity and interest of the student. Obviously the course in question would not be one on the metaphysical foundations of modern science; yet the teacher can hardly ignore completely the influence of new scientific concepts on contemporary thinking about the structure of the universe or the nature and destiny of man. Nor can one fail in all honesty to identify at least vaguely those philosophic problems which have arisen when man has sought to examine critically the basis of his knowledge about "the external world." Perhaps in collaboration with a colleague from the department of philosophy the instructor would wish to suggest the reading of extracts from the writings of certain philosophers. If so, the existence of more than one school of thought should certainly be emphasized.

As I shall show in subsequent chapters, a discussion of the evolution of new conceptual schemes as a result of experimentation would occupy a central position in the exposition. This being so, there would be no escape from a consideration of the difficulties which historically have attended the development of new concepts. Is a vacuum really empty, if so, how can you see through it? Is action at a distance imaginable? These questions at one time in the forefront of scientific discussion are well worthy of careful review. The Newtonian theory of gravitation once disturbed "almost all investigators of nature because it was founded on an uncommon unintelligibility." It no longer disturbs us because "it has become a common unintelligibility." To what extent can the same statement be made about other concepts which have played a major part in the development of modern science? When we say that the chemists have "established" that chlorophyll is essential for photosynthesis and that they also have "established" the spatial arrangements of the carbon, hydrogen, and oxygen atoms in cane sugar, are we using the word "establish" in two different senses? These and similar questions should be explored in sufficient degree to make the students aware of some of the complexities which lie hidden behind our usual simplified exposition of the basic ideas of modern science in an elementary course.

However, I cannot emphasize too often that the course in question must *not* be concerned with the fruits of scientific inquiries, either as embodied in scientific laws or theories or cosmologies, or in the applications of science to industry or agriculture or medicine. Rather, the instructor would center his attention on the ways in which these fruits have been attained. One might call it a course in "scientific method" as illustrated by examples from history, except that I am reluctant to use this ambiguous phrase. I should prefer to speak of the methods by which science has been advanced, or perhaps we should say knowledge has been advanced, harking back to Francis Bacon's famous phrase, the advancement of learning.[2]

[2] From *On Understanding Science* by James B. Conant. Copyright © 1947 by Yale University Press. Used by permission.

Before attempting to summarize this essay, we should conceive—or construct—a hypothetical purpose for our labor. (We should never, as mentioned earlier, write in a vacuum, but always with a definite occasion and audience in mind—a rhetorical stance.) Let us say, then, that we are taking notes on Conant's projected science course for a paper we are preparing on science education today (its distinctive function, present status). We will use Conant's proposal as an illustration of one of several innovative suggestions offered by educators. The limited length of our paper makes it imperative, however, that we "boil down" this proposal to a short paragraph. How can we do this without distorting its essential features?

One way to begin is by isolating key terms and concepts. As indicated above, the title is a helpful clue, for it contains the words "tactics" and "strategy." Is not Conant proposing that the introductory science course concern itself with the tactics and strategy of science—its long and difficult struggle to break through to new areas of knowledge—rather than with the "fruits" of such struggles—scientific knowledge, neatly classified into systems and codified into laws? Is not Conant proposing further that we use a "case history" method (note how many times this term appears); i.e., that we study specific historical instances in which scientific discoveries were made. Students in introductory science should be able to observe these discoveries "in process," says Conant, as if they were watching a drama unfold before them. In watching these discoveries "take place," students will learn the true nature of the scientific enterprise, as they do *not* learn it in the conventional course.

We are not yet summarizing Conant's proposal, only exploring it to discover its main contours. We note, then, that the word "difficult" recurs frequently along with various synonyms that refer to the assembling of scientific precepts.

> The *necessary fumblings* of even intellectual giants when they are also pioneers. . . .
>
> One comes to understand what science is by seeing how *difficult* it is in fact to carry out glib scientific precepts.

Note the juxtaposition here of "difficult" and "glib." In a sense this sums up the difference between the course Conant would institute (one that would demonstrate how *difficult* it is to arrive at scientific precepts) and the conventional course that, as Conant sees it, is a *glib*, packaged presentation of scientific facts.

> I should wish to show the *difficulties* which attend each new push forward. . . .
>
> I should hope to illustrate the *intricate* interplay between experiment, or observation, and the development of new concepts. . . .
>
> I should . . . show the *hazards* which nature puts in the way of those who would examine the facts impartially. . . .
>
> There would be no escape from a consideration of the *difficulties* which historically have attended the development of new concepts.
>
> Make the students aware of some of the *complexities* which lie hidden behind our usual simplified exposition of the basic ideas of modern science in an elementary course.

Here again we note the juxtaposition of the two approaches: Conant's emphasis on *complexities* (difficulty) as against the *simplified* (and therefore falsified) conventional presentation.

The last paragraph of Conant's essay, though not a formal recapitulation, nonetheless sums up his case: "I cannot emphasize too often that the course in question must *not* be concerned with the fruits of scientific inquiries. . . . Rather [with] the ways in which these fruits have been attained." Clearly this is the central theme of Conant's essay, the main point of his argument in favor of a new type of science course. Recognizing this, we must plan to organize our summary around this point, adding whatever further information we "interpret" as important. Thus the summary of Conant's proposal (as it appears in the hypothetical paper on "Science Education Today") may read as follows:

> Conant proposes a new type of introductory science course that concerns itself *not* with the "fruits" of scientific inquiry (a presentation of scientific fact, neatly formulated into theory and law), but rather with the *way* these fruits have been attained—what Conant calls the "Tactics and Strategy of Science." Rejecting the "usual simplified exposition" of the usual introductory course, which makes science seem static and "glib," Conant calls for a "case history" approach: a close study of a few historical examples of scientific discovery that would give students a realistic picture of how the scientific method works in actual practice: the countless difficulties and "necessary fumblings" that accompany every scientific advance, as well as the ultimate triumphs. Conant's introductory course would emphasize the difficulties and complexities of the scientific enterprise—also its tentativeness and ongoing dialectic. For science is always advancing, says Conant: "One conceptual scheme for a time is adequate and then is modified or displaced by another."

Summarizing Data

Just as we will frequently find occasion for summarizing ideas and concepts, so we will find occasion to summarize a body of data that is relevant to our purposes and usable in our writing, provided it can be "boiled down" to one ninth or tenth of its original length: provided, that is, it can be seen in terms of its most significant and relevant points of information. Data may be of many kinds (factual, technical, sociological, statistical, historical), and it may be taken from many sources (a report, study, survey, reference work). In any case, summarizing data requires that we analyze what the data "adds up to"—giving not a long list of facts and figures, but rather a short indication of what they *mean.* A good working example of data summary may be seen in Margaret Bryant's book-length survey of *Current American Usage.* Based on information gathered over a ten-year period, this book presents its findings in the form of individual entries for each particular usage containing the accumulated evidence *for* and *against* it. Accompanying each entry is a concise summary, to give "the hurried reader a quick reference guide."

YOU, INDEFINITE

Data: Indefinite *you* is employed most frequently when one wishes to express a principle or philosophy, referring to people in general, as in "*You* can never tell what's going to happen" and "*You* never find what *you* want when *you* look for it." Written examples are: "In 'Jane,' however, he has no more conscience than *you* can find in Somerset Maugham . . ." (Brooks Atkinson, *The New York Times,* Feb. 10, 1952, Sec. 2, 1) and "And I suppose the point to be made is that, whereas *you* can have such tendencies . . . as *you* have . . . in the later Mann *you* find . . ." (*Kenyon Review,* Winter, 1952, 150).

Indefinite *you* often occurs with *if* or *as if,* as in "Differences can be nourishing if *you* don't waste time and energy fighting them" (Hannah Lees, "How to Be Happy Though Incompatible," *Reader's Digest,* May, 1957, 46) and "Each pain was something all-encompassing now, as if someone were taking *you* and shaking you . . ." (Julie Harris, "I Was Afraid to Have a Baby," *Reader's Digest,* Apr., 1957, 44). This usage with the conjunction is more frequent in written English than in common speech. According to one study (Altman), it occurred 29% of the time in written English and 10% in spoken English, whereas the use of *you* to express a general principle occurred much more frequently in spoken English. Another investigator (R. Thomas) showed that it is often found in expository writing.

Indefinite *you* is normally found in more informal writing, the type that meets the reading taste of the general public. More direct and less formal than *one,* it is established in current usage.

We and *they,* like *you,* are also established in standard usage as indefinite pronouns in informal English, as in "*We* never can tell what will happen in the future" and "*They* don't know any history today." This means "One never can tell . . ." and "One doesn't know . . ." French *on* and German *man* serve the same purpose and would be used in translating each one. See also *agreement, indefinite pronouns and they, indefinite.*

Summary: Indefinite you is common in Modern English and occurs both in speech and in expository writing.[3]

Summarizing Plot

The ability to write a plot summary or synopsis underlies much writing about literature, for we cannot discuss a literary work such as a novel or play unless we are sure that the reader knows its "story line"—the sequence of events that constitute its action. We may relate the events in chronological order, adding neither interpretive asides nor explanations of the work's structure or underlying logic—only its "happenings" as they happen.

Thus in "outline" versions of major works of literature, the summary confines itself to a bare recital of unfolding events—as in the following one-paragraph summary of Chapter XXII in Book I of *Don Quixote.*

Don Quixote saw trudging towards him in the road twelve convicts linked together by a chain, manacled, and accompanied by four armed guards. Be-

[3] From *Current American Usage* by Margaret Bryant.

cause these men were obviously not going to their destination of their own free will, the Don believed that this was a situation which called for the services of a knight-errant. He rode up and asked each convict what crime he had committed, receiving honest answers in return. Despite these accounts of roguery, the Don according to his duty as a knight-errant, requested the guards to free the men. When they refused, he attacked them. The convicts, seizing this opportune moment, broke their chain and proceeded to stone the guards who finally took to their heels. Sancho, fearing that a posse of the Holy Brotherhood would set upon himself and his master, advised the Don to get away as fast as possible. But Don Quixote gathered the criminals around him and commanded them to present themselves to his lady Dulcinea del Toboso. However, unwilling to risk apprehension and already suspicious of the sanity of a man who would free convicts, they began to pelt the Don with stones. When they had felled him, they stripped him and Sancho of a goodly portion of their clothing, then departed leaving the Don in a sullen mood and Sancho trembling for fear of the Holy Brotherhood.[4]

Naturally all narrative detail such as dialogue, description, and reflection are omitted from a one-paragraph summary. What is left is a bare-bones account of the action—a helpful tool if used to chart one's way through a long and involved novel such as *Don Quixote,* which contains many more details and episodes than one could possibly keep track of without a chapter-by-chapter outline. Such outlines are available in various "outline series," such as the one cited above. Some of these publications are accurate and reliable; others are filled with errors and distortions of the original text. In any case it is far better to make your own outlines, for in outlining a work, as mentioned earlier, you come to see its shape and the progressive unfolding of its purpose on a far deeper and more intimate level than reading alone can yield—or reading of someone else's summary. Approached in this way, then, as a note-form, the section-by-section plot summary is a helpful study aid. Also useful is the overall plot summary which sweeps across the terrain of an entire novel, reducing it to two pages, or even a single paragraph, as in the following:

Don Quixote de la Mancha, the history of, a satirical romance by Miguel Cervantes, the first part of which appeared in 1605 and the second in 1615. A kindly and simple-minded country gentleman has read the romances of chivalry until they have turned his brain. Clad in a suit of old armor and mounted on a broken-down hack which he christens Rozinante, he sets out on a career of knight-errantry, assuming the name of Don Quixote de la Mancha. For the object of his devotion he chooses a village girl, whom he names Dulcinea del Toboso and as squire he takes an ignorant but faithful peasant, Sancho Panza. The ordinary wayfarers of the Spanish roads of the seventeenth century are transformed by the knight's disordered imagination into warriors, distressed damsels, giants, and monsters. For instance, he tilts on one occasion, at the sails of a group of wind-mills, thinking them living creatures, and his attempts to right fictitious wrongs and win chivalric honor among them lead him and his squire into ludicrous and painful situations. Yet amidst their discomfitures

[4] Paul B. Bass, *A Complete Critical Outline of Don Quixote* (Boston, Mass.: Student Outlines Co., 1957), pp. 32–33.

Don Quixote retains a dignity, a certain nobility, and a pathetic idealism, and Sancho a natural shrewdness and popular humor which endear them to the reader. In the second part the interest is fully sustained, and variety is introduced by the sojourn of the pair with a duke and duchess and Sancho's appointment as governor of the imaginary island of Baratoria. At the end, Don Quixote, as the result of a dangerous illness, recovers his senses, renounces all books of chivalry, and dies penitent. The book was begun as an attack on the absurdities of the late chivalric romances, not on the essential chivalric ideals. As the work progresses it becomes a picture of human nature, its absurdities and its aspirations, its coarse materialism and lofty enthusiasm.[5]

The length of a summary does not determine its excellence. A good summary is as long as it *needs* to be in order to fulfill the writer's purpose. It may be objective and analytic or subjective and interpretive, again depending on the writer's purpose. He may not want to intrude any judgments or comments on the work, but simply tell it "as it is"—in brief space.

It is more common and generally preferable for the writer to weave into the recital of bare facts an interpretive description of the work's underlying logic and theme. He usually does not summarize just to summarize, but rather to provide plot background for a literary review or literary analysis. In such cases the length of the plot summary varies according to how important plot is in the development of the writer's main theme, how much space is available, and how much plot there is to summarize. Some stories have weak, virtually nonexistent plots, as the writer of the following summary tells us:

> *Adolphe,* a romance by Benjamin Constant. The story has very little incident or action. The whole plot may be summed up in a few words: Adolphe loves Eleonore, and can be happy neither with her nor without her. The beauty of the author's style and the keenness and delicacy with which he analyzes certain morbid moods of the soul have placed this work among the masterpieces of French literature. The romance is almost universally believed to be an autobiography, in which Constant narrates a portion of the adventures of his own youth.[6]

A summary that provides a background for a literary paper should not be a mere recital of happenings (first this happened, then this, then this). Rather, it should explain *why* things happen as they do, how events are significant, how they contribute to the pattern of the total work. The literary plot summary, in other words, should go beyond the superficial story line to analysis and interpretation. In such a summary the writer weaves in his own view of the plot, even as he recounts the bare facts. This deeper dimension of plot summary can be seen in the brief three-sentence introduction to the interpretation of "Happy Birthday" (pp. 171–72) wherein the writer uses interpretive adjectives like "private" emotions of an "inconspicuous" couple, "emotional tension," and "conflicting" responses. In using these adjectives, the writer is giving us a perspective on the plot in addition to a mere digest.

[5] Taken from *Thesaurus of Book Digests* edited by Hiram Haydn and Edmund Fuller. © 1949 by Crown Publishers, Inc. Used by permission of Crown Publishers, Inc.

[6] From *The Reader's Digest of Books,* edited by Helen Rex Keller. Copyright, 1929, by The Macmillan Company and reprinted with their permission.

Summarizing Events

As mentioned earlier, the weekly news magazines and "The News of the Week in Review" section of the *New York Times* are devoted specifically to summarizing events in time—a week, a month, or more. Such a summary requires seeing events in terms of highlights and the broad sweep of change. This kind of perspective is fundamental to a good "capsule" summary of the news, a form that helps the busy reader find out quickly what is happening or what has happened in the world.

The following highly ambitious summary, for example, attempts (in 500 words) to touch upon major historic events, "surprises," and trends during the sixties, and also to provide prophecies for the seventies. More than that, the writer "sums up" the decade in a single term: paradox.

THE PARADOX OF THE SIXTIES

JAMES RESTON

This has been a century of stunning surprises, yet the resident seers and magicians here seem to think the seventies will be menacing but manageable. It is a puzzler. The mood of the capital about present problems is pessimistic, but the forecasts for the coming decade are fairly optimistic.

No major war, retreat from Vietnam, probably a controlled war in the Middle East with the big powers on the sidelines, endless local and tribal conflict in Africa and maybe even in Latin America, more spheres of influence or Monroe Doctrines for the Soviet Union in Eastern Europe and for China in Southeast Asia; more people, more inflation, more trouble—in short, more of the same—but nothing apocalyptic. This seems to be the forecast of many thoughtful people in the capital.

The Historical Record

There is very little in the history of these last sixty years to justify this assumption that the human race has run out of spectacular stupidities. These sixty years started with the decline of the British and French and ended with the triumph of the Mets—with two tragic wars and endless barbarities and futilities in between.

Herman Kahn and Anthony J. Wiener have kept the boxscore on the astounding surprises that took place in the first and second thirds of the century. It started, they note, with parliamentary democracy in pretty good shape, and Christianity on the rise. The Western world felt fairly optimistic and secure. Then in the first third of the century, the following:

The Russo-Japanese War; the First World War, which devastated Europe; the collapse of the five major dynasties (Hohenzollern, Habsburg, Manchu, Romanov and Ottoman); the rise of Communism and the Soviet Union and Fascism; the Great Depression; and the intellectual influence of Bohr, de Broglie, Einstein and Freud.

The Big Surprises

The second third of the century produced even more surprises: The Second World War; mass murders and evacuations beyond all previous dreams of human depravity; the collapse of the old empires; the reunification and centralization of China and its development of nuclear weapons; the emergence of two superpowers (the U.S. and the U.S.S.R.), five large powers (Japan, West Germany, France, China and Britain; the new confrontation of Washington and Moscow in the cold war; and the emergence of new techniques, new post-Keynesian and post-Marxian economic theories.

Why, then, after all these apocalyptic events—why now when Washington is depressed about its frustrations over Vietnam, inflation, the blacks, the rebellious university whites—should thoughtful men and women here be taking a comparatively calm and even optimistic view of the seventies?

The Major Trends

Maybe it is merely wishful thinking or lack of imagination, and maybe the optimists are wrong, for there are many others who think the country and the world are hopelessly lost and divided and headed for chaos. But this does not seem to be the view of most reflective and experienced minds in the capital.

In fact, the majority seems to be suggesting that the sixties, for all the violence, defiance and confusion, were just violent and defiant and confused enough to force a reappraisal of past assumptions, and make the major powers think about adopting new attitudes and policies in defense of their vital interests.

Within their own geographical spheres of influence, the great powers are still demanding control, and in contested areas like the Middle East, they are still competing for influence in the most dangerous way, but on the big questions, which could produce a world and nuclear war, they are finally talking with a little more common sense.

The major trends elsewhere are also a little more rational. Europe is talking seriously again about cooperation and even economic integration; the war in Vietnam is not escalating but de-escalating; the Soviet Union is just worried enough about China's belligerent tone to reduce tensions in the West and avoid trouble on both fronts at the same time.

Accordingly, at least some observers think they see a new balance of power developing at the turn of the decade. The Congress is challenging the President's right to make war as he chooses; the Communist parties of the world are challenging Moscow's use of power against Czechoslovakia; the militant blacks and military students in the United States are finding that violence by the minority produced counterviolence by the white majority.

So while all these struggles still go on, there is a feeling here that maybe they can be contained in the seventies, mainly because we learned in the sixties that violence doesn't always pay off, either at home or abroad.[7]

ASSIGNMENTS

I. Summarizing Ideas

Note: Visualize the following writing assignments as answers to essay questions on an examination.

[7] From the *New York Times*, December 21, 1969.

A. Like Mills' essay "On Liberty," Milton's *Areopagitica* is a defense of free press, a protest against censorship, specifically (in Milton's case) against the licensing of books and pamphlets—a practice established by law in seventeenth-century England. Read and reread the following passage from *Areopagitica* (written in Milton's eloquent and somewhat difficult prose style); distill from it its central idea; then compare it (200–250 words) with the central idea in Mill's statement reprinted above. Are the two men saying essentially the same thing? Explain.

Good and evil we know in the field of this world grow up together almost inseparably; and the knowledge of good is so involved and interwoven with the knowledge of evil, and in so many cunning resemblances hardly to be discerned, that those confused seeds which were imposed upon Psyche as an incessant labour to cull out, and sort asunder, were not more intermixed. It was from out the rind of one apple tasted, that the knowledge of good and evil, as two twins cleaving together, leaped forth into the world. And perhaps this is that doom which Adam fell into of knowing good and evil, that is to say of knowing good by evil. As therefore the state of man now is; what wisdom can there be to choose, what continence to forbear without the knowledge of evil? He that can apprehend and consider vice with all her baits and seeming pleasures, and yet abstain, and yet distinguish, and yet prefer that which is truly better, he is the true warfaring Christian.

I cannot praise a fugitive and cloistered virtue, unexercised and unbreathed, that never sallies out and sees her adversary, but slinks out of the race, where that immortal garland is to be run for, not without dust and heat. Assuredly we bring not innocence into the world, we bring impurity much rather; that which purifies us is trial, and trial is by what is contrary. That virtue therefore which is but a youngling in the contemplation of evil, and knows not the utmost that vice promises to her followers, and rejects it, is but a blank virtue, not a pure; her whiteness is but an excremental whiteness. Which was the reason why our sage and serious poet Spenser, whom I dare be known to think a better teacher than Scotus or Aquinas, describing true temperance under the person of Guion, brings him in with his palmer through the cave of Mammon, and the bower of earthly bliss, that he might see and know, and yet abstain. Since therefore the knowledge and survey of vice is in this world so necessary to the constituting of human virtue, and the scanning of error to the confirmation of truth, how can we more safely, and with less danger, scout into the regions of sin and falsity than by reading all manner of tractates and hearing all manner of reason? And this is the benefit which may be had of books promiscuously read. . . .

B. In a statement of no more than 200 words sum up each of the following:

1. The evidence cited in James O'Kane's "Whither the Black Odyssey?" (pp. 352–62) to support the writer's thesis that problems of black Americans are not basically racial.
2. Allan Gilbert's argument for abolishing college lectures ("College Lectures Are Obsolete," pp. 301–04).
3. The "facts" about American Indians as presented by Oliver LaFarge ("The American Indian: Truth and Falsehoods," pp. 185–86).
4. Ronald Hilton's "Ten Commandments for the New Behavioral Scientist" (pp. 266–68).

II. Summarizing Data

A. Write summaries (three to six lines) for each of the following entries in *Current American Usage:*

AS . . . AS, SO . . . AS

Data: About the middle of the last century, one study (Rucks) shows, only 11.7% of the writers used *as . . . as* in negative statements whereas 88.3% used *so . . . as* ("She is not *so* pretty *as* her sister"); but today the situation is quite different; there has been a substantial shift to 53.6% using *as . . . as* and 46.4% using *so . . . as.* Two other studies (Winburne, Tavin) cited evidence such as the following: ". . . efficiency does not always pay *as* well *as* chance . . ." (*The Atlantic Monthly,* May, 1956, 16) and "There is not *as* much of it *as* there was . . ." (*Yale Review,* Autumn, 1955, 114); on the other hand, "But the effect was not quite *so* 1910 *as* it may sound" (*Harper's,* March, 1956, 82) and "Never had Great Britain been *so* prosperous *as* in 1955 . . ." (*The Atlantic Monthly,* May, 1956, 10).

The use of *as . . . as* in the affirmative is well established. *As . . . as* has also become involved in an almost uncountable number of word patterns or stereotypes; *as* bright *as* day, *as* clean *as* a bone, *as* cunning *as* a fox, *as* dry *as* dust, *as* easy *as* not, *as* good *as, as* soon *as, as* sure *as* fate, *as* tight *as* a drum, not *as* young *as* she used to be (to mention a few). Occasionally one also encounters *so . . . as* in the affirmative, as in "Seldom has a novel opened *so* laboriously . . . and yet carried *so* forceful an impact . . . *as* this fictionized chronicle . . ." (*The New York Times Book Review,* Apr. 1, 1956, 17, cited by Rucks). Perhaps the inverted verb selects *so . . . as,* because the head word in the sentence, *seldom,* inverts the subject-verb order in the manner of *never.*

PREPOSITION AT END OF CLAUSE OR SENTENCE

When John Dryden in the seventeenth century decided, on the analogy of Latin, against the propriety of placing a preposition at the end of a clause or a sentence, he set up a prejudice which has persisted to the present time.

Data: Actually, a number of constructions require the final preposition:

The final preposition may be part of the verb, especially in passive constructions, as in ". . . hardly any wind for us to *contend with*" (*Holiday,* June, 1953, 70); ". . . a recess *was* tacitly *agreed to*" (*New York Post,* May 28, 1953).

If the relative pronoun serving as the object of a preposition is omitted, the preposition invariably comes last, as in "It was the lumber company's watchman I went up there to call *on*" (*Holiday,* June, 1953, 45); cf. ". . . watchman *on whom* I went up there to call"; "Pride, dignity, conventionality became poor rags to *wrap* one's loneliness *in*" (*Ladies' Home Journal,* Mar., 1953, 110); cf. ". . . *in which to wrap* one's loneliness."

If *that* or *as* is the relative, the preposition comes last: ". . . plans *that* he really does not look *at* . . ." (*Saturday Review,* Apr. 2, 1955, 30). Observe that if *at* is removed from the end of the preceding example, *that* must be replaced by *which:* ". . . plans *at which* he really does not look . . ."

The preposition may come last because the clause it is in may be the object of a preposition, as in "Many a marriage might be saved by a timely look at what it was built *on*" (*Ladies' Home Journal*, Apr., 1953, 25), where the clause *what it was built on* is the object of the preposition *at*.

One construction, however, on which usage may vary, is illustrated in "News . . . is . . . those things that happen *about* which people are curious" (*Saturday Review*, Jan. 1, 1955, 9). Here the preposition could have come at the end, thus: ". . . which people are curious *about*," as it actually does in the sentence "I recognized one which three of my partners had been working *on* . . ." (*ibid*, Oct. 2, 1954, 18). This sentence, likewise, could have been written: "*on* which three of my partners had been working. . . ." Quantitative evidence on this construction, as it occurs in a study of formal written English (Russell), shows an overwhelming preference for the preposition before its object: in almost 94% of the instances. In informal written English and in conversation, other studies (Dunlap, Frost, Hessel, Spanier, R. Thomas, Zavin) show that one finds more instances of the preposition at the end of the clause or sentence than in formal English. One also frequently finds the preposition at the end in questions: "But isn't this exactly what the ostrich was counting on?" (*New York Herald Tribune*, Nov. 30, 1952) and "What are we afraid of?" (*Life*, May 18, 1953, 172).[8]

B. Write a digest or "abstract" (200 words) of Virginia Woolf's "The Duchess of Newcastle" (pp. 346–51).

III. Summarizing Plot

In a paragraph of no more than 100–150 words summarize the plot of Irwin Shaw's "The Girls in Their Summer Dresses" (pp. 177–81).

IV. Summarizing Events

A. Write a set of three summaries (200 words each) of the week's news events, under the following headings: national news, international news, and any special heading that is "in the news" this particular week (a particular country, a "shake-up" in government, a political figure). For sample summaries, see one of the weekly news magazines or "The News of the Week in Review" section of the *New York Times*.

B. Write an essay (500 words) summarizing events of the seventies to date.

C. Another event that regularly requires accurate and concise paraphrasing is the speech made by a prominent person. See how accurately you can summarize the following speech delivered by educator James B. Conant as a keynote address before the Conference on Unemployed, Out-of-School Youth in Urban Areas (Washington, D.C., May 24, 1961). Visualize yourself as a television reporter telling the audience what Dr. Conant said *that day* in Washington. Assume that your allotted air time permits no more than 350 words (a page and a half) of script.

[8] From *Current American Usage* by Margaret Bryant.

SOCIAL DYNAMITE IN OUR LARGE CITIES: UNEMPLOYED, OUT–OF–SCHOOL YOUTH

I appreciate the opportunity of serving as Keynote speaker and chairman of this workshop Conference on Unemployed, Out-of-School Youth in Urban Areas sponsored by the National Committee for Children and Youth. It is a sobering responsibility. I make this statement principally because I am convinced that the problem you ladies and gentlemen are here to discuss poses a serious threat to our free society. I submit that the existence in the slums of our large cities of thousands of youths ages 16–21 who are both out of school and out of work is an explosive situation. It is social dynamite.

In preparation for this Conference, a few special studies were conducted in slum areas of large cities to find out what the facts really were. In a slum section composed almost entirely of Negroes in one of our largest cities the following situation was found. A total of 59 percent of the male youth between the ages of 16 and 21 were out of school and unemployed. They were roaming the streets. Of the boys who graduated from high school 48 percent were unemployed in contrast to 63 percent of the boys who had dropped out of school. In short, two-thirds of the male dropouts did not have jobs and about half of the high school graduates did not have jobs. In such a situation, a pupil may well ask why bother to stay in school when graduation for half the boys opens onto a dead-end street?

An even worse state of affairs was found in another special study in a different city. In a slum area of 125,000 people, mostly Negro, a sampling of youth population shows that roughly 70 percent of the boys and girls ages 16–21 are out of school and unemployed. When one stops to consider that the total population in this district is equal to that of a good-sized independent city, the magnitude of the problem is appalling and the challenge to our society is clear.

In the slum area where over half the male youth are unemployed and out of school we are allowing a grave danger to the stability of our society to develop. A youth who has dropped out of school and never has had a full-time job is not likely to become a constructive citizen of his community. Quite the contrary. As a frustrated individual he is likely to be anti-social and rebellious. Some of this group of youths will end as juvenile delinquents. I suggest that full employment would have a highly salutary effect. Moreover, I offer the following hypothesis for professional social workers and sociologists to demolish; namely, that the correlation between desirable social attitudes (including attitudes of youth) and job opportunities are far higher than between the former and housing conditions, as measured by plumbing facilities, heating, and space per family.

Leaving juvenile delinquency aside, the existence of gangs of unemployed out-of-school youth in some neighborhoods of our large cities creates social problems acute enough by themselves. The adverse influence of the "street" is largely a consequence of the existence of these gangs. I doubt if anyone familiar with a slum district would deny that, if all the male youth by some miracle were to find employment, the social climate would change dramatically for the better. Some juvenile delinquents would remain, gangs might not wholly disappear, but the whole attitude of the neighborhood would alter in such a way as to make more effective the teachers in every classroom.

Consider for a moment the long-run consequence of persistent failure of underprivileged youth to find work. Out of work and out of school since they turned 16, these youths behave in ways that may have serious political consequences, similar behavior of youth in smaller cities would be far less serious. It is a matter of geography in the last analysis. Three factors are significant: first, the total size of the group of youth to whom I am referring—the larger the group, the more dangerous; second, the density of the population—the number of frustrated youth per block; third, the isolation of the inhabitants from other kinds of people and other sorts of streets and houses.

I know there are those who maintain that, on the average, Negro children are inferior to white children in academic ability. I have seen no evidence to support any such contention. In considering the relative abilities of whites and Negroes, let us examine the situation in an all-white slum in a city of considerable size. A careful study of a group of children in grade 4 of one such school showed that their average achievement level was a full year below their grade placement—a typical situation in any slum area.

The principal [of this school] writes, . . . "The parents of at least one-third of the children are either in penal institutions, are on probation, or have prison records. At least 100 children are on probation to the Juvenile Court . . .

"Less than 10 percent of the children have private doctors or dentists. A dental examination of 900 children in the fall of 1959 reveals only forty-five free of cavities. The eyes of every child in the school were examined and about 300 showed some vision defects, and thirty had such serious vision loss that they were referred for partially-seeing teaching. At least one-third of the children are on welfare rolls or are recipients of very small social security and/or veteran benefits checks."

I am quoting from an official report which, in acknowledging the generally low achievement of the white children in this school, makes the interesting statement that "there is no reason to believe that these students as a group are inherently or genetically less capable than average students, but apparently because of some types of experiences in their lives they have been unable to develop their intellectual skills." *I should argue strongly that to date we have no evidence to indicate that the assumption* [made above] *should not be broadened to include both white and Negro students.* [italics his.] I start with the belief that, given a satisfactory socio-economic background and educational opportunity, Negro children can be just as successful in academic work as any other group.

Visits to a wealthy suburb and impoverished slums only a few minutes away jolt one's notions of the meaning of equality of opportunity. On the one hand, there is likely to be a spacious, modern school staffed by as many as 70 professionals for 1,000 pupils; on the other hand, one finds a crowded often dilapidated and unattractive school staffed by 40 professionals for 1,000 pupils. Expenditure per pupil in the wealthy suburban school is likely to be over $1,000; often it is less than half that in the slum school. To my mind, in view of the problems one finds, conditions in the slum school necessitate more staff and more money than in the suburban school.

The growth of Negro slums in big cities is alarming. I wish that I could do more than direct attention. For without being an alarmist, I must say that when one considers the total situation that has been developing in the Negro slums since World War II, one has reason to worry about the future. The building up of a mass of unemployed and frustrated Negro youth in congested areas of a city is a social phenomenon that may be compared to the piling up of inflammable material in an empty building in a city block. Potentialities for trouble—indeed, possibilities of disaster—are surely there.

I have so far referred only to white and Negro slums. In addition, a few words are necessary to point out that in some cities, New York in particular, there are slum areas inhabited by recent arrivals from Puerto Rico. In these sections, the problems are similar to those I have described but complicated by the difference in language. Unlike the American Negro from the South, these recent arrivals bring with them a set of social mores closely associated with their own methods of communication. At the same time, they often, if not always, come with children where schooling has been bad. These problems [of language] are so special I shall not attempt to discuss them here. Add to these tasks the possibilities of interracial hostility and gang warfare between Negroes and Puerto Ricans and the resentment of both toward the whites and one has a veritable witches' brew which comes to boil with unsavory vehemence in certain schools in certain areas—particularly in the junior high school years. The amazing feature of the whole situation is that pupils make any progress in schools in certain areas of the city.

In closing, I should like to express my own views on a very few of the subjects just mentioned about which I feel strongly. In the first place, there are those who would say that what goes on in the schools should not have any direct connection with the community or the employment situation. I completely reject this idea. The school, the community, and the employment picture are and should be closely tied together. *I submit that in a heavily urbanized and industrialized free society the educational experience of youths should fit their subsequent employment.* This should be so whether a boy drops out of school in grade 10, after graduation from high school, or after graduation from college or university. In any case, there should be a smooth transition from full-time schooling to a full-time job.

When we examine the situation at the high school level, we find that in many high schools a half or more of the graduates seek employment immediately on graduation, only in a few cities does one find an effective placement service. The obligation of the school should not end when the student either drops out of school or graduates. At that point the cumulative record folder concerning a student's educational career is usually brought to an end. It should not be. To my mind, *guidance officers, especially in the large cities, ought to be given the responsibility for following the post-high school careers of youth from the time they leave school until they are 21 years of age.* It is with the unemployed out-of-school youths that I am especially concerned—especially the boys, for whom the unemployment problem is more severe than for girls. This expansion of the school's function will cost money and will mean additional staff; but the expense is necessary, for vocational and educational guidance must be a continuing process to help assure a smooth transition from school to work. What I have in mind suggests, of course, a much closer relationship than now exists between school, employers, and labor unions, as well as social agencies and employment officers.

In short, there is much that schools are doing but much more that they should do. Money in many instances is the key—remedial reading teachers, smaller classes, guidance counselors cost money.

But even if the schools were to improve their services drastically, there should remain what seems to me the crux of the situation—the presence or absence of employment opportunity. Whereas I have indicated my conviction that the problems of Negro education are no different from those of all underprivileged socio-economic groups, the problems of Negro employment are distinctly different. The enforcement of anti-discrimination laws has proved a most difficult undertaking. I have heard it said that only those projects which are supported by public funds can really be operated on a truly non-discriminatory basis. Therefore, it seems to me that unless local management and labor take up the challenge, it may be necessary for Congress to appropriate funds for public work programs to alleviate the problem of unemployment among youth 16 to 21 in the large cities. In view of the past discriminatory employment practices by both management and labor, action at the federal level may become a necessity. Even if there were no discrimination, it might become a necessity if the private sector of the economy is unable to provide sufficient jobs.

In conclusion, let me repeat my sense of shock as I contemplate conditions in our big cities with respect to youth in slum neighborhoods. The problems are the result of a social situation the roots of which run back to the days of slavery and the result of an economic problem which is in part a reflection of the total unemployment situation and is in part a result of racial discrimination among labor unions and employers. To improve the work of the schools requires an improvement in the lives of the families who inhabit these slums, but without a drastic change in the employment prospects of urban Negro youth, relatively little can be accomplished. I close by urging that our large-city problems be analyzed in far more detail than in the past and with far greater degree of frankness. Neighborhood by neighborhood we need to know the facts, and when these facts indicate a dangerous social situation the American people should be prepared to take drastic measures before it is too late.[9]

[9] Reprinted by permission of James B. Conant.

20 WHAT CASE CAN BE MADE FOR OR AGAINST X?

Aristotle said: "If it is a disgrace to a man when he cannot defend himself in a bodily way, it would be odd not to think him disgraced when he cannot defend himself with reason." It is reason—and *mainly* reason—we must marshal when we ask the question "What case can be made *for* or *against* X?" In trying to build a case, we move beyond plain exposition into the more active and aggressive realm of argumentation, an ancient and honored form of discourse wherein the arguer tries not merely to explain but to defend or refute what logicians call a "proposition," i.e., a statement about which there may be and usually is conflict and controversy. Unlike a plain statement of fact (John Smith is the mayor of Squedunk), a proposition cannot be summarily looked up, verified, and established once-and-for-all. Instead, a proposition is debatable: it may or may not be true (The mayor of Squedunk is a crook and should be thrown out of office). In making this judgment, in asserting this proposition, the writer must assume the burden of proof; he must marshal evidence and exert rigorous reasoning in defense of his cause.

Thus an argument for or against any proposition represents one individual's attempt to substantiate his own reasons for believing as he does. In presenting his case, he hopes to convince his readers (or listeners) that he is right and to win them to his side. In order to do this he must, of course, make sense; his facts must be believable and his logic unassailable. In addition he must be persuasive: he must make an appeal on a personal and emotional level; he must seem sincere, genuinely committed to his cause, responsible, well meaning, open-minded, fair, and clearly on the side of the good.

Is and Ought Propositions

Basically we may distinguish two kinds of propositions: the *is* proposition (an assertion of opinion or value) and the *ought* proposition (a proposal for action). You will note in the illustrative essays in this chapter that most arguments combine the two types, thereby establishing the fundamental causal relationship that underlies most argumentation:

> Because A *is* the case, B *ought* to be done.

An example of this logical formulation can be found in Woodrow Wilson's historic address to Congress in 1917, asking for a declaration of war against Germany.

> Because Germany's aggressive submarine action against American commerce *is* an act of warfare against both the United States and mankind [an assertion of opinion or value], America *ought* to enter World War I [a proposal for action] which action would make the world "safe for democracy" [the projected conclusion].

President Wilson's aim in this classic example of "making a case" for a specific action was to win the assent of members of Congress, to convince them that what he asserted was true and just, worthy of whole-hearted and unconditional support. To achieve his end, he drew upon many of the traditional methods of argumentation, even following—roughly—the three-part structure of the classical oration, as outlined below:

THE STRUCTURE OF ARGUMENT

I. *INTRODUCTION*

The introduction may consist of a single sentence or of several paragraphs, including one or more of the following:

A. *Exordium:* The beginning or opening words, designed to win attention and good will by introducing the case in an interesting and favorable light (a quotation, personal reference, story)
B. *Exposition or narration:* An account of the history of the case (what gave rise to the present problem; how the issues developed)
C. Direct statement of the case (the *proposition* to be proved or defended)
D. Division of proofs: An *outline* of how the evidence will be presented ("first I will explain . . . and then I will demonstrate")

II. *BODY OF ARGUMENT*

A. *Confirmation* of one's case by presenting evidence [1] in its favor:

1. facts
2. reasons
3. statistics
4. testimony of experts
5. opinions

[1] Evidence may be defined as whatever constitutes support for the proposition.

6. reports
7. examples
8. logical reasoning (deductive and inductive)
9. analogy

B. *Refutation* of opposing views by demonstrating that they are:

1. untrue
2. illogical
3. self-contradictory
4. ambiguous (terms not defined)
5. dishonest (a *deliberate* attempt to deceive)
6. absurd

C. *Concession* of points to the opposition that must *fairly* be conceded; reply to them and offer of alternate positions

III. *CONCLUSION*

A. *Recapitulation* and *summary* of argument: To repeat is to reinforce points, and to make certain they have not been misunderstood.

B. *Peroration:* A final, heightened appeal for support

Note how President Wilson's address falls into this pattern.

WOODROW WILSON ASKS CONGRESS TO DECLARE WAR [2]

INTRODUCTION

Gentlemen of the Congress:

Exordium

I have called the Congress into extraordinary session because there are serious, very serious, choices of policy to be made, and made immediately, which it was neither right nor constitutionally permissible that I should assume the responsibility of making.

Narration

On the third of February last I officially laid before you the extraordinary announcement of the Imperial German Government that on and after the first day of February it was its purpose to put aside all restraints of law or of humanity and use its submarines to sink every vessel that sought to approach either the ports of Great Britain and Ireland or the western coasts of Europe or any of the ports controlled by the enemies of Germany within the Mediterranean. That had seemed to be the object of the German submarine warfare earlier in the war, but since April of last year the Imperial Government had somewhat restrained the commanders of its undersea craft in conformity with its promise then given to us that passenger boats should not be sunk and that due warning would be given to all other vessels which its submarines might seek to destroy, when no resistance was offered or escape attempted, and care taken that their crews were given at least a fair chance to save their lives in their open boats. The precautions taken were meager and haphazard enough, as was proved in distressing instance after instance in the progress of the cruel and unmanly business, but a certain degree of restraint was observed. The new

[2] Address delivered to a joint session of the two houses of Congress, April 2, 1917.

policy has swept every restriction aside. Vessels of every kind, whatever their flag, their character, their cargo, their destination, their errand, have been ruthlessly sent to the bottom without warning and without thought of help or mercy for those on board, the vessels of friendly neutrals along with those of belligerents. Even hospital ships and ships carrying relief to the sorely bereaved and stricken people of Belgium, though the latter were provided with safe conduct through the proscribed areas by the German Government itself and were distinguished by unmistakable marks of identity, have been sunk with the same reckless lack of compassion or of principle.

(Note listing of details to support the case against Germany)

I was for a little while unable to believe that such things would in fact be done by any government that had hitherto subscribed to the humane practices of civilized nations. International law had its origin in the attempt to set up some law which would be respected and observed upon the seas, where no nation had right of dominion and where lay the free highways of the world. By painful stage after stage has that law been built up, with meager enough results, indeed, after all was accomplished that could be accomplished, but always with a clear view, at least, of what the heart and conscience of mankind demanded. This minimum of right the German Government has swept aside under the plea of retaliation and necessity and because it had no weapons which it could use at sea except those which it is impossible to employ as it is employing them without throwing to the winds all scruples of humanity or of respect for the understandings that were supposed to underlie the intercourse of the world. I am not now thinking of the loss of property involved, immense and serious as that is, but only of the wanton and wholesale destruction of the lives of noncombatants, men, women, and children, engaged in pursuits which have always, even in the darkest periods of modern history, been deemed innocent and legitimate. Property can be paid for; the lives of peaceful and innocent people cannot be. The present German submarine warfare against commerce is a warfare against mankind.

IS Proposition (1)

It is a war against all nations. American ships have been sunk, American lives taken, in ways which it has stirred us very deeply to learn of, but the ships and people of other neutral and friendly nations have been sunk and overwhelmed in the waters in the same way. There has been no discrimination. The challenge is to all mankind. Each nation must decide for itself how it will meet it. The choice we make for ourselves must be made with a moderation of counsel and a temperateness of judgment befitting our character and our motives as a nation. We must put excited feeling away. Our motive will not be revenge or the victorious assertion of the physical might of the nation, but only the vindication of right, of human right, of which we are only a single champion.

When I addressed the Congress on the twenty-sixth of February last I thought that it would suffice to assert our neutral rights with arms, our right to use the seas against unlawful interference,

IS
Proposition (2)

our right to keep our people safe against unlawful violence. But armed neutrality, it now appears, is impracticable. Because submarines are in effect outlaws when used as the German submarines have been used against merchant shipping, it is impossible to defend ships against their attacks as the law of nations has assumed that merchantmen would defend themselves against privateers or cruisers, visible craft giving chase upon the open sea. It is common prudence in such circumstances, grim necessity indeed, to endeavor to destroy them before they have shown their own intention. They must be dealt with upon sight, if dealt with at all. The German Government denies the right of neutrals to use arms at all within the areas of the sea which it has proscribed, even in the defense of rights which no modern publicist has ever before questioned their right to defend. The intention is conveyed that the armed guards which we have placed on our merchant ships will be treated as beyond the pale of law and subject to be dealt with as pirates would be. Armed neutrality is ineffectual enough at best; in such circumstances and in the face of such pretensions it is worse than ineffectual: it is likely only to produce what it was meant to prevent; it is practically certain to draw us into the war without either the rights or the effectiveness of belligerents. There is one choice we cannot make, we are incapable of making: we will not choose the path of submission and suffer the most sacred rights of our nation and our people to be ignored or violated. The wrongs against which we now array ourselves are no common wrongs; they cut to the very roots of human life.

OUGHT
Proposition: United States should declare war

With a profound sense of the solemn and even tragical character of the step I am taking and of the grave responsibilities which it involves, but in unhesitating obedience to what I deem my constitutional duty, I advise that the Congress declare the recent course of the Imperial German Government to be in fact nothing less than war against the government and people of the United States; that it formally accept the status of belligerent which has thus been thrust upon it; and that it take immediate steps not only to put the country in a more thorough state of defense but also to exert all its power and employ all its resources to bring the Government of the German Empire to terms and end the war. . . .

[In the next four paragraphs, omitted here, Wilson reviews the specific ways in which the country should mobilize: increase armed forces, raise taxes.]

BODY OF ARGUMENT (Marshalling of reasons in support of propositions)

While we do these things, these deeply momentous things, let us be very clear, and make very clear to all the world what our motives and our objects are. My own thought has not been driven from its habitual and normal course by the unhappy events of the last two months, and I do not believe that the thought of the nation has been altered or clouded by them. I have exactly the same things in mind now that I had in mind when I addressed the Senate on the twenty-second of January last; the same that I had in mind when I addressed the Congress on the third of February

Reason (1): to vindicate peace against autocratic power

and on the twenty-sixth of February. Our object now, as then, is to vindicate the principles of peace and justice in the life of the world as against selfish and autocratic power and to set up amongst the really free and self-governed peoples of the world such a concert of purpose and of action as will henceforth insure the observance of those principles. Neutrality is no longer feasible or desirable where the peace of the world is involved and the freedom of its peoples, and the menace to that peace and freedom lies in the existence of autocratic governments backed by organized force which is controlled wholly by their will, not by the will of their people. We have seen the last of neutrality in such circumstances. We are at the beginning of an age in which it will be insisted that the same standards of conduct and of responsibility for wrong done shall be observed among nations and their governments that are observed among the individual citizens of civilized states.

We have no quarrel with the German people. We have no feeling towards them but one of sympathy and friendship. It was not upon their impulse that their government acted in entering this war. It was not with their previous knowledge or approval. It was a war determined upon as wars used to be determined upon in the old, unhappy days when peoples were nowhere consulted by their rulers and wars were provoked and waged in the interest of dynasties or of little groups of ambitious men who were accustomed to use their fellowmen as pawns and tools. Self-governed nations do not fill their neighbor states with spies or set the course of intrigue to bring about some critical posture of affairs which will give them an opportunity to strike and make conquest. Such designs can be successfully worked out only under cover and where no one has the right to ask questions. Cunningly contrived plans of deception or aggression, carried, it may be, from generation to generation, can be worked out and kept from the light only within the privacy of courts or behind the carefully guarded confidences of a narrow and privileged class. They are happily impossible where public opinion commands and insists upon full information concerning all the nation's affairs.

Reason (2): to band together with other democratic nations

A steadfast concert for peace can never be maintained except by a partnership of democratic nations. No autocratic government could be trusted to keep faith within it or observe its covenants. It must be a league of honor, a partnership of opinion. Intrigue would eat its vitals away; the plottings of inner circles who could plan what they would and render account to no one would be a corruption seated at its very heart. Only free peoples can hold their purpose and their honor steady to a common end and prefer the interests of mankind to any narrow interest of their own.

Reason (3): analogy to Russia's "shaking off" of

Does not every American feel that assurance has been added to our hope for the future peace of the world by the wonderful and heartening things that have been happening within the last few weeks in Russia? Russia was known by those who knew it best to autocratic power

have been always in fact democratic at heart, in all the vital habits of her thought, in all the intimate relationships of her people that spoke their natural instinct, their habitual attitude towards life. The autocracy that crowned the summit of her political structure, long as it had stood and terrible as was the reality of its power, was not in fact Russian in origin, character, or purpose; and now it has been shaken off and the great, generous Russian people have been added in all their naïve majesty and might to the forces that are fighting for freedom in the world, for justice, and for peace. Here is a fit partner for a League of Honor.

Reason (4): German spying

One of the things that has served to convince us that the Prussian autocracy was not and could never be our friend is that from the very outset of the present war it has filled our unsuspecting communities and even our offices of Government with spies and set criminal intrigues everywhere afoot against our national unity of counsel, our peace within and without, our industries and our commerce. Indeed it is now evident that its spies were here even before the war began; and it is unhappily not a matter of conjecture but a fact proved in our courts of justice that the intrigues which have more than once come perilously near to disturbing the peace and dislocating the industries of the country have been carried on at the instigation, with the support, and even under the personal direction of official agents of the Imperial Government accredited to the Government of the United States. Even in checking these things and trying to extirpate them we have sought to put the most generous interpretation possible upon them because we knew that their source lay, not in any hostile feeling or purpose of the German people towards us (who were, no doubt as ignorant of them as we ourselves were), but only in the selfish designs of a government that did what it pleased and told its people nothing. But they have played their part in serving to convince us at last that that government entertains no real friendship for us and means to act against our peace and security at its convenience. That it means to stir up enemies against us at our very doors the intercepted note to the German Minister at Mexico City is eloquent evidence.

Reason (5): constant threat to security

We are accepting this challenge of hostile purpose because we know that in such a government, following such methods, we can never have a friend; and that in the presence of its organized power, always lying in wait to accomplish we know not what purpose, there can be no assured security for the democratic governments of the world. We are now about to accept gauge of battle with this natural foe to liberty and shall, if necessary, spend the whole force of the nation to check and nullify its pretensions and its power. We are glad, now that we see the facts with no veil of false pretense about them, to fight thus for the ultimate peace of the world and for the liberation of its peoples, the German peoples included: for the rights of nations great and small and the privilege of men everywhere to choose their way of life

(This line would become a rallying cry for all the Allied Forces)

and of obedience. The world must be made safe for democracy. Its peace must be planted upon the tested foundations of political liberty. We have no selfish ends to serve. We desire no conquest, no dominion. We seek no indemnities for ourselves, no material compensation for the sacrifices we shall freely make. We are but one of the champions of the rights of mankind. We shall be satisfied when those rights have been made as secure as the faith and the freedom of nations can make them.

Just because we fight without rancor and without selfish object, seeking nothing for ourselves but what we shall wish to share with all free peoples, we shall, I feel confident, conduct our operations as belligerents without passion and ourselves observe with proud punctilio the principles of right and of fair play we profess to be fighting for.

I have said nothing of the governments allied with the Imperial Government of Germany because they have not made war upon us or challenged us to defend our right and our honor. The Austro-Hungarian Government has, indeed, avowed its unqualified indorsement and acceptance of the reckless and lawless submarine warfare adopted now without disguise by the Imperial German Government, and it has therefore not been possible for this government to receive Count Tarnowski, the Ambassador recently accredited to this government by the Imperial and Royal Government of Austria-Hungary; but that government has not actually engaged in warfare against citizens of the United States on the seas, and I take the liberty, for the present at least, of postponing a discussion of our relations with the authorities at Vienna. We enter this war only where we are clearly forced into it because there are no other means of defending our rights.

CONCLUSION
Recapitulation

It will be all the easier for us to conduct ourselves as belligerents in a high spirit of right and fairness because we act without animus, not in enmity towards a people or with the desire to bring any injury or disadvantage upon them, but only in armed opposition to an irresponsible government which has thrown aside all considerations of humanity and of right and is running amuck. We are, let me say again, the sincere friends of the German people, and shall desire nothing so much as the early re-establishment of intimate relations of mutual advantage between us,—however hard it may be for them, for the time being, to believe that this is spoken from our hearts. We have borne with their present government through all these bitter months because of that friendship,—exercising a patience and forbearance which would otherwise have been impossible. We shall, happily, still have an opportunity to prove that friendship in our daily attitude and actions towards the millions of men and women of German birth and native sympathy who live amongst us and share our life, and we shall be proud to prove it towards all who are in fact loyal to their neighbors and to the government in the hour of test. They are, most of them, as true and loyal Americans as if they had never known any other fealty or allegiance. They will be prompt to stand with us in rebuking and restraining the few who may be of a different mind and purpose. If there should be disloyalty, it will be dealt with with a firm hand of stern repression; but, if it lifts its head at all, it will lift it only here and there and without countenance except from a lawless and malignant few.

Peroration

It is a distressing and oppressive duty, Gentlemen of the Congress, which I have performed in thus addressing you. There are, it may be, many months of fiery trial and sacrifice ahead of us. It is a fearful thing to lead this great peaceful people into war, into the most terrible and disastrous of all wars, civilization itself seeming to be in the balance. But the right is more precious than peace, and we shall fight for the things which we have always carried nearest our hearts,—for democracy, for the right of those who submit to authority to have a voice in their own governments, for the rights and liberties of small nations, for a universal dominion of right by such a concert of free peoples as shall bring peace and safety to all nations and make the world itself at last free. To such a task we can dedicate our lives and our fortunes, everything that we are and everything that we have, with the pride of those who know that the day has come when America is privileged to spend her blood and her might for the principles that gave her birth and happiness and the peace which she has treasured. God helping her, she can do no other.

Locating the Issues

It is not our business here to dwell on the intrinsic merits of this historic argument—or on the merits of any of the illustrative arguments presented in this chapter; we shall simply note some of their logical and rhetorical features so that we may be better equipped to make our own arguments concerning problems that confront us today. One contemporary argument, drawn from the field of education, is found in the more informal essay that follows—Allan H. Gilbert's spirited and sometimes snappy case against a hallowed academic tradition, the college lecture. Here again *is* and *ought* propositions are combined:

> Because, in an age of mass printing and sophisticated audio-visual aids, the lecture system of teaching *is* obsolete [assertion of opinion and value], college lectures *ought* to be abolished [proposal for action].

Note that here again the classic three-part division of argument is visible: introduction, body, conclusion. Note also how carefully Gilbert has isolated the issues involved in this controversial topic.

"Issues" may be defined as the main points of difference or opinion upon which the writer builds his case. Thus, locating the issues on any given subject is an important first step in argumentation—indeed is its very core—since the body of the argument is generally organized according to a systematic consideration of issues, each one coming up for review and, wherever possible, proof.

COLLEGE LECTURES ARE OBSOLETE

ALLAN H. GILBERT

INTRODUCTION

The advertising pamphlet of a well-known American university recently showed a picture of a professor presenting chemistry to some hundreds of students. Except for the costumes and the ugly angularity of the room, it might have been an academic scene in 1450, before the invention of printing. In 1766 Dr. Johnson remarked:

Narration

> I cannot see that lectures can do as much good as reading the books from which the lectures are taken.

And in 1781 he still thought:

Quoting authority

> Lectures were once useful, but now, when all can read, and books are so numerous, lectures are unnecessary.

Proposition (implicitly stated)

Yet after two hundred years, the modern professor has not overtaken Dr. Johnson. He has not discovered that printing has been invented—not to mention xerox, etc. The old-time methods are good enough for him. Academic photographers are especially amusing in that they delight in showing the most blatantly up-to-date subjects, such as physics, presented as in Abelard's Paris. Obviously this applies not to the occasional public lecture, but to the twice-a-week throughout the term.

BODY

WHAT IS WRONG ABOUT LECTURES?

Systematic review of issues:

1. Even a good speaker will not always be correctly heard by his audience. Horns toot, students cough. And sometimes professors mumble. Even in the notes of graduate students the well-known Professor Fredson Bowers has appeared as Fritz and Brower, and Nike of Samothrace as the Decay of Sammy's Face.

(First from a negative point of view;

2. What is written on a blackboard—often in professorial scribble—cannot be perfectly copied. Time presses, even modern lighting is not all-revealing; perfect vision is not universal.

Then from a positive— the remedy)

3. A student trying to take excellent notes cannot think about their content; he must not lag. He is like the telegrapher of whom Edison tells. The man received, in dots and dashes, the news of Lincoln's assassination; when he went out on the street, he learned that such news had been reported. In the days of monotype composition for newspapers, I knew the man who set the gossip column for the local paper. When the paper appeared, he read it as something new to him. Such must be the mind of the student who takes notes so good that he can attain the ideal of giving back in his blue book what the lecturer has said. The Welsh professor of mediaeval literature, Dr. Ker, is said to have remarked: "How can I give less than 90 for my own words?"

4. Lectures prepared long since and read from yellowed paper cease to call on the professor's brain. His class in the morning

need not call him from the idiot box in the evening. The chairman of a department in which I served once read the same lecture to a class for the third successive time. . . . It is reported of a Harvard professor that he moved to the door and put his hand on the knob for his last sentence. No student could catch him. Revision would disarrange the schedule and desecrate the sentences which, through many repetitions, the professor has come to regard as truth. He is a human tape recorder. The students are tape-receivers. . . .

5. The college lecturer seldom has a prepared audience. How often can a lecturer on Shakespeare, for example, be sure that his hearers have read the play on which he speaks? If he can read aloud, he may read to his class with profit, but then he ceases to be a lecturer. The unprepared audience (or the audience not eager to learn the subject, and not impatient of failure to help them do so) affects the lecturer. He wishes to break through their boredom. So he tends to become an entertainer, giving a show. There is much in the story that the faculty of a well-known college for men opposes the admission of women because—evidently being old fogies—they imagine they would be deprived of the bawdy jokes supposed to amuse their captive audiences. But how often do professorial jokes illustrate the subject in hand? Or the popular lecturer turns to oratory. Newspaper pictures of some popular teachers who recently have gathered publicity by dismissal, show them making gestures suited to the soap box or the pulpit. An academic Savonarola or Billy Sunday or Graham may rouse in a few hearers an emotional desire to learn. Such a desire, when it lasts, prepares a youth to study and to seek aid from a teacher, but it is not teaching. Colleges, like the rest of life, need their share of emotion, but their primary business is intellectual. A man given over to his own convictions and beliefs is not a teacher because he cannot see both sides of a subject.

6. Especially for commuting students, attendance at lectures is a serious burden. If the teacher has lectures prepared, let them be mimeographed. Then the student can study them at home. Or let the professor require the student to read the books from which the lectures are drawn. They can be bought for less money than commuting requires; and the student is not wasting his time in a bus or automobile.

7. In the lecturer's audience, the student tends to become a mere numbered unit, deprived of power to question, much less to object. He is trained to accept the dicta of the professor—a habit worse than that of going to the library to find "a book"—author unobserved—from which to copy. At least the library offers more than one book, and even the most facile pedagogue is likely to take more pains with dicta to be printed than with those merely to be pronounced in the uncritical isolation of the lecture hall, before students who—if they wish good marks—will not murmur pub-

licly against what they are told. The lecture inculcates passivity of mind. The student is a spectator, with no part in the game, except that he selects the lecture course because it is called a crip.

8. The book, even when mimeographed, is better than any student's notes. There are no hiatuses for sickness, empty pens, noise. As Dr. Johnson said: "If your attention fails and you miss part of a lecture, you are lost; you cannot go back as you can upon a book."

Furthermore, the best lectures are most likely to attain printing. If a professor has lectures better than any printed book or even group of printed books, can he be defended for restricting them to his own university, instead of giving them to mankind? Are we to suppose that there are in America a hundred sets of lecture notes superior to anything in print? Is not the student better off with A. C. Bradley's own vindication of Falstaff—however absurd it is—than with the Shakespeare professor's diluted version of it? If the professor cannot do better than the authors on his reading list, why not omit the lectures and attend to the reading list?

9. Something can be said for the living presence of the lecturer. But this is again revivalistic; the college lecturer is supposed to be teaching a subject. There is, too, a presence behind the written word, usually stronger, though less immediate, than that on the platform. Does the student come to college for the personality of Professor X, or to learn? Indeed the professor who gives a course in himself is handicapped by the insignificance of his subject. "A good book is the precious life blood of a master spirit." How often are lecture-writers such spirits?

10. The important poets have been so richly annotated that even the most expert scholars can now add little detailed comment. Fortunate is the lecturer on Milton who can improve on Professor Hughes' notes. The lesser authors have been carefully worked. How many teachers of Herrick can correct any of Professor Patrick's notes, or explain difficulties he has not elucidated? As to more general comment, a lecturer may indeed warn his pupils against much that has been written on great authors, but how many lecturers are capable of anything else than riding with the tide? Poetry exists to be read; the lecture pushes it into the class of something to be talked about rather than experienced. (Non-lecture teaching is somewhat less subject to this danger.)

THE REMEDY

Perfect teaching will appear when we have teachers who have entered into their subjects and students eager to learn. With these, we would not need to bother about systems. Without them, not much can be done. We have always had, and always shall have, lawyers not aware of the nature of law, generals unaware of the nature of war, professors of physics who have not found out what their subject is, teachers of Chaucer and Dante who do not, as Benedetto Croce has said, sympathize with their authors. Yet something external can be done against lecturitis.

Citing authority

Let a teacher who sufficiently believes in his own greatness put his lectures in print to be revised frequently as he grows wiser. Then he can abandon his robes of glory, and the student will have more accurate statements and clearer diagrams, which he can copy at his leisure, if that will implant them in his memory.

In a normal lecture course, let us suppose thirty lectures per term, and 150 students. At that rate, each student gets of the professor's public time 1/150 of thirty hours, or 1/5 of an hour. If the professor abandons his rostrum, he has time to meet each student individually for ten minutes a term. The student is warned to prepare. The assistants who gather about such courses are consulted on what the student may profitably ask. Some students would treasure throughout life the memory of ten minutes' serious talk with an eminent professor.

I know students at some of our large places who have gone through their four years without ever speaking on their studies with a man of professorial rank. Such undergraduates deal with junior teachers, graduate students, some of them brilliant, but many of them destined to be mediocrities or failures. Yet from the class of a thousand, the hundred and fifty with the best records can still meet the eminent professor. Such a teacher, relieved from the strain of the large lecture—not entirely removed by the loud speaker—would usually be willing to go beyond the hundred and fifty. If freed from the ceremonial lecture, the pupil has two hours a week free for studying books, mimeographed or printed, and scientific specimens. He does not—in the computer age—spend thirty hours a term writing by hand. Nothing good in the present system need be abolished. The students in the big class can still be divided into small sections, presided over by the best junior teachers the college will pay for.

CONCLUSION

Recapitulation

The survival of the lecture, for nearly five hundred years after the invention of printing, exhibits the unimaginative, unobserving professorial mind. Hidebound professors still read lectures to three or four students, even to one. This seems more ludicrous in nuclear physics than in the humanities, but does not reveal a more imperceptive mind. John Philip Holland, the father of the submarine, said that naval officers (who yield little to professors in holding to what has been) disliked the submarine because it provided no quarter deck to strut on. Do professors cling to lectures because they offer a rostrum to strut on and a lectern to sprawl over? [3]

Peroration

Lively and provocative as this argument is, are there not logical grounds on which its indictment of the lecture system could be challenged? Are all lectures *necessarily* read "from yellowed paper"? Are all lecturers *neces-*

[3] From *CEA Critic*, October 1967. Reprinted with the permission of the author and the College English Association.

sarily "human tape recorders"? Are all students *necessarily* "human tape-receivers"? Are mimeographed copies of a lecture read by the student privately in the library *necessarily* more profitable than personal delivery in a lecture? (May not students fall asleep in the library as well as the lecture hall?) What about the creative lecturer (is there such a person?) who communicates fresh insights in such a contagious manner that the student "catches fire"—as he could not from the printed page? And can you say more about the possibilities and value of a class "dynamic"—live, person-to-person encounter? Does the lecture *have* to be an extended monologue? Is Gilbert talking about *some* kinds of lectures and lecturers or *all* kinds (see below on generalization, pp. 308–09). Do you think a writer convinced of the merits of a lecture system could challenge Gilbert's position and, using a different set of descriptive terms and examples, write an equally lively and provocative case *for* the college lecture?

Deduction and Induction

Admittedly there is no "best way" of making a case for or against something. The "best way" depends on the particular subject and situation at hand, the particular readers being addressed, and the particular purpose in the writer's mind. These factors are relative. What is constant and predictable is the line along which argument inevitably proceeds, i.e., according to two basic types of reasoning that characterize the way our minds work. They are *deduction*—inferring a particular fact from a general truth (e.g., since deciduous plants are known to shed their leaves in winter, I can expect the deciduous dogwood that I planted in my yard last spring to shed its leaves this winter) and *induction*—moving from particular facts to generalizations (e.g., since I tasted thirty green apples and each one was sour, I conclude that all green apples are sour). In actual experience the two modes run into one another, as Thomas Huxley demonstrated in his essay "Thinking Scientifically" (pp. 80–81).

Thus:

	1. You examine thirty green apples.
	2. Each one is sour.
(induction)	3. You generalize: green apples are sour.
	4. You pick up apple thirty-one, which is also green.
(deduction)	5. You infer that this apple—which you have not yet tasted—will also be sour.

Interdependent as they are, each mode of reasoning has distinctive features and therefore should be examined individually.

Deduction

In deductive reasoning we lay down certain statements we know or strongly believe are true (premises); we then use these premises to get to other statements (conclusions). Deduction, then, involves a closely linked *chain of reasoning:*

		A B
major premise:	All men are mortal	Men are mortal
		C A
minor premise:	Socrates is a man	John is a man
		C B
conclusion: ∴	Socrates is mortal	John is mortal

The line of reasoning in this syllogism (as a three-part statement of this kind is called) is logically valid because given the two premises, the conclusion necessarily follows. In fact, the conclusion merely states *explicitly* what is already stated *implicitly* in the premises. The conclusion can then be said to derive logically and formally from the premises; in this case it points to the axiomatic truth that "things equal to the same thing are equal to each other."

There are formal rules for syllogisms, but we need not go into them here. Our interest is in compositional logic, not in logic per se. Furthermore, common sense—that inborn quality of mind that enables us to follow a logical line of reasoning even if we have never heard the word "logic" before—will often alert us to logical errors. We can tell, for example, that thinking is askew when the premises state that some of X is undesirable, and the inference drawn is that all of X is undesirable:

Some men are cruel
John is a man
∴ John is cruel

Obviously, John might not belong in the group of "cruel men." The conclusion changes "some" to "all."

The leap from "some" to "all" is an especially common fallacy; most people will not specify "some" even when they mean it. Instead they will say—ambiguously—"men are cruel." Such a statement is patently unfair. It can create ill feeling toward whole groups, when in truth only some members are blameworthy: because some students cheat on examinations, we should not conclude—as a sensationalized exposé-type magazine story might maintain—that "college kids are dishonest."

Similarly, common sense tells us that another gross error has been committed in the following statement:

All men are mammals
All monkeys are mammals
∴ All men are monkeys

Logicians call this the "fallacy of the undistributed middle";[4] but here again we need not name the logical flaw to see that it has been committed: things belonging to the same general class are not necessarily identical. In this case, the fact that men are mammals and monkeys are also mammals simply means that they, along with many other animals, share a larger biological category, as the logician's circular diagram shows:

[4] In logic the term "distributed" means *all* members of the class designated. Thus the "fallacy of the undistributed middle" means that the middle term in the syllogism (monkeys) does not refer to *all* members of the class.

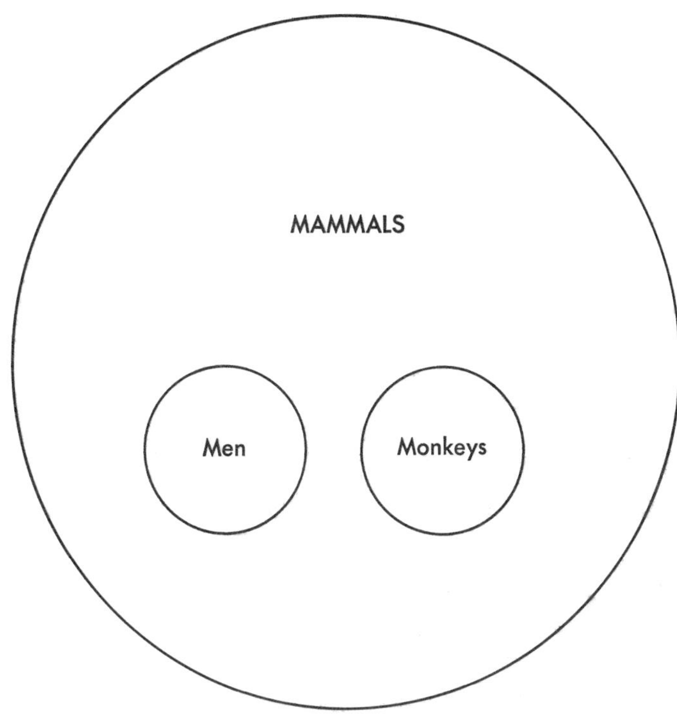

No one fails to spot the fallacy of the undistributed middle in this example (we *know* men are not monkeys!); but the fallacy is not usually so easy to detect. Indeed it may be (and frequently is) used in a subtle and insidious way to create spurious arguments, such as guilt by association:

Communists support the ABC Plan
Jack Smith supports the ABC Plan
∴ Jack Smith is a communist

(See the diagram on the next page.)

"Syllogism" is a logician's term, but the process of thought that it describes is hardly specialized; whenever anyone infers one idea from another, he is using a syllogism. If the reasoning is correct, the syllogism is valid, i.e., the conclusion follows logically from the premises. But is it true? That is quite another question since it is possible for a syllogism to be *valid* (correct in its formal reasoning) but factually *false*.

Thus the following two syllogisms are valid (i.e., given the premises the conclusions may logically be inferred); yet the first one is nonsense and the second is patently false because the premises are false:

All boys are unicorns
All unicorns are girls
∴ All boys are girls

All people are weaklings
All weaklings are fools
∴ All people are fools

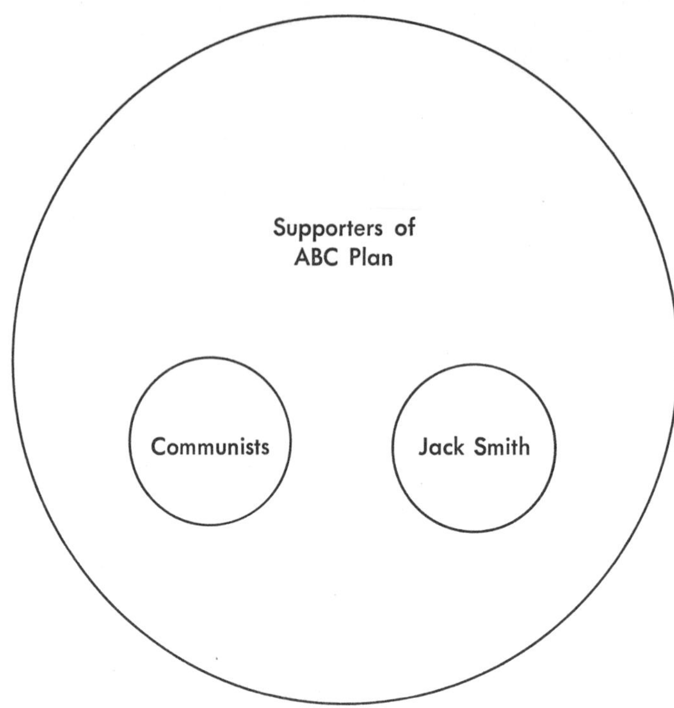

Clearly it is important to examine the premises of an argument before making a judgment. If someone accuses a congressman of accepting graft, for example, by arguing that "it is a widely known fact that congressmen take graft, so why should this member of Congress be any different?" it should be obvious immediately that the basic premise is open to question. *Is* it widely known and is it a *fact* that all congressmen accept graft? The attack conceals a faulty syllogism:

All congressmen take graft
Mr. X is a congressman
∴ Mr. X takes graft

Yes, the reasoning is valid; but the major premise is false, thereby dictating that the conclusion will be false.

Induction

As noted above, when we reason inductively we follow the scientific method of moving from particular facts that are objectively verifiable (what we can test, observe, or experience) to a broad generalization. We see the sun rise in the east and set in the west . . . once . . . twice . . . three times . . . four . . . five . . . six . . . seven. Finally we take the "inductive leap," the assertion of the general truth that the sun rises in the east and sets in the west, and in all *likelihood* can be counted on to do so tomorrow, the next day, the day after that. (The scientist works with probability, not certainty; thus all scientific truths must be considered probable rather than absolute.)

A good inductive leap can be made only when a sufficient number of particular instances have been observed. This number varies from situation to situation, the perfect induction being one in which every member of the class of things to which the proposition refers has actually been observed. This is clearly impossible in many cases and unnecessary in most cases; a fair sampling of typical instances chosen at random usually leads to a reliable enough generalization. For example, fifteen sour green apples certainly provide a reasonable basis for the generalization "green apples are sour." Yet if all the apples tasted came out of one orchard, or even one group of orchards located in one section of the country, we have to wonder, "Is it just *these* green apples that are sour? Perhaps green apples in other sections of the country are as sweet as red ones." A fair sampling of apples, then, should include apples from different parts of the country, thereby eliminating the possibility that special geographical or climatic conditions produce sour green apples.

Scientific investigators require a relatively large "fair sampling"—perhaps hundreds, thousands, or in some cases tens of thousands of subjects (especially in medical research)—before any generalizations can safely be drawn.

In any induction, the danger to guard against is that of hasty generalizations made without a sufficient number of examples, perhaps the most widespread fallacy in popular thinking. Like the error in deductive reasoning that takes us from "some" to "all," this error in inductive reasoning can produce prejudice and bias. Or perhaps it runs concomitant with it. A person who is already prejudiced against a minority group (blacks, Jews, Mexicans) is predisposed to conclude after noting even a few "offenses" in the group that "that's the way they *all* are."

Interestingly, the tendency to "wild generalization" has been analyzed psychologically as a form of exhibitionism:

> The exhibitionist desires to attract attention to himself. No one pays much attention to such undramatic statements as "Some women are fickle," or that some are liars, or "Some politicians are not better than they ought to be." But when one says that "all women are liars" this immediately attracts notice.[5]

Argument by Analogy

Still another mode of reasoning, often regarded as a form of induction, is reasoning by analogy—the drawing, in one inductive leap, of a crucial comparison.

In urging the United States to join the Allied cause in the First World War, Woodrow Wilson pointed to the fact that Russia had done so. In comparing his proposed action for the United States with Russia's earlier action Wilson was making an analogy, telling Congress that just as Russia wisely joined the Allied cause, so should we. The reasoning here proceeds from one specific instance to a similar specific instance, the implication being that what was a

[5] Lionel Ruby, *The Art of Making Sense* (Philadelphia: J. B. Lippincott Co., 1968), pp. 254–55.

good action for one country will be a good action for another, that there is a lesson to be learned from the Russian action.

There is no doubt that analogical reasoning serves as an important function in argumentation. It makes a point simply and economically (if Russia found it impossible to deal with Germany, why should the United States find it any easier?). Analogy is also vivid and may strike a strongly persuasive note when all direct reasoning fails. The story is told, for example, of the union organizer in the early days of the labor movement who, after reciting all rational reasons for joining the movement, finally won a prospective member by drawing a vivid and amusing analogy: "The top crowd's pressin' down! The bottom crowd's pressin' up. Whaddayou wanna be, a hamburger?"

Aside from its dramatic impact, the value of inductive analogy can be determined only by closely examining the two things being compared. Are they in fact similar in the essential characteristics relating to the conclusion? *Does the generalization underlying the analogy stand up to logical analysis?* In his book, *Thinking Straight*, Monroe Beardsley points to what he calls a "simple and crude example" of how analogy may mislead.

> One old gambit of the temperance orator was to say: "The delicate membranes of the stomach are like the delicate membranes of the eye; if you want to see what alcohol does to your stomach, just pour some gin in your eye." Now we may grant that there are *some* resemblances between eye tissue and stomach tissue: the question is whether these are *relevant* resemblances. In other words, the question is whether there is some true generalization like "Everything that hurts the eye will hurt the stomach" that will allow us to infer that if gin hurts the eye it will also hurt the stomach.
>
> So we might reply to him, "So you mean that *everything* that hurts the eye will also hurt the stomach?" He may wish to narrow the suggested generalization from "everything" to "every liquid," or in some other way. But unless he is willing to subscribe to *some* relevant generalization, he simply hasn't got what it takes to draw the conclusion he wants. We are therefore justified in saying to him, "If your argument proved anything, it would prove just as well that lemonade, vinegar, and hot coffee are bad for the stomach because they will hurt the eye. Doesn't that show that there must be important *differences* between the eye and stomach, so that what is true of one is not necessarily true of the other?" [6]

The important thing to remember about analogy, then, is that just because two things are alike in some respect they are not necessarily alike in others. Mental processes and bodily processes, for example, are comparable but not identical; therefore the following analogy represents a deceptive argument in behalf of censorship: "We don't allow poisonous substances to be put into our foods, so why should we permit books to be published that will poison the minds of our citizens?" Do you see the dangerously authoritarian generalization that underlies this argument? It is just as unsound, although less obviously so, as the old defense of monarchy that maintained

[6] Monroe C. Beardsley, *Thinking Straight*, 3rd edition, © 1966. Reprinted by permission of Prentice-Hall, Inc., Englewood Cliffs, New Jersey.

that since the earth revolved around the sun, circular motion was "natural"; consequently, by analogy, monarchy was a "natural" form of government because the subjects revolved around their monarch.[7]

Standing alone to prove a point, analogy cannot be trusted; it is useful only as a supplement to factual evidence mounted in support of a proposition. In the following essay,[8] for example, note how effectively the writer uses analogies to illuminate and reinforce his contention that in its own terms and within the context of its own premises, Marxist theory does not "stand up" to analysis: instead, it denies itself.

MARXISM

W. T. JONES

We have criticized Marxism as a theory of social causation because, of course, it was put forward as a definitive account of social change. Just as in physics a "law" is supposed to describe a necessary pattern of behavior that makes prediction and control possible, so the formula of dialectical materialism was supposed to reveal a necessary sequence of social relations. Marx the social scientist believed that what men do is not the product of "free will" but merely the expression of economic forces over which they have no control and which develop according to a purely deterministic sequence.

But Marx was not only a social scientist; he was a reformer. Now, suppose for the sake of argument that dialectical materialism is the "scientifically correct" formula describing the social process. Since the overthrow of bourgeois capitalism is inevitable, what is the point of agitating for its overthrow? If we take Marx seriously as a social scientist, Marx the reformer looks about as silly in writing his *Manifesto* urging the workers of the world to unite as we would look inviting a falling stone to fall a little faster. Of course, Marx could reply that the economic forces at work in the society of which he was a part determined that he would fight for the revolution, just as they determined that somebody else with a different economic background would fight against it. But this plunges Marxism—the theory—into the struggle about which it theorizes. It is not just a question of whether or not it is silly to try to further an inevitable end (e.g., induce the stone to fall faster), but whether, if the course of events is inevitable, "end" has anything more than a purely subjective meaning.

On the other hand, when Marx the reformer spoke, Marx the social scientist took a back seat, and we get a wholly different conception of the function of the theory and of its claim to truth. Marx the reformer was aware that the objective truth of a theory is no measure of its utility as a rallying point for aspiration and endeavor. (The Arian and orthodox theories of the Trinity are cases in point.) For Marx the reformer, Marxism was not a theory of social causation; it only pretended to be for propagandistic purposes. It was actually a call to the working class to rise and overthrow their masters, and it should be judged on the basis of its effectiveness in producing a class war from which the proletariat emerge victorious.

[7] Example cited in Bernard F. Huppé and Jack Kiminsky, *Logic and Language* (New York: Alfred A. Knopf, 1956), p. 204.

[8] Note also the use of analogy in the long paper on argumentation, "Whither the Black Odyssey?" pp. 352–62.

But why, then, did Marxism pretend to be a theory of social causation? Because, given the time, the place, and the circumstances (e.g., the "vogue" of science), men want to be assured that what they are fighting and dying for has been "scientifically" proved to be true—just as purchasers of soap or cigarettes like to be assured that "science" shows the product they use to be superior. In another age, in another country, revolutionists would not formulate their program in terms of dialectical materialism, but in terms, say, of a crusade to free the Holy Places from the infidel. It just happens that in the present age the former type of formula appeals and so provides the oppressed classes with a rationale for the revolutionary acts which one wants them to perform.

This presents a totally different picture of the social process. Far from being rigorously determined, it now appears that free will and indeterminism are predominant factors. Action, it would seem, can always alter the course of events. This would appear to rule out a science of social causation, but Marx the reformer would not be distressed: *qua* reformer, he had no interest in theory as theory. Thus, in his *Theses against Feuerbach,* Marx stated quite explicitly, "The question whether human thought can achieve objective truth is not a question of theory but a *practical* question. In practice man must prove the truth, i.e., the reality, power, and this-sidedness of his thought. The dispute over the reality or unreality of thought which is isolated from practice is a purely *scholastic* question." From this point of view, a theory proves itself true by its success in bringing about the state of affairs it describes—dialectical materialism would be a "true" theory if it incited the workers to rise and make an end of bourgeois capitalism.

It will be seen, then, that Marxism falls apart. It is impossible to ignore, as some have done, these pragmatic aspects of Marxism, but it is ridiculous to maintain, as others have, that this is the only "true" Marx. From a purely pragmatic point of view, dialectical materialism is encumbered with all sorts of impedimenta which can hardly have appealed to the working class but which Marx and Engels took very seriously—and took seriously not because they held them to be good propaganda but because they held them to be "true." This duality of point of view has persisted in Marxism to this day. On the one hand, we find a rigid and authoritarian dogmatism masquerading as a science of social causation; on the other, an extremely flexible and Machiavellian *Realpolitik,* designed to bring events which refuse to be determined by dialectic into conformity with the "fore-ordained" pattern. But it is only fair to say that Marxism is not unique in this respect; it is not the first philosophy that has combined doctrinaire self-assurance about ends with a cynical attitude toward means.[9]

Common Logical Fallacies

Before citing further examples of argumentation, it will be helpful to consider some common logical fallacies, recognizing that logical flaws are not necessarily *rhetorical* flaws. In fact logical flaws may be extremely effective in their impact on the reader. Lies, if they are bold enough, generate drama and excitement; emotional appeals often "touch the heart" so deeply that

[9] From *A History of Western Philosophy,* by W. T. Jones, copyright 1952, by Harcourt Brace Jovanovich, Inc. and reprinted with their permission.

the understanding is ignored. But these, of course, are tricks designed to fool and blind the reader. Since we consider the ethics of rhetoric later on (in Chapter 24, "The Limits of Language") we need not go into these matters here. Suffice it to say that the good argument is logically sound and intellectually honest; the good argument bases it case on reason and uses emotion only to reinforce reason; the good argument not only makes a case in behalf of its subject, it also illuminates it so that the reader—whether he agrees or disagrees with the argument—will at least learn more about the issues.

Checklist of Fallacies

CIRCULAR REASONING

To assume in the premise what you are supposedly trying to *prove* in the course of your argument is to argue in a circle—or "beg the question." It has been observed that "the function of logic is to demonstrate that because one thing or group of things is true, another must be true as consequence."[10] But in a circular argument there is no progression; the same thing is said in different words: "We shall always be free in America because we have a democratic form of government." This statement establishes nothing because the idea of freedom is already assumed in the word "democratic."

EQUIVOCATION

To equivocate is to change the meaning of a word in the course of an argument or to use an ambiguous word in two different senses (whether deliberately or unintentionally)—as in the following:

> Science has discovered many laws of nature. This is proof that there is a God, for a law implies the existence of a law-giver, and God is the great Lawgiver of the universe.

Observe the confused and careless use of the word "law": it is first used with the scientific meaning of uniform behavior in nature; it is then used prescriptively to refer to regulations enforcible by a higher authority.[11]

(See further discussion, Chapters 1 and 24.)

EVADING THE ISSUE

This fallacy takes several forms:

1. *Distraction*

The course of an argument may be turned away from the main issues by raising extraneous considerations, such as emotions or sentiments. Thus in making a case for the democratic form of government, the arguer may eulogize George Washington and the other founding fathers, extolling their personal courage and foresight. Such distractions may divert the adversary's attention and make him forget the real issues.

[10] See Robert Gorham Davis, "Logic and Logical Fallacies," in the *Harvard Handbook for English* (Harvard University, 1947).

[11] Example drawn from Lionel Ruby, *The Art of Making Sense* (Philadelphia: J. B. Lippincott Co., 1968), pp. 32–33.

2. *Ad hominem*

Another way to evade the issue is by directing the argument against the character of the man making the case, rather than against the case itself. This fallacy is common and sinister ("You cannot trust Smith's reform bill because he has had questionable leftist leanings . . . and there is the divorce . . . and that suspicious suicide attempt. . . .").

3. *Name Calling*

Here is still another evasive "smear" tactic (and verbal trick): calling an opposing view by a "bad name," thereby suggesting that it is in reality bad. Thus an attempt to improve welfare legislation may be labelled "starry-eyed idealism" or "sheer romanticism," which will turn our government into a "welfare state." (See also pp. 418–22.)

4. *Appeal to Pity*

When General Douglas MacArthur, pleading his case before the American people, cited the old refrain "Old soldiers never die, they just fade away," he was resorting to the popular (and often successful) ruse of making himself pitiful in order to win sympathy. Obviously this is another way of evading substantive issues by focusing on "poor old me."

FALLACIOUS APPEAL TO AUTHORITY

To cite a Nobel Prize-winning chemist as an authority on civil rights legislation is to misunderstand the meaning of the word "authority." An authority's opinion is meaningful only when it concerns his special field of competence; otherwise the so-called authority is simply an ordinary citizen like the rest of us—neither more wise nor more foolish.

FALLACY OF THE UNDISTRIBUTED MIDDLE

(See "Deduction," pp. 305–08.)

FALSE ANALOGY

(See "Argument by Analogy," pp. 309–12.)

HASTY GENERALIZATION

(See "Induction," pp. 308–09.)

NON SEQUITUR

When a conclusion does not follow from its premises, there has obviously been a serious "slip" in the deductive reasoning process.

All artists are creative
Jackson is an artist
∴ Jackson should be pensioned

This broken line of reasoning can be mended and made to conform to a logical pattern, but it must be thought through carefully. What the individual probably wants to say, and is obliged to say if his conclusion is to be rendered valid, is:

All creative artists deserve to be pensioned
Jackson is a creative artist
∴ Jackson should be pensioned

Both syllogisms contain the same conclusion; but in one case it does not follow from the premises, and in the other it does. To correct a non sequitur, we must remember that a conclusion is valid not in and of itself but within the context of its own terms, i.e., the body of the syllogism.

OVERSIMPLIFICATION

This is a root fallacy in which the arguer ignores the complexities of a problem so that he may solve it more easily.

1. *Either . . . Or*
This is a device in which the arguer states that there are two and only two alternatives in a given situation: *Either* you vote for the mayor's tax reform bill *or* you permit the city to become bankrupt. No intermediate choices are allowed, although in fact there may be many other possibilities available.

2. *Post Hoc, Ergo Propter Hoc* ("After this, therefore because of this")
An error in cause-effect analysis described earlier (see p. 113).

PERSONIFYING ABSTRACTIONS

This fallacy represents both oversimplification and verbal distortion. It suggests that "Science tells us. . . ." or "History teaches. . . ." or "Poets believe. . . ." as if each of these were a single person speaking with one voice, instead of a complex abstraction representing many different points of view (Chapter 24, "The Limits of Language").

Substantiating the Argument

Argumentation is by far the most demanding and comprehensive form of discourse, not only because it requires rigorous reasoning and persuasive tactics but also because it frequently embraces other forms: definition, description, comparison, analysis, narration, characterization, interpretation, reflection, and evaluation. All of them may enter into argumentation. Indeed, it is quite possible that in the course of answering question 20 "What case can be made for or against X?" we may include every form of writing cited—and some that are not mentioned.

In "making a case," then, we should try to raise as many pertinent points as possible, for it is the *content* of the argument—the evidence that substantiates our position—as well as the rigor of our *reasoning* that will establish and hopefully *prove* our case. The following essay, for example, is a brief but compelling argument in behalf of raising safety standards in American coal mines. It is a compelling argument because the writer cites facts and figures as well as personal feeling and experience. He clearly knows what he is talking about; he checked his information with the International Labor Office; he obtained production figures and accident rates for American and foreign mines. He moves through his subject with assurance because he is thoroughly familiar with it; he does not lapse into nebulous generalities, nor does he simply play on emotion. Instead he combines objective data with first-hand accounts of what life is like in a coal mine. It is grim, and we are made to see how and why it is grim. We are also made to feel, with the writer, a deep compassion for the miner, whose fears are rooted in the realities of an inherently hazardous situation, but whose pride (the writer himself projects this attitude) persists in the face of all dangers. By the time we have finished reading this piece we have a deeper understanding of the coal miner's situation.

LIFE, AND DEATH, IN THE COAL MINES

DUANE LOCKARD

INTRODUCTION

NARRATION

Nearly thirty years ago, 350 feet beneath a West Virginia mountain, I stood paralyzed with fear when a greasy haulage motor caught fire. Having heard endless mine lore from my father and grandfather, I knew that fire in a mine was death, especially when the mine was not rockdusted to reduce the explosiveness of coal dust. I knew many miles of volatile coal dust lay in the tunnels of that mine, since I was at that moment preparing to spray the walls with tons of an incombustible matter.

We worked 24 hours that Saturday and Sunday rockdusting because the boss said the state mine inspector was coming Monday and the mine had to be prepared for him. The fire burned itself out, but not before it impressed me as deeply as any fright I ever experienced, including wartime air combat.

BODY

This memory returns as I observe the current maneuvers to prevent the raising of U.S. coal mine safety standards.

Citing vital statistics as evidence

Mining is dangerous and always will be; no other industry levies a higher toll in lives and disabling accidents. To produce half a billion tons of bituminous coal last year cost the lives of 307 miners; 88 of them died in explosions and an equal number were crushed in roof falls. Besides these fatalities another 9,500 men suffered serious injuries. And an undetermined number breathed the decisive quantity of coal dust that assured their lingering death of asphyxiation from pneumonoconiosis or "black lung."

Conceding an opposing point . . . and modifying it

Apologists for the industry point to the reduction in the number of accidents in recent decades, and it is true that since 1930 the number of accidents has declined from 100,000 to about 10,000. Not all the reduction is due to safety advances, however, for 135,000 miners now produce as much coal as did half a million during World War II.

Comparative statistics as evidence

Does the production of coal necessitate such a cost in lives? Coal can be and long has been mined in other countries with lower accident rates. On the average Western European nations having mining fatality rates that are a third to a half of those for the United States.

Citing authority

The International Labor Office reports that American mining fatality rates are matched only by those for Canada, Taiwan, Korea and Turkey among the 22 nations for which it has data.

Morocco and Southern Rhodesia have rates only half as high as ours, while India, Czechoslovakia, Poland, Great Britain and Yugoslavia have rates that are lower still.

Quoting authority

Is this because American mines are more dangerous than others? I posed this question to a British mining official. He replied that on the contrary, "British mines are inherently more dangerous than yours and therefore our safety standards have to be all the higher. . . . Our rockdusting standards are very high and rigidly enforced. I believe our standards of electrical safety are higher than in the U.S. Indeed, most American machinery—if not all—that has been installed over here has had to be redesigned on the electrical side."

He concluded, "It sounds as if I'm being beastly and critical of your mining people and I would hate to be so, because we have a lot to learn from them in some matters while still trying to retain our safety standards. We have learned by experience, much of which has been bitter, and I am quite sure that it is the inherently greater danger in our mines that makes us the more careful and creates our higher standards."

Citing personal experience

Mining has changed greatly since I left it, but that dreaded top still hangs overhead always ready to avenge its loss. I recall once that my father asked me to stop shoveling while he sounded the roof with his pick-handle, listening carefully. Coal began to snap and fly just as he shouted a warning and we ran from the coal face. Within seconds the half-filled coal car, the tracks, some tools (but not the lunch buckets—I saw to their safety) disappeared in a roar of rubble and a cloud of dust. A thick layer of slate had given way, splintering huge safety posts like twigs as it came down.

CONCLUSION

Every miner is aware of this risk, as he is of explosions, and his body bears blue scars to mark each injury by a hank of coal. I never knew a miner lacking in fear of the mine nor one without a certain compensating pride.

Peroration

Too many of these brave men will be killed even with the best of safety rules, but in this technologically advanced nation need we have so much blood on our coal? [12]

The Satiric Attack

The essay that follows demonstrates that in argumentation an indirect attack may be even more effective than a direct attack. The arguer may discredit a view, in other words, by seeming to agree with it, and thereby allowing it to betray its own absurdity. Thus the suggestion made by the following essayist—that we "pep up" the old classics by abridging and simplifying them—is in reality a satiric attack on this very procedure, a mocking evaluation of the attempt to make complex works seem easy, to "happy things up, swing a little."

[12] From the *New York Times,* June 21, 1969. © 1969 by The New York Times Company. Reprinted by permission.

LET'S PEP UP THOSE OLD CLASSICS

DAVID E. SHERMAN

The novel, an art form whose imminent demise is predicted hourly in literary publications, has recently had two significant reprieves. In New York, there appeared a fast-paced 60-cent edition of Henry Fielding's classic, *Tom Jones*. This obliging volume omits all "the parts that lack interest for the modern reader"—meaning Fielding's trenchant commentaries on eighteenth-century English morality—and simply furnishes a zippy plot line.

In Paris, there appeared a 368-page digest "for the modern reader" of another classic, Victor Hugo's gigantic *Les Misérables*. Such passages as the Battle of Waterloo and descriptions of the sewers of Paris—which made the book famous—are omitted altogether. Other downbeat bits, like the death of the hero, Jean Valjean, have been bypassed. The book, now fast and clean as a hound's tooth, or a used Edsel, has a happy ending. (Although a moss-packed literary society brought suit to confiscate the edition, no one suggested the obvious next step: drop Hugo's name and retitle the book *Les Joyeuses*.)

Then along come a couple of cubes named James J. Lynch and Bertrand Evans with a book called *High School English Textbooks: A Critical Examination* (Little, Brown). These gloom-dispensers purport to see a clear and present danger, for instance, in the fact that in one textbook Charles Dickens's fusty old back number, *David Copperfield*, was sensibly cut to a handy 22 chapters and retitled *One Boy's Life*.

What these literary spoilsports do not seem to realize is that to interest the modern reader you have to talk his language, happy things up, swing a little. For example, these versions of classics everybody knows:

A Dane and His Dad. This could become a family comedy about an excitable kid from Denmark. His mom and his Uncle Fred treat his cantankerous but kindly father for a nasty carache and, cured, Dad goes off to Stockholm on business. The boy has a dream that Dad is in some kind of trouble, but when he tells his girl about it she thinks she sees Dad's ghost, screams and falls into the water. The boy rescues her and then almost cripples an old family friend he catches peeking at the subsequent smooching. Of course it turns out it wasn't a ghost at all. It was Dad himself, who had hung around to keep an eye on things. A good thing he did too, because at the end of the book he's on hand to see his boy win the school fencing championship.

A story called *Love Is a Crime?* could—if properly simplified—do a great deal for international understanding by illustrating some universal truths about today's teen-agers. In this one, a mixed-up Russian lad named Harry (his last name is Raskolnikov) gets in wrong for pinching cigarets from an old woman who runs a small but prosperous candy store in downtown Moscow. A good-hearted cop, Inspector Petrovitch, tries to put Harry straight but the boy takes up instead with Sonia, an attractive kid who is supporting her family as a waitress. It is she who talks Harry into going straight. He comes clean, gets 30 days, and when he gets out marries Sonia. The inspector is best man and the old woman gives the boy a job in a branch she's opening in Odessa.

There's another one, *Bye-bye to Battle*. In this one a boy named Fred Henry is working in the officers' PX in Rome during the war. It's a rugged job, but he has a girl, a lovely nurse named Cathy Barkley, from one of your fine old English families. Fred gets transferred to a line outfit and, during a retreat of the enemy at a town called Caporetto, which is very colorfully described, he gets a million-dollar wound in the ankle. He is sent to a field hospital and who should be there but Cathy. They get married and move to Lausanne where they have a healthy, bouncing child and Fred buys a motel.

But the big switcheroo—too many happy endings can be a drag—is *Ten Years to Get Home*. It's about a Marine colonel who gets his discharge and starts home to his wife Penny. A number of frankly fanciful episodes happen to him en route—he mets one-eyed monsters, and a beautiful lady who runs a pig farm. Everyone else in his outfit is killed. This is downbeat enough, but when he finally gets home he finds that Penny, who has been making ends meet by weaving blankets, is besieged by a bunch of 4-Fs who convince her the husband has deserted her. He turns up with a big smile and open arms. "Baby," he says, "it took a long time but I'm here." "You're not kidding it took a long time, Buster," says Penny. "I sold out last night to the highest bidder. Get lost."

Who says the novel has to die? [13]

Testing the Argument

Whatever case we may make *for* or *against* any subject, we should test our argument against the following questions:

1. Have we defined the terms? (Chapter 1, "What Does X Mean?" Chapter 24, "The Limits of Language")
2. Have we established exactly what the argument is about, i.e., have we stated the proposition *clearly* and indicated precisely what issues are to be defended and refuted?
3. Are facts and assumptions correct?
4. Have we offered sufficient evidence—facts, statistics, illustrations, testimony—that will further illuminate and substantiate each point as well as the overall position? (Chapter 22, "Gathering Information")
5. Are generalizations fair and reliable?
6. Do conclusions follow logically from the premises?
7. Have we cited reliable authorities?
8. Have we been as *precise* as possible in the treatment of the subject?
9. Is the presentation "artful," rhetorically effective, clear, well-organized?

   It is well to remember that in no form of writing is it more important to use the strengths of language "to the best possible effect." Stylistic failings such as undefined terms that create ambiguity, confusing grammatical constructions, vague allusions, pompous, clumsy, overlong sentences are guaranteed to alienate those who might otherwise be convinced. (Bad writing, in other words, can kill a case as surely as lack of evidence or fallacious reasoning.)
10. Is the tone (whether serious or satiric) appropriate to the subject, the audience, the occasion, and the purpose we are trying to achieve?
11. Have we examined *every* important aspect of the case? Aristotle

[13] "Let's Pep Up Those Old Classics," by David E. Sherman, *Life* Magazine, October 9, 1964 © 1964 Time, Inc. Reprinted by permission.

maintained that we should be able to argue on either side of a question—not because we are without personal conviction or commitment, but because only then can we feel certain that no aspect of the case has escaped us. Only then can we anticipate the reader's (or listener's) objections and by anticipating them either avoid them or prepare an advance refutation.

12. Is the approach reasonable rather than dogmatic, rigid, unnecessarily (and irritatingly) disputacious?

In considering the last question, we might also consider the rule of that eminently practical and successful diplomat, Benjamin Franklin, who, recognizing that an overconfident and imperious manner may "lose the day," wrote the following in his autobiography:

> I made it a rule to forbear all direct contradictions to the sentiments of others, and all positive assertion of my own. I even forbade myself . . . the use of every word or expression in the language that imported a fix'd opinion, such as *certainly, undoubtedly,* etc., and I adopted, instead of them, *I conceive, I apprehend,* or *I imagine* a thing to be so or so; or it *so appears to me at present.* When another asserted something that I thought an error, I deny'd myself the pleasure of contradicting him abruptly, and of showing immediately some absurdity in his proposition; and in answering I began by observing that in certain cases or circumstances his opinion would be right, but in the present case there *appear'd* or *seem'd* to me some difference, etc. I soon found the advantage of this change in my manner; the conversations I engag'd in went on more pleasantly. The modest way in which I propos'd my opinions procur'd them a readier reception and less contradiction; I had less mortification when I was found to be in the wrong, and I more easily prevail'd with others to give up their mistakes and join with me when I happened to be in the right.
>
> And this mode, which I at first put on with some violence to natural inclination, became at length so easy, and so habitual to me, that perhaps for these fifty years past no one has ever heard a dogmatical expression escape me. And to this habit (after my character of integrity) I think it principally owing that I had early so much weight with my fellow-citizens when I proposed new institutions, or alterations in the old, and so much influence in public councils when I became a member; for I was but a bad speaker, never eloquent, subject to much hesitation in my choice of words, hardly correct in language, and yet I generally carried my points.

ASSIGNMENTS

I. Discuss the advantages and possible disadvantages of Benjamin Franklin's advice, as cited above. Do his rules preclude the kind of *confident* assertion necessary to win the reader's agreement and assent? Explain the psychological value of Franklin's approach.

II. A. Evaluate Woodrow Wilson's address to Congress from the point of view of its factual content, soundness of logic, and persuasive tactics.

B. Write an essay (750–1,000 words) in which you make a case for some political program, policy, or piece of legislation that you support and would like to persuade others to support. (Try to move the reader to *action*, as President Wilson moved Congress to action.)

III. A. In an essay (750–1,000 words) reply to Allan H. Gilbert's essay "College Lectures Are Obsolete." Support the position or assert a contrary position in favor of the lecture system.

or

B. Write an essay (750–1,000 words) attacking another aspect or procedure of our educational system that you consider obsolete or otherwise inadequate (the grading system, required courses, awarding of degrees, formal class meetings). Be sure to locate specific issues and, in both cases, be sure to include in the body of your argument not only evidence in behalf of your case, but evidence refuting points of opposition.

IV. Analyze the following argument by pointing out weaknesses in inductive and deductive reasoning and any other logical fallacies you may note on both sides.

TEACHER CERTIFICATION

TEACHER: I suppose I should begin by admitting that, after making a successful career of teaching in elementary and high school for many years, I have finally been driven out by the totalitarian methods of the educational hierarchy, with their nagging requirements and hamstringing restrictions.

DEAN: You refer to . . . ?

TEACHER: I refer, among other things, to the enormous proliferation of teacher-training programs, topheavy with "how-to" courses in educationism and pedagogy, and the whole certification racket. To get a raise in rank and pay, it doesn't matter how good you are, or how much experience you have—you have to keep going back every summer, or winter nights, to take more and more of these "Mickey Mouse" courses on how to teach. Then automatically, as you pile up the credits—all you need is a C—you get your raise. It is a system designed for the incompetent and the drudge.

DEAN: I don't know what you mean by "Mickey Mouse."

TEACHER: That's what the students call them, because they are so easy. In one course I took, Education 201: Human Development, there were twenty-four hours of school observation. Lesson 1 was to make a diagram of the classroom, noting size and position of door, windows, lights, and so forth. What a bore! Genuinely superior teachers will simply not submit to these humiliating requirements, and I predict that we are on the verge of an even more drastic decline—a terrifying descent—in the quality of our teaching. I shudder to think how the next generation will be taught.

DEAN: How do you know that the good teachers will refuse to submit to these requirements? Maybe the ones who get out or stay out are simply the poor students who are afraid they cannot pass the courses. You can't go by their opinion, when it's evidently based on a fear of doing advanced work.

TEACHER: There is one way to tell who good teachers are: anyone who would be willing to bow to the educationists and accept the system of piling up hours of credits doesn't have the brains and ability to be a good teacher. Why, Admiral Rickover once said that even Albert Einstein could not legally be a teacher of first-grade arithmetic, because he never had enough credits for courses in education.

DEAN: Well, Einstein always said he was not very good at arithmetic, anyway. And of course the Admiral did not examine the teacher certification codes of the various states. The truth is that any superintendent of schools in any state could have hired Dr. Einstein immediately under the temporary provisional certification structure.

TEACHER: But at the end of the year, Einstein would get a little note saying that if he wished to continue to teach in that state, he would have to take six credit hours of education in the summer, or something like that. Imagine that poor old man having to put his intellect on a course in audio-visual aids, telling what kind of chalk works best on a blackboard, and what kind of colored balls make the best demonstration materials for teaching subtraction. It's pathetic.

DEAN: Your argument is fallacious. You seem to say that if the certification system allowed Einstein to teach in the first grade, it would be acceptable; but it does not, therefore it is not acceptable. The fallacy here is that Einstein might not want to teach in the first grade, and anyway he was unique.

TEACHER: What worries me most is that as teacher training is more and more dominated by educationism, it becomes harder and harder to maintain standards in schools. So many of the principals are ex-coaches, and such like, because they were the ones who had time to take all the education credits. One teacher I know resigned when her principal turned over her physics laboratory to a driver-training course and student activities. Pupils take less and less history, mathematics, languages, and so forth. What is happening to the standards?

DEAN: Of course we maintain standards. There is no slackening in the number of hours of work pupils have to take, or the number of days they have to go to school. We have rules in force. And remember that we must also maintain standards for the teachers—that is the purpose of education requirements, to prevent untrained people from ruining the minds of our pupils. For many years the states have recognized the need for accrediting professional personnel in veterinary medicine, chiropody, library science, and many other fields. Can you honestly say that the man who treats our dumb animals must undergo a more careful program of preparation and certification than the man who is responsible for molding the minds of our youth?

TEACHER: That is what concerns me—the idea of "molding minds," as though they are like putty in the hands of the teacher. I am amazed at the extent to which educationist thinking has taken over the accents of authoritarianism and tyranny. But it's all of a piece with the educationists' work. What worries me most is the way the national and state educational associations, putting the bite on their members to build up huge slush funds for lobbying, have manipulated the state legislatures to protect their interests. They have built up a closed shop—that's what it comes down to. Though we have organized to counteract them—our organization is called We The Parents (WTP)—and strongly solicited our members for contributions to support our effort to persuade legislators, we have not been able to accomplish much against the entrenched educationist powers.

DEAN: I hate to hear you speak that way. We educators welcome constructive criticism, of course, but these pernicious attacks can only undermine public confidence in the teaching profession and bring harm upon our teachers, schools, pupils, and the national welfare.

TEACHER: A lot the educationists care about the general welfare! We all know there is a serious teacher shortage; and we know how restrictive the certification requirements are. It is evident that it is these very requirements, which drive good people out of the profession and prevent new teachers who come into the state from teaching, that cause the shortage. It is the closed-shop principle.

DEAN: But certification cannot be the cause of the teacher shortage. The shortage is recent—it grew with the coming to school of the war babies. Before that, teachers were begging for jobs. Yet the certification standards have not been tightened. How do you account for that?

TEACHER: I don't think you need to put me on the witness stand for cross-examination. Some causes take a long time to achieve their effects, you know. But that's not my main point. I'm not against having teachers go back to school, take more courses, refresh their knowledge. I am against the fact that when they do go back to school, they are not supposed to take real content-courses, but only method-courses.

DEAN: Now this is a gross distortion of the facts, as I could prove to you if you were willing yourself to take the 135 education courses taught at our state university. We *have* content-courses, just as we have method-courses; and we encourage our returning teachers to get credit in subjects like history, mathematics, science, languages, that are related to what they are teaching. We see no inherent opposition between content-courses and method-courses; in fact, we see no basic distinction between them, for every course, if it does anything at all, has a content, doesn't it? If something is taught, then something must be learned.

TEACHER: It is learned, if the pupils are capable of learning. But you know yourself that the students who are attracted to schools of education are generally the poorest students. Why, aside from the two friends of mine I mentioned earlier, the three teachers I got to know best in my last school had low I.Q.'s, and were admitted to state education colleges with College Board scores of under 400.

DEAN: I don't agree with your evidence here. The best test of ability in studying is the grade a student gets; education students get just as good grades in their courses as other students do in theirs; it follows that they are just as good students.

TEACHER: My argument is perfectly clear and convincing. All poor students avoid taking many courses in the hard subjects, such as mathematics, philosophy, economics; most education students avoid taking many courses in these subjects; therefore, most education students are poor.

DEAN: I can see that your prejudice against educators and students of education goes far too deep to allow rational arguments to prevail upon you, and so, with sadness and regret, I suggest that we draw this discussion to a close.[14]

[14] Monroe C. Beardsley, *Thinking Straight,* 3rd edition, © 1966. Reprinted by permission of Prentice-Hall, Inc., Englewood Cliffs, New Jersey.

V. A. Analyze the analogies in W. T. Jones' essay "Marxism." Indicate in what ways they enhance the argument.

B. In an essay (500–750 words) make a case against any –ism of your choice (atheism, romanticism, racism) by showing that it is either self-contradictory (a logical flaw) or self-defeating (a moral flaw). Use analogies to develop your argument.

VI. In an essay (500–750 words) present a case for or against a subject of your choice, using the methods of ridicule and irony, as in "Let's Pep Up Those Old Classics."

VII. Outline and evaluate the rhetorical effectiveness and logical soundness of the essays in this chapter.

VIII. Read the following brief essay by Dr. Frederick Wertham and, choosing your own topic, write an essay using the same format: presentation of points in support of your position, followed by a parenthetic rebuttal.

THE COMICS—VERY FUNNY

FREDERICK WERTHAM

What is the case for the comic books? Various points are adduced in favor of them. It is said:

That they reflect the children's minds and if there is something wrong with them, it must be the child's fault, and the child must have been neurotic or disturbed or unstable in the first place. (That reminds me of the owner of the dog that had killed a rabbit, who claimed in court that the rabbit had started the fight.) . . .

That there are good comic books. (That reminds me of the story of the polite clergyman who was asked about a bad egg which he had just started to eat: "Isn't it good?" "Madam," he answered, "parts of it are excellent.")

That the children identify themselves with the good figures in the comic books. (That is like saying that the spectators in the Grand Guignol who watch the rape, murder, and violence identify themselves with the gendarme who breaks into the room a few seconds before the curtain falls. There are comic books in which girls are bound and burned, sold as slaves, thrown to the animals, and rescued only at the last moment by a good and faithful elephant. Do the experts of the comic-book industry claim that the children identify themselves with the elephant?) . . .

That comic books must be all right because they are so widespread. (That is like saying that infantile paralysis is all right because so many children have it.)

That comic books should be left as they are, because curbing them would mean interference with free speech. (As if censoring what adults read has anything to do with planning for children the kind of reading matter that will not harm them.)

That comic books are a healthy outlet. (On the contrary, they stimulate unhealthy sexual attitudes: sadism, masochism, frigidity.) [15]

[15] From *Saturday Review,* May 29, 1948. Reprinted by permission of Frederick Wertham.

Suggested Topics:

automation
monogamy
pornography
the CIA
making the punishment fit the crime
marijuana
electoral college
euthanasia
the jury system
psychoanalysis
vivisection
intelligence of dolphins
women's rights
smoking
bullfighting
weddings
insecticides
controlling the weather
watching television
the war on poverty
censorship of press
a volunteer army
buying guns
conscientious objectors
miscegenation laws

II WRITING A LONG PAPER: RESEARCH AND ORGANIZATION

21 THE LONG PAPER

For our purposes we have regarded the short paper (500–1,000 words) as one that takes its impulse from a single question, confining itself—since the contemplated scope of the paper is limited—to answering that one question.

In this chapter we shall examine longer and more complex forms of writing in which the answer to one question involves the writer in many subsidiary questions. Specifically we shall consider four longer papers: an extended analysis, a description-narration, an extended characterization, and an extended argument. Each of these provides an illustration of a possible term paper. In the assignment section following each illustrative piece is a suggested topic for a term paper on a similar subject and of comparable scope, i.e., one that takes its major impulse from one question but which requires the writer, in the course of "extending" his subject, to answer many of the other twenty questions posed in earlier chapters. It will be helpful to begin by describing the term paper itself.

Form and Function of the Term Paper

A so-called term paper is a strictly academic form, named for the period of time in which the paper must be completed. It is essentially a long paper —a relatively thorough study of an aspect of a given subject—averaging 3,000–6,000 words (although it can be much longer) and requiring some research (this too varies from course to course). Instructors in every discipline are likely to assign term papers on the justifiable assumption that they require more independent, intensive, and creative effort than any other single unit of work asked of the student throughout the semester. Certainly it is true that when you prepare a term paper you are in charge of your own destiny: you generally select your own topic, locate appropriate reference materials, abstract from them what you need, and reassemble your data to conform to the new statement you wish to make, expressed in your own style. No single piece of work, then, requires more imagination and patience, more sustained intellectual effort, more persistence and rhetorical skill than this full-term research and writing project; nor does any single piece of work give the instructor a better measure of your ability to relate meaningfully and articulately to some aspect of the discipline in question.

The following essays are in forms suitable for a term paper. Indeed one way to "hit upon" a subject for a paper of your own is to examine these pieces; you may be moved to write a similar piece on a different subject, or you may be moved to write a piece which is essentially a reply to the piece you have just read.

Extended Analysis

WHAT IS PAIN?

W. K. LIVINGSTON

Every feeling person knows from personal experience what pain is, yet scientists have found it extraordinarily difficult to agree on a satisfactory definition for it. The question is not a metaphysical one. It has profound bearing on the search for ways to relieve pain and on basic human fears. Probably no subject in medical science interests people more than this one. They like to hear about new anesthetic agents, analgesic drugs and nerve operations to control pain; about "pain clinics" for the study of rare pain phenomena; about laboratory investigations of the physiology and psychology of pain. And pain is one of their chief concerns when they go to the doctor. They frequently question their physicians about the pains of cancer, heart disease and other feared maladies. They ask about their own immediate pains—how long they will last, how much worse they can get. In particular, they ask about the pain of dying.

There can be no definite answers to such queries until we learn the answers to certain more specific problems. The most penetrating questions about pain come from children rather than adults. A child's fear of the unknown is closely coupled with his experiences of pain. Whenever he has to face some new ordeal, his invariable query is, "Will it hurt?" If he sees some person with a disabling injury, he tries to imagine how it would feel to have the same injury. He wants to know how much it hurts to break a leg, to have a tooth pulled, to undergo a surgical operation, to be wounded in battle. His sympathy goes out spontaneously to injured people and injured animals. It even extends to inanimate objects to which he ascribes a personality. His curiosity about pain is insatiable. He wants to know how much it hurts a fish to be caught on a hook or to flop around in a boat, and he may even insist that the writhing of an angleworm impaled on the hook is evidence of great pain.

From *Scientific American*, Vol. 188, No. 3 (March 1953). Reprinted with permission.

Naive as the child's questions may sound, they are fundamental. Transcribed into more formal terms, some of them might read: How far down the scale of animal life is there a conscious perception of pain? Are an animal's reactions to injury an accurate measure of pain? Is physical pain ever devoid of psychological factors? Can human pain be measured objectively? Why do certain emotional states make pain more tolerable, while others make it worse? Is pain compatible with unconsciousness? Does an anesthetic agent abolish pain or does it merely erase its memory? How often is death painful?

It is doubtful that these questions will ever be answered by anything better than speculation or personal opinion until there is some agreement as to what pain is. I have used the question, "What is pain?" for my title because I believe its answer is fundamental to understanding the phenomenon and is the only basis on which one can build his own philosophy about it.

INJURY WITHOUT PAIN

First let us consider a couple of specific cases to clarify the nature of the problem. A young woman is giving birth to her first baby. Her labor pains have become so severe that her obstetrician orders an anesthetic. She is given just enough to keep her in a state of "analgesia," meaning that she feels no pain but remains conscious. In this condition the woman ceases to complain about her pains or else talks about them in a dispassionate fashion, in spite of the fact that the force of the uterine contractions is steadily increasing. She answers questions and carries out the requests of the obstetrician in lending her assistance to the delivery of the baby. The only signs that she is not fully conscious may be a slight slurring of speech and the uninhibited nature of some of her remarks. A casual observer would say that she is mildly drunk. The remarkable feature of her analgesic state is that her pain perception should be so profoundly depressed while other perceptions and the "thinking" part of her brain are still functioning. When the delivery is over, she reports that under the anesthetic she felt no pain. That settles the matter for her, but it does not answer the observer's question of whether or not pain was present. We can see the problem more clearly by imagining what would have happened to this woman if the anesthetic had been deepened.

With just a slight increase in dosage the woman might have entered a state of excitement in which she was practically unconscious but the body would make heroic efforts to escape the stimulus. She would scream and struggle each time her uterus contracted. She would no longer cooperate with the obstetrician and her talk would become incoherent. If the anesthetic were further deepened, she would stop talking and struggling, but each contraction of the uterus would be accompanied by a rise in her blood pressure, a quickening of the heartbeat and other physical responses. A light touch on the cornea of her opened eye would make the lids twitch. If the anesthetic were deepened still more, these body responses would disappear one by one in an orderly sequence. Finally, the vital centers controlling the heartbeat and respiration would become depressed and her heart and breathing would stop, though for a brief time her nerves might still be capable of transmitting sensory signals. She would not yet be "dead," for strenuous measures might revive her, but after some minutes all possibility of resuscitation would be gone.

At what particular stage in this progression from complete consciousness to death did her pain disappear? Was it after the first few whiffs of the anesthetic, after her complaints of pain ceased, after she stopped struggling, after the disappearance of her corneal reflex, after the cessation of her heartbeat or only after she was irretrievably dead?

The second case presents a similar question under different circumstances. A fisherman is sitting in one of a line of boats stretching from one sand spit to another at the mouth of a river. He suddenly feels a smashing strike, and as he lunges back to set the hook, a large salmon breaks out of the water, sinking the hook in its mouth. He realizes that his best chance for landing the salmon lies in getting ashore before his line runs out or becomes entangled with the lines of other fishermen in the neighboring boats. Fighting the salmon as he goes, he starts crossing from boat to boat to reach the spit. Once there, he runs far out on the beach and after a hard struggle lands his salmon. As he winds up his line, he looks down and sees that the wet sand under his right shoe is reddening. Then he notices a long rent in his trousers and is surprised to discover a deep cut in his leg. By the time he has improvised a dressing for this wound he has found other injuries: skin scraped off three knuckles, a friction burn on his right thumb and two massive bruises on his left thigh. He realizes that these injuries must have been sustained while he was crossing the line of boats. Yet he cannot recall having felt the slightest pain at the time.

There is nothing particularly unusual about this incident: people often are injured in battle or automobile accidents without being aware of it until afterwards. I have selected this case because the man was not dazed or in shock. He says he had "no pain." I would agree with him. I am unwilling to call anything pain unless it is perceived as such. In my opinion the woman in childbirth had no pain of any consequence after the first few whiffs of anesthetic.

The two cases make plain the fact that to resolve the issue we need a clear-cut decision as to what we mean by the words "pain" and "perception." One reason pain is so difficult to define is that it has so many different aspects. The word is derived from the Latin *poena,* meaning a penalty or punishment. The ancients thought of pain as something inflicted by the gods on anyone who incurred their displeasure. There is an echo of that attitude in the common lament: "What have I ever done that I must suffer this way?" The interpretation of pain varies with the point of view of the investigator or the sufferer. To the sociologist pain and the threat of pain are powerful instruments of learning and social preservation. To the biologist pain is a sensory signal which warns the individual when a harmful stimulus threatens injury. To a man with an incurable cancer, pain is a destructive force: his suffering began too late to serve as an effective warning and it did not stop after the warning had been given. To the physiologist pain is a sensation like sight or hearing, but he tends to ignore its conscious, perceptual aspects, because consciousness has, as yet, no physiological equivalents; one might say that he is studying the pain "signal." To the psychologist, on the other hand, the important thing about pain is the brain's translation of the signal into a sensory experience. He finds pain, like all perceptions, to be subjective, individual and modified by degrees of attention, emotional states and the conditioning influence of past experience.

To the layman the sensation of pain, which he has known all his life, seems a perfectly straightforward, noncontroversial matter. "Hot" and "sharp" were among the first words he learned; his earliest memories are associated with the pain of accidental injury and of parental discipline. When he was hurt, he struggled and cried out. He accepts these reactions as the natural manifestations of physical suffering. Experience has taught him that many different kinds of stimuli can cause pain, even those, such as heat, which are distinctly pleasant in moderate intensities. All parts of his body are sensitive to pain and he assumes that other people are equally sensitive. He knows that pain is caused by physical injury and believes that its intensity is proportional to the force of a blow, the heat of an iron or the depth of a wound.

This concept of pain as a physical quantum, measurable in terms of stimulus intensity or the body's response to injury, is a reasonable everyday interpretation. But there are many situations where it does not apply. Bullet wounds are usually painless, partly because the impact of the missile can temporarily paralyze nerve conduction. Superficial wounds usually are more painful than deep ones, because the skin is much more richly supplied with sensory nerve endings than are the deeper tissue. The internal organs can be cut, crushed, burned without causing the slightest distress. Then also there are enormous individual variations in sensitivity to pain. At one extreme are patients with such conditions as causalgia, facial neuralgia or postherpetic pain—conditions in which the skin becomes so sensitive that the lightest touch or even a breath of air precipitates an acute exacerbation of pain. At the other extreme are those unfortunate children who are constantly injuring themselves because they were born without the normal susceptibility to pain. Such a child may lean casually against a hot stove without showing signs of distress.

In the majority of instances pain *is* proportional to the injury. Therefore we are surprised when it differs noticeably from what we would have expected. We wonder why some insignificant-looking scar should give severe pain, or why a serious injury is not noticed in the excitement of an automobile accident. We attribute such exceptions to "psychic" causes and wish we had some reliable objective method for measuring pain.

A SCALE OF PAIN

Attempts have been made to develop an objective scale of pain in terms of stimulus intensity. The stimulus used for eliciting pain may be an electric current, heat or some kind of pressure. These experiments show that most normal people have about the same threshold for pain. For instance, the average normal person begins to feel pain when heat applied to the skin reaches around 220 millicalories per square centimeter per second. For most people the threshold is within 5 per cent of that figure. This amount of heat will redden the skin after repeated tests, and it is close to the level of heat at which cells are irreversibly damaged.

Although people are fairly uniform in their perception threshold, they vary greatly in their tolerance of pain—that is, the amount of heat above the threshold that they will bear before pulling away from the testing instrument. A stoical person may endure heat which actually burns the skin. Once this burning point has been passed, the pain actually lessens, even though the heat level is raised, because the burning process destroys the sensory fibers in the skin, and the deeper tissues have fewer such fibers. Thus one might call the burning level the pain "ceiling."

In one method for measuring pain the levels of stimulus intensity between the threshold and the ceiling have been divided into 10 equal steps, called "dols," from the Latin *dolor,* meaning pain. This "dol scale" in the hands of experts has proved of some value in testing the efficacy of analgesic drugs, since it provides a rough measure of the ability of a given drug to raise the threshold for pain perception. But the method is unreliable when attempts are made to measure human pains or to use test subjects who have not had intensive training in sensory discrimination. There are too many sources of error in the measurements and too many psychological factors involved to permit anyone to claim that this instrument truly measures pain. Even with trained subjects a placebo or some other form of suggestion may raise the pain threshold almost as much as does an analgesic drug.

Every thoughtful person will agree that the intensity of pain is not always proportional to the stimulus. He remembers injuries of his own that went unnoticed in the excitement of a fight, a competitive game or a serious accident. He may recall a toothache that seemed intolerable during the night when no help was available but which had almost disappeared the next morning when he reluctantly climbed into the dentist's chair. Nor are body responses reliable indices of pain. A dog will yelp and struggle as wildly from fear as from physical injury. The flopping about of the body of a decapitated chicken cannot mean that it suffers pain.

Such commonplace occurrences as these are what raise the question: "Is awareness of pain essential to its being called by that name?" The answer that my colleagues and I have made to this question is based, in part, on our clinical investigations of pain. We conduct a pain clinic in which we study selected patients with pains that are peculiarly resistant to treatment. Whenever our treatment is successful, we search for objective evidence to confirm the patient's subjective sense of improvement. In the experimental laboratory we are trying to locate the site where analgesic and anesthetic drugs act on the nervous system and to trace pain signals from, for example, the tooth of an anesthetized cat to its brain. . . .

I believe that the interpretation of all sensory information is modified by the same factors that apply to visual perception. I am sure that this is true of pain perception. The interpretation an individual makes of a specific pain signal is an intrinsic part of the perception and a determining factor in its emotional tone.

A father is playing with his son at bedtime. The boy is almost undressed and the father holds out his pajamas. As the last garment comes off, the boy pushes the pajamas aside and dashes across the room. As he passes, the father slaps his bare bottom. The sting surprises the child and he looks back to see how the blow was meant. If the father is laughing, the chances are good that the boy laughs too, as if the slap were a pleasant part of the play. If the father looks and acts as if he meant the blow as a punishment, the boy clutches himself and howls as if badly hurt.

No physician doubts that the severity of a pain is modified by the patient's interpretation of it. If the patient has a morbid fear of cancer, every pain he develops is intensified because it suggests the onset of cancer. The pain that a child experiences is often conditioned by the fears, attitudes and afflictions of his parents. Indeed, parental influences may be decisive factors in determining the amount of pain their children will suffer from minor injuries throughout the rest of their lives. . . .

PAIN AS PROTECTION

This presentation has indicated some of the difficulties encountered in any investigation of pain. We are handicapped from the outset by the lack of a clear-cut definition of the entity we are to study. The few definitions for pain that have been proposed tend to emphasize its protective function and make no mention of its harmful potentialities. The best of these definitions was suggested years ago by the English physiologist Sir Charles Sherrington. He said that pain was "the physical adjunct of an imperative protective reflex." This statement says a great deal in few words, but it hardly defines pain, since it tells nothing of its nature beyond the fact that it is "psychical." The statement also conveys the impression that the important protective factor is the reflex, to which pain is merely an "adjunct." As far as the lower animals are concerned, this is probably true. But for thinking human beings pain assumes a much greater significance than it does for lower animals.

What are some of man's defenses against injury and how intimately are they related to one another? The simplest and most familiar is the withdrawal reflex. A man standing beside a hot stove happens to touch it with one hand. His arm muscles jerk the hand away before he has time to feel any pain or to know what is happening. If he had fallen against the stove his muscular reflexes would have been more widespread and powerful. They would have taken the violent and irrepressible form that Sherrington refers to as the "imperative protective reflex." Perhaps the best example of their violence is seen at times during the excitement stage of anesthesia induction. The patient is just dropping off into unconsciousness when some inadvertent noxious stimulus sets off his muscular reflexes. The fact that consciousness has faded seems actually to heighten the response. It is as if all restraints had been removed and the nerve signal could produce its maximal effects.

The muscular reflexes are the body's first line of defense against injury. In many situations they effectively break contact with the offending stimulus. The withdrawal reflex takes place over the shortest possible route from the site of injury to the spinal cord and back again to the local musculature. The speed of the reflex tends to reduce tissue damage to a minimum.

A second line of defense is represented by visceral reflexes that involve the vital organs and glands of internal secretion. We are all familiar with the increase in the heartbeat and in respiration, the dilation of the pupils and the sense of tension throughout the body that accompanies pain. These are the more obvious manifestations of a chain reaction that mobilizes all of our resources to meet what may be an emergency situation. If the emergency is real, these preparations for "fight or flight" can spell the difference between life and death. They account for the almost superhuman feats of strength and agility that men sometimes perform in a crisis.

The third line of defense is the voluntary response to a situation. A noxious stimulus initiates a signal which is translated by the brain into a pain perception. Having felt the pain, the individual can find its source and decide on the basis of experience how to deal with the situation.

In the sense that a reflex response is much faster than a voluntary one, it affords a better protection against injury. But reflexes are always stereotyped and often totally inappropriate to the situation. They occur whether they can serve any useful purpose or not, and they may waste the body's resources. Under conditions of sustained or repeated injury the body may be so depleted that it no longer can withstand infection and new stresses. As a matter of fact, actual tissue injury need not be present to cause this exhaustion. Fear can do exactly the same thing. Often the threat of pain does a person more harm than the injuries that taught him to fear it.

The intimate relationship among these three lines of body defense, all activated by the same noxious stimulus, makes it easy to confuse them with one another. In our desire to find a method for measuring pain, we are tempted to identify pain with the measurable associated mechanisms—the noxious stimulus, the body response or the signal pattern on its way to the sensorium. To do so, I believe, is an error. As Sherrington says, pain is a psychical process. It represents some activity of the brain which cannot be fully accounted for as yet by experimental observations. The signal pattern is doubtless a part of the mechanisms from which perceptions are secondarily derived, but the process itself is beyond the reach of our present recording techniques. It seems to me to be just as misleading to identify pain with the signal pattern as it would be to identify an act directed by human intelligence with a reflex. Furthermore, clinical experience indicates that the psychic and physical factors that determine the intensity of a pain are inseparable components of a single sensory experience. It is so difficult to eliminate psychological factors from the simplest test for pain that I doubt we shall ever find a satisfactory method of objective measurement.

PAIN AND DEATH

Returning to the original question—What is pain?—I believe that we can accept the "common sense" answer. Pain is a perception. To be "perceived" means to be "felt." Certainly what counts most with my patient and what counts with me as his physician is the amount of pain he feels. When a patient needs a surgical operation and asks me to perform it, he does not ask how deeply the knife will cut, nor would he be concerned if I were to tell him that pain signals would continue to traverse his nervous system after he had gone to sleep. What he asks is, "How much will it hurt me?" He is really asking how much of the inevitable tissue injury he will consciously experience as pain.

Anything that depresses brain function impairs pain perception. It doesn't seem to make much difference whether the depression is due to drugs, excessive fatigue or any of the many factors that deprive the sensitive brain cells of their supply of oxygen. The brain cells involved in pain perception are selectively depressed by anesthetic and analgesic drugs, so that this sensation falls in intensity before other sensory perceptions are seriously impaired.

I am convinced that neither a dying man nor a person undergoing anesthesia feels any pain, though their groans and body movements, those physical manifestations which we so naturally associate with pain, may seem to support the contrary view.

With these convictions I can tell the man who fears death will be painful that dying is merely the closing event in a sequential loss of function which accompanies brain depression. Just as an exhausted mountain climber gratefully lies down on the rocks and goes to sleep under conditions that would be intolerable to him in his normal state, so a dying man may welcome death because it offers his exhausted body rest. Before all his senses fail, before he loses all power of speech and movement, before his heart stops beating, long before

his nerves lose their capacity to transmit pain signals, the ability of his brain to translate these signals into pain perception has been lost. For pain is a product of consciousness in which the essential element is awareness.

Commentary

The above article is basically an extended analysis—it examines the component parts, causes and consequences, types, and function of pain. The article includes elements of narrative. It considers specific case histories and describes personal responses. It also contains interpretation. It considers pain as both a physical and a mental phenomenon. In addition, as the title leads us to expect, the article provides a definition of the key term, gets its derivation from the Latin *poena*—and equates "pain" with "perception." Note the formal structure embedded in the definition: [1]

	Genus	Differentia
pain is	a product of consciousness	in which the essential element is awareness

Although many questions are raised in this piece, note that the main thrust of analysis is never blurred. The author single-mindedly pursues the question with which he set out: What is that psychological-physiological state known as "pain"? He also asks, What can we know about it? What is the present status of our knowledge? This last question gives the piece its timeliness since it leads to a consideration of recent experimental findings.

ASSIGNMENTS

I. Suggested Topic: What Is Fear?

In a manner similar to W. K. Livingston's piece on "pain," write an extended analysis (3,000–5,000 words) of the most powerful and devastating of all emotions—fear. What does the word mean? What is its derivation? What are the component parts of fear? What are its causes and consequences? What are the different types of fear? Compare normal fear with neurotic fear; distinguish between fear and phobia, fear and anxiety, fear and panic; consider the function of fear, current theories and experimental evidence; offer case histories and illustrations. In this paper you are called upon to define, analyze, compare, describe, narrate, interpret.

For a discussion of research procedure and library resources, read Chapter 22, "Gathering Information." For a "List of Possible Sources" for the topic "What Is Fear?" see pp. 387–88.

II. Additional topics suitable for an extended analysis (3,000–5,000 words).

What Is Courage?
What Is Homosexuality?
What Is Insomnia?
What Is ESP (Extra Sensory Perception)?

[1] See formal definition in Chapter 1, "What Does X Mean?"

What Is Pornography?
What Is Sleep?
What Is Intelligence?
What Is Hypnosis?
What Is Fatigue?
What Is Imagination?

Description-Narration

In Chapter 4, "How Did X Happen?" Winston Churchill's essay "The Battle of Hastings" is cited as an example of a historical event rendered in narrative form, i.e., with the drama and excitement of a story. In the following account of another historical event, the assassination of Abraham Lincoln, drawn from Carl Sandburg's celebrated biography of Lincoln, we see a more extended example of this same form, a description-narration.

THE ASSASSINATION OF LINCOLN

CARL SANDBURG

The play proceeds, not unpleasant, often stupid, sprinkled with silly puns, drab and aimless dialogues, forced humor, characters neither truly English nor truly American nor fetching as caricatures. The story centers around the Yankee lighting his cigar with an old will, burning the document to ashes and thereby throwing a fortune of $400,000 away from himself into the hands of an English cousin. The mediocre comedy is somewhat redeemed by the way the players are doing it. The audience agrees it is not bad. The applause and laughter say the audience is having a good time.

Mrs. Lincoln sits close to her husband, at one moment leaning on him fondly, suddenly realizing they are not alone, saying with humor, "What will Miss Harris think of my hanging on to you so?" and hearing his: "She won't think anything about it."

From the upholstered rocking armchair in which Lincoln sits he can see only the persons in the box with him, the players on the stage, and any persons offstage on the left. The box on the opposite side of the theatre is empty. With the box wall at his back and the closely woven lace curtains at his left arm, he is screened from the audience at his back and from the musicians in the orchestra pit, which is below and partly behind him.

The box has two doors. Sometimes by a movable cross partition it is converted into two boxes, each having its door. The door forward is locked. For this evening the President's party has the roominess and convenience of double space, extra armchairs, side chairs, a small sofa. In the privacy achieved he is in sight only of his chosen companions, the actors he has come to see render a play, and the few people who may be offstage to the left.

This privacy however has a flaw. It is not as complete as it seems. A few feet behind the President is the box door, the only entry to the box unless by a climb from the stage. In this door is a small hole, bored that afternoon to serve as a peephole—from the outside. Through this peephole it is the intention of the Outsider who made it with a gimlet to stand and watch the President, then at a chosen moment to enter the box. This door opens from the box on a narrow hallway that leads to another door which opens on the balcony of the theatre.

Through these two doors the Outsider must pass in order to enter the President's box. Close to the door connecting with the balcony two inches of plaster have been cut from the brick wall of the narrow hallway. The intention of the Outsider is that a bar placed in this cut-away wall niche and then braced against the panel of the door will hold that door against intruders, will serve to stop anyone from interfering with the Outsider while making his observations of the President through the gimleted hole in the box door.

At either of these doors, the one to the box or the one to the hallway, it is the assigned duty and expected responsibility of John F. Parker to stand or sit constantly and without fail. A Ward Lamon or an Eckert on this duty would probably have noticed the gimleted hole, the newly made wall niche, and been doubly watchful. If Lincoln believes what he told Crook that afternoon, that he trusted the men assigned to guard him, then as he sits in the upholstered rocking armchair in the box he believes that John F. Parker in steady fidelity is just outside the box door, in plain clothes ready with the revolver Pendel at the White House had told him to be sure to have with him.

In such a trust Lincoln is mistaken. Whatever dim fog of thought or duty may move John F. Parker in his best moments is not operating tonight. His life habit of never letting anything trouble him is on him this night; his motive is to have no motive. He has always got along somehow. Why care about anything, why really care? He can always find good liquor and bad women. You take your fun as you find it. He can never be a somebody, so he will enjoy himself as a nobody—though he can't imagine how perfect a cipher, how completely the little end of nothing, one John F. Parker may appear as a result of one slack easygoing hour.

"The guard . . . acting as my substitute," wrote the faithful Crook later, "took his position at the rear of the box, close to an entrance leading into the box. . . . His orders were to stand there, fully armed, and to permit no unauthorized person to pass into the box. His orders were to stand there and protect the President at all hazards. From the spot where he was thus stationed, this guard could not see the stage or the actors; but he could hear the words the actors spoke, and he became so interested in them that, incredible as it may seem, he quietly deserted his post of duty, and walking down the dimly-lighted side aisle, deliberately took a seat."

The custom was for a chair to be placed in the narrow hallway for the guard to sit in. The doorkeeper Buckingham told Crook that such a chair was provided this evening for the accommodation of the guard. "Whether Parker occupied it at all, I do not know," wrote Crook. "Mr. Buckingham is of the impression that he did. If he did, he left it almost immediately, for he confessed to me the next day that he went to a seat, so that he could see the play." The door to the President's box is shut. It is not kept open so that the box occupants can see the guard on duty.

Either between acts or at some time when the play was not lively enough to suit him or because of an urge for a pony of whiskey under his belt, John F. Parker leaves his seat in the balcony and goes down to the street and joins companions in a little whiff of liquor—this on the basis of a statement of the coachman Burns, who declared he stayed outside on the street with his carriage and horses, except for one interlude when "the special police officer (meaning John F. Parker) and the footman of the President (Forbes) came up to him and asked him to take a drink with them; which he did."

Thus circumstance favors the lurking and vigilant Outsider who in the afternoon gimleted a hole in the door of the President's box and cut a two-inch niche in a wall to brace a bar against a door panel and hold it against interference while he should operate.

The play goes on. The evening and the drama are much like many other evenings when the acting is pleasant enough, the play mediocre and so-so, the audience having no thrills of great performance but enjoying itself. The most excited man in the house, with little doubt, is the orchestra leader, Withers. He has left the pit and gone backstage, where, as he related, "I was giving the stage manager a piece of my mind. I had written a song for Laura Keene to sing. When she left it out I was mad. We had no cue, and the music was thrown out of gear. So I hurried round on the stage on my left to see what it was done for."

And of what is Abraham Lincoln thinking? As he leans back in his easy rocking chair, where does he roam in thought? If it is life he is thinking about, no one could fathom the subtle speculations and hazy reveries resulting from his fifty-six years of adventures drab and dazzling in life. Who had gone farther on so little to begin with? Who else as a living figure of republican government, of democracy, in practice, as a symbol touching freedom for all men—who else had gone farther over America, over the world? If it is death he is thinking about, who better than himself might interpret his dream that he lay in winding sheets on a catafalque in the White House and people were wringing their hands and crying "The President is dead!"—who could make clear this dream better than himself? Furthermore if it is death he is thinking about, has he not philosophized about it and dreamed about it and considered himself as a mark and a target until no one is better prepared than he for any sudden deed? Has he not a thousand times said to himself, and several times to friends and intimates, that he must accommodate himself to the thought of sudden death? Has he not wearied of the constructions placed on his secret night ride through Baltimore to escape a plot aimed at his death? Has he not laughed to the overhead night stars at a hole shot in his hat by a hidden marksman he never mentioned even to his boon companion Hill Lamon? And who can say but that Death is a friend, and who else should be more familiar of Death than a man who has been the central figure of the bloodiest war ever known to the Human Family—who else should more appropriately and decently walk with Death? And who can say but Death is a friend and a nurse and a lover and a benefactor bringing peace and lasting reconciliation? The play tonight is stupid. Shakespeare would be better. "Duncan is in his grave . . . he sleeps well."

Yes, of what is Abraham Lincoln thinking? Draped before him in salute is a silk flag of the Union, a banner of the same design as the one at Independence Hall in Philadelphia in February of '61 which he pulled aloft saying, "I would rather be assassinated on this spot than surrender it," saying the flag in its very origins "gave promise that in due time the weights would be lifted from the shoulders of all men, and that all should have an equal chance." Possibly his mind recurs for a fleeting instant to that one line in his letter to a Boston widow woman: "the solemn pride that must be yours to have laid so costly a sacrifice upon the altar of freedom." Or a phrase from the Gettysburg speech: "we here highly resolve that these dead shall not have died in vain."

Out in a main-floor seat enjoying the show is one Julia Adelaide Shephard, who wrote a letter to her father about this Good Friday evening at the theatre. "Cousin Julia has just told me," she reported, "that the President is in yonder upper right hand private box so handsomely decked with silken flags festooned over a picture of George Washington. The young and lovely daughter of Senator Harris is the only one of his party we see as the flags hide the rest. But we know Father Abraham is there like a Father watching what interests his children, for their pleasure rather than his own. It had been announced in the papers he would be there. How sociable it seems like one family sitting around their parlor fire. Everyone has been so jubilant for days that they laugh and shout at every clownish witticism such is the excited state of the public mind. One of the actresses whose part is that of a very delicate young lady talks about wishing to avoid the draft when her lover tells her not to be alarmed 'for there is to be no more draft' at which the applause is loud and long. The American cousin has just been making love to a young lady who says she'll never marry for love but when her mother and herself find out that he has lost his property they retreat in disgust at the left hand of the stage while the American cousin goes out at the right. We are waiting for the next scene."

And the next scene?

The next scene is to crash and blare as one of the wildest, one of the most inconceivably fateful and chaotic, that ever stunned and shocked a world that heard the story.

The moment of high fate was not seen by the theatre audience. Only one man saw that moment. He was the Outsider. He was the one who had waited and lurked and made his preparations, planning and plotting that he should be the single and lone spectator of what happened. He had come through the outer door into the little hallway, fastened the strong though slender bar into the two-inch niche in the brick wall, and braced it against the door panel. He had moved softly to the box door and through the little hole he had gimleted that afternoon he had studied the box occupants and his Human Target seated in an upholstered rocking armchair. Softly he had opened the door and stepped toward his prey, in his right hand a one-shot brass derringer pistol, a little eight-ounce vest-pocket weapon winged for death, in his left hand a steel dagger. He was cool and precise and timed his every move. He raised the derringer, lengthened his right arm, ran his eye along the barrel in a line with the head of his victim less than five feet away—and pulled the trigger.

A lead ball somewhat less than a half-inch in diameter crashed into the left side of the head of the Human Target, into the back of the head, in a line with and three inches from the left ear. "The course of the ball was obliquely forward toward the right eye, crossing the brain in an oblique manner and lodging a few inches behind that eye. In the track of the wound were found fragments of bone, which had been driven forward by the ball, which was embedded in the anterior lobe of the left hemisphere of the brain."

For Abraham Lincoln it was lights out, good night, farewell and a long farewell to the good earth and its trees, its enjoyable companions, and the Union of States and the world Family of Man he had loved. He was not dead yet. He was to linger in dying. But the living man could never again speak nor see nor hear nor awaken into conscious being.

Near the prompt desk offstage stands W. J. Ferguson, an actor. He looks in the direction of a shot he hears, and sees "Mr. Lincoln lean back in his rocking chair, his head coming to rest against the wall which stood between him and the audience . . . well inside the curtains"—no struggle or move "save in the slight backward sway."

Of this the audience in their one thousand seats knew nothing.

Major Rathbone leaps from his chair. Rushing at him with a knife is a strange human creature, terribly alive, a lithe wild animal, a tiger for speed, a wildcat of a man bareheaded, raven-haired—a smooth sinister face with glaring eyeballs. He wears a dark sack suit. He stabs straight at the heart of Rathbone, a fast and ugly lunge. Rathbone parries it with his upper right arm, which gets a deep slash of the dagger. Rathbone is staggered, reels back. The tigerish stranger mounts the box railing. Rathbone recovers, leaps again for the stranger, who feels the hand of Rathbone holding him back, slashes again at Rathbone, then leaps for the stage.

This is the moment the audience wonders whether something unusual is happening—or is it part of the play?

From the box railing the Strange Man leaps for the stage, perhaps a ten-foot fall. His leap is slightly interrupted. On this slight interruption the Strange Man in his fine calculations had not figured. The draped Union flag of silk reaches out and tangles itself in a spur of one riding-boot, throwing him out of control. He falls to the stage landing on his left leg, breaking the shinbone a little above the instep.

Of what he has done the audience as yet knows nothing. They wonder what this swift, raven-haired, wild-eyed Strange Man portends. They see him rush across the stage, three feet to a stride, and vanish. Some have heard Rathbone's cry "Stop that man!" Many have seen a man leap from a front seat up on the stage and chase after the weird Stranger, crying "Stop that man!"

It is a peculiar night, an odd evening, a little weird, says the audience to itself. The action is fast. It is less than half a minute since the Strange Man mounted the box railing, made the stage, and strode off.

Offstage between Laura Keene and W. J. Ferguson he dashes at breakneck speed, out of an entrance, forty feet to a little door opening on an alley. There stands a fast bay horse, a slow-witted chore boy nicknamed John Peanuts holding the reins. He kicks the boy, mounts the mare; hoofs on the cobblestones are heard but a few moments. In all it is maybe sixty or seventy seconds since he loosed the one shot of his eight-ounce brass derringer.

Whether the Strange Man now riding away on a fast bay horse has paused a moment on the stage and shouted a dramatic line of speech, there was disagreement afterward. Some said he ran off as though every second of time counted and his one purpose was to escape. Others said he faced the audience a moment, brandished a dagger still bloody from slashing Rathbone, and shouted the State motto of Virginia, the slogan of Brutus as he drove the assassin's knife into imperial Caesar: "*Sic semper tyrannis*"—"Thus be it ever to tyrants." Miss Shephard and others believed they heard him shriek as he brandished the dagger: "The South is avenged!" Others: "The South shall be free!" "Revenge!" "Freedom!"

Some said the lights went out in the theatre, others adding the detail that the assassin had stabbed the gasman and pulled the lever, throwing the house into darkness. Others a thousand miles from the theatre said they saw the moon come out from behind clouds blood-red. It is a night of many eyewitnesses, shaken and moaning eyewitnesses.

The audience is up and out of its one thousand seats, standing, moving. Panic is in the air, fear of what may happen next. Many merely stand up from their seats, fixed and motionless, waiting to hear what has happened, waiting to see what further is to happen. The question is spoken quietly or is murmured anxiously—"What is it? What has happened?" The question is bawled with anger, is yelled with anguish—"For God's sake, what is it? What has happened?"

A woman's scream pierces the air. Some say afterward it was Mrs. Lincoln. The scream carries a shock and a creeping shiver to many hearing it. "He has shot the President!" Miss Shephard looks from the main floor toward the box and sees "Miss Harris wringing her hands and calling for water." There are moanings. "No, for God's sake, it can't be true—no! no! for God's sake!"

Men are swarming up to the edge of the stage, over the gas-jet footlights onto the stage. The aisles fill with people not sure where to go; to leave would be safe, but they want to know what has happened, what else they may see this wild night. Men are asking whether some God-damned fool has for sure tried to shoot the President. Others take it as true. The man who ran across the stage did it. There are cries: "Kill him! Shoot him!" On the stage now are policemen, army officers, soldiers, besides actors and actresses in make-up and costume. Cries for "Water, water!" Cries for "A surgeon! a surgeon!" Someone brings water. It is passed up to the box.

An army surgeon climbs to the stage and is lifted up and clambers over the railing into the box. Some two hundred soldiers arrive to clear the theatre. The wailing and the crazy chaos let down in the emptying playhouse—and flare up again in the street outside, where some man is accused of saying he is glad it happened, a sudden little mob dragging him to a lamppost with a ready rope to hang him when six policemen with clubs and drawn revolvers manage to get him away and put him in jail for safekeeping.

Mrs. Lincoln in the box has turned from the railing, has turned from where she saw the wild-eyed, raven-haired man vanish off the stage, sees her husband seated in the rocking chair, his head slumped forward. Never before has she seen her husband so completely helpless, so strangely not himself. With little moaning cries she springs toward him and with her hands keeps him from tumbling to the floor. Major Rathbone has shouted for a surgeon, has run out of the box into the narrow hallway, and with one arm bleeding and burning with pain he fumbles to unfasten the bar between wall and door panel. An usher from the outside tries to help him. They get the bar loose. Back of the usher is a jam of people. He holds them back, allowing only one man to enter.

This is a young-looking man, twenty-three years old, with mustache and sideburns. Charles A. Leale, assistant surgeon, United States Volunteers, who had left the army General Hospital at Armory Square, where he was in charge of the wounded commissioned officers' ward, saying he would be gone only a short time. Rathbone shows Dr. Leale his bleeding arm, "beseeching me to attend to his wound," related Leale later. "I placed my hand under his chin, looking into his eyes an almost instantaneous glance revealed the fact that he was in no immediate danger, and in response to appeals from Mrs. Lincoln and Miss Harris, who were standing by the high-backed armchair in which President Lincoln sat, I went immediately to their assistance, saying I was a United States army surgeon."

Leale holds Mrs. Lincoln's outstretched hand while she cries piteously: "Oh, Doctor! Is he dead? Can he recover? Will you take charge of him? Do what you can for him. Oh, my dear husband! my dear husband!" He soothes her a little, telling her he will do all that can possibly be done.

The body in the chair at first scrutiny seems to be that of a dead man, eyes closed, no certainty it is breathing. Dr. Leale with help from others lifts the body from the chair and moves it to a lying position on the floor. He holds the head and shoulders while doing this, his hand meeting a clot of blood near the left shoulder. Dr. Leale recalls seeing a dagger flashed by the assassin on the stage and the knife wound of Rathbone, and now supposes the President has a stab wound. He has the coat and shirt slit open, thinking to check perhaps a hemorrhage. He finds no wounds. He lifts the eyelids and sees evidence of a brain injury. He rapidly passes the separated fingers of both hands through the blood-matted hair of the head, finding a wound and removing a clot of blood, which relieves pressure on the brain and brings shallow breathing and a weak pulse. "The assassin," Leale commented later, ". . . had evidently planned to shoot to produce instant death, as the wound he made was situated within two inches of the physiological point of selection, when instant death is desired."

Dr. Leale bends over, puts a knee at each side of the body, and tries to start the breathing apparatus, attempts to stimulate respiration by putting his two fingers into the throat and pressing down and out on the base of the tongue to free the larynx of secretion. Dr. Charles Sabin Taft, the army surgeon lifted from the stage into the box, now arrives. Another physician, Dr. Albert F. A. King, arrives. Leale asks them each to manipulate an arm while the presses upward on the diaphragm and elsewhere to stimulate heart action. The body responds with an improvement in the pulse and the irregular breathing.

Dr. Leale is sure, however, that with the shock and prostration the body has undergone, more must now be done to keep life going. And as he told it later: "I leaned forcibly forward directly over his body, thorax to thorax, face to face, and several times drew in a long breath, then forcibly breathed directly into his mouth and nostrils, which expanded his lungs and improved his respirations. After waiting a moment I placed my ear over his thorax and found the action of the heart improving. I arose to the erect kneeling posture, then watched for a short time and saw that the President could continue independent breathing and that instant death would not occur. I then pronounced my diagnosis and prognosis: 'His wound is mortal; it is impossible for him to recover.' "

Commentary

Basing his account on historical fact, carefully rendered down to the smallest detail, Sandburg has given us a chillingly vivid account of this famous horror scene from history—the assassination of President Lincoln. We see him sitting in his box seat, his wife next to him whispering fondly in his ear. At that same moment a nameless Outsider is peering through the barrel of his derringer pistol. We know what is coming, yet Sandburg manages to build suspense. How does Sandburg create the almost palpable sense of immediacy and stark reality that transports us back to Ford's Theater, watching and waiting for *it* to happen: the assassination of a president? Sandburg draws on two important devices here:

1. He uses the present tense, thereby creating for us the feeling that we are present at the event. Indeed, almost every verb puts us into a vividly reconstructed present where events are unfolding before our eyes: Lincoln *leans* back in his rocker, Major Rathbone *leaps* from his chair, a woman's scream *pierces* the air.

2. He weaves in countless small details that lend further authenticity to the description. As readers we believe this account because the writer has painted such a full picture, even allowing us a glimpse of the action onstage, and the thoughts that might—or could—have been going through Lincoln's unsuspecting mind.

More than this the writing is impeccable in terms of sentence structure, rhythm, variety in sentence length, choice of words, and general flow. We would do well to study this essay for its rhetorical excellence.

ASSIGNMENTS

I. Suggested Topic: The Assassination of Malcolm X.

Since the assassination in 1865 of Abraham Lincoln, there have been, unfortunately, many other "memorable" assassinations, several occurring in our own time. One is the assassination of Malcolm X, a leader of the black revolution (Ossie Davis, "Why I Eulogized Malcolm X," pp. 118–19). A man with a criminal past (by his own admission a thief, drug peddler, procurer), Malcolm X ultimately converted to the religion of Islam, which he then served with passionate intensity. At first a hate-preacher himself (hate the whites), he was beginning to embrace a more compassionate view of humanity when he was shot down by an assassin's bullet, thereby fulfilling his own prediction that he would not live to see his autobiography in print. How did this tragedy happen? How can it be described? What were its causes and consequences? What was its larger significance? Can any comment be made on the nature of the assassin? These are some of the questions that a term paper (4,000–5,000 words) on this subject should encompass. It is essentially a description-narration; but it is also an analysis-interpretation.

For a discussion of research procedure and library sources, read Chapter 22, "Gathering Information." For a "List of Possible Sources" for the topic "The Assassination of Malcolm X," see p. 388.

II. Additional topics suitable for a description-narration (4,000–5,000 words).

The Assassination of Mahatma Gandhi
The Assassination of John F. Kennedy
The Assassination of Martin Luther King
The Assassination of Robert Kennedy

Extended Characterization

Like the short "sketch," the extended characterization focuses on a single individual, posing the question, "What kind of person is this?" What makes him (or her) "tick"? The extra length of the extended study enables the writer to probe more deeply into the complexities of his subject and to compose a fuller portrait: richer in descriptive detail, illustrative episode, and possible interpretations. Even so, like the 500 word sketch, the 5,000 word character study should have a unifying thread; it should point to the quality or qualities that define the person and provide a "key" to his character (Chapter 15, "What Kind of Person Is X?").

In the following essay, Virginia Woolf paints a memorable picture of the little-known Duchess of Newcastle, a lady whose ruling passion was her "desire for fame," and her distinguishing quality her dauntless eccentricity.

THE DUCHESS OF NEWCASTLE

VIRGINIA WOOLF

". . . All I desire is fame," wrote Margaret Cavendish, Duchess of Newcastle. And while she lived her wish was granted. Garish in her dress, eccentric in her habits, chaste in her conduct, coarse in her speech, she succeeded during her lifetime in drawing upon herself the ridicule of the great and the applause of the learned. But the last echoes of that clamour have now all died away; she lives only in the few splendid phrases that Lamb scattered upon her tomb; her poems, her plays, her philosophies, her orations, her discourses—all those folios and quartos in which, she protested, her real life was shrined—moulder in the gloom of public libraries, or are decanted into tiny thimbles which hold six drops of their profusion. Even the curious student, inspired by the words of Lamb, quails before the mass of her mausoleum, peers in, looks about him, and hurries out again, shutting the door.

But that hasty glance has shown him the outlines of a memorable figure. Born (it is conjectured) in 1624, Margaret was the youngest child of a Thomas Lucas, who died when she was an infant, and her upbringing was due to her mother, a lady of remarkable character, of majestic grandeur and beauty "beyond the ruin of time." "She was very skilful in leases, and setting of lands and court keeping, ordering of stewards, and the like affairs." The wealth which thus accrued she spent, not on marriage portions, but on generous and delightful pleasures, "out of an opinion that if she bred us with needy necessity it might chance to create in us sharking qualities." Her eight sons and daughters were never beaten, but reasoned with, finely and gayly dressed, and allowed no conversation with servants, not because they are servants but because servants "are for the most part ill-bred as well as meanly born." The daughters were taught the usual accomplishments "rather for formality than for benefit," it being their mother's opinion that character, happiness, and honesty were of greater value to a woman than fiddling and singing, or "the prating of several languages."

Already Margaret was eager to take advantage of such indulgence to gratify certain tastes. Already she liked reading better than needlework, dressing and "inventing fashions" better than reading, and writing best of all. Sixteen paper books of no title, written in straggling letters, for the impetuosity of her thought always outdid the pace of her fingers, testify to the use she made of her mother's liberality. The happiness of their home life had other results as well. They were a devoted family. Long after they were married, Margaret noted, these handsome brothers and sisters, with their well-proportioned bodies, their clear complexions, brown hair, sound teeth, "tunable voices," and plain way of speaking, kept themselves "in a flock together." The presence of strangers silenced them. But when they were alone, whether they walked in Spring Gardens or Hyde Park, or had music, or supped in barges upon the water, their tongues were loosed and they made "very merry amongst themselves, . . . judging, condemning, approving, commending, as they thought good."

The happy family life had its effect upon Margaret's character. As a child, she would walk for hours alone, musing and contemplating and reasoning with herself of "everything her senses did present." She took no pleasure in activity of any kind. Toys did not amuse her, and she could neither learn foreign languages nor dress as other people did. Her great pleasure was to invent dresses for herself, which nobody else was to copy, "for," she remarks, "I always took delight in a singularity, even in accoutrements of habits."

Such a training, at once so cloistered and so free, should have bred a lettered old maid, glad of her seclusion, and the writer perhaps of some volume of letters or translations from the classics, which we should still quote as proof of the cultivation of our ancestresses. But there was a wild streak in Margaret, a love of finery and extravagance and fame, which was for ever upsetting the orderly arrangements of nature. When she heard that the Queen, since the outbreak of the Civil War, had fewer maids-of-honour than usual, she had "a great desire" to become one of them. Her mother let her go against the judgement of the rest of the family, who, knowing that she had never left home and had scarcely been beyond their sight, justly thought that she might behave at Court to her disadvantage. "Which indeed I did," Margaret confessed; "for I was so bashful when I was out of my mother's, brothers', and sisters' sight that . . . I durst neither look up with my eyes, nor speak, nor be any way sociable, insomuch as I was thought a natural fool." The courtiers laughed at her; and she retaliated in the obvious way. People were censorious; men were jealous of brains in a woman; women suspected intellect in their own sex; and what other lady, she might justly ask, pondered as she walked on the nature of matter and whether snails have teeth? But the laughter galled her, and she begged her mother to let her come home. This being refused, wisely as the event turned out, she stayed on for two years (1643–45), finally going with the Queen to Paris, and there, among the exiles who came to pay their respects to the Court, was the Marquis of Newcastle. To the general amazement, the princely nobleman, who had led the King's forces to disaster with indomitable courage but little skill, fell in love with the shy, silent, strangely dressed maid-of-honour. It was not "amorous love, but honest, honourable love," according to Margaret. She was no brilliant match; she had gained a reputation for prudery and eccentricity. What, then, could have made so great a nobleman fall at her feet? The onlookers were full of derision, disparagement, and slander. "I fear," Margaret wrote to the Marquis, "others foresee we shall be unfortunate, though we see it not ourselves, or else there would not be such pains to untie the knot of our affections." Again, "Saint Germains is a place of much slander, and thinks I send too often to you." "Pray consider," she warned him, "that I have enemies." But the match was evidently perfect. The Duke, with his love of poetry and music and play-writing, his interest in philosophy, his belief "that nobody knew or could know the cause of anything," his romantic and generous temperament, was naturally drawn to a woman who wrote poetry herself, was also a philosopher of the same way of thinking, and lavished upon him not only the admiration of a fellow-artist, but the gratitude of a sensitive creature who had been shielded and succoured by his extraordinary magnanimity. "He did approve," she wrote, "of those bashful fears which many condemned, . . . and though I did dread marriage and shunned men's company as much as I could, yet I . . . had not the power to refuse him." She kept him company during the long years of exile; she entered with sympathy, if not with understanding, into the conduct and acquirements of those horses which he trained to such perfection that the Spaniards crossed themselves and cried "Miraculo!" as they witnessed their corvets, voltoes, and pirouettes; she believed that the horses even made a "trampling action" for joy when he came into the stables; she pleaded his cause in England during the Protectorate; and, when the Restoration made it possible for them to return to England, they lived together in the depths of the country in the greatest seclusion and perfect contentment, scribbling plays, poems, philosophies, greeting each other's works with raptures of delight, and confabulating doubtless upon such marvels of the natural world as chance threw their way. They were laughed at by their contemporaries; Horace Walpole sneered at them. But there can be no doubt that they were perfectly happy.

For now Margaret could apply herself uninterruptedly to her writing. She could devise fashions for herself and her servants. She could scribble more and more furiously with fingers that became less and less able to form legible letters. She could even achieve the miracle of getting her plays acted in London and her philosophies humbly perused by men of learning. There they stand, in the British Museum, volume after volume, swarming with a diffused, uneasy, contorted vitality. Order, continuity, the logical development of her argument are all unknown to her. No fears impede her. She has the irresponsibility of a child and the arrogance of a Duchess. The wildest fancies come to her, and she canters away on their backs. We seem to hear her, as the thoughts boil and bubble, calling to John, who sat with a pen in his hand next door, to come quick, "John, John, I conceive!" And down it goes—whatever it may be; sense or nonsense; some thought on women's education—"Women live like Bats or Owls, labour like Beasts, and die like Worms, . . . the best bred women are those whose minds are civilest"; some speculation that had struck her perhaps walking that afternoon alone—why "hogs have the measles," why "dogs that rejoice swing their tails," or what the stars are made of, or what this chrysalis is that her maid has brought her, and she keeps warm in a corner of her room. On and on, from subject to subject she flies, never stopping to correct, "for there is more pleasure in making than in manding," talking aloud to herself of all those matters that filled her brain to her perpetual diversion—of wars, and boarding-schools, and cutting down trees, of grammar and morals, of monsters and the British, whether opium in small quantities is good for lunatics, why it is that musicians are mad. Looking upwards, she speculates still more ambitiously upon the nature of the moon, and if the stars are blazing jellies; looking downwards she wonders if the fishes know that the sea is salt; opines that our heads are full of fairies, "dear to God as we are"; muses whether there are not other worlds than ours, and reflects that the next ship may bring us word of a new one. In short, "we are in utter darkness." Meanwhile, what a rapture is thought!

As the vast books appeared from the stately retreat at Welbeck the usual censors made the usual objections, and had to be answered, despised, or argued with, as her mood varied, in the preface to every work. They said, among other things, that her books were not her own, because she used learned terms, and "wrote of many matters outside her ken." She flew to her husband for help, and he answered, characteristically, that the Duchess "had never conversed with any professed scholar in learning except her brother and myself." The Duke's scholarship, moreover, was of a peculiar nature. "I have lived in the great world a great while, and have thought of what has been brought to me by the senses, more than was put into me by learned discourse; for I do not love to be led by the nose, by authority, and old authors, *ipse dixit* will not serve my turn." And then she takes up the pen and proceeds, with the importunity and indiscretion of a child, to assure the world that her ignorance is of the finest quality imaginable. She has only seen Des Cartes and Hobbes, not questioned them; she did indeed ask Mr. Hobbes to dinner, but he could not come; she often does not listen to a word that is said to her; she does not know any French, though she lived abroad for five years; she has only read the old philosophers in Mr. Stanley's account of them; of Des Cartes she has read but half of his work on Passion; and of Hobbes only "the little book called *De Cive*," all of which is infinitely to the credit of her native wit, so abundant that outside succour pained it, so honest that it would not accept help from others. It was from the plain of complete ignorance, the untilled field of her own consciousness, that she proposed to erect a philosophic system that was to oust all others. The results were not altogether happy. Under the pressure of such vast structures, her natural gift, the fresh and delicate fancy which had led her in her first volume to write charmingly of Queen Mab and fairyland, was crushed out of existence.

> The palace of the Queen wherein she dwells,
> Its fabric's built all of hodmandod shells;
> The hangings of a Rainbow made that's thin,
> Shew wondrous fine, when one first enters in;
> The chambers made of Amber that is clear,
> Do give a fine sweet smell, if fire be near;
> Her bed a cherry stone, is carved throughout,
> And with a butterfly's wing hung about;
> Her sheets are of the skin of Dove's eyes made
> Where on a violet bud her pillow's laid.

So she could write when she was young. But her fairies, if they survived at all, grew up into hippopotami. Too generously her prayer was granted:

> Give me the free and noble style,
> Which seems uncurb'd, though it be wild.

She became capable of involutions, and contortions and conceits of which the following is among the shortest, but not the most terrific:

The human head may be likened to a town:
The mouth when full, begun
Is market day, when empty, market's done;
The city conduct, where the water flows,
Is with two spouts, the nostrils and the nose.

She similised, energetically, incongruously, eternally; the sea became a meadow, the sailors shepherds, the mast a maypole. The fly was the bird of summer, trees were senators, houses ships, and even the fairies, whom she loved better than any earthly thing, except the Duke, are changd into blunt atoms and sharp atoms, and take part in some of those horrible manoeuvres in which she delighted to marshal the universe. Truly, "my Lady Sanspareille hath a strange spreading wit." Worse still, without an atom of dramatic power, she turned to play-writing. It was a simple process. The unwieldy thoughts which turned and tumbled within her were christened Sir Golden Riches, Moll Meanbred, Sir Puppy Dogman, and the rest, and sent revolving in tedious debate upon the parts of the soul, or whether virtue is better than riches, round a wise and learned lady who answered their questions and corrected their fallacies at considerable length in tones which we seem to have heard before.

Sometimes, however, the Duchess walked abroad. She would issue out in her own proper person, dressed in a thousand gems and furbelows, to visit the houses of the neighbouring gentry. Her pen made instant report of these excursions. She recorded how Lady C. R. "did beat her husband in a public assembly"; Sir F. O. "I am sorry to hear hath undervalued himself so much below his birth and wealth as to marry his kitchen-maid"; "Miss P. I. has become a sanctified soul, a spiritual sister, she has left curling her hair, black patches are become abominable to her, laced shoes and Galoshes are steps to pride—she asked me what posture I thought was the best to be used in prayer." Her answer was probably unacceptable. "I shall not rashly go there again," she says of one such "gossip-making." She was not, we may hazard, a welcome guest or an altogether hospitable hostess. She had a way of "bragging of myself" which frightened visitors so that they left, nor was she sorry to see them go. Indeed, Welbeck was the best place for her, and her own company the most congenial, with the amiable Duke wandering in and out, with his plays and his speculations, always ready to answer a question or refute a slander. Perhaps it was this solitude that led her, chaste as she was in conduct, to use language which in time to come much perturbed Sir Egerton Brydges. She used, he complained, "expressions and images of extraordinary coarseness as flowing from a female of high rank brought up in courts." He forgot that this particular female had long ceased to frequent the Court; she consorted chiefly with fairies; and her friends were among the dead. Naturally, then, her language was coarse. Nevertheless, though her philosophies are futile, and her plays intolerable, and her verses mainly dull, the vast bulk of the Duchess is leavened by a vein of authentic fire. One cannot help following the lure of her erratic and lovable personality as it meanders and twinkles through page after page. There is something noble and Quixotic and high-spirited, as well as crack-brained and bird-witted, about her. Her simplicity is so open; her intelligence so active; her sympathy with fairies and animals so true and tender. She has the freakishness of an elf, the irresponsibility of some non-human creature, its heartlessness, and its charm. And although "they," those terrible critics who had sneered and jeered at her ever since, as a shy girl, she had not dared look her tormentors in the face at Court, continued to mock, few of her critics, after all, had the wit to trouble about the nature of the universe, or cared a straw for the sufferings of the hunted hare, or longed, as she did, to talk to some one "of Shakespeare's fools." Now, at any rate, the laugh is not all on their side.

But laugh they did. When the rumour spread that the crazy Duchess was coming up from Welbeck to pay her respects at Court, people crowded the streets to look at her, and the curiosity of Mr. Pepys twice brought him to wait in the Park to see her pass. But the pressure of the crowd about her coach was too great. He could only catch a glimpse of her in her silver coach with her footmen all in velvet, a velvet cap on her head, and her hair about her ears. He could only see for a moment between the white curtains the face of "a very comely woman," and on she drove through the crowd of staring Cockneys, all pressing to catch a glimpse of that romantic lady, who stands in the picture at Welbeck, with large melancholy eyes, and something fastidious and fantastic in her bearing, touching a table with the tips of long pointed fingers in the calm assurance of immortal fame.

Commentary

Like Sandburg's description-narration, Virginia Woolf's essay is a brilliant example of prose writing: vivid and rhythmical, as disciplined and aesthetically satisfying as poetry. The notion that a "vein of authentic fire" runs through the Duchess' behavior (this, of course is Mrs. Woolf's interpretation) is supported by ample illustrations: though flamboyant, the Duchess is no phony. By drawing on the vast reservoir of the Duchess' own writings, Mrs. Woolf evokes the unique flavor of this amusing and amazing woman whose erratic personality, we are told, "meanders and twinkles through page after page" of her own work. (Note the precise verbs that describe so appropriately the special quality of the Duchess herself.)

In this extremely sensitive and sympathetic portrait, we can see what a wide range of questions Mrs. Woolf has addressed to her subject: she has asked about the causes (i.e., the early childhood influences) and the consequences of the Duchess' behavior; she has compared the Duchess with other ladies of the period; she has probed into the deeper meaning and significance of the Duchess' "crack-brained" yet somehow "noble" life style.

ASSIGNMENTS

I. Suggested Topic: Robert Schumann.

As Virginia Woolf has explored the personality of the Duchess of Newcastle, study and write (3,000–5,000 words) about the composer Robert Schumann, whose idyllic love affair with Clara Schumann was marred by his steadily advancing mental illness. Try to find the motivational source (the key that turns the lock) of this highly talented but tormented figure out of musical history.

For a discussion of research procedure and library resources, read Chapter 22, "Gathering Information." For a "List of Possible Sources" for the topic "Robert Schumann," see p. 388.

II. Additional topics for an extended characterization (4,000–5,000 words).

George Sand
Isadora Duncan
Mme de Staël
Mary Wollenstonecraft
Harriet Beecher Stowe
John Brown
Ludwig van Beethoven
Pablo Picasso
Albert Schweitzer

Extended Argumentation

Most good examples of argumentation are at least 3,000–5,000 words long, since it requires that many words to develop issues, marshal evidence, and construct a convincing case. The following article, written by a sociologist, argues that the black man's plight is a consequence of class and ethnic factors rather than simply of race.

WHITHER THE BLACK ODYSSEY?

JAMES M. O'KANE

In recent years it has become academically fashionable to analyze and interpret the plight of the lower-income black in urban ghettoes as though this were an entirely novel situation in American life. Reference has been made to the "problem of the black," as one which is intrinsically unique and fundamentally different from the predicament of all previously lower-income minority groups.

This mode of analysis implies that the difficulties which this black urbanite faces as a result of his inferior position on the lowest rungs of the social ladder are infinitely more complex, more paradoxical, and less amenable to solution than anything encountered by the Irish, the Pole, the Jew, and the Italian. The problem's specific interpretation in these terms has consequently resulted in social scientists abandoning, or at least side-stepping, the socio-historical relationships relevant to the routes of upward mobility for minority groups in American life.

The resultant myopic interpretation has subsequently led social observers to view the problem of the lower-income black as essentially a *racial* problem. Hence the black has been differentiated from previous lower-class minority groups on the basis of so-called racial differences and distinctions. The argument runs as follows: the black cannot be likened to the immigrant groups of the nineteenth century simply because of his ascribed *racial* qualities. The

From *The Drew University Magazine*, Vol. 3, No. 3 (Spring 1969). Reprinted by permission. Originally published as "Ethnic Mobility and the Lower-Income Negro: A Socio-Historical Perspective" in *Social Problems*, Vol. 16, No. 3 (Winter 1969). Reprinted by permission of The Society for the Study of Social Problems.

former slave status and legal disenfranchisement from American social life have necessitated the realization that the black is in a category distinct from all previous societal rejects. His situation and problems are unique; they are literally larger and more incomprehensible than anything of a similar vein witnessed in our history, and the old answers will be irrelevant to the amelioration of the Negro's situation.[1]

Such a position betrays not only a pessimistic, but also a tempo-centric view of the lower-income black and his supposed uniqueness at the bottom of urban society. Yet, *how* different is this urban black from his Italian counterpart of sixty years ago? *How* distinct is the so-called female centered household of the lower-income black from that of the Irish a century ago? *How* different is the inequality and discrimination which the black ghettoite presently faces from that of his Jewish predecessors? Basically the differences are secondary. To become absorbed in analyzing only the differences between these groups implies a certain degree of ignorance of the structural supports of ethnic and class mobility which have been similar for all the minority groups in American urban life.

Presently it might indeed be more fruitful to view the plight of the lower-income urban black in terms of *class* and *ethnic* factors rather than *racial* factors. The social unrest and turmoil evident in the urban ghettoes are consequences of lower-class membership and, to that degree, are not specifically related to racial factors. John and Lois Scott in a recent article have paraphrased this relationship:

> Most racial antipathy in America is not pure racism but derives from the disdain of higher classes for those below them. The tragedy of race in this country . . . is that visible genetic differences, superficial in themselves, have become generally reliable clues to a person's class position—his education, his income, his manners. . . . Events of the last 20 years have done much to modify the legal and political aspects of this subordination, but the more general effects of the past remain: black Americans are disadvantaged and poor, and their culture—so much a "culture of poverty"—is offensive to more affluent classes.[2]

The lower-income black thus represents the most recent ethnic group in urban America and, like his forerunners from other ethnic minorities, has migrated from agricultural poverty to industrial poverty. Essentially he has moved from the lowest position in an agricultural caste society to the lowest position in an urban class system; in the former environment caste characteristics exerted primary importance while in the latter they are secondary and of limited consequence in either defining or labeling the plight of the black.

The black, like all the lower ethnic minorities in America's past, comes from an agricultural background. He has been forced from the land and consequently drawn to the cities primarily because of agricultural technology and

[1] *The Report of the National Advisory Commission* has subscribed to this approach, stating: "Racial discrimination is undoubtedly the second major reason why the Negro has been unable to escape from poverty. The structure of discrimination has persistently narrowed his opportunities and restricted his prospects. Well before the high tide of immigration from overseas, Negroes were already relegated to the poorly paid, low status occupation. . . . European immigrants, too, suffered from discrimination, but never was it so pervasive as the prejudice against color in America which has formed a bar to advancement, unlike any other." *Report of the National Advisory Commission on Civil Disorders* (New York: Bantam Books, 1968), pp. 278–79.

[2] John F. Scott and Lois H. Scott, "They Are Not So Much Anti-Negro as Pro-Middle Class," *New York Times Magazine,* 24 March 1968, p. 46.

impoverishment which have destroyed his economic usefulness in an agricultural society. In this respect he differs little from the Irish, the Pole, and the Southern Italian. To observe that each came from a different historical, social, and cultural heritage does not alter the fact that their primary reasons for migration were similar.

So also with the lower-income black. It is of little concern to the unemployed Harlemite that his great-grandfather was a slave. His concerns are with survival in a modern urban metropolis. To dwell solely on the past glories and past humiliations of the black, of his African heritage, of his slave status and freedom from bondage, is an irrelevant point. All the immigrant minorities had similar exposures to cultural pride and historical trauma, yet this heritage had little to do with their realistic position in poverty. Each of these minorities also fought and pushed its way into a dominant American society which had made it quite evident that the group concerned was not socially acceptable. The Irish, the Jews, and the Italians—all faced the reality of exclusion from the dominant middle-class society, yet each in turn maneuvered its way into the economic, political, and social mainstream. There is no reason to suggest that the black will not do similarly, for if the lessons of history are correct, he will be successful.

Yet how is the black slum dweller to move away from his socially inferior lower class position? Through what methods will he be able to partake of the status and affluence of the middle class dominant groups? What routes of upward social mobility lie open to him? The historical and social realities of America's past suggest answers to these questions, for, strangely enough, the lessons of our own history provide us with the clues necessary for the understanding of the present situation.

One factor remains constant: no minority group ever achieved acceptance through dependence upon the benevolence and good will of the dominant American society. Each of the immigrant groups started at the bottom of American society and eventually forged its way into economic, political, and —ultimately—social equality with the dominant society. They had not been invited, and it has been adequately documented that their presence was ridiculed and resented in America. Naturally there were those few voices in the established society which bemoaned the cruel and harsh treatment of the immigrant minorities, yet these dissenters from middle-class propriety were too few and too powerless to effect any real change. Hence, the Irish and the Jews, the Italians and the Slavs—all faced the same basic dilemma of removing themselves from the poverty of the lower class and simultaneously gaining a foothold in the door of the socially accepted classes.

However, the socially approved routes of upward mobility bear little semblance to the daily reality of life in the slums. Being economically and socially ostracized, the newcomers were forced into seeking routes of upward mobility which were not totally explainable in terms of the Horatio Alger form of success. Prejudice and discrimination prevented these minority groups from succeeding in the acceptable manner and consequently other forms or modes of mobility evolved. But what were these routes of mobility? What form did they take?

Each of the minority groups utilized three core modes of movement from the lower classes to the dominant society, each of which is interrelated and interdependent. These can be identified as labor, crime, and politics. Each of these offered a route of upward mobility to the newcomers and their children. This is not to imply that no other modes were present. Hence, for specific ethnic groups such as the Irish, the clergy became an "occupational" source of prestige and power. For other groups, particularly the black and Puerto Rican, professional sports and entertainment became alternative methods of success.[3]

Yet these alternative forms served as corollary forms of mobility while the primary forms remained labor, crime and politics. In discussing the progress of the immigrants and their relationship to the Anglo-Saxon Establishment, E. Digby Baltzell in *The Protestant Establishment* writes, "as the traditional ways to wealth and respectability in business or the professions were more or less monopolized by Protestant Americans of older stock, many of the more talented and ambitious members of minority groups found careers in urban politics, in organized crime, or for those of the Catholic faith, in the hierarchy of the church."[4] Thus the analysis of ethnic upward mobility somehow encompasses the relationships between these three factors of labor, crime, and politics.

LABOR

The economic expansion of the nineteenth century provided the most obvious channel of upward mobility for the recent immigrants, for it was this industrial expansion which required the abundant supply of cheap and unskilled labor. Each of the ethnic minorities had been forced through societal exclusion to work at the most menial and underpaid types of employment—digging canals, working in the garment sweatshops, building subways and railroads, working in unskilled construction, and literally thousands of other tasks which had been deemed economically and socially unfit for the dominant classes. Yet these jobs provided the newcomer with a relative degree of economic security, a ray of hope perhaps not for himself but possibly for his children. Certainly he was mistreated and underpaid, yet his meager, but growing, savings and primitive accumulation enabled him to initiate the ever-so-slow process of mobility from the ethnic slum and the conditions of pauperization. In time, each of the minorities accepted this pattern and subsequently realized that the American norms of thrift, hard work, advancement and progress were integral parts of the American ethos. As Handlin points out, they were the keys to status and respectability in the new nation and the immigrant's desire for upward mobility necessarily required the internalization of these ideals.[5] Hence, labor in the unskilled and semi-skilled professions provided the immigrant with a beginning from which he could at least maintain himself and his immediate family. Physical labor was in economic demand and it furnished the newcomer with the "tool" necessary for an entry into the labor market.

[3] Oscar Handlin writes, "In the theatre, art, music and athletic worlds, talent was more or less absolute; and discrimination was much less effective than in other realms. This accounted for the high incidence among Negroes and Puerto Ricans to seek these pursuits as a way up; and it accounted also for the popularity and high status among them of prize fighters, musicians and the like, a popularity of which the incidence of reference in magazines and newspapers is a striking index." Oscar Handlin, *The Newcomers* (Garden City: Doubleday, 1962), p. 72.

[4] E. Digby Baltzell, *The Protestant Establishment* (New York: Vintage, 1966), p. 49.

[5] Handlin, p. 19.

The plenitude of unskilled labor enabled the immigrant to place himself, however unequally, on the lowest rung of the social class ladder, but at least he was on the ladder. Hence stable unskilled employment became the basic requirement for the subsequent mobility of all the nation's ethnic minorities. Without such economic usefulness, upward mobility would have been conceivably impossible. Yet this marginal employment did not function in a social vacuum, for simultaneously there existed and prospered two other modes of ethnic mobility—ethnic crime and ethnic politics.

ETHNIC CRIME AND ETHNIC POLITICS

It would be fruitless and unrealistic to speak of the ethnic political movements of the nineteenth and early twentieth centuries without realizing the close connection between these movements and the criminal organizations of that era. Ethnic crime and ethnic political structures formed a symbiotic relationship which is perhaps best epitomized by the success of Tammany Hall in New York City. In his book, *The Gangs of New York,* the noted social observer Herbert Asbury comments on this relationship:

> The political geniuses of Tammany Hall were quick to see the practical value of the gangsters, and to realize the advisability of providing them with meeting and hiding places, that their favor might be curried and their peculiar talents employed on election days to assure government of, by and for Tammany. . . . The underworld thus became an important factor in politics, and under the manipulation of the worthy statement the gangs of the Bowery and Five Points participated in a great series of riots which began with the spring election disturbances of 1834 and continued, with frequent outbreaks, for half a score of years.[6]

Ethnic crime and ethnic politics thus formed a working alliance which dates from the earlier part of the nineteenth century and has continued to the present. In New York, the Irish ranked as the most noteworthy of the early immigrant groups in both politics and crime, and their political and criminal expertise has subsequently been duplicated and imaginatively expanded by the Jews and the Italians. As each of these groups attained success and renown in politics and crime, so also did the entire ethnic group maneuver into the dominant society. Once established, in the new acceptable class, the ethnic group no longer depended on the functional relation of crime and political structure and, correspondingly, the lower ranks of the political structure and underworld activities came into the hands of those groups still struggling to remove themselves from the lower class. As Daniel Bell has phrased it, crime is the "American way of life." [7]

New immigrant groups wasted little time in realizing the potential value of success, not only in the political sphere, but simultaneously in the criminal sphere, for political affiliations and connections provided the legal immunity so essential to the survival of criminals. In turn the influence of the gangster could be noted in his provision of financial backing for political ventures, in his physical "support" for the growing trade union movement, and, perhaps most important of all, in his power to dissuade unwelcome individuals and groups

[6] Herbert Asbury, *The Gangs of New York: An Informal History of the Underworld* (New York: Knopf, 1929), p. 37.

[7] Daniel Bell, "Crime as an American Way of Life," *Antioch Review,* 13 (Sept. 1953), 131–54.

from political competition with the forces in power. Realistically, then, it remains historically and socially significant that some of the earliest leaders of urban political machines were, at the same time, the leaders of the more important gangs of that era.

Commenting on this symbiotic relationship between political parties and gangsters, Richard Cloward and Lloyd Ohlin write, in *Delinquency and Opportunity:*

> The gangsters and racketeers contributed greatly to the coffers of political parties and were rewarded with immunity from prosecution for their various illegal activities. As the political power of the ethnic or nationality group increased, access to legitimate opportunities became enlarged and assimilation facilitated. . . . Blocked from legitimate access to wealth, the immigrant feels mounting pressures for the use of illegal alternatives.[8]

Accordingly, a working relationship emerged in each of the ethnic groups between crime and politics. As Oscar Handlin and Will Herberg both discuss, illegality provided an attractive means of upward mobility and social advancement, and its success was insured through an established, though sometimes tenuous and uneasy relation to the local neighborhood political structure. The vast majority of the specific ethnic groups worked their way out of the lower classes by saving their "pennies and dimes" and eventually, in two or three generations, their descendants achieved middle-class status and respectability.[9]

Productive labor was but one factor. Concurrent with it there existed the profound impact of ethnic crime and politics which supplied the finances and the political acumen necessary for the mobility of the entire group. Ethnic consciousness and ethnic solidarity were thus created, the cultural heroes of each of these groups being both the political bosses and the gangsters. These "models" demonstrated to the masses of the lower class that an individual could achieve success and power and that the ethnic group itself, as a collective entity, constituted a force with which the dominant elites would have to reckon.[10]

IMPLICATIONS

What about the black? How do the channels of employment, crime, and politics affect his opportunities for upward mobility? What relationship, if

[8] Richard Cloward and Lloyd Ohlin, *Delinquency and Opportunity* (Glencoe: Free Press, 1960), p. 196.

[9] Handlin, p. 26; see also Herberg's discussion of the immigrant groups and political development, in Will Herberg, *Protestant, Catholic, Jew* (Garden City: Doubleday Anchor, 1960), p. 17.

[10] Boss Joseph Maloney, Alderman of "Cornerville" bitterly recognized this stating, "Then the Italians will always vote for one of their own. We recognized them when we didn't need to. They didn't have many votes, and we could have licked them every-time, but we gave them Italian representatives. We did it for the sake of the organization. But they wouldn't stick by us. The Italian people are very undependable. You can't trust them at all. They play a dirty game too. I estimate that now there are between eight hundred and a thousand repeaters in Cornerville every election. I've tried to stop that, but you can't do it. You can't tell one Italian from another." William Whyte, *Street Corner Society* (Chicago: U. of Chicago, 1955), p. 95. See also, Baltzell, p. 217, for a discussion of Al Capone as a folk hero and his relationship to the American value of non-conformity.

any, exists between the lessons of historical mobility and the conditions of black lower-income life?

The answers to these questions are both interrelated and complex; it would be an oversimplification and, indeed, a gross misrepresentation of reality to say that the black should pursue these routes of mobility. The fact remains that he *is* pursuing these routes. It takes no profound insight to see that in crime and politics the black has been working his way into the higher positions of power. Yet, like the Jew and the Italian before him, he has been forced to contend with the established criminal and political elites, for mobility in the political and the criminal realm is demonstrably as difficult, if not more so, than mobility in the occupational realm. Thomas Pettigrew, in an article entitled, "Negro American Crime," has written ". . . as with other minority groups who find discriminatory barriers blocking their path towards the mainstream of success-oriented America, many Negroes turn to crime. Crime may thus be utilized as a means of escape, ego-enhancement, expression of aggression, or upward mobility." [11]

Political considerations are also operative. The recent black political successes in Gary, Indiana and Cleveland, Ohio underscore the contention that the traditional path of ethnic political power is being utilized. Among both black militants and moderates there is a growing awareness that the key to success lies not in violence and disorder but rather in political mobility. In a recent interview, in *The New York Times,* Timothy Still, the late president of the United Community Corporation of Newark, stated:

> Newark is a city that is 60 percent colored, and we are going to inherit this city. And so we cannot let fools destroy the city we are going to inherit. The guys who were trying to start all this trouble were those who were lost, hopeless, those who had no chance. I can understand their feelings, but you can't destroy the whole city. It is *our* city, and we are not going to let you do that.[12]

Still's comments point to the increasing recognition on the part of the black community of the need for political awareness and political power. Black power and black consciousness thus can be considered as necessary intermediary means to the politicalization of the black population.[13] If present demographic projections hold true, the major urban centers of America will be predominantly black and consequently the population base for black political leverage will be present. Ethnic solidarity thus becomes the key to the subsequent political power and political mobility of the entire group. Again, the lessons of America's past are in evidence, for the black is presently actualizing what other minorities historically have accomplished.

A closer examination of the employment route, however, reveals the presence of one all-important factor which has blocked the potential for upward mobility for the black. Unlike all his predecessors, the lower-income black faces one enduring fact of contemporary economic structure—the relative disappearance of unskilled occupations. The lower-income Negro increasingly

[11] Thomas Pettigrew, "Negro American Crime," in *A Profile of the Negro American* (Princeton: Van Nostrand, 1964), p. 156.

[12] Fred Cook, "It's Our City, Don't Destroy It," *New York Times Magazine,* 30 June 1968, p. 31.

[13] For a recent appraisal of the relationship between black power and the Negro community see, Seymour Leventman, "Black Power and the Negro Community in Mass Society," paper presented at the annual meeting of the American Sociological Association, Boston, August, 1968.

can be classified as economically useless.[14] Economic and technological developments since World War II have eliminated precisely those positions which the black might have utilized as leverage for subsequent mobility. Without these jobs he cannot even hope to climb the class ladder. Without them he has little chance of removing himself from the lower class, for employment in these occupations constitutes the barest minimum necessary for ethnic mobility. In *Problems and Prospects of the Negro Movement,* Herbert Hill has emphasized this factor:

> Optimistic assumptions regarding the Negro's progress in American society must be re-examined in the light of the Negro's current economic plight. The great mass of Negroes, especially in the urban centers, are locked in a permanent condition of poverty. This includes the long-term unemployed as well as the working poor, who have only a marginal economic existence and who increasingly are forced into the ranks of the unemployed.[15]

Hence, structural considerations of employment and its impact upon the black has created the present societal chaos so evident in our urban centers. An analysis of the condition of unemployment over the past two decades reflects this structural problem—one which statistically is growing more chronic over the years. Unemployment statistics illustrate the situation of the nonwhite worker, and his plight has increased significantly from the plight of the white worker since 1948, the first year when such statistics were available for persons over 16 years of age.

However, class factors are evident in the employment situation confronting the black. The unavailability of unskilled jobs does not affect the middle-class black and, to that degree, its members participate in the economic and social prosperity so characteristic of contemporary American society. The black has been victimized not primarily by his color, nor by his former slave status, but by his lower-class position. In this he remains no different from his Puerto Rican, Mexican-American, or Appalachian white counterpart. All are substantially represented in the lower class, and upward mobility is increasingly very difficult due to the economic structural forces beyond their control. Thus, the degree that unemployment in the unskilled jobs diminishes, to the same degree will the lower-income black be cut-off from the possibilities of upward mobility.

The recent urban disorders in scores of cities have underscored this problem of class. In many of the cities, the rioters demonstrated the same hostility towards middle-class black as they did towards white policemen, firemen, and business proprietors. It should also be emphasized that lower-income blacks were not the only group to participate in urban disorders, for New York City, in the summer of 1967, and Paterson, New Jersey, in the summer of 1968, witnessed small scale outbreaks among the lower-income Puerto Rican community.

The rigidity of lower-class positioning and the increasing uncertainty of upward mobility thus create tensions in those individuals cut-off from the prospects of improving their societal lot. Given the proper environment, these

[14] For an interesting article dealing with the economics of uselessness of the lower-income Negro see, Sidney M. Willhelm and Edwin Powell, "Who Needs the Negro?," *Transaction,* 1 (Sept.–Oct., 1964), 3–6.

[15] Herbert Hill, "Racial Inequality in Employment: The Patterns of Discrimination," in *Problems and Prospects of the Negro Movement,* eds. R. Murphy and H. Elinson (Belmont, California: Wadsworth, 1966), p. 86.

TABLE 1

UNEMPLOYMENT RATE FOR NON–WHITE WORKERS AS PERCENT OF RATE FOR WHITE WORKERS, 1948–1967
(Persons 16 years and over)

Year	Unemployment Rate		Non-white Rate as Percent of White
	White	Non-white	
1948	3.2	5.9	169
1949	5.6	8.9	159
1950	4.9	9.0	184
1951	3.1	5.3	171
1952	2.8	5.4	193
1953	2.7	4.5	167
1954	5.0	9.9	198
1955	3.9	8.7	223
1956	3.6	8.3	231
1957	3.8	7.9	208
1958	6.1	12.6	207
1959	4.8	10.7	223
1960	4.9	10.2	208
1961	6.0	12.4	207
1962	4.9	10.9	222
1963	5.0	10.8	216
1964	4.6	9.6	209
1965	4.1	8.1	198
1966	3.3	7.3	221
1967	3.4	7.4	218

Source: *Manpower Report, 1967,* U.S. Department of Labor (Washington, D.C.: Government Printing Office, 1967).

tensions erupt in violence and destruction. As the Riot Commission has pointed out, the typical rioter was *better* educated, *better* informed, and geographically *more stable* than the non-rioter of the same neighborhood.[16] He perhaps had more reason to hope for subsequent upward mobility, yet the inevitable workings of an economic structure which cannot, or will not, use his labor has confronted him with the realities of the American class structure. His behavior bears the marks of vengeance, of lashing back at a society which has promised him much yet has removed the routes to the rewards. It may be surmised that the non-rioter comprises an American variation of the Marxian "lumpenproletariat"—that group which has been so suppressed that appeals to revolution and retaliation become meaningless and hollow.

The problems and the styles of life encountered in the lower-income black are not basically distinguishable from those of other ethnic groups, past or present. Certainly his family structure, his beliefs and his values are different from those of the middle class. Yet, how distinct are these same traits from other lower-income ethnic groups such as the Puerto Rican? The similarities found in our current lower-class ethnic minorities greatly outweigh the differences and to magnify the differential styles and values of these respective

[16] *The Report of the National Advisory Commission on Civil Disorders,* pp. 128–35.

groups is to place undue emphasis for poverty and deprivation on the wrong factors.

Currently, the black comprises the most important ethnic group in the urban lower class. His problems and tragedies are those of preceding ethnic minorities, yet the profound economic changes in American society have greatly complicated his status and his potential for mobility. These changes have produced the disorders of Watts, Detroit, Newark, and Washington. In turn the unskilled black's relative economic marginality has created the impetus for the proliferation of many of the socio-psychological problems of the ghetto with its underlying culture of poverty, its irrelevant educational system, its so called multi-problem families, and its forced exclusion from affluent America through economic dysfunction.

Racial considerations add little to the analysis of these issues; all too often they act as smokescreens which mask the real problems. If race and racial considerations exerted primary importance, it would increasingly be difficult to interpret the values and styles of life of the black *middle-class* population. These values are vastly different from the black lower class, yet they are essentially similar to the values and life styles of the white middle-class population. The gap thus exists between the classes, not the races; it is between the white and black middle class on one hand, and the white and black lower class on the other. Skin color and the history of servitude do little to explain the present polarization of the classes.

Social class thus assumes a primary position in defining and explaining the relationship between upward mobility and the behavior of specific ethnic groups, while racial stigmatization can be considered as relatively secondary in importance. Class differentials, not racial differentials, explain the presence and persistence of poverty in the ranks of the urban black. It thus becomes superfluous to speak of the problem in moral terms, in the rhetoric of brotherly love and social equality. However noble these answers may be, they ignore the reality of ethnic mobility, for no group has ever achieved parity unless it followed the well-traversed route of labor, crime, and politics. Only *after* each of the groups achieved relative success and power in these ventures were they "accepted." Social acceptance and social integration were the last steps, and perhaps the easiest steps, in the long journey from the bottom. In contemporary America, many well-meaning individuals and groups have placed the cart before the horse. They have argued for social acceptance first, from which ultimately should come economic equality, political power, etc., rather than the converse. To argue in this manner merely aggravates the situation, for it deflects the forces of change from the economic and structural considerations and wastes them in moral reform and spiritual catharsis.

The Head Starts, the community action programs, the educational pilot projects function yet they remain unrelated to the roots of the problem of poverty in the black ghettoes. The facts speak for themselves: none of the existing programs attack the problem at its structural foundation, employment. What difference does it make if all these programs do not create employment for the presently unskilled? What contribution is made by a Job Corps that trains youth for non-existing jobs? What difference does it really make for a lower-income Negro to get a high school diploma when the available statistics suggest that his unemployment rate remains disproportionately higher than whites with or without the diploma? These are the crucial questions which must be answered if the black is to move in American society. His odyssey is essentially no different from that of previous ethnic minorities; it only remains for American society to provide the employment necessary to make the journey productive and rewarding.

BIBLIOGRAPHY

Asbury, Herbert. *The Gangs of New York: An Informal History of the Underworld.* New York: Alfred A. Knopf, 1929.

Baltzell, E. Digby. *The Protestant Establishment.* New York: Vintage Books, 1966.

Bell, Daniel. "Crime as an American Way of Life." *Antioch Review,* 13 (Sept. 1953), 131–54.

Cloward, Richard, and Lloyd Ohlin. *Delinquency and Opportunity.* Glencoe, Ill.: The Free Press, 1960.

Cook, Fred. "It's Our City, Don't Destroy It." *New York Times Magazine,* 30 June 1968, pp. 31 ff.

Handlin, Oscar. *The Newcomers.* Garden City, N.Y.: Doubleday Anchor Books, 1962.

Herberg, Will. *Protestant, Catholic, Jew.* Garden City, N.Y.: Doubleday Anchor Books, 1955.

Hill, Herbert. "Racial Inequality in Employment: The Patterns of Discrimination." *Problems and Prospects of the Negro Movement.* Eds. R. Murphy and H. Elinson. Belmont, Calif.: Wadsworth Co., 1966.

Leventman, Seymour. "Black Power and the Negro Community in Mass Society." Paper presented to the Annual Meeting of the American Sociological Association, Boston, August 1968.

Pettigrew, Thomas. *A Profile of the Negro American.* Princeton, N.J.: Van Nostrand Co., 1964.

Report of the National Advisory Commission on Civil Disorders. New York: Bantam Books, 1968.

Scott, John, and Lois H. Scott. "They Are Not So Much Anti-Negro as Pro-Middle Class." *New York Times Magazine,* 24 March 1968, pp. 46 ff.

Whyte, William. *Street Corner Society.* Chicago: University of Chicago Press, 1955.

Willhelm, Sidney, and Edwin Powell. "Who Needs the Negro?" *Transaction,* 1 (Sept.–Oct. 1964), 3–6.

OTHER SOURCES CONSULTED *

Baltzell, E. Digby. *Philadelphia Gentlemen, The Making of a National Upper Class.* Glencoe, Ill.: The Free Press, 1958.

Bell, Daniel. *The End of Ideology.* Glencoe, Ill.: The Free Press, 1960.

Cahan, Abraham. *The Rise of David Levinsky.* New York: Harper and Brothers, 1917.

Glazer, Nathan, and Daniel Moynihan. *Beyond the Melting Pot.* Cambridge, Mass.: The M.I.T. Press, 1963.

* This list refers to works consulted and in some cases actually read by the writer, but not used directly in the article.

Gordon, Milton. *Assimilation in American Life.* New York: Oxford University Press, 1964.

Hansen, Marcus Lee. *The Problem of the Third Generation Immigrant.* Rock Island, Ill.: Augustana Historical Society, 1938.

Higham, John. *Stranger in the Land: Patterns of American Natavism 1860–1925.* New Brunswick, N.J.: Rutger University Press, 1955.

Hofstadter, Richard. *The Age of Reform.* New York: Vintage Books, 1960.

Liebow, Eliot. *Tally's Corner.* Boston: Little, Brown and Company, 1967.

Solomon, Barbara. *Ancestors and Immigrants: A Changing New England.* Cambridge, Mass.: Harvard University Press, 1956.

Commentary

In this piece, as in the shorter examples of argumentation cited in Chapter 20, "What Case Can Be Made For or Against X?" the structure of the argument follows the conventional form: introduction, body, and conclusion. Note too that in supporting his case for an ethnic approach to black problems, the writer touches on many questions:

1. He describes the past and present status of the blacks.
2. He compares their problems and life style with that of other minority groups.
3. He traces the causes and consequences of their problems.
4. He summarizes opposing views.
5. He explains how other minorities have achieved upward mobility (a process analysis).
6. He cites numerous facts: details, statistics.
7. He interprets these facts in the light of his proposition.

After supporting his main IS proposition throughout the body of his argument (namely that the black man is victimized not so much by his color but by his lower-class status, i.e., his poverty), the writer moves on at the end of his argument to infer from the IS proposition an OUGHT proposition (the problems of the black *ought* to be attacked not on a social level but at its roots, i.e., at the level of employment). The writer draws to a conclusion with a series of provocative rhetorical questions ("Why bother training blacks for non-existent jobs?"). He concludes with a brief recapitulation of his position: "[The black man's] odyssey is essentially no different from that of previous ethnic minorities; it only remains for American society to provide the employment necessary to make the journey productive and rewarding."

ASSIGNMENTS

I. Suggested Topic: Whither the Black Odyssey: A Reply.

If you disagree with this interpretation—if you believe that the present problems faced by the black ghetto-dweller are qualitatively different from those faced by other dispossessed minority groups in this country; if you believe that his African heritage and former slave status have created in the black American a distinct identity that cannot be dealt with apart from the racial issue; and if you believe that we are more likely to solve the problems of poverty and deprivation among the blacks by approaching the problem from a racial rather than economic point of view—you could write a reply to this article in which you explain how and why the position of blacks differs from that of other minorities in our nation's history. How can blacks expect to achieve "upward mobility" if this is their goal? What are their aspirations? How may they best achieve them? The author of "Whither the Black Odyssey?" has called upon many sources to support his position, as his footnotes and bibliography indicate. In order to write a substantial reply (4,000–5,000 words) you must do the same.

For a discussion of research procedure and library resources, read Chapter 22, "Gathering Information." For a "List of Possible Sources" for the topic "Whither the Black Odyssey: A Reply," see p. 389.

II. Additional topics suitable for an extended argumentation (4,000–5,000 words). Make a case for an unorthodox interpretation and solution to one of the problems confronting us today:

urban blight
inflation
rising crime rate
rising divorce rate
drug abuse and addiction
the Middle East conflict
the Vietnam war

22 GATHERING INFORMATION

The Importance of Facts

In an article entitled "What Every Writer Must Learn," the poet John Ciardi pointed out that "good writers deal in information. . . . [even poets] are gorgeously given to the fact of the thing." Ciardi supports his case for the fact by citing two such different poets as the "mystical" Gerard Manley Hopkins and the down-to-earth Robert Frost. For instance, Hopkins' images are deeply grounded in fact: ". . . And blue bleak embers, ah my dear, / Fall gall themselves, and gash gold vermilion" (i.e., "Coal embers in a grate, their outside surfaces burned out and blue-bleak, sift down, fall through the grate, strike the surface below or the side of the grate, and are gashed open to reveal the gold-vermilion fire still glowing at their core").

Likewise it may be said of Frost's poem "Mending Wall" (too widely reprinted to need reprinting here) that within its flawless rhythm and exultant theme, which deals symbolically with human isolation and kinship, there is "as much specific information about stone walls as one could hope to find in a Department of Agriculture pamphlet."

The important point to be made here is that even the poetic nature is not antagonistic to fact. Indeed, every writer who wants his piece to have substance and texture builds upon solid information that he has obtained from one or more of the following sources:

1. remembering
2. observing
3. thinking
4. research

We shall consider these sources separately, noting how the writer may best proceed in each case, noting also that most often he turns to more than one source for his materials.

Remembering Facts

We saw in Chapter 17, "What Is My Memory of X?" that novelist Thomas Wolfe could remember with shattering clarity events of his childhood and early youth: they came back to him unsolicited, in their minutest, most vivid detail. Because the rest of us do not have this gift of total recall, we must make a conscious and sustained effort to conjure up the past so that we can reproduce it again on paper with a degree of reality and vividness.

Take a typical "memorable event," for example: let us say you once almost drowned. That *should* provide the ingredients for an exciting narrative account—but maybe not. It depends on how accurately you can recall specific details. The careless amateur barely tries, for he is satisfied to work off the top of his head, setting down a general outline of "what it was like." But the careful writer strains to remember and render in vivid images the specific sensations and impressions associated with the original experience—the water bubbling in his ears as he was going down . . . down . . . the sound of voices in the distance . . . (how did they sound—*exactly*?). The careful writer knows that he can make his experience live again on paper only if he activates those small telling details that capture its essence. Thus, he will spend hours gathering information from the deepest recesses of his own memory. He knows that it is all buried there *somewhere* and that if he persists in his digging he will recover it. He knows too that this is not an easy task but a formidable discipline.

Interestingly, many conscious procedures, even rituals, have been worked out by people who want, for a variety of reasons, to prod their memories. Two of these are worth mentioning here, for they may be adapted to the writer's purpose. They arise from the "group workshops in creativity" and "direct experience workshops" conducted by psychotherapist Ira Progoff.[1] Although these workshops have a larger than literary purpose ("They are designed," says Dr. Progoff, "to expand awareness and evoke the unlived creative potential of the individual"), their methods can be applied to retrieving one's past experience so that it may be recreated realistically on paper. In his workshop sessions, Dr. Progoff tries, as he says, "to help the individual extend the time dimension of his personality so that he can feel the movement and direction of his life from the outside." Thus at one recent workshop session Dr. Progoff addressed the group as follows:

> Let's put ourselves in adolescence . . . , make it early adolescence, pre-sexual awareness. Ask yourself "How did I feel then? Were there any special experiences that stand out in my mind? Funny? Sad? Strange? How did I feel about myself? About life? About my relation to life? What was my image of myself in those days?" Let yourself be carried back . . . relax and think . . . try to remember . . . people . . . images . . . events. . . . Just speak out when you *do* remember. . . . Tell us what it was like.

We can simulate a creativity workshop by assembling a small group of people (five or six classmates, let us say) who will systematically set out to

[1] Dr. Progoff, formerly a special lecturer on depth psychology at Drew University, now director of Dialogue House in New York City, has conducted workshops at universities and study centers across the country.

evoke memories, their own and one another's. Actually there are many ways to conduct such a session: each participant might simply free associate, letting his mind wander at will and telling his own story as he thinks of it, or as other people's stories remind him of his own. (Mutual reminding is an important factor and a substantial aid in this process.) Then again the session might be structured by having one person present a problem, like the following (also used in a recent workshop session):

> There's an intersection: two roads going in different directions; one road is taken, one is not. Relax and think of yourself on the road, any kind of road that will lead into a crossroad. Get the feeling of being there, walking along, thinking, feeling, coming to the intersection, trying to decide which way to go . . . *which way will it be?* What happens? What is there on the road you finally take? *Why* do you take it? Just speak out as it comes to you on that road. . . .

There is still another way student writers may adapt workshop methods to their own purpose—by keeping an intensive journal (as workshop members call it): a psychological notebook in which they enter significant images or thoughts, flashes of memory, dreams, ideas, feelings, fears. "The purpose of the notebook," says Dr. Progoff, "is to give the individual a tangible procedure by which he can enter the depth of himself and [thereby] re-experience his existence from an inward point of view." It is this tangible procedure of reexperiencing one's existence *inwardly* that can be most helpful to the writer. He should make daily entries in his notebook; then, after a few days, read the entries at his leisure, ponder their significance, try to recover those half-forgotten details that are often the key to a whole experience.

Take that most trite of trite topics, for example, which students and teachers alike ridicule as a nonsubject—"My Summer Vacation." Everyone expects a paper written under this heading to be slapdash and dull, *but does it have to be?* Is a visit to the Grand Canyon dull, for example, if it is seen with the seeing eye? If the writer has really looked? If he has experienced it genuinely in his own person and remembered it not only in terms of the outward spectacle (which may be overly familiar to some people) but of his own inward response as well? When approached in this way—with a sense of the self at the center of the experience ("Let me tell you, reader, what it was like: I have a purpose in writing this piece")—an account of one's summer vacation at the Grand Canyon, or anywhere, will not be a bore to the writer or the reader.

One last point should be mentioned in this section. The student who writes an essay that *authentically* recreates one of his own experiences gains not only the instructor's commendation but also, and more important, he gains for *himself* a portion of his own life seen again from a deeper and more meaningful perspective. And in doing this he is, in a sense, *extending* his life; for it may be that he will see his experiences for the first time in their true shape; it may be that he will probe for the first time into their true and full significance.

Observing Facts

Just as memory may be probed and prodded, so the power of observation may be extended and sharpened by making a conscientious and deliberate effort to gain more than a general impression of something—a place, event, person, object. Anyone can get a general impression merely by being there. But this is not enough for the writer; in fact, to merely look is not enough, as we have pointed out earlier in Chapter 2, "How Can X Be Described?" and Chapter 14, "How Did X Happen?" Looking must be *purposive;* all senses must be alert to precise details—the exact color, texture, shape, smell, temperature, or tactile sensation of a place or an object; the exact appearance of a person, his facial grimaces, hand gestures, body movements, his tone of voice, the exact event as it occurred and the way people reacted to it and to each other. These are the raw materials that must register in your consciousness if you are to gather facts from observations and write a realistic account of how something happened, or what someone or something was like. Not everyone is a highly sensitive receptor, to be sure, but everyone can at least *try* to see more than he would ordinarily see if he made no special effort.

Actually, observation, like charity, begins at home, in our immediate surroundings. Because the professional writer realizes this, he is—in an important sense—always "on duty," always gathering information, making mental notes, noticing this or that detail that might provide him with material at some future time.

Let us say that you have decided to write a piece about a single special place—the campus library. Since you are a steady visitor and pass it daily, you regard this as a relatively simple, straightforward assignment. Are you ready, then, to sit down and start writing? Not at all. Not until you have looked at it with the conscious intention of seeing this structure with fresh eyes, as if you had never seen it before. Only then will you discover that in truth *you have never seen it before,* not in any richness or sharpness of detail. Chances are that on each previous visit—numerous as they were—you only glossed over its general contour and main features. In just this way New Yorkers observe their own huge New York Public Library on Fifth Avenue and Forty-second Street. Naturally, everyone notices the stately white columns that frame the entrance, and the famous reclining stone lions. But how many observers note that there are precisely *six* columns and that the lions are *angled* slightly toward one another? How many of those who look, look still more closely—over the heads of the lions—at the maxims engraved on the building itself: BUT ABOVE ALL THINGS TRUTH BEARETH AWAY THE VICTORY (on the right), and BEAUTY OLD YET EVER NEW, ETERNAL VOICE AND INWARD WORD (on the left). The careful observer will note still another detail: over the revolving doors of the main entrance are three plaques pointing out that this library is in actuality *three separate libraries* housed in one building, a fact that most New Yorkers are unaware of, even though it appears in bold lettering on the face of the building that many thousands of them pass every day of the week.

A famous teacher of the art of observation was Louis Agassiz, the great nineteenth-century naturalist, who began his course in zoology by presenting his students with a dead fish, insisting that they *look at it.* And so they would for an entire morning, after which Agassiz would return, asking "Well, what is it like?" As the students recited what they had seen (fringed gill-arches, fleshy lips, lidless eyes), Agassiz's face would reflect disappointment. "Keep looking," he would finally say—and leave them to their observations for the afternoon. One student who had been looking for days and days and days, later described the experience as follows:

> I was piqued. I was mortified. Still more of that wretched fish! But now I set myself to my task with a will, and discovered one new thing after another, until I saw how just the Professor's criticism had been. The afternoon passed quickly; and when, towards its close, the professor inquired:
>
> "Do you see it yet?"
>
> "No," I replied, "I am certain I do not, but I see how little I saw before."
>
> "That is next best," said he, earnestly, "but I won't hear you now; put away your fish and go home; perhaps you will be ready with a better answer in the morning."[2]

For eight solid months Agassiz would entreat his pupils to "look at your fish"; he had them compare it with other fish in the same family, note resemblances and differences, detect the orderly arrangement of parts, and finally see the parts in relation to the whole and the whole in relation to an overall principle or law. Indeed, the lesson in looking ended only after Agassiz had warned his students never to be satisfied with isolated observations, no matter how apt they might be, for as Agassiz believed, "facts are stupid things until brought into connection with some general law."

Thinking: Drawing Inferences and Interpretations

In order to see a "general law" behind a set of particular details, we must carry the process of observation a step further: we must go beyond *looking* to *thinking;* we must observe and analyze each particular, and then move on through a chain of reasoning to a valid and correct inference about the nature of the whole. To draw an inference, to see one truth as following from another: this is still another way of gathering information for a piece of writing.

Not everyone is equally adept at formulating original interpretations, but as was suggested in the section on argumentation, everyone of normal intelligence is capable of moving in a logical progression from one thought or observation to another. William Blake aspired to see the world in a grain of sand—an essentially poetic insight, to be sure; but more than that *cerebral,* arrived at through rigorous thinking and through a leap or inference from the facts as observed in a simple grain of sand to a larger encompassing Truth of Nature.

We have already made a brief survey of logical procedures in Chapter 20, "What Case Can Be Made For or Against X?" At this point it is simply worth repeating that we do not have to be logicians to think logically. All that is needed is a practical compositional logic that enables us to interpret

[2] Samuel H. Scudder, "Look at Your Fish," *Every Saturday,* 4 April 1874.

materials correctly, to make sound and interesting conjectures, to draw provocative *defensible* conclusions, and—at the higher reaches—to weld old ideas into new patterns: to reassess, recreate, and synthesize. Such is the work of the creative thinker and writer. An extraordinary example of this creativity is the French essayist, Michel de Montaigne (1533–92), who at the age of forty-seven shut himself up in his library "with only his own thoughts," so that he might spend the rest of his life committing his musings to paper (thereby creating the essay form). Was Montaigne a man of vast erudition? In his own words, he never "bit his nails" over Aristotle or mastered any single branch of knowledge. "What does it avail us," he once asked, "to have a stomach full of food if it does not digest, if it does not become transformed within us, if it does not increase our size and strength?" Thus Montaigne's erudition was characterized not so much by a vast store of accumulated knowledge (he was convinced everything had already been thought) but rather by the way he *transformed knowledge* through his own mental operations—his inferences and interpretations.

Research

The fourth method of gathering information for expository writing is through research. To be a good researcher you must be part scholar, part reporter—you must be able to locate within the libraries accessible to you those printed and manuscript sources that contain the facts you need, and you must have a kind of nose for news, the ability to see which of the facts you encounter in your reading best serve your purpose and which must be discarded because they do not contribute to the special thesis of your piece. This screening process is evidence that invention does not end when research begins. For even as you are gathering the special information that will constitute the substance of your paper, you are at the same time rounding it out and reshaping it. You may even revise your original thesis somewhat in the light of the materials you collect during this active research period; although you will try not to revise it too *drastically*—not unless the emerging facts show that your central thesis is not true or that it will not work. Otherwise the central thesis or intention of your paper serves as your guide to what is relevant and therefore usable in the materials you uncover, and what is not.

Most often in gathering information for a research paper you will get more materials than you use. This may seem wasteful, but it is really a necessary part of research procedure, because you are learning about your subject, developing a perspective on your materials and an awareness of the context from which they are drawn. Without this broader view, you may not be able to distinguish what is relevant from what is not; what should and should not be included. Furthermore, all the facts that you know about your subject—even those that do not appear in the finished piece—contribute to its total impact, for they give you confidence in your knowledge of your subject and authority in your writing.

At the same time you must not allow yourself to get bogged down in research. There is a point at which you must decide "this is enough"—even if it does not seem *quite* enough. For in most cases no matter how conscientiously you have explored your subject, there will always be some aspect of it you would like to pursue further, something else you would like to know. There is no end to research (as you will discover) and so—arbitrarily but firmly—you must call an end to it and move on to the writing. Hopefully, of course, you will begin writing (however tentatively) while you are still doing research—setting up a possible beginning, a strong conclusion, or some self-contained middle section.

The necessity of limiting research to what is *feasible* within the allotted time has been aptly commented upon by Charles Schultz, creator of the famous "Peanuts" comic strip. Because Schultz believes that a comic strip should constantly introduce the reader to "new areas of thought and endeavor," which "should be treated in an authentic manner," he is constantly engaged in research:

> I never draw about anything unless I feel I have a better than average knowledge of my subject. This does not mean that I am an expert on Beethoven, kite-flying, or psychiatry, but it means that as a creative person, I have the ability to skim the surface of such subjects and use just what I need.

To skim the surface of a subject and dip down only where and when there are usable materials—i.e., information pertinent to your purpose—this is a skill every student-writer should try to cultivate so that he may cope with the thousands of pages contained in the hundreds of volumes he will be consulting during his undergraduate and graduate years.

Major Reference Sources

Let us now move into the library itself to see what major reference sources are available and how the precise source you need can best be located when you need it. This is an important aspect of research technique: that you be able to find what you want as quickly as possible, without wasting time looking up information that bears only a peripheral relationship to your subject. Library materials are roughly of two kinds: primary and secondary. "Primary" refers to basic, first-hand sources: original manuscripts, letters, diaries, journals, notebooks, research reports written by the researchers themselves, statistics issued by the people who compiled them, reports of interviews, and so on. Articles and books are considered primary if the content is essentially original with the authors. Secondary materials are largely derivative in that they are assembled from a variety of outside sources. Thus all major reference works such as encyclopedias and almanacs are secondary; so are essays, articles, and books whose major purpose is to report on, analyze, or interpret the findings of original researchers. Actually many works are primary in one sense, secondary in another—i.e., they offer their own findings and interpretations built upon someone else's findings and interpretations. Thus the terms "primary" and "secondary" are relative rather than absolute. Though primary sources are obviously more reliable, undergraduate students work most of the time with secondary sources.

We shall make a brief survey here of the major reference sources [3] you are

[3] The main emphasis in the following discussion is on *categories* of reference works, with only representative examples of the works themselves, since a listing of all reference sources would occupy a whole volume. Indeed there is such a volume available in all libraries as the standard and annotated guide to reference materials.

likely to need during the academic years ahead—and in later years as well, when your professional work or your duties as a citizen (determined to *write* that Letter to the Editor, and not just talk about it!) may send you to the reference room of your local library to gather information on a given subject.

It will be helpful to begin with a definition of a reference book, and then in the following sections to group such books (along with booklets, pamphlets, periodicals, etc.) into eight main headings. First a definition:

> A reference book, as generally understood, is a book to be consulted for some definite information rather than for consecutive reading. In such books, the facts are usually brought together from a vast number of sources and arranged for convenient and rapid use.
>
> Reference tools serve the inquirer in two ways. They may supply the information directly, as in encyclopedias, directories, almanacs, and similar works, or they may point the way to the place where the information is found, the function of the many ingenious bibliographies and indexes now available.[4]

A reference book differs from an ordinary book, then, in that it is not read sequentially. The researcher turns to it with a special purpose in mind, thumbing as quickly as possible to *that place* that will provide the information he needs. As the definition above points out, there are two broad types of reference works: those that give direct information about a subject and those that tell you where to find information. The first two categories listed below (general and special references) concern themselves exclusively with direct sources of information, the logical place in most instances to begin research.

I. GENERAL REFERENCE BOOKS

When the writer has finally found his topic and is ready to gather information, he is wise to turn at the outset to the most general sources available, for they will provide a helpful overview of the subject, a description of its essential nature and its scope. More than that, they will verify whatever

---

Winchell, Constance M. *Guide to Reference Books.* 8th ed. Chicago: American Library Association, 1967.

First Supplement, 1965–1966. Second Supplement, 1967–1968.

For a handy, quick guide suitable for his own reference shelf, every student should buy one of the following inexpensive paperbacks:

Barton, Mary Neill, and Marion V. Bell. *Reference Books: A Brief Guide for Students and Other Users of the Library.* 6th ed. Baltimore: Enoch Pratt Free Library, 1966.

Galin, Saul and Peter Spielberg. *Reference Books: How to Select and Use Them.* New York: Random House, 1969.

Gates, Jean Key. *Guide to the Use of Books and Libraries.* New York: McGraw-Hill Book Company, 1969.

McCormick, Mona. *Who-What-When-Where-How-Why Made Easy.* A *New York Times* Book. Chicago: Quadrangle Books, 1971.

Morse, Grant W. *A Concise Guide to Library Research.* New York: Washington Square Press, Inc., 1967.

Murphy, Robert W. *How and Where to Look It Up.* New York: McGraw-Hill Book Company, 1958.

[4] Mary Neill Barton and Marion V. Bell, *Reference Books: A Brief Guide for Students and Other Users of the Library* (Baltimore: Enoch Pratt Free Library, 1966), p. 7.

facts the writer has on hand and fill in further details, thereby bringing him up-to-date on his subject and either reinforcing his interest in it, or (equally helpful) discouraging him, if his preliminary study shows that the subject is not as promising as it seemed. It is important for the writer to learn as soon as possible that a projected topic will not work or that it is not worth his time and energy.

A. ENCYCLOPEDIAS

The best all-around reference work—and the best known—is the encyclopedia, which provides background materials for almost any field of knowledge. Do you want to know about white supremacy in Africa? the fiscal crisis of Catholic parochial education? the world's consumption of raw materials? All these questions call for initial consultation with a broad, all-encompassing treatment of the subject. This is exactly what the encyclopedia offers in the form of a relatively short, condensed article, in many cases written by a specialist and signed.

The best general encyclopedias include the following:

Encyclopædia Britannica: A New Survey of Universal Knowledge. 24 vols. Chicago: Encyclopædia Britannica, Inc., 1970.
Supplemented annually by the *Britannica Book of the Year.*

Encyclopedia Americana (International Edition). 30 vols. New York: Encyclopedia Americana Corp., 1970.
Supplemented annually by the *Americana Annual.*

Chamber's Encyclopædia. New rev. ed. Oxford and New York: Pergamon Press, 1967.
Supplemented annually by Chamber's *Encyclopædia World Survey.*

Collier's Encyclopedia. 24 vols. New York: Crowell-Collier, 1970.
Supplemented by *Collier's Year Book.*

Special Note:

Whatever encyclopedia you use, several facts are worth remembering:

1. Although the major encyclopedias are not thoroughly revised each year, most of them undergo a process of continuous revision whereby each edition embodies some changes. In most cases, therefore, the information gathered from a reputable encyclopedia is relatively up-to-date. For absolute up-to-the-minute information, however, obviously you must consult a periodical—an abstract, article, or news report. (These are described below under "Periodical Indexes and Abstracts.")

2. Every encyclopedia contains an explanation of its own code: its abbreviations, a key to the initials on the signed articles, index conventions, etc. This code should be consulted at the outset of research so that the information that is gathered may be fully understood.

3. The major encyclopedias contain bibliographies (lists of other works on a given subject or other places where information may be obtained), plus a detailed index, usually located in the last volume. Researchers are not always aware of these supplementary aids; the main index, in particular, is often ignored by the student who hurriedly turns to the alphabetically-located main entry where, in truth, most of the needed information can be found. But not all. The index enables you to see at a glance *all* the material available on your subject.

Proper use of the encyclopedia also involves cross-referencing. If your topic is the chateau country of France, for example, you should follow each of the suggested cross-references to individual chateaux as they are mentioned in the main entry (Amboise, Chenonceaux) and then you should proceed still further—on your own—to look up other entries that *might* provide more information: you might investigate individual kings, for example, who built or restored chateaux (Charles VIII, Louis XII, Francis I) or you might turn to the individual towns in which chateaux are located. Your ingenuity at cross-referencing may determine whether your paper contains simply the usual and expected information, or that extra dimension that raises it above the ordinary.

B. BIOGRAPHICAL WORKS

If your topic involves a prominent person or persons (a historical character, an inventor, a literary figure), then you must begin your research by compiling biographical data. General biographical works may be universal in scope (like the first two listed below) or they may be limited to individuals of a particular nationality, geographical location, or professional position. For our purposes (in fact for most purposes) the main distinction depends on whether the person in question is living or dead.

PERSONS LIVING

Current Biography, 1940–date. New York: Wilson, 1940–date.
Published monthly and cumulated into annual volumes, each of which contains lively profiles of about 400 new personalities.

Who's Who, 1849–date. London: Black, 1849–date.
Published annually, this famous dictionary of notable living Englishmen and a few distinguished persons of other countries gives brief facts and addresses.

Who's Who in America, 1899/1900–date. Chicago: Marquis, 1899–date.
This American counterpart of the British *Who's Who* is published every other year, along with a supplementary *Who's Who of American Women,* 1958–date. (See also separate volumes of *Who's Who* that cover different regions of the United States: *Who's Who in the East, Who's Who in the South and Southwest, Who's Who in the Midwest,* and so on. See also volumes covering various other nations such as *Who's Who in Australia, Who's Who in Modern China, Who's Who in Latin America.*)

Other contemporary biographical sources are organized according to profession and include such volumes as the following:

American Men and Women of Science
The Directory of American Scholars
Twentieth Century Authors
Contemporary Authors
(Includes many little-known authors not listed elsewhere)
Dictionary of Scientific Biography

PERSONS NO LONGER LIVING

Dictionary of American Biography. 20 vols. New York: Scribner, 1928–1958.
Also includes Index and Supplements I and II.
Long, detailed articles, written by prominent scholars and accompanied by a bibliography of sources (most of them primary), chronicle the lives and accomplishments of distinguished Americans. See also *Facts About the Presidents* and *American Authors* (1600–1900).

Dictionary of National Biography. Ed. Leslie Stephen and Sir Sidney Lee. London: Smith, Elder and Co., and Oxford University Press, 1885–.

The British counterpart of (and model for) the *Dictionary of American Biography* (D.A.B.), the D.N.B. is the most complete and accurate guide to the lives of important Britons of the past.

(See also such helpful sources as *Who Was Who, British Authors of the Nineteenth Century, British Authors Before 1800, European Authors, 1000–1900.*)

PERSONS LIVING AND DEAD

Webster's Biographical Dictionary. Springfield, Mass.: G. & C. Merriam Company, 1963.

Chambers's Biographical Dictionary. New ed. New York: St. Martins, 1962.

(See also entries under individual names in the general encyclopedias and see *Biography Index*, described below under "Periodical Indexes and Abstracts.")

C. DICTIONARIES

At the outset of research it is wise to look up key terms in order to find out their conventional boundaries of meaning. Will you want to stay within these boundaries or will you want to use certain terms in an unorthodox sense—either more or less restricted than usual? As we saw in Chapter 1, "What Does X Mean?" we can vary word usage provided we indicate at the outset that we are using the term in a special sense, one that meets the particular needs of the paper.

Before we can make any such statement, however, we must see what the dictionary—preferably one of the large unabridged dictionaries—has to say; we may even find it necessary to find out how the meaning of a particular word has changed over the years: maybe a past meaning will be specially relevant to our purpose; maybe it will be worth adopting or adapting. To provide information of this kind there are four great standard dictionaries: three are general, one historical.

Webster's Third New International Dictionary of the English Language. 3rd ed. unabridged. Ed. Philip Gove. Springfield, Mass.: Merriam, 1961.

One of the great English dictionaries—the first to be published under the direct and commanding influence of modern linguistic science—*Webster's Third* contains almost half a million words, 100,000 of which are new entries or new meanings for older entries. Some early critics maintained that this dictionary would *never* replace Webster's more traditional Second Edition (1934). But it has.

The Random House Dictionary of the English Language. Unabridged ed. Ed. Jess Stein. New York: Random House, 1966.

A computer-produced, highly legible dictionary containing 260,000 words.

The American Heritage Dictionary of the English Language. Ed. William Morris. New York: American Heritage Publishing Co., Inc., and Boston: Houghton Mifflin Co., 1969.

An entirely new and highly readable dictionary, copiously illustrated.

New English Dictionary on Historical Principles. Ed. Sir James A. H. Murray. 10 vols. and supplement. Oxford: Clarendon Press, 1888–1933. Reissued, 1933, in 13 vols. under the title *Oxford English Dictionary.*

(See also the one-volume *Oxford University Dictionary*, 3rd ed., revised with addenda and corrections. Oxford: Clarendon Press, 1959.)

This great dictionary, the most scholarly lexicographical achievement in the English language, which took years of cooperative scholarship to complete, was compiled on a different plan and serves a different purpose from that of the ordinary dictionary. It traces the history of every word in the language (its meaning, spelling, pronunciation) from the time it first appeared as an English word (perhaps 800 years ago) to the present, giving illustrations of its usage at the various stages of its career.

D. YEARBOOKS AND ALMANACS

Yearbooks and almanacs, published each year, contain a wealth of general information and statistics, much of it based on primary materials drawn from government bulletins and abstracts.

Facts on File, A Weekly Digest of World Events with Cumulative Index. New York: Facts on File, Inc., 1930–date.

An extremely helpful, time-saving weekly digest of the news, arranged under such headings as world affairs, arts, economy, science, education, religion. It has been said that *Facts on File* is a *current* encyclopedia, keeping the reader abreast of the latest developments in all fields, particularly in the United States. (See also *Keesing's Contemporary Archives,* a weekly diary of world events, published in London, but world-wide in scope.)

The New York Times Encyclopedic Almanac. New York: The New York Times, 1970–date.

Comprehensive and reliable, this recently introduced encyclopedic almanac offers all the useful features of an almanac (statistics on every phase of American life, from the Supreme Court to sports) based on the research and educational resources of the *New York Times.* Issued annually.

Information Please Almanac: Atlas and Yearbook. Planned and supervised by Dan Golenpaul Associates. New York: Simon & Schuster, 1947–date.

Statesman's Year-Book: Statistical and Historical Annual of the States of the World. London: Macmillan, 1864–date.

An exceptionally useful manual containing information and statistics on the governments of the world—their rulers, constitutions, forms of government, population, commerce, state finance, defense, production, industry.

(See also the Worldmark *Encyclopedia of the Nations* (1967), which provides supplementary materials to the *Statesman's Year-Book* and presents helpful information on the newer countries and on famous persons in each country's history. See also yearbooks for individual countries and continents, such as *Europa Year Book, Canadian Almanac and Directory, South American Handbook.*)

E. ATLASES AND GAZETTEERS

There are general and special atlases, some of which are listed below:

GENERAL

Hammond Medallion World Atlas (1966)
Rand McNally Commercial Atlas (revised annually)
Rand McNally New Cosmopolitan World Atlas (1968)
McGraw-Hill International Atlas (1964)
The Times Atlas of the World (1967)

SPECIAL

Atlas of American History
Atlas of World History
Atlas of the Historical Geography of the United States
Atlas of the Sky

A gazetteer is a dictionary of places that provides information about history, population, trade, industry, cultural institutions, natural resources. See, for example:

Columbia-Lippincott Gazetteer of the World (1962)
Webster's Geographical Dictionary (1966)
The Times Index-Gazetteer of the World (1966)

F. BOOKS OF CURIOUS FACTS

Odd bits of out-of-the-way information can be located in such books of "curious facts" as those listed below:

Douglas, George William. *The American Book of Days.* Rev. ed. New York: Wilson, 1948.
An account of the history and observance of American holidays, local festivals, and anniversaries of such events as the world's first balloon ascension. (For the British equivalent see Chambers, Robert. *Book of Days, A Miscellany of Popular Antiquities.* 2 vols. Edinburgh: Chambers, 1863–64.)

Kane, Joseph Nathan. *Famous First Facts.* 3rd ed. New York: Wilson, 1964.
Records famous "firsts" in the United States: events, discoveries, inventions, etc.

Funk & Wagnalls Standard Dictionary of Folklore, Mythology and Legend. 2 vols. Ed. Maria Leach. New York: Funk & Wagnalls, 1949–50.
A vast and comprehensive work dealing with all aspects of world culture: gods, heroes, tales, customs, beliefs, songs, dances, demons, folklore of animals and plants.

Walsh, William Shepard. *Curiosities of Popular Customs and of Rites, Ceremonies, Observances, and Miscellaneous Antiquities.* Philadelphia and London: Lippincott, 1898.
Descriptions of popular customs and celebrations in different countries of the world.

Walsh, William Shepard. *Handy Book of Curious Information Comprising Strange Happenings in the Life of Men and Animals, Odd Statistics, Extraordinary Phenomena and Out-of-the-Way Facts Concerning the Wonderlands of the Earth.* Philadelphia and London: Lippincott, 1913.
(See also *Walsh's Handy Book of Literary Curiosities,* 1909.)

Wheeler, William Adolphus. *Familiar Allusions: A Handbook of Miscellaneous Information.* 5th ed. Boston: Houghton, 1890.
Radford, E., and M. A. Radford. *Encyclopedia of Superstitions.* Ed. and rev. by Christina Hole. London: Hutchinson, 1961.
(See also *A Treasury of American Superstitions.*)

II. GENERAL BIBLIOGRAPHIES

Formal bibliographies are very much like subject guides in that they also list books and other written materials according to author and subject. Thus Winchell's *Guide to Reference Books* also functions as an annotated bibliography, for it includes brief notes and comments about each title listed. A formal bibliography (one that is published independently, not merely appended to a scholarly article or an encyclopedia entry) is an end in itself, a listing, rigorously and systematically organized, of the literature on a given subject.

A bibliography, then, is a list and nothing but a list. As such it is extraordinarily useful, for it indicates how much material exists on a subject and where it is available. It also suggests—either implicitly in the title of the work listed or explicitly in an annotation—which articles and books bear most directly on a topic. Thus a good bibliography saves you time and effort, for it helps you to begin your research with the most useful and pertinent works. Equally important, it enables you to check the literature on your subject so that you will know what has already been done and what remains to be done.

There are several master bibliographies every student should be familiar with and refer to early in his research.

Bibliographic Index: A Cumulative Bibliography of Bibliographies. New York: H. W. Wilson Company, 1938–.
An indispensable tool for anyone compiling a bibliography in a particular subject, especially if the subject is somewhat obscure.

World Bibliography of Bibliographies. 4th ed., revised and enlarged. Ed. Theodore Besterman. Geneva: Societas Bibliographica, 1965–66.
A monumental work that includes 117,000 separately published bibliographies arranged according to subject.

Subject Guide to Books in Print: An Index to the Publishers' Trade List Annual. New York: Bowker, 1957–. Annual.

United States Catalog. 4th ed. New York: Wilson, 1928. Supplemented by *Cumulative Book Index,* 1928–date. New York: Wilson, 1933–date.

Library of Congress Catalog. Washington, D.C.: Library of Congress, 1955–.

III. SPECIAL REFERENCES

In addition to general references, there is a large body of special reference works devoted to individual fields such as history, political science, and literature. Each of these fields has its own corpus of materials—encyclopedias, handbooks, indexes, abstracts, almanacs, yearbooks, dictionaries and so on—that can be located through a general reference guide like Constance Winchell's standard *Guide to Reference Books* or one of the smaller "pocket guides." These overall subject guides are the single, most helpful aid to the researcher, for they acquaint him with the major writings in his chosen field, listing not only encyclopedias and handbooks but also bibliographies, abstracts, and periodical indexes that tell him where he can find further information (discussed below under Periodical Indexes).

Exactly how many subject areas have their own reference shelf of special materials? It would be impossible to list them all, for there are separate reference works devoted to almost every discipline, activity, profession, occupation, and recreation known to man; there are handbooks and encyclopedias concerned with every field and every field-within-a-field that one can possibly imagine—and many that could not be imagined because they are so small and specialized, so remote and improbable.

We can only give some of the more common Subjects (or categories) under which special references are likely to be listed:

SUBJECT HEADING	REPRESENTATIVE REFERENCE WORKS
Philosophy	*Encyclopedia of Philosophy*
Psychology	*Annual Review of Psychology*

SUBJECT HEADING	REPRESENTATIVE REFERENCE WORKS
Religion	*Encyclopedia of Religion and Ethics* (See separate encyclopedias for Catholic, Jewish, etc.)
Social Sciences	*Sources of Information in the Social Sciences* *International Encyclopedia of the Social Sciences* *Dictionary of Sociology* *Biennial Review of Anthropology* (See separate reference works in political science, economics, law, education, etc.)
Physical Sciences	*The Harper Encyclopedia of Science* *Encyclopedia of Science and Technology* *A Guide to the Literature of Chemistry* *The International Dictionary of Applied Mathematics* *Encyclopaedic Dictionary of Physics* *Glossary of Geology and Related Sciences*
Natural Sciences	*The Encyclopedia of Biological Sciences* *Gray's Manual of Botany* *Mammals of the World* *Glossary of Genetics and Other Biological Terms*
Technology	*Encyclopedia of Science and Technology* *A Guide to Information Sources in Space Science and Technology* (See separate reference works under medical science, engineering, agriculture, business, etc.)
Fine Arts	*Encyclopedia of World Art* *Guide to Art Reference Works* *Grove's Dictionary of Music and Musicians* *Encyclopedia of Jazz*
Literature	*The Reader's Adviser: A Guide to the Best in Literature* (See also bibliographies, dictionaries, directories, handbooks, biographies, criticisms, history, drama, poetry, fiction, etc.; see also national literatures: English, American, French, etc.)
Language and Linguistics	*The World's Chief Languages* *Language in Culture and Society* *A History of the English Language* [5] *Dictionary of Linguistics*
History	*An Encyclopedia of World History* *Oxford Classical Dictionary* (See under historical periods: ancient, medieval, etc.; also national histories: English, American, etc.)

IV. PERIODICAL INDEXES AND ABSTRACTS

When you want to find out the latest information on a given subject (the influence of drugs on mental alertness, critical opinion of a current pro-

[5] This book, by scholar-historian Albert Baugh, is an example of a textbook so comprehensive that it may be and often is regarded as a reference work.

duction of *King Lear*, new facts about the moon, and so on), you must turn to periodical indexes that list articles, reports, reviews, essays, news stories, speeches, bulletins, and editorials that have been printed in periodical form —in journals, magazines, and newspapers. In some cases, you may want to turn to this resource immediately, for what is new about your subject may be the most important thing you need to learn; it may be the core of your paper and your reason for writing it.

This is what you can expect from the periodical indexes, then: to be put in touch with the most recent and up-to-date information. In that special type of index known as an "abstract," you will also find a brief summary of what is contained in the articles and essays.

Major periodical indexes can be divided into general and specialized (according to subject areas).

A. GENERAL INDEXES

The Readers' Guide to Periodical Literature. New York: Wilson, 1905–date.
Social Sciences and Humanities Index. New York: Wilson, 1907–date.
Formerly known as *Readers' Guide to Periodical Literature Supplement,* 1907–19; and as *International Index,* 1920–65.
Essay and General Literature Index. New York: Wilson, 1900–date.
Book Review Digest. New York: Wilson, 1905–date.
Book Review Index. Detroit: Gale Research, 1965–date.

B. SPECIAL SUBJECT INDEXES

Here again, as in the section on special subject reference works, it is impossible to list all the separate indexes devoted to particular subjects. To locate the particular one most useful to your purpose, it is wise to consult one of the general guides to the literature such as Winchell's *Guide to Reference Books* (mentioned earlier), or the less formal but eminently readable *How and Where to Look It Up.*

A few representative subject indexes are listed below:

Applied Science and Technology Index. New York: Wilson, 1958–date.
Formerly *Industrial Arts Index,* 1913–58.
Art Index. New York: Wilson, 1929–date.
Business Periodicals Index. New York: Wilson, 1958–date.
Education Index. New York: Wilson, 1929–date.
Index of Religious Periodical Literature. Ed. American Theological Library Assn. Princeton, N.J.: Princeton Theological Seminary, 1953–date.
The Music Index. Detroit: Information Service, Inc., 1949–date.
Public Affairs Information Service Bulletin. New York: Public Affairs Information Service, 1915–date.
Psychological Index, 1894–1935. 42 vols. Princeton, N.J.: Psychological Review Co., 1895–1936.
(Continued by *Psychological Abstracts*)

C. ABSTRACTS

Abstract of English Studies
America: History and Life: A Guide to Periodical Literature (with abstracts)
Biological Abstracts
Chemical Abstracts
Historical Abstracts
Now being published in two parts: *Modern Abstracts, 1775–1914;* and *Twentieth Century Abstracts, 1914–1970.*

Mathematical Reviews
Mineralogical Abstracts
Psychological Abstracts
Religious and Theological Abstracts
Science Abstracts (physics and electrical engineering)
Sociological Abstracts

V. GOVERNMENT PUBLICATIONS

The United States government is probably the largest and most versatile publisher in the world, printing and processing in a single year more books, booklets, periodicals, newsletters, leaflets, films, and filmstrips; more annual reports, research documents, transcripts (of Congressional hearings, for example), manuals, handbooks, bibliographies, indexes, dictionaries, catalogues, checklists, and statistical compilations than any single commercial publisher anywhere—or any foreign government.

Few people, students or ordinary citizens, are aware of the enormous amount of information available to them through the Government Printing Office, either free or at very low cost. A brief listing of recent titles suggests how far-ranging this information is: *Science and the City, Mini-gardens for Vegetables, Family Budgeting, The Nature of Ocean Beds, Raising Racoons, Home Construction, Space, National Parks, Living Death: the Truth About Drug Addiction, FDA* (Food and Drug Administration) on *Oral Contraceptives, Story of the Mississippi Chocktaws, Pocket Guide to Japan, Fables from Incunabula to the Present.* In truth, there are few fields not touched upon by government publications, especially in the areas of history, travel, and the social, physical, and biological sciences.

To tap this rich source of information, most of it first-hand primary source material, authoritative and up-to-date, the student researcher should be familiar with the main bibliographies and indexes issued by the government and some of the more recent and important guides.[6]

U.S. Superintendent of Documents
Monthly catalogue of United States Government Publications, 1895–date.

Price Lists of Government Publications. Washington, D.C.: Government Printing Office, 1898–date.

U.S. Bureau of the Census. *Statistical Abstract of the United States.* Washington, D.C.: Government Printing Office, 1878–date.

This matchless compendium of statistics covers the political, social, economic, and industrial organization of the country, including vital statistics, and figures on population, immigration, finance, employment, etc. It is the basic source of statistical information of all kinds from which most other sources (yearbooks, almanacs) get their information.

Jackson, Ellen. *Subject Guide to Major United States Government Publications.* Chicago: American Library Association, 1968.

Covers important government publications from the earliest period to the publication date, arranged by subject.

[6] It should be pointed out that libraries organize their government materials differently: some catalogue them in the regular card catalogue, as they would any other library material; other libraries may keep them in a separate file, or official United States government depository, classifying them as "Government Documents," or "Government Publications." The reference librarian can explain the system used in the individual library.

Leidy, W. Philip. *A Popular Guide to Government Publications.* 3rd ed. New York: Columbia University Press, 1968.
Covers the most popular government publications issued 1961–66, arranged by subject.

Schmeckebier, Lawrence F., and Roy B. Eastin. *Government Publications and Their Use.* 2nd rev. ed. Washington, D.C.: Brookings Institute, 1969.
Contains descriptions of catalogues and indexes, bibliographies, Congressional publications, constitutions (federal and state), court decisions, presidential papers, etc.

VI. PAMPHLETS

Pamphlets deserve to be treated in a separate category because, like government publications, they are often ignored by the student researcher who is unaware of their importance, or even their existence. Pamphlets serve the important function of bridging a time gap until current information on a given topic can be gathered into book form.

Many reputable organizations and institutions, such as the Mental Health Association, the public affairs offices of colleges and universities, and the Civil Liberties Union, regularly publish pamphlets in order to keep the public abreast of their activities and achievements.

The best way to locate a pamphlet dealing with a given subject is through the Pamphlet or Vertical File of the library, or in the regular card catalogue under the appropriate subject heading if your library integrates pamphlets into its general collection. You can expect to find materials on current and controversial subjects such as racial conflicts, drug addiction, alcoholism, civil disobedience, antiwar protest, conservation, pollution, etc. Much of this material reflects the underlying and pressing conflicts of American society and of the world at large, treated in a timely fashion.

In working with pamphlets the student should be particularly alert for evidence of bias. Extremist political groups, both left and right, for example, often distribute pamphlets that *seem* to be informative but are really propagandist. These should be viewed with appropriate suspicion.

Some of the more noteworthy pamphlet series are cited below:

Public Affairs Pamphlets
Published by the nonprofit Public Affairs Committee to keep the American public informed on vital economic and social problems.

Headline Series
Published by the nonprofit, nonpartisan Foreign Policy Association to stimulate wider interest in world affairs.

Editorial Research Reports
Individual monographs dealing with vital contemporary issues.

National Industrial Conference Board
Another nonprofit fact-finding laboratory, this Board publishes studies on scientific research in the fields of business economics and management.

American Universities Field Staff Publications
A continuing series on current developments in world affairs issued by the nonprofit American Field Staff, Inc.

National Bureau of Economic Research
Publishes scientific reports on current economic problems.

Center for the Study of Democratic Institutions
A nonprofit, nonpartisan educational institution, the Center publishes articles dealing with basic problems in a democratic society.

VII. CARD CATALOGUE

The card catalogue is exactly that—a catalogue of 3 x 5 index cards, filed alphabetically in pull-out drawers that line the walls of the main circulation room in your library. This catalogue is the index to the library, for each card represents a library holding—a book, booklet, periodical—and contains such vital facts as author, title, subject, publisher, place and date of publication, number of pages. For each library holding there are usually three cards: one indexed under the author's name, one under the title of the book, the third under the subject. (A typical card is shown on page 384.)

It would be impossible to overestimate the importance of the card catalogue because it tells you not merely what has been published on your subject but what is actually available in your own library.

Learning how to use the card catalogue is hardly difficult. It requires no special sleuthing to turn to the "Man-Mut" drawer to locate books on the subject of "money"; or the "Gut-Hil" drawer for a novel by "Hemingway"; or "Fez-Fos" if the title of the novel you want is *For Whom the Bell Tolls*. What does take some thought, however, is tracking down *all* the material in the library that pertains to your subject, for this is not always evident from a first quick look under the obvious main headings. Here again you must be aware of various subheadings under which relevant works may be listed. Some subheadings are indicated on the main entry card itself as illustrated on page 384 (e.g. Education—U.S.—Hist.) For further information you can refer to these subject cards. In addition to being ingenious about subheadings, you must be imaginative and knowledgeable enough about your subject to figure out alternate designations. If it is "cinema techniques" you want to know about, for example, then surely you should think of turning to "Motion Pictures," "Film," or perhaps "Movies." By referring to *Subject Headings . . . of the Library of Congress*, a large volume owned by most libraries and installed near the card catalogue, you will get an idea of the variety of cross-references possible for most subjects.

One of the main limitations of the card catalogue is that it generally includes only the main subject matter of a book, not all the subjects discussed in the book. Thus, as one librarian-author reminds us, "a book on North American Indians might contain a very useful discussion of wampum, but few card catalogues would have a subject card for this book indexed under wampum."[7] What to do, then, to tap resource material *within* books themselves?

> There are a number of other guides to a library's contents which you should learn to use. For example, you may find that your reference librarian has his own card catalogue, developed out of his own experience. That is, he will have carded for his own use the best sources of information on many different subjects. These may include subjects which are important but about which few or no special books have been

[7] Robert W. Murphy, *How and Where to Look It Up* (New York: McGraw-Hill Book Company), p. 33.

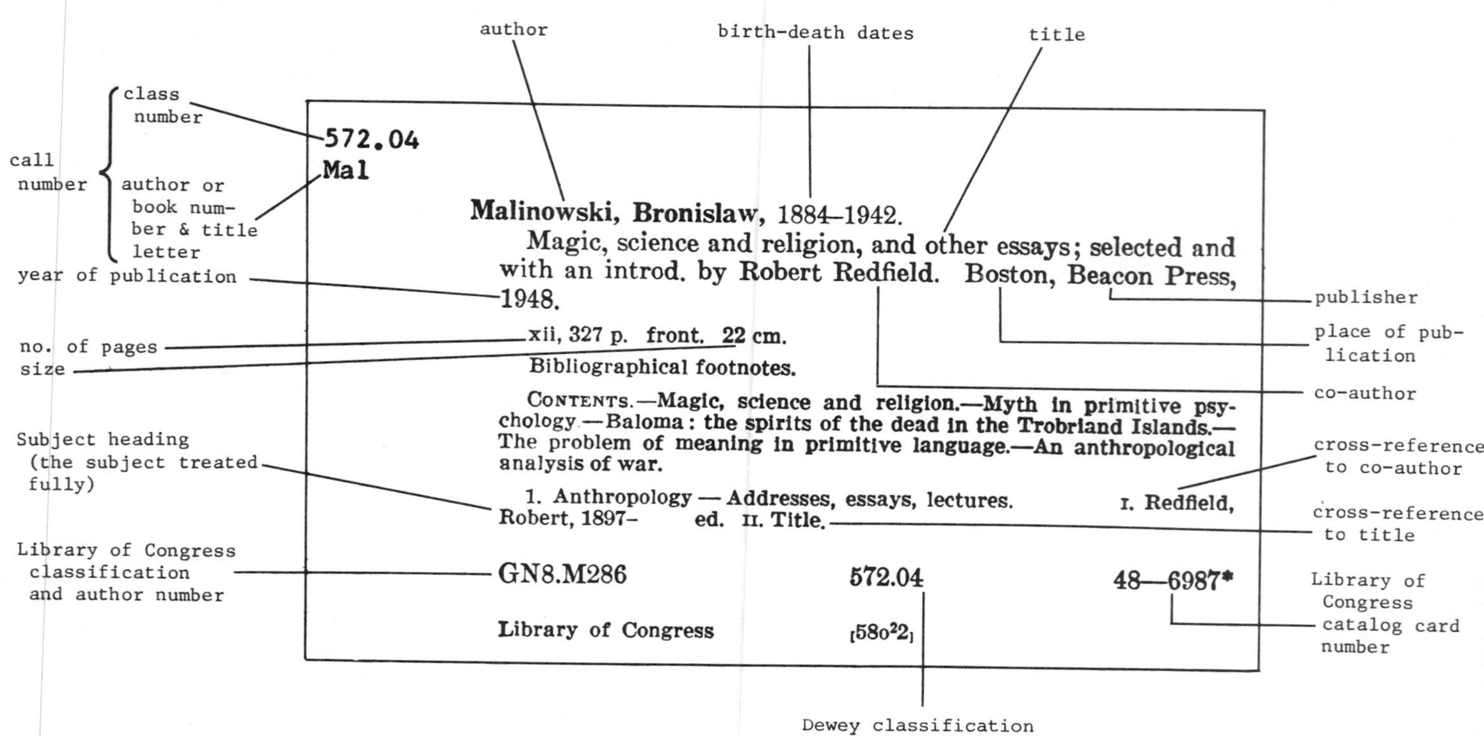
572.04
Mal

Malinowski, Bronislaw, 1884–1942.
Magic, science and religion, and other essays; selected and with an introd. by Robert Redfield. Boston, Beacon Press, 1948.
xii, 327 p. front. 22 cm.
Bibliographical footnotes.
CONTENTS.—Magic, science and religion.—Myth in primitive psychology.—Baloma: the spirits of the dead in the Trobriand Islands.—The problem of meaning in primitive language.—An anthropological analysis of war.
1. Anthropology — Addresses, essays, lectures. I. Redfield, Robert, 1897– ed. II. Title.
GN8.M286 572.04 48—6987*
Library of Congress [58o2]

> written. Through his years of answering people's queries he has found sources containing the needed information, and he has carded these sources. Most librarians will be glad to let you use their special card files.
>
> In addition, . . . most special collections in libraries have their own card catalogues, both complementing and supplementing the main catalogue. In a number of such catalogues the index of subjects is considerably more detailed than it is in the main library catalogue.[8]

Helpful as it is to become aware of special catalogues, the student researcher should concentrate on the regular catalogue, especially that single main entry card that generally provides him with enough information to decide whether or not a book is worth fetching from the stacks. *Note date of publication:* Maybe the work is too old to be useful. *Note author:* Is he known to you? Is he reputable? Is his book likely to be a trustworthy treatment of the subject? *Note publisher:* Is it a reputable press or a fly-by-night, pay-for-it-yourself "vanity" press that publishes *anything?* *Note number of pages:* Maybe the book is too long or too short for your purposes. *Note the exact wording of the title and subtitle:* Maybe the tone of the book is all wrong.

Final Note: Having become acquainted—on your own—with the main resources of the library, you need not feel guilty about addressing difficult questions directly to the reference librarian in charge, whose job is to guide the researcher in areas where he cannot guide himself. Indeed reference librarians are themselves repositories of vast information concerning the resources of the particular library in which they work and of the resources to be found in the local area as well as the nation at large. When necessary, they can help the researcher obtain materials through interlibrary loan, or, if this is not possible, they may suggest alternate materials. Do not hesitate, then, to consult the reference librarian when you are in need, but try to conduct your research independently up to that point.

Gathering Information for Short Papers

The weekly, biweekly, or semiweekly writing assignment that usually runs from 500 to 1,000 words often requires library research. Let us take an average 500–750 word paper (two to three pages) and call it a "short" paper. It is different from a "long" paper mainly because its scope is limited to one aspect of a subject.

Information for this average writing assignment can be gathered in approximately three to four hours of library research, with an equal amount of time allowed for writing the paper and revising. Thus the average writing assignment requires from six to eight or nine hours of total effort. Since virtually all writing assignments have a deadline, they are thereby self-limiting: what needs to be done, in other words, becomes a function of what *can* be done within the prescribed time. It is well to keep this in mind, for it puts the paper in perspective and helps the student-writer to make a realistic assessment of how much he can hope to cover and what he can accomplish. (Even a work of art, as someone once noted, is "never finished, but abandoned.")

[8] Ibid.

Let us consider how you might go about gathering information for four possible topics, each an answer to a specific question: [9]

1. How Does X Compare to Y?

   Title: The Peace Corps—Then and Now

   LIST OF POSSIBLE SOURCES:

   Encyclopedia Americana

   Government Publications
   (See "Federal Depository" in school library, which contain recent reports, pamphlets, bulletin, programs, etc.)
   Public Affairs Information Service Bulletin (PAIS)
   New York Times Index
   Readers' Guide

2. What Is the Present Status of X?

   Title: A New View of the Soul [10]

   LIST OF POSSIBLE SOURCES:

   Encyclopedia of Philosophy (1967)
   The Dictionary of Religious Terms (1967)
   Encyclopedia of Religion and Ethics (1908–27)
   The New Schaff-Herzog Encyclopedia of Religious Knowledge (1951)
   Handbook of Denominations in the United States (1965)
   Religious and Theological Abstracts (1958–date)

3. How Is X Made or Done?

   Title: How Man Makes Snow

   LIST OF POSSIBLE SOURCES:

   Science News Yearbook (annual)
   Encyclopædia Britannica
   McGraw-Hill Encyclopedia of Science and Technology
   (see supplementary yearbooks)
   or
   Van Nostrand's Scientific Encyclopedia (1968)
   Weather and Climate (1958)
   Applied Science and Technology Index
   Readers' Guide

4. What Case Can Be Made For or Against X?

   Title: The Case Against Multiple Choice Tests

[9] Not all references listed need be consulted in each instance; sometimes one or two provide sufficient information. Although it is obvious, it might also be mentioned that in most cases you should also look into the card catalogue under appropriate headings. Although you may not have time to read a whole book on a subject, you may find separate chapters directly pertinent to your purpose.

[10] This topic could be treated briefly (see Bertrand Russell, "On the Status of the Soul?" pp. 160–62) or it could easily be extended into a long piece dealing with different concepts of the soul at different periods in history or among different religions. See *Handbook of Denominations in the United States* and encyclopedias and dictionaries of the various religions.

LIST OF POSSIBLE SOURCES:

Encyclopedia of Educational Research
Mental Measurements Yearbook
Psychological Abstracts
Education Index
Readers' Guide
See card catalogue under "Educational Tests," "Testing," etc.

Gathering Information for Long Papers

The long papers cited in Chapter 21, "The Long Paper"—"What Is Pain?" "The Assassination of Lincoln," "The Duchess of Newcastle," and "Whither the Black Odyssey?"—were written only after the writers had spent not merely three or four hours but perhaps thirty or forty hours in the library. The student writing a term paper may not be able to devote that much time to this assignment, but he should plan on at least fifteen to twenty hours of research for a paper that will run between three and five thousand words. It is impossible, of course, to set exact specifications; the demands of the subject vary, as does the background information of the writer. Suffice it to say that these figures are roughly indicative of the investment that must be made in a paper of any substance and scope.

Following is a list of possible sources for term paper topics suggested in Chapter 21. They will give an indication of the extent of research necessary for a typical term paper.

Term Paper 1: An Extended Definition

Title: What Is Fear?

1. For definition of key term "fear":

   Webster's Third
   A Compound Dictionary of Psychological and Psychoanalytic Terms (1958)
   Oxford English Dictionary

2. Background information:

   Dictionary of Psychology (1964)
   Encyclopedia of Mental Health (1965)
   International Encyclopedia of the Social Sciences (includes subjects related to psychology)
   (Sources of this type generally provide informal bibliographies.)

3. Guides and formal bibliographies:

   The ABC Guide to Recent Publications in the Social and Behavioral Sciences (American Behavioral Scientist)
   The Harvard List of Books in Psychology. 3rd ed. Cambridge, Mass.: Harvard University Press, 1964.
   Subject Guide to Books in Print (See under "Psychology" and possible subheading, "Fear.")

4. Periodical indexes and abstracts

   Psychological Index
   Psychological Abstracts
   Social Sciences and Humanities Index
   (These indexes will lead to authoritative articles in professional journals such as the *American Journal of Psychology, Journal of General Psychology, Psychological Review,* etc.)

Readers' Guide (for articles in national magazines)
Ulrich's International Periodicals Directory (for reference to a wider range of periodicals)

5. Card catalogue
   Check under "Psychology" and "Fear"
6. Government publications
7. Pamphlets

Term Paper 2: A Description-Narration

Title: The Assassination of Malcolm X
(Since this topic is of relatively recent occurrence [1965], the researcher will need to use recent references.)

1. Biographical sources
   Current Biography
   Who Was Who in America
   Biography Index
2. Newspaper and magazine accounts
   New York Times Index
   Readers' Guide
3. Essays and commentaries in journals, anthologies, etc.
   Essay and General Literature Index
   Social Science and Humanities Index
   America: History and Life: A Guide to Periodical Literature
4. Card catalogue
   See under Malcolm X: Biography, Bibliography.
5. Miscellaneous pamphlets
   Negro Year Book
   Encyclopedia of Islam

Term Paper 3: An Extended Characterization

Title: Robert Schumann: The Triumph and Tragedy

1. Encyclopedias and dictionaries
   Harvard Dictionary of Music (1956)
   Grove's Dictionary of Music and Musicians (1954, with supplement, 1969)
   Encyclopedia of Concert Music (1959)
   The International Cyclopedia of Music and Musicians (1964)
   (These references contain bibliographies.)
2. Biographical dictionaries and guides
   Baker's Biographical Dictionary of Musicians (1965)
   Great Composers, A Biographical and Critical Guide (1966)
3. Bibliographies and indexes
   Music Reference and Research Materials: An Annotated Bibliography (1967)
   Music Index
   Social Sciences and Humanities Index
   See also *Subject Guide to Books in Print*

4. Card catalogue
   Check for individual biographies

Term Paper 4: An Extended Argument

Title: Whither the Black Odyssey? A Reply

1. General background survey

   Encyclopedia Americana

2. Guides and handbooks

   The Negro in the United States: A Research Guide (1965)
   The American Negro Reference Book (1966)
   The Negro Almanac (1970)

3. Card catalogue: see under:

   Negroes and/or blacks
   Negroes. History
   Negroes. Bibliography
      Under this last heading you are likely to find such pertinent materials as the following:
      Work: A Bibliography of the Negro in Africa and America (1928)
      Bibliography of Negro History (1963)
      The Negro in the United States: A Selected Bibliography (1970)

4. Indexes

   Index to Periodical Articles by and about Negroes, 1950–date.
   Public Affairs Information Service
   America: History and Life
   New York Times Index
   Readers' Guide
   Psychological Abstracts
   Sociological Abstracts

5. Miscellaneous

   Government Publications
   Pamphlets
   Negro Yearbook

Note-Taking

The importance of familiarizing oneself with the library's major reference tools cannot be overstated; but it must be admitted at the same time that the vast resources of the Library of Congress itself will be of little use to the student who does not know how to extract from them the information he needs in order to develop his particular topic into a sound and informative paper. To do this he must know how to take good notes, for they are obviously the foundation on which the paper itself will be constructed. When the time comes to sit down and write the paper—when a certain point must be made, or certain data provided—the student who has taken good notes will simply thumb through them and there the needed information will be, ready to take its rightful place in the total piece. *The writing process is a lot easier when the writer has taken accurate, ample, and well-organized notes.* When he has not, he is in serious trouble, for without good notes it is impossible to write a good research paper, just as it is impossible to build a strong and attractive building if the individual bricks are not themselves strong and attractive.

It is worthwhile, then, to devote special attention to note-taking, a skill closely related to writing in that the good note-taker does not mindlessly copy a paragraph of text, word for word. On the contrary, he actively *thinks* about what he reads and tries to figure out exactly what it means and how it may contribute to his topic. Only after he has figured out its possible usefulness to his purpose is he ready to put pencil to pad—preferably a small 3 x 5 or 5 x 8 pad (or cards) where he can enter separate points on separate pages, thereby saving himself the trouble later on of leafing through the dense, cluttered, and unclassified materials of a notebook.

Each note should be written in the researcher's own words (unless the passage deserves to be quoted verbatim) and carefully labeled (in the upper right-hand corner of the page, or wherever the writer chooses—according to the special category of information that it deals with). Thus a note card or page may read as follows: [11]

Card 1

Poe / Early Years

The only major American writer of his time to spend part of childhood at school in England. Apparently healthy: a good athlete; boxer; represented his school at racing competition; story often told of how he could swim up to six miles, against the tide and under a hot June sun. Also a top student with a "keen disciplined mind." Yet as reminiscences from school-mates indicate, he was "not popular in the usual sense of the word." (p. 84)

Quinn's EAP, pp. 65-85

[11] Note that in each case the writer uses a short-hand method of citation. The full citation for each of these would be included on a 3 x 5 bibliography card.

Quinn, Arthur Hobson. Edgar Allen Poe, A Critical Biography. New York: Appleton-Century-Crofts, 1941.

Chivers' Life of Poe. Ed. Richard Beale Davis. New York: E. P. Dutton & Co., 1952.

Poe, Edgar Allen. "The Philosophy of Composition," Graham's Magazine (Apr. 1846), rpt. in James A. Harrison, ed., The Complete Works of Edgar Allen Poe. Vol. XIV. New York: AMS Press, Inc., 1965, pp. 193-208.

Card 2

```
                                   Poe / Personal Appearance

Neat and tidy, nervous in manner.  Slender and dark:  "His hair
was dark as a raven's wing.  So was his beard--which he always
kept shaved." (p. 53)  Broad forehead; long slender neck which
"made him appear, when sitting, rather taller than he really
was." (p. 54)  Slender arms and hands, gracefully tapered:  "In
fact, his hands were truly remarkable for their roseate softness
and lily-like, feminine delicacy." (p. 56)  Oval face, violet
eyes with long lashes, strong chin, even white teeth:  "really
handsome...especially when he smiled." (p. 57)  Strange smile:
"...there was this peculiarity about his smile...it did not
appear to be the result of gladness of heart altogether...but
...of that apollonian disdain which seemed to say, what you
'see through a glass darkly, I behold through the couched eyes
of an illuminated Seer.'"

                          - Chivers' Life of Poe, pp. 53-58
```

Card 3

```
                                   Poe / Theory of Poetry

Poe saw "Beauty" as the proper province of the poem and
"Sadness" as the proper tone:
                 Beauty of whatever kind, in its supreme
                 development, invariably excites the
                 sensitive soul to tears.  Melancholy
                 is thus the most legitimate of all the
                 poetical tones.

                               Philos. of Comp., p. 198
```

By classifying his notes as he goes along the researcher is actually creating order out of the chaos of materials that confront him; without this preliminary organizing he would probably be overcome by the incredible bulk of sheer verbiage. He cannot take it *all* down; he does not need it all. He only needs what relates to his topic and presumably he has made at least a tentative decision about his topic and its main headings. His notes will pick up these headings then; perhaps even break them down into smaller subheadings (e.g., Poe/Early Years/ Relationship with mother), so that he can later arrange like page headings into separate groupings (an early years group subdivided into "relationship with parents," "school," "early influences"; a "theory of poetry" group; a "marriage" group; a "drinking problem" group; a "financial reverses" group). When notes are organized in this way, it is relatively easy for the writer to see the total paper taking shape, even before he has begun writing. He can also judge his materials more easily: see where he has enough information (on Poe's theory of poetry, let us say) and where there are confusing "gaps" (Was Poe a dipsomaniac or a drunkard? Is there a difference between the two?). Thus it becomes possible, simply by examining a particular grouping of notes, to see that in one area more information is needed, whereas in other areas the research is apparently complete.

The conscientious note-taker will, as mentioned earlier, probably end up with more notes than he actually uses, but if he has been reasonably selective along the way, he will not pile up an unscalable mountain of information.

Beyond what has already been said about being a thoughtful rather than a passive note-taker, there are a few principles of note-taking that should be mentioned:

1. Avoid taking notes to soon—during the preliminary background reading period in encyclopedias, for example. You may want to get down certain basic facts, figures, and dates about your subject, but beyond this it is generally best to hold your pencil until you have the overall feel of your subject. More specialized references, which you will turn to later, will probably provide more timely and profound information; *then* you will want to begin note-taking in earnest, but not before.
2. Read reference materials at different rates and levels of intensity, depending on how promising they seem. It may be necessary to merely skim page after page of a book, without taking a single note; then you may come upon a section or a separate article so relevant and reliable that you must pause two or three times per page to take notes.
3. Just as you deal with different types of references, so you must take different types of notes: you may simply record relevant facts or ideas, summarizing them in your own words (p. 390); another type of note may be a direct word-for-word copy of a quotation you would like to use; still another may include not only the data gleaned from reading, but your own comment on it: your own responses and observations as they strike you during your reading. It is wise to jot these down immediately, while the thought is with you; it is also wise to set off your own remarks in brackets, or in some other way, so that you can distinguish later what your authority said and what you said.
4. In general, try to compress and summarize information that you take down from a reference source so that later, when you are ready to use this information, you will have no alternative but to fill out the idea in your own words. This reduces the possibility of inadvertent plagiarism (see the next section, "Avoiding Plagiarism").
5. Very important: the first time you use a new source, make out a complete citation slip on which you enter *all* the documentary information you will need for footnotes and bibliography (Davidson, Edward H. *Poe: A Critical Study*. Cambridge, Mass.: Harvard University Press, 1957). Having done this, you need not repeat all the information about the work on each page of notes; in fact, some simple code like "Davidson, p. 8" or "David., p. 8" or "David./8" or even "D/8" is sufficient—so long as you understand your own abbreviations. (Some people devise such cryptic codes that they themselves later forget what they stand for.)
6. Finally, a suggestion that may seem trivial but is actually important: never take notes on both sides of the paper. Unfailingly, when you are at the writing stage, looking for a specific point of information, it will be on the *other* side of whatever side of the page you are looking

at—where you cannot find it! To avoid a frustrating shuffle back-and-forth from one side of a sheet to another, then, write on one and only one side of a note page.

Avoiding Plagiarism

Plagiarism is an ugly practice which most students try to avoid, but may inadvertently commit if they are not aware of what plagiarism *is*. There should be no uncertainties on this score, however, for the offense is serious. Indeed plagiarism is literally a crime, a form of theft in which one person steals the words of another—in ignorance, perhaps, of the fact that "phraseology, like land and money, can be individual personal property, protected by law."[12] Plagiarism can also involve ideas: a writer can steal someone else's ideas, put them into his own words, and say they are his. But they are *not* his and courtesy as well as honesty requires that this fact be acknowledged with a simple phrase such as "according to":

> *According to Northrop Frye*, the writer's ability to shape life into a literary form comes not from life but from previous contact with literature. This point is made in Frye's essay "Nature and Homer."

Even if it seems to you, after having read it, that you could have thought of that idea yourself, remember that you *did not*—and that you therefore owe a credit line to Mr. Frye, whether you have used his exact words or not. You have borrowed his idea. The conscientious writer is always on guard against violations of this kind. He will be aware, for instance, that it was not anybody-at-all or nobody-in-particular, but *specifically* H. L. Mencken who maintained that "no quackery has ever been given up by the American people until they have had a worse quackery to take its place." This observation, with its fine cynical edge, is passed along by Gilbert Seldes, in *The Stammering Century*, a history of quacks and cultists in nineteenth-century America. Seldes credits Mencken with the statement even though it is not a direct quotation and Seldes is not even certain whether Mencken made the remark in print or in private conversation.

Another subtle and often unwitting form of plagiarism involves *slightly changing* someone else's statement (substituting a different word here and there, shifting phrases, inverting clauses) and then presenting the passage as one's own. Here again it is important to recognize that this is not permissible. A paraphrase in your own language and style still deserves to be credited.

Most students realize, as mentioned above, that they must use quotation marks when an exact sentence or two is picked up, but they may not realize that this holds true even for a simple phrase, in fact even for a single word: if that word is significant, it should be placed in quotes. It was the critic, Gilbert Murray, for example, who wrote an essay called "Literature and Revelation." Anyone following Murray in this, i.e., anyone treating literature as "revelation" and introducing the term as such into his writing—with all the richness of meaning that accompanies it—should credit Murray: "An-

[12] Craig B. Williams and Allan H. Stevenson, *A Research Manual* (New York: Harper & Row, 1963), p. 126.

other way to view literature, as Gilbert Murray has pointed out, is as "revelation." (A footnote should indicate precisely in what article Murray said this.)

It is possible, of course, for a writer to arrive independently at an idea such as Murray's. "I just thought up that idea myself," a student might say. "I wrote about literature as revelation because that's the way I saw it. I don't even know who Gilbert Murray is." The point to be made here is that the student *should* know; he should know who has written on his chosen subject before he did; he should have read Murray's essay as part of a routine check of the literature in the *Essay and General Literature Index* or one of the literary bibliographies listed according to topic. For after all it stands to reason: very few ideas are totally original. The honest and conscientious writer—student and professional alike—realizes this and therefore always begins a piece of writing by searching the literature to see what has already been said on his projected subject. By conducting this preliminary search of the literature, he gains two advantages: he stimulates his own thinking and possibly learns something new; he also finds out what has already been written. Knowing this, he will not naïvely present as new and original an idea that is, in fact, old and familiar (as many seemingly fresh ideas turn out to be). This does not mean that no one can write about literature as revelation because Murray has already done so. It *does* mean that anyone writing on the subject should know what Murray said at an earlier date, and go on from there.

To summarize: credit should be given in the following instances—either in a footnote or in the body of text:

1. When you have directly quoted someone else
2. When you have used someone else's ideas or opinions (unless they are common knowledge)
3. When you have used someone else's examples
4. When you cite statistics or other facts gathered by someone else
5. When you present evidence or testimony taken from someone else's argument

Footnotes and Bibliography

Footnotes and bibliographies provide the writer with a set procedure for crediting his sources, telling the reader exactly where he has obtained information relating to his subject. In order to simplify and standardize the process of documentation, writers generally use one of two established forms, that set forth in the University of Chicago's *A Manual of Style* or that in *The MLA* (Modern Language Association) *Style Sheet.* These two do not differ radically from one another, nor is one better than the other. The writer simply chooses the one that serves his purpose better (writers in the sciences tend toward the University of Chicago style, those in the humanities toward the MLA). The student should decide which one he wants to use (or is required to use) and use it consistently throughout.

The undergraduate writer need not concern himself with the intricacies of footnoting but simply learn the basic forms he will need to document his term papers. The following section should provide adequate guidance.

Footnotes

As mentioned above ("Avoiding Plagiarism," pp. 393–94), all information taken from a source, whether it is summarized, paraphrased, or quoted, should be documented in a footnote. Footnotes should be numbered consecutively throughout the paper and be placed at the bottom of the page on which the reference occurs or in a list at the end of the paper. (The instructor will probably indicate his preference in this matter.)

Footnotes are also used for explanations and additional comments that the author wishes to include but that he feels would interrupt the flow and continuity of thought in his text. (See p. 495 for an example of an informational footnote.) The writer is free to develop his own style for this kind of footnote.

Documentary footnotes should include the following information, listed in the order cited.

BOOKS

Author's or authors' names in normal order

Title of book underlined (If reference is to a particular section of a book, as in footnote 8 below, it precedes the book title and is enclosed in quotation marks.)

Editor's or translator's name in normal order (See exception in footnote 6 below.)

Edition used if several have been published

Series name if any

Place, publisher, and date of publication

Volume number in Roman numerals

Page number or numbers (If a volume number precedes a page number, the abbreviations "p." or "pp." are not used.)

ENCYCLOPEDIAS

Author's or authors' names in normal order (If the author is identified.)

Title of article exactly as it appears in the encyclopedia

Name of encyclopedia underlined

Latest copyright date

Volume number in Roman numerals

Page number or numbers without "p." or "pp."

PERIODICALS

Author's or authors' names in normal order

Title of article in quotation marks (If no author is specified, this item comes first.)

Name of periodical underlined

Volume number in Arabic numbers (See exception in footnote 2 below.)

Date of issue in parentheses (See exception in footnote 2 below.)

Page number or numbers without "p." or "pp." (If the volume number is not cited, "p." or "pp." precede the page number.)

For the conventions of punctuation in footnotes see the examples below.

Examples of the most common types of documentary footnotes are cited below. Their form is based on *The MLA Style Sheet.*

SAMPLE FOOTNOTES—FIRST REFERENCES

BOOKS

[1] Kenneth B. Clark, *Dark Ghetto: Dilemmas of Social Power* (New York: Harper & Row, 1965), p. 14.
[one author]

[2] George Eaton Simpson and J. Milton Yinger, *Racial and Cultural Minorities: An Analysis of Prejudice and Discrimination,* 3rd ed. (New York: Harper & Row, 1965), p. 345.
[two authors; book that has gone through several editions]

[3] Emmette S. Redford et al., *Politics and Government in the United States,* 2nd ed. (New York: Harcourt Brace Jovanovich, 1968), p. 385.
[four or more authors]

[4] Bertolt Brecht, *Collected Plays,* ed. Ralph Manheim and John Willett (New York: Pantheon, 1970), I, 63.
[edited work; work in more than one volume]

[5] Carl Sandburg, *Abraham Lincoln, The War Years* (New York: Harcourt Brace Jovanovich, 1939), II, 95.
[work in more than one volume]

[6] Brooks Atkinson, ed., *The Sean O'Casey Reader: Plays, Autobiographies, Opinions* (New York: St. Martin's Press, 1968), p. 797.
[another way to handle an edited work]

[7] André Boucourechliev, *Schumann,* trans. Arthur Boyars, Evergreen Profile Book 2 (New York: Grove Press, 1959), p. 47.
[translation; book in a series]

[8] Linda Harrison, "On Cultural Nationalism," in *The Black Panthers Speak,* ed. Philip S. Foner (Philadelphia: J. B. Lippincott & Co., 1970), p. 151.
[article in an edited collection]

Encyclopedias

[1] "Schumann, Robert Alexander," *Encyclopædia Britannica,* 1971, XIX, 1188.
[unsigned article; title is given as it appears in the encyclopedia]

[2] Daniel Gregory Mason, "Robert Schumann," *The International Cyclopedia of Music and Musicians* (New York: Dodd, Mead & Co., 1958), p. 1684.
[signed article]

MAGAZINES

[1] Joseph Stanley-Brown, "My Friend Garfield," *American Heritage,* 22 (Aug. 1971), 52.
[signed article]

[2] "Pity the Poor Porpoise," *Newsweek,* 6 Sept. 1971, p. 60.
[unsigned article; weekly magazine]

Note: *The MLA Style Sheet* suggests abbreviating the titles of periodicals such as *PMLA* (*Publications of the Modern Language Association*). Your instructor will tell you whether such abbreviations are desirable or acceptable in your paper.

NEWSPAPERS

[1] Russell Baker, "A Timid Question," *New York Times,* 31 Aug. 1971, p. 33.
[signed article]

[2] *New York Times,* 31 Aug. 1971, p. 18.
[unsigned article]

Government Bulletins

[1] *The Foreign Assistance Program: Annual Report to the Congress for Fiscal Year 1970* (Washington, D.C.: Government Printing Office, 1971), p. 22.

[2] *Preserving Our Air Resources,* New York State Department of Health, 1968, p. 10.

SAMPLE FOOTNOTES–SECOND REFERENCES

Second or later references should be as brief as is consistent with clarity. Following are some acceptable forms for these references. (The second references follow the order of the first references above, but second references are not given for all the works cited under First References.)

BOOKS

[1] Clark, p. 15.
[only one book by Clark is referred to in the paper]

[2] Ibid.
[reference is to the same page of the same book cited just above]

[3] Ibid., p. 22.
[reference is to the same book just cited above but to a different page]

[4] Clark, *Dark Ghetto,* p. 15.
[two or more books by Kenneth B. Clark are referred to in the paper; therefore it is necessary to use a short title to distinguish between them–the use of the short title is now preferred to the old and elusive op. cit.]

[5] Kenneth B. Clark, p. 22.
[another author named Clark is referred to in the paper; therefore it is necessary to distinguish between the two names]

[6] Simpson and Yinger, p. 346.

[7] Redford et al., p. 386.

[8] Brecht, p. 65.

[9] Sandburg, p. 96.

[10] Sandburg, III, 86.
[a different volume of Sandburg is being cited]

Encyclopedias

[1] "Schumann, Robert Alexander," p. 1189.

[2] "Schumann, Robert Alexander," *Encyclopædia Britannica,* p. 1189.
[repetition of the name of the encyclopedia is necessary if an article with the identical title from another encyclopedia is used]

MAGAZINES

[1] Stanley-Brown, p. 53.

[2] Stanley-Brown, "My Friend Garfield," p. 53.
[repetition of the title is necessary if more than one article by Stanley-Brown is referred to]

[3] "Pity the Poor Porpoise," p. 60.

NEWSPAPERS

[1] Baker, p. 33.

[2] *New York Times,* p. 18.
[if more than one issue of the *New York Times* is referred to it would be necessary to repeat the date as in the first sentence]

GOVERNMENT BULLETINS

[1] *The Foreign Assistance Program,* p. 23.

[2] *Preserving Our Air Resources,* p. 9.

Bibliographies

The form of bibliographies is the same as that for footnotes with the following exceptions:

1. The name of the author (or of the first author if there are more than one) is given last name first (Brown, Frank). Entries in a bibliography are listed in alphabetical order by author. Frequently a bibliography is subdivided into "Books Consulted," "Periodicals," "Encyclopedias," etc.
2. If the work is in more than one volume, the number of volumes is given.
3. No page references are given for books, but full page references are given for articles in periodicals and encyclopedias.
4. A bibliography may be titled simply "Bibliography" or if the writer prefers "List of Works Consulted," "Sources," etc. (See p. 362 for an example.)

The following bibliographic entries cover most of the common usages:

BOOKS

Atkinson, Brooks, ed. *The Sean O'Casey Reader: Plays, Autobiographies, Opinions.* New York: St. Martin's Press, 1968.

Boucourechliev, André. *Schumann.* Trans. Arthur Boyars. New York: Grove Press, 1959. (Evergreen Profile Book 2)

Brecht, Bertolt. *Collected Plays.* Ed. Ralph Manheim and John Willett. Vol. I. New York: Pantheon, 1970.

Clark, Kenneth B. *Dark Ghetto: Dilemmas of Social Power.* New York: Harper & Row, 1965.

Harrison, Linda. "On Cultural Nationalism." *The Black Panthers Speak.* Ed. Philip S. Foner. Philadelphia: J. B. Lippincott & Co., 1970.

Redford, Emmette S. et al. *Politics and Government in the United States.* 2nd ed. New York: Harcourt Brace Jovanovich, 1968.

Sandburg, Carl. *Abraham Lincoln, The War Years.* 4 vols. New York: Harcourt Brace Jovanovich, 1939.

Simpson, George Eaton, and J. Milton Yinger. *Racial and Cultural Minorities: An Analysis of Prejudice and Discrimination.* 3rd ed. New York: Harper & Row, 1965.

ENCYCLOPEDIAS

Mason, Daniel Gregory. "Robert Schumann." *The International Cyclopedia of Music and Musicians.* New York: Dodd, Mead & Co., 1958, pp. 1683–87.

"Schumann, Robert Alexander." *Encyclopædia Britannica,* 1971.

MAGAZINES

"Pity the Poor Porpoise." *Newsweek,* 6 Sept. 1971, p. 60.

Stanley-Brown, Joseph. "My Friend Garfield," *American Heritage,* 22 (Aug. 1971), 49–53, 100–01.

NEWSPAPERS

Baker, Russell. "A Timid Question." *New York Times,* 31 Aug. 1971, p. 33.

New York Times, 31 Aug. 1971, p. 18.

Government Bulletins

The Foreign Assistance Program: Annual Report to the Congress for Fiscal Year 1970. Washington, D.C.: Government Printing Office, 1971.

Preserving Our Air Resources. New York State Department of Health, 1968.

ASSIGNMENTS

I. Preparing Bibliographies

A. Prepare a bibliography of general references you would consult in order to write a short essay (500–750 words) on one of the following topics:

1. Why the Taj Mahal Was Built
2. A Brief History of the Alligator
3. Four Types of American Prisons
4. Carrie Nation: A Character Study
5. The Facts About Smoking
6. The Function of Hormones
7. The Present Status of Pop Art
8. What Is Propaganda?
9. The Poverty Program: Then and Now
10. A Critical Estimate of Edward Albee

B. Prepare a bibliography of eight to twelve reference works you would consult in preparation for writing a term paper on one of the following:

1. The Case Against Capital Punishment
2. A Critical Estimate of Tennessee Williams
3. Hiroshima in Retrospect (an analysis and evaluation of causes and consequences)
4. The Lincoln and Kennedy Assassinations: A Comparative Study

II. Take notes on the following essays. Treat them as if they were source materials for a paper you are writing on a related subject:

1. John C. Pallester, "Grasshoppers" (p. 52)
2. David Randolph, "Five Basic Elements of Music" (pp. 66–67)
3. John Kord Lagemann, "How to Get More Work Done" (pp. 88–89)
4. W. H. Auden, "The Function of a Critic" (pp. 102–03)
5. George Stade, "Football—The Game of Aggression" (pp. 168–70
6. Oliver LaFarge, "The American Indian: Truth and Falsehoods" (pp. 185–86)
7. Ronald Hilton, "Ten Commandments for the New Behavioral Scientist" (pp. 266–68)
8. W. K. Livingston, "What Is Pain?" (pp. 330–37)
9. Virginia Woolf, "The Duchess of Newcastle" (pp. 346–51)
10. James M. O'Kane, "Whither the Black Odyssey?" (pp. 352–63)

23 ORGANIZING THE PAPER

Having found his topic and gathered sufficient information (invention), the writer faces his next and in some ways most bedeviling challenge, *how to handle his materials:* how to sort, select, and classify categories of information; how to isolate main points and weave in supporting details; how to determine what should go where—and why. This second stage of the writing process is referred to in classical rhetoric as "disposition" or "arrangement"—the organization of the whole into an orderly sequence of parts. Whether he does it on paper in carefully worked-out detail or only roughly in his head, the writer must plan his paper so that it will flow smoothly and logically from one point to another, moving steadily in its intended direction.

Natural Order

Earlier in examining the questions that generate topics, we noted that some kinds of writing are, in a sense, self-organizing. A simple analysis, for example, breaks a subject down into its component parts or types that are then—quite naturally—listed in the form of a series (one, two, three, four, and so on). Similarly, an analysis of a process (how something is done or made) is inevitably organized chronologically (first this, then this, then this). A description is usually arranged in terms of space (left to right, north to south), and narration naturally organizes itself in terms of time (sequence, flash-back, and so on). In such cases the materials determine, if not dictate, how they should be developed. The writer need only recognize the imperatives of his topic and fulfill them; the piece organizes itself.

Logical Order

This is not always the case, however. In constructing a comparison, for example (Chapter 10, "How Does X Compare to Y?"), the writer must make a conscious decision about its structure: Should he compare the totalities X and Y (comparison of wholes)? Should he break them down and systematically examine elements of each (comparison of parts)? Should he compare likenesses and differences (comparison of parts)? The choice is open and the decision rests on the logical determinations of the writer: Which ordering principle will best promote his purpose by exhibiting his points in their clearest and sharpest light?

Similarly in the organization of "The Changing Patriotism" (pp. 162–64) Loudon Wainwright has clearly imposed a logical order on his materials, one that evolved as he contemplated the question, "What is the present status of patriotism?" This main question led to subordinate questions such as "What was patriotism like in the past?" "How do people today respond to patriotic speeches and celebrations like the Fourth of July?" "What is the effect of dissent?" "What is their significance?" These and many other questions are raised during the course of this essay, all of them organized—roughly—under three main headings.

Structure of "A Changing Patriotism"

Introduction

Hillside: the "tribal ritual" of patriotism described

I. What is patriotism today? question raised by July 4, 1967 celebration)
   A. Speaker refers to Vietnam
   B. Author approves of reference
   C. It sets him wondering

II. Old-style patriotism is waning
   A. People are divided
   B. Simple calls to patriotism backfire
   C. "Flag-wavers" heighten dissent (by pressing issue)
      1. Legislature acted hysterically about flag-desecrators
      2. Johnson's speech to Jaycees was demagogic

III. We have today a new-style patriotism (a broader conception)
   A. Dissenters are loyal
   B. "Cussers and doubters" are part of American tradition

Conclusion

Hillside: we should commemorate those who inspired the tribal ritual of patriotism (the signers of the Declaration of Independence)—the "cussers and doubters" of their day

In this essay, as in most exposition and all argumentation, the ordering of parts is purely logical. The writer works out his own pattern of ideas—establishing causal connections, making inferences, drawing conclusions. If the reasoning process is sound, then the essay will seem as inevitably ordered as the steps of a natural process.

The Working Outline

A practical approach to organization is expressed in such reminders as E. B. White's, "Before beginning to compose something, gauge the nature and extent of the enterprise and work from a suitable design." White's reasoning is simple and convincing:

> Design informs even the simplest structure whether of brick-and-steel or of prose. You raise a pup tent from one sort of vision, a cathedral from another. This does not mean that you must sit with a blueprint always in front of you, merely that you had best anticipate what you are getting into.[1]

Journalist John Gunther also believed in anticipating "what you are getting into." Before he had set down a single page of his voluminous *Inside Asia,* he projected thirty-five chapters; he ended up with thirty-six. "It is always a good thing," he suggested, "to have a firm structure in mind."

This is helpful advice, and it should be followed as closely as possible, for without a structure or goal in mind, the writer resembles the harried gentleman who jumped on his horse and rode off in all directions.

Humor aside, let us face a deeper, more sobering truth about organization: it is not accomplished—as some people think—with a strict outline that captures once-and-for-all the shape of the final paper. "One's plan is one thing," said Henry James, "and one's result another." For invention is an ongoing process, as mentioned earlier. It spills over into the research stage and the organizing and writing stages as well. The writer continues to make discoveries. Writing itself is discovery, and the outline, to cite James again, is but "the early bloom of one's good faith." One must allow for, indeed expect, later blooms as well. In this sense the outline should be viewed not as a permanent form but as a working guide, pointing the way in a given direction, but amenable to change when the writer happens on new and better possibilities.

Keeping this in mind, let us see how we may draw up an outline for a representative term paper topic—perhaps an extended analysis of hypnosis (Assignment II, Chapter 21, "The Long Paper," pp. 337–38) that will include information on function, present status, and value. Whether the paper is to be 2,000 or 10,000 words, certain inevitable categories will suggest themselves:

1. definition (What constitutes the hypnotic state?)
2. history (The phenomenon of hypnosis as observed through the centuries)
3. hypnotic technique
4. hypnotic behavior
5. uses of hypnotism (medicine, dentistry, psychotherapy)
6. abuses and dangers of hypnotism (unqualified hypnotists)
7. autohypnosis
8. individual susceptibility to hypnosis
9. recent experimental evidence
10. posthypnotic suggestion

[1] William Strunk and E. B. White, *The Elements of Style* (New York: The Macmillan Co., 1959), p. 57.

11. misconceptions about hypnosis
12. current scientific opinion of hypnosis

Certainly these twelve categories will be useful during the note-taking stage when the writer groups his information under specific headings. Later on, however, when he organizes his material, he will undoubtedly find twelve categories unwieldy and overlapping, not a workable ground plan for his piece. Thus he will have to condense the categories into three or four main headings into which he will list various subheadings. Thus the working outline may look something like this:

Tentative Title: "What Is Hypnotism? or The Continuing Mystery of Hypnosis"

Introduction: a general statement about hypnotism, a subject that has intrigued and mystified men for centuries, and that still remains largely "in the shadows" despite the probings of modern science

I. What hypnotism is (brief description of psychological and physiological state)

II. History
    A. Ancient observations, superstitions, etc.
    B. Eighteenth and nineteenth centuries: beginning of scientific study (Mesmer, Charcot)

III. Hypnotism today: what we know
    A. The hypnotic trance
        1. How induced
            a. Classical techniques (gazing at fixed object, etc.)
            b. Drugs (sodium pentathol, etc.)
            c. Autohypnosis
        2. How subject reacts
    (cite examples)
            a. Hypnotic anaesthesia (insensitivity to pain)
            b. Hallucinations
            c. Age regression
            d. Unusual muscular strength and rigidity
            e. Organic effects (blisters, etc.)
            f. Social behavior
        3. Posthypnotic suggestions
    B. Hypnotic "subjects'
        1. Variations in individual susceptibility
        2. Variations in how "far" people go under hypnosis
            a. Antisocial acts (crime, etc.)
            b. Destructive acts
    C. Uses of hypnotism
        1. Medicine

(*weave in evidence from recent scientific studies*)

2. Dentistry
3. Psychotherapy

(*cite examples*)

D. Abuses and possible dangers

(*weave in stories to illustrate*)

1. Hypnotism as "entertainment"
2. Unqualified hypnotists (unable to awaken subject, etc.)

Conclusion: summary of significance of hypnotism; speculation on possible future applications

A working outline not only helps to channel ideas as you write, but also to check beforehand on their logical progression. Does section three logically follow section two, or should the order be reversed? Should part of the introduction be transferred to the conclusion? Is the first part of the middle section too long in comparison to the second part? And so on. By studying the outline carefully, much as an architect studies his blueprint, you can see whether the structure is likely to hold together: whether the parts are clearly and consistently related and whether they are soundly and strategically developed, each in its due and proper proportion. By checking and improving a paper in the outline stage you can save yourself hours of reworking and rewriting later on.

Intuitive Order

There is still another method of organizing a piece of writing—by intuition, i.e., according to an internal "voice" and rhythm that dictates how a subject is to be treated. What should be said first, second, third? What is the proper point of view, the appropriate tone, the right words. The structure of such a piece follows the contours of the writer's musings, which may have their own natural logic. Similarly the mood is established not by any premeditated plan, but simply by following feelings and setting them down as they are felt—with no conscious organization. Approached in this way, as critic Herbert Read tells us, an essay is an informal "attempt at the expression of an idea or a mood or feeling lurking unexpressed in the mind . . . an attempt to create a pattern in words which shall correspond with the idea, mood or feeling." [2]

Read tells us further that this process is comparable to musical improvisation; it is also "the counterpart of the lyric in poetry." Thus we have such pieces—free and spontaneous—as Logan Pearsall Smith's "Trivia," or J. B. Priestley's "On a Mouth-Organ." Obviously it is the writer's intimate relationship to his subject and his desire to explore with the reader an essentially "inner experience" that make an intuitive ordering of materials not only appropriate but inevitable. For in such cases, as in the writing of a poem, it is in the act of writing itself that the writer discovers what he wants to say.

It should be added here that only certain subjects and certain informal forms lend themselves to this approach; a term paper, for example, would *not* fall into this category.

[2] Herbert Read, *Modern Prose Style* (Boston: Beacon Press, 1952), p. 66.

Getting Started

Many students complain that getting started is the most difficult job in writing. One way to overcome the difficulty is to plan an opening for the paper, since this section is least likely to come naturally. It is an important section, however, for it is the place where the attention of the reader must be captured. A provocative introduction that arouses curiosity or establishes the importance of the subject will encourage him to read on into the body of the piece. Provided it is not a mere trick to entice the reader—provided it creates an honest and appropriate expectation of what will follow—a provocative introduction may be viewed as a valid and valuable rhetorical device.

There are many types of introductions. Note that each of the examples cited below prepares the reader for the piece by raising a central issue, making a meaningful observation, creating a mood, or defining a key term.

1. A quotation or meaningful allusion:

"I have traveled a good deal in Concord," said the stationary pilgrim Henry Thoreau. Today his descendants move from country to country instead, some seeking wisdom, some seeking academic credit, some only fun. Indeed, a latter day Children's Crusade is upon us. No crusaders are sold into slavery, but nobody can say whether any will reach Jerusalem.

Hans Rosenhaupt, "The New Children's Crusade, or Going to Jerusalem on a Grant"

William Congreve's opinion that hell has no fury like a woman scorned can fairly be expanded by the alteration of a word. For "woman" read "author"; the cries of exasperation from aggrieved writers come shrieking down the centuries.

Ivor Brown, "Critics and Creators"

Pascal once remarked that the entire face of the world was changed by the shape of Cleopatra's nose. Almost two thousand years later the entire face of history was nearly changed by the shape of another nose. In the fall of 1831 the twenty-two-year-old divinity student, Charles Darwin, was about to sail as an unpaid naturalist on his Majesty's ship, the *Beagle*. But Captain Fitzroy, who commanded the *Beagle*, hesitated to take Darwin along because he judged, from the shape of Darwin's nose, that the young man had "neither the mentality nor the energy" to become a good scientist.

Henry Thomas and Dana Lee Thomas, "Charles Robert Darwin"

2. A short narration:

Nine days before his death Immanuel Kant was visited by his physician. Old, ill and nearly blind, he rose from his chair and stood trembling with weakness and muttering unintelligible words. Finally his faithful companion realized that he would not sit down again until the visitor had taken a seat. This he did, and Kant then permitted himself to be helped to his chair and, after having regained some of his strength, said "Das Gefühl für Humanität hat mich noch nicht verlassen"—"The sense of humanity has not yet left me." The two men were moved almost to tears. For, though the word *Humanität* had come, in the eighteenth century, to mean little more than politeness or civility, it had, for Kant, a much deeper significance, which the circumstances of the moment served to emphasize: man's proud and tragic consciousness of self-approved and self-imposed principles, contrasting with his utter subjection to illness, decay and all that is implied in the word "mortality."

Historically the word *humanitas* has had two clearly distinguishable meanings. . . .[3]

Erwin Panofsky, "The History of Art as a Humanistic Discipline"

A young medical student at Pisa was kneeling in the Cathedral. There was silence over the vast auditory save for the annoying rattle of a chain. A sacristan had just filled a hanging oil lamp and had carelessly left it swinging in the air. The tick-tack of the swinging chain interrupted the student's prayer and started him upon a train of thought that was far removed from his devotions.

Suddenly he jumped to his feet, to the amazement of the other worshipers. A flash of light had descended upon him in the rhythm of the swinging lamp. It seemed to him that this rhythm was regular, and that the pendulum of the rattling chain was taking exactly the same time in each of its oscillations although the distance of these oscillations was constantly becoming less and less.

Was this evidence of his senses correct? If so, he had hit upon a miracle. He must rush home and find out immediately whether he had suffered an illusion or discovered one of the great truths of nature.

When he arrived home, he hunted up two threads of the same length and attached them to two pieces of lead of the same weight. He then tied the other ends of the threads to separate nails and was ready for his experiment. He asked his godfather, Muzio Tedaldi, to help him in this experiment. "I want you to count the motions of one of the threads while I count the motions of the other."

The old man shrugged his shoulders. "Another of Galileo's crazy ideas," he mumbled to himself. But he agreed to help.

Galileo took the two pendulums, drew one of them to a distance of two hands' breadth from the perpendicular, and then let them go simultaneously. The two men counted the oscillations of the two threads, and then compared notes. The total was exactly the same—one hundred counts in each case. The two threads, in spite of the great difference in their starting points, had arrived at the same point at the same time.

And thus, in the swinging motion of the cathedral oil lamp, Galileo had discovered the rhythmic principle of nature which today is applied in the counting of the human pulse, the measurement of time on the clock, the eclipses of the sun and the movement of the stars.[4]

Henry Thomas and Dana Lee Thomas, "Galileo Galilei"

[3] From *Meaning in the Visual Arts* by Erwin Panofsky. Copyright © 1955 by Erwin Panofsky. Reprinted by permission of Doubleday and Company, Inc.

[4] From *Living Biographies of Great Scientists* by Henry Thomas and Dana Lee Thomas. Copyright 1941 by Doubleday & Company, Inc. Reprinted by permission of the publishers.

3. A provocative question, observation, or line of dialogue:

The attitude of some citizens is like that of a mother who said to her son, "Why do you want to be a physicist, John? Isn't there enough trouble in the world already?"

Joel H. Hildebrand, "The Care and Feeding of Creative Young Minds"

"Now tell me," said the lady, "all about yourself."

J. B. Priestley, "All About Ourselves"

4. A definition of a key term:

"Alienation," a term once confined to philosophy, law, psychiatry and advanced literary criticism, has entered the daily vocabulary. Newspaper editorials refer without quotes or elucidation to the alienation of the slum dweller, the drug addict, the vanguard painter; popular fiction writers rely on readers to recognize the symptoms of alienation as a motive for adultery or murder. Alienage, or strangeness, is understood to be not only a condition (as of foreigners) but a process. As they say in the health drives, it can happen to anyone.

Harold Rosenberg, "It Can Happen to Anyone"

5. A striking contrast:

Not often in the story of mankind does a man arrive on earth who is both steel and velvet, who is as hard as rock and soft as drifting fog, who holds in his heart and mind the paradox of terrible storm and peace unspeakable and perfect.

Here and there across centuries come reports of men alleged to have these contrasts. And the incomparable Abraham Lincoln, born 150 years ago this day, is an approach if not a perfect realization of this character.

Carl Sandburg, "Lincoln, Man of Steel and Velvet"

6. A direct statement:

Where the reader may be assumed to have interest in the subject—some knowledge—the writer may announce his purpose directly, with no preparation or build up:

The film "Hiroshima, Mon Amour," which is getting a good deal of attention in this country, deserves to be viewed—and reviewed—from a number of perspectives. But I have noticed that reviewers have all tended *not* to explore its moral substance, what the vernacular would call its "message." This is remarkable when a film's message is expressed as urgently as this one's is, and even more remarkable when it is expressed with success *cinematically,* when it is perfectly fused with a web of images and sounds. Here is a film that contradicts the widely-held assumption that messages and good esthetics are incompatible.

Amitai Etzioni, "Hiroshima in America"

It might well dismay the intelligent reader to be informed at the outset that the years 1600–60 were an age of transition. But while every period in history deserves, and doubtless has received, that illuminating label, there are some periods in which disruptive and creative forces reach maturity and combine to speed up the normal process of change. In the history of England, as in that of Europe at large, the seventeenth century is probably the most conspicuous modern example, unless we except our own age, of such acceleration.

Douglas Bush, "The Background of the Age"

Critics permit themselves, for this or that purpose, to identify literature with great books, with imaginative writing, with expressiveness in writing, with the non-referential and non-pragmatic, with beauty in language, with order, with myth, with structured and formed discourse—the list of definitions is nearly endless—with verbal play, with uses of language that stress the medium itself, with the expression of an age, with dogma, with the *cri de coeur,* with neurosis. Now of course literature is itself and not another thing, to paraphrase Bishop Butler; yet analogies and classifications have merit. For a short space let us think of literature as sentences.

Richard Ohmann, "Literature as Sentences"

Ending the Paper

At one point in her adventures in Wonderland, Alice is advised to "begin at the beginning, keep going until you get to the end, and then stop." In some cases it is possible for the writer to do exactly the same thing: to stop when he has finished saying what he wants to say. His piece (this is especially applicable to a short paper) ends where his last thought ends, creating its own sense of completeness and finality. In other cases, however (usually in a long paper), a formal conclusion of some kind is needed: a recapitulation of the main points; a heightened restatement of the thesis or argument (what the ancients called a "peroration"); a summing-up quotation; a reference to an idea or event mentioned earlier (as in the cyclic return to the hillside in "A Changing Patriotism"). Any one of these devices (and there are many other suitable equivalents) signals to the reader that the piece is coming to an end—*pay close attention; here are my final words on the subject.*

Unquestionably the end is an emphatic position, for the final words impress themselves more forcibly on the reader's mind than any others. Similarly the mood at the end of a piece strongly influences—if not determines—the reader's final feeling about what he has read.

Since there are no standard endings, the writer must depend on his own judgment in ending his paper. He must compose a conclusion that is appropriate to the subject and purpose of his piece. One helpful procedure is to set aside, at an early stage of research or writing, some information or a passage of quoted material that might serve as a concluding statement. This ending should not open up a whole new aspect of the subject (it is too late for that), nor should it raise additional questions that the writer cannot answer. Rather the ending should tie the paper together so that the reader experiences a sense of satisfaction, both rational (a unit of discourse has reached a logical conclusion) and emotional (the end *feels* like the end).

ASSIGNMENTS

I. Indicate (in outline form) the structure of the following essays:

Bruce Catton, "Grant and Lee" (pp. 148–51)
A. M. Rosenthal, "No News From Auschwitz" (pp. 164–66)
George Stade, "Football—the Game of Aggression" (pp. 168–70)
Allan H. Gilbert, "College Lectures Are Obsolete" (pp. 301–04)
W. K. Livingston, "What Is Pain?" (pp. 330–37)
Virginia Woolf, "The Duchess of Newcastle" (pp. 346–51)
James M. O'Kane, "Whither the Black Odyssey?" (pp. 352–63)

II. Evaluate the opening and closing paragraphs of the above essays. What special devices for opening and closing are used? Are they effective? Can you suggest alternate opening and closing paragraphs that would be equally, or perhaps even more, effective?

III PRINCIPLES OF STYLE: A GUIDE

24 THE LIMITS OF LANGUAGE

Language Is Removed from Reality

In his Second Meditation, the French philosopher René Descartes complained that "words often impede me." It is difficult to imagine what unutterable insights, what wordless thoughts (if such is possible) this most original of thinkers was contemplating when he made the paradoxical complaint—*words often impede me*—a complaint to be echoed a hundred years later in a great comic-tragic line by T. S. Eliot: "I gotta use words when I talk to you."

Yes, we all "gotta use words." Philosophers and scientists have demonstrated that without the ordering convention of words, we would be overwhelmed by what William James called the "booming, buzzing confusion" of real life—the world Out There where nothing stands still long enough to be named; where "Stately Nature" is in actual, measurable fact a dynamic ongoing process, and so-called "objects" are really "events" flowing into each other by insensible gradations. Our words are still-cameras that artificially freeze reality, making us believe that it conforms to the linear, cause-effect structure of our language. But it does not. Language is removed from reality and, in fact, imposes a pattern on reality that is essentially a distortion. Semanticist Alfred Korzybski vividly illustrates this point:

> If we take something, anything, let us say the object . . . called "pencil" and enquire what it represents . . . we find that the "scientific object" represents an "event," a mad dance of "electrons," which is different every instant, which never repeats itself, which is known to consist of extremely complex dynamic processes of very fine structure, acted upon by and reacting upon, the rest of the universe, inextricably connected with everything else and dependent on everything else. If we enquire *how many characteristics* we should ascribe to such an event, the only

> possible answer . . . is that we should ascribe to an event infinite numbers of characteristics . . .[1]

Clearly it is impossible to ascribe to an event an infinite number of characteristics: there is not enough time; there are not enough words. In order to cope with the world Out There, then (and the world within as well, for there is a "mad dance of 'electrons'" going on within as well as outside us), we must change it; we must somehow stop the world long enough to make contact with it and with each other. We must select and simplify—and this is precisely what we do—with the help, first of all, of our senses that compress time, mass, motion, light, and sound so that we are cut off from much of what is going on. What is, in reality, an incessant process, we see simply as an object. And we call that object by a name, thereby simplifying still further. These dancing atoms we designate "rock"; that vast mass of gases spinning in space we designate "star"—and so on. We name these things, in other words, as if they were fixed entities, unchanging from one moment to the next.

But obviously *the word is not the thing;* only a pale and distorted version of the thing. The thing itself is beyond our grasp to know or talk about. In addition to scientists, philosophers, and semanticists, poets and writers emphasize this point; for they too sense that in talking about the world—as opposed to directly experiencing it—we somehow shape it into something different;

> In the way you speak
> You arrange, the thing is posed
> What in nature merely grows.[2]
>
> Wallace Stevens, "The Idea of Order at Key West"

Similarly a character in a Virginia Woolf novel laments the artificial and deceptive tidiness that language imposes upon actual experience:

> [How] tired I am of phrases that come down beautifully with all their feet on the ground! Also, how I distrust neat designs of life that are drawn upon half sheets of notepaper. I begin to long for some little language such as lovers use, broken words, inarticulate words, like the shuffling of feet on the pavement.

Life is indeed more a shuffling on pavement than a neat landing with both feet solidly on the ground. Note that in indicating this truth, the writer has abandoned ordinary language in favor of metaphor, which, as we shall see later, is often more effective in describing certain kinds of insights and experiences than a direct statement:

> Words strain,
> Crack and sometimes break, under the burden,
> Under the tension, slip, slide, perish,
> Decay with imprecision. . . .[3]
>
> T. S. Eliot, "Burnt Norton" in *Four Quartets*

[1] Alfred Korzybski, *Science and Sanity,* 3rd ed. (Lakeville, Conn.: Institute of General Semantics, 1948), p. 387.

[2] Copyright 1936 and renewed 1964 by Holly Stevens Stephenson. Reprinted from *The Collected Poems of Wallace Stevens* by permission of Alfred A. Knopf, Inc.

[3] From *Four Quartets* by T. S. Eliot. Reprinted by permission of Harcourt Brace Jovanovich, Inc.

Words Are Generalizations

It is the nature of language, then, to both help and hinder us in our attempt to know the world. It helps by freezing the infinite, ongoing process of reality into fixed, finite objects. It also helps by enabling us to generalize about these objects, for, as we pointed out above, we could not have a name for every separate object in the world; every idea, every thought that passes through the mind of every man; every feeling, every sensation, every emotion, etc. To make our world intelligible, we must bunch things together into categories so that every word (with the exception of proper nouns) is a class word or generalization, representing not one particular idea, object, or person but a whole class of ideas, objects, or persons.

Thus verbs are class words; each one points to a class of actions characterized by certain features: "to jump" is to engage in an action marked by a propulsive leap from the ground, repeated in bobbing, bouncing up-and-down movements of the legs and entire body. All actions sharing these particular features are thereby classified, categorized, abstracted, and generalized in the verb "jump." Likewise, nouns name a cluster of qualities that "sum up" an object, for example, a *dog:* a furry, barking, four-legged, carnivorous mammal; domestic, etc. Every noun represents a list of qualities that, according to the abstracting process of our own minds, a group of objects have in common. Even function words like "and" and "to" perform a class function in that "and" joins together like grammatical elements and "to" indicates relationship.

Words, then, are simply "convenient capsules of thought" that tell us what the members of a class have in common ("house"); but do not tell us anything about the differences (how my house differs from yours and a dozen other houses on the street). As T. S. Eliot observed, "The particular has no language."

Here is a curious predicament indeed. Our most important means of communication is characterized by the most frustrating of limitations: its generalizing tendency is always drawing us away from the particular thing we want to say. To achieve particularity, we must actively and constantly counteract this inherent resistance of language; we must use all the devices against it that we can command, else we shall end up in realms of abstraction wherein no one knows exactly what anyone else is talking about. This happens all too often when we deal with abstract words such as the word "nature." It was once demonstrated that Western philosophers were using this word in no less than thirty-nine different senses and that it was on occasion being used two or three different ways on the same page. What, then, is meant by "nature"? Anyone using words at this level of abstraction should follow Cicero's counsel that every rational discourse begin with a definition.

We should also note here that this generalizing tendency of language has played into the hands of the prejudiced by enabling them to make sweeping statements and judgments about whole groups of people, treating them as if they were a single entity rather than an aggregate of individuals ("All Southerners are reactionary"). A group may be identified on the basis of race, religion, political affiliation, geographical location, nationality—whatever. The fallacy lies in not seeing that each member of a group—*any* group —is different from every other member, is indeed unique. Semanticist Alfred

Korzybski has suggested—as an exercise—that we remind ourselves of this fact by adding index numbers to our general nouns. Then we would see, he tells us, that cow_1 is not cow_2; $Italian_1$ is not $Italian_2$; Jew_1 is not Jew_2; $politician_1$ is not $politician_2$—and so on. Beyond such obvious and harmless generalizations, then, as "cows give milk" or "Jews are a minority group," we should avoid sweeping pronouncements.

Language Is Subjective

Another limit of language is that it is one of the most intensely subjective of media. No one can speak with total objectivity; there is no such thing as neutral language. The first person singular, whether or not it appears explicitly as "I," is implicit in every statement we make. Thus physicist P. W. Bridgeman observed:

> When I make a statement, even as cold and impersonal a statement as a proposition of Euclid, it is I that am making the statement, and the fact that it is I that am making the statement is part of the picture which is not to be discarded. And when I quote you it is I that am doing the quoting.[4]

"We never get away from ourselves," concludes Bridgeman. "The brain that tries to understand is itself part of the world that it is trying to understand." No wonder then that we never "transcend the human reference point." Words are always filtered through the mind and emotions of the person using them, so that he and he alone endows them with their special meaning for that situation; he has something "in mind." What is it? How can we find out? In a sense we cannot. Not totally. As the late news commentator Edward R. Murrow once remarked, "We are all prisoners of our own experience." During the lifetime each of us has spent with words we have related them in personal ways to our own experiences; we have made them our own. Consequently, no two people respond to the same word in precisely the same way.

At the sound of the word "car," for instance—to cite a relatively insignificant but typical example—you and I would immediately focus our attention on a four-wheeled vehicle—a "car." There is no special ambiguity in the term. Still, from the moment the word is pronounced, it might evoke an utterly different image in your mind and mine; an utterly different internal response. For you—let us say—are a racing fan. Thus the mere mention of "car" sets your pulse beating faster as you recall (all in a flash and perhaps not even consciously) moments of high adventure and excitement on the speedway . . . sleek racers whipping past like bullets . . . etc. To me, prone to car sickness, the same word "car" would instantly conjure up a touch of nausea.

In their classic study of semantics, *The Meaning of Meaning,* C. K. Ogden and I. A. Richards constructed a "triangle of meaning" to illustrate the subjectivity of language. Semanticist Bess Sondel later "animated" and commented upon the diagram as follows:

[4] P. W. Bridgeman, "The Way Things Are," in *The Limits of Language,* ed. Walker Gibson (New York: Hill and Wang, 1962), p. 42.

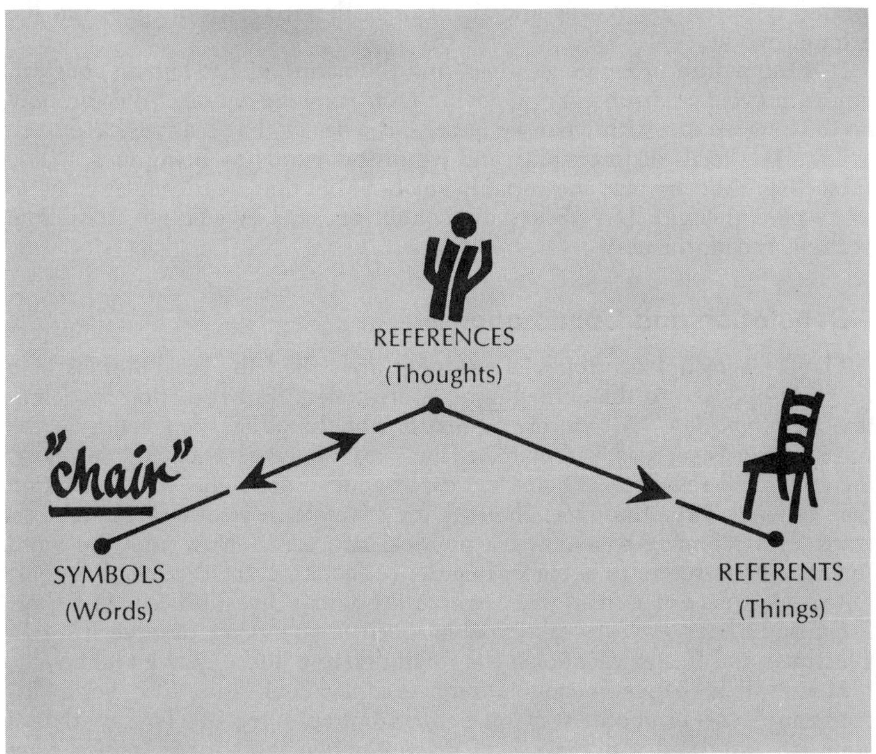

At the peak of the "triangle" is a human being. Here is either the user of words—the person who has selected the words—or the recipient of the words who must, from his perspective, entertain those words.

There is no base in this "triangle."
There is no direct relation between words and things.

Consider yourself at the peak of that "triangle." As you use the word "chair," if your thoughts and mine are directed to the same object out there in the world, then you and I come together—we communicate through the use of the word "chair." We "understand" each other.[5]

But let us say that your thoughts and mine are *not* directed toward the same object. As we have seen, words are so general they cannot automatically conjure up identical "referents" in different minds. Before they are referred outward to the real thing, words make a trip through the nervous system of a human being. Thus, as the triangle of meaning makes clear, the circuit of meaning is not completed until words are filtered through the mind of an individual. The thought, then, stands between the word and the thing, even as the animated fellow at the peak of the triangle is spatially

[5] Bess Sondel, *The Humanity of Words* (New York: World Publishing Co., 1958), pp. 48–49.

located between the Words and the Things they refer to out there in the external world.

It is the nature of language, then, and the nature of the human constitution to prevent us from ever achieving *total* communication. We can only do the best we can with what we have, and what we have, as we have seen, is flawed. Words distort reality and we distort words by being inescapably subjective. We are also inescapably emotional in that words never come to us as pure thought, but always as thought encased in emotion, sensation, attitude, mood, memory.

Denotation and Connotation

These associated overtones of meaning are called the *connotations* of a word, as opposed to the agreed-upon, more-or-less formal dictionary definition or *denotation.* All words, no matter how bloodless they seem on the surface—words such as "circular" or "flat"—are nonetheless capable of evoking emotional responses. Some words, of course, are richer in connotation than others. Take the word "house," for example, a relatively straightforward term referring to a place, a physical structure. Now take the word "home"; it too refers to a place, but the connotations of this word suggest the special place it is: the place where the family lives; where, as Robert Frost said, "they have to take you in—even if you don't deserve it." On Christmas and Easter vacations, you do not go to a house; you go home.

Many words change in connotation over a period of time. The word "discriminate," for example, was once an admirable term. To say that a man had taste and a fine sense of discrimination was to pay him a compliment. Today, however, it might suggest that the man was a bigot; he discriminates against minority groups. Similarly the word "propaganda" once suggested a reliable and trustworthy source of information; whereas now it implies slanting and deception. One may play semantic games by juggling with the connotations of words, as in Bertrand Russell's famous "I am firm; you are stubborn; he is pig-headed." Of course Russell was joking—but also making a point. All three terms have more-or-less the same *core* meaning (denotation); by cleverly manipulating the *overtone* of meaning (connotation), the user can shade his statement into a commendation or a criticism. Consider the following pairs of words, which once again have essentially the same denotation. But do they mean the same thing?

debate	dispute
relax	loaf
reflect	daydream
carefree	unconcerned
statesman	politician
sweet	saccharine
childlike	childish
antique	old-fashioned
slender	skinny
voluptuous	fat
restrained	repressed
chatting	yakking
intellectual	egghead

In most contexts the connotations of the words in the left column would be favorable, whereas those in the right would be less favorable. You can see how useful and dangerous a tool connotation can be in the hands of those who would like to misinform without really lying. To cite a small and relatively innocuous example from the mass media: during the 1940s a news magazine, openly Republican in policy, would refer repeatedly to Democratic President Truman's friends as "cronies" (suggesting backroom, poker-playing types). Later, when Republican President Eisenhower was in office, however, the magazine spoke solemnly and respectfully of the president's "long-time associates" (suggesting dignified colleagues in high political office).

One of the strangest, most tragic accounts of mistaken connotation comes out of the Second World War. It involves a reply reportedly received from the official news agency of Japan in response to the surrender ultimatum issued by the Allies at Potsdam. The reply contained the Japanese word *mokusatsu,* which the Domei agency translated into the English word "ignore," thereby implying that the Emperor's regime would not consider surrender under any circumstances. In truth, however, the word *mokusatsu* suggests that one is not flatly dismissing or *ignoring* but only "reserving an answer until a decision is reached." If this careless translation of *mokusatsu,* which failed to incorporate the special connotations of this word, did in fact "confirm America's resolve to drop the atomic bomb, the error may well have been the most costly linguistic blunder in human history." [6]

Extending the Limits

Conceding the limits of language represents a proper first step toward extending the limits, for in recognizing them we can begin counteracting them as well; we can begin making effective compensations. Aldous Huxley once noted that although no complete solution is possible for the problems posed by language, the alternative need not be despair (the either-or fallacy). We can approach a language problem, the ambiguity of words, for example, "armed with suitable equipment to deal with it." In this way ambiguous words may be "considerably clarified"; a more modest goal than absolute clarity, to be sure, but with this advantage—it is obtainable.

Aristotle said that "it is the mark of an educated man to look for precision in each class of things just so far as the nature of the subject admits." No better counsel could be adopted by the writer: that from the first he fight the generalizing tendency of language; that in all his writing he always be as precise as his subject permits. For as we have shown above, without precision there is no possibility of communication. Sometimes we *think* we are communicating because words are going back and forth. But this is no test of communication; people can and often do talk at cross-purposes, answering questions that have not been asked, attacking arguments that have not been proposed. In other words, people can and often do talk *at* each other, without realizing that they are not talking about the same thing, without even knowing precisely what they *are* talking about:

[6] Michael Girsdansky, *The Adventure of Language,* rev. and ed. Mario Pei (New York: Fawcett Publications, 1967), p. 88.

"The Heart sees farther than the Head," says Debater A.

"Oh, no," protests Debater B. "That's a blatantly Romantic notion."

"I don't think it's at all Romantic. It's an Experiential Truth that's been Demonstrated time and time again."

"I regard it as Immature and Dangerous. All Thought and Action should be Controlled by the Head."

Is there a real argument going on here? Who can tell? Who can even know what the debaters are talking about until they specify what they mean by such abstractions as "Romantic" (one of the most protean terms in all of literature, criticism, history, art, and popular usage). And what is an "Experiential Truth," as used in this context? In what sense "Dangerous?"

In "A Note on Methods of Analysis," Professor Herbert J. Muller warns us against discussions of this kind:

> The assertion that the Heart sees farther than the Head gets us nowhere, until we specify what kind of thing it sees better, under what circumstances, for what purposes—always remembering that heart and head see in conjunction, and are not engaged in a seeing contest.

The crucial test of communication, then, is not whether words are going back and forth, but whether ideas are being exchanged. Is there a "crossing-over" between one mind and another? A giving and receiving, not just a *giving* of information? For after all, communication is a circular and not a linear process. The case for precision cannot be made too emphatically—or too early. Thus it has been included here as one means of extending that most serious of all limits of language: its tendency to raise us to realms of abstraction where no one knows precisely what anyone else is talking about.

In *The Meaning of Meaning*, Ogden and Richards set up a "new science of symbolism" in which they rejected all general words that have no "concrete referent"—i.e., object, situation, or event that could be pointed to as the external "thing" for which the word stands. Such words ("faith," "loyalty," "beauty") are not real symbols, said Ogden and Richards, but only expressions of emotion, not appropriate or usable in a "language of fact."

> This distinction between symbolic and emotive language is not intended by these authors to depreciate emotive language. Emotive language is conceded by Ogden and Richards to have its usefulness in the communication process. It may be used, they say, to evoke desired attitudes in others or to incite others to action of one kind or another. But emotive language has no place in the new science of symbolism.
>
> Ogden and Richards are interested only in the correspondence of words and thoughts and things, and the language of science is set up as the exemplar of their theories. In the language of science, the words refer specifically and definitely and accurately to things, and this without the intrusion of the reporter's attitudes. A reporter doesn't say *It's hot today.* He says *The temperature is ninety degrees according to that thermometer.* The language of science is symbolic language at its best.[7]

[7] Sondel, p. 44.

Obviously Ogden and Richards set standards for a "language of fact" that the nonscientist may find overly rigid and restrictive (and that some scientists, like Bridgeman, quoted on p. 416, do not agree with). Even so, the expository writer, whose primary purpose is to inform and explain, should make careful note; for by observing rigorous standards of fact he will sharpen his prose. He will also develop the important habit of distrusting the lofty abstractions and sweeping generalizations that give the *sound* of meaning but not the substance.

Using Language to Deceive

To review briefly: we have seen that the nature of language plus our own natures as species Man are such that communication can never be more than approximate; we never deliver an idea directly (mind-to-mind) without contamination. Under the best of circumstances and with the best of intentions our words can constrain, constrict, and even distort meaning. Imagine, then, what happens when circumstances are *not* of the best and when intentions are *not* honest, when, on the contrary, a deliberate attempt is being made to deceive, i.e., to mislead and misinform.

This is the problem to which the professional semanticist addresses himself, for he recognizes that we use language not only to formulate our highest ideals and aspirations but also to justify our basest motives and our meanest behavior. Thus semanticists like Stuart Chase warn against "the tyranny of words": linguistic manipulations by advertisers, propagandists, demagogues, who try to control our behavior by stirring emotion rather than thought, thereby eliciting an uncritical conditioned response. In these cases language is being used for directive rather than communicative purposes; for words that convey absolutely no information may direct us, as by hypnosis, to vote for candidate A rather than B ("He's the one!"), or to buy a car that will make you "Feel like a Million" (Super-Duper-Hyper-Ultra-Extra-High-Power-Deluxe-Double-Bonus . . . etc.).

Developing Semantic Sophistication

Our only protection against manipulations of this kind is our own semantic sophistication: we must be able to see through verbal tricks; we must recognize that language lends itself to subtle misrepresentation and sinister manipulation. If we are not aware of this, we will surely be victimized by it. Note how the dictator in the following story has misused and abused language to promote his own dark purposes:

> A dictator rules a land. In the morning he orders that the able-bodied men of three villages be required to crush rock and construct roads of it. They are to work indefinitely and without pay. All other villagers, old men, all women and children, are lined up and machine-gunned. All of the villagers' goods are confiscated.
>
> In the evening the dictator speaks over the radio, telling of his morning's work. He says, "I have readjusted the population proportion in the north. I have arranged for the more rapid and efficient improve-

ment of our country's transportation system. I have arranged to have available a greater per capita supply of the basic necessities of life.

The populace cheers.[8]

Obviously, the populace does not know what it is cheering *for*. People think they have been given the facts, but in truth they have been grievously misled. They are both uninformed and misinformed.

In our reading and listening, then—as in our writing—we must develop semantic sophistication; we must test words against the rigorous standards of fact (referent). Unless we do we become symbol worshippers. It is easy to become a symbol worshipper because most of the time most of us do not and cannot adhere to the strict language of fact that scientists and semanticists recommend. Instead we may get so caught up in the connotations of a word that we refuse to accept a fact that does not concur with our feelings. Thus a young woman was heard to protest a news story about a lady who had murdered her child, maintaining that it was "impossible for a *Mother* to do such a thing!"

We can extend the semantic limits of language only by extending the limits of our own critical intelligence. We must not allow ourselves to be mesmerized by words. If we understand how language works and how it may be worked against us, then and only then can we hold our own against those who would deceive and mislead. The ultimate aim is to bring about a more intelligent use of language for human ends.

Writing Versus Speech

There remains but one aspect of language to touch upon: the special limits of writing (words on paper), as opposed to speech (words in the air). Both are language, of course, and both are therefore subject to the limits inherent in the medium itself and in ourselves. But writing deserves special attention, for it is a special way of using language that has its own obvious strengths (it endures, for one thing, while speech drifts off into empty space), and its own not-so-obvious, very serious limitations.

Writing is flat, one-dimensional. Try raising your voice on paper. Well, maybe you can manage that with upper case: LOOK, I'M RAISING MY VOICE. Very good. Now try raising your eyebrows. Ah, you are stuck! But surely you are familiar with this gesture; it is so expressive that it has become part of our language: to raise one's eyebrows is to be disapproving, skeptical—or something like that. It is impossible to translate into words the unstudied eloquence of that gesture—or other gestures like it: lowering one's eyes, closing them, lifting, narrowing, fluttering, rolling, winking. One can carry on an extended "conversation" with the eyes.

This is true of all the expressive features that supplement the spoken word: facial expressions (pursing the lips in stubborn defiance); body movements (a shrug of the shoulders); and most important, variations in the voice ("Is he *crazy?*" versus "Is *he* crazy!"). Loudness, stress, pitch, pause: all these expressive features, and many more, enter into every spoken sentence and impart to it a distinctive tone and point of view—all of which

[8] John Lord, *Experiments in Diction, Rhetoric Style* (New York: Holt, Rinehart and Winston, 1960), p. 61.

are absent on the written page where words stand alone, bearing the full brunt and burden of meaning.

Thus written English, an "artificial dialect of speech," as linguist Harold Whitehall called it, "must be so managed that it compensates for what it lacks." To begin with it must be more carefully organized than talk, for in discussing a subject orally, we may shift back and forth, digress, repeat ourselves, and even fall into contradiction. The other person is there to issue a direct challenge ("But you said earlier it was an ethical question, and now you're saying it's basically psychological"); or to ask a question ("I don't understand what you mean by 'diminishing returns.' Would you explain that term?"); or to pick up cues ("That half-smile on your face suggests that you are not completely serious. . . ."). The reader, sitting alone with his article or book, has no such opportunity to observe signs, or to ask for further information; nor does the writer have a second chance to clarify a point or to safeguard a meaning. What he has not made clear the first time, he will never make clear—and that is that!

Thus the writer must be more painstaking than the speaker. As Quintilian said centuries ago: the writer must aim not merely "at being possible to understand, but at being impossible to misunderstand." And this he must do in the absence of personality and without the assistance of gestures, tone of voice, timing. In truth, the writer can never make up for the many deficiencies of writing as compared to speaking; he can only make amends. Specifically he can try to anticipate the readers' questions and possible points of confusion; he can also organize his material carefully so that point follows point in reasonable, understandable, logical sequence.

Still a third consideration: the writer must be more concise and compressed than the speaker. A group of people can enjoy two or three hours of conversation, during which time tens of thousands of words pass back and forth; but few people would be willing to spend an equal number of hours reading an equivalent number of words on a subject, if their book did not provide substantially more information than their conversation. For the writer, then, economy is an imperative: *every word must tell.*

Of course writing has its advantages as well as its shortcomings. For the reader there is the opportunity to move slowly or rapidly—as he wishes, also to reread what he does not understand or would like to understand better. Reading is a private and in some ways more thoughtful activity than listening; certainly it provides an opportunity for greater concentration.

From the writer's point of view, too, there are obvious advantages to writing. There is the possibility of revision: what he does not say well in his first rough draft, the writer can improve in a later polishing; and the reader will never know the earlier, less successful effort. In conversation or impromptu speech, we think as we talk, talk as we think—at the rate of about 200 to 300 words a minute. The pace of writing can be adjusted to the needs of the writer. He can think, brood, rearrange, reclassify, rephrase, and delete as he goes along—a stuttering and stammering process that would be totally unacceptable in speech.

ASSIGNMENTS

I. Language and Reality:

A. It has been observed that nothing ever happens "again"; the word "again" is a verbal fiction. In a paragraph (150–200 words), explain why this is so, citing other verbal fictions in our language, indicated at the same time why most words distort reality.

B. Virginia Woolf distrusted language because, as she said, it draws neat designs of life on notepaper. In a short essay (150–250 words), explain what you think she means by this, comment on her metaphor, and indicate your own sense of how well or poorly language represents (re-presents) life.

II. The Generalizing Tendency of Language:

A. There are various ways to make language more precise: by quantifying (i.e., instead of saying it was a "large" crowd, say "about 2,000 people"); by exemplifying, illustrating, explaining, defining, describing. Using one of the opening sentences suggested below (all generalizations), write a paragraph (150–250 words) in which you provide specific referents for the general term or suggest specific applications to specific situations:

1. Lincoln claimed that all *progress* may be laid to *discontent.*
2. "A hungry man," said Montaigne, "would be very foolish to seek to provide himself with a fine garment, rather than a good meal: we must speed to what is *most urgent.*"
3. Balthasar Gracián once wrote that women are *realists* and men are *romanticists.*
4. The show was *wonderful.*
5. Everyone should *work.*
6. "*Pleasure*" is the main motive for human *action.*

B. Write two versions of a paragraph based on an activity (such as *eating, dancing, writing poetry*) or a concept (*loyalty, beauty, justice*). In version one, use as many general and emotive words as you wish; in version two, confine yourself exclusively to "the language of fact."

III. Demonstration:

To what extent are we "prisoners of our own experience"? Write a one-paragraph "response" to one or more of the following terms and compare your response with that of another student who has written on the same subject.

auto racing	a dog
divorce	hearing a sermon
falling in love	making a mistake
death	fighting a lost cause
writing a paper	wounded vanity
ballet	lying
reading poetry	apologizing
a second chance	parting
a salesman	dissent

IV. Connotations:

A. Consider the following words, all with good connotations. Cite for each a *bad* counterpart: a word that means approximately the same thing denotatively but *not* connotatively.

cautious	individualist
courageous	clever
retaliation	dissent
compromise	leader
liberty	cooperation
subtle	independent
chatting	intellectual
satisfied	patriotism
passion	reformer
discuss	nonconformist

B. After conducting a detailed study of dictionaries and *Roget's Thesaurus,* Ossie Davis, Negro author and actor, concluded that "the English language was his enemy."

> In *Roget's,* he counted 120 synonyms for "blackness," most of them with unpleasant connotations: blot, blotch, blight, smut, smudge, sully, begrime, soot, becloud, obscure, dingy, murky, threatening, frowning, foreboding, forbidden, sinister, baneful, dismal, evil, wicked, malignant, deadly, secretive, unclean, unwashed, foul, blacklist, black book, black-hearted, etc. Incorporated in the same listing were words such as Negro, nigger, and darky.
>
> In the same *Roget's,* Mr. Davis found 134 synonyms for the word "white," almost all of them with favorable connotations: purity, cleanness, bright, shining, fair, blonde, stainless, chaste, unblemished, unsullied, innocent, honorable, upright, just, straightforward, genuine, trustworthy, honesty, etc. "White" as a racial designation was, of course, included in this tally of desirable terms.
>
> No less invidious than black are some of the words associated with the color yellow: coward, conniver, baseness, fear, effeminacy, funk, soft, spiritless, poltroonery, pusillanimity, timidity, milksop, recreant, sneak, lily-livered, etc. Oriental people are included in the listing.[9]

Commenting on this report, Norman Cousins speaks of a language of "prejudice," which not only reflects the way we think about minorities in this country, but actually influences our thoughts:

> People in Western cultures do not realize the extent to which their racial attitudes have been conditioned since early childhood by the power of words to ennoble or condemn, augment or detract, glorify or demean. Negative language infects the subconscious of most Western people from the time they first learn to speak. Prejudice is not merely imparted or superimposed. It is metabolized in the bloodstream of society. What is needed is not so much a change in language as an awareness of the power of words to condition attitudes. If we can at

[9] From Norman Cousins, "The Environment of Language," *Saturday Review,* April 8, 1967. Copyright 1967 Saturday Review, Inc. Reprinted by permission.

least recognize the underpinnings of prejudice, we may be in a position to deal with the effects.[10]

Write an essay (500–750 words) in which you add your own observations on an alleged "language of prejudice," indicating also whether you agree or disagree with the idea that this language "infects the subconscious" of a nation and thereby promotes prejudice.

[10] From Norman Cousins, "The Environment of Language, *Saturday Review,* April 8, 1967. Copyright 1967 Saturday Review, Inc. Reprinted by permission.

25 CHOOSING WORDS

Despite the limitations of language (as discussed in the previous chapter), words are the writer's only tool, the basic "stuff" of his medium. It is not surprising then that the professional writer (by his own testimony) is forever preoccupied with and even obsessed by words, not simply their meaning but their sound, shape, texture, configuration, rhythm. Like strains of melody presenting themselves unbidden to the composer, words whirl about in the writer's mind, resound in his inner ear, impinge on his consciousness—as if they were palpable beings with lives of their own. Indeed, some writers even personify words, as the Mexican poet Octavio Paz has done in his observation that

> the easiest thing in the world is to break a word in two. At times the pieces continue to live with a frantic life, ferocious, monosyllabic. It's wonderful to throw that handful of newborns into the circus: they jump, they dance, they bound and rebound, they scream tirelessly, they raise their colored banners.

The ordinary person does not have this almost mystical affinity for words; he does not see them as "colored banners," but rather as conveyors of meaning. And properly so, for it is here that our concern should begin: with words that convey meaning most simply, clearly, and forcefully. Thus, as Lincoln said in his second Inaugural Address:

> With malice toward none, with charity for all, with firmness in the right as God gives us the right, let us strive on to finish the work we are in, to bind up the nation's wounds, to care for him who shall have borne

> the battle and for his widow and his orphan, to do all which may achieve and cherish a just and lasting peace among ourselves and with all nations.

Note the simplicity of the diction here; each word is *right* because it is appropriate not only to the speaker, but also to his subject and to the occasion for the address. There are no long, pretentious adjectives, no vague terms, no clichés, no fiery declamations. Indeed the inspired eloquence of the utterance—its absolute "rightness" and rhythm—can best be appreciated when we read a more formal but patently flat paraphrase:

> We want to terminate this conflict and have an equitable peace. We do not desire a vindictive peace but one that will restore the country to unity. We believe that we are right and are determined to gain the victory and have a fair peace. After the cessation of hostilities we must not forget to take care of the veterans and the dependents of those unfortunate killed or wounded in the struggle.

We cannot—on order or even on exhortation—increase our sensitivity to words or enlarge our word-stock. As we read and pay attention to words, as words assume a prominent place in our thinking ("In the beginning was the Word, . . ."), then and only then will the right word be available when it is needed, only then will the struggle for that word seem worthwhile. In the meantime, however, the writer can improve his writing by committing himself to certain broad categories of words: to the natural word, as opposed to the pretentious or trite; to the specific word as opposed to the ambiguous; to the exact word as opposed to the approximate. We shall consider each of these in turn.

The Natural Word

Bertrand Russell once advised the young writer never to use a long word if a short one will do. This somewhat sweeping dictum ignores those notable exceptions where a long word has a better sound or helps to establish a better rhythm in the sentence. Even so, the general principle has merit. Certainly we should avoid such pomposities as that reported of Dr. Johnson who, Boswell tells us, remarked casually, and naturally, of a comedy he had just seen that "It has not wit enough to keep it sweet." Disturbed by the simplicity of his statement, Dr. Johnson hastily amended it to "It has not vitality enough to preserve it from putrefacation."

We can forgive Dr. Johnson the lapse he viewed as a correction, for the sonorous, elevated style he used was acceptable in his time, or at least tolerated. Today, however, it is unthinkable, absurd. Modern prose style, as it has been evolving over the past fifty years, is straightforward and relaxed, designed to capture the rhythms of everyday speech, to serve the reader rather than to impress him, to talk to him rather than to pontificate. The modern prose stylist, as Bonamy Dobrée points out in *Modern Prose Style*, "is trying to be more honest with himself." He is aiming at a style "that will faithfully reflect [his] mind as it utters itself naturally."

In this sense, the unknown author of Ecclesiastes was writing in a modern vein when he composed the following famous verse:

> I returned, and saw under the sun, that the race is not to the swift, nor the battle to the strong, neither yet bread to the wise, nor yet riches to men of understanding, nor yet favour to men of skill; but time and chance happeneth to them all.

In his essay "Politics and the English Language" George Orwell praises this passage as an example of "good English"—simple, direct, concrete, smoothly flowing, harmonious, *natural.* By way of contrast Orwell offers a stiff, jargon-ridden variation, written by an imaginary but "typical" bad writer, a stylist of "the worst sort":

> Objective considerations of contemporary phenomena compel the conclusion that success or failure in competitive activities exhibits no tendency to be commensurate with innate capacity, but that a considerable element of the unpredictable must invariably be taken into account.

"This is a parody," Orwell admits, "but not a very gross one." He goes on to explain why Ecclesiastes is preferable:

> It will be seen that I have not made a full translation. The beginning and ending of the sentence follow the original meaning fairly closely, but in the middle the concrete illustrations—race, battle, bread—dissolve into the vague phrase "success or failure in competitive activities." This had to be so, because no modern writer of the kind I am discussing—no one capable of using phrases like "objective consideration of contemporary phenomena"—would ever tabulate his thoughts in that precise and detailed way. . . . Now analyse these two sentences a little more closely. The first contains forty-nine words but only sixty syllables, and all its words are those of everyday life. The second contains thirty-eight words of ninety syllables: eighteen of its words are from Latin roots, and one from Greek. The first sentence contains six vivid images, and only one phrase ("time and chance") that could be called vague. The second contains not a single fresh, arresting phrase, and in spite of its ninety syllables it gives only a shortened version of the meaning contained in the first.[1]

In an attempt to be "formal" and to seem properly "authoritative," many of us are trapped into writing stiff, dehumanized prose such as that which Orwell parodies. We must guard against it, repress any impulse to use a word such as "transpire," for example, when we simply mean "take place." We must also repress the tendency to write phrases like "objective consideration of contemporary phenomena" or "commensurate with innate capacity" or "considerable element of the unpredictable." One need only read these passages aloud and *listen* to them to know that they are hardly faithful reflections of "the mind as it utters itself naturally."

[1] George Orwell, *Shooting an Elephant and Other Essays* (New York: Harcourt Brace Jovanovich, 1945), pp. 84–85.

The Concrete Word

We have already discussed the generalizing tendency of language (see pp. 415–16), which leads us away from clear, unambiguous statement. We saw that one word like "nature," for example, may have as many as thirty-nine specific referents. In addition to raising semantic problems and even dangers, general and abstract terms cause rhetorical problems, for they create dense, lifeless prose lacking in precision and energy. We cannot avoid such prose altogether, for a certain amount of classifying of ideas and experiences is necessary to all discourse. Nonetheless, every time we choose a word we can make a determined effort to be as specific and concrete as the subject will allow. In his *Philosophy of Style,* Herbert Spencer suggests that we avoid sentences like the following: "In proportion as the manners, customs, and amusements of a nation are cruel and barbarous, the regulations of their penal code will be severe."

Instead, says Spencer, we should write a sentence like the following: "In proportion as men delight in battles, bull-fights, and combats of gladiators, will they punish by hanging, burning, and the rack."

The point to keep in mind is that the average person does not think in general or abstract terms but in concrete particulars. Thus when he encounters generalizations or abstractions, the reader tends to translate them into specific images of his own choosing, filling in what the writer has only suggested, rather than specified. The conscientious writer, of course, does not want his readers filling in his prose for him. Thus he writes in concrete images of *his* own choosing. It is no accident that in Antony's speech over Caesar's body, Shakespeare—who wanted to excite in his audience the utmost horror—has Antony talk in the most highly particularized language: "those honorable men [not who merely *killed* Caesar, but] whose *daggers* have *stabbed* Caesar." [2]

The following examples illustrate another way in which the general may be rendered more specific, the abstract more concrete, by adding details:

Example: My father and I argue about everything.
Improvement: My father and I argue about everything from politics and civil rights to the relationship between parents and children.

Example: She looked sensational.
Improvement: She looked sensational in her new purple knit pantssuit, long dangling earrings, and brown leather thong-sandals.

The Right Word

No one can use words with any exactness unless he is painstaking; the first word that comes to mind is not always the best one. Often a writer realizes this and tries to clarify his meaning by adding "that is to say," "in century rhetorician Hugh Blair observed, but he "never just hit[s] the

[2] Richard Whately, *Elements of Rhetoric* (Boston and Cambridge: James Munroe and Company, 1854), p. 322.

thing."[3] The precisely right word used in precisely the right place will "hit the thing"; it will say once-and-for-all what needs to be said—with no "nervous restatements."

It is difficult to discuss "right" words in the abstract, for they depend on specific writing situations. Some general principles, however, may be set down.

1. Make certain that the word you choose is literally correct and used idiomatically (i.e., in the customary way). In the following examples the writers have made nearly right but ultimately wrong choices:

Example:	Her selfishness is prevalent throughout the story.
Improvement:	Her selfishness is *evident*. . . .
Example:	There is a sadness that emits from the character's every action.
Improvement:	There is a sadness that *issues*. . . .
Example:	I banged my fist on the table, thereby instilling pain throughout my arm.
Improvement:	I banged my fist on the table, thereby *inflicting*. . . .
Example:	They are utterly ignorant to her fears.
Improvement:	They are utterly ignorant *of* her fears.
Example:	I found his poems unmeaningful.
Improvement:	I found his poems *meaningless*.
Example:	He became bitter when the job he was promised never happened.
Improvement:	. . . never *materialized*.
Example:	The fishing trip had a remedial effect on their spirits.
Improvement:	The fishing trip had a *restorative* effect. . . .

2. Choose a word that is appropriate in tone and level of usage (formal, informal, colloquial, slang). Although modern prose style tends to be informal and relaxed, the writer should not introduce words that are clearly out of place in the context of his piece. Certainly anyone with the slightest sensitivity to words and how they are used will recognize that the verb in the following sentence is ill-chosen.

Plato's dialogues stuff the student's mind with new ideas.

The verb "stuff" in this sentence clearly has the wrong tone and the wrong connotation. The hungry man may *stuff* his mouth with food and the camper may *stuff* his bag with equipment, but the reader of Plato does not have his mind *stuffed*.

Similarly in the following sentence there is an awkward combination of formal and somewhat stiff language with the plain and informal and the slangy and rather trite.

> One must remember that despite the multitudinous tasks that confront the average student, he must somehow get his work done; he cannot permit himself to goof-off, even for a day.

Today there are no fixed rules governing correctness; slang expressions and colloquialisms are often included in so-called formal writing. As the

[3] Hugh Blair, *Lectures on Rhetoric and Belles Lettres* (Brooklyn: Printed by Thomas Kirk, 1812), Lecture X.

National Council of Teachers of English announced in 1952, "All usage is relative." This is to say that the correct or best expression always depends on many factors: what is being said (a description of a soccer scrimmage or stoic philosophy); how it is said (written or spoken); to whom it is said and on what occasion (a bull session with a roommate or a presentation of a paper before a graduate seminar). Ultimately the writer must exercise his own taste and judgment; his sense of what is appropriate, acceptable, and comfortable in a given "ambience" (surrounding atmosphere or environment).

Two recent reference works may be consulted by writers who cannot make up their minds about a specific usage:

Margaret Nicholson, *A Dictionary of American-English Usage* (New York: Oxford University Press, 1957).

This American adaptation of H. W. Fowler's *Modern English Usage* strikes a sensible balance between strict purism and absolute permissiveness.

Margaret Bryant, *Current American Usage* (New York: Funk & Wagnalls, 1962).

A survey of 240 disputed points of usage, this book is readable and extremely helpful because it is based on how words are *in fact* being used today, rather than on how the author feels they *should* be used.

3. Choose a word that has suitable connotations. Your own sensitivity to words, and the care you exercise in selecting them must be your guide here.

Example:	In their simple-mindedness children are free of racial and religious prejudice.
Problem:	The word "simple-mindedness" suggests that children are ignorant, that they simply do not understand the complexities of the situation—and if they did, they too would be prejudiced!
Improvement:	In their *innocence* children are free of racial and religious prejudice. (The word "innocence" is preferable here because it suggests [as the writer wanted to suggest] purity and lack of contamination rather than stupidity.)
Example:	In his novels Faulkner lashes out against racial prejudice.
Problem:	The term "lashes out" implies violence and lack of control.
Improvement:	In his novels Faulkner *attacks* racial prejudice. (The word "attacks" does not carry the connotation of uncontrollable fury but rather of a more measured, thoughtful, and even *righteous* action against an opposing evil.)

4. Whenever possible choose the *single exact* word in place of a series of words.

Example:	He was introducing considerations that had nothing to do with the case.
Improvement:	He was introducing *extraneous* considerations.

Example: They cut themselves off from the main group.
Improvement: They *detached* themselves from the main group.
Example: There are many factors contributing to the deficiencies in my writing, the most outstanding one being my unwillingness to work.
Improvement: Many factors contribute to my writing deficiencies, most notably my *laziness*.

5. Avoid ill-sounding combinations of words. Although the good reader reads silently, he nonetheless "hears" in his inner ear the sounds of the words. Inadvertent rhymes and words that have the same sound but different meanings (homonyms) are distracting and should be avoided.

   Example: Another explanation of his motivation can be found in his observation that. . . .
   Problem: Too many *–tion* endings.
   Example: Those who lean toward leniency. . . .
   Problem: Awkward repetition of *lean* sound.
   Example: The sole purpose of his soul-shattering address was. . . .
   Problem: Homonyms.
   Example: It must be clear that the fear of the atmosphere. . . .
   Problem: Inadvertent rhyme.

6. Avoid awkward variations. "Repetition is bad," said Mark Twain, "but inexactness is worse." Guard against using an inexact or awkward variation of a word simply to avoid repetition.

   Example: Having considered Faulkner's vision, let us now go on to a consideration of the characters who exemplify the theory.
   Improvement: Repeat the word "vision" in place of "theory."

7. Avoid quaint and archaic terms. The writer cannot be nostalgic about language without jarring the reader.

   Example: We should treat the medium of writing with respect, nay with reverence.
   Improvement: We should treat the medium of writing with respect, *even* (or "as well as" or "indeed") reverence.

8. Avoid clichés.

   Example: It was a deep dark secret that I would not for the life of me have revealed to a soul; certainly not to any Tom, Dick, or Harry that happened by, like a ship passing in the night.

Clichés

A cliché may be defined as an expression that was once original and apt—a new and vivid metaphor, perhaps—but that acquired "an unfortunate popularity," and was used and used and used and used. The *Oxford English*

Dictionary calls the cliché "a stereotyped expression, a commonplace phrase." We might add to this definition the adjectives "trite," "hackneyed," "overworked," "worn out"—"a coin so battered by use as to be defaced."[4]

Clichés appear in many varieties.

> Some are foreign phrases (*coup de grâce; et tu, Brute*). Some are homely sayings or are based on proverbs ("You can't make an omelet without breaking eggs," *blissful ignorance*). Some are quotations ("To be or not to be, etc."; "Unwept, unhonored, and unsung"). Some are allusions to myth or history (*Gordian knot, Achilles' heel*). Some are alliterative or rhyming phrases (*first and foremost, high and dry*). Some are paradoxes (*in less than no time, conspicuous by its absence*). Some are legalisms (*null and void, each and every*). Some are playful euphemisms (*a fate worse than death, better half*). Some are figurative phrases (*leave no stone unturned, hit the nail on the head*). And some are almost meaningless small change (*in the last analysis, by the same token*).[5]

We cannot banish clichés altogether from our speech and writing; but they should be weeded out with patience and diligence before they destroy all possibility of meaningful discourse. For stock phrases are the enemy of thought; we repeat them mechanically without thinking about what we are saying. Thus the cliché can lead to a kind of mass No-Think.

Because the reader or listener participating in the No-Think of the cliché expects the language to proceed according to a set pattern, we can extract real humor by twisting or reversing the pattern and thereby defeating the set expectation. Thus wits have said, "She's as pure as the driven slush." "You pays your money and you takes your Joyce." "It is better to have loved and lost than never to have lost at all." "None but the brave desert the fair." "Bachelors never make the same mistake once." "Work is the curse of the drinking class."

Bergen Evans has said of these anticlichés that they are "golden transmutations of some of the world's dullest lead."

Figures of Speech

As discussed earlier (Chapter 24, "The Limits of Language") language is an abridgment of reality. There are not enough words in any one language or in the sum total of all languages to express the infinite variety of man's ideas, feelings, and experiences. Because we instinctively recognize this, we try to expand and strengthen our power of expression by creating new ways of saying what we mean, specifically through the use of "figures of speech"—saying one thing in terms of something else.

[4] George Baker cited in Eric Partridge, *A Dictionary of Clichés* (New York: E. P. Dutton & Co., 1963), p. 2. This is a book everyone should own for it lists more than 2,000 words, phrases, and familiar expressions that are better "left unsaid": to "lend an ear," "cook someone's goose," "make the supreme sacrifice"; to be "up in arms," "fit for a king," "on the horns of a dilemma," "under the thumb of," or "in the lap of the gods."

[5] Theodore Bernstein, *The Careful Writer* (New York: Atheneum, 1965), p. 104.

I think a poet is just a tree—
it stands still and rustles its
leaves; it doesn't expect to lead
anyone anywhere.

Boris Pasternak

The bases of figures of speech are comparison and association, and their purpose is not merely ornamental: it is to add freshness, vividness, and immediacy to our utterance.

When I say, for instance, "That a good man enjoys comfort in the midst of adversity"; I just express my thought in the simplest manner possible. But when I say, "To the upright there ariseth light in darkness"; the same sentiment is expressed in a figurative style; a new circumstance is introduced; light is put in the place of comfort, and darkness is used to suggest the idea of adversity. In the same manner, to say, "It is impossible, by any search we can make, to explore the divine nature fully," is to make a simple proposition. But when we say, "Canst thou, by searching, find out God? Canst thou find out the Almighty to perfection? It is high as heaven, what canst thou do? deeper than hell, what canst thou know?" This introduces a figure into style; the proposition being not only expressed, but admiration and astonishment being expressed together with it.

(Blair, Lecture XIV)

Because figures of speech issue from the deepest recesses of the imagination, they cannot be learned. The writer can simply note the figures of other writers and hope that in sensitizing himself and giving free play to his own imagination he too will be inspired to create word-pictures. Let us examine, then, some of the more common forms of figurative language.

Metaphor (identification of one thing with another)

To an imaginative person, what is a map? The silhouette of a chimera or a spot of colour? Trivial comparisons are futile, so be careful. What is South America? A pear upside down.

Adolfo Costa Du Rels, *Bewitched Lands*

In his financial operations, Monsieur Grandet was part tiger and part boa constrictor. He would crouch in ambush watching his prey until it was time to spring with open jaws; then, having swallowed the gold, he would slowly digest it, like a snake, impassive, methodical, cold to any human touch. (Note also the simile here: *like* a snake . . . See below.)

Honoré de Balzac, *Eugénie Grandet*

Living was a field of grain blowing in the wind on the side of a hill. Living was a hawk in the sky. Living was an earthen jar of water in the dust of the threshing with the grain flailed out and the chaff blowing. Living was a horse between your legs and a carbine under one leg and a hill and valley and a stream with trees along it and the far side of the valley and hills beyond.

Ernest Hemingway, *For Whom the Bell Tolls*

No man is an island, entire of itself; every man is a piece of the continent, a part of the main.

John Donne, *Meditation XVII*

Rhetorical question

If gold ruste, what shall iren do?

Geoffrey Chaucer, *The Canterbury Tales,* Prologue

Implicit or submerged metaphor

Youth is the time to go flashing from one end of the world to the other both in mind and body; to try the manners of different nations; to hear the chimes at midnight.

Robert Louis Stevenson

Outside the weather was winter, the trees medieval presences arching gray through gray.

John Updike, "Museums and Women"

About the middle of the nineteenth century, in the quiet sunshine of provincial prosperity, New England had an Indian summer of the mind; and an agreeable reflective literature showed how brilliant that russet and yellow season could be.

George Santayana, *Character and Opinion in the United States*

A kind of splendid carelessness goes with surpassing power. The labor of the file was not for Aeschylus as it was not for Shakespeare.

Edith Hamilton, *The Greek Way to Western Civilization*

Simile (comparison of one thing with another joined by "like" or "as")

Unfortunately Justice is like a train that's nearly always late.

Yevgeny Yevtushenko, *A Precocious Autobiography*

His whole appearance had an amazing, sparkling freshness, like a newly cut bunch of lilacs and the morning dew still in their leaves.

Yevgeny Yevtushenko, *A Precocious Autobiography*

Their prose—Tolstoy's sentences, heavy as blocks of granite; Chekhov's rhythms, soft as autumn leaves; Dostoievsky's moaning and quivering like telegraph wires at night—revealed itself to me in all its beauty of language and depth and richness of meaning.

Yevgeny Yevtushenko, *A Precocious Autobiography*

Human potentialities, so poignant and literally crucial in adolescence really are trapped and vitiated in a mass society. But American society, just because it is so very mass is attached to mass institutions like a factory to its parking lot, or a church to its graveyard.

Edgar Z. Friendenberg, *Coming of Age in America*

Personification (attributing human characteristics to inanimate objects or ideas)

Wit is a lean creature with a sharp inquiring nose, whereas humor has a kindly eye and comfortable girth.

Charles Brooks, "Wit and Humor"

Falseness withered in her presence, hypocrisy left the room.

Adlai Stevenson, eulogizing Eleanor Roosevelt

The songbirds might all have been brooded and hatched in the human heart. They are typical of its highest aspirations, and nearly the whole gamut of human passion and emotion is expressed more or less fully in their varied songs. Among our own birds there is the song of the hermit thrush for devoutness and religious serenity; that of the wood thrush for the musing, melodious thoughts of twilight; the song sparrow's for simple faith and trust, the bobolink's for hilarity and glee, the mourning dove's for hopeless sorrow, the vireo's for all-day and everyday contentment, and the nocturne of the mockingbird for love. Then there are the plaintive singers and the half-voiced, inarticulate singers. The note of the wood pewee is a human sigh; the chickadee has a call full of unspeakable tenderness and fidelity. There is pride in the song of the tanager, and vanity in that of the catbird. There is something distinctly human about the robin; his is the note of boyhood.

"John Burroughs' America: Selections from the Writings of the Hudson River Naturalist"

Death came for her, ashamed of itself.

Bertolt Brecht, *Brecht on Brecht*

ASSIGNMENTS

I. A. Render the following sentences in concrete or specific terms that will create a more vivid impression in the reader's mind.

1. She seemed happy.
2. She seemed lovely.
3. She seemed intelligent.
4. She seemed rebellious.
5. She seemed tired.
6. She seemed angry.
7. She seemed restless.
8. She seemed frightened.
9. She seemed nervous.
10. The countryside was beautiful.
11. The city was awful.
12. The campus was in a turmoil.
13. The dormitory was noisy.
14. The room was crowded.
15. He had the patience of Job.

B. Improve the following sentences by changing a word or words.

1. The park is rather circular, with momentous oak trees.
2. The reversal of Robert Jordan in *For Whom the Bell Tolls* is Frederic Henry in *A Farewell to Arms.*
3. Thomas Wolfe was abhorred by what he saw in society.
4. One notices the author's occupation with this theme.
5. He carries out his life in accordance with Faulkner's vision of fate and moral responsibility.

6. The memory of Ben's death was so vivid that Wolfe was able to duplicate it in his novel with all its poignancy.
7. The most beneficial source was *The International Index*.
8. The room seemed to him to have too much in it.
9. Many writers are too flowery and superfluous so that the point they are trying to convey is lost in the garbage of irrelevant material.
10. For a complete terminology of a word, see an unabridged dictionary.
11. Oftentimes I yearn for the good old days.
12. The speaker of the poem relates how he felt the loss of the pleasures he had once enjoyed.
13. Hemingway looked very deeply into the nature of courage.
14. He was admired for his stubborn principles.
15. Mrs. Compson's last speech in *The Sound and the Fury* reiterates our assumptions about her.
16. Most high school students are all the same.
17. Words are one of the most essential sophistications man has devised.

C. Try to revitalize the following clichés by creating a "play" or "twist" on the words.

1. Home is where the heart is.
2. It never rains, but it pours.
3. The more the merrier.
4. As ye sow, so shall ye reap.
5. Hell hath no fury like a woman scorned.
6. All work and no play makes Jack a dull boy.
7. A fool and his money are soon parted.
8. Spare the rod and spoil the child.
9. People who live in glass houses shouldn't throw stones.
10. Beggars can't be choosers.

26 IMPROVING SENTENCES

The Writer's "Style"

We learn in school how to compose paragraphs and essays, but we master the sentence in early childhood, long before we are even conscious of the learning process. Whether it issues from our tongue or pen, the sentence "appears" as a spontaneous creation, occurring within the individual consciousness, a result of a lifetime's experience with language, not just the needs of the moment. Thus no one can tell someone else how to write a sentence, for by the time a person is writing sentences (certainly by the time he has reached college), a habit pattern has already been established. The writer calls this habit pattern his "style," his characteristic way of expressing himself, and however unsatisfactory and frustrating he may find it ("I know I don't write well"), he tends to cling to the way he has written before (the *tried* though not necessarily *true*). This is natural and should be admitted at the outset. What we can hope to do, and what this chapter will try to accomplish, is to indicate specific ways in which the student writer, beginning with the sentence he has written, can rewrite it to better effect so that it will be a more accurate and successful rendition of what he himself wants to say.

It is a formidable job, improving one's sentences, but it can be done by anyone who takes the trouble to contemplate them critically—i.e., to see how they actually work on paper and what options are available for effective change and revision. Only in this way can a writer improve his writing style. For the rhetorical strengths that contribute to what we call "readability" operate principally on the level of the sentence. No matter how apt and interesting a subject is, no matter how carefully it is visualized and organized, no matter how soundly it is developed, it cannot be turned into a good essay unless the writer has embodied each element of thought in a clear, tight, reasonably smooth-flowing, easy-to-follow series of forceful, graceful sentences.

Logically we may think in paragraphs or units of thought, but concretely we spin out our ideas sentence by sentence—subject / verb / object by subject / verb / object. This is the typical English prose sentence that we vary instinctively as we feel a need for change in rhythm and pace. The reader receives ideas sentence by sentence, reaching out from subject to predicate and trying to remember the various modifications and qualifications set down along the way. For every sentence advanced beyond the primer stage of "See John run!" contains more than a bald subject committed to a particular action. There are always conditions and descriptions woven into the assertion that deepen and enrich its core meaning.

Dr. Samuel Johnson said that "most men think indistinctly and therefore cannot speak with exactness." To some extent this is true, but it is also true that the writer's special function when he is writing is to overcome this human shortcoming. Before setting down his thoughts on paper, the writer has a special obligation to probe his mind until he sees his ideas clearly as a distinct and unified whole. It is then his special obligation to try out different forms for each sentence to see which one most exactly reproduces the idea as it exists in his mind. Only after he has made clear thinking *visible on paper* is he justified in claiming the time and attention of a reader.

We shall approach our subject by considering six basic rhetorical features of the sentence that provide a foundation for clarity and readability: unity, coherence, emphasis, economy, vigor, and rhythm. Upon this foundation each writer can build those subtler qualities of prose tone and style that best suit the needs and purposes of his own piece and his own person. For it is true—and deserves to be repeated—that every writer, student as well as professional, is entitled to his own style, just as everyone is entitled to his own personality, of which writing style is a reflection. The only imperative is that style begin with the minimum rhetorical proficiency without which a piece of writing, no matter how modest in purpose or limited in scope, is doomed to failure. It should also be mentioned that throughout this chapter suggestions and illustrations will be cited from the lectures of the eighteenth-century rhetorician Hugh Blair, whose observations on writing and on the improvement of style, although published in 1783, have yet to be bettered—or even equaled.

Working Toward Unity

A sentence, however complicated by modifications and qualifications, should be essentially about *one* thing.

> For the very nature of a Sentence implies one proposition to be expressed. It may consist of parts, indeed; but these parts must be so closely bound together as to make the impression upon the mind of one object, not of many.
>
> (Blair, Lecture XI)

Thus the reader, who can accommodate only one idea at a time (this being a universal human limitation), can grasp the writer's one idea before moving on to the next. A sentence is unified, then, if it clearly conveys its one main idea; a sentence is not unified if it tries to crowd in so many details that no single idea emerges as *the* idea of the sentence. Similarly a sentence is not unified, nor can it produce a unified effect, if its parts are illogically arranged or if there is needless shifting within the sentence from one subject to another. We shall now consider each of these impediments to sentence unity.

Overcrowding

Actually when we talk about unity we are concerned with something inside the writer: his conception, his idea as it forms in his mind and takes shape on paper. Is it *an* idea—i.e., *one unified idea*—and does it take a clearly defined shape? Or do many ideas—only vaguely related and equally vaguely expressed—crowd into one another to form an amorphous mass that buries rather than exhibits its meaning? This is what happened in the following sentence:

> We think that there is footloose in society, in the enthusiasms with which people become missionaries for the various things in which they take a deep personal interest; a great capacity for helping the other fellow along, and we believe that any leisure-time service should consider its function not alone to the promotion of specific activities, such as athletics, or the arts, but that we should consider as a leisure-time field, in which a great many will find happy outlets for their energies, the pursuit of information or of intellectual culture, not as a matter of schooling but as a matter of post-school avocational interest, and that others can only be served by affording organized outlets for their own leisure enjoyment, in being helpfully identified with causes and movements which are appealing to them, in capacities of service to their group as individuals, or to society at large.
>
> "Youth . . . Leisure for Living"

To convert this gibberish into a meaningful statement the writer must first isolate his main point, focus it sharply, and state it clearly. Then he must organize the details so that they follow in an orderly sequence. At the same time he must eliminate meaningless generalities ("post-school avocational interest"). Having done all this, the writer is ready to convert his "notes" into an intelligible written statement. In this case he will need more than one sentence:

Improvement: Most people appear to enjoy helping other people: notice how the enthusiast (say the fly fisherman) tries to convert others to his pastime. Why shouldn't a leisure-time agency utilize this natural missionary impulse by building into its regular program of athletic and cultural activities a program of social service? This would provide an organized outlet for people who want to "do good" for others—individuals in their own community or society at large.

Piled-up Phrases

Like the overcrowded sentence (of which it is a variation), the sentence with too many prepositional phrases, one piled on top of the other, confuses the reader because no single coherent idea emerges. There is no rule concerning the number of prepositional phrases that can be comfortably accommodated in a sentence. Suffice it to say that a long string of phrases generally produces a loose, rambling effect. In such cases the writer should eliminate some of the phrases and replace others with single adjectives or adverbs.

Example: Words are the efforts made by man to crystallize his ideas and thoughts in order to express them in a manner suitable to the mind of a rational creature.

Improvement: Words represent man's effort to crystallize and express his ideas in a rational manner. (Or simply "rationally")

Illogical Arrangement

Long rambling sentences are not the only violators of unity. A short sentence such as the following also fails to convey meaning because the hodgepodge arrangement of words on paper simply does not add up to one unified, well-thought-out idea:

> If one moves into the sentient, aware sense of intellectual self-development, here too are found barriers to attainment.

Meaningless, confused, illogical, roundabout sentences such as we have been discussing (they are almost impossible to classify because they take so many bizarre forms) generally issue from one of two problems: either the writer's own thoughts are tangled in his own mind, not sorted out and understood; or they are not coming out on paper as he envisions them. In either case the writer must work with the sentence itself, examining it critically word-for-word and asking, "Does it make the clear, logical, unified statement that I have in mind? If not, how can I make it say what I want it to say and not something else?" Only after he has answered these questions can the writer begin to revise his sentences so that they will convey meaning effectively, so that they will not fall apart in the reader's mind. In the case of the sentence cited above, the writer has to rethink the idea itself because the form it took on paper does not make a logical statement.

Another kind of illogical arrangement that may be classified as a violation of unity grows out of a careless, illogical combination of subject and predicate. Rhetoricians call this "faulty predication," a very common problem, illustrated by the following:

> The first step in hiking is comfortable shoes and light clothing.

The writer of this sentence should have asked himself, as he critically reread his first draft, "Are shoes and clothing steps in hiking?" Of course not. The sentence should read:

> The first step in preparing for a hike is to get comfortable shoes and light clothing.
>
> or

> Before setting out on a hike, one should put on comfortable shoes and light clothing.

Admittedly neither of the improved versions is a model of rhetorical splendor, but at least it states a simple idea clearly and accurately, whereas in the original sentence the predicate does not sensibly complete the meaning initiated by the subject.

Similarly in the following sentence the writer does not say what he means; nor can he possibly mean what he says because it is nonsense:

> The abnormal psychology of a human being falls into two distinct divisions: the organic and the functional psychoses.

What is wrong here? Once again there is a faulty predication, compounded, in this case, by a careless and illogical opening phrase—"the abnormal psychology of a human being." We may speak of "abnormal psychology," and we may speak of "the psychology of a human being," but we cannot unite the two in the phrase "the abnormal psychology of a human being." There is no such thing; it has no meaning. More than that, the vast field of abnormal psychology does not fall into the two simple divisions indicated here—organic and functional. These are the categories of psychoses, which represent but one aspect of the total field of abnormal psychology. Thus we can only try to reconstruct what the writer probably *means* to say here but does not actually say:

> There are two fundamental types of psychoses: organic and functional.
>
> or
>
> All psychoses may be classified as either organic or functional.

Working Toward Coherence

A sentence is a sequence of separate words and word clusters. How these words are arranged on paper determines what they mean. A careful and skillful arrangement in which the separate parts fit together to form a cohesive structure is clear; an arrangement in which the parts are loosely and haphazardly thrown together or set down as they happen to enter the writer's mind is unclear, perhaps incomprehensible. Working toward coherence, then, means improving the structure of the sentence so that the parts hold together in such a way that the meaning flows logically and smoothly from one sentence element to the next, thereby enabling the reader to follow and grasp the exact contour of the writer's thoughts as well as its bare substance.

To be able to improve the structure of a sentence, however, we must first understand its dynamic. How does the sentence work? How is it composed? Here we may turn to a modern rhetorician, Francis Christensen, who has formulated what he calls "a generative rhetoric of the sentence" in which he demonstrates that writing a sentence is essentially an "additive" process, i.e., a building or adding on to a basic unit.[1] In the paragraph, the

[1] Francis Christensen, "A Generative Rhetoric of the Sentence," in *Notes Toward a New Rhetoric* (New York: Harper & Row, 1967), pp. 1–23.

basic unit is a topic or lead sentence; in the sentence it is a main clause. Like the topic sentence, the main clause is generally stated in general or abstract terms to which the writer adds specific modifiers (subordinate clauses, adjective clusters, verb clusters, prepositional phrases) that expand and enrich the meaning of the predication. Thus the "cumulative sentence," like the "cumulative paragraph," comes into being through the addition or accumulation of specific details.[2]

Christensen points out that "What you wish to say is found not in the noun but in what you add to qualify the noun. . . . The noun, the verb, and the main clause serve merely as a base on which the meaning will rise. The modifier is the essential part of any sentence."[3] The sentence, then, like the paragraph, frequently exhibits "levels of generality." An example will make this clear:

> 1 He dipped his hands in the bichloride solution and shook them, (main clause)
>
> 2 a quick shake, (noun cluster)
>
> 3 fingers down (absolute—i.e. a verb cluster with its own subject)
>
> 4 like the fingers of a pianist above the keys. (prepositional phrase)
>
> Sinclair Lewis (cited in Christensen, p. 9)

Here is another longer example:

> 2 Calico-coated (adjective cluster)
>
> 2 small-bodied (adjective cluster)
>
> 3 with delicate legs and pink faces in which their mismatched eyes rolled wild and subdued (prepositional phrase)
>
> 1 they huddled, (main clause)
>
> 2 gaudy, motionless and alert, (adjective series)
>
> 2 wild as deer, (adjective cluster)
>
> 2 deadly as rattlesnakes, (adjective cluster)
>
> 2 quiet as doves. (adjective cluster)
>
> William Faulkner (cited in Christensen, p. 9)

[2] Basically there are six ways in which we may add to or expand a minimal sentence:

1. Compounding the base or "head" term in a subject / verb / complement pattern:
   Example: Fresh fruit is good.
   Head word: fruit
   Expansion: Fresh fruit and vegetables are good.
2. Juxtaposing appositive phrases to the head term:
   Expansion: Fresh fruit, a rare treat in any season, is good.
3. Using verbals or verbal phrases (participles, gerunds, infinitives) in the subject / verb / complement pattern:
   Expansion: Oozing its natural juices, fresh fruit is good.
4. Using noun clauses to serve as the subject or complement in the subject / verb / complement pattern:
   Expansion: Whoever eats fresh fruit says that it is good.
5. Using an adjective or adjective clause to modify the head term of the subject or complement in the subject / verb / complement pattern:
   Expansion: Wherever it comes from, fresh fruit is good.
6. Using an adverb or adverb clause to modify the verb in the subject / verb / complement pattern:
   Expansion: Fresh fruit is always good.

[3] Christensen, p. 25.

It may seem strange to see the sentence "laid out" in this almost mathematical manner, but it is important to recognize that a well-constructed sentence lends itself to schematization. For any well-constructed sentence has a plan or design. The practiced writer frequently creates the design spontaneously as a product of his own well-ordered and trained mind, accustomed to bending words to his will. Just as frequently, however, the design is a result of the careful reworking and polishing of a rough first draft.

In any case, it is well to keep Christensen's schema in mind, for it describes more accurately than the traditionally "diagrammed sentence" how we actually write: we accumulate information as we go along (word follows word on the page; they unite into clusters, phrases, clauses); detail builds on detail; separate parts combine to form a total statement—a sentence.

We may join assertions. This is the simplest example of the "additive process."

> I eat / and / I drink.

Or we may amplify a basic point through a series of modifying details.

> The girl / who had won the scholarship / was celebrating / at a house party / when her parents arrived / to congratulate her.

The possible methods of expanding a sentence are legion. The writer should experiment with various alternatives to determine which works best in a given situation. Most important he should aspire to coherence—a sentence in which the main clause and its added elements flow smoothly and logically into one another, with no interruption or obstacle.

To begin working toward coherence of this kind we must avoid the pitfalls listed below, each of which involves carelessness or misplacement of an added element.

Misplaced Modifiers

It was a misplaced modifier that created the amusing song title of some years ago, "Throw Mama from the Train a Kiss." Similarly it was a misplaced modifier (plus a few missing words) that produced the following almost unbelievable letter, addressed to the welfare service at the Lackland Air Force Base and written by a serviceman's wife: "In accordance with your instructions, I have given birth to twins in the enclosed envelope."

Since word order is the principal grammatical process of the English language (the difference in meaning between "Dog bites man" or "Man bites dog" is simply a matter of how identical words are positioned), it is vital that the writer arrange his words on paper so that they show accurate relationships. Modifiers should be near the terms they modify; related ideas should be in close proximity, otherwise they may "latch on" to some other sentence element where they will not make sense.

Notice how easily the following sentences—each containing a misplaced modifier—can be improved either by repositioning the modifier or by restructuring the sentence slightly so that the reader can readily see what words and word groups are intended to go together:

Example: He saw an accident which he reported yesterday.
Problem: What does "yesterday" modify—the accident or the time of the report?
Improvement: He saw an accident yesterday that he immediately reported.

Example: She was the kind of girl who could accept the fact that she was pigeon-toed with a smile.
Improvement: She was the kind of girl who could accept with a smile [good naturedly] the fact that she was pigeon-toed.

Example: He was born while the Korean War was in progress in the United States.
Improvement: He was born in the United States while the Korean War was in progress.

The dangling modifier is a form of a "misplacement."

Example: Having just returned from a long cruise, the city seemed unbearably hot.
Problem: (In *A Dictionary of American-English Usage,* Margaret Nicholson cites this as an example of the famous [and often inadvertently funny] danging participle.) "The city had not been on the cruise," Nicholson points out—thereby voicing the English teacher's classic protest. Participles must be attached to the noun responsible for the action or they will "dangle." On this ground she revises the sentence to read:
Improvement: Having just returned from a long cruise, we found the city unbearably hot.

A prohibitive attitude toward the dangling participle will be familiar to almost all students, for the construction has long been universally condemned. Unfairly so, according to many contemporary writers on usage and style who point out that in most instances the so-called dangling modifier (it may be a gerund or an infinitive as well as a participle) is often modifying the entire main clause, not just the single noun subject. Thus, according to Bergen and Cornelia Evans in *A Dictionary of Contemporary American Usage,* (N.Y.: Random House, 1957), it is not misleading or unclear to say "Looking at the subject dispassionately, what evidence is there?" They claim that "this is the idiomatic way of making statements of this kind and any other construction would be unnatural and cumbersome."

The general principle to follow here is simply this: if the meaning is obscured or made absurd by a dangling modifier, it should be rewritten so that the sentence makes immediate sense. The reader should never be required to reread the sentence in order to get it right. Thus, in order to be absolutely free of ambiguity, a sentence such as the following, "After finishing college, my family moved to New York," should be improved to read "After I finished college, my family moved to New York."

Mixed Construction

There are times when a writer begins a sentence with one construction in mind and then, somewhere along the way, carelessly or inadvertently shifts to another.

Example: Students know that in getting together to discuss a problem how they can avoid violence.
Improvement: Students know that in getting together to discuss a problem they can avoid violence.

The second version of this sentence is an improvement because the second half of the sentence fulfills the expectation raised in the first half—namely that the subordinating conjunction "that" will be followed by a new subject and predicate. These grammatical terms may mean little or nothing to the average reader who has either forgotten or never really understood grammatical terminology, but the reader nonetheless responds to structural signs whether or not he can identify them.

Thus a reader unconsciously knows that in a sentence beginning "I believe that . . ." a subject and predicate will follow.

I believe that someone is knocking at the door.
or
I believe that Harry will call.
not
I believe that how hard you try is good.

In this last sentence, as in the original example cited above, the subordinating conjunction "that" is followed by a second subordinating conjunction "how." The result is momentary but nonetheless real confusion in the reader's mind, for halfway along in the sentence the signals he has been picking up and responding to have been abruptly shifted. The implied promise of the sentence has not been fulfilled; the reader's expectations have been thwarted.

It is important to avoid this kind of awkwardness in sentence construction. Actually it is carelessness rather than ignorance that creates such problems, for all native speakers have a deep awareness of the basic structure of English. If you doubt this, consider Lewis Carroll's famous "Jabberwocky" poem from *Through the Looking-Glass.*

'Twas brillig and the slithy toves
Did gyre and gimble in the wabe:
All mimsy were the borogoves,
And the mome raths outgrabe.

You may recall that when Alice hears these lines she says: "Somehow it seems to fill my head with ideas—only I don't know exactly what they are!" Actually, the ideas are *patterns*—the structural or grammatical meanings that stand out unmistakenly because the lexical meanings have been obliterated; i.e., the words themselves do not mean anything; but the *form* of the words and their arrangement within the line stir the mind to vague recognition. Let us see how this works. First of all, there are certain real words that frame the nonsense words. The verse starts with "it was." 'Twas ______. Ask yourself, what kind of word could possibly follow " 'Twas" in this particular line? Certainly not a verb. " 'Twas *walked?*" Nobody would ever combine such words in English. Our intuition leads us to such expressions as "it was *lovely,*" or "it was *dangerous,*" or "it was *special.*" Which is to say that "brillig" is probably an adjective and "slithy" is obviously another adjective followed by the noun "toves."

'Twas beautiful and the happy girls
Did dance and frolic in the snow:

Some such statement is being made here. We know it; we feel it. It could not be otherwise. Whatever particular words you might choose to fill in here, they would all have the same *form:* they would be adjective, adjective, noun / verb, verb, noun. The same principles apply to the next two lines:

All mimsy were the borogoves,
And the mome raths outgrabe.

All (adjective) were the (noun),
And the (adjective) (noun) (verb).

All happy were the carolers,
And the young boys jumped.

How do we know and why do we feel that these kinds of words fit into these particular places? As modern linguists tell us,[4] we are responding here to the structural or grammatical meanings that we learned as children, long before we could read or write. We heard words in certain positions within an utterance: the subject came first, followed by an action, then an object or adjective. We learned to identify the territories where we could expect to hear one or another *form* arising. In other words we learned the basic grammatical process of the English language: word order.

We also learned that certain kinds of words changed in set ways; some might have an *s* sound attached to the end, and when they did certain other words would change their form to *agree with* them. Thus we feel that "borogoves" is plural; it has an *s* ending, and the verb that precedes it is a verb that goes with a plural noun. If "borogoves" were singular, the verb preceding it would be "was," not "were" (the borogove was; the borogoves were).

It does not matter what the individual word denotes here: "borogoves" could mean "cars" or "handkerchiefs." In either case—in *any* case—the *structural* or *grammatical* meaning (the terms are interchangeable) remains constant: an *s* ending signals plurality, and an alteration in verb form signals a particular relationship between the verb and the noun. Collectively these changes in form are known as "inflection." Inflection is the second most important structural device in the English language.

There is still a third formal device. Function words such as "the," "and," "by" have no concrete meaning when they stand alone but serve an important function within the context of a sentence. Here they help to indicate how full words such as "water" and "sink" are related: The water is *in* the sink; the shoes are *under* the bed. Function words are *determiners* or *formal markers* that help us to identify other words in the sentence and indicate how other words are functioning: as verbs? nouns? adjectives? After all, what a word *is* depends on how it functions in the sentence: one may *jump* across a puddle (verb); one may take a big *jump* (noun); or one may watch a referee at a basketball game toss up a *jump* ball (adjective).

[4] See W. Nelson Francis, "Revolution in Grammar," *Quarterly Journal of Speech,* October 1954.

When we find a "the" or "a" preceding words such as "toves" or "wabe," we know that they are words to which an *s* can be added, words that we, using traditional terminology, call "nouns." Thus when we substitute for "borogoves" we automatically do so with another noun. Similarly by using the function word "and" at the beginning of the fourth line—"and the mome raths outgrabe"—the writer is telling us that the fourth line conveys a parallel assertion to the assertion in line three, "All mimsy were the borogoves." The past tense "were" (rather than "are") in line three is therefore carried over, by virtue of the connective "and" (a conjunction) to line four. The "borogoves" "were" and the "mome raths" also appear to have completed some action in the past.

The purpose of this long explanation has been to demonstrate that you need not be familiar with the complexities of English grammar to write well-constructed sentences. What you must do is follow your own unconscious knowledge of how words are "signaled" so that you may fulfill the reader's expectations.

Miscellaneous Shifts

We have seen that any change in the pattern of a sentence that surprises the reader and stops him—even for a fraction of a second—or that disappoints an expectation set up in the early part of the sentence is a violation of coherence, the kind of "sticking together" of the parts that makes the sentence a sound, consistent, and easy-to-read unit. In addition to shifts in the basic pattern of the sentence that produce hybrid constructions, there are other kinds of shifts. They are not as obviously bad as those described above, but equally unnecessary and undesirable because they break up the flow and therefore the coherence of the sentence. These are shifts in voice, tense, mood, and person: we shall consider each of them in turn.

Shift in Voice

Example: When the townspeople heard that the mayor had resigned, a general meeting was called.

Problem: In the above sentence the writer has needlessly shifted from active to passive voice—and this, in turn, has involved a shift in subject from "townspeople" to "meeting." Both of these shifts interfere with the smooth, natural flow of the sentence.

Improvement: When the townspeople discovered that the mayor had resigned, they called a general meeting.

(See "Using Active Voice," p. 463.)

Shift in Tense

Example: They come into the room and began opening up the books that are sitting on the table.

Problem: The writer shifts carelessly from present to past to present tense.

Improvement: They come into the room and begin opening up the books that are sitting on the table.

or

They came into the room and began opening up the books that were sitting on the table.

Shift in Mood

Example: First discuss the problem; then you should take action.

Problem: A needless shift in mode or mood—from imperative, which issues a command or request, to subjunctive, which expresses obligation.

Improvement: First discuss the problem; then take action.

Shift in Person

Example: A student should know the provisions of the Civil Rights Act, for one cannot be a good citizen unless you keep up with current legislation.

Problem: The writer shifts from "student" to "one" to "you."

Improvement: A student should know the provisions of the Civil Rights Act, for he cannot be a good citizen unless he keeps up with current legislation.

or

You should know the provisions of the Civil Rights Act, for you cannot be a good citizen unless you keep up with current legislation.

Blair sums up the case against unnecessary shifts by pointing out that

> During the course of the Sentence, the scene should be changed as little as possible. We should not be hurried by sudden transitions from person to person, nor from subject to subject. There is commonly, in every Sentence, some person or thing, which is the governing word. This should be continued so, if possible, from the beginning to the end. . . . Should I express myself thus:
>
> > After we came to anchor they put me on shore, where I was welcomed by all my friends who received me with the greatest kindness.
>
> In this Sentence, though the objects contained in it have a sufficient connexion with each other, yet by this manner of representing them, by shifting so often both the place and the person, *we* and *they* and *I* and *who*, they appear in such a disunited view that the sense of connexion is almost lost. The Sentence is restored to its proper unity . . . in . . . the following manner:
>
> > Having to come to anchor, I was put on shore, where I was welcomed by all my friends and received with the greatest kindness.[5]

Unclear Reference

Still another violation of sentence coherence grows out of unclear pronoun reference, a common flaw in student writing. "Reference" suggests that the meaning of a pronoun depends on its antecedent. Strictly speaking, a pronoun is a word used in place of a noun; therefore unless the reader knows precisely what noun or noun clause, what overall idea the pronoun is replacing, the sentence will be neither clear nor coherent.

[5] Note dangling modifier here. Do you find it offensive? See discussion on page 446.

Example: The women were stopped and questioned by company guards. They then went to the police who refused to protect them. This attitude has also been reported in other towns.

Problem: The direct antecedent of "they" in the second sentence is "guards." Yet (as we realize on a second reading) the pronoun is *supposed* to refer to "women." Still another problem: "This attitude" is not clear. Does the writer mean this "hostile" attitude—or what? In this sentence sequence the pronoun references do not provide a clear and definite guide to meaning because the writer has been careless about antecedents of the personal pronoun and has not supplied enough information to indicate precisely what the demonstrative adjective "this" refers to. It is up to the writer to say *specifically* what he means here. The reader should not be asked to "fill in" a noun and adjectives.

Improvement: After being stopped and questioned by company guards, the women went to the police, who refused to protect them. A similar indifference on the part of the police has been reported in other towns.

Note another unclear, ambiguous reference.

Example: Jim's father was president of the college, which gave him considerable prestige.

Problem: Does "him" refer to Jim's father? Technically it does, but is that what the writer means? (The reference of "which" is also vague.)

Improvement: Because his father was president of the college, Jim enjoyed considerable prestige.

Unnecessary Splits

Sentence flow or coherence is impaired by the careless separation or splitting of words that belong together, as in the following examples:

Subject Split from Its Verb

Example: Zodomirsky, shocked and grieved at the death of Mariana, becomes a monk.

Improvement: Shocked and grieved at the death of Mariana, Zodomirsky becomes a monk.

Verb Split from Its Object

Example: She sipped slowly and contentedly the warm cocoa.

Improvement: Slowly and contentedly she sipped the warm cocoa.

Verb Split from Its Auxiliaries

Example: He had long ago known the lady.

Improvement: He had known the lady long ago.

or

Long ago he had known the lady.

It should be pointed out here that all splits are not bad. Sometimes, as in the following sentence, the writer deliberately suspends his predication, without losing the flow or continuity of thought.

> "Alienation," a term once confined to philosophy, law, psychiatry, and advanced literary criticism, has entered the daily vocabulary.

Generally speaking, a sentence can be neither coherent nor logical if the writer has not provided precise connectives, i.e., conjunctions such as "and," "but," "or," "therefore," "since," "although," "consequently." These words indicate how the parts of the sentence are related in the writer's mind. Thus the reader looks to these words for a sign of what direction the sentence will take. These words prepare him for what is to come; if used accurately, they predict the writer's intent.

To demonstrate, here is a simple exercise in logical predication: [6]

I read the book (,) (;)
and
or
because
however
therefore
after
although
consequently

Each of the words following "I read the book" suggests the type of particulars that will follow:

and—Like the plus sign (+) in arithmetic, the coordinating conjunction "and" suggests an addition of comparable (or coordinate) importance:

> I read the book and I enjoyed it.
> or
> I read the book and I wrote a letter.

As Frank C. Flowers tells us,

> In both sentences, the added clauses involve balanced AGENT–ACT sequences. The balance would be disturbed logically if the sentence were to read "I read the book, and Tom is a senior." The two thoughts do not seem to "add" as parts of a normal context. There seems to be no reason why these two expressions should be joined. Logicians would say of the second thought "*non sequitur*" . . . "it does not follow logically."

or—This coordinating conjunction signals that an alternative rather than a simple addition is about to follow:

> I read the book, or at least *tried* to read it.

because—This subordinating conjunction anticipates a causal relationship:

[6] Adapted from Frank C. Flowers, "Logic and Composition," in *Practical Linguistics for Composition* (New York: The Odyssey Press, 1968), pp. 77–83.

I read the book because it was assigned.

Here again the connective prepares the reader for a particular type of statement—a reason *why*. Should this explanation fail to appear in the second half of the sentence, the sentence "falls apart" in the reader's mind (as it has in the writer's):

I read the book because sun-tan lotion prevents sunburn.

however—This connective (called a conjunctive adverb) functions like the simple conjunction "but"; it predicts a qualification or contrast to what might be expected:

I read the book, but I did not enjoy it.
or
I read the book; however I did not enjoy it.

therefore—This conjunctive adverb tells the reader that what he has just read provides a reason for what he is about to read.

I read the book; therefore I understand these issues.

after—Connectives such as "after" and "before" obviously alert the reader to the introduction of a time element:

I read the book after I had talked to the professor.
or
I read the book after dinner.

although—Like "however," this conjunction foretells qualification and contrast, a possible reversal of expectations:

I read the book, although I did not want to.

consequently—Like "therefore," this term signals reason and result, suggesting (however faintly) a time element—i.e., the consequences resulting over a period of time:

I read the book; consequently I was able to lead the class discussion on Friday.

Because the basic logic or coherence of the sentence rests heavily on the precision of connectives, the writer should choose his terms carefully, recognizing that his choice "signals" to the reader the direction of his sentence. The following list presents most of the common connectives, classified according to the relationships they establish with the subsequent added element.

Relationship	*Connective*
Additive	and, also, in addition, besides, furthermore, moreover, likewise, namely, specifically
Alternative	or, nor, neither . . . nor
Comparison	than, as . . . as, likewise
Condition	if, unless, whether, as long as, provided that
Contrast and Concession	but, yet, although, though, even though, however, on the other hand, while, conversely, nevertheless, granted that, so long as, whereas

Relationship	*Connective*
Effect	then, consequently, accordingly, so . . . that
Intensification	indeed, actually, really, rather, likewise
Manner	as if, as though, so, how
Place	where, wherever, there, here
Purpose	in order that, so that
Reason	because, why, since, for, therefore, as, hence
Result	so . . . that, hence, thus, accordingly, then, therefore, as a result
Time	when, whenever, after, before, since, as, as long as, as soon as, while, until, then

Weak Connectives

In addition to using connectives precisely, the writer should avoid small, loose connectives that detract from the force or impact of a statement.[7] As an example, we may look at Wilson Follett's observation in *Modern American Usage* on the use of "as."

> The novice's resort to *as* with the meaning *since* or *because* is always feeble. It makes trivial what follows. Webster (1934 edition) remarks: "*As* assigns a reason even more casually than *since*." What is worse, the untrained or heedless writer turns to this weak subordinating link to introduce a co-ordinate clause or what should be his main clause. In either case he ruins emphasis. *It was a comparatively unproductive year, as he was dogged by ill health and domestic worries.* For *as* read *for*.

Similarly the word "so" is a loose connective, more suited to rambling conversation than to writing.

> *So* I told him I was *so* angry I could barely contain myself . . . and *so* he finally admitted he was *so* sorry he could hardly stand it . . . and *so* I said "forget it" . . . *so* we made up and *so* I'm seeing him again tonight. . . .

Where "so" is used as an intensifier ("I was *so* happy") it can usually be eliminated without loss, for like most so-called intensifiers ("I really was happy," "I truly was so so very happy") it does not work.[8] In fact it may produce a reverse effect by creating uneasiness and suspicion. "Exactly *how* happy is *so* happy?" the reader may wonder. "Why is the writer being vague and seemingly inarticulate? And why does he keep saying 'really' and 'truly'? Is he afraid we will not believe him? Is he trying to convince himself?"

The use of "so" to introduce a clause of purpose or a clause of result is equally ineffective, although the usage is clearly established in informal conversation.

> I wanted to see the town so I asked them to take me along.
> The glass was broken so I had to get another.

[7] For a discussion of "imprecise connectives," see pp. 452–54.
[8] See under, "Avoid ineffective intensifiers," p. 457.

Even here the link provided by "so" is weak and can be made more emphatic by using "so that."

The glass was broken so that I had to get another.

Better still, the first half of the sentence can be subordinated.

Because (or since) the glass was broken, I had to get another.

Working Toward Economy

Loose writing is often said to be a reflection of loose thinking; if so, verbosity is a root flaw. Frequently, however, loose writing is a sign not so much of loose thinking as of not enough work, specifically not enough reworking and revising of the original sentence. For that first spontaneous overflow simply cannot be trusted to serve its purpose efficiently, i.e., to convey meaning in a clear, concise, and effective manner. "With years of practice," as editor Norman Cousins has observed, "a man may be able to put down words swiftly and expertly. But it is the same kind of swiftness that enables a cellist, after having invested years of effort, to negotiate an intricate passage from Haydn."[9]

Those of us who are not experts will probably need more than one try at most sentences, for people are naturally wordy. Indeed as George Orwell has observed in "Politics and the English Language," "It is easier—even quicker once you have the habit—to say *In my opinion it is not an unjustifiable assumption that* than to say *I think*."

We cannot very well trim our conversation as we go along, nor can we go back and edit it. When we write, however, we can and must do exactly that: we must return to the sentences we have written and rework, recast, rewrite them until they are lean, crisp, and concise, free of what Flaubert called "fatty deposits." Such "tight" sentences have far more impact on the reader: "'Beware the anger of a quiet man' is superior to 'A quiet man's anger is especially to be feared,' for the same reasons and in the same way that a short, straight shaft is better than a long, crooked one in most machine operations."[10]

Admittedly it is always harder to condense than to write; still there are concrete ways to go about the "boiling down" process: we can eliminate unnecessary words; and we can condense long sentence elements into shorter ones (independent clause to subordinate clause, subordinate clause to phrase, phrase to word).

Eliminating Unnecessary Words

Avoid indirect expressions

Example: Probably the *Encyclopædia Britannica* would avail one with the choicest information since it spends almost five pages expounding upon Shelley. (20 words)

[9] Norman Cousins, *Present Tense: An American Editor's Odyssey* (New York: McGraw-Hill Book Company, 1967), p. 479.

[10] Jackson Burgess, "Sentence by Sentence," *College Composition and Communication* 14 (Dec. 1963).

Improvement: The *Encyclopædia Britannica,* with five full pages on Shelley, is probably the best source.
(14 words)

Example: Without words and what they communicate both connotatively and denotatively, man would be reduced to the level of lower primates.
(20 words)

Improvement: Without language man would be reduced to the level of the lower primates.
(13 words)

Example: The agnostic is one who holds that he has no knowledge of God; indeed that the human mind is incapable of knowing whether there is or is not a God.
(30 words)

Improvement: An agnostic maintains that the human mind has no way of knowing [or "cannot know"] whether or not God exists.
(14–17 words)

Avoid useless repetition

Example: He sees not only the world of man, but instead he also sees the world of God.

Improvement: He sees both the world of man and the world of God.

Example: The main portion of the story dealt with Robert Peel's political life, an aspect of his life that was very active.

Improvement: The main portion of the story dealt with Robert Peel's very active political life.

Example: The average person in high school is a combination of both of these types, having a balance of both of these types of characteristics.

Improvement: The average high school student combines the characteristics of both types.

Avoid negative phrasing

Example: I find myself not in complete agreement with you.
Improvement: I disagree with you.

Example: I do not have much faith in his honesty.
Improvement: I distrust him.

Example: She was not very often on time.
Improvement: She usually arrived late.
or
She usually was late.

Example: I do not expect to be misunderstood.
Improvement: I expect to be understood.

Avoid loose, inexact verbs

Example: He felt that the best way to avoid temptation was to get her to leave.

Improvement: He felt that the best way to avoid temptation was to make her leave.

Avoid ineffective intensifiers ("really") and qualifiers ("rather")

Example: *A Farewell to Arms* was the novel which really first made Hemingway a commercial success.
Improvement: *A Farewell to Arms* was Hemingway's first commercially successful novel.

Example: The most powerful force in all the world is love.
Improvement: The most powerful force in the world is love.

Example: He was a somewhat quiet man.
Improvement: He was a quiet man.

Avoid anticipatory phrases such as "it is," "there was"[11]

Example: It is for the above mentioned reasons that I abandoned the project.
Improvement: For the above mentioned reasons I abandoned the project.

Example: There were crowds of people milling about.
Improvement: Crowds of people were milling about.

Example: The reason that he voted for the independent candidate was that he had an antiwar record.
Improvement: He voted for the independent candidate because he had an antiwar record.

Avoid redundance

Example: Her dress was pink in color.
Improvement: Her dress was pink.

Example: The professor introduced a new innovation.
Improvement: The professor introduced an innovation.

Avoid deadwood (words that carry no meaning)

Example: In many cases students are now working along the lines of discussing controversial issues with the administration.
Improvement: Many students are now discussing controversial issues with the administration.

Example: He is working in the interest of political unity.
Improvement: He is working toward political unity.

Example: That society is an interesting one.
Improvement: That society is interesting.

Example: She was aware of the fact that he had not returned her paper.
Improvement: She was aware that he had not returned her paper.

Below is a list of common "deadwood" expressions that pad rather than add to the meaning of a sentence.

along the lines of
to the extent that
the fact that

[11] This principle generally applies, although with notable exceptions: specifically when the extra words contribute to the rhythm of the sentence or when they help to build the sentence toward an appropriately emphatic climax.

seems to me to be
of the character that
on the level of
in the interest of
of the nature of
owing to the fact that
with reference to
tends to be
may be said to be

Note how easily many of these useless and cumbersome expressions can be abbreviated.

at that time	then
at some future time	after
in the event that	if
is aware of	knows
by virtue of	through
owing to the fact that	because
in spite of the fact that	despite
he is a man who	he
is likely to	may
was of the opinion that	believed
the question as to whether	whether
to be desirous of	to want
the great percentage of	most
to be deficient in	to lack
in a slow manner	slowly
there is no doubt that	undoubtedly
it may be assumed that	supposedly
as an example or an example is	for example
to take into consideration	to consider

Condensing Long Sentence Elements

Reduce predications

Example: If we follow such a policy it may have the desired effect of convincing the U.S.S.R. that we mean business.

Improvement: Following this policy may convince the U.S.S.R. that we mean business.

Subordinate independent clauses

Example: Honor was important to both Stamm and Zodomirsky and as a result of it they were both hurt.

Improvement: Because honor was important to both Stamm and Zodomirsky, they were both hurt.

Example: In many cases, people have trouble finding ways to use up idle time. This is especially true of Sundays when they have been removed from the cares of work.

Improvement: Many people have trouble filling in idle time, especially on Sundays when there is no work.

Example: It has been shown throughout history that some men are ahead of their time. Such is the case with Galileo and Newton.

Improvement: Throughout history some men, like Galileo and Newton, have been ahead of their time.

Example: In the second section complications are introduced by Mariana. She begs Zodomirsky not to duel. This begging causes Zodomirsky to face a conflict between his honor as a man and his love for Mariana.

Improvement: In the second section complications are introduced by Mariana who begs Zodomirsky not to duel, thereby creating in him a conflict between honor and love.

Reduce clause to phrase or adjective

Example: Einstein, who was one of the most brilliant men of all time, behaved in a manner that was warm and human.

Improvement: Einstein, one of the most brilliant men of all time, was a warm human being.

Example: After his working day was completed, he stopped in at the same tavern which he visited nightly.

Improvement: Every night after he finished work, he stopped in at [or "went to"] the same tavern.

Example: I picked up the papers which were on the desk.

Improvement: I picked up the papers on the desk.

Example: He was introducing considerations which have nothing to do with the case.

Improvement: He was introducing extraneous considerations.

Reduce phrase to adjective

Example: This passage from the Bible is noted for its style which is simple and eloquent.

Improvement: This biblical passage is noted for its simple eloquence.

In summary it may be said of economy that we should aspire to spareness and leanness of style, taking care not to err in the other extreme whereby style becomes so spare as to be telegraphic. Here Blair suggests the happy medium.

> We shall always find our Sentences acquire more vigour and energy when . . . retrenched: provided always that we run not into the extreme of pruning so very close, as to give a hardness and dryness to style. For here, as in all other things, there is a due medium. Some regard, though not the principal, must be had to fullness and swelling of sound. Some leaves must be left to surround and shelter the fruit.
>
> (Blair, Lecture XII)

Working Toward Emphasis

In a properly emphatic sentence every word and every group of words are given what Blair calls "due weight and force"—i.e., what the writer considers most important is made to seem most important and what he considers less important is, accordingly, made to seem less important.

These messages or clues as to what is centrally at issue in the sentence and what is of secondary or subordinate significance can to some extent be built into the grammatical construction of the sentence. Main ideas can be placed in the main clause and subordinate ideas can be placed in the subordinate clause that does not compete with the main proposition but feeds into it. Important elements can also be positioned in a sentence so that they stand out, thereby making a deeper impression on the reader's mind.

We shall consider these grammatical constructions in turn.

Putting Main Idea in Main Clause

It is an oversimplification to say that the main idea should always be placed in the main clause, and subordinate points in the subordinate clause; but it nevertheless represents a helpful technique that can be easily demonstrated. If, for example, you have two points of information to present in a sentence—(1) that you were walking in the park, and (2) that you saw a thief steal a woman's purse—you certainly would want to emphasize the second point for that is clearly the *news* of the sentence: that you were witness to a theft. Thus you would be wise to subordinate the background information by placing it into a subordinate rather than in a coordinate position:

Example: I was walking in the park and I saw a man snatch a woman's purse.

Problem: This coordinate construction distributes importance equally to both halves of the sentence. Actually, however, the two halves are not equal and should *not* be made to seem so. One clause, in other words, should be made subordinate.

Improvement: As I was walking in the park, I saw a man snatch a woman's purse.

This second form makes it clear that you just *happened* to be walking in the park at the time of the "incident." The incident itself, the *point* of your statement and the part that you will develop in succeeding sentences, is that you saw a purse snatched. By embodying the greater importance of this point in your grammatical construction, you are focusing your reader's attention where it belongs and moving him toward completion of the story you have initiated.

In general, ideas should not be indiscriminately connected by the coordinating conjunction "and." This produces a loose, unemphatic statement that—at the extreme—can sound childlike: "I was walking in the park and I saw a man take a lady's purse and I ran to a policeman and he asked me what the man looked like and I said he was very tall and. . . ."

Using Emphatic Positions

A writer may also achieve proper emphasis in a sentence by the positioning of important elements as Blair tells us:

> [Still another principle] for promoting the Strength of a Sentence . . . is to dispose of the capital [important] word or words in that place of the Sentence where they will make the fullest impression. That such capital words there are

in every Sentence on which the meaning principally rests, every one must see; and that these words should possess a conspicuous and distinguished place is equally plain. Indeed, that place of the Sentence where they will make the best figure, whether the beginning or the end or sometimes even in the middle cannot, as far as I know, be ascertained by any precise rule. This must vary with the nature of the Sentence. . . . For the most part, with us, the important words are placed in the beginning of the Sentence. So Mr. Addison:

> The pleasures of the imagination, taken in their full extent, are not so gross as those of sense, nor so refined as those of the understanding.

And this, indeed, seems the most plain and natural order, to place that in the front which is the chief object of the proposition we are laying down. Sometimes, however, when we intend to give weight to a Sentence, it is of advantage to suspend the meaning for a little, and then bring it out full at the close:

> Thus [says Mr. Pope] on whatever side we contemplate Homer, what principally strikes us is his wonderful invention.
>
> (Preface to Homer) (Blair, Lecture XII)

The beginning of the sentence and the end, then, are the emphatic positions, especially the end. For in the unfolding of a sentence, as in the unfolding of a total essay, the last words stand out and impress themselves most forcibly on the reader. The writer who does not take advantage of this, who allows his sentence to trail off with empty qualifying phrases, insignificant afterthoughts, or small weak monosyllables such as "it," "was," "done," "is," "etc.," is not only ignoring an extremely important psychological resource but is also creating a sense of anticlimax, of a sentence closing after its natural and proper end.

Example: The advances of the future must be made in the moral as well as the technological sphere, according to the commencement speaker.

Improvement: According to the commencement speaker, the advances of the future must be made in the moral as well as the technological sphere.

Example: Hawthorne was haunted throughout his life by the evil deeds his ancestors had done.

Improvement: Hawthorne was haunted throughout his life by the evil deeds of his ancestors.

Example: The word is the basic unit of language and what we communicate with.

Improvement: The word is the basic unit of language with which we communicate.

Note that in the above example the final preposition has been moved to a less prominent middle position. This was done, not because the final preposition is in itself bad as the old rule proclaims ("Never end a sentence with a preposition"), but rather because it is a small unemphatic word that ends the sentence weakly. Actually, where idiom demands it, a final preposition is acceptable:

I did not know what to put it in.

Where idiom does not demand a final preposition, however, it should be avoided, along with all small "inconsiderable words" as Blair terms them: adverbs, participles, conjunctions.

> For besides the want of dignity which arises from those monosyllables at the end, the imagination cannot avoid resting for a little on the import of the word which closes the sentence; and as those prepositions [etc.] have no impact of their own but only serve to point out the relations of other words, it is disagreeable for the mind to be left pausing on a word which does not by itself produce any idea nor form any picture in the fancy.
>
> (Blair, Lecture XII)

Transposing Normal Word Order

Because the normal and familiar pattern of the English sentence is subject / verb / object (*I don't like him*), any variation in this pattern calls attention to itself and thereby emphasizes the point being expressed (*Him I don't like*). The second sentence intensifies the predications because it wrenches subject and object out of their expected positions. The subject no longer opens the sentence; the object no longer follows the verb. Instead the word "him" opens the sentence—an unusual location for a pronoun in the objective case. Clearly, then, this sentence informs the reader that this is no ordinary dislike, just as this is no ordinary sentence. The inexperienced writer might try to get his point across by using weak intensifiers (*I really dislike him very very much*); the simple transposition of pronouns is far more economical and successful.

Achieving emphasis through transposition is not necessarily a conscious process. The strength of our feelings often dictates a spontaneous switching of terms:

> That I cannot believe!
> Oh, the troubles I've had!
> Never will I do that again!

We can also make conscious use of this device in such simple transpositions as the ones listed below, all of them effective as emphasizers of what might otherwise be mundane observations.

> Cold was the night.
>
> Come winter and we'll see the fall of snow.
>
> Of this plan, he knew nothing.
>
> [referring to Big Ben striking] First a warning, musical; then the hour, irrevocable.
>
> Virginia Woolf, *Mrs. Dalloway*

Working Toward Vigor

Closely allied to economy and emphasis is vigor: a lean, tightly constructed sentence with movement and energy built into its structure. Such a sentence, as Bishop Whately told us long ago,[12] will "stimulate attention,

[12] Whately, p. 318.

excite the Imagination, and . . . arouse the feelings." Chances are that along with its other strengths this sentence will be written in the active rather than in the passive voice and will contain a strong, substantial verb rather than weak, colorless verbs such as "is," "was," "does," and "has."

Using Active Voice

"Voice" indicates whether the subject of a sentence acts or is acted upon, whether the subject is the doer of the action or the receiver.

I hit the ball.

This is active voice because "I," the subject, is the actor or doer.

The ball was hit.

This is passive voice because the subject, "ball," receives the action of being hit. Actually to be complete, the sentence should read, "The ball was hit by me."

Once we are aware of the distinction between active and passive voice, we cannot fail to see that in general the active voice is more lively and assertive than the passive, which tends—as the term "passive" suggests—to lack immediacy.

Example: The test was taken by the students.
Improvement: The students took the test.

Example: College students were recruited by the township and a new project was begun.
Improvement: The township recruited college students and set up a new project.

Example: In economics the student is taught that there is a law of diminishing returns.
Improvement: In economics the student learns the law of diminishing returns.

Sentences in the active voice are stronger and more emphatic for two reasons. First, they are more economical: the active voice generally requires fewer words. Second, the *real* subject is emphasized because it is also the *grammatical* subject: "students" in the first sentence cited above is the *real* subject of the sentence, not "test." But we should also recognize that in some cases the passive voice is preferable: when the doer of the action is unknown (*The house was robbed*); when the receiver of the action, rather than the doer, has to be emphasized (*Shoplifters will be prosecuted*); and in formal report writing, where it is conventional for a writer to be anonymous (*The test was run and the following results obtained*).

Despite these important exceptions, the writer should try, whenever possible, to strengthen and enliven his sentences by converting unnecessary and awkward passives into the active voice.

Concentrate Activity in Verbs

The second way to invigorate a sentence is to concentrate its action in substantial, well-chosen verbs, avoiding wherever possible weak verbs such as "is," "was," "has," and "does." Shakespeare habitually used strong verbs rather than the weak "state of being" forms ("is" and "was"). When he did use them, he exacted from them their deepest existential meaning: "To be or not to be, that is the question."

The careless writer often uses a weak, roundabout verb form or inadvertently wastes the action of the sentence on a noun.

Example:	He felt an obvious hatred for the new recruit.
Improvement:	He obviously hated the new recruit.
Example:	Thoreau became a complete recluse from society in his shack at Walden Pond.
Improvement:	Thoreau secluded himself in his shack at Walden Pond.
Example:	In this anthology are some of the best Haiku and Tanka verse ever written.
Improvement:	This anthology contains some of the best Haiku and Tanka verse ever written.
Example:	There were two contributing factors to this situation.
Improvement:	Two factors contributed to this situation.
Example:	There was a car moving in circles around the speedway.
Improvement:	A car moved in circles around the speedway. or A car circled the speedway.

Note that when we exploit the peculiar power of the verb to invigorate a sentence, we have at the same time tightened the sentence, i.e., reduced the number of words and phrases. We have also pinpointed the action of the sentence on one vivid verb, instead of wasting it on a noun (*Thoreau became a recluse*) or a participle (*a car moving*).

Choose Concrete, Specific Words

Still a third way to promote vigor in the sentence is to use words that are specific and concrete rather than general and abstract (*the tall, red-haired soldier at the end of the line* rather than *that man over there*). (See Chapter 25, "Choosing Words".)

Working toward Rhythm

Although rhythm is normally associated with poetry, it is a feature of prose writing as well. Indeed anyone who has ever listened to a sentence read aloud knows that it is a unit not only of meaning but also of rhythm and sound. Actually there is no better guide to good writing than the ear because what sounds good usually reads well. Conversely what is jarring, overly intricate, or unpronounceable is usually hard to read and just as hard to understand. Thus it is wise for the student writer to test his sentences on his ear, to *listen* to the sound of the words—both individually and in combination—and to *feel* their rising and falling action. For, as one writer has noted,

> an author who would please or move his readers will often wish to do so by sound as well as sense. Here rhythm becomes important. Feeling tends to produce rhythm; and rhythm, feeling. Further, a strong

> rhythm may have a hypnotic effect, which holds the reader, as the Ancient Mariner held the wedding guest; prevents his attention from wandering; and makes him more suggestible.[13]

It should be admitted that basically prose rhythm defies strict analysis and is probably "dictated by some inner pressure, hardly felt at the time, just as the rhythms of poetry seem to come into the head almost unbidden." [14] We may speculate that rhythm is associated with physical sensations: the writer's rate of breathing, heartbeat, pulse, metabolism. Similarly for the reader, a good sentence meets what Flaubert called "the needs of respiration." The sentence must "breathe" correctly—provide pauses where needed, change of pace, slowing down, speeding up.

Certainly the musical quality of the sentence cannot be denied, but neither can it be described easily in a short space. It will suffice to quote Blair once again, for his observations on "harmony"—though brief—are germane:

> Let us consider agreeable sound, in general, as the property of a well-constructed Sentence. . . . This beauty of musical construction in prose, it is plain, will depend upon two things; the choice of words, and the arrangement of them.
>
> I begin with the choice of words; on which head, there is not much to be said, unless I were to descend into a tedious and frivolous detail concerning the powers of the several letters, or simple sounds, of which Speech is composed. It is evident, that words are most agreeable to the ear which are composed of smooth and liquid sounds, where there is a proper intermixture of vowels and consonants; without too many harsh consonants rubbing against each other; or too many open vowels in succession, to cause a hiatus, or disagreeable aperture of the mouth. It may always be assumed as a principle, that whatever sounds are difficult in pronunciation, are, in the same proportion, harsh and painful to the ear. Vowels give softness; consonants strengthen the sound of words. The music of Language requires a just proportion of both; and will be hurt, will be rendered either grating or effeminate by an excess of either. Long words are commonly more agreeable to the ear than monosyllables. They please it by composition, or succession of sounds which they present to it: and, accordingly, the most musical languages abound most in them. Among words of any length, those are the most musical, which do not run wholly either upon long or short syllables, but are composed of an intermixture of them; such as, *repent, produce, velocity, celerity, independent, impetuosity*.
>
> The next head, respecting the Harmony which results from a proper arrangement of the words and members of a period, is more complex, and of greater nicety. For, let the words themselves be ever so well chosen, and well sounding, yet, if they be ill disposed, the music of the Sentence is utterly lost. . . . In English, we may take, for an instance of a musical Sentence, the following from Milton, in his Treatise on Education:
>
> > We shall conduct you to a hill-side, laborious indeed, at the first ascent; but else, so smooth, so green, so full of goodly prospects, and melodious sounds on every side, that the harp of Orpheus was not more charming.

[13] F. L. Lucas, *Style* (New York: Macmillan, 1962), p. 215.

[14] Marjorie Boulton, *The Anatomy of Prose* (London: Routledge and Kegan Paul Ltd., 1954), p. 68.

> Every thing in this Sentence conspires to promote the Harmony. The words are happily chosen; full of liquid and soft sounds; *laborious, smooth, green, goodly, melodious, charming:* and these words so artfully arranged, that were we to alter the collocation of any one of them, we should, presently, be sensible of the melody suffering. For, let us observe, how finely the members of the period swell one above another. "So smooth, so green,"—"so full of goodly prospects, and melodious sounds on every side;"—till the ear, prepared by this gradual rise, is conducted to that full close on which it rests with pleasure;—"that the harp of Orpheus was not more charming."
>
> (Blair, Lecture XIII)

Rhythm and harmony are matters too complex to contemplate here with any thoroughness. We shall simply consider four basic rhetorical devices that contribute to the rhythmic and euphonious arrangement of sentence elements: (1) parallel construction; (2) balanced antithesis; (3) order of climax; (4) variation in sentence length, pattern, and type.

Parallel Construction

More than any other single resource at the writer's disposal, parallel construction—repetition of sentence elements (*I came, I saw, I conquered*)—provides a basis for rhythm in prose. Listen to these familiar words from Lincoln's Gettysburg Address: ". . . we cannot dedicate, we cannot consecrate, we cannot hallow this ground." Rhythmically, this sentence approaches poetry, as we can hear by noting the measured beat in each clause:

/ × × / × ×
we cannot dedicate,

/ × × / × ×
we cannot consecrate,

/ × × / × × /
we cannot hallow this ground.

Or, if you wish to stress different syllables:

× / / / × ×
we cannot dedicate,

× / / / × ×
we cannot consecrate,

× / / / × × /
we cannot hallow this ground.

The casting of like ideas in like grammatical form improves sentences on almost every count: it tightens, enlivens, and unifies; it also makes the sentence more emphatic and coherent since likeness of form enables the reader to recognize more readily likeness of content. For each item in a parallel series announces itself as a companion to the others—a comparable action: *They were walking, running, leaping* (three participles).

Because the meaning of such a sentence is reinforced by its structure and rhythm, a direction issued in parallel form is easier to grasp and therefore to follow.

Walk, do not run, to the nearest exit. (two verbs in the imperative)

Similarly, a longer sentence that contains a series of observations or many details and qualifications is held together by a framework of parallelism.

> The only advice . . . that one person can give another about reading is to take no advice, to follow your own instincts, to use your own reason, to come to your own conclusions.
>
> Virginia Woolf, *The Second Common Reader*

(Note the series of four infinitives: *to take . . . , to follow . . . , to use . . . , to come. . . .*)

> Jealousy of Mr. Elliot had been the retarding weight, the doubt, the torment. That had begun to operate in the very hour of first meeting her in Bath; that had returned, after a short suspension, to ruin the concert; and that had influenced him in every thing he had said and done, or omitted to say and do, in the last four-and-twenty hours.
>
> Jane Austen, *Persuasion*

(Note that in the first sentence above the three complements of "had been" are nouns presented in order of rising intensity: "weight," "doubt," "torment." In the second longer sentence, the parts are held in place by the three long "that" clauses, in the last of which there is parallelism within the parallel: *every thing he had said and done, or omitted to say and do. . . .*)

Parallelism combined with repetition of key words clearly produces an especially tight and emphatic rhythmic unit.

> No fact, however interesting, no image, however vivid, no phrase, however striking, no combination of sounds, however resonant, is of any use to a poet unless it fits: unless it appears to spring inevitably out of its context.
>
> Northrop Frye, "New Directions from Old"

The careless and inexperienced writer is apt to overlook both the semantic and rhythmic significance of arranging like ideas in parallel form. He does not realize that when the items themselves correspond to each other the reader expects to find the words in corresponding form and is disappointed if they are not.

Example: They liked to go to the movies, hiking in the mountains, and on long rainy days they would sleep the whole afternoon.

Problem: The writer has expressed three comparable activities in three different grammatical forms: an infinitive phrase, a participial phrase, and a clause.

Improvement: They liked to go to the movies, to hike in the mountains, and on long rainy days to sleep the whole afternoon.

or

They liked going to the movies, hiking in the mountains, and—on long rainy days—sleeping the whole afternoon.

Example: The course grade is based on three factors: what you do in the final examination, writing a term paper, and class work.

Problem: Here again, three ideas of equal importance are expressed in three different grammatical forms: a relative clause, a participial phrase, and a single noun.

Improvement: The course grade is based on three factors: a final examination, a term paper, and class work.

Balanced Antithesis

It has long been recognized that when two ideas stand in opposition to one another, the contrast or tension between them (the *is* versus the *is not;* the *either . . . or*) can be emphasized by setting them forth in a form of parallelism called "balanced antithesis."

> Either we live by accident and die by accident; or we live by plan and die by plan.
>
> Thornton Wilder, *The Bridge of San Luis Rey*

> The tragedy of life is not that man loses but that he almost wins.
>
> Heywood Brown

> Talent, Mr. Micawber has; money, Mr. Micawber has not.
>
> Charles Dickens, *David Copperfield*

(Note that Dickens has achieved further emphasis here by inverting normal word order.)

The force and binding power of balanced antithesis rest basically on parallel constructions in which key words are repeated in an opposite context. Note the impact, for example, of President Kennedy's famous statement.

> Ask not what your country can do for you; ask what you can do for your country.

One way to emphasize a balanced antithesis is to pair words through alliteration:

> Both poems are didactic: one preaches, one praises.

> Yonder is one whose years have calmed his passions but not clouded his reason.
>
> Samuel Johnson, *Rasselas*

Herbert Read tells us that "used with discretion [balanced antithesis] adds point and vivacity to expression; but when abused it becomes tedious and artificial."[15] This point is worth remembering.

Order of Climax

> But in a larger sense we cannot dedicate, we cannot consecrate, we cannot hallow this ground.

In addition to casting this sentence in a parallel construction, note that Lincoln carefully organized its three verbs in climactic order, moving from

[15] Herbert Read, *English Prose Style* (Boston: Beacon Press, 1955), p. 40.

the least commitment ("to dedicate" is to set aside ground); to a deeper commitment ("to consecrate" is to declare the ground sacred); to the very deepest commitment ("to hallow" is to perpetually honor the ground as holy). Thus, Lincoln fulfilled the requirements of a rhythmic as well as a properly emphatic statement; he did not allow his sentence to fall off at the end. Indeed he has arranged the verbs so that they would grow both in meaning and in rhythmic impact. The importance of rising action cannot be overstressed, for it rests on the natural human expectation that items in a series will intensify as they progress. Surely it was this recognition that led Jane Austen in the sentence cited earlier to describe jealousy in progressively more oppressive terms: first as a "retarding weight," then as a "doubt," and finally as a "torment." To reverse the order (a "torment," a "doubt," a "retarding weight") would create an anticlimax—a let-down instead of a build-up. Thus as Blair tells us, the writer should always make certain that the "members" of a sentence

> Go on rising and growing in their importance above one another. This sort of arrangement . . . is always a beauty in composition. From what cause it pleases is abundantly evident. In all things we naturally love to ascend to what is more and more beautiful, rather than to follow the retrograde order. Having had once some considerable object set before us, it is with pain we are pulled back to attend to an inferior circumstance. . . . The same holds in melody . . . : that a falling off at the end always hurts greatly. For this reason particles, pronouns, and little words, are as ungracious to the ear, at the conclusion, as I formerly showed they were inconsistent with strength of expression. It is more than probable that the sense and sound here have a mutual influence on each. That which hurts the ear seems to mar the strength of meaning; and that which really degrades the sense, in consequence of this primary effect appears also to have a bad sound.
>
> (Blair, Lecture XIII)

Variation in Sentence Length, Pattern, and Type

A succession of declarative sentences written in the conventional subject / verb / object order, with an average length of fourteen to twenty words, or two lines apiece, would produce a droning monotone. After a while the sameness of rhythm and pattern, the lack of emphasis, would dull if not deaden the reader's senses and send his attention elsewhere.

Note the tiresome succession of short, choppy sentences in the following paragraph:

> Hemingway's works abound in war, violence, and death. Hemingway had first hand experience with all three. He took in two world wars. He also participated in smaller wars. They made him see death without disguise. He had no heroic illusions. [Note gap in thought here.] Life and death were intermingled in the minds of his characters.

Most writers intuitively vary sentence length because the mind in the process of composition tends to express itself in unequal "waves" of thought. Note in the following paragraph, for example, how John Steinbeck's sentences range from three words to forty-two:

Sentence length: average, short, average, short, average, long, average, short

> When I was very young and the urge to be someplace else was on me, I was assured by mature people that maturity would cure this itch. When years described me as mature, the remedy prescribed was middle age. In middle age I was assured that greater age would calm my fever and now that I am fifty-eight perhaps senility will do the job. Nothing has worked. Four hoarse blasts of a ship's whistle still raise the hair on my neck and set my feet to tapping. The sound of a jet, an engine warming up, even the clopping of shod hooves on pavement brings on the ancient shudder, the dry mouth and vacant eye, the hot palms and the churn of stomach high up under the rib cage. In other words, I don't improve; in further words, once a bum always a bum. I fear the disease is incurable.[16]

Similarly most writers tire of the typical declarative sentence and vary the pattern of their prose with the addition of a rhetorical question, an imperative, an exclamation.

> I hate to hear people saying, "He is young, he must wait; he will get plenty of chances." How do they know? Could Keats have waited, or Shelley, or Byron, or Burns?
>
> J. A. Spender

Still again writers tire of the usual subject / verb / object pattern and automatically alter it so that sentences open differently—sometimes with the subject, sometimes with a prepositional phrase, an adverb, a subordinate clause.

> Sometimes in history, a nation collapses not because of its own flaws but because of the attacking nation's tremendous strength. Was this but the latest example? For years, from Berlin, I had watched Nazi Germany's mercurial rise in military might, which the sleeping democracies in the West did little to match. I had followed, too, at firsthand, Hitler's cynical but amazingly successful diplomacy, which had so easily duped the West and paved the way for one quick military conquest after another. But still the French debacle was quite incomprehensible. Not even the German generals I had talked with in Berlin expected it.[17]

The most dramatic wrenching of normal word order occurs in the so-called suspended sentence wherein the writer postpones his predication to the end of the sentence, thereby achieving a kind of "suspense."

> The fighter who stays in the ring as long as he can stand on his feet, the man who keeps his business alive while his clothes are threadbare and his stomach empty, the captain who clings to his ship while there is a plank left afloat—that is Washington.[18]

[16] John Steinbeck, *Travels with Charley in Search of America* (New York: Viking Press, 1962), p. 1.

[17] William Shirer, *The Collapse of the Third Republic* (New York: Simon and Schuster, 1969).

[18] W. E. Woodward, *George Washington, the Image and the Man* (New York: Horace Liveright, Inc., 1926), p. 295.

Because the reader does not know what a suspended sentence is about until he has reached the end, he will surely get lost or simply give up along the way unless the writer establishes a rhythmic unity that holds the sentence together and moves it toward its climax. This can be achieved only by observing strict parallelism, as in the following example:

> How is it that I, who had the biggest Big League Gum collection in the East, who can still recite the lineup of the 1931 World Series (though there isn't much demand for it), who missed supper rather than miss the ball scores on WOR at 7 P.M., who never read the great novels because of a boyhood spent reading baseball news and "The Baseball Magazine" instead—how is it that I, the despair of my parents for an addiction that shut out almost every other field of knowledge, the bane of my sisters for the simulated major league doubleheaders that I played against the side of the house every day with a rubber ball, can hardly bring myself to follow the game today? [19]

Sentences like these gain enormously in emphasis and vigor by virtue of their suspension—the "long and steady climb upward over successive terraces of clauses," [20]—followed by the final swift descent to the point of the sentence, its predication. Certainly the reader is caught up in the cadence of such a sentence, so that a whole new dimension of rhythmic as well as mental response is elicited.

Not all sentences, it should be said, are as dramatically suspended as the above examples. Frequently the writer introduces a short delay, using words that may seem unnecessary but that serve a rhythmic purpose.

> **It was not until the other day, when I returned on a visit to Coney Island, that I recalled an important episode of my youth which had been buried all these years.**
>
> **Isaac Rosenfeld, in "Coney Island Revisited"**

A hasty editor might complain about the seemingly useless "It was" opening of the above sentence. But if he studies it more carefully he will see that this normally poor construction works here; it enables the writer to build a short rhythmic suspense that is more effective than the direct and economical and flat alternative:

> I recalled an important, long-buried episode of my youth the other day when I returned on a visit to Coney Island.

It is commonly supposed, and to some extent true, that a series of short, simple sentences conveys an impression of speed, whereas longer sentences, as Herbert Read tells us, "give an air of solemnity and deliberation to writing." [21] Actually long sentences may move swiftly, provided they are well constructed and flow smoothly and harmoniously from one word group to another. Take the two virtuoso examples that follow:

[19] William Zinsser, *Pop Goes America* (New York: Harper & Row, 1963), p. 155.
[20] Stephen Potter, *Our Language* (London: Books, Ltd., 1950).
[21] Read, *English Prose Style*, p. 35.

1. This sentence closes Lytton Strachey's biography of Queen Victoria:

> Perhaps her fading mind called up once more the shadows of the past to float before it, and retraced, for the last time, the vanished visions of that long history—passing back and back, through the cloud of years, to older and ever older memories—to the spring woods at Osborne, so full of primroses for Lord Beaconsfield—to Lord Palmerston's queer clothes and high demeanor; and Albert's face under the green lamp, and Albert's first stag at Balmoral, and Albert in his blue and silver uniform, and the Baron coming in through a doorway, and Lord M. dreaming at Windsor with the rooks cawing in the elmtrees, and the Archbishop of Canterbury on his knees in the dawn, and the old King's turkey-cock ejaculations, and Uncle Leopold's soft voice at Claremont, and Lehzen with the globes, and her mother's feathers sweeping down towards her, and a great old repeater-watch of her father's in its tortoise-shell case, and a yellow rug, and some friendly flounces of sprigged muslin, and the trees and the grass at Kensington.
>
> Lytton Strachey, *Queen Victoria*

This long sentence moves back steadily in time, as the writer imagines the queen's "fading mind" is moving back through memory to retrace the "vanished visions" of her long life. As her memories pass "back and back, through the cloud of years," so this single sentence moves back and back in one continuous flow of images: spring woods, Lord Palmerston's queer clothes, Albert's first stag, Victoria's mother, her father, the trees and the grass at Kensington. One long life is thus encompassed in one long tightly organized sentence that captures in its unity the unity and rhythm of the life it describes.

2. Here is another seemingly endless descriptive sentence, this one suspended:

> If the eyes are too big, and they are twice too big, and if they surround a nose that cannot be subdivided, and if the body parts might have been assembled by a weary parent on Christmas Eve, and if the teeth are borrowed from a rabbit soliciting carrots, and if the voice could summon sentry dogs, and if she does not walk so much as lurch, glide and jerk in continuing peril of collapsing like a rag doll dismissed by a bored child, and if on top of that she is saddled with being Judy Garland's first of three children by her second of five marriages, then how can the bearer of these oddments, how can this girl put together in the Flea Market, how can Liza Minnelli, at 23, threaten to become the major entertainment figure that she is becoming? [22]

This sentence is clearly an amusement as well as a description. By piling if-clause upon if-clause, the writer has tried to intensify his mystery ("Who is this strange creature?" we wonder), and by building on a repetitive "and if . . . and if," he has established an almost breathless musical refrain, moving us, we are led to expect, to some sort of crescendo. Instead, the sentence falls off at the end, contrary to conventional principles of emphasis and harmony. Nonetheless, the sentence succeeds almost despite it-

[22] Thomas Thompson, "Judy's Daughter Wants to be Liza," *Life,* 17 October 1969.

self, for it brings us down to earth, again rhythmically. The subject, after all, is not of momentous import (note that most of the words are short and simple); the writer's weak ending seems to tell us that he knows he has been a bit overdramatic, but he has been writing in a spirit of fun. There is clearly a tongue-in-cheek element in this sentence. It is in itself a little essay, light and playful in tone.

Forging a Better Style

As Blair tells us in the following passage, the best way to forge a better style is to write slowly and carefully, never aiming directly for speed. At the same time, we must not be too plodding.

> Many rules concerning style I have delivered, but no rules will answer the end, without exercise and habit. At the same time, it is not every sort of composing that will improve style. This is so far from being the case, that by frequent, careless, and hasty composition, we shall acquire certainly a very bad style; we shall have more trouble afterwards in unlearning faults, and correcting negligences, than if we had not been accustomed to composition at all. In the beginning, therefore, we ought to write slowly and with much care. Let the facility and speed of writing, be the fruit of longer practice. Says Quintilian, with the greatest reason, "I enjoin, that such as are beginning the practice of composition, write slowly and with anxious deliberation. Their great object at first should be, to write as well as possible; practice will enable them to write speedily. By degrees, matter will offer itself still more readily; words will be at hand; composition will flow; every thing as in the arrangement of a well-ordered family, will present itself in its proper place. The sum of the whole is this; by hasty composition, we shall never acquire the art of composing well; by writing well, we shall come to write speedily."
>
> We must observe, however, that there may be an extreme, in too great and anxious care about words. We must not retard the course of thought, nor cool the heat of imagination, by pausing too long on every word we employ. There is, on certain occasions, a glow of composition which should be kept up, if we hope to express ourselves happily, though at the expense of allowing some inadvertencies to pass. A more severe examination of these must be left to be the work of correction. For, if the practice of composition be useful, the laborious work of correcting is no less so: it is indeed absolutely necessary to our reaping any benefit from the habit of composition. What we have written, should be laid by for some little time, till the ardour of composition be past, till the fondness for the expressions we have used be worn off, and the expressions themselves be forgotten; and then, reviewing our work with a cool and critical eye, as if it were the performance of another we shall discern many imperfections which at first escaped us. Then is the season for pruning redundances; for weighing the arrangement of sentences; for attending to the juncture and connecting particles; and bringing style into a regular, correcting and supported form. This *"Limœ Labor,"* must be submitted to by all who would communicate their thoughts with proper advantage to others; and some practice in it will soon sharpen their eye to the most necessary objects of attention, and render it a much more easy and practicable work than might at first be imagined.
>
> **(Blair, Lecture XIX)**

Punctuation Chart

The following chart shows the main principles of sentence punctuation:

1. Sentence. Sentence.
2. Main clause; main clause.
3. Main clause, {and / or / but / for} main clause.
4. Main clause; {so / therefore / however / then} main clause.
5. Main clause subordinate clause.
6. Subordinate clause, main clause.
7. Main clause subordinate clause; main clause.
8. Main clause; subordinate clause, main clause.

ASSIGNMENTS

I. Compose appropriate second halves for the sentence below, using each of the connectives and indicating what kind of relationship each of them signals.

I went to class (,) (;)

and
because
however
therefore
after
although
consequently
or
but
hence
since
so that
so . . . that
indeed
likewise
moreover
specifically
yet
as if

II. Locate the weakness in the following sentences and wherever possible improve them:

1. Just as scientific progress has dispelled the belief that an "evil spirit" causes the headache, so has it replaced the former cure of boring holes in the skull with aspirin.

2. There are more single women than men in the United States, according to the Census Bureau.

3. Most of the churches have large congregations that are rather wealthy.

4. In 1870 Pavlov conducted an investigation of the pancreatic nerves and was awarded a gold medal for it.

5. One old cottage in particular attracted my attention. It was a huge white structure with four gables, one at each corner.

6. Milton, who was one of the most scholarly men of all time, devoted a good part of his life to activities in the sphere of politics.

7. She began singing in a coffeehouse in Boston at the age of nineteen.

8. The author's central purpose is a view of human behavior.

9. It is important to keep in mind what sin and guilt meant in Hawthorne's use.

10. He was a man of heroic soul, keen intellect, and quiet wit.

11. There is a noticeable lack of friends in his life.

12. On returning to the deck, the sea became dark and turbulent.

13. The French engineers proposed an alternative plan. Their plan called for the construction of a semicircular dam two hundred fifty feet wide which cost eighty million dollars.

14. Today's American woman is envied by other women. The main basis for this is her supposed freedom to live as she chooses. This may include such things as travel, studying in college and graduate school, and even day-to-day attire.

15. There are two basic means of communication of which one is speaking and the other is the use of the written word.

16. The English hate frogs, but the French love frogs and hate the English, and cut off their hind legs and consider them a great delicacy.

III. Comment on the following passages and indicate what factors contribute to their rhetorical effectiveness.

1. When youth is gone, every man will look back upon that period of life with infinite sorrow and regret. It is the bitter sorrow and regret of a man who knows that once he had a great talent and wasted it, of a man who knows that once he had a great treasure and got nothing from it, of a man who knows that he had strength enough for everything and never used it.

Thomas Wolfe

2. The world of Homer is unbearably sad because it never transcends the immediate moment; one is happy, one is unhappy, one wins, one loses, finally one dies. That is all. Joy and suffering are simply what one feels at the

moment; they have no meaning beyond that; they pass away as they came; they point in no direction; they change nothing. It is a tragic world but a world without guilt for its tragic flaw is not a flaw in human nature, still less in an individual character, but a flaw in the nature of existence.

W. H. Auden, Introduction to *The Portable Greek Reader*

3. Our literature is filled with young people like myself who came from the provinces to the Big Cave, seeking involvement in what one always thought from the outside was a world of incomparable wonder, hoping for some vague kind of literary "fulfillment." In the 1960s, as always since New York became our literary and journalistic marketplace, there would be thousands of them clustered around the great axis of publishing, newspapering, and broadcasting, starting out at minuscule salaries, living in unfamiliar, claustrophobic walk-ups, fighting the dread and alien subways twice a day, coming to terms with the incredible noise and crowdedness. Most of them would not "make it"; the more resourceful and talented might.

Why did we come? Not because the materials for our work did not exist in those places we knew best. Not merely for fame and money and success, for these also some of us could have had, and perhaps in more civilized ways, in places far removed from New York. Not even because we wanted to try ourselves in the big time, and out of curiosity to see how good the competition was. We had always come, the most ambitious of us, because we *had* to, because the ineluctable pull of the cultural capital when the wanderlust was high was too compelling to resist.

Willie Morris, *North Toward Home*

4. I who am blind can give one hint to those who see—one admonition to those who would make full use of the gift of sight: Use your eyes as if tomorrow you would be stricken blind. And the same method can be applied to the other senses. Hear the music of voices, the song of a bird, the mighty strains of an orchestra, as if you would be stricken deaf tomorrow. Touch each object you want to touch as if tomorrow your tactile sense would fail. Smell the perfume of flowers, taste with relish each morsel, as if tomorrow you could never smell and taste again. Make the most of every sense; glory in all the facets of pleasure and beauty which the world reveals to you through the several means of contact which Nature provides. But of all the senses, I am sure that sight must be the most delightful.

Helen Keller, *Three Days to See*

5. They went down to the camp in black, but they come back to the town in white; they went down to the camp in ropes, they came back in chains of gold; they went down to the camp with their feet in fetters, but came back with their steps enlarged under them; they went also to the camp looking for death, but they came back from thence with assurance of life; they went down to the camp with heavy hearts, but came back with pipe and tabor playing before them.

John Bunyan: *Life and Death of Mr. Badman*

6. We sailed early in January, and for nearly a year we wandered from country to country. I saw Egypt. I saw the Pyramids, at noon and at sunset,

by moonlight, and at sunrise. I saw the Tombs of the Kings, and the great Temple at Karnak. I saw the lovely vanished Temple of Philae. I saw the coast of Asia Minor, and the harbor of Smyrna. I sailed on the Aegean Sea. I saw the Isles of Greece, and the Acropolis. I saw the Golden Horn in the sunrise, and the minarets and the cypresses of Constantinople. I saw Italy. I saw Switzerland. I saw Paris. I saw London. I saw England in summer. I saw the frozen lakes of Norway, and the midnight sun over the ice fields.

Ellen Glasgow, *The Woman Within*

27 WRITING PARAGRAPHS

The Paragraph as a Cage of Form

When we talk about writing the paragraph, we are talking about the act of writing itself, the actual at-the-desk, word-by-word, sentence-by-sentence writing situation. The writer is not now thinking about rhetorical principles, but rather about the rush of ideas whirling about in his mind. How can he commit them to paper, capture them, as Archibald MacLeish says, in a "cage of form"? MacLeish's image refers to poetry, but it applies equally to the paragraph, for it is in the paragraph—the major message unit of the piece—that the writer unfolds his ideas, one-by-one, as his mind dictates and his pen flows.

In this sense it may be said that we write in paragraphs. Admittedly the writing process proceeds sentence-by-sentence, but the sentence is never writen in isolation, only within the context of the paragraph. Certainly we think in paragraphs, or units of thought that we block out as we write, indenting every so often when it seems "time." Interestingly this intuitive approach works well, for studies have shown that most people instinctively begin a new paragraph at the right place: where there is a change or turn of thought, a shift from one phase of the subject to another.

Looked at in terms of its basic function, the paragraph is both a convenience and a convention. Physically it serves an important purpose by breaking up a solid mass of print that would otherwise tire the reader's eye and tax his patience (line after line in unvarying succession; ideas flowing into one another indiscriminately and without pause). A little white space and periodic indentations break the monotony and provide brief resting places for the eye.

Recognized as a logical and rhetorical unit as well as a mechanical structure, the paragraph has been described as "a small group of thoughts that hang together."[1] Although they are part of a larger whole, these thoughts generally constitute a self-contained unit that makes sense by itself. Each paragraph or series of paragraphs marks off a stage in the development of the writer's thought. Thus each paragraph in a well-written essay can be justified as such: the writer made it a paragraph because it is a meaningful unit of the total discourse. Paragraph indentations, then, help the reader by indicating the organization and development of the writer's thought as it moves from one aspect of the subject to another.

Paragraph Divisions

Many paragraphs dictate their own boundaries, especially if the writer is working from an outline. In a short paper each heading often turns out to be one or two paragraphs; in a longer paper the subheadings frequently constitute or at least suggest paragraph divisions. Paragraph breaks may also be determined by the topic itself. In the simple analysis that follows, for example, note that the first sentence is, in fact, an introductory paragraph listing the three elements that make up the whole; each of these elements is then discussed in its own paragraph, followed by an extended paragraph of commentary. The essay concludes with another one-sentence paragraph.

STUDYING MUSIC IN INDIA

RAVI SHANKAR

Guru, vinaya, sadhana—these three words form the heart of the musical tradition of India.

Guru, as many people now know, means master, spiritual teacher, or preceptor. We give a very important place to the *guru,* for we consider him to be the representation of the divine. There is a saying—

Pani piye chhanke
Guru banaye janke

—which means that one should drink water only after it has been filtered, and one should take a *guru* only after one feels sure of the decision. The choice of the *guru,* to us, is even more important than choosing a husband or a wife. A potential disciple cannot make a hasty decision to take just any teacher as his *guru,* nor should he break the bond between *guru* and *shishya,* once the *ganda* or *nara* ceremony, the initiation, which symbolically binds the two together for life, has taken place.

Vinaya means humility; it is the complete surrendering of the self on the part of the *shishya* to the *guru.* The ideal disciple feels love, adoration, reverence, and even fear toward his *guru,* and he accepts equally praise or scoldings. Talent, sincerity, and the willingness to practice faithfully are essential qualities of the serious student. The *guru,* as the giver in this relationship, seems to be all-powerful. Often, he may be unreasonable, harsh, or haughty, though the ideal *guru* is none of these. Ideally, he should respond to the efforts of the disciple and love him almost as his own child. In India, a Hindu

[1] Boulton, *The Anatomy of Prose,* p. 41.

child, from his earliest years, is taught to feel humble toward anyone older than he or superior in any way. From the simplest gesture of the *namaskar,* or greeting (putting the hands palm to palm in front of the forehead and bowing), or the *pranam* (a respectful greeting consisting of touching the greeted person's feet, then one's own eyes and forehead with the hands held palm to palm) to the practice of *vinaya* or humility tempered with a feeling of love and worship, the Hindu devotee's vanity and pretension are worn away. . . .

The third principal term associated with our music is *sadhana,* which means practice and discipline, eventually leading to self-realization. It means practicing with a fanatic zeal and ardent dedication to the *guru* and the music. If the student is talented, sincere, faithful to his *guru* and devoted in his practicing, and if the *guru* is teaching with utmost dedication and not being miserly with his knowledge, there is a distinct pattern for learning Indian music. The student must begin by acquiring the most basic techniques of the voice or instrument. In vocal music, this skill is achieved by assiduously practicing first one note, trying to produce correct breathing, voice, and pitch control. Students both of vocal and of instrumental music then learn scales and *paltas* (also called *alankars*). *Paltas* are short melodic figures performed in sequential order within a scale and *tala* framework in different tempi. Then, the *sargams* must be learned—the various fixed compositions sung to the note-names. In some fixed compositions *talas* and tempi can be varied, and in others no *tala* is used at all. The student also learns various other fixed compositions called *bandishes,* which include songs in different styles sung to a meaningful text, slow or fast instrumental pieces (*gats*), or some melodic phrases in a variety of melodic motions and tempi (*tans*).

This elementary training, for a talented and persevering student, should last not less than five years, very much like the elementary training for any Western musical discipline. This means the student should practice every day for at least eight hours. In Western music, of course, the student has a visual advantage. That is, much of his learning can be taken from books, without the close supervision of a teacher. But with Indian music, for the first five or six years, the student relies completely on the guidance of his *guru.* This is because the *guru* teaches everything to the *shishya* individually and directly, according to our ancient oral traditions, for very rarely do we use textbooks or manuals. Then, little by little, the student learns to improvise, and he works at it until he feels free and confident within a *raga.* From this point on, the aspiring musician must draw completely from within himself—from his own methodical musical training and his feelings and inspirations. As his musicianship grows, he acquires first a high degree of proficiency in the technical side of playing and then an ability to follow his imagination in whatever musical direction it leads. His technique must be highly enough developed to enable him to render instantaneously the mental pictures that flash before his mind's eye. It is such an exhilarating feeling to grasp a fresh idea and perform it spontaneously! Even after the student has become a fairly proficient performer and has created his own musical personality, he goes back to his *guru* from time to time for an evaluation of his development and to be inspired by new ideas. A true *guru* never stops growing musically and spiritually himself and can be a constant source of inspiration and guidance to the loving disciple.

So, starting from the very beginning, I would estimate that it requires at

> least twenty years of constant work and practice to reach maturity and a high standard of achievement in our classical music.[2]

The above represents a fairly typical series of paragraphs: the average length of the paragraphs is 150 to 200 words, with a two-line introductory paragraph and a four-line concluding paragraph to break the monotony of a succession of equal blocks.

Paragraphing does not always correspond so neatly to joints in the structure of thought, for in addition to logic there are many considerations that enter into the division of prose into paragraphs. Indeed, "thought movement itself," as rhetorician Paul C. Rodgers has pointed out, "submits to very flexible partitioning; hence the size of a given logical paragraph frequently reflects secondary influences."[3] The narrow-column format of a newspaper, for example, and the reader's demand that he be able to skim the page and get the news almost at a glance, require short, varied paragraphs. (They should all be short but not *equally* short.) Normally the writer should not fragment his ideas, however, by chopping them up into a series of very short paragraph units. We can see immediately that a typewritten page containing four or more paragraphs needs reworking: either the writer has not developed his ideas sufficiently or he has failed to respect their unity and flow.

Strictly formal considerations may also enter into paragraph division, "as when paragraphs are paired off for contrast or comparison or knit into some larger pattern involving paragraphs as units."[4]

Similarly a paragraph may be set off for a particular purpose: as an introduction, a conclusion, or a transition from one aspect of thought to another. Such paragraphs may contain only one or two sentences, but they nonetheless deserve to stand alone.

Finally, we must consider emphasis, rhythm, and tone. A short paragraph, for example, isolates a piece of information and thereby stresses it; it may also contribute to the rhythmic sweep of the essay and the particular tone the writer hopes to establish. A philosophic essay may contain relatively long, detailed paragraphs that reinforce the unity, flow, and continuity of thought; a light essay may embody its scattered and tentative ideas in shorter, less formally structured paragraphs. As always, the writer must consider not only his subject but the reader as well. Will a demandingly long and bulky paragraph discourage him? If so, it may be advisable to divide a normal unit of thought into two units, as the writer of the following narrative has done, clearly to increase readability:

> In any journey there are three separate and recognizable stages. First there is the setting-out, the more-or-less anxious business of organizing the expedition and getting it off complete and on time. Then there is the journey itself, with its satisfying sense of achievement in each mile travelled. This is the most peaceful stage for the travellers, since we hand ourselves over as so much baggage to be passively transported. Even in a motor-car which we drive ourselves we are only a part of the steering-wheel: we have only to propel the

[2] From *My Music, My Life* by Ravi Shankar. Copyright © 1968, by Kinnara School of Indian Music, Inc. Reprinted by permission of Simon and Schuster, Inc.

[3] Paul C. Rodgers, Jr., "A Discourse-Centered Rhetoric of the Paragraph," *College Composition and Communication*, 17 (Feb. 1966), 5.

[4] Ibid.

car; and even driving across London in the rush hour is wonderfully soothing, for instance, with getting a family off on summer holiday.

The third stage of the journey is less definite and more variable. It begins imperceptibly as we near the end, and we recognize the transition by a growing impatience to arrive. We are no longer travelling, but impatiently covering the distance which still separates us from where we want to be. However it is not the number of miles remaining which decides our impatience: it is their proportion of the whole. On a journey of a hundred miles, at forty-nine we are still placid travellers.

Nan Fairbrother, *The House in the Country*

Similarly the writer of the following piece has promoted readability by distributing a single idea ("Sebastiana was devoted to Tanguy, in a silent, inarticulate way") over four relatively short paragraphs, each bringing out a different nuance of feeling:

Sebastiana was devoted to Tanguy, in a silent, inarticulate way. She watched over him and took care of him. Every day, during the midday break, everyone saw her arrive with "the kid's" dinner. She had a half-hour's walk each way to bring him his food, but she was determined he must get something hot inside him. She always managed to get something which she considered a "luxury"—a slice of ham, perhaps, or a little cheese. She arrived proudly carrying her bundle and sat on a big stone, in the shade, beside Tanguy. Other workers used to have jokes at her expense, and tell her she was "past the age for that kind of thing." She let them talk, and did not even take the trouble to reply. She was desolate at seeing Tanguy so ill and dejected, and she continued to look after him with extraordinary tenderness.

She spent a great deal of time finding classical music for him in the radio programs, pretending to adore Bach and Beethoven. In the evening, after Tanguy had come home, they would sit before dinner in the little courtyard and chat. When he was reading the paper or listening to music, she sat quietly, without moving or speaking.

They never expressed their affection openly. Sebastiana's love remained dumb; like Gunther, she never gave external reality to her tender feelings except through the unimpeachable eloquence of her actual behavior. She lived for Tanguy as she would have lived for her own son, watched over him while he slept, took care of his clothes, gave him the kind of food he liked best (as far as she could), and tried to find amusements for him. On Sundays they sometimes picnicked on the beach, well away from the crowd.

He told her about everything. She listened in silence and smiled at him tenderly. All her understanding came from her heart, for she was the maternal instinct personified. Tanguy, on his part, loved and admired her because she was fair and honest. He loved her uncalculating generosity and her tranquil expression. She was sensible rather than clever, but she almost always knew what was right.[5]

In summary, then, it may be said that paragraph divisions proceed primarily by logic and secondarily by physical, rhythmical, tonal, formal, and

[5] From *Child of Our Time* by Michael del Castillo. Copyright © 1958 by Frederick Muller, Ltd. Reprinted by permission of Alfred A. Knopf, Inc.

other rhetorical criteria. There is no simple formula by which to describe the architecture of the paragraph. "To indent," as Rodgers concludes, "is to interpret."

Paragraph Unity

Insofar as the average paragraph treats a relatively self-contained idea, we may accept the common view of the paragraph as a miniature essay, which, like the full-length essay, answers a specific question posed by the writer. If the essay itself is a unified whole, then the individual questions posed at the paragraph level are but aspects of the larger questions posed by the piece. Whether each question is explicitly raised in the topic sentence, or merely implied in the direction of the discourse at a certain stage of its development, the writer confronts the same imperative: to answer *that* question that he has raised and no other. In the paragraph, then, as in the essay, the writer is obliged to work toward unity—singleness of subject. The substance of the paragraph (like the substance of the total piece) should be about what it is supposed to be about; it should make the points the writer set out to make and not some other points that happen to occur to him as he is writing. It should, in other words, stick to its subject and not wander off into digressions or irrelevant side issues. A paragraph is unified when it contains only those elements that contribute to the realization of its main idea.

We may say without reservation that no quality is more central to good exposition than unity, for it is only through a series of unified paragraphs, clearly and systematically related to one another, that a good piece of writing—whether a short essay or a long book—can result.

It is worthwhile, then, to consider the problem of paragraph unity in detail and to examine some representative paragraphs. Take the following paragraph, for example, drawn from an article on cabaret life in contemporary Germany. At the point in the article where this paragraph occurs, the writer clearly wanted to draw a contrast between East and West Berlin cabarets. Note how she characterizes the contrast in her first sentence—"striking and pathetic"—and how she then presents details that relate directly to reasons why the contrast exists and in what it consists.

> The difference between West Berlin cabarets and the one cabaret in East Berlin is striking and pathetic. To begin with, the Distel is not a cabaret at all, but a little theater; there are no little tables; and since smoking is not allowed and one cannot order drinks, coffee, or frankfurters during the performance, the whole *gemutlich* atmosphere is lost. No one feels impelled to join in the choruses, or even to laugh very loudly. There is a feeling of discipline—not to be confused with the universal Central European solemnity about the arts—which is infinitely out of place and depressing, for the cabaret is just the place where discipline should be thrown to the wind.
>
> Sarah Gainham, "The Political Cabarets"

Here is a longer paragraph written by a Shakespearean scholar. Note that once again the main idea is stated in the first sentence of the paragraph;

it is then restated more specifically in the second and third sentences, followed by examples. This, as we shall see, is a recurrent paragraph pattern: idea followed by illustrations or examples.

> The easiest way to bring home to oneself the nature of the tragic character is to compare it with a character of another kind. Dramas like *Cymbeline* and the *Winter's Tale,* which might seem destined to end tragically, but actually end otherwise, owe their happy ending largely to the fact that the principal characters fail to reach tragic dimensions. And, conversely, if these persons were put in the place of the tragic heroes, the dramas in which they appeared would cease to be tragedies. Posthumus would never have acted as Othello did; Othello, on his side, would have met Iachimo's challenge with something other than words. If, like Posthumus, he had remained convinced of his wife's infidelity, he would not have repented her execution; if, like Leontes, he had come to believe that by an unjust accusation he had caused her death, he would never have lived on, like Leontes. In the same way the villain Iachimo has no touch of greatness. But Iago comes nearer to it, and if Iago had slandered Imogen and had supposed his slanders to have led to her death, he certainly would not have turned melancholy and wished to die. One reason why the end of the *Merchant of Venice* fails to satisfy us is that Shylock is a tragic character, and that we cannot believe in his accepting his defeat and the conditions imposed upon him. This was the case where Shakespeare's imagination ran away with him, so that he drew a figure with which the destined pleasant ending would not harmonise.
>
> A. C. Bradley, *Shakespearean Tragedy*

Clearly, then, unity in the paragraph is achieved when the writer recognizes and respects the thrust of his own idea, whether it is explicitly stated or only implied. The following passage from George Orwell's "Such, Such Were the Joys" demonstrates vividly how every detail in a unified paragraph contributes to the total effect—in this case an image of "disgust":

> Whoever writes about his childhood must beware of exaggeration and self-pity. I do not want to claim that I was a martyr or that Crossgates was a sort of Dotheboys Hall. But I should be falsifying my own memories if I did not record that they are largely memories of disgust. The overcrowded, underfed, underwashed life that we led was disgusting, as I recall it. If I shut my eyes and say "school," it is of course the physical surroundings that first come back to me: the flat playing-field with its cricket pavilion and the little shed by the rifle range, the draughty dormitories, the dusty splintery passages, the square of asphalt in front of the gymnasium, the raw-looking pinewood chapel at the back. And at almost every point some filthy detail obtrudes itself. For example, there were the pewter bowls out of which we had our porridge. They had overhanging rims, and under the rims there were accumulations of sour porridge, which could be flaked off in long strips. The porridge itself, too, contained more lumps, hairs and unexplained black things than one would have thought possible, unless someone were putting them there on purpose. It was never safe to start on that porridge without investigating it first. And there was the slimy water of the plunge bath—it was twelve or fifeen feet long, the whole school was supposed to go into it every morning, and I doubt whether the water was changed at all frequently—and the always-damp tow-

els with their cheesy smell: and, on occasional visits in the winter, the murky sea-water of the local Baths, which came straight in from the beach and on which I once saw floating a human turd. And the sweaty smell of the changing-room with its greasy basins, and, giving on this, the row of filthy, dilapidated lavatories, which had no fastenings of any kind on the doors, so that whenever you were sitting there someone was sure to come crashing in. It is not easy for me to think of my schooldays without seeming to breathe in a whiff of something cold and evil-smelling—a sort of compound of sweaty stockings, dirty towels, faecal smells blowing along the corridors, forks with old food between the prongs, neck-of-mutton stew, and the banging doors of the lavatories and the echoing chamber-pots in the dormitories.[6]

The most common violation of unity is the inclusion of material in one paragraph that should either be in a separate paragraph or dropped altogether. The best way to test for unity is to reread the first draft of each paper to make certain that no extraneous material has crept in during the writing stage. It is necessary to be very critical at this time, examining each point of information and each turn in the development of thought to make sure that it belongs where it is and that each point picks up the preceding point and leads to the next in a natural, logical movement. Indeed it may be said of every structural element (sentence, paragraph, essay, chapter, book) that it is never a haphazard concourse of ideas but rather "a careful record of a mind moving toward a preconceived goal." It is this principle in action, the meticulous development of a single idea through its various stages, that gives a work organic unity—oneness of aim in all its parts.

Developing the Paragraph

In addition to sticking to his subject, the writer must say enough about it to give the reader a sense of inclusiveness, a clear, well-rounded, and reasonably complete picture of the matter at hand. As Edgar Allan Poe said of the poem and short story, so we may say of any piece of prose writing, that "a certain degree of duration"—or bulk—is necessary to produce a given effect. Poe's frequent purpose in his fiction was to produce an emotional effect such as horror or fear; the expository writer tries to produce in his reader something quite different—the intellectual effect or "state" of understanding. In both cases, however, duration or "extended treatment" is required—i.e., systematic development of an idea beyond the mere mention of it. The question of development, then, is concerned with fullness of information, fleshing out the bare bones of thought so that the reader knows precisely what the writer means.

We cannot generalize about how much the reader should be told at any given stage of exposition. The writer himself must decide, paragraph by paragraph, how best to amplify a unit of meaning so that the reader is not left with unanswered questions and gaps in thought and reasoning. To avoid these problems, the writer must provide supporting data that will fill in the boundaries of an idea: details, facts, examples, analogies, anecdotes, reasons,

[6] From "Such, Such Were the Joys" in *Such, Such Were the Joys* by George Orwell, copyright, 1945, 1952, 1953, by Sonia Brownell Orwell. Reprinted by permission of Harcourt Brace Jovanovich, Inc. and Martin Secker & Warburg.

illustrations, quotations. These are the supporting materials of paragraph development, and although they may be arranged in an indefinite number of ways, there are certain recurrent patterns that the writer should be familiar with. Some of these are discussed and illustrated below.

General to Specific

Irritatingly simplistic as it may seem, there is truth in the notion of the paragraph as a block of prose introduced by a topic sentence containing a general idea that is developed in the remaining sentences of the paragraph through specific details, examples, reasons, and so on. Studies of professional writing indicate that this deductive pattern of paragraph development (i.e., movement from a general statement to specific examples or explanations of that statement) does in fact characterize much of English prose. Note, for example, how the following paragraphs, drawn from different sources, exemplify this "general to specific" principle of order:

1. General idea developed by specific examples

An "example" is a representative member of a group; therefore examples serve to illustrate a general principle and—if they are plentiful enough—to support and possibly prove it.

> Many of the Founding Fathers were passionate lovers or practitioners of music. Jefferson used to rise at five in the morning to practice the violin; his expense books record many a purchase of "the latest minuets" and of fiddle strings for string-quartet sessions; and he was well acquainted with the technique and construction of various instruments. Samuel Adams organized the people of Boston into secret singing clubs to stir up enthusiasm for independence. And Thomas Paine wrote at least two fine songs, "The Liberty Tree" and "Bunker Hill." In addition to having made a famous ride, Paul Revere might go down in history as having been the engraver of the first volume of original hymns and anthems ever published in this country. And Benjamin Franklin—most versatile of all—not only was a writer of ballad verses and a music publisher, but even invented a new musical instrument—the glass Armonica, for which Gluck, Mozart, and Beethoven composed a number of pieces.
>
> Elie Siegmeister, "Music in Early America"

> A surprising number of the people of Hiroshima remained more or less indifferent about the ethics of using the bomb. Possibly they were too terrified by it to want to think about it at all. Not many of them even bothered to find out much about what it was like. Mrs. Nakamura's conception of it—and awe of it—was typical. "The atom bomb," she would say when asked about it, "is the size of a matchbox. The heat of it is six thousand times that of the sun. It exploded in the air. There is some radium in it. I don't know just how it works, but when the radium is put together, it explodes." As for the use of the bomb, she would add, "Shikata ga nai," a Japanese expression as common as, and corresponding to, the Russian word "nicheve": "It can't be helped. Oh, well. Too bad." Dr. Fujii said approximately the same thing about the use of the bomb to Father Kleinsorge one evening, in German: "Da ist nicht zu machen. There's nothing to be done about it."
>
> John Hersey, *Hiroshima*

2. General idea developed by specific details

Details consist of the component parts that make up a whole—the individual steps in a procedure, the particular aspects of an image or impression. Details include factual data of all kinds: statistics, evidence, direct quotations. They answer the questions "how?" and "what?"

Scientists have learned to supplement the sense of sight in numerous ways. In front of the tiny pupil of the eye they put, on Mount Palomar, a great monocle 200 inches in diameter, and with it see 2000 times farther into the depths of space. Or they look through a small pair of lenses arranged as a microscope into a drop of water or blood, and magnify by as much as 2000 diameters the living creatures there, many of which are among man's most dangerous enemies. Or, if we want to see distant happenings on earth, they use some of the previously wasted electromagnetic waves to carry television images which they re-create as light by whipping tiny crystals on a screen with electrons in a vacuum. Or they can bring happenings of long ago and far away as colored motion pictures, by arranging silver atoms and color-absorbing molecules to force light waves into the patterns of the original reality. Or if we want to see into the center of a steel casting or the chest of an injured child, they send the information on a beam of penetrating short-wave X rays, and then convert it back into images we can see on a screen or photograph. Thus almost every type of electromagnetic radiation yet discovered has been used to extend our sense of sight in some way.

George R. Harrison, "Faith and the Scientist"

He had altered. His eyes had lost a little of the brilliance which used to strike one so forcibly, and his face was no longer ascetically thin. His hair had turned white, of course, and this made his beard look less sparse. The body covered by the sand-colored tunic was as frail as ever; but his cheeks had filled out and taken on a pinkness which gave him a somewhat artificial air. There was still a strong hint of mischief in his expression, however, and his dry laugh supplied the finishing touch—he looked and sounded like some old scholar whose wisdom had led him to discover the virtues of poverty. . . .

Jean Lacouture, *Ho Chi Minh*

3. General idea developed by specific reasons

There are three kinds of reasons: opinions, judgments, deductions. Reasons answer the question "Why?" (in contrast to a detail, which is a step in a procedure, a fact, a part of a whole, the "how" or "what" of the thing discussed).

Reasons are acceptable and respectable only if they are founded on established fact, close observation or experience, or logical analysis.

The life of a student in India is much more difficult than anything we know in this country. Lack of material resources hampers most of the students at every turn. An overwhelming majority of them live at home, if they have homes, in conditions—by any standards we know—of miserable poverty. Often they have too little to eat, very little to wear, almost never any money to spend on the small things which we take so much for granted in our country.

More serious is the fact that they can rarely afford to buy books for study, nor do their libraries have resources remotely comparable with those of our institutions. Beyond this, instruction is frequently anything but inspiring, and study is constrained and limited because the student is required by law to pass an annual examination which puts a high premium on memory work—an examination, set by an outside examining authority, to which each year many more are called than can possibly be chosen. And if a student persists in the face of repeated difficulty and finally in time earns a degree, there is the further debilitating consideration that his chances of finding an appropriate job are frighteningly slim. Yet so great is his inner drive and so bright his hope that the Indian student desires education beyond all else, and perseveres.

Nathan M. Pusey, *The Age of the Scholar*

In outward appearance Canada is very definitely a North American, not a European land. It possesses the vast spaces and distances that are likely to be one of the strongest impressions of the European who visits the United States. And many regions of Canada suggest northward extensions of the United States. We have, to be sure, no equivalent for the distinctive French community, closely knit by bonds of race and religion, that one finds in the Province of Quebec. But the tranquil prosperous farming country of the Upper St. Lawrence is not very different from the neighboring districts of New England and New York. And Canada's prairie provinces—Manitoba, Saskatchewan, Alberta—have much in common with Kansas and Iowa and the Dakotas.

William Henry Chamberlain, "Canada and Ourselves"

4. General idea developed by specific illustration

An illustration is a narrative example or anecdote that embodies an idea in an action. In illustration, in other words, something happens (the distinguishing mark of all narration). The writer may develop his point with one paragraph-length illustration or with several short ones.

"Omit needless words!" cries the author on page 17, and into that imperative Will Strunk really put his heart and soul. In the days when I was sitting in his class, he omitted so many needless words, and omitted them so forcibly and with such eagerness and relish, that he often seemed in the position of having short-changed himself, a man left with nothing more to say yet with time to fill, a radio prophet who had outdistanced the clock. Will Strunk got out of this predicament by a simple trick; he uttered every sentence three times. When he delivered his oration on brevity to the class, he leaned forward over his desk, grasped his coat lapels in his hands, and in a husky, conspiratorial voice said, "Rule Thirteen. Omit needless words! Omit needless words! Omit needless words!"

William Strunk and E. B. White, *Elements of Style*

Never in the history of English letters has there been a more dedicated participant in the literary feuds of his day than the great and cantankerous Dr. Samuel Johnson, who stomped noisily through eighteenth-century London, demolishing arguments and smashing reputations with enormous vigor and gusto. Usually his verbal abuse was enough to smite the unworthy, but sometimes the impatient Doctor resorted to physical violence. ("There is no arguing with

Johnson," the novelist, Oliver Goldsmith, said, "for when his pistol misses fire he knocks you down with the butt end of it.") Once, when a waiter used his dirty fingers instead of the proper tongs to drop a lump of sugar into the Doctor's tea, Johnson tossed the glass through the window and was about to do the same with the waiter, when a friend appeared and calmed him. On another occasion, the manager had placed a chair on a side stage especially for Dr. Johnson's use. Another man, finding the seat empty, sat in it, and then made the unpardonable error of failing to relinquish it to its rightful holder. Faced with this effrontery, the powerful Dr. Johnson simply picked up the chair, with the man still in it, and threw both chair and occupant into the pit.

Myrick Land, *The Fine Art of Literary Mayhem*

Clearly the particularizing of general ideas clarifies and enlivens a subject as well as developing it. Factual details and an analysis of reasons give texture to writing and lend substance, authenticity, and authority to general observations. Examples embody the generalization and thereby illuminate it; indeed nothing is more encouraging to the reader plowing through difficult material than the two words "for example," since the example frequently clears up the straight exposition that preceded it. Similarly an anecdote or illustration enlivens discourse by "acting out" ideas and facts in the form of a story.

Some particularizing procedures are simpler than others. For example, take the paragraph on the Founding Fathers' love of music, cited above, and observe how easily it can be diagrammed, since each sentence is, in fact, an example of the general idea set forth in the topic sentence.

General idea: Founding Fathers loved music

Jefferson . . .
Adams . . .
Paine . . .
Revere . . .
Franklin . . .

The paragraph on the scientists' ability to supplement the sense of sight—also cited above—is only a little more complex. Here again each sentence following the opening sentence provides concrete information as to *how* scientists perform their feats. Only in the last sentence does the writer repeat his generalization. Thus the paragraph (a kind of "sandwich") may be diagrammed as follows:

General idea: Scientists supplement sight in numerous ways

Way 1
Way 2
Way 3
Way 4
Way 5

Terminator: Summing up restatement

Not all paragraphs are as neatly representative of a type as these. Many writers mix supporting examples, reasons, and details, as in the following paragraph by Norman Podhoretz. In it he explains, through a series of vividly recounted details, presented anecdotally, precisely why he finds Norman Mailer "extraordinary."

The better I got to know Mailer personally—and we became very close friends—the more extraordinary I found him. He was, as the saying goes, a walking bag of contradictions: pugnacious in temperament and yet of a surpassing sweetness of character; foolish beyond belief about people, and yet unbelievably quick to understand the point of what anyone was up to; obsessed with fame, power, and rank, and yet the freest of any man I had ever encountered of snobbishiness in any of its forms. Like most famous writers, he was surrounded by courtiers and sycophants, but with this difference: he allowed them into his life not to flatter him but to give his radically egalitarian imagination a constant workout. He had the true novelist's curiosity about people unlike himself—you could see him getting hooked ten times a night by strangers at a party—and his respect for modes of life other than his own was so great that it often led him into romanticizing people and things that might legitimately have been dismissed as uninteresting or mediocre. He would look into the empty eyes of some vapid upper-class girl and announce to her that she could be the madam of a Mexican whorehouse; or he would decide that some broken-down Negro junkie he had met in a Village dive was a battalion-commander at heart. Mailer assumed in the most straightforward way that everyone was out for all the power he could get at every minute of the day, and that from the most casual confrontation between two people, one emerged with a victory and the other with a defeat; he even had a hypochondriacal theory involving the birth and death of cells to cover for the assumption. He himself wanted everything: he would "settle for nothing less" than making a revolution in the consciousness of his time, *and* earning millions of dollars, *and* achieving the very heights of American celebrityhood. He respected the position of celebrityhood precisely as he respected people, sometimes romanticizing a particular "office," but never making the more common and worse mistake of underestimating how much it took to get anywhere big in America or pooh-poohing the qualities of mind and character required for staying on top.[7]

Similarly the following paragraph mixes its supporting materials by incorporating into an extended illustration a mass of statistical data that if presented directly would be dull. When presented within the frame of a story, however, the facts and figures come alive. Indeed it is the concreteness and specificity of the illustrative story—dealing with a family in a specific place, paying a stated amount of money for a single prefabricated ranch house—that demonstrates the truth of the general observation presented here.

Investigating home-buying habits in the Midwest, I found that most home buyers do not compute the burden they are undertaking when a home is offered to them on a long-term mortgage. In Toledo, Ohio, a salesman and his wife proudly showed me their customized pre-fab ranch house which they said they had just bought for $19,500. Did they have a mortgage? Yes, it was a

[7] From *Making It,* by Norman Podhoretz. Copyright © 1967 by Norman Podhoretz. Reprinted by permission of Random House, Inc.

thirty-year kind for $17,000. How much was their interest rate? The husband said, "Gosh, I don't know . . . 4½ per cent I think." His wife thought it was 6 per cent. Their difference in guesses could make a difference of nearly $6,000 in the total cost. Actually, it turned out, they were paying 5½ per cent interest. The one thing they did know was that their monthly payment was $96.53. We quickly multiplied that figure by the 360 months they had committed themselves to pay it, and added on the $2,500 cash down payment. The result was a figure that plainly dismayed them: $37,250.80. That was the real price of their home, not $19,500.

Vance Packard, *The Waste Makers*

Levels of Generality

The paragraph pattern of "general to specific" has recently been amended by the rhetorician Francis Christensen who has observed that in the paragraphs of professional writers, as in their sentences (Chapter 26, "Improving Sentences"), a far more subtle pattern is actually at work—an "additive" or "cumulative" method of expanding the paragraph at "varying levels of generality." [8] This means that one sentence (usually the first, "topic" sentence) will contain a statement that provides a base for discussion; the sentences that follow represent an ebb and flow between the general and the particular. It will be rewarding to examine this method, for it clarifies still further how paragraphs work. To be sure, Christensen's inductive approach is not the only possible approach to paragraph analysis today,[9] but it is demonstrably practical. It enables us to see the many shapes paragraphs take and to appreciate the variability and viability of the form. Such insights surely enable us to use the form with greater control and skill.

Strictly speaking, the well-constructed, well-developed paragraph may assume an indefinite number of forms: it is clearly impossible to encompass *all* possible paragraphs in a single description. But basically, Christensen tells us, the paragraph is "a sequence of structurally related sentences."

> By a sequence of structually related sentences I mean a group of sentences related to one another by coordination and subordination. If a first sentence of a paragraph is the topic sentence, the second is quite likely to be a comment on it, a development of it, and therefore subordinate to it. The third sentence may be coordinate with the second sentence (as in this paragraph) or subordinate to it. The fourth sentence may be coordinate with either the second or third (or with both if they themselves are coordinate, as in this paragraph) or subordinate to the third. And so on.[10]

The typical paragraph, then, opens with a "base" or topic sentence to which other sentences are added; the first may simply be a comment, the second an example, the third another example (detail or reason), the fourth another comment, and so on. The significant point Christensen makes is

[8] Christensen, pp. 52–81.

[9] Christensen's trail-breaking work on the paragraph has stimulated such further investigations as the following: Paul C. Rodgers, Jr., "A Discourse-Centered Rhetoric of the Paragraph," *College Composition and Communication,* 17 (Feb. 1966), 2–11, and Francis Christensen, "Symposium on the Paragraph," *College Composition and Communication,* 17 (May 1966), 60–88.

[10] Christensen, p. 57.

that the movement of the paragraph is not necessarily in a straight line from general to specific. Indeed, he says, "Following a paragraph is more like a dance than a dash. The topic sentence draws a circle, and the rest of the paragraph is a pirouette within that circle."

In the properly unified paragraph, then, all the sentences deal with the same subject but at various levels of generality. A comment, for example, will be subordinate to the base sentence on which it is commenting; an explanation or example of the comment will be subordinate to the comment, and so on. The paragraph moves and takes shape in terms of how each added sentence relates—either coordinately or subordinately—to the sentence that precedes it. We can see that the topic sentence is like the base clause of the additive sentence (Chapter 26, "Improving Sentences") in that "it is the sentence on which all the others depend: the sentence whose assertion is supported or whose meaning is explicated or whose parts are detailed by the sentences added to it."

If the added elements all have the same structure and the same relationship to the topic sentence, then Christensen calls the sequence in that paragraph "coordinate," and likens the paragraph to a two-level sentence:

Two-Level Sentence

1 [Lincoln's] words still linger on the lips—
  2 eloquent and cunning, yes
  2 vindictive and sarcastic in political debate,
  2 ripping and ribald in jokes,
  2 reverent in the half-formed utterance of prayer.

Alistair Cooke (cited in Christensen, p. 59)

Coordinate Sequence Paragraph

Note that in this type of paragraph all supporting sentences are structurally alike (note, also, that the Founding Fathers paragraph on page 490 follows this same pattern).

1 This is the essence of the religious spirit—the sense of power, beauty, greatness, truth infinitely beyond one's own reach, but infinitely to be aspired to.
  2 It invests men with pride in a purpose and with humility in accomplishment.
  2 It is the source of all true tolerance, for in its light all men see other men as they see themselves, as being capable of being more than they are, and yet falling short, inevitably, of what they can imagine human opportunities to be.
  2 It is the supporter of human dignity and pride and the dissolver of vanity.
  2 And it is the very creator of the scientific spirit; for without the aspiration to understand and control the miracle of life, no man would have sweated in a laboratory or tortured his brain in the exquisite search after truth.

Dorothy Thompson (cited in Christensen, p. 59)

In a subordinate sequence the sentences added to the topic sentence are structurally different and have different relationships to the topic sentence and to each other. Christensen compares this type of paragraph to a multilevel sentence:

Multilevel Sentence

1 A small Negro girl develops from the sheet of glare-frosted walk,
 2 walking barefooted,
  3 her brown legs striking and recoiling from the hot cement,
   4 her feet curling in,
    5 only the outer edges touching.

(cited in Christensen, p. 60)

Subordinate Sequence Paragraph

1 The process of learning is essential to our lives.
 2 All higher animals seek it deliberately.
  3 They are inquisitive and experiment.
   4 An experiment is a sort of harmless trial run of some action which we shall have to make in the real world; and this, whether it is made in the laboratory by scientists or by foxcubs outside their earth.
    5 The scientist experiments and the cub plays; both are learning to correct their errors of judgment in a setting in which errors are not fatal.
     6 Perhaps this is what gives them both their air of happiness and freedom in these activities.

J. Bronowski (cited in Christensen, p. 60)

By viewing the paragraph as a linked sequence of sentences—as in the above examples—Christensen provides us with a quick and useful test of paragraph unity, one which we can easily apply to our own writing. For as we reread the first draft of a paragraph we have written, we can ask, "Does every sentence (i.e., every link in the sequence) connect with the sentence that precedes it and the sentence that follows?" If not, if a sentence is neither coordinate with any sentence above nor subordinate to the sentence immediately preceding it, then it does not belong in the paragraph (it breaks the sequence) and should either be moved elsewhere, or set off in parentheses. In these cases, as Christensen puts it, "the paragraph has begun to drift from its moorings, or the writer has unwittingly begun a new paragraph."

Purely coordinate or subordinate paragraph sequences are, as we might expect, not as common as a mixed sequence in which subordinate elements are added to a basically coordinate sequence or vice versa. Some examples follow.

Mixed Sequence, based on coordination

1 The atmosphere that stirs expectation, that tantalizes the secret hunches that all theater-goers have, is composed of many things, some tangible and some not so very.
 2 Titles count.
  3 ("Sixth Finger in a Five Finger Glove" is not a good title; "The Strong Are Lonely" is not a good title; "Bells Are Ringing" is a good title.)

2 Personalities count.
3 (I've always liked that nice Walter Pidgeon.)
2 Subject matter counts.
3 (Do I want to see a play tonight about treachery in a prison camp?)
2 Timing counts.
3 (I may want to see a play about treachery in a prison camp next year, or I may have wanted to see one last year, but—tonight?)
2 Circumstances count.
3 (Is it Eugene O'Neill's last play, and what did he say about his family?)
2 Curiosity counts.
3 (What in heaven's name can "The Waltz of the Toreadors" be like?)
2 The curve of the moon counts.

Walter Kerr, "How to Beat the Critics"

Mixed Sequence, based on coordination

1 It is commonplace that most artists of outstanding originality and creative power have met lack of appreciation or abuse in their lifetimes.
2 We know that Beethoven's latest and finest works seemed to his contemporaries to be meaningless meanderings of senility aligned with deafness, that Rembrandt's paintings were judged to be "Gothic and crude" by the autocrats of good taste in France.
2 We know the obloquy which the Post-Impressionist painters were required to face.
3 Even in 1925 Cézanne was described by one American critic as "commonplace, mediocre, and a third-rate painter," and in 1934 his work was characterized by another as "meager and unfulfilled art," while an English critic of some prominence has published his judgement that when you have seen one you have seen them all.
2 We know the indignation which was aroused at the beginning of the century by the new enthusiasm for African sculpture.
2 We remember the bewildered ridicule of "modern" music—Stravinsky and Bartók, even of Scriabin and Sibelius—which is now accepted and "placed."
2 We remember the controversies aroused by D. H. Lawrence and James Joyce, the repudiation of Eliot, Pound, Auden.
[Coda] This is not a new thing in critics who have led the vociferous opposition to the new. (This sentence represents a summing up of the sense of the paragraph—a conclusion.)

Harold Osborne, *Aesthetics and Criticism*

Mixed Sequence, based on subordination

1 Whether we like it or not, ours is an Age of Science.
2 It is also, like every other epoch of history, an Age of Private Experience.

3 In this second half of the twentieth century what can a writer do about these inescapable historical facts?

3 And what, as a conscientious literary artist and a responsible citizen, ought he to do about them?

4 His first duty, of course, is to write as well as he can.

5 Much of our experience comes to us, so to say, through the refracting medium of art.

6 If that art is inept, our experience will be vulgarized and corrupted.

6 Along with unrealistic philosophy and religious superstition, bad art is a crime against society.

4 The writer's next duty is to learn something, if only superficially and in patches, about the methods and results of advancing science.

5 This knowledge should then be correlated with private experience and the shared traditions of culture, and the amalgam should be treated as a new kind of raw material for the creation of new varieties of the familiar literary forms.

Harper's

Mixed paragraphs such as these are especially interesting and worthy of close study, for as Christensen says, they suggest "careful calculation of what could be left to the reader and what must be made more explicit." Obviously those points that contain several subordinate sentences are being treated at greater length because the writer feels that they need clarification or emphasis. The inclusion of subordinate categories of information (details, examples) provides the additional "mass" that tells the reader "take note: this is difficult; it needs further explaining" or "this is important and therefore should be lingered over."

The determination of how much the reader must be told at any point—where an added subordinate sentence is necessary or where another coordinate statement might clarify or emphasize an important idea—is left to the judgment of the individual writer. There is no formula that spells out the proper proportions of a paragraph. Even so, the writer can benefit enormously by familiarity with the "additive" approach, for very often all that is needed to improve a passage of prose is further development or amplification at a given level. Thus, says Christensen, "there is nothing arbitrary or unnatural about urging the student to add levels, usually of a lower order of generality, in order to produce a texture rich enough to contain and display his subject." [11]

Similarly John Lord tells us in his study of the paragraph that "all good writing is a constant weaving up and down between the concrete and the abstract, as well as a constant forward movement from a beginning through a middle to an end." [12]

Although, as we have seen, most paragraphs open with a topic sentence, it may occur earlier—in the preceding paragraph.

[11] "Symposium on the Paragraph," p. 62.

[12] John Lord, *The Paragraph: Structure and Style* (New York: Holt, Rinehart and Winston, 1964), p. 73.

1 The mystical artist always sees patterns.

Preceding paragraph

2 The symbol, never quite real, tends to be expressed less and less realistically, and as the reality becomes abstracted the pattern comes forward.

¶3 The wings on Blake's angels do not look like real wings, nor are they there because wings belong to angels.

New paragraph

4 They have been flattened, stylized, to provide a curving pointed frame, the setting required by the pattern of the composition.

3 In Hindoo art and its branches, stylization reaches its height.

4 Human figures are stylized far beyond the point of becoming a type; they too are made into patterns, schematic designs of the human body, an abstraction of humanity.

3 In the case of an Easter rug all desire to express any semblance of reality has gone.

4 Such a work of art is pure decoration.

5 It is the expression of the artist's final withdrawal from the visible world, essentially his denial of the intellect.

Edith Hamilton (Cited in Christensen, pp. 72–73)

To cite a final example, it is worth noting also that a paragraph may stand on its own with no topic sentence per se; in fact no announced statement of its theme—as in the following:

2 In Spain, where I saw him last, he looked profoundly Spanish.

3 He might have passed for one of those confidential street dealers who earn their living selling spurious Parker pens in the cafés of Málaga or Valencia.

4 Like them, he wore a faded chalk-striped shirt, a coat slung over his shoulders, a trim, dark moustache, and a sleazy, fat-cat smile.

4 His walk, like theirs, was a raffish saunter, and everything about him seemed slept in, especially his hair, a nest of small, wet serpents.

3 Had he been in Seville and his clothes been more formal, he could have been mistaken for a pampered elder son idling away a legacy in dribs and on drabs, the sort you see in windows along the Sierpes, apparently stuffed.

2 In Italy he looks Italian; in Greece, Greek: wherever he travels on the Mediterranean coast, Tennessee Williams takes on a protective colouring which melts him into his background, like a lizard on a rock.

2 In New York or London he seems out of place, and is best explained away as a retired bandit.

3 Or a beach comber: shave the beard off any of the self-portraits Gauguin painted in Tahiti, soften the features a little, and you have a sleepy outcast face that might well be Tennessee's.

Kenneth Tynan (Cited in Christensen, pp. 71–72)

In this paragraph, the three level 2 sentences are clearly coordinate, but there is, as Christensen notes, "no superordinate sentence to umbrella them; that is, there is no level 1, no topic sentence. With paragraphs such as this the topic can usually be inferred from the preceding paragraph." Indeed, very often the structure and impetus of an idea carries over from paragraph to paragraph so that no formal transition or topic sentence is needed.

In summary, then, it may be said about this most crucial subject of development (the *heart* of writing) that each paragraph unit (or each series of units) should have sufficient "duration" to do full justice to its subject; it should also develop its thought (answer its question) systematically, with a variety of materials that give the paragraph substance and texture (levels of generality); and it should not drop the thought (leave that aspect of the answer) until, as Herbert Read says, it has been "seen in all profitable lights."[13] Further, these thoughts should be developed at a steady, reasonably accelerated pace so that the writing *flows* in an ongoing progression. To quote Read once again:

> There is about good writing a visual actuality. It exactly reproduces what we should metaphorically call the contour of our thought. The metaphor is for once exact: thought has a contour or a shape. The paragraph is the perception of this contour or shape.
>
> The writer has toward his materials, words, the same relation that an artist, say a modeller, has toward his material, clay. The paragraph is a plastic mass, and it takes its shape from the thought it has to express: its shape *is* the thought."[14]

Achieving Coherence

Coherence literally means "sticking together." Thus a piece of writing is coherent when all its parts stick together, when the individual words, phrases, and sentences are so arranged and connected that a clear pattern of thought emerges. The word "pattern" is important here. Words, like pictures, must fall into a pattern before they can be recognized and understood. Indeed, in a sense, words *are* pictures of a state of affairs. To continue this analogy ask: Would we recognize a picture if it had no visible order, proportion, or composition, if the parts were not firmly held together by the canvas backbone? Indeed we would not only not recognize it, we would not even call it a picture but a jigsaw puzzle that had to be reassembled into a meaningful visual whole.

The reader who is, as E. B. White once said, "always in trouble" has no time and certainly no inclination to play games, to reassemble verbal parts; he must accept the writer's composition as he reads it. If there are missing pieces (important points not mentioned) or corners cut so that the pieces do not interlock (gaps in thought, puzzling jumps from one idea to another), then the reader cannot see the shape of the writer's thought. The writer sees it; he knows exactly what he is trying to say and where he is trying to go, but the reader has only a vague notion; instead of walking beside the writer, turning and bending with his turns and bends, stepping briskly at

[13] Read, *English Prose Style* (Boston: Beacon Press, 1955), p. 54.
[14] Ibid., p. 61.

the pace he has set, the reader must stumble along, losing his way here, picking it up again there, following a parallel path—if he is lucky.

The conscientious writer, then, tries to communicate more than the basic raw material of his ideas; he tries to communicate relationships: Why does point three follow point two and not vice versa? Does the example cited at the end of the paragraph illustrate the whole paragraph or only the last point? Is the second point the cause or the effect of the first? And what does reason three have to do with reason two? Are they of equal importance or is one subordinate to the other? The conscientious writer allows for no guesswork; he makes certain not only that the reader shares the main idea of his paragraph (unity), but also that he follows his particular train of thought—that it flows smoothly from beginning to end (coherence).

Coherence in writing is accomplished basically in three ways:

1. By ordering or arranging material in a logical sequence.
2. By providing transitions from one idea to another.
3. By maintaining a consistent tone and point of view.

We have already discussed the most common ordering principle: the deductive or analytic—i.e., movement from the general to varying levels of the specific. It is worth mentioning here that this order is occasionally reversed so that the paragraph opens with a series of specific details that culminate in a general statement. This is an inductive or synthetic paragraph. The following is an example:

> The Manus teach their children very young the things which they consider most important—physical skill, prudery and respect for property. They teach them these things firmly, unrelentingly, often severely. But they do not teach them respect for age or for knowledge; they enjoin upon them neither courtesy nor kindness to their elders. They do not teach them to work; they regard it as quite natural if a child refuses to rescue a lost necklace from the sea, or retrieve a drifting canoe. When a new house is thatched the children clamber over the scaffolding, shouting and useless. When they catch fish they do not bring them home to their parents; they eat them themselves. They are fond of young children and enjoy teaching them, but refuse to take any responsibility for them. They are taught to control their bodies but not their appetites, to have steady hands but careless tongues. It is impossible to dose them with medicine, for all their lives they have spat out anything which they disliked. They have never learned to submit to any authority, to be influenced by any adult except their beloved but not too respected fathers. In their enforced servitude to their older brothers and uncles, they find neither satisfaction nor pride. They develop from overbearing, undisciplined children into quarrelsome, overbearing adults who make the lagoon ring with their fits of rage.[15]

In addition to the ordering principles of general to specific and specific to general, there are other orders that determine a paragraph pattern: time, space, and order of emphasis.

Time Order

Material can be arranged according to *when* it happened (past or present, early to late, old to new), or in what order it should be done (first do this,

[15] Margaret Mead, *Growing Up in New Guinea* (New York: William Morrow and Company, 1930), pp. 212–13.

then that, and finally this). Narration, historical accounts, the steps in a process, directions or instructions have to be presented in the order in which they happen or should happen.

As an example of this type of ordering here is an account of the final moments in the life of Mary, Queen of Scots. The writer takes us to the scaffold and allows us to witness the event as it happened—minute by minute:

> She laid her crucifix on her chair. The chief executioner took it as a perquisite, but was ordered instantly to lay it down. The lawn veil was lifted carefully off, not to disturb the hair, and was hung upon the rail. The black robe was next removed. Below it was a petticoat of crimson velvet. The black jacket followed, and under the jacket was a body of crimson satin. One of her ladies handed her a pair of crimson sleeves, with which she hastily covered her arms; and thus she stood on the black scaffold with the black figures all around her, blood-red from head to foot.[16]

It should be mentioned that chronological order does not necessarily imply a strictly natural order of events, i.e., an uninterrupted movement forward in time. Like Homer, the writer may begin *in medias res* with an important or exciting event and weave in background by interrupting the ongoing development of the story to dip into the past for some crucial or illuminating details. In other words, the writer may organize his material in whatever time sequence best suits the subject and purpose of his paragraph (or essay), as long as the presentation proceeds in an orderly manner that the reader can follow.

Spatial Order

Just as some material lends itself to a presentation in time, other material calls for a presentation in space. Here again there are no rigid rules prescribing one spatial pattern over another. It is important that the writer visualize the effect he is trying to achieve and that he then set about achieving that effect in a systematic manner. He should be clear in his own mind where the narrator stands (point of view), and proceed according to a natural or logical principle of progression (left to right, far to near, ugly to beautiful). Note that in the following paragraph from *The Adventures of Huckleberry Finn*, Mark Twain blends a time and space pattern. Huck is a stationary observer, describing what he sees as the day breaks over the water.

> The first thing to see, looking away over the water, was a kind of dull line —that was the woods on t'other side; you couldn't make nothing else out; then a pale place in the sky; then more paleness spreading around; then the river softened up away off, and warn't black any more, but gray; you could see little dark spots drifting along ever so far away—trading-scows, and such things; and long black streaks—rafts; sometimes you could hear a sweep creaking; or jumbled-up voices, it was so still, and sounds come so far; and by and by you could see a streak on the water which you know by the look

[16] James Anthony Froude, "The Execution of Mary Queen of Scots," *History of England from the Fall of Wolsey to the Defeat of the Spanish Armada* (New York: AMS Press, 1969).

of the streak that there's a snag there in a swift current which breaks on it and makes that streak look that way; and you see the mist curl up off the water, and the east reddens up, and the river, and you make out a log cabin in the edge of the woods, away on the bank on t'other side of the river, being a wood-yard, likely, and piled by them cheats so you can throw a dog through it anywheres; then the nice breeze springs up, and comes fanning you from over there, so cool and fresh and sweet to smell on account of the woods and the flowers; but sometimes not that way, because they've left dead fish laying around, gars and such, and they do get pretty rank; and next you've got the full day, and everything smiling in the sun, and the song-birds just going to it!

Order of Climax or Emphasis

As mentioned earlier, when presenting a series of items or ideas, it is generally best to arrange them in ascending order of importance or value. The rhetorical justification rests on what appears to be a law of human nature—that we intuitively build to a climax—passing from the "least" to the "most"—the last-mentioned item impressing itself most forcibly on our minds. Thus if a third or fourth item is weak, we say that it is anticlimactic; we have built up to something and "fallen off." Attempting to order his materials emphatically, the writer may begin with a specific fact or situation and unfold the subject by degrees, working steadily toward a culmination or resolution. Or he may simply move from what is expected and obvious to what is unexpected and surprising—as in the following paragraph:

> As Americans are drawn more and more into overseas travel and service abroad, we are advised to be ready for something called "culture shock." Culture shock, roughly defined, is the total psychological discomfort one feels in foreign situations where every human function is dealt with somewhat differently. Big differences, such as language, are obvious; it is not too hard to make allowances for them and adjust to them. But the many, many tiny differences between life in the United States and life abroad—like the taste of the coffee, the value of time, or the smells—are more insidious. Bit by bit, their effects pile up in the pit of the emotions until they all become too much to be endured. Suddenly, unexpectedly, we have had it.
>
> Donald Lloyd, "The Quietmouth American"

It should be mentioned here that the "building up" order of climax is not always suitable. Sometimes one item is so obvious and all-important that it must be stated at the outset, just as an overwhelmingly strong reason in support of an argument often must be presented first if it is not to be conspicuous by its absence, thereby distracting the reader who may keep wondering why the writer doesn't say the *obvious*. Thus in the following paragraph, the writer quite properly presents his most important explanation first:

> Some people are astonished to find that such primitive transportation as dog traction is still used. Why? Probably the most important reason is economy. A dog team can be assembled without expenditure of too much money. Pups appear in the normal course of events. The team becomes self-supporting

since it enables the owner to become a more efficient hunter, especially of seals and caribou. The environment furnishes food for the team and food and clothing for the hunter and his family. A vehicle such as a weasel, snow-buggy, or motor toboggan requires cash capital for the initial investment and for spare parts, gasoline, and oil. Most Eskimos are relatively wealthy in meat and animal products but desperately poor in money. A recent comparison of motor toboggans and dog teams in the Canadian Arctic showed that, considering weight only of food or fuel needed per mile, the dog teams were more efficient. And—very important—a team can be started in thirty-below-zero weather without preheating, using explosive ether for starting fluid, or "burning" one's hands on the cold steel.

Transitional Expressions or Devices

The word "transition" means passing over. Thus transitional guides are connectives (symbols, words, phrases; sometimes whole sentences and paragraphs) that make possible a smooth "passing over" from one idea to the next. Transitions are made by referring to what has been said before, establishing cause-effect connections, looking ahead to what will be said, referring to the present, marking time and place, qualifying, comparing, contrasting. These and other common transitional devices are briefly described below in categories that necessarily overlap to some extent:

Referring: as we have seen, on the whole, as mentioned above, as stated previously, as I have said, it would seem then

Looking ahead: then, later, next, after, afterward, thereafter, finally, now, consequently, to sum up

Establishing causal connections: the result, in conclusion, to conclude, because, for, since, consequently, accordingly, hence, thus, therefore

Time markers: now, then, later, soon, before, next, afterward, finally, meanwhile, thereafter, at the same time

Place markers: here, there, at this point, below, beside, next to, behind, in front, outside, inside

Comparing and establishing degree: and, similarly, in like manner, in the same way, just as, so . . . that, also, more than, less than, beyond this

Qualifying, conceding, or contrasting: but, nevertheless, on the other hand, however, despite this, still, on the contrary, conversely, if, as if, granted that, unless, whether, anyhow, although, even though, yet

Adding and intensifying: first, second, third; a, b, c; 1, 2, 3; to repeat, in addition, moreover, and, also, still, again, similarly, furthermore, finally, really, indeed

Introducing an illustration: thus, to illustrate, for example, for instance

Repeating a key word: This device keeps the main idea before the reader's attention and carries the thread of meaning throughout a passage.

Using synonyms: Instead of repeating a key word so that it becomes monotonous, the writer may use suitable synonyms that continue the same thought.

Using proper pronoun reference: Another substitute for the repetition of key nouns and another way of connecting ideas is to use pronouns in place of nouns.

Maintaining same subject throughout paragraph: It is often possible to continue the same subject from sentence to sentence, thereby maintaining a steady focus throughout the paragraph. The reader moves smoothly and swiftly from one predication to another without mentally shifting gears.

Establishing repetitive or parallel sentence patterns: In addition to repeating key words and ideas the writer may repeat the grammatical structure of his sentences, thereby reinforcing the unity of his thoughts and promoting their flow.

Linking of last sentence of one paragraph with first sentence of next: This is a natural, frequently intuitive method of maintaining coherence between paragraphs. Sometimes connecting words are needed (such as "then again" or "on another occasion"), but sometimes the direction of the thought provides its own continuity.

Note in the following paragraph (also cited earlier) how many transitional words and devices have been used to "tie up" the paragraph into a cohesive whole: to keep the reader aware throughout of the writer's intent, to let him know what is coming next (an additional bit of information, a contrast, an effect):

	The life of a *student* in India is much more diffi-	
	cult than anything we know in this country. Lack of	
Repetition	material resources hampers most of the *students* at	
Pronoun	every turn. An overwhelming majority of *them* live	
reference	at *home,* if *they* have *homes,* in conditions—by any	
	standards we know—of miserable poverty. Often	
Intensification	*they* have too *little* to eat, *very little* to wear, almost	Parallel phrases
and word	never any money to spend on the small things which	
repetition	we take so much for granted in our country. *More*	Comparison
	serious is the fact that they can rarely afford to buy	(degree)
	books for study, nor do their libraries have resources	
	remotely comparable with those of our institutions.	
Comparison and	*Beyond this,* instruction is frequently anything but in-	
pronoun	spiring, and study is constrained and limited because	
reference	the student is required by law to pass an annual ex-	
	amination which puts a high premium on memory work	
	—an *examination,* set by an outside examining au-	Repetition
	thority, to which each year many more are called	
	than can possibly be chosen. *And* if a student per-	Conjunction
Additive/time	sists in the face of repeated difficulty *and finally* in	(additive)
marker	time earns a degree, there is the *further debilitating*	Comparison
	consideration that his chances of finding an appropri-	(degree) and synonyms
	ate job are frighteningly slim. *Yet so* great is his in-	Conjunction
Repetition	ner drive and *so* bright his hope that the Indian stu-	(contrast)
parallel	dent desires education *beyond* all else, and perse-	Comparison
structure	veres.	

Now let us examine a passage of prose and observe how many transitional signals (thirty-five) the writer has included to keep his reader moving steadily in the right direction—from beginning to end—in a straight line of connected statements, each following logically from the one preceding it and each telling the reader accurately what he can expect next (an "and" suggesting another item of equal value; a "however" suggesting contrast; a "because" anticipating a reason).

First read the passage as it appeared in print; then read an analytic version that labels the transitions.

But the plays we are concerned with here pursue ends quite different from those of the conventional play and therefore use quite different methods. They can be judged only by the standards of the Theatre of the Absurd, which it is the purpose of this book to define and clarify.

It must be stressed, however, that the dramatists whose work is here presented and discussed under the generic heading of the Theatre of the Absurd do not form part of any self-proclaimed or self-conscious school or movement. On the contrary, each of the writers in question is an individual who regards himself as a lone outsider, cut off and isolated in his private world. Each has his own personal approach to both subject matter and form; his own roots, sources, and background. If they also, very clearly and in spite of themselves, have a good deal in common, it is because their work most sensitively mirrors and reflects the preoccupations and anxieties, the emotions and thinking of an important segment of their contemporaries in the Western world.

This is not to say that their works are representative of mass attitudes. It is an oversimplification to assume that any age presents a homogeneous pattern. Ours being, more than most others, an age of transition, it displays a bewilderingly stratified picture: medieval beliefs still held and overlaid by eighteenth-century rationalism and mid-nineteenth-century Marxism, rocked by sudden volcanic eruptions of prehistoric fanaticisms and primitive tribal cults. Each of these components of the cultural pattern of the age finds its characteristic artistic expression. The Theatre of the Absurd, however, can be seen as the reflection of what seems the attitude most genuinely representative of our own time's contribution.

The hallmark of this attitude is its sense that the certitudes and unshakable basic assumptions of former ages have been swept away, that they have been tested and found wanting, that they have been discredited as cheap and somewhat childish illusions. The decline of religious faith was masked until the end of the Second World War by the substitute religions of faith in progress, nationalism, and various totalitarian fallacies. All this was shattered by the war. By 1942, Albert Camus was calmly putting the question why, since life had lost all meaning, man should not seek escape in suicide.[17]

Place marker	But the plays we are concerned with *here pur-*	
	sue ends quite different from *those* of the conven-	Pronoun reference
Causal connection	tional play and *therefore use* quite different meth-	Parallel, "pursue"
Pronoun reference	ods. *They* can be judged only by the standards	

[17] From *The Theatre of the Absurd* by Martin Esslin, copyright © 1961, 1968, 1969 by Martin Essling. Reprinted by permission of Doubleday & Company, Inc.

of the Theatre of the Absurd, which it is the purpose of *this* book to define and clarify.

It must be stressed, *however,* that the dramatists whose work is *here* presented and discussed under the generic heading of the Theatre of the Absurd do not form part of any self-proclaimed or self-conscious school or movement. *On the contrary,* each of the *writers* in question is an individual who regards himself as a lone outsider, cut off and isolated in his private world. *Each* has his own personal approach to both subject matter and form; his own roots, sources, and background. *If* they *also,* very clearly *and* in spite of *themselves,* have a good deal in common, *it* is *because their* work *most* sensitively mirrors and reflects the preoccupations and anxieties, the emotions and thinking of an important segment of their contemporaries in the Western world.

This is not to say that their works are representative of mass attitudes. It is an oversimplification to assume that any age presents a homogeneous pattern. *Ours* being, *more than most others,* an age of transition, *it* displays a bewilderingly stratified picture: medieval beliefs *still* held and overlaid by eighteenth-century rationalism and mid-nineteenth-century Marxism, *rocked* by

Demonstrative adjective

Contrast

Place marker

Contrast

Synonym (for "dramatists")

Pronoun reference

Parallel structure

Qualifying condition

Additives

Reflexive pronoun

Causal connection

Pronoun reference

Comparison of degree

Additive "and"s plus parallel structure

Transitional phrase (looking back)

Pronoun reference

Pronoun reference

Comparison of degree

Pronoun reference

Additive and time marker

Parallel to "held and overlaid"

sudden volcanic eruptions of prehistoric fanaticisms and primitive tribal cults. *Each of these* components of the cultural pattern of the age finds *its* characteristic artistic expression. The Theatre of the Absurd, *however*, can be seen as the reflection of what seems the attitude most genuinely representative of our own time's contribution.

Pronoun reference

Contrast

The hallmark of *this attitude* is its sense that the certitudes and unshakable basic assumptions of former ages have been [swept away, that they have been tested and found wanting, that they have been discredited as cheap and somewhat childish illusions.] The decline of religious faith was masked until the end of the Second World War by the substitute religions of faith in progress, nationalism, and various totalitarian fallacies. *All this* was shattered by the war. By 1942, Albert Camus was calmly putting the question why, since life had lost all meaning, man should not seek escape in suicide.

Demonstrative adjective plus repetition of "attitude"

Parallel "that" clauses

Pronoun reference

Consistency of Tone

Still a third factor entering into a coherent paragraph (or essay) is the tone—or tone of voice—that emerges from the written page. It is the voice of the writer, selecting, arranging, spinning out his story in terms of how he feels about it (angry, amused, disdainful, admiring, and so on). However bloodless the subject, all writing is, as pointed out in the introduction to this book, a *human* activity. Therefore there is always a voice involved in a passage of prose, however formal or muted it may be.

Simply stated, tone is a function of the writer's attitude toward his subject and his readers. How does he want them to take his statement: as a formal explanation, a personal impression, an emotional attack, a lament, a joke? For it is patently true and universally recognized that it is not merely what the writer says but the *way* that he says it that enters into the total meaning of a piece of writing and either reinforces or violates its coherence.

The writer who wishes to maintain a consistent tone and point of view must begin with mechanical decisions concerning who is speaking (a first-person "I"? an impersonal "one"? an unbiased "he"?) and then consider whether the statement should be made in the present or past tense, the active or passive voice. On a deeper level the writer must consider who his reader is and having visualized him, will know what kind of usage would be most appropriate (should he say "conflagration" or "fire"?). On a still deeper level the writer must define the particular effect he is trying to create with his words (should he call a lady "thin," "skinny," or "scrawny"?). These mechanical and semantic considerations must be accompanied by the writer's searching of his own mind to ensure that he has a clear idea of how *he* feels about what he is saying and how he wants his readers to feel and think.

Note in the following scatterbrained account of New York City that the writer fails to maintain consistency either in tone or point of view: he shifts in person from "I" to "one" to "you"; he changes tenses and voice throughout; he gasps colloquially over a "hunk of engineering" and then comments pompously on what is "therapeutically preferable." The paragraph is poorly written on many counts, not the least of which is failure to establish and maintain an appropriate tone.

> Although I was born and raised in New York, it still seems to me an exciting city. One can see beautiful sights no matter where you travel, especially up the West Side Highway where I saw the George Washington Bridge eloquently span the Hudson River from New York to New Jersey. What a hunk of engineering! All kinds of recreational activities are offered by New York: at Madison Square Garden you could be a spectator of almost any sport one is interested in: basketball, hockey, boxing. As for participating sports (which are, psychiatrists maintain, therapeutically preferable) I can't imagine any that you wouldn't be able to take up: bowling, tennis, horseback riding, ad infinitum. A veritable cornucopia of cultural activities also await the visiting New Yorker: theatres where thespians from all over the country—nay, the globe—exhibit their talents in plays that rival the splendor of the glorious age of Greek drama; museums which I had the opportunity to visit all my life and were always educational and are also interesting; concerts which are always well-attended by New Yorkers as well as a multitude of outsiders who will be eager to see their favorite artists in the flesh. No kidding, New York is an exciting city.

As a more sustained and successful example of tone, examine the following series of three paragraphs on the subject of "why men marry." The sentences are short and clipped, the words carefully chosen for their biting edge. The writer does not say in so many words that men would be better off *not* marrying, but does he leave any doubt that that is precisely what he thinks?

> Men marry for a variety of reasons, few of them self-appreciated and self-apprehended. The reasons they believe they marry for are seldom the real

ones. Men, even quite young men, often marry for no other reason than that they are lonely and seek a consoling companionship. Older men frequently marry not because they are immediately lonely or seek companionship but because they fear loneliness in their later years. This is particularly—almost inevitably—true in cases where the man is alone in the world, without living parents or close relatives. He is, like a child, afraid of the dark that lies ahead. Love, money, all the other usual theoretical considerations, have nothing to do with his marrying or with the women he marries. He just wants to get married, and that is that.

"Love at first sight—there is no other kind of love, for all men's analysis," an eminent Viennese psychologist has lately observed. Although the illustrioso's remark has been widely ridiculed, there is a deal of truth in it. If it isn't love, or at least something quickly leading to love, at first sight, it isn't love. It may be respect or admiration, or understanding, or camaraderie, or animal magnetism, or anything else of the sort, but it is not love. And it is this first sight, impromptu emotional galvanism that often draws men into marriage without the slightest sober reflection on such matters as have occupied the Viennese Professor Baber's solemn inquiry. A man's eye has much oftener propelled him into wedlock than his heart, and both combined have sucked him into matrimony twenty thousand times oftener than his cerebrum.

Men also marry out of disappointment. The beaten man, the humiliated man, the disappointed man, the man who has taken it on the chin in one way or another, is a veritable gull for almost any woman gunning for a mate. And this is even more true in the case of women. The woman who has been hurt, the woman who has been disappointed, is ready to take on the first even faintly eligible man who comes her way.[18]

There is no simple or single formula for maintaining an appropriate tone throughout a unit of writing; the writer's own sensitivity plus a keen awareness of rhetorical stance (the writer's relation to his subject and his audience) must be the guide.[19] It is worth mentioning, however, that the tone of modern prose style is, on the whole, natural and informal, for, as mentioned earlier, most expository writers today are using the rhythms of normal, everyday speech.

With these principles as a general guide, the writer must check for violations of tone in the paragraphs of the piece he is writing. If a flippantly irreverent term—ill-suited to the context of his subject—slips into a sentence during the writing stage, it should be deleted during a later rewriting or revision. So too should a ponderous or overly elaborate phrase be eliminated from a light informal piece, or a strongly emotional outburst be toned down in a serious argument.

Choice of words and phrases, levels of usage, length and rhythm of sentences, juxtaposition of details, and other such rhetorical devices combine to produce the special tone of the paragraph. It is up to the writer to forge the tone he feels is appropriate, and, having forged it, he should—in the name of coherence—maintain that tone throughout, as in the following examples:

[18] From *The World of George Jean Nathan*, edited by Charles Angoff. Reprinted by permission of Mrs. George Jean Nathan.

[19] See page 9.

Straight exposition: objective, informative, and detached

As the paragraph evolved throughout the centuries from simple graphic mark to complex verbal structure, the word *paragraph* itself came to have three major and distinct meanings. Its earliest meaning signified a graphic mark or character in a variety of forms placed in the margin or in the text itself to direct attention to a particular part of the text. Later the paragraph came to be understood as a division of discourse introduced either by a paragraph mark or indentation. The word now designates a prose structure capable of organic internal arrangement.

Virginia Burke, *The Paragraph in Context*

Informal exposition: subjective, witty

One can argue over the merits of most books, and in arguing understand the point of view of one's opponent. One may even come to the conclusion that possibly he is right after all. One does not argue about *The Wind in the Willows.* The young man gives it to the girl with whom he is in love, and if she does not like it, asks her to return his letters. The older man tries it on his nephew, and alters his will accordingly. The book is a test of character. We can't criticize it, because it is criticizing us. As I wrote once: It is a Household Book; a book which everybody in the household loves, and quotes continually; a book which is read aloud to every new guest and is regarded as the touchstone of his worth. But I must give you one word of warning. When you sit down to it, don't be so ridiculous as to suppose that you are sitting in judgment on my taste, or on the art of Kenneth Grahame. You I don't know. But it is you who are on trial.

A. A. Milne, Introduction to *The Wind in the Willows*

Nonfiction narration: reflective, personal

There are in this world some very strange individuals whose thoughts are even stranger than they are.

In our house in Warsaw—No. 10 Krochmalna Street—and sharing our hallway, there lived an elderly couple. They were simple people. He was an artisan, or perhaps a peddler, and their children were all married. Yet the neighbors said that, despite their advanced years, these two were still in love. Every Sabbath afternoon, after the *cholent,* they would go for a walk arm in arm. In the grocery, at the butcher's—wherever she shopped—she spoke only of *him:* "He likes beans . . . *he* likes a good piece of beef . . . *he* likes veal . . ." There are women like that who never stop talking about their husbands. He, in turn, also would say at every opportunity, "My wife."

Isaac Bashevis Singer, "The Sacrifice," *In My Father's Court*

Critical review: breezy, sarcastic

Her (Bette Davis') first husband lacked professional drive and had to be divorced. Her second husband, toward whom she still feels tender, died. She paid alimony to get shet of her third. She and her fourth husband, Gary Merrill, were happy for a long time. But he fell out of love with her, she says, because "for three years I was solely a wife and mother." She had become a confirmed homebody with cleaning rag and stirring spoon, like Old Mother

Hubbard or Old Dutch Cleanser. Now Miss Davis is thoroughly disillusioned. "Power is new to women," she says with the solemn authority of a sociologist, but she does see a "swing towards a matriarchal society." Three swings out, I hope.

Brooks Atkinson, *Brief Chronicles*

ASSIGNMENTS

I. A. Analyze the paragraphs below in terms of

1. topic sentence (if there is one)
2. main idea or purpose of paragraph
3. basic materials of development
4. ordering principle (general to specific, specific to general)
5. transitional devices
6. tone and point of view
7. pace

B. In order to see their structure more clearly, try to diagram these paragraphs (as the Founding Fathers paragraph is diagrammed) or to arrange and number them according to Christensen's "level of generality."

1. It is a miracle that New York works at all. The whole thing is implausible. Every time the residents brush their teeth, millions of gallons of water must be drawn from the Catskills and the hills of Westchester. When a young man in Manhattan writes a letter to his girl in Brooklyn, the love message gets blown to her through a pneumatic tube—pfft—just like that. The subterranean system of telephone cables, power lines, steam pipes, gas mains and sewer pipes is reason enough to abandon the island to the gods and weevils. Every time an incision is made in the pavement, the noisy surgeons expose ganglia that are tangled beyond belief. By rights, New York should have destroyed itself long ago, from panic or fire or rioting or failure of some vital supply line in its circulatory system or from some deep labyrinthine short circuit. Long ago the city should have experienced an insoluble traffic snarl at some impossible bottleneck. It should have perished of hunger when food lines failed for a few days. It should have been wiped out by a plague starting in its slums or carried in by ships' rats. It should have been overwhelmed by the sea that licks at it on every side. The workers in its myriad cells should have succumbed to nerves, from the fearful pall of smoke-fog that drifts over every few days from Jersey, blotting out all light at noon and leaving the high offices suspended, men groping and depressed, and the sense of world's end. It should have been touched in the head by August heat and gone off its rocker.[20]

2. The line between the fancy and the plain, between the atrocious and felicitous, is sometimes alarmingly fine. The opening phrase of the Gettysburg address is close to the line, at least by our standards today, and Mr. Lincoln knowingly or unknowingly, was flirting with disaster when he wrote "Four

[20] From pp. 24–25 in *Here is New York* by E. B. White. Copyright 1949 by E. B. White. By permission of Harper & Row, Publishers.

score and seven years ago." The President could have got into his sentence with plain "Eighty-seven," a saving of two words and less of a strain on the listeners' powers of multiplication. But Lincoln's ear must have told him to go ahead with four score and seven. By doing so, he achieved cadence while skirting the edge of fanciness. Suppose he had blundered over the line and written, "In the year of our Lord seventeen hundred and seventy-six." His speech would have sustained a heavy blow. Or suppose he had settled for "Eighty-seven." In that case he would not have got into his introductory sentence too quickly; the timing would have been bad.

William Strunk and E. B. White, *The Elements of Style*

3. Out on Safaris, I had seen a herd of Buffalo, one hundred and twenty-nine of them, come out of the morning mist under a copper sky, one by one, as if the dark and massive, iron-like animals with the mighty horizontally swung horns were not approaching, but were being created before my eyes and sent out as they were finished. I had seen a herd of Elephant travelling through dense Native forest, where the sunlight is strewn down between the thick creepers in small spots and patches, pacing along as if they had an appointment at the end of the world. It was, in giant size, the border of a very old, infinitely precious Persian carpet, in the dyes of green, yellow, and black-brown. I had time after time watched the progression across the plain of the Giraffe, in their queer, inimitable, vegetative gracefulness, as if it were not a herd of animals but a family of rare, long-stemmed, speckled gigantic flowers slowly advancing. I had followed two Rhino on their morning promenade, when they were sniffing and snorting in the air of the dawn—which is so cold that it hurts in the nose—and looked like two very big angular stones rollicking in the long valley and enjoying life together. I had seen the royal lion, before sunrise, below a waning moon, crossing the grey plain on his way home from the kill, drawing a dark wake in the silvery grass, his face still red up to the ears, or during a midday-siesta, when he reposed contentedly in the midst of his family on the short grass and in the delicate, spring-like shade of the broad Acacia trees of his park of Africa.[21]

4. What are qualities that make language live? *Feeling* is one. A writer's ability to feel life deeply, to be responsive to it. Then *power over language*, the gift to use words significantly and to form them in ways to give them meaning and impact. Also the quality of *style*, a writer's personal way with words, as intimate a part of a good writer as the size and shape of his nose. *Knowledge* is another quality that elevates writing into literature, so that the reader is memorably informed and made aware of new worlds. *Insight* is still another quality—a writer's ability to illuminate experience, to light up the dark places so that the reader sees life more clearly. And lastly what Dobie calls *perspective*, so that in reading one is aware of relationships both in space and time.

Lawrence Clark Powell, *The Little Package*

5. Acts of conscientious objection in our own times have passed beyond the original grounds of protest against military service. Young people, sown like dragon's teeth by the winds of war in the 1940's, band together to do battle

21 From *Out of Africa*, by Isak Dinesen. Copyright 1937 and renewed 1965 by Rungstenlundfonden. Reprinted by permission of Random House, Inc. Reprinted by permission of Putnam & Company Ltd., British Commonwealth publishers.

with what they feel to be the intolerable terms of contemporary life—germ war, cold war, the arms race, discrimination. Middle-aged men, remembering that they once went to war to "make the world safe for democracy," have felt obliged in the 1960's to oppose the course of events, the felt terrors of the times. This "quiet war" is an intense one. Determined to work some change in society, to violate laws if necessary, the new conscientious objector is more militant than his forebears. No longer is he willing to stand aside, to say, in effect, "I cannot join with you, but I will not stop you from doing as you see fit." Today, conscientious scruple is demanding that the objector attempt to turn his society from the course it has selected. With sit-ins, lie-ins, teach-ins, peace vigils, freedom marches, work stoppages, tax refusals, men of conscience attempt to change the status quo. Thoreau is heard in the land as never before: "If [injustice] is of such a nature that it requires you to be the agent of injustice to another, then, I say, break the law. Let your life be a counter friction to stop the machine."

Lillian Schlissel, *Conscience in America*

6. The Negro's search for equality has followed closely the classic pattern of most revolutions. Crane Brinton, Harvard's distinguished professor of history, notes in his study of the subject that there are at least three principal requisites for the birth of a revolution. First, revolution most often takes place in a society that is economically progressive, but in which the fruits of progress are not distributed evenly throughout the population. This is certainly true of U.S. society, and of the Negro's place in it. Secondly, the government should either be corrupt or else ineffective in trying to institute reforms. The Federal government today is hardly corrupt, nor is it ineffective. But it certainly did very little to help the Negro during the ninety years between emancipation and the beginning of his American revolution. A third condition is that the upper classes, and especially the upper-class intellectuals, have enough leisure to develop social consciousness and take up causes. Leisure born of rising affluence, of course, is a mark of American society today, and the Negro has in fact drawn much support from upper-class sympathizers and intellectuals (he has, however, perhaps drawn more from young college students). Brinton also found that a revolution flourishes best when the country is not involved in any international conflict, which tends to distract attention from the cause. This is one condition lacking in the Negro revolution, since the United States has become deeply involved in war in Vietnam. In fact, the Vietnam war is cited by civil-rights leaders as one very specific reason why the Negro's revolt has slowed: many of those who once worried about the Negro's plight now worry about the war.[22]

7. The chronicler of Petrarch's life must record high hopes coupled with bitter disappointments. The poet spent a lifetime lyricizing an idealized and unattainable love, finally concluding that "Commerce with women, without which I had sometimes thought I could not live, I now fear more than death. . . . When I reflect on what woman is, a temptation quickly vanished." He worked for the restoration of an imperial Rome, only to decide that it was a city which sold for gold the blood of Christ. He wanted an ivory tower in which to write masterpieces, but wandered restlessly through a dozen towns on a lifetime

[22] From *Black and White* by William Brink and Louis Harris. Copyright © 1966, 1967, by Newsweek, Inc. Reprinted by permission of Simon and Schuster.

odyssey, which Bishop retraced in preparing his book. (Mrs. Bishop's pen impressions of these towns illustrate and enhance the volume.) He sought to emulate Virgil by rallying Italy to greatness with an epic poem on Scipio Africanus, only to have contemporaries hoot at it and tempt him to burn it. He strove for immortality through erudite works in Latin, but he won it with Italian rimes to a woman he had never touched.

Robert J. Clements, "Laurels in Lieu of the Lady"

8. The rehearsal studio of a ballet company is something of a cross between a convent and a prize fight gym. Before the dancers go into action, they paw a resin box in a corner, like fighters, and when they make their way about the room between classes or rehearsal sessions, they are apt—even the most petite of ballerinas—to walk with a pugilist's flat-footed but springy gait, shoulders swaying with a bit of swagger, arms hanging loosely. There is the acrid sweat smell of the gym, and the same formidable presence of lithe, steel-muscled, incredibly trim and capable bodies ruthlessly forcing themselves to become even trimmer and more capable. But there is also an aura of asceticism, of spirituality—a spirituality achieved paradoxically, by means of single-minded concentration of the body. The mirror covering one whole wall from ceiling to floor would seem to speak of gross vanity, but the dancers, though they may have embarked on their careers from vain motives, have learned to rid themselves of conceit when they work. They use the mirror dispassionately, measuring their reflected selves with almost inhuman objectivity against the conception of an ideal to which they have dedicated their lives. The ideal, of course, is that of a particular kind of beauty, a centuries-old, thoroughly artificial way of moving, which, when shaped into ballets by a choreographer, becomes art of a special sort—an elusive, evanescent art, as fleeting as fireworks or soap bubbles, that nevertheless has the power not only to entrance beholders but even, in some mysterious manner, to convey an experience of lasting significance.[23]

9. The attitude toward slavery of those much-admired classical Greeks is curious. Certainly there were great thinkers among the Athenians, but the lot of the slave never engaged their sympathy. Reading Plato's *Republic* or Aristotle's *On Politics,* one can easily come to think what nasty people those Greeks were. Somehow they just could not see that the "slave mentality" that they so despised was the product, not of the kind of people made into slaves, but of the system. As the great sociologist, William Graham Sumner, remarked in *Folkways,* "If any man, especially a merchant, who went on a journey incurred a great risk of slavery, why was not slavery a familiar danger of every man, and therefore a matter for pity and sympathy?" The woes of slavery were certainly often enough pictured in the tragedies, but the inequities of the system never worried the philosophers.

L. Morston Bates, "On Being Mean"

10. The parlor, a room in which to have conversation, not only derived etymologically from the French verb *parler,* but took its airs and graces from what was called in the early part of the last century "the French taste." In polite urban circles anything French was considered more fashionable than anything

[23] From p. 3 in *Balanchine* by Bernard Taper. Reprinted by permission of Harper & Row, Publishers.

English, and it was not until late in the century, when the "parlor" had become the butt of ridicule and rich Americans were buying titled Englishmen as husbands for their daughters, that the British expression "drawing room" came into polite usage in America. In general the parlor meant a room set apart for formal occasions; for entertaining acquaintances, rather than intimate friends, and clergymen on their rounds of parish calls. The word was ubiquitous, and even in the log houses of the frontier, which consisted of two square cabins joined by a breeze way or dog-trot, the room in which the family entertained guests (as opposed to the "family room," where the family cooked and ate and some of it slept) was called the parlor.

"The Parlor," *American Heritage*

II. Study the paragraphs in the following selections. Note how each paragraph functions in terms of the whole unit of discourse. Note also the main idea, method of development, ordering principle, transitional devices, tone, and pace of the individual paragraphs.

1. The lyrical fragment "Kubla Khan" (fifty-odd rhymed and irregular verses of exquisite prosody) was dreamed by the English poet Samuel Taylor Coleridge on a summer day in 1797. Coleridge writes that he had retired to a farm near Exmoor; an indisposition obliged him to take a sedative; sleep overcame him a few moments after he had read a passage from Purchas describing the construction of a palace by Kubla Khan, the emperor who was made famous in the West by Marco Polo. In the dream the lines that had been read casually germinated and grew; the sleeping man perceived by intuition a series of visual images and, simultaneously, the words that expressed them. After a few hours he awoke with the certainty that he had composed, or received, a poem of about three hundred verses. He remembered them with singular clarity and was able to write down the fragment that is now part of his work. An unexpected visitor interrupted him and afterward he was unable to remember any more. To his no small surprise and mortification, although he still retained "some vague and dim recollection of the general purport of the vision, yet, with the exception of some eight or ten scattered lines and images, all the rest had passed away like the images on the surface of a stream into which a stone has been cast, but, alas! without the after restoration of the latter!" Coleridge wrote.

Swinburne felt that what he had been able to salvage was the supreme example of music in the English language, and that to try to analyze it would be like trying to unravel a rainbow (the metaphor belongs to John Keats). Summaries or descriptions of poetry whose principle virtue is music are useless and would only defeat our purpose; so then let us merely remember that Coleridge was given a page of undisputed splendor in a dream.

Although the case is quite extraordinary, it is not unique. In the psychological study *The World of Dreams* Havelock Ellis has compared it to the case of the violinist and composer, Giuseppe Tartini, who dreamed that the Devil (his slave) was playing a prodigious sonata on the violin; when the dreamer awoke he played *Trillo del Diavolo* from memory. Another classic example of unconscious cerebration is that of Robert Louis Stevenson; as he himself has related in his "Chapter on Dreams," one dream gave him the plot of *Olalla* and another, in 1884, the plot of *Jekyll and Hyde*. Tartini undertook to imitate the music he had heard in a dream. Stevenson received outlines of plots from his dreams. More akin to Coleridge's verbal inspiration is the inspiration attributed by the Venerable Bede to Caedmon (*Historia ecclesiastica gentis Anglorum*, IV, 24). The case occurred at the end of the seventh century in the missionary and warring England of the Saxon kingdoms. Caedmon was an uneducated herdsman and was no longer young; one night he slipped away from a festive gathering because he knew that they would pass the harp to him and he knew also that he could not sing. He fell asleep in the stable near the horses, and in a dream someone called him by name and told him to sing. Caedmon replied that he did not know how to sing, but the voice said, "Sing about the origin of created things." Then Caedmon recited verses he had never heard before. He did not forget them when he awoke, and was able to repeat them to the monks at the nearby monastery of Hild. Although he did not know how to read, the monks explained passages of sacred history to him and he ruminated on them like a clean animal and converted them into delightful verses. He sang about the creation of the world and man and the story of Genesis; the Exodus of the children of Israel and their entrance into the Promised Land; the Incarnation, Passion, Resurrection, and Ascension of the Lord; the coming of the Holy Spirit; the teaching of the Apostles; and also the terror of the Last Judgment, the horror of Infernal Punishments, the delights of Heaven, and the graces and punishments of God. He was the first sacred poet of the English nation. Bede wrote that no one equaled him because he did not learn from men, but from God. Years later he foretold the hour of his death and awaited it in sleep. Let us hope that he met his angel again.[24]

2. There is one word which, if we only understand it, is the key to Freud's thought. That word is "repression." The whole edifice of psychoanalysis, Freud said, is based upon the theory of repression. Freud's entire life was devoted to the study of the phenomenon he called repression. The Freudian revolution is that radical revision of traditional theories of human nature and human society which becomes necessary if repression is recognized as a fact. In the new Freudian perspective, the essence of society is repression of the individual, and the essence of the individual is repression of himself.

The best way to explore the notion of repression is to review the path which led Freud to his hypothesis. Freud's breakthrough was the discovery of meaningfulness in a set of phenomena theretofore regarded, at least in scientific circles, as meaningless: first, the "mad" symptoms of the mentally deranged; second, dreams; and third, the various phenomena gathered together under the title of the psychopathology of everyday life, including slips of the tongue, errors and random thoughts.

Now in what sense does Freud find meaningfulness in neurotic symptoms, dreams and errors? He means, of course, that these phenomena are determined and can be given a causal explanation. He is rigorously insisting on unequivocal allegiance to the principle of psychic determinism; but he means much more than that. For if it were possible to explain these phenomena on behavioristic principles, as the result of superficial associations of ideas, then they would have a cause but no meaning. Meaningfulness means expression of a purpose or an intention. The crux of Freud's discovery is that neurotic

[24] From *Other Inquisitions* by Jorge Luis Borges, translated by R. L. Simms. Reprinted by permission of University of Texas Press.

symptoms, as well as the dreams and errors of everyday life, do have meaning, and that the meaning of "meaning" has to be radically revised because they have meaning. Since the purport of these purposive expressions is generally unknown to the person whose purpose they express, Freud is driven to embrace the paradox that there are in a human being purposes of which he knows nothing, involuntary purposes, or, in more technical Freudian language, "unconscious ideas." From this point of view a new world of psychic reality is opened up, of whose inner nature we are every bit as ignorant as we are of the reality of the external world, and of which our ordinary conscious observation tells us no more than our sense organs are able to report to us of the external world. Freud can thus define psychoanalysis as "nothing more than the discovery of the unconscious in mental life."

But the Freudian revolution is not limited to the hypothesis of an unconscious psychic life in the human being in addition to his conscious life. The other crucial hypothesis is that some unconscious ideas in a human being are incapable of becoming conscious to him in the ordinary way, because they are strenuously disowned and resisted by the conscious self. From this point of view Freud can say that "the whole of psychoanalytic theory is in fact built up on the perception of the resistance exerted by the patient when we try to make him conscious of his unconscious." The dynamic relation between the unconscious and the conscious life is one of conflict, and psychoanalysis is from top to bottom a science of mental conflict.

The realm of the unconscious is established in the individual when he refuses to admit into his conscious life a purpose of desire which he has, and in doing so establishes in himself a psychic force opposed to his own idea. This rejection by the individual of a purpose or idea, which nevertheless remains his, is repression. "The essence of repression lies simply in the function of rejecting or keeping something out of consciousness." Stated in more general terms, the essence of repression lies in the refusal of the human being to recognize the realities of his human nature. The fact that the repressed purposes nevertheless remain his is shown by dreams and neurotic symptoms, which represent an irruption of the unconscious into consciousness, producing not indeed a pure image of the unconscious, but a compromise between the two conflicting systems, and thus exhibiting the reality of the conflict.

Thus the notion of the unconscious remains an enigma without the theory of repression; or, as Freud says, "We obtain our theory of the unconscious from the theory of repression." To put it another way, the unconscious *is* "the dynamically unconscious repressed." Repression is the key word in the whole system; the word is chosen to indicate a structure dynamically based on psychic conflict.[25]

3. The Kingdom of Didd was ruled by King Derwin. His palace stood high on the top of the mountain. From his balcony, he looked down over the houses of all his subjects—first, over the spires of the noblemen's castles, across the broad roofs of the rich men's mansions, then over the little houses of the townsfolk, to the huts of the farmers far off in the fields.

It was a mighty view and it made King Derwin feel mighty important.

Far off in the fields, on the edge of a cranberry bog, stood the hut of the

Cubbins family. From the small door Bartholomew looked across the huts of the farmers to the houses of the townsfolk, then to the rich men's mansions and the noblemen's castles, up to the great towering palace of the King. It was exactly the same view that King Derwin saw from his balcony, but Bartholomew saw it backward.

It was a mighty view, but it made Bartholomew Cubbins feel mighty small.

Dr. Seuss, *The Hats of Bartholomew Cubbins*

TOPIC INDEX

Accuracy: in factual reporting, 184; in "how-to" writing, 87
Addison, Joseph, 134
Adventures of Huckleberry Finn, The, 499
Agassiz, Louis, 58, 368–69
Analogy, 146–47; in argumentation, 309–12; figures of speech, 434–37
Analysis: of cause-effect relationships, 107–31 (*See also* Causal analysis; Causation); chronological (*See* Process analysis); by classification of types, 132–44; by comparison, 145–59; of present versus past, 160–67; of component elements, 59–70; of concepts and ideas, 61–64; of consequences or effects, 124–31; definition of, 59; of directions ("how-to" instructions), 85–96; extended, 330–38: outline for, 402–04; by functions, 97–106; logical principles of, 64–65; organization of essays in, 59, 64; of personality in character study, 218–36; of physical structures, 59–61; of processes (*See* Process analysis)
Anticlichés, 434
Argumentation, 18, 117, 121, 292–325; by analogy, 309–12; approach to, 320; Benjamin Franklin on, 320; causal analysis as, 117–19; deductive reasoning in, 305–08, 314–15; evidence in, 293*n;* extended, 352–64; inductive reasoning in, 305, 308–09; is and ought propositions in, 293, 295–96, 300, 363; issues in: definition of, 300, discernment of, 300–05, evasion of, 313–14; logic in, 305–09: fallacies in, 306–09, 312–15, syllogisms in, 306–08, 314–15; satiric attack as, 317–19; structure of, 293–94, 363: examples of, 294–304, 316–17; substantiation of, 315–17; testing of, 319–20
Aristotle, 9, 18, 19, 107, 292, 319–20, 419
Atkinson, Brooks, 508–09
Auden, W. H., 266, 480
Austen, Jane, 467, 469
Autobiographical narration, 199–202

Balanced antithesis, 10, 468
Balzac, Honoré de, 435
Barton, Mary Neill, 372
Bates, L. Marston, 512
Beginnings, types of, 405–08
Bell, Marion V., 372
Bernstein, Theodore, 434
Bibliography: documentary format for, 398–99; of major reference sources (*See* Reference sources)

Blair, Hugh, 430–31, 435, 440, 450, 459, 460–61, 462, 465–66, 469, 473
Book reviews, 264–68, 274; criteria for, 265–66; function of reviewer in, 266; unfavorable criticism in, 266–68 (*See also* Critical writing; Literary criticism)
Boswell, James, 218, 428
Bradley, A. C., 484
Brecht, Bertolt, 437
Bridgeman, P. W., 416
Brink, William, 511*n*
Brooks, Charles, 436
Broun, Heywood, 468
Brown, Ivor, 405
Bryant, Margaret, 432
Bunyan, John, 477
Burke, Kenneth, 3, 9
Burke, Virginia, 508
Bush, Douglas, 408

Capote, Truman, 204
Carroll, Lewis, 447
Causal analysis, 107–31; as argumentation, 117–19, 292; by causation, 107–23; conditions and, 113–14; by consequences, 124–31; humor in, 113, 129–30; personal reasons as, 117–20; *post hoc, ergo propter hoc* fallacy in, 113, 315; speculation as, 114–17; sufficiency principle in, 110–13; uniformity principles in, 107–10, 120
Causation: conditions and, 113–14; law of, 107–08, 114; sufficiency principle of, 110–13; uniformity principle of, 107–10, 120; "universal" principle of, 107
Chamberlain, William Henry, 488
Character study, 218–36; as analysis of personality, 218–33; description and narration in, 219; extended, 346–51; of family member, 218–27; of friend or well-known person, 227–29; of historical figure, 229–32; "key" to, 218, 227, 346; in narrative form, 219, 223–25; of remembered people, 256–58; of "type," 232–33
Characters of Vertues and Vices, 233
Chase, Stuart, 421
Chaucer, Geoffrey, 436
Christensen, Francis, 443–44, 491–93, 495, 497
Ciardi, John, 41, 365
Cicero, 14, 17, 25, 415
Clarity, 3, 8–9, 87, 423
Classification, 132–44; as analysis, 132; basis of, 132, 133; complete types of, 134–38; complex, 140–42; cross-ranking in, 133–34; Dewey decimal system, 134; dichotomous, 134; organization of essay in, 138–40; by purpose, 133–34; for rhetorical reasons, 137–40; scientific, 134
Clements, Robert J., 511–12
Clichés, 433–34; humor in, 434
Coherence, achievement of, 497–511; by consistency of tone, 505–11; impediments to, 445–52; methods for (listed), 498; by order of arrangement: climactic, 500–01, general to specific, 486–91, spatial, 499–500, specific to general, 498, time, 498–99; by paragraph pattern, 498–99, 513–16; in sentence structure, 443–55: connectors and, 452–55; by transitional expressions and devices, 501–05
Comparison, 145–59; by analogy, 146–47; basis of, 146; definition of, 145*n;* figures of speech, 434–37; in observation, 369; organization of essay in, 151–54; of persons, 145–53; of present status with past, 160–67; rhetorical advantages of, 154; similarity and difference in, 147–51; of "wholes" and "parts," 151
Conceptual analysis, 61–64
Confessions of a Disloyal European, 255
Connectives, 452–55; common, 453–54; as transitional devices, 501–04; weak, 454–55
Connotation, 418–19, 422, 432–33; and "language of prejudice," 424–26; in *Roget's Thesaurus,* 425
Consequences as starting point for causal analysis, 124–30
"Courtship" devices, rhetorical, 9–10
Cousins, Norman, 425–26, 455
Creativity, 11, 370; analysis of creative process, 71–75; group workshops in, 366–67; invention, art of, 15–22
Critical writing, 264–71, 274; book reviews, 264–68; critic and his role in, 261, 264, 266, 268; general reviews, 268–71: of movies, 270–71, of recordings, 269–70, of restaurants, 269; objective data in, 268; subjective standards in, 261, 264–66
Current American Usage, 432

Dangling modifiers, 446, 450*n*
Data, summarization of, 279–80, 286–87
Davis, Ossie, 425
Deadwood expressions, 457–58
Deductive paragraph, 486–91
Deductive reasoning, 305–08, 314–15
Definition, 25–40, 415; development of:

by citing different meanings, 28–29, by citing examples, 30, by citing origins, 32–33, by contrast with what it is not, 31, by enlarging meaning, 33–34; experiential, 35–38; formal, 34–35; as introduction, 27; meaning of, 26–27; rhetorical stance in, 38; structure in, 28; subject possibilities in, 27–28
Del Castillo, Michael, 486
Depth psychology, 15*n*, 366–67
Descartes, René, 413
Description, 41–58; in character study, 219–20; chronologically arranged, 71–73, 75–76; creating mood in, 42–44, 56; detail selection in, 43–46, 251–52; order and point of view in, 43, 46, 400; sensory, 41–51, 53–56; technical, 51–53; tone in, 47–51; words, evocative, in, 42
Description-narration, 338–45
Details, use of, 43–46, 251–52, 345, 366, 368–69, 487
Dewey decimal system, 134
Diary as narration, 211–13
Dickens, Charles, 468
Dictionary of American-English Usage, A, 432, 446
Dictionary of Clichés, A, 434*n*
Dictionary of Contemporary American Usage, A, 446
Dinesen, Isak, 510
Directions (*See* "How-to" writing)
Dobrée, Bonamy, 428
Documentation, 394–99; bibliographies, format for, 398–99; footnotes, format for, 395–98
Don Quixote, 280, 281
Donne, John, 435
"Dream Children: A Reverie," 260
Du Rels, Adolfo Costa, 435

Ecclesiastes, 428–29
Economy, 7, 87, 423; in sentences, 455–59
Einstein, Albert, 11–12
Electric Kool-Aid Acid Test, The, 204
Elements of Style, The, 7, 488, 509–10
Eliot, T. S., 57, 413, 414, 415
Emphasis: and coherence, 500–01; in sentences, 459–62, 468–69
Endings, 408
English Prose Style, 468, 471, 497
Esslin, Martin, 503
Etzioni, Amitai, 407
Evaluation, 261–72; of books, 264–68; of human behavior, 261–64; objective data in, 268; of one's own writing, 5, 10; purpose of, 261; role of writer in, 261, 264, 266, 268; subjective standards in, 261, 264–66 (*See also* Critical writing; Literary criticism)
Evans, Bergen, 434, 446
Evans, Cornelia, 446
Excellence: Can We Be Equal and Excellent Too? 27*n*, 142*n*

Fact, "language" of, 420–22
Facts: in argumentation, 292, 293, 315–17; observing, 368–69; remembering, 366–67; researching, 365, 370–89
Factual reporting, 184–98; John Gunther on, 198; organization of essays in, 191–95: one-two-three format, 185–86, question and answer method, 192–95; range of purposes in: to clear up misconceptions, 185–86, to entertain, 188–89, to make social comment, 189–91, to satisfy natural curiosity, 186–88; range of subjects in, 184
Fairbrother, Nan, 481–82
Fallacies, logical, 306–08, 312–15; in causal analysis, 113, 315; checklist of, 313–15; in classification, 133–34; "fallacy of undistributed middle," 306–08; false premises, 307–08; hasty generalization, 309; *post hoc, ergo propter hoc*, 113, 315
Familiar essay (*See* Personal essay)
Fielding, Henry, 44–45
Figures of speech, 434–37; metaphor, 435, 436; personification, 436–37; rhetorical question, 436; simile, 436
Flaubert, Gustave, 6, 455, 465
Flowers, Frank C., 452
Follett, Wilson, 454
Footnotes: documentary, 395–98; use of, 353*n*, 355*n*
Forster, E. M., 16
Franklin, Benjamin, 320
Friendenberg, Edgar Z., 436
Frost, Robert, 365, 418
Froude, James Anthony, 499
Frye, Northrop, 467
Fuller, Edmund, 282*n*
"Function of a Critic, The," 266
Functional analysis: of institution, 97–102; organization of essay in, 102; of professional person, 102–04

Gainham, Sarah, 483
"Galileo Galilei," 406
Gardner, John W., 27
Generalization: in argumentation, 304–05; in deductive reasoning, 306–08, 369; as exhibitionism, 309; hasty, 309; in induc-

Generalization (*continued*)
tive reasoning, 305, 308–09; tendency of language toward, 415–16, 424; uniformity principle of causation, 110
"Generative Rhetoric of the Sentence, A," 443–44
Gibbon, Edward, 10
Glasgow, Ellen, 477
Golding, William, 16
Group workshop methods, 366–67
Guide to Reference Books, 372*n*, 377, 378, 380
Gunther, John, 402

Hamilton, Edith, 436
Hand, Learned, 35, 40
Harris, Louis, 511*n*
Harrison, George R., 487
Haydn, Hiram, 282*n*
Hazlitt, William, 247
Hemingway, Ernest, 435
Henry, Patrick, 6
Hersey, John, 486
"Heuristic" for generating writing ideas, 18–22
Hildebrand, Joel H., 407
Historical characterization, 229–32
Historical narration, 209–10
Historical-social analysis, 75–76
History of the English-Speaking Peoples, 209
History of Western Philosophy, A, 25
How and Where to Look It Up, 372*n*, 380, 383–84
"How-to" writing, 8–9, 85–96; on acquiring skill, 85–86; cardinal virtues of, 86–87; carried too far, 91; humor in, 89–90, 93–95; in narrative form, 93–95; as process analysis, 85, 96; as set of directions, 85; on technical procedure, 96; variety in, 87–90
Humor: in anticlichés, 434; in cause-effect relationships, 113, 129–30; in "how-to" writing, 89–90, 93–95; as protest, 242–43
Huxley, Aldous, 419

Immediacy in narration, 205–09
Imperatives, 86, 87
In the American Grain, 229
In Cold Blood, 204
Indirect expressions, 455–56
Inductive paragraph, 498
Inductive reasoning, 305, 308–12, 369
Inflection, 448
Information, gathering of, 365–99; for long papers, 387–89; by observation, 368–69; by remembering, 366–67; by research, 365, 370–89; for short papers, 385–87; by thinking, 369–70 (*See also* Reference sources; Research)
Inside Asia, 402
Inspiration, 17, 21
Intensifiers, ineffective, 454–55, 457
Interpretation, 369–70; of activity, 168–70; differentiated from analysis, 170; in literary criticism: of poetry, 174–76, 182–83, of short stories, 170–72, 177–82, of symbols, 172–74
Introductions, types of, 405–08
Invention, art of: classical approaches to, 17–18; finding subjects for, 14–22; new "heuristic" for, 18–19; question procedure for, 19–22
Irony: in argument, 317–19; in descriptive tone, 47–51; in social commentary, 189–91, 197

"Jabberwocky," 447
James, William, 147, 275
"John Burrough's America: Selections from the Writings of the Hudson River Naturalist," 436–37
Johnson, Samuel, 84, 428, 440, 468

Kazantzakis, Nikos, 8, 202, 259
Keller, Helen, 477
Keller, Helen Rex, 282*n*
Kennedy John F., 8, 10, 468
Kerr, Walter, 493–94
Kitzhaber, Albert, 5*n*, 11
Korzybski, Alfred, 413–14, 416

Lacouture, Jean, 487
Lamb, Charles, 260
Land, Myrick, 488–89
Language: abstraction tendency in, 420; connotation and denotation, 418–19, 422, 425–26, 432–33; extending limits of, 419–21; generalizing tendency of, 415–16, 424, 430; grammatical patterns in, 447–49; limits of, 413–26; and reality, 413–18, 434; semantic sophistication and, 421–22; subjectivity of, 416–18; symbolic and emotive, 420–21, 422; test of communication in, 419–20; "triangle of meaning," 416–18; used to deceive, 421; words as generalizations, 415–16; writing versus speech, 422–23
"Language of fact," 420–22
"Language of prejudice," 425–26
Lectures on Rhetoric and Belles Lettres, 431*n*

Levels of generality, 444, 491–98
Library research: Dewey decimal system, 134; for long papers, 387–89; major reference sources (lists), 371–85; primary and secondary materials, 371; for short papers, 385–87 (*See also* Reference books; Research)
Life on the Mississippi, 47
Lincoln, Abraham, 8, 35, 427, 466, 468–69
Literary criticism: interpretation in, 170–83: of poetry, 174–76, 182–83, of short stories, 170–72, 177–82, of symbols, 172–74; of one's own writing, 4–5, 10 (*See also* Book reviews; Critical writing)
Literary plots, synopsis of, 280–82
Lloyd, Donald, 500
Logic: in analysis, 64–65, 107–14; in argumentation, 305–09: fallacies in, 306–09, 312–15, syllogisms in, 306–08, 314–15; in formal definition, 34–35; as information-gathering technique, 369–70
Long paper, 329–409; description-narration, 338–45; extended analysis, 330–37; extended argumentation, 352–64; extended characterization, 346–52; form and function of term paper, 329–30; organization of, 400–09: outline as working guide, 402–04; plagiarism pitfalls, 393–94; research for, 387–89: crediting sources, 394–99, note-taking, 389–93 (*See also* Documentation; Research)
Lord, John, 421–22, 495
Lucas, F. L., 3, 465*n*

MacArthur, Douglas, 314
McCarthy, Mary, 218
MacDonald, Dwight, 91*n*
MacLeish, Archibald, 478
Maurois, Andre, 8
Mead, Margaret, 498
Meaning of Meaning, The, 416, 420
Memory: probing of, 15*n*, 251: group workshops for, 366–67, psychological notebook as means of, 367; quality of, 249–59 (*See also* Reminiscences)
Mencken, H. L., 393
Metaphor, 435, 436
Millikan, Robert Andrew, 17
Milne, A. A., 243, 512
Modern American Usage, 454
Modern Prose Style, 428
Modifiers, misplaced, 445–46, 450*n*
Montaigne, Michel de, 370
Mood, creating of, 42–44, 56, 202
Mood essay, 237–42
Morris, Willie, 476–77
Muller, Herbert J., 420
Murphy, Robert W., 372*n*, 383–84
Murray, Gilbert, 393
Murrow, Edward R., 416

Narration, 199–217; autobiographical, 199–202; in characterization, 219, 223–25; diary as, 211–13; historical, 209–10; "how-to" writing as, 93–95; illustrative anecdote, 488–89; immediacy in, 205–09; interpretation of, 170–72, 177–82; point of view in, 204–05; of remembered childhood experiences, 252–55; as social comment, 205–09; structure in, 202–04, 214, 400
Nathan, George Jean, 506–07
Natural events as subjects: for causal analysis, 107–10; for factual reporting, 186–88
News events, summarization of, 283
Nicholson, Margaret, 432, 446
Notebook, psychological, 367
Note-taking for research paper, 389–93
Notes toward a New Rhetoric, 443–44, 491–95

Observation, art of: Agassiz as teacher of, 368–69; as sources of information, 365, 368–69
Ogden, C. K., 416, 420–21
Ohmann, Richard, 408
"On Liberty," 274, 285
Order: in description, 43, 46; in "how-to" writing, 87; intuitive, 240, 404; logical, 401; natural, 400; in process analysis, 71–73, 75–76; in sentences, 442–43, 447–48, 460–62 (*See also* Emphasis; Point of view)
Order of climax, 468–69, 500–01
Organization, 400–09; of analytic essays, 59, 64; of argumentation, 293–94, 363; beginnings, 405–08; chronological: of process analysis, 71–73, 75–76, 400; of classification, 138–40; of comparison, 151–54; of definition, 28; endings, 408; of factual reporting, 191–95; of narration, 202–04, 400; outline as working guide for, 402–04 (*See also* Order)
Orwell, George, 429, 455, 488–89
Osborne, Harold, 494
Outline: as summarizing aid, 280–81; as working guide, 402–04
Oxford English Dictionary, The, 433

Packard, Vance, 490–91
Panofsky, Erwin, 405–06
Paragraph, 478–516; "additive" approach to, 491–95; as "cage of form," 478–79; coherence in, 497–509; development of, 476–97: particularizing procedures for, 486–91; divisions and boundaries of, 479–83; "duration" of, 485, 497; forms of: coordinate sequence, 492, deductive, 486–91, inductive, 488, mixed sequence, 493–95, subordinate sequence, 492–93; Francis Christensen, on, 491–97; functions of, 478–79; general to specific pattern in, 486–91; levels of generality in, 491–97; as logical and rhetorical unit, 478–79; topic sentence in, 444, 483, 491–92, 495–97; unity in, 483–85
Parallel construction, 466–68
Parker, Dorothy, 5
"Parlor, The," 512–13
Partridge, Eric, 434*n*
Pasternak, Boris, 434–35
Payne, Robert, 12
Paz, Octavio, 427
Periodic (suspended) sentence, 10, 470–71
Peroration, 294, 408
Personal essay, 237–48; "appreciation" as, 243–44; familiar style in, 237, 240, 247; Hazlitt on, 247; Herbert Read on, 240, 404; humor in, 242–43; intuitive order in, 240, 404; as mood vehicle, 237–40; protest as, 242–43; rhetoric in, 245
Personality analysis in character study, 218–33
Personification, 315, 436–37
Philosophy of Style, 430
Physical analysis, 59–61
Plagiarism pitfalls, avoiding, 393–94
Podhoretz, Norman, 490
Poe, Edgar Allan, 485
Poetry, 365, 404; comparison in, 157–59; interpretation of, 174–76, 182–83
Point of view: in description, 43, 46; in narration, 204–05; physical, 43, 46; psychological, 47–51; and spatial order, 499–500
"Politics and the English Language," 429, 455
Potter, Simeon, 10
Pound, Ezra, 3
Powell, Lawrence Clark, 510
Present status: *now* versus *then* as subject material, 160–67
Process analysis, 71–84; of creative activity, 71–75; of historical-social developments, 75–76; "how-to" writing as, 85, 96; of natural or technical operations, 76–79; organization of essay in, as chronological progression, 71–73, 75–76; of thinking, 80–81
Progoff, Ira, 15*n*, 366, 367
Protest, personal essay as, 242–43
Psychological notebook, 367
Punctuation chart, 474
Pusey, Nathan M., 487–88

Questions as instruments for invention, 19–22; addressed to subject-topic, 21–22; checklist of, 19–21

Rapoport, Anatol, 36
Read, Herbert, 240, 404, 468, 471, 497
Reference books, 372–82; definition of, 372; major reference sources, 371–85; on usage, 432
Reference Books: A Brief Guide for Students and Other Users of the Library, 372
Reference sources, 371–85; atlases and gazetteers, 376–77; bibliographies, general, 377–78; biographical works, 374–75; card catalogues, 383, 385; "curious facts" books, 377; dictionaries, 375–76; encyclopedias, 373–74; government publications, 381–82; pamphlets, 382–83; periodical indexes and abstracts, 379–81; special references, by subject, 378–79; yearbooks and almanacs, 376
Reminiscences, 249–60; of childhood experiences, 251–55; of episodes, 255–56; in narrative form, 252–56; of people, 256–58; and recall of facts, 366–67
Report to Greco, A, 202, 254, 259
Reportorial writing (*see* Factual reporting)
Research, 370–99; crediting sources, 394–99; for long papers, 387–89; major reference sources, 371–85; note-taking, 389–93; primary and secondary materials, 371; setting limits on, 370–71; for short papers, 385–87
Reviews (*See* Book reviews; Critical writing; Evaluation)
Rhetoric: basic principles of, 6–10; "courtship" devices, 9–10; definitions of, 3; "generative rhetoric of the sentence," 443–44; limits of language, 413–26; as responsible writing, 3–4
Rhetorical question, 436
Rhetorical stance, 9, 38, 191, 278, 507
Rhythm in sentences, devices for, 464–73;

balanced antithesis, 10, 468; order of climax, 468–69; parallel construction, 466–68; variations, 469–73
Richards, I. A., 416, 420–21
Rodgers, Paul C., Jr., 481, 483, 491*n*
Rosenberg, Harold, 407
Rosenfeld, Isaac, 471
Rosenhaupt, Hans, 405
Ruby, Lionel, 309*n*, 313*n*
Russell, Bertrand, 25–27, 418, 428

Sandburg, Carl, 407
Santayana, George, 436
Saroyan, William, 249
Satire: as argumentation, 317–19; in descriptive tone, 47–51
Saturday Review, 425
Schlissel, Lillian, 511
Schultz, Charles, 371
Seldes, Gilbert, 393
Semantics: developing sophistication in, 421–22; "language of fact," 420–22; "language of prejudice," 425–26; "new science of symbolism," 420; and tone, 506; "triangle of meaning," 416–18; used to deceive, 421
Sentences, 439–77; "additive process" in, 443–45: six expansion methods, 444*n;* as basis of individual "style," 439–40; coherence in, 443–55: connectives and, 452–54, impediments to, 445–52; economy in: eliminating unnecessary words, 455–58, shortening long sentence elements, 458–59; emphasis in, 459–62; Francis Christensen on, 443–44; Hugh Blair on, 440, 450, 459–62, 465–66, 469; modifiers in, 444–46, 450*n;* multilevel, 493; order in, 442–43, 447–48, 460–62; periodic (suspended), 10, 470–71; punctuation chart, 474; rhythm in, 464–73; structural meanings in, 447–48; suspended (periodic), 10, 470–71; topic, 444, 483, 491–92, 495–96; two-level, 492; unity in, 440–43: impediments to, 441–43; vigor in, 462–64
Seuss, Dr., 515–16
Shakespeare, William, 44, 430, 463–64
Shirer, William, 470
Short papers: gathering information for, 385–87; writing of, 25–325
Short stories, interpretation in criticism of, 170–72, 177–82
Siegmeister, Elie, 486
Simile, 436
Singer, Isaac Bashevis, 508
Social commentary: factual reporting as, 189–91; in narrative form, 205–09
"Social Value of the College Bred, The," 275
Sondel, Bess, 416–17, 420
Speculation as causal analysis, 114–17
Spencer, Herbert, 430
Spender, J. A., 470
Steinbeck, John, 214, 469–70
Stevens, Wallace, 414
Stevenson, Adlai, 436
Stevenson, Robert Louis, 436
Strachey, Lytton, 472
Strunk, William, 7, 488, 509–10
Student writer, 4–5, 10–11, 154
Style, 7–10; familiar, 247; of writer as individual, 439–40
Subjectivity: in causal analysis, 114–20; in critical writing, 261, 264–66; in definition, 35–38; of words, 416
Subjects: Aristotle's four categories of, 18; checklist of, 15–16; classical approaches to, 17–18; finding and developing, 14–22; limiting scope of, 16–17: factors in (list), 17; questions as instruments for invention, 19–22: addressed to subject-topic, 21–22, checklist of, 19–21
"Such, Such Were the Joys," 484
Sufficiency principle of causation, 110–13
Summarization, 273–91; basis of, 274; of data, 279–80; of events, 283–84; of ideas, 274–79; of literary plots, 280–82
Suspended (periodic) sentence, 10, 470–71
Swiss Family Robinson, The, 16
Syllogisms: basic form of, 306; enthyme form of, 84; fallacies in, 306–08: false premises, 307–08, non sequitur conclusions, 314–15, "undistributed middle," 306–08
Symbols: interpretation of, 172–74; semantics and "new science of symbolism," 420–22
"Symposium on the Paragraph," 491*n*, 495
Synopsis of literary plots, 280–82

Table Talk: Opinions on Books, Men, and Things, 247
Taper, Bernard, 512
Technical description, 8–9, 51–53
Term paper (*See* Long paper)
Thinking: analysis of process of, 80–81; logical, 305–15; as source of information, 365, 369–70
Thinking Straight, 310
Thomas, Dana Lee, 405, 406
Thomas, Henry, 405, 406

Thompson, Thomas, 472
Through the Looking-Glass, 34, 447
Thurber, James, 5
Tom Jones, 44
Tone: consistency of, and coherence, 505–11; in description, 47–51; as psychological point of view, 47–51; as social commentary, 189–91
Transitional devices, 73, 76, 501–05
Travels with Charley, 214, 470
"Triangle of meaning," 416–18
Twain, Mark, 47, 113, 433, 499–500

Uniformity principle of causation, 107–10, 120
Unity: of effect in description, 51; in paragraphs, 483–85; in sentences, 440–43
Updike, John, 436
Usage, 431, 454; reference books on, 432

Verbosity: deadwood expressions, 457–58; "fatty deposits," 6, 455; indirect expressions, 455–56; redundance, 457
Verbs, 456, 463–64
Vigor in sentences, 462–64

Wainwright, Loudon, 401
"What Every Writer Must Learn," 365
What To Do Till the Doctor Comes, 87
White, E. B., 7, 12–13, 27, 36, 402, 488, 497, 509–10
Wicker, Tom, 146*n*
Wilder, Thornton, 468
Winchell, Constance M., 373*n*, 377, 378, 380
Wind in the Willows, The, 243
Wolfe, Thomas, 476
Wolfe, Tom, 49, 204
Woodward, W. E., 470
Woolf, Virginia, 414, 462, 467
Word order, 448
Words, 427–38; to avoid, 433; clichés, 433–34; concrete and specific, 430, 464; connotation of, 418–19, 422, 425–26, 432–33; figures of speech, 434–37; as generalizations, 415–16; natural, 428–29; and reality, 413–14, 417–18; right, 430–33; subjectivity of, 416; symbolic and emotive, 420–21, 422
Writing: basic qualities of excellence in, 6–8, 10; compared with speech, 422–23; "courtship devices" in, 9–10; developing ability for, 4–6; finding subjects for, 14–22; as human activity, 3–13, 505; inspiration and, 17, 21; rhetorical stance in, 9; student writer and, 10–11

Yevtushenko, Yevgeny, 436

Zinsser, William, 471
Zorba the Greek, 8

SELECTIONS INDEX

Abrams, Meyer H., 30
Addison, Joseph, 33–34, 134
Agee, James, 53–55
All Trivia (excerpts), 240–42, 246–47
Allen, Frederick Lewis, 68–70
Allport, Gordon W., 36–38
"American Indian: Falsehoods and Truths, The," 185–86
"anyone lived in a pretty how town," 174–75
Areopagitica (excerpt), 285
Armstrong, Donald B., 87*n*
"As . . . As, So . . . As," 286
"Assassination of Lincoln, The," 338–44
Auden, W. H., 102–03

Baker, Russell, 155–56
Bass, Paul B., 280–81
Beardsley, Monroe C., 310, 321–23
"Beginner's Recipe for Walking," 85–86
Bell, Daniel, 97–98
Bennett, Arnold, 114–17
"Birthday Party," 170–71
Bishop, Louis Faugeres, 60–61
Bliven, Bruce, 108–10
Bohannan, Paul, 132–33
Book of Popular Science, The (excerpts), 52, 60–61, 76
Borges, Jorge Luis, 513–14
"Brain Transplantation and Personal Identity," 124–27
Brown, Norman O., 514–15
Brush, Katherine, 170–71
Bryant, Margaret, 280, 286–87
Buchwald, Art, 129–30

Carnegie, Dale, 91
Catton, Bruce, 148–51
"Changing Patriotism, A," 162–64
Cheyney, Edward P., 76*n*
Churchill, Winston, 209–10
Ciardi, John, 98–100
Claiborne, Craig, 269
"Classification System," 135–37
Coffin, Robert P. Tristram, 219–20
Cohen, B. Bernard, 171–72
"College Lectures Are Obsolete," 301–04
"Comics—Very Funny, The," 324
Complete Critical Outline of Don Quixote, A (excerpt), 280–81
"Composing a Ballet," 71–72
"Composition of Blood, The," 60–61
Conant, James B., 276–77, 287–91
Copland, Aaron, 137–38
"Credo of the Intellectuals (1920's), The," 68–70

cummings, e. e., 174–75, 225–26
Current American Usage (excerpts), 280, 286–87

Davis, Ossie, 118–19
"Death Be Not Proud," 157
"Definition of Philosophy, A," 25–26
"Delay," 246–47
DeMille, Agnes, 71–72
"Democracy," 36
"Detaching from Reality," 155–56
"Development of Intelligence: Heredity or Environment?" 111–13
"Diary of Carolina Maria de Jesus," 211–12
Dickens, Charles, 46
Didion, Joan, 189–91
"Different Types of Composers," 137–38
"Directory of Dining," 269
"Dissatisfaction," 241
"Do Not Go Gentle into That Good Night," 158–59
Donne, John, 157
Douglas, William O., 45
"Duchess of Newcastle, The," 346–51

"Egg, The," 172–74
Emerson, Ralph Waldo, 103–04
"Evil Eye, The," 241

"Fine, Family-Size Enterprise: *Gypsy Girl* with Hayley Mills, A," 270–71
"Five Basic Elements of Music," 66–67
"Football—the Game of Aggression," 168–70
Fordham, Frieda, 139–40
"Four Episodes," 255–56
Fragment of Autobiography, A (excerpt), 198
Francis, W. Nelson, 28–29
Franklin, Benjamin, 96
Frye, Northrop, 153–54
"Function of a Critic, The," 102–03

Gardner, John W., 140–42
Gehman, Richard, 227–29
"George Washington," 230–32
Gilbert, Allan H., 301–04
"Girl in the Tobacconist Shop, The," 205
"Girl of the Year, The," 50–51
"Girls in Their Summer Dresses, The," 177–81
Golden, Harry, 221–22
Golding, William, 243–44
Goode, Ruth, 85–86
"Grandfather," 226–27
"Grant and Lee: A Study in Contrasts," 148–51
"Grasshoppers," 52
"Green Ivory," 241
Gregory, Dick, 200–02
Gunther, John, 198

Hall, Joseph, 233
Hallock, Grace T., 87*n*
"Hanging, A," 205–09
Hart, Moss, 252–54
Hazlitt, William, 247
Hebb, Donald Olding, 111–13
Hilton, Ronald, 266–68
Hoffer, Eric, 262–64
"House Beautiful," 47–49
"House of Usher, The," 56
"How I Write," 73–75
"How to Be Efficient with Fewer Violins," 90
"How to Control Bleeding by Pressure Bandage," 87
"How to Get More Work Done," 88–89
"How to Make Lightning Rods," 96
"How to Stop Worrying," 91
Hughes, Ted, 182–83
"Hurricanes," 186–88
Huxley, Thomas Henry, 80–81

"In the Battle of Hastings," 209–10
"Insert Flap A," 93–95
"Interpretation of 'Birthday Party,' An," 171–72
"Interpretation of e. e. cummings' 'anyone lived in a pretty how town,' An," 174–76

James, William, 100–02
Jones, W. T., 311–12
"Jung's Psychological Types," 139–40

Kazantzakis, Nikos, 202–03, 254–55

"Lady (for a) Day," 227–29
LaFarge, Oliver, 185–86
Lagemann, John Kord, 88–89
Lee, Laurie, 251–52
Lehmann, Rosamund, 205
"Let's Pep Up Those Old Classics," 318–19
Lewis, C. S., 32–33
Life Against Death (excerpt), 514–15
"Life, and Death, in the Coal Mines," 316–17
Livingston, W. K., 330–37
Lockard, Duane, 316–17

Love, Sex, and Being Human (excerpt), 133
Ludwig, Emil, 152–53

"Many Kinds of Excellence, The," 140–42
"Marihuana," 192–95
"Marrying Absurd," 189–91
"Marxism," 311–12
"Memorable Summer, A," 252–54
Mill, John Stuart, 274–75
Millikan, Robert Andrew, 62–64
Milton, John, 285
Montaigne, Michel de, 188–89
"Moon, The," 246
"Moonrise over Monument Valley," 42–43
"My Average Uncle," 219–20
"My Father," 225–26
"My Uncle Koppel and Free Enterprise," 221–22
Myrdal, Jan, 255–56
"Myth and Folk Tale," 153–54

"Nature of Prejudice, The," 36–38
Nevins, Allan, 31
"Night in a Calabrian Village, A," 202–03
"Night in a Maine Motel, A," 214–15
"No News from Auschwitz," 164–66
"Not Poor, Just Broke," 200–02
"Not So Rich As You Think: A Review," 264–65

"October," 56
"Of the Liberty of Thought and Discussion," 274–75
"Of Thumbs," 188–89
O'Kane, James M., 352–64
"On a Mouth-Organ," 238–40
"On the Status of the Soul," 160–62
"Orphan, The," 256–58
Orwell, George, 205–09
Other Inquisitions (excerpt), 513–14

Pallester, John C., 52
"Paradox of the Sixties, The," 283–84
"Patient Man, A," 233
Perelman, S. J., 93–95
"Playful Mood, The," 262–64
Poe, Edgar Allan, 56
"Preposition at End of Clause or Sentence," 286
Priestley, J. B., 238–40
"Process of Riveting, The," 78–79
Puccetti, Roland, 124–27

"Quality of Memory, The," 249–50

Randolph, David, 66–67
"Report to Greco, A," 254–55
Reston, James, 283–84
"Role of the Scholar, The," 103–04
Rosenthal, A. M., 164–66
Rousseau, Jean Jacques, 128–29
Russell, Bertrand, 25–26, 73–75, 160–62

St. Clair, David, 213
Sandburg, Carl, 338–44
Saroyan, William, 172–74, 223, 225
Schickel, Richard, 270–71
Schorer, Mark, 147–48
"Shady Grove, Alabama, July 1936," 53–55
"Shameful Act, A," 128–29
Shankar, Ravi, 479–81
Shaw, Irwin, 177–81
Sherman, David E., 318–19
Short History of England, A (excerpt), 75–76
"Shrinkage," 246
Smith, Logan Pearsall, 240–42, 246–47
"Social Dynamite in Our Large Cities: Unemployed, Out-of-School Youth," 288–91
"Social Value of the College Bred, The" (excerpt), 100–02
"Spirit of Modern Science, The," 62–64
"Spreading 'You Know,' The," 242–43
Stade, George, 168–70
Stallman, R. W., 174–76
"Stanley and Livingstone," 152–53
Steinbeck, John, 214–15
"Story of Carolina Maria de Jesus, The," 213
"Studying Music in India," 479–81
"Subtitles for Old Books," 129–30
Sussman, Aaron, 85–86
"Swiss Family Robinson," 243–44

"Tactics and Strategy of Science, The," 276–77
"Teacher Certification," 321–23
"Ten Commandments for the New Behavioral Scientist—A Review," 266–68
Theophrastus, 232
"They," 241
"Things to Write," 241–42
"Thinking Scientifically," 80–81
Thinking Straight (excerpts), 310, 321–23
Thomas, Dylan, 158–59
"Thought-Fox, The," 182–83
"Three Meanings of Grammar," 28–29
Thurber, James, 242–43
Trivia (excerpts), 240–42, 246–47

Twain, Mark, 47–49
"Two Beggars," 45
"Two 'Southern' Writers," 147–48

"Uncle Aram and the Poem," 223–25
"Under an Umbrella," 240–41
"Unseasonable Man, The," 232

"View from Rochester Bridge," 46
"Village School, The," 251–52

Wainwright, Loudon, 162–64
"Way Things Work: A Thermostat, The," 77–78
Weeks, Edward, 264–65
Wertham, Frederick, 324
"What Is a College Education For?" 96–102
"What Is History?" 31
"What Is Pain?" 330–37
"What Is a Pedant?" 33–34
"What Is a Symbol?" 30
White, E. B., 36
"Whither the Black Odyssey?" 352–64
"Why a Classic Is a Classic," 114–17
"Why I Eulogized Malcolm X," 118–19
"Why Is the Sky Dark at Night?" 108–10
Wiesel, Eli, 256–58
Williams, Martin, 269–70
Williams, William Carlos, 230–32
Wilson, Woodrow, 294–300
"Wizardry of Oz Smith, The," 269–70
Wolfe, Thomas, 56, 249–50
Wolfe, Tom, 50–55
"Woodrow Wilson Asks Congress to Declare War," 294–300
Woolf, Virginia, 346–51
"World A and World B," 32–33

Yeats, William Butler, 226–27
"You, Indefinite," 280
Young, John V., 42–43

3
C 4
D 5
E 6
F 7
G 8
H 9
I 0
J 1